A Bride In Exile

by:

G. W. Court Jr.

When I Return, Will I Find Faith?

A Twenty-First Century Letter To the Church at...Everywhere

Permissions

To My Wife and Precious Children,

> Thank you for the sacrifices you've made;
> For coping with my passion, and for
> Being patient with this project.
> He knows and rewards.

To My Family and Friends,

> I couldn't find a book that rightly expressed
> All the exciting things that He has been
> Showing me. So I went ahead and
> Wrote one of my own.

And to the Brethren,

> Seek after it. Embrace it.
> Demonstrate it!
> Truth.

"So it shall be when all of these things have come upon you, the blessing and the curse which I have set before you, and you call *them* to mind in all nations where the LORD your God has banished you, and you return to the LORD your God and obey Him with all your heart and soul according to all that I command you today, you and your sons, then the LORD your God will restore you from captivity, and have compassion on you, and will gather you again from all the peoples where the LORD your God has scattered you."

Deuteronomy 30:1-3

Table of Contents

Foreword   ix
Prologue   xi
Form, Function & Faith

1   All We Like Sheep   19
2   Destiny and Desire   33
3   Conduct Becoming   53
4   Signed in Blood   91
5   Yea, Hath God Said?   135
6   Divided We Stand   191
7   Who is this G-d?   213
8   Body Parts   261
9   Sacreligiosity   289
10   Cleaning House   329
11   Abuses of Power   375
12   Pandora's Box   413

     Sincerely Yours,   479
     End Notes   493
     Chapter Divisions   503
     Acknowledgments   507
     Additional Resources   508

Preface

The Owner of the vineyard is coming to gather in His harvest. The Rich Man is returning to His estate. The Landowner is coming to distribute our wages. In all these prophetic parables, His arrival brings mixed results. Everything depends on whether or not the Master is loved.

There is coming a time when He will be returning. That, He has assured. For some, it will be a time of great joy; for others, great woe. When He does, much like what was done at the Temple, our God is going to clean house on a very imposing scale. Jesus did a little 'Father's house dusting' with some hastily braided cord, but that's only a sneak preview of what needs to be done and, upon His return, will be.

Part of that refurbishment is going to require the correction of false practices and errant theologies—to get the stench of worthless sacrifices out and the graffiti of friendly bloodshed off the walls. It is the end result that will have the most significance. We will end up with only one religion, one truth and one faith. The question for you to contemplate is whether or not it will be yours?

O LORD, my strength and my stronghold, and my refuge in the day of distress, to You the nations will come from the ends of the earth and say, "Our fathers have inherited nothing but falsehood, futility and things of no profit." (Jeremiah 16:19)

If you have a saving faith, these words should not come from your mouth because you certainly have been given some truth. They will, however, surely be spoken by many who thought they were living well, being nice, doing good deeds, being faithful, and most importantly...loving their god. Can you hear the shock and frustration in their voices? They had no idea! Maybe, to a lesser degree, there are areas in which we have no idea. What losses are they contemplating as they look back over their lives and see how what they believed affected how they lived, and how they lived is about to affect their eternal future?

I, with firm conviction, believe the reason this tragic reality check is coming is due to past generations and our inability (or unwillingness) to tell the whole truth—so help us God! The "full-gospel" many of our leaders seem to profess as the modus operandi for ensuring a scripturally supported lifestyle is dangerously lacking in, well…gospel. We have been instructed to love our Master, but we're really not sure how.

Let me promptly state some points regarding this book before you too quickly assume it's not for you, and potentially inherit some of that all too readily available…nothing.

If you desire the same old, ineffective, ear-tickling kind of cookie-cutter book, then maybe you'd be right. I promise this is nothing like that. This book is about facing and conquering spiritual, life-threatening illnesses. Indiscriminate with its candor, it crosses all party lines, isn't impressed with your ministry status, and is ecumenical in audience. Like at a surgeon's table, it is going to shine a very bright light on things that need to be exposed for what they are and we will use the Light of the World to do it.

I realize I am breaking promotional protocol by saying such things, but I am not a bait-and-switch kind of guy. I believe there is no more a desperately needed and life-giving message (besides the Word this is drawn from) in print today. According to market research, I am now out of time to convince you that this is in fact for you. I really hope you will sit down and at least read through the introduction, before you make that errant assumption.

Introduction

Form, Function and Faith

This book is really just a *tough-love* letter; the purpose of which is to assist His Chosen with her preparations during our earth-bound, divine engagement. But, I warn you forwardly now. If sedentary Christianity is your cup of tea, I hope you like it hot. I believe the stakes are just too high to play games, so this will be a hard-hitting, "if the shoe fits" kind of read. If you picked up this book looking for someone to play footsies with your soul, you'll need to go find some other author.

There are some things my spirit is really grieved over. I have spoken with, counseled with, prayed for and observed the fruits of too many lives that supposedly have embraced the concept of needing a savior, yet are defeated, depressed and ineffective. It doesn't have to be this way and I am just as commissioned to help prove it as are we all.

We all also have watched the enemy of our souls have a field day with unsuspecting family, friends and believers in general. We have seen the same person approach the "altar of salvation" over and over again in unending confusion and frustration. We have seen the influence of "revivals" have more negative than positive impact. We have heard enough "amen-ed" drivel dripping off the teeth of wolves in sheep's clothing, bellowed from the trusted pulpits of *our* (certainly not *your*) places of worship to write a book. So I have. It is time for some stuff to get dealt with. The days of silence being a religious virtue are over. I'm praying this book will awaken those who slumber, and give courage and ammunition to fight the good fight. For we are not just called to receive forgiveness; we are called to be victorious.

My greatest reason though, for dealing with all this, is to solidify and clarify *the Faith*, and our capacity, so as to properly lead and teach the Truth to our loved ones and any others whom the Lord puts in our path. We must endeavor to spare them from having to go through the treacherous gauntlet of seeking *a religion*. Now I can't speak for you, but I was once (and if not very careful could be again) both kinds of these aforementioned people: an inheritor and giver of lies.

I have always believed, even in my darkest (and lost) hours, that the man of the home has a most profound responsibility; an *almost* impossible one to achieve. A man must wear many hats, but the one that represents the priesthood is the one that I, and many of us, had or have no idea how to wear. I could be damned to destruction and I alone would have to deal with that. But if I ended up bringing my family with me— well, I don't even have the words.

Now add to that those we deal with every day, or even the once-in-a-while opportunities with strangers, to whom we might get to serve some spiritual meat, or perhaps an evangelistic message. Are you telling them the truth? Are you sure? Can we say as Paul did, "Be imitators of me, as I am of Christ"? Should we go ahead and invite them to our own churches, or send them somewhere else? Wherever we send them, do we warn them ahead of time of the 'might be' inconsequential errors in their theology? Do you even notice them? Would they even notice, or does any of it really matter? Because, after all, God doesn't really care about *how* we love Him; what matters is how we feel! Hmm?

Do you know why you believe what you believe and practice what you practice? If you are a parent, do you know how to sow the right answers to the questions that are forming, into the fertile soil of the young minds of your children? As a fellow soldier, do you know how to defend yourself (and the weak) against the fists of fury our adversary is incessantly swinging? As a Christian, are you ineffective in your witness because you cannot see how duplicating yourself could do any good for the Kingdom?

As I began to mature in my walk of faith, and build my family as well, I started to take inventory of all the concerns that have arisen along my journey. I realized at some point in time I was going to have to make a choice. Do I cloak my soul with a lead shield, to hide from the x-ray vision our children seem to see inconsistency (hypocrisy) so clearly with; or, do I draw some tough conclusions and stand firmly upon them?

My wife and I had been actively involved in one ministry or another in the church (that is how we met) since prior to our union— fifteen plus years, I guess. For what does that qualify me? Very little. I am barely a blip on the radar screen. I want to get it out in the open that I do not have a Doctorate, and unless *hard knocks* develops more than a continuing education program, it's hard to foresee that I ever will. All I have is an impressive looking diploma on my wall that says Associates of Christian Counseling from a small, Protestant, charismatic, pentecostal, and evangelical university from which I graduated "Summa cum Laude."

I obtained that because I wanted to respond to the calling I had on my life to serve the Lord of Lords, and the Body. Although I cannot attribute to it skeleton key powers for opening doors of opportunity, I am glad I obtained it. It gave me a good base-line to which I could compare and build upon, as time moved forward. Hindsight is an odd thing though, for it often delivers its greatest benefit upon perceived malfunction. A few years after that shingle was hung, I added one more year's worth of seminary education when working toward obtaining a Bachelor in Divinity, through a Baptist seminary. Yes, I wanted more knowledge, as well as credibility, as well as a job in the ministry.

It's quite amazing how much you can think you know, even when you know you don't know. After all, I had read the Word multiple times over. I went to a private, Christian school for my middle school years. I attended many Christian youth camps. I was faithfully raised in church, with services at least twice a week. I served in nearly every way conceivable, up to and including pastoral positions, and was even a decorated Royal Ranger. Additionally, my professors and pastors had worked diligently to put the 66-piece puzzle together for me, as they try to do for all of us. But here and there I noticed the pieces didn't quite fit. So, in typical childlike fashion, I just smiled and smashed them firmly and solidly out of place. One just assumes the reason they are "up there," and the rest of us are "down here," is because they are "in the know". (Wherever that is?) Looking back though, having come to this place—the place I hope to share with you through the foolishness of preaching through words on paper—I can confidently say it was all part of a well-orchestrated plan from above; or more accurately, from within.

How paradoxical it is that in this day of enlightenment, truth can be as subjective in the church as it is in the world. I have my suspicions how (which of course I'll share throughout the book), but how do you think that we got to the place where there can be so many differing versions of it? Is there actually more than one version of truth? Did God ever say there are a thousand ways to Him? Why are we divided into so many denominational factions? How can the Body of the Christ have brethren so opposed in their views that they will not even break bread with one another; and yet, all equally declare the kingdom's righteousness, peace and Joy? Yes, it is true. It will end someday. However, I believe you and I should and can be agents of change up until that great and glorious day. Though sadly, some things will likely get much worse before they get better.

Together, we are going to excavate down through the centuries, and sometimes millennia old layers man has buried it under, and we are going to get to the truth that has been right under our noses this whole time, but that few are willing to dig hard enough to reveal. By doing this, instead of waiting around for Jesus to come and force-fix us all up, we'll see clearly just what it is He is wanting from us now. Let's prepare ourselves in advance of His arrival. You never know. Maybe we can help speed it along!

To accomplish this, one unavoidable thing we will have to do is examine some of the mainstream teachings and practices we often find ourselves scaled over with, while not even knowing it. But not to worry, this will not be an exhaustive dissertation on obscure and boring subjects. At the same time, I will give you plenty of scriptural support for whatever I teach. I make no apologies for my love of Scripture. It's the light for our paths. My intent is to stir up the unaware soul and get it thinking; maybe get you flabbergasted—hopefully causing you to seek out your own answers. I am just acting as flint striking a rock, but you the reader will be responsible for the fuel.

It is my intent to do this in a scholarly, but coherent and digestible manner. I enjoy the "lofty" as much as anyone, but I have found that it tends to effect little change in those who think they've been eating filet mignon, when in reality they've never left the bottle. I do not propose that you necessarily are this person, but I once was and many still are. Therefore, I will attempt to balance my speaking 'to your mind' with also speaking 'to your heart.' I have tried to build my cases on readily available research, and from easily accessible sources that are themselves supported elsewhere as well. After all, a source is only as good as its believability and credibility.

My soul's ultimate desire is to propagate a radical change in your (and anyone else's I can reach) intensity of relationship with your Maker. Of this, there will be no doubt. You see, I've had a born-again experience. But I'm not talking about the entry-level one that you're hopefully also familiar with. I'm referring to a "scales falling from my eyes," Pauline[1] sort; the kind that knocks you off your own horse. The major differences being that: I already was a believer in The Way, I wasn't out aggressively persecuting people, and our ideological views were somewhat reversed. The ironic thing is that we both thought we were doing the Lord's work, when in reality we were in many ways working against Him. I believe this same level of awakening is coming to us all eventually, but the exciting part is that it can actually be accomplished *before* our appointment to die.

Disclaimer

If you are the theological type, as I desire to almost be, have no fear. I will give you plenty to react to. There will be times you will think I have simply gone *too far*. That may be true, when held up against the mainstream, milk-toast messages that are *far too* prevalent today. I, however, am not ashamed of the Gospel...the biblical one. There will also be times you will want to jump up and cheer, because you've been waiting for someone to say it like it is. Go ahead! Nobody will tease you. Just promise me that if you do react excitedly, in a public place, you'll hold up the cover. I've self-published this, so I can use all the advertisement help I can get.

If you have been given this book by someone who is reaching out to you in hopes to get you to understand from where they are coming, please do them the honor of hearing them out, by your reading this in its entirety. People want to be validated in the eyes of those they care about, but that's only part of the story. The part that may open your eyes to something very rich may be towards the back.

Some of you will flat-out reject portions. Others of you will be liberated, and they know that. I'm sure they are hoping for anything in between. So, after prayerful consideration, they have chosen to go out on a thin limb and take the chance that you may be ready to see the truths presented in here. The risk to them is that if you do reject what it says, you will possibly reject them also. Not so much because of the content of this book, but because much of this book reflects the contents of their heart. I will also go out on the limb with them and suggest they themselves may not support absolutely everything in this book. So follow up with them afterwards. For the giver, their road to life has gotten somewhat narrower, and they are just looking for another traveling companion.

This has also been written with the preconceived angle that you have more than just a superficial knowledge of things Christian. If you are a new believer, this book will likely be somewhat difficult for you. We will be dealing with spiritual issues that are generally avoided, potentially divisive, and beyond the fundamentals. I definitely do not want that to deter you from reading it though. I have attempted to disseminate the material in more a thematic method, than systematic. It is principle and pattern driven. That is how the Bible functions. I believe, if this can assist in setting you on the right track now, or at least give you a heads up regarding the potential pitfalls you will face, you will at the least avoid a lot of confusion. At the most, it will prevent debilitating error from sinking its teeth into your mind. Go ahead and give it a college try!

All that being said...who am I to accomplish this? You've probably never heard my name. I do not speak a variety of languages. I won't even use big words from a thesaurus I don't know the meaning of to try and validate my cause. I am literally a lowly tent-maker who hopes to perform some curative maintenance on the Body. And really, without your contrasting and comparing what I say against the truth of Scripture, concurrently praying through the provocative and somewhat controversial topics presented, you will benefit far less. You should not indiscriminately assume what I write to be true. If you do, as you will see, you will have defeated the purpose of this book. I also intend to make it as clear as possible, through my writing style, when I am giving an opinion.

It is quite probable that something in here is mistaken. I am fully human. I have been known to be a smidge philosophical, but I will try to hold that back—no promises though! I also intend to stand firm on that which I have confidence in, regardless of political correctness or public opinion.

Finally, but most importantly, you need to know these things about me: I am not a member of the Church of the Nazarene, although I follow One. I am not an ethnic Jew, although I'm married to one and am the disciple of another. I am not a Jehovah's Witness, but I'll tell anyone I can. I am not sectarian, denominational, prejudiced, or trying to start an official anything. I don't even have a license to share the Gospel; not because I don't respect accountability, but because I have not yet found a religious organization to which I would pledge my allegiance, from where the Apostles would have gotten theirs. I am simply an unworthy, grafted-in, citizen of the Commonwealth of Israel. Hopefully, you are too!

I am, however, wholly accountable to my Savior, the God-Man called Jesus, in whom all the fullness of deity dwells. He is the Word come into a tabernacle of flesh; the God of Abraham, Isaac, and Jacob. I pray that your spirit bears witness to this, and to it, you testify as well.

I believe His voluntarily shed blood upon the tree is the only means by which I can obtain redemption. I believe His self-professed resurrection after three days and nights in Joseph's Sepulcher, along with the witnessed signs and wonders, as well as the abundant, fulfilled prophecies testify to all His teaching's truthfulness and His identity.

I believe we can know the power of resurrection. Unfortunately, we have an adversary among us as well, whose intent is to steal, kill, and destroy our hopes for that, and I will as necessary refer to him by his given Hebrew name HaSatan (the Adversary). I intend to expose some of his finest and most insidious works, regardless of their location.

I also believe it is possible to personally know the will of the Father, (which is not as much a mystery as most think), and that we can joyfully obey Him. By doing so, we likewise will then be able to step on the *real* serpents (deceivers) and scorpions (demons), who seek to thwart our capacity for obedience and blessing, without incurring harm.

"He led you through the great and terrible wilderness, *with its* fiery serpents and scorpions and thirsty ground where there was no water." [2]

"Behold, I have given you authority to tread on serpents and scorpions, and over all the power of the enemy, and nothing will injure you." [3]

Just like our Savior did!

"And I will put enmity between you and the woman, and between your seed and her seed; He shall bruise you on the head..." [4]

But...

"The God of peace will soon crush Satan under **your** feet. The grace of our Lord Jesus be with you." [5]

That is, of course, when we know the Truth.

1

All We Like Sheep

Since ancient days, the existence of God, His attributes (at least some), and plan of redemption have been freely demonstrated to all whose eyes were open to see. Many were privileged with sight, but chose to reject their vision. They preferred illusions. Yet, there has always been a believing remnant that's beheld clearly, preserved through every culture, civilization and generation. As crazy as it seems from a logical perspective, God has chosen to use man, fallen and frail as we are, to be a vessel through which eyes help get opened, and His desire expressed; whether it be done through living example, signs and wonders, or via preaching.

There have been a variety of creeds, many thousands of books, and multiple millions of sermons written, presented, and absorbed by masses of starving, young spiritual hatchlings. In most cases, these are the means by which we learn and grow in knowledge as believers. That is not necessarily a bad thing, but it is only a part of what is discipleship. The "bad thing" arises from the fact that many never move past mastering the art of *passive* learning, thereby never moving into the role of *active* disciple. Eyes often open…and then they dim.

The modern American religious experience is commonly composed of a token visit to a local church, followed by a race to a local cafeteria, where the latest gossip on so-and-so soon spreads at florescent light-speed. If the pastor is fortunate, a small percentage of the congregation will have paid enough attention to warrant having gathered, and given enough offering to keep the lights on. The vast majority of times, the message given will be inspirational and contain enough truth to improve the state of those who choose to actively listen. But due to that human factor again, certain of those messages have negatively (and perpetually) influenced the course of our life's journeys.

Most errors are of minor consequence; others are toxic at the least. Generally, we have confidently been told what we are to believe, from our earliest childhood. We've accepted those teachings with perhaps the same confidence of our parents and attempted to, in essence, "Take hold of the plow, and never look back (Luke 9:62)."

Jesus said to the Pharisees in Mark 7:9, "You are experts at setting aside the commandment of God in order to keep your tradition." Paul told us in Colossians 2:8, "See to it that no one takes you captive through philosophy and empty deception, according to the tradition of men, according to the elementary principles of the world, rather than according to Christ." What we see here is a clear admonishment to be on the lookout for teachings that contradict truth, or cause us to disobey.

The mistake that some make is their perception of tradition only acknowledges expressions of custom and style. On the contrary, tradition often includes *belief*. Take, for example, prejudices. They are most often a learned characteristic—not always purposed to perpetuate damage to the next generation, but thoughtlessly passed down through the parent/s or guardian. To look upon a people group as being inferior, or of less value as compared to another, based solely upon look, race, creed, etc., cannot be rationally or scientifically substantiated. Yet, it is believed.

Another group of silly but seriously accepted beliefs are what are known as superstitions. Without listing the abundant and obvious, it is thought by the adherent that an action, rationally and logically ineffective upon reality, influences the natural course and patterns of life. These also are scientifically and evidentially devoid of truth, but believed.

What about fairy tales, wives' tales and those little white lies? As children, we believed many things that weren't true because we didn't have the intellectual mechanisms to filter out fallacious information. We used to believe in super-heroes; that a Warner Bros. company named ACME produced the coolest gadgets (if we could just get a catalogue); and that when we flapped our arms hard enough we actually lifted off the ground a bit. Here's the crux of the matter: If we don't grow up spiritually, we will still believe in fairy tales; or, even worse yet, we'll jump from our high places only to discover we really can't fly.

I say all this to set the stage for you to be willing to conclude that just as it's possible to be wrong by intellectual immaturity, we as believers can be wrong due to spiritual immaturity. I know. Not you, and not me either. Concluding we are wrong about anything can certainly be a bittersweet revelation. Maybe you've heard the phrase, "You must be willing to be wrong, if you desire to be right." Well, perhaps not, because I might have just made it up. But it's true! I'm not going to ask you to "open your mind" to the idea, because that carries a new-age connotation. I am, however, going to ask you to be as intellectually honest as possible. It's the least you should be. If this book causes you to reexamine some of your beliefs, hopefully I will have done a good thing. Ideally, it will strengthen your present resolve. However, in the event of conflict, you will have to wrestle with the material—possibly resulting in effective change. Either result is profitable.

Stop for a minute and think back in time. Can you remember an incident when you discovered that something of significance you had an emotional investment in was exposed for what it was, that turned out to be a lie? Maybe it was your Santa Claus revelation. Perhaps it was when the dramatic, "I love you!" from your sweetheart was shortly followed with notice that he/she had been cheating on you. Maybe someone pulled you into his or her pipe dream, only to find out it was a nightmare gone up in blinding smoke. We have all been misled at one point or another.

Millions, if not billions of dollars each year are pilfered by illegitimate scammers that prey on the gullibility (oftentimes desperation) of the hopeful. People buy lottery tickets (some with large portions of their welfare) not because they hate to hold on to their non-appropriated funds, but because somewhere along the line they bought the marketing line that says, "Because someone has to win, it might as well be you!" We are a smelly and misguided bunch of dopey sheep that have the habit of following anyone with a mesmerizing staff…even if over a cliff.

Lies in Disguise

It's really kind of a paradoxical dilemma. We are designed to require leadership, but it's often our leadership that leads us astray. Let me give you a practical example many can probably relate to: The theory of evolution, as taught by our elementary educators.

Do you remember from your science books the picture of "Java Man"? He was the very *advanced* ape, almost sapien, with the big, shelf-like eyebrow ridge and over-sized teeth. Do you know from what he was conceived? A cursory scan of any encyclopedia or the web will tell you. A man named Eugene Dubois, a Dutch scientist, around 1892, was digging in Indonesia and happened across some old bones. To be exact, there was one femur (thighbone), a skullcap section, and three teeth. Yes, that's right. Nowhere near the substantiating evidence required to reconstruct the image that many were led to believe once walked the earth.

Or, do you remember the pictures of Haeckel's "matching" embryos? You know, the one where the fish, and the salamander, and the

All We Like Sheep

tortoise, and the pig, and the rabbit, and the human, and a couple others were presented at three different stages of their embryonic development as being essentially identical? Are you aware that those were complete fraud? Do you know that the drawings were altered to look the way they do, with full knowledge of the deception? Did you know that they were exposed as fakes, as far back as the 1860's?[1] Then tell me why are they presented as fact? Why are they still in our books at all? Okay, I'll tell you. Transparency causes exposure. Science is supposed to be transparent, but it is often ideologically murky. Great lengths to block exposure must be undertaken, even if it requires complete fraudulence, when the ideological agenda is in jeopardy. This is especially true when self-serving, humanistic motivations are involved. Thus, science has proven something evolutionary after all! A life-initiating evolutionary process is an ideologically driven concept. How people authenticate religion, and how science comprehends the cosmos, have a lot in common.

But these are not the greatest deceptions. These are mere examples of the myriads of lies, or half-truths, or white lies, or ignorant beliefs that are thrown at us from very early on. If you remember those pictures, when you first saw them, did you not wonder? Even if you were raised by wise and religiously indoctrinating parents, it was easy to imagine that scenario was reasonable and possible. I clearly remember looking at the images of those embryos for the first time and thinking how neat and amazing the whole idea was. But I remember thinking that they didn't substantiate evolution at all. I, in contrast, gave credit to our Creator for having the power to take a similar blob of cells, direct their course of meiosis and mitosis, and change things that started out looking the same into whatever He wanted for an outcome. I thought that was pretty neat, and for that my God was pretty cool. My teacher said nothing whatsoever of their illegitimacy, so why would I have thought otherwise?

Please read carefully into what I just said. I took a lie at face value, wrapped it up with some preconceived notions about my Creator, justified it into the pretty picture I was comfortable with and then never looked back. Maybe, in other ways, that has happened to you too. Did you know they were a fake?

So, after all that, what is *your* great deception? I obviously can't accurately answer that for you. You have been given one though, and maybe more. They're unique for each of us. It could be as simple as having been told you were "good for nothing" enough to believe it. Or, it could be as complicated as having an astronomer for a dad, who raised you to believe in the probability of extra-terrestrial life, and that you were the illegitimate child of "mother nature" (forgive my lack of capitalization). Either one will steal from the abundant potential of your life.

Somewhere along your journey you were handed a map, whose highways didn't end up where they were pictured. Maybe the map was actually correct, but your compass was off from true North a couple degrees. As any adventurer will tell you, even a few, seemingly insignificant millimeters off per-meter-traveled, over a long distance, will result in being miles away from the intended destination. The Spirit of the Holy One wants to keep you on track. It is never too late to shine the light of His navigating Word onto your beliefs, to assure your direction and illuminate the potholes on the road you're now traveling.

Most likely, it's the ones you have trusted the most that have helped to lead you astray at times. It's an unfortunate and ironic reality. Granted, it is usually unknowingly and unintentional. They are the ones we most listen to; the ones with the most influence. They are the ones we would least expect to misguide us and for good reason. I believe that in reality, the majority of false teaching is perpetuated by people with good and sincere intentions, who are ignorant of the errors they themselves profess. That's the optimistic side of me trying to beat up the pessimistic side of me that knows there are a great many charlatans out there as well.

I will now continue to contribute to that optimism and add that if genuinely good people really knew they were wrong, they would appreciate correction. Proverbs 15:32 says, "He who neglects discipline despises himself, but he who listens to reproof acquires understanding." and in 10:17, "He is on the path of life who heeds instruction, but he who ignores reproof goes astray." Only if it was that easy.

Our War

You need to come to grips with the fact that it is the war between Truth and Deception (whose first, infamous battle took place in the heavenly coup d'état), that you were drafted into upon your birth. It's inescapable. Actually, the more one tries to avoid it, our enemy's relentless pursuit of victory gains ground. Ignorance will gain you very little in this life. Remember how there is armor we are supposed to put on? Let's take a quick look again at that Sunday school lesson from yesteryear.

Put on the full armor of God, so that you will be able to stand firm against the schemes of the devil. For our struggle is not against flesh and blood, but against the rulers, against the powers, against the world forces of this darkness, against the spiritual *forces* of wickedness in the heavenly *places*. Therefore, take up the full armor of God, so that you will be able to resist in the evil day, and having done everything, to stand firm. Stand firm therefore, HAVING <u>GIRDED YOUR LOINS WITH TRUTH</u>, and HAVING PUT ON THE BREASTPLATE OF RIGHTEOUSNESS, and having shod YOUR FEET WITH THE PREPARATION OF THE GOSPEL OF PEACE; in addition to

All We Like Sheep

all, taking up the shield of faith with which you will be able to extinguish all the flaming arrows of the evil *one*. And take THE HELMET OF SALVATION, and the sword of the Spirit, which is the word of God. (Ephesians 6:11-17)

First, I would like to draw your attention to all the CAPITAL letters throughout the text. Those are references to the not often recognized parallel passages in Isaiah 59, that tell us that these same items were and still are donned by our Messiah Himself. If He deemed it a good idea to do so, being our living illustration and all, should we not also?

Secondly, stated just a couple of verses before this portion is one of the biggest reasons that He had to come at all. Look at this!

Yes, <u>truth is lacking</u>; and he who turns aside from evil makes himself a prey. Now the LORD saw and it was displeasing in His sight that there was no justice. (Isaiah 59:15; Italic emphasis mine.)

Did you notice that all but one of those earlier listed, capitalized pieces of armor are defensive? Do you see how they are necessary to thwart the attacks of deception? Did you also notice that you are responsible for putting them on, and that Truth is the very first piece of equipment you need? After all, our greatest enemy's mightiest weapon is his lying tongue. Looking back in history, the Dark Ages, as they were justly called, occurred because these pieces of armor were stripped off the Lord's potential army before they even had a chance to fight! How? The Truth of the Word was either unavailable or misrepresented to the common layperson. The only purely offensive weapon we carry, the Sword of the Spirit, had its edge dulled. This generation is not the time for a relapse into darkness. Remember this statement in Hosea 4:6a, "My people are destroyed for lack of knowledge"? I am going to great lengths to establish a critical point. Lack of Truth corrupts us. Without it, there is an absence of justice. Ultimately, it can kill us. At the very least, it will hinder us from growing up and becoming mature citizens of His kingdom.

We should all desire truth at any cost—irrelevant of its consequences, societal impact, or personal sacrifice. Many a man has laid his life down to uphold truth. Did they die in vain? Fear of truth is certainly not of the Spirit. Romans 8:15 says, "For you have not received a spirit of slavery leading to fear again, but you have received a spirit of adoption as sons by which we cry out, Abba! Father!" Demonstrating that Jesus is Truth personified, Proverbs 8:12 says, "I, wisdom, dwell with prudence, and I find knowledge *and* discretion."

Inheritance

O LORD, my strength and my stronghold, and my refuge in the day of distress, to You the nations will come from the ends of the earth and say, "Our fathers have inherited nothing but falsehood, futility and things of no profit." (Jeremiah 16:19)

Yes, I've already quoted this verse. Repetition is the master of all teachers. Yet, one of the hardest things for us to learn as we mature from childhood to adolescence is that our parents are flawed, and that we reflect them. That they are humans with the capacity to make mistakes seems impossible when we are little children. In our earliest years, any parent could have told us just about anything and we would have believed them.

For me, it seems like my rude awakening came via being disciplined for something I didn't do. Do you remember yours? Perhaps not. We tend not to remember difficult and emotionally challenging times from our childhood. Why would we want to? Additionally, we were conditioned from our earliest years to not question authority. If a *big* person, to whose care we had been entrusted demanded something, we assumed it to be a valid command and were obedient, most of the time. Mom and Dad took us to school and told us to "respect our teachers" and "do what they say." If we went to church, we were dropped off into the tutelage of both young workers and seemingly ancient teachers, who would never mislead us. We were in church, golly gee.

How about this all too familiar declaration, "God said it, I believe it, and that settles it for me!" Although I am not opposed to this concept, there are inherently two problems encountered regarding it. First, our parents and teachers, through divine osmosis, carried the same authority. And secondly, does that which is spoken on His behalf, through the human conduit, actually agree with what "The Word" Himself says?

Or, along the same line, does the doctrine of your church line up with what Moses, the Prophets, Jesus, and the Apostles taught? Well, do you know? Do you really even care? Would you know if what your pastor was preaching last Sunday was truly accurate? I mean after all, the sermon was funny, illustrative, poignant, etcetera. Do you know how your denomination, congregation or church started, or who the founding presbyters/ministers/prophets/false-prophets/evangelists were, and what they believed? Again, I ask you, does it even matter? I believe it does! With my whole heart, I do; and you should too! It is, after all, your spiritual health and life we are talking about here. The sad reality is most do not. I don't know about you, but it would seem to me that cults, extreme-fringe movements, wolves, false-prophets, and teachers would

All We Like Sheep

have a lot less power to flourish, influence, and destroy lives if we would resoundingly answer yes to this last paragraph's questions.

As a result, we are (*would be*) no longer to be children, tossed here and there by waves and carried about by every wind of doctrine, by the trickery of men, by craftiness in deceitful scheming. (Ephesians 4:14)

"Wait a minute, that's not fair!" you say. "I can't go to Bible school. I'm not called to the ministry! I don't want my faith to be all clouded up with theology. Doctrine is for the doctorate. If I can't trust my pastor, whom can I trust? No church is going to be perfect. You have to settle somewhere. God judges my heart, not my mind. I'm not accountable for what my church does!" Must I go on? Does any of this sound familiar? You may very well not be this kind of thinker. Bless Abba for that! You are actually a rarer breed than you might think. Overwhelmingly, the vast majority of pew-warming individuals pay little attention to the "details".

Actually, I believe the Bible has a lot more practical answers to everyday life than many have been allowed to recognize. Let me ask you though, of the times that you did notice the little, textual discrepancies, how did you respond to them? Did you do what you should have done, or what we are all accustomed to doing? Did you go home and study to bring clarity? Did you ask the teacher/pastor to have a private word with him/her to explain it? Or, did you think to yourself that would be wrong, and recklessly glazed it over?

A Couple "What ifs?"

Presented illustratively, do you think that if James the Just overheard Simon Peter telling a small crowd of onlookers, "If you give one thousand denari to us, Jesus will bless it and you will soon get ten thousand denari back," that he would not have emphatically corrected him? He possibly would have said something as forthright and obvious as, "Where do you think we are going to get that kind of money, Peter? Why are you getting that man's hopes up, when you know full well money doesn't grow on olive trees?" I can hear Peter's response now, "Not us James, but He can do it. He can do anything! You just have to have faith!" (Incorporate author's sarcastic tone here).

What about if Paul saw Timothy laying hands on someone, while blowing in his face and laying him out "in the Spirit"; then picking him up and then blowing him down again, and then up, and then down again—followed by the passing around of a plate? (I know I've gotten someone's gut churning now). Would Paul not have rushed over and asked him what in the world he was doing, quickly followed up with an apology to the confused and unsuspecting man? It seems a little more out of sorts when applied to our apostolic fathers, doesn't it? What has happened to us that brought us to the place where we exalt our leaders so highly, we can neither correct nor question their actions or words? Maybe I am coming out of the gate too fast.

What are we afraid of? Does iron not sharpen iron anymore? Wouldn't a committed leader want to know if they are operating inappropriately, so they may become more competent in ministry? I, by no means am condoning rushing up to your pastor at your next opportunity, to beat him up with critical analysis. Firstly, you'd better do your correcting in love. Secondly, you had better know your stuff; for if you walk out of that office not having effectively made your point, you will likely not be appreciated any more for your "wise insight". Thirdly, who are you? Are you a respected individual within your church/synagogue/fellowship? If not, become one and leave correcting up to someone who is; otherwise, you may never become one. If you just can't let it go, as it is required in both the Mosaic and Apostolic teachings (Deuteronomy 19:15; 2nd Corinthians 13:1), get yourself two or three witnesses to support you. (This really is a good idea in all cases anyway.)[2]

Have you ever wondered if the deeper doctrinal questions you've had over the years were answered, whether or not you'd be where you are today, both spiritually and in regards to fellowship? Let me give you an example.

Have you ever struggled with whether or not the "God-Head" was really composed of three, separate and distinct persons? Essentially, in many cases (though many will argue otherwise), three independent but united in purpose gods acting as one (a.k.a. Trinity). Or is He, as the Hebrew Sh'ma declaratively states in Deuteronomy 6:4, "Hear, O Israel! The LORD is our God, the LORD is <u>One</u>!" a single, supreme deity, and that is all! Or, with perhaps a more concise, alternate conception is He, YHVH, one God, revealing Himself in three distinct manifestations as a triune, monotheistic plurality. And I might add, who manifests through progressive revelation, in various forms, with humanly conceived and imposed limitations. Of course this sounds confusing. What else would you expect when trying to define God?

What about the "man" who came to visit Abraham, had lunch with him, and told him Sarah was going to have a baby? Was He the pre-incarnate Christ? And if so, since He had flesh, does that mean He came in the flesh before He came in the flesh?

Obviously, this is a hot–button topic. People will declare you a heretic over this and similar doctrines. Actually, people have been killed for even questioning this. There are well-written decrees and creeds

All We Like Sheep

arguing for all three and more. But in most fellowships, you must think in one particular way to get along. There's little room for discussion. So, if you enjoy where you are, you may not want to bring this topic up, especially if you do have questions and want to keep the peace.

But what if you did bring it up, or any other third rail you're willing to step onto? What if you believe that the Bible you read is telling you that Christians and Jews and the whole world alike were going to go through the future coming "Great Tribulation" together? Maybe you are of the persuasion that some of the tribulation-attributed prophecy already has taken place. Could you share that with your church family without castigation? What about there being no "rapture" of "the church" at all? What then? Would you be labeled too extreme to be taken seriously, even though it is a legitimate, scriptural debate? Who wants that?

Maybe you've spent your life wishing you could "speak in tongues," but your church tells you it is not a gift for us today. After all, so many people are doing it, and it sure seems super-spiritual. You'd be so much more mature wouldn't you? Not only that, but you've heard another church teach that it is the "evidence" of the baptism of the Holy Spirit. Without that, you might not even get into heaven, right?

But wait! You can't find one single verse that says that. In fact, you find it to be quite the opposite. So, instead of trusting God's Word, you choose to mourn your loss, assume you are a "less-than" believer for reasons you never find answers to, and keep asking relentlessly, depressingly for it.

Maybe you're one of the more fortunate and have the gift. Have you ever seriously contemplated the validity of the tongues you already speak; i.e., "Do all those sounds I'm making really mean something in another language?" Have you ever noticed that within small, intimate groups, the members who do speak in tongues have similar sounding words and phrases? Perhaps you're one whose always been told by your denomination that tongues are the evidence of the manifestation of a demon? What is the truth? And what's all that "getting slain" commotion about anyway?

These are just a few examples of the kind of issues we will take up in greater detail as this book moves along. It is going to be an interesting ride, I assure you. More than that, I want it to be liberating. If we can't fly, and there is no Super Man or Tooth Fairy, and the ACME manufacturing company doesn't make all those cool gadgets, and your dad can't really beat up everyone else's dad, and picking your nose won't make your brain leak out, and closing your eyes won't make you invisible, what other kinds of things might we have believed as kids? More specifically, what "not quite right" things do we still believe, things that we have brought with us from our spiritual infancy, that had we known otherwise, would have altered the course of our spiritual development?

Have I provoked you yet to pondering a little on your current state? What if you acted upon your suspicions and sought out definitive answers? Where would they lead you? If you sought out similar thinking people, where would you find them? If you're like most, you don't even ask the questions anymore. Are you at least willing to admit that it's possible you believe incorrectly about something, maybe even something significant?

Maybe I haven't made you ponder that. Maybe these last examples seem obscure and meaningless to you. Perhaps it is your assessment that since we can't really know right from wrong absolutely, or because doctrinal disputes are often divisive, that it's a waste of energy to concern yourself with such things. Maybe you are not so sure you want to know, because of the potential consequences. What if I stepped up the ramifications of taking false teachings at face value? What if I reminded you of the Kool-Aid® of Jim Jones? How about the fires of the Branch Davidians? Oh, alright. Let's make it less cultish and ridiculous.

Do you remember the story of Korah? In Numbers 16:32, we see the results of his deception, "...and the earth opened its mouth and swallowed them up, and their households, and all the men who belonged to Korah with *their* possessions." Why did this happen? Because his followers bought his personal deception. Read the story again if you must. His followers might not have found it all that hard to trust in his self-appointed right to the priesthood. Talk about going down with the ship.

Is this still too impractical for you? How about Ananias and Sapphira (Acts 5, New Testament)? Just a little deception on their part, in attempts to save a little money, ultimately cost them everything. How about *some* of those extremely obedient Pharisees? Most were pretty on track according to behavior. Today (disregarding prejudice) they would be considered upright and benevolent citizens by the general populace; but in truth could be white-washed tombs heading for destruction. They'd be out there evangelizing away, traveling great distances, and giving alms to the poor; yet all the while creating sons of hell out of their proselytes.

How about those who trusted in (no need to mention any names) famous pastors and evangelists, who after significant personal investment ended up finding their leaders and sometimes themselves in prison? How about the followers of certain priests and pastors who end up with their children being molested by them? Where was our discernment then? We are all capable of temporary blindness. But even after the spittle-formed mud is applied, we still need to open our own eyes and wash up a bit.

Do you really think all those aforementioned people, had they known the truth of what was coming, would have still headed in the exact, same direction? Do you think any one of those who lost their lives would

All We Like Sheep

have confessed their knowledge of being members of an evil cult, while they were yet alive? What is the likelihood, a member of the aforementioned woke up one morning during their childhood and declared, "One day, when I get older, I will join a foolish man's coup, and end up being consumed by the earth in God's wrath"? Did they think, "When a servant of HaSatan whispers in my ear, 'Lie to the Disciples,' I will do so, with no fear of reprisal," or, "Let's buy a twelve thousand dollar time-share to a Christian resort that will soon go bankrupt"? I know, I know; none of us would ever find ourselves in those positions.

Whether you're a pastor, teacher, parent, or human, you should always be willing to be proven wrong, unless proven otherwise; especially since *all* of you teach someone at some point. For, as Matthew 18:6 says,

"But whoever causes one of these little ones who believe in Me to stumble, it would be better for him to have a heavy millstone hung around his neck, and to be drowned in the depth of the sea."

And in Matthew 5:19, "Whoever then shall break one of these commandments, the least, and shall <u>teach</u> others to do so, he shall be called least in the Kingdom of Heaven. But whoever <u>keeps</u> and <u>teaches</u> *them*, he shall be called great in the Kingdom of Heaven."

Please don't let the same, intellectual pride and reasoning that has ruined the lives of so many, hold you back from the hidden treasures that are found in our Christ! Scripture tells us the way we learn spiritual things:

Whom shall he teach knowledge? And whom shall he make to understand doctrine? *Them that are* weaned from the milk, *and* drawn from the breasts. For precept *must be* upon precept, precept upon precept; line upon line, line upon line; here a little, *and* there a little. (Isaiah 28:9 & 10, KJV)

But shortly following this, in verse twenty-two, Scripture says:

Now therefore be ye not scoffers, lest your <u>bands</u> be made strong; for an extermination wholly determined have I heard from the Lord, the GOD of hosts, upon the whole land.

You can be one of two kinds of people: those who hear, accept, apply, mature, and are saved; or, those who hear, reject, mock, and are bound to destruction. The latter do so, based on preconceived and foolish notions. Nobody really throws themselves headlong into an eternity of miserable banishment without first thinking it's either not really possible, or they have no choice. Yet neither is true! Oh, how much that should tell us.

We generally grow in knowledge by processing and accepting a fact to be true or false. Then over time, to add weight to our position, we selectively infuse more information into our arguments. Lies gain credence by locating the weakest areas in our foundation, and then proceed to build their strongholds there. As both sides are simultaneously whispering into our ears, we then allow compromises to take place in our minds until we fully embrace one or the other. All in all, we represent the summation of the traditional thoughts we have received and uphold.

Yes, I do believe there is a great, universal deception, working against all mankind. It began its ruthless propaganda campaign nearly at the beginning of time. We are about to travel back there together and see if we can draw some conclusions as to what it is. But before we do, there are just a few more preparations to make. I know. Let's get on with it already, right?

To get to the truth, wherever and whatever it is, you have to stop only seeking substantiation for what you already believe. Slow down. I'm not saying what you believe is wrong. I'm actually saying that, in many cases, there may be more to why you're right than you know. I know that sounds precarious, but our faith does not mature the way today's pseudo-science operates, where a hypothesis becomes a "law" even before the experiments are complete, and whatever evidence does not support the theory gets thrown out.

So to avoid making that mistake, I must make a special request of you. Treat this book differently. For whatever reason, and I am not immune to this practice, when we see questions in the midst of some text, we treat them automatically as though they are all rhetorical, and have no need to be answered. Try not to do that here. Even if just quickly in your mind, answer them yourself. Don't wait for me to do it for you. Contemplate them. See if what you think agrees with what I will eventually say, or what is commonly thought. Be honest with yourself and analyze your own understanding. It may be the necessary first step for any breakthrough you may need.

On that same note, when Scripture is given, even if you know the portion well, please don't give it a cursory glossing over. Read it as if for the first time. If you just sweep over it as if you already have it memorized, you're not doing yourself any good. We should never get tired of hearing God's voice. If I just reference a text and you are not familiar with it, look it up. There is no shame in that. Sometimes a verse that you've read a hundred times has a way of coming to life in an unexpected way, when put into its right perspective. Don't miss out on that opportunity.

What our goal needs to be now, as *the Day* approaches all the closer, is to go back down to the basements of our souls, to look for the

All We Like Sheep

breaching and out-of-square cinderblocks and shore them up. Because if we don't, and we leave our faith weak and shifting, when those "full-of-hot-air" winds start blowing past the lips of our adversary, he may very well huff, and puff, and blow our houses down. Since cornerstones are laid at the very beginning, that is where we will likewise start.

It is time to get our heads out of the proverbial sand and stop pretending we don't see what's going on around us. Our faith and its eternality are not child's play. Pastors putting their hands over their eyes will not make the church invisible, nor put our adversary's diametric weapon back in its scabbard. We, as believers, are responsible to reflect the truth through our lives and our fellowships, and we are failing too often. Let's change things, and let's start with ourselves. All right! Grab your jackhammers and proceed to chapter two.

2

Destiny and Desire

As a whole we have, as far as humanity goes, blown it from the launch. Adam (earthy, ruddy, man) and his wife Chavvah (hhah-vaw; life-giver)—yes, that's her true name—succumbed to the craftily arranged and deceitful words of HaSatan (meaning: the Adversary), and really fouled things up. At that moment in newly created time there was but one single command to follow, one bit of basic instruction, and that was simply to not ingest any meat from a particular fruit-bearing tree, in the center of a garden known as Eden (meaning: delight).

Imagine that! Having only one, easy, straightforward rule to follow in life. How seemingly 'delightful'? It should have been that way for all of us, right? Well, let's think about that for a bit. I'm going to toss something at you that may seem like a side-step, but not to worry. Did Jesus's death come as a tragic back-up for a mission gone badly? Was it a last ditch effort to compensate for the inadequacy of God's providential planning skills? Well, some among us may answer *yes*, although they may never do so that openly. Those questions are inadvertently answered yes when it is thought that He didn't foresee the sin coming; but, if He did see it coming, when? Was it just prior to the actual ingestion; or, was it long before He spoke this planet into existence? (Whatever long equates to?)

Destiny and Desire

The Stage

When "the Word who became flesh" was walking around in the garden asking, "Where are you?" (Genesis 3:9) did He not know? Or in 3:11, when He asked if they had eaten of the tree of which He had commanded them not to, had He no clue? I'm going to take a chance and answer for you. "Of course not!" So maybe what we see here is really Act 1, Scene 2 of the screenplay titled, "The Truman Show of Creation." Could this be the first illustrated sermon with two, unknowingly recruited actors that had been given a set, but had no idea they were being recorded?

Going back to the earlier thought line, when did God know He would inevitably have to indwell a human body and kill it to save this race of humans? Before time began? So why did He still make this place called Terra Firma, put a peculiar garden in the middle of it, and plant a tree in the middle of that, to be kept by people who would break the one and only, unbelievably easy-to-keep rule they were given? Time is ticking...... Love! Pure and simple. His construct is so permeated with love that He initiated a plan to physically associate with, and suffer for, a being He had not yet even made. Amazing!

Moving forward now, we come to the place where He walks around the garden pretending He has no idea what's going on and plants the question, "Have you eaten of...?" Do you know why He made this rhetorical inquiry? To get Adam to confess—the first part of our restoration process. He is always taking the initiative and seeking us. If we don't acknowledge our problems, we will never find solutions! "If we confess our sins, He is faithful and righteous to forgive us... (1st John 1:9)." But like we so often do, Adam accepted part of the blame and projected the other part anywhere he could get it to go. In this case, he had only one option, his helpmate...well, kind of. Actually, although most of us were taught that in Sunday school, that's not exactly what happened. Careful reading actually shows he blamed it on God Himself. Look at Genesis 3:12, "The man said, 'The woman whom <u>You gave</u> *to be* with me, she gave me from the tree, and I ate.'"

Here's an angle you may not have heard preached. He was right! Not for the projection of blame per se, but from a technical perspective. From Adam's viewpoint, had Chavvah not been there, he may never have eaten the fruit. He was right. But to be equitable, Adam was the one who originally received the order directly from God, not Chavvah. Now, before you women out there start getting squirmy, please give me a second to redeem myself.

There are two different ways that this portion of the narrative can be interpreted. The first is that Adam did not actually hear the serpent's lies himself. He heard them *through* Chavvah. Notice that the narrative doesn't say in v.4, "The serpent said to *them*...," it says, "to *her*." Perhaps Adam was *with* her there, in the sense of the two being one, and a short time had lapsed before he ate also.

The second way this could be interpreted would be that they were both together there while the serpent spoke, and Adam observed the whole event go down as if on the sideline. HaSatan just chose to focus in on her. I wonder why. If she was the "weaker vessel," how would HaSatan have known that? Regardless, Adam didn't demonstrate the best of leadership skills. He probably had not read any of John Maxwell's material yet. You would think he would have stopped her from going through with this risky act, if he was caring and all. Ah, but wait! There is an overlooked component to this second picture, to which I just referred. Adam wasn't her 'leader' at this time. As far as they were concerned, they were equal partners; one flesh—equal strength. The hierarchical system didn't appear on the scene until after the fall!

> To the woman He said, "I will greatly multiply your pain in childbirth, in pain you will bring forth children; yet your desire will be for your husband, and <u>he will rule over</u> you." (Genesis 3:16)

Perhaps Adam simply waited to see the results from her disobedience, and saw none. At that point, why not eat? She looked at him, smiled a slightly crooked smile and handed the fruit over. Perhaps she thought that because she didn't receive the direct order, she might not die after all. There is no doubt Adam was just as guilty as she was, as God blamed him (Romans 5:14). But maybe his attachment to her pushed him to do it, more than the 'reward' that was promised for the act. Regardless, I think the thing that most needs to be seen, that's going on between the lines of this narrative, is that neither Adam nor Chavvah knew the reality of what the result of their fall would be. If they had, they never would have "eaten the forbidden".

And Then Came Death

Perception vs. Reality is synonymous in spiritual matters with Deception vs. Truth. The ultimate reality of sin is its consequential death.

> Romans 6:23, "For the wages of sin is death, but the free gift of God is eternal life in Christ Jesus our Lord."

If you don't fear death, sin's consequences alone have little power to effect change. Adam and Chavvah were clueless as to what physical

Destiny and Desire

death was. They had never seen it before. For nothing, probably not even a flower had yet died. Just as we really have no clue as to what spiritual death is, we've just been told a few details that clearly lead us to believe we don't want it. Look around and you'll see plenty of examples of people who know of the *potential* consequence for sin, but do not change accordingly. Even our government has advertised to, "Just say no!" These same people, with true understanding, would quickly reverse their course. Things of the Spirit (Ruach) are true. Things from our adversary are lies. This is what Jesus has to say about HaSatan regarding this matter, as recorded by the Apostle John, in his gospel:

He was a murderer from the beginning, and does not stand in the truth because there is no truth in him. Whenever he speaks a lie, he speaks from his own *nature,* for he is a liar and the father of lies (8:44).

That's the way he's always been and always will be—even into his everlasting destruction. Do you now see how deception works its craft? It's not necessarily the temptation itself that causes us to break God's rules. It's the deception that aligns itself with temptation and tells us there is no real consequence. HaSatan's ultimate deception is that sin and death are of no consequence. Selah. One of the many missions the Spirit has is to awaken to us the perception that physical death does lead to the ultimate spiritual reality. This being, that depending on your relationship with God, you will either be eternally separated from Him, or enjoined to Him in perpetual paradise. Those crazy kids in Eden took just a little bite of fruit. And for it, they died. And for that, we all die.

Therefore, just as through one man sin entered into the world, and death through sin, and so death spread to all men, because all sinned. (Romans 5:12)

So hold on, back up a minute and then move forward. After these two were booted from paradise, two warrior cherubim with flashing and flaming swords were placed on the east side of the garden to keep them and any future visitors out. Couldn't He have placed a few more around the whole garden, and kept the serpent out from the very beginning? I'm sorry to have to be the one to tell you this, but in case you hadn't conceived this, Adam and Chavvah were *destined* to fall. That is not the same as *desired.* They wouldn't have without the Deceiver there. And in order for him to have gotten there, he had to become stripped of his glory and undergo his own banishment from citizenship in Heaven. If this wasn't anticipated, someone was losing control.

Who Fell First?

HaSatan, as I'm sure you are all aware, did not start out as the adversary of all that is good and holy. He began his existence as a rather remarkable creature. Quite possibly, he was the leader of a band called "The Heavenly Host". Here's some trivia relief: His name was not Lucifer. The word rendered Lucifer in English is actually 'Helel' in the Hebrew text. It denotes a "bright and shining object" as well as "to bring praise." (This is part of where the worship leader idea comes from). With *helel* being a root part of the phrase "hallelujah," you can easily see its connection. The fact is that Scripture doesn't explicitly name him.

In St. Jerome's Latin Vulgate, the Latin word for "Light Bearer" was used, Lucifer (*Luc*=Lux, meaning: "light"; and *ferre* meaning: "to bring".) This was then transferred to the KJV, which is really the only currently published Bible translation that continues to use it. The name Lucifer was ascribed to the planet Venus in Roman mythology before its current name. The funny thing is, the name's usage in Isaiah 14:12 does not even refer to HaSatan at all, but to an actual king of Babylon, probably Nebuchadnezzar.

So was HaSatan created with The Mighty One's foreknowledge that he would eventually "bite the hand of the One who made him"? It is inconceivable to be otherwise. God knew that HaSatan would be the 'Judas of the Host'. Yet, He still created him. Why? It was also part of the plan! God wanted a creature (man) who would return love voluntarily to Him. But for that to happen, this creature would have to choose to love Him, and not be created preprogrammed to robotically serve Him.

In order for there to be voluntary love, which would entail voluntary obedience, there had to be an opposing force to love, against which the creature-man would voluntarily war. Certainly, the other creature (HaSatan) alone would not suffice to interact with millions and millions of people, so therefore untold numbers of cohorts would be made capable of following his leadership. And so they did. If you think that the first two humans, and the great adversary, accidentally found themselves in the center of a garden, in the center of creation, in direct proximity to the only temptation they had, you really shouldn't play roulette, if you know what I mean. Now, I would like to offer an opinion on this part of the drama, based mostly on inference.

Look back at the temptation. What was the allure? The first part, "Your eyes will be opened and you will be like God!" sounds wonderfully glamorous, but it is insignificant really. They already were made in His image, and they didn't know their eyes were closed. Notice as well, that HaSatan is actually tempting her with *his personal* evil desire, "to be like God"; the very thing at which he failed. It's the second part that's most

Destiny and Desire

intriguing, and the most telling. In order for, "and you will know 'good' (Hebrew; *tov*--a good thing, happiness, prosperity) and 'evil'" (Hebrew, *ra*--evil, distress, misery) to be tempting, a couple things would seem to be necessary.

The first, which adds support to these concepts, is that at the time of their temptation, I think Adam and Chavvah were relatively newly created and therefore somewhat naïve. But this is purely speculation. It *appears* they had not yet had children, although her "great increase" in labor pain is an interesting phrase. The lack of dialogue or narrative, prior to the fall, causes suspect. And the fact that they did not yet know evil, even with a liar and a murderer skulking around their garden, is curious. How long would HaSatan have waited before ambushing God's creation? Had those two understood that "being fruitful and multiplying," along with their fellowshipping with the One who walked in the garden with them, was already going to fulfill the "knowing good" part, the temptation wouldn't have worked. Similarly, had they known what evil was, because they had no concept, it also would not have been very tempting.

The second is that there was apparently such a thing as evil to be known. And, just as intellectually challenging to contemplate is that Adam and Chavvah were made perfect and innocent, but apparently capable of being enticed to reject the authority of the very One who made them, and seduced by something they knew nothing of. Sounds a bit similar to HaSatan's experience, doesn't it?

Here is the irony of this situation: The 'naked truth' of this temptation was that, in actuality, it was a barely tempting temptation that ultimately succeeded in wreaking such havoc on mankind. We cannot become the Mighty One, and we all know that. I think they knew that better than anybody ever will. And evil, whatever it was, was in contrast to good; so they logically shouldn't have wanted that.

This persuades me to believe that if enough fellowship time had gone by, and they had developed a working knowledge of evil, or the danger HaSatan posed, Adam and Chavvah would most certainly have been strong enough to easily overcome this simple challenge. There is an obvious lesson, if not many, in that for us.

The means by which they could have thwarted temptation; the means all mankind can thwart it, is to know and wield the truth. Example: If someone told you to put water in your car's gas tank, and that it would run fine, you obviously wouldn't believe them. Not because you, or anyone you know had tried it before, but purely because of your basic knowledge of combustion. There is no one on this planet crafty enough to convince you that H_2O is flammable, hopefully.

Shame Shame Shame

Moving further into this depiction we find that these two, newly enlightened ones discovered their nakedness, and it bothered them. An interesting consideration is, with all preconceptions aside, regardless of their body shape, color, age, etc., there is really no philosophical explanation for their 'naked' shame. Psycho-scientists may disagree, but without bringing in aesthetic judgments regarding bodily characteristics, there really is no case for our current, *normal* shame of nakedness. There has never been a *civilized* society whose cultural normalcy was not garbed, and even pagan, tribal communities generally cover their most private parts, even if barely.

Before you toss our sexual nature into the mix, it really is not part of the original equation. Adam and Chavvah were not embarrassed by their attraction to each other. They had after all become quite familiar with each other. What they were embarrassed about was that someone else (namely God) would see them in their corrupted state.

In case you were starting to panic, I am not a nudist, nor do I condone the behavior. But that's only because the fall eventually brought perversion into existence. If we were perfect in our morality, and had no sin-nature, none of us (regardless of our body types) would have anything about which to be ashamed. I am, however, tired of the vanity and meaninglessness of 'trend', that goes along with cloaking our shame.

I bring all this shame-oriented thinking up to expose an imbedded support for further validity to this story. The mere fact that there is physical shame in humanity, and the fact that we are told how it came about through naturalistically disassociated means, bears witness to its own authenticity. It's curious how a supposed, continually advancing society has not been able to 'evolve' its way out of this inherent sin ramification. Think about it. Anytime shame is felt as a result of being naked, it is a throwback to the garden scene. Oh, how wise is our Creator!

So how do they respond? They go find some sorely inadequate leaves and bind them together enough to cover themselves. How I would love to explore with you more of the teachings that have been drawn from this story, but there are just far too many. This next part is so rich and deep though, it can't be avoided. Those fig leaves could not possibly have covered them from their shame, nor could they have atoned for their disobedience. They were not an acceptable covering! So God does what He always knew He was going to have to do—lead Adam through the process of shedding blood. An innocent animal (certainly one or more of the yet to be appointed, qualified-for-sacrifice animals), had to surrender its life to pay the price for their first sin (transgression of a law; 1st John 3:4).

Destiny and Desire

Adam and Chavvah watched as the breath of life (nephesh), which was recently breathed into creation, vanish like a vapor—as the light dimmed in the eye of the creature that had been just recently named. Try to feel their anguish? Can you empathize with their guilt? What a roller coaster of emotion they must have been experiencing. One day, they were walking in Paradise, side-by-side with their Creator; and the next they were shamefully watching the blood of propitiation seep deep into the rich earth. Little did they know that He who was with them now, would someday watch His own blood do the very same thing.

Then, to top it all off, God made garments from the pelts of the sacrificed creatures, to create a more appropriate cover for them. But that's not all the pelts did. They became a daily, worn reminder of the consequence of transgression. Consider this: God valued those animals He sacrificed, albeit not with the intensity or depth He loves us with, but in a way that would grieve Him. Is it possible that this pre-incarnate Messiah may have wept the first tears ever shed, as He demonstrated the penalty of sin, and the shadow of the future price of His redeeming all mankind? I can see it. I think so. All this could have been avoided so easily, but then again, it was meant to be. It had to be! There was no other way to fashion a bride who would choose to love the Bridegroom. There was no other way to take the unfathomable and transcendent form of the love of God, and reveal it to fallen and finite man.

So, why this author's entire commentary on the fall? Because I want you to see the origin of the 'Law' and its most fundamental purpose—to save life, and keep chaste the Bride through obedience to it. And I want you to see, and consider this carefully, that it is often the restraining instruction itself that we find ourselves rebelling against, more than just our desire for any gain wrought through the rebellion.

HaSatan accomplished his mission through deception. Have you ever noticed that he never clearly lied, in an obvious and blatant way? He actually, in the three critical components of his dialogue, attacked with a "reformed" truth.

Con #1, as seen in Genesis 3:1, "Now the serpent was more crafty than any beast of the field which the LORD God had made. And he said to the woman, 'Indeed, has God said'; "You shall not eat from any tree of the garden?"

This is just a question. It may be based on a false premise, but a question is like a feeling, it is neither right nor wrong in itself. In fact, this question should have triggered intuition on Chavvah's part, telling her that either this creature didn't know what it was talking about, or that something very shady was going down.

Something I personally want to know is why she didn't ask its name? Adam and Eve were the ones responsible for naming the creatures, and surely, this one wasn't seen by them previously, or had it been? She seemed rather comfortable with it, doesn't she? This is, after all, a talking beast. Perhaps they were used to hearing creatures speak. But how did it know anything about the tree restriction at all? Were all the creatures told not to eat of that tree?

Con #2, in Genesis 3:4, "The serpent said to the woman, 'You surely will not die!'" Ultimately, they did of course, some 900 plus years later! HaSatan was correct in the punishment's immediacy from a physiological perspective, because the purpose of creation was far grander than just Adam and Chavvah. A global civilization was the plan, and Adam and Chavvah had not yet conceived enough children. They were to accomplish much more before their demise. But from a spiritual perspective, the higher meaning, they surely did die (temporarily). And of course, that was the greater goal of the deceiver. If he could get Adam to sin, God's creation would appear a failure. Also, from him and through him, sin would be perpetuated; which as far as HaSatan knew, would put creation in an unrecoverable state. (I believe HaSatan had a general overview of the purpose of creation, as deduced from Matthew 8:29, which may partly explain his actions.) Perhaps HaSatan wanted in on something, for which he was not intended. But he could never have conceived of Immaculate Conception, or deity level self-sacrifice. Abba always has a winning plan!

Con #3, in 3:5, "For God knows that in the day you eat from it your eyes will be opened, and you will be like God, knowing good and evil." Actually all true! And that's exactly what happened.

Now keep in mind, death had not manifested evidence as of yet. Therefore, it's possible that this is another support for believing this drama occurred shortly after creation. If God said, "Touch or Eat and die," how could HaSatan come along and just say, "Nope, ain't gonna happen!" and have it be believed? Death was incomprehensible! Not all the ramifications for disobedience are. Often they are not. That does not render them unjust though. Nor does it demonstrate ignorance as license for law-breaking.

We Fall Down

The ploy through which deception gets accomplished, in the spiritual realm as well as in the physical, is via the taking of a lie and repackaging it to appear as something true, valid, or authentic. To do that, truth has to be the wrapping paper. Nobody would ever believe a blatant lie. Certainly, if it was understood to be a lie from the beginning, it either had to be appealing enough to consider, or completely misunderstood. HaSatan uses both tactics. He masquerades as an angel of light, but he is

Destiny and Desire

kness. How many lives has he destroyed with these lies: "This one ̣a of heroin won't kill you!" or, "You won't get a disease from ̍ou don't need protection." or, "It's just a date. I love my wife and ᴀ..., ̣ I really enjoy being with this woman. She just makes me feel special and desired." Sure, the odds are that you won't die. But again, it's our spiritual lives we are talking about here! There are no favorable enough odds! The fact we let him convince us to gamble with the only eternal thing we possess is quite telling, and disconcerting.

HaSatan works on us by breaking down the boundaries that would ordinarily keep us sheltered and on track. If he can't change the rules, because they are "written in stone," then he will attempt to strip us of their memory, or cause us to believe they have no authority over us. Then bam! Just like that, we fall. If HaSatan can't strip us of our intentions to obey, then he'll simply strip us of our understanding of how to do it. It makes perfect sense really. There are those among us who preach that we will *only* be judged against the backdrop of our conscience, and that currently there are no active stipulations to receiving the blessings promised in our covenant relationship with God, except having faith. What do you think? How were Adam and Chavvah judged? They certainly believed in God. They had one, single mitzvah (law) to obey. If they were judged only for their act, in relation to the severity of its offense, I would say God was extraordinarily unjust. They just ate a little non-kosher fruit; I mean...come on! And, if they were judged for their conscience alone, I would say the same thing. I believe they knew it was wrong, but had no idea of the extent. What I am proposing here is that the law, "Do not eat!" became part of the evidence required for conviction. It was the part that had to be obeyed in order for them to remain in a state of innocence. That law was weightier as evidence than the partially eaten fruit itself. Without that law officially stated it would seem that their conscience alone would not have had the capacity to create the desire to be rebellious.

...for sin, taking an opportunity through the commandment, deceived me and through it killed me. So then, the Law is holy, and the commandment is holy and righteous and good. (Romans 7:11 & 12)

And similarly, the obedience of that law, no matter how insignificant, would have avoided a truly severe judgment. The judgment did more than bring about their ultimate death. It impacted their and our lives as well, both physically and spiritually, and all of creation too.

As far as physically, it affected their lifestyle as well as their environment. They had to work the land, and the land would work against them. The very scenery of their habitation would lose some of its splendor. True pain was introduced into childbirth. The relationship of man vs. beast would change, and more. But the over-all, most terrible part of the judgment would be the change of communion between man and his maker. The intimacy of their walking together in the garden would then shift to intermittent contacts as needed. And that basically remained true throughout the process of the world being populated, annihilated, repopulated, and still continues right through to today.

Adam and Chavvah, it would seem, were "born again" when they watched the slaughter of the animals on their behalf, grieved over the cost of their transgression (law-breaking), and asked for forgiveness from the first acting High Priest. Although it is not portrayed in Genesis (Hebrew: *bereshit*, beginnings), it is safe to presume that during this first sacrifice Adam and Chavvah were also instructed on how they and future generations would then have to perform this act for themselves, from then on. Their knowledge of this would have always been on the forefront of their minds, as they contemplated obedience vs. disobedience during the remainder of their lives.

Specifically, we are not told of other pre-Mosaic, mitzvoth (plural form of mitzvah [command]) Adam was subject to. Due to the fact that Adam, Chavvah, and their soon coming children would now know evil, there would absolutely need to be some boundaries set. For, because of the fall and its effect on creation, not all that was perfect and good remained that way. Surely, if in a perfect paradise and pre-sinful state there was a law, for fallen civilization there would have to be plenty more. That just stands to reason. So looking back to the very beginning of time, the need for instruction has been established as always necessary for the creation called man. Let's now think of these commands as boundaries.

In retrospect, how do you feel about my presenting a case suggesting Adam and Chavvah being destined to fall? Does it make you uncomfortable? Does it fly in the face of your conception of God somehow? "...for they stumble because they are disobedient to the word, and to this *doom* they were also appointed (1st Peter 2:8b)." Out of context or not, Peter conceived of such things. Is it possible that some of your seeming-to-be troubles in life are the result of failed tests that were allowed to be put before you by the Lord Himself, with advanced knowledge of the outcome? Tests that you *could* have passed, but didn't? It is truly something to contemplate isn't it? Even if so, however, your failures in no way diminish God's love. God still loved Adam and Chavvah.

What if your failure ultimately becomes God's success though? What if your failure was required to better create the opportunity to express His love and patience and mercy towards you? Would that make you feel better? It does me! What if all the commands (boundaries) given

Destiny and Desire

to us by God, were designed and given to man to create the same opportunity for us to know Him that way? Wouldn't that make His *commandments* a gift to us and not a curse? Yes, it would. Did the Lord curse Adam and Chavvah by telling them not to eat the forbidden fruit? No, He didn't! Now, what you might be thinking is, "But James 1:13 & 14 says God doesn't tempt anyone, we are tempted by our own lusts and desires." Yes, and these verses also need to be taken into consideration.

You shall not listen to the words of that prophet or that dreamer of dreams; for the LORD your God is 'testing' you to find out if you love the LORD your God with all your heart and with all your soul. (Deuteronomy 13:3)
You shall remember all the way which the LORD your God has led you in the wilderness these forty years, that He might humble you, 'testing' you, to know what was in your heart, whether you would keep His commandments or not. (Deuteronomy 8:2)

The Hebrew word for 'test', and the Greek word for 'tempt' are practically identical in meaning. When it comes to God, He can do nothing sinful, right? So in Him, the line of demarcation between temptation and testing is in the motivation. He does not tempt! But He sure does test. And since He writes the examining questions, He can even make them extremely difficult to answer, if He so desires. He created the opportunity for sin, but did not sin in doing so. Likewise, He has all privilege and authority to place a test in front of us He knows in advance that we'll fail. Foreknowledge is not forced-knowledge.

Deeper thought: If Adam and Chavvah were being tempted by God, then James is a liar. So that can't be. If Adam and Chavvah lusted for knowledge, or coveted the powers of God, and that drove them to eat the fruit, they had already failed the test before they wrote their name in the upper, right-hand corner. And that would then be the actual, first moral transgression. If God 'tested' them beyond what they could handle (as a superficial examination would support), then Paul lied. Remember, "...we are tempted by our own lusts and desires."

In the original Greek, the words 'lust' and 'desire' are not both present in the verse, just 'epithumia', which *can* mean both. The 'desire' is negatively associated with the lust. However, because the laws to not covet or lust had not yet been written, they could not be formally found guilty of them; nor was that likely their downfall anyway. "For apart from the law, sin is dead (Romans 7:8)." HaSatan is the tempter, not our Abba! God was the tester, the prover. HaSatan's motivations are to cause us to sin, with the purpose to destroy us. God tests to refine and improve. It might seem like semantical double-talk, but it's truly all in the details.

This might be a theological thorn in some of your sides, but it's a good time to bring up an essential understanding. Because of the interchangeability of 'test' and 'tempt' as the meaning behind the Greek word *peirazo*, there is a significant ramification in some famous portions of Scripture.

"Jesus went into the desert for 40 days to be *tested* by the devil" is a perfectly viable translation. "He was tested in all ways such as we," is likewise. It has always struck me odd that some of Jesus's followers want to support the idea that He could have sinned, but didn't. In my mind, the 'Impeccability of Christ' is a no-brainer. If He could have sinned then, what's to say He cannot sin *now?* I don't need to 'feel' like Jesus could have sinned to bring Him down to a more relational level with myself. I believe Jesus was a fleshly vessel for God. And although it's difficult to accept that divinity needed to have diaper changes, I submit He could not sin. Period! He felt the pain of hunger and sorrow; but He did nothing, nor spoke anything, outside the Father's will. If it was the Father's will for Him to be the sinless, spotless Lamb, how could He have sinned? To logically prove my point, try imagining if He accidentally had. And to further establish this fact, I present to you Psalm 95:9.

(NASU) "When your fathers <u>tested</u> Me, they tried Me, though they had seen My work."

(KJV) "When your fathers <u>tempted</u> me, proved me, and saw my work."

(YLT) "Where your fathers have <u>tried</u> Me, have proved Me, yea, have seen My work."

Jesus came as the second Adam, and passed the tests the first Adam failed. Have you ever noticed their tests were essentially the same? Comparing the desert and the garden varieties, presented thematically they look like this:

Adam's Test 1: HaSatan purports, "You can't trust the words you think you heard."

Adam responds, "Yeah, I can digest your words."

Jesus's Test 1: HaSatan proposes, "You can't honestly think you are The Word!"

Jesus responds, "I will eat only my Father's bread of life!"

Adam's Test 2: HaSatan states, "You won't eat and die!"

Adam responds, "Okay. Down the hatch!"

Jesus's Test 2: HaSatan says, "You won't jump and die."

Jesus reflects, "Exactly. I'm going to the tree."

Adam's Test 3: HaSatan asks, "Don't you want all knowledge and power?"

Adam responds, "Yes! I think I would."

Destiny and Desire

Jesus's Test 3: HaSatan asks, "Don't you want all you can see?" Jesus counters, "Nope! Absolutely not *your* way!"

I'm pretty confident God doesn't have a lust or desire problem. I consider it an impossibility for Him to have been able to sin for another reason as well. Jesus Himself raised the bar of righteousness even higher than Moses did during His Sermon on the Mount (Matthew 5). He taught sin occurs at the thought level. If Jesus gave serious consideration to HaSatan's temptations in the desert, according to His own standards, He was a sinner. Let's get back on track now.

If you are (or plan to become) a parent, would you ever suggest that the highest form of love you could show your children would be to give them anarchy? Would at any time, the idea of having a rule-free environment in your home, sound potentially constructive? I ask you as reasonable people, why do we go to such great lengths to adopt and defend a practically rule-free, autonomous faith? How did we get to the place where presumably the highest form of spiritual maturity is found where specific codes of conduct are the least needed?

A Moral Constitution

The premise that "law" is bad and "grace" is good is hopelessly false. There has never been a civilly decent and prosperous society that did not require governance by rules. The vehicle for any country's success as a society is its adherence to a moral constitution. Its basic construct is an outline of initial suppositions labeled 'articles'. Each article is then broken down into the particulars, as to how to enforce and enact the articles, with amendments and subsections. If these subsections were not clearly expressed, you would ultimately have a covenant of notions, which by themselves would be weak to institute virtuous, human conduct. [Point to ponder: Ironically, it is the freest nation in the world, which has the most laws governing it.] Looking at the text of Mark 12:28-31, Jesus, when asked this test question by a scribe, "What is the greatest commandment?" answered in this way: He cited from the "Sh'ma" (Israel's Declaration of Monotheism), and then He cited the passages of Deuteronomy 6:5 and Leviticus 19:18.

And Jesus answered him, "The first of all the commandments *is*, Hear, O Israel; The Lord our God is one Lord: "AND YOU SHALL LOVE THE LORD YOUR GOD WITH ALL YOUR HEART, AND WITH ALL YOUR SOUL, AND WITH ALL YOUR MIND, AND WITH ALL YOUR STRENGTH. The second is this, YOU SHALL LOVE YOUR NEIGHBOR AS YOURSELF." There is no other commandment greater than [these]." (Note: 'these' are considered unified and inseparable.)

May I ask you a confrontational question? It is true that these commandments were expressed in various ways and at different times throughout Scripture; but, since they weren't expressed back-to-back (actually years apart), was the first not in force until the second was clearly given? Or was the second unnecessary until the first was given?

These laws (mitzvoth) are what the Law (Moses) and the Prophets hang upon (Matthew 22:40). That means, if you remove love from the law equation, everything goes out of balance. That also means love is the central and pivotal point on which the Law hinges. If God's universal government was a house, love would be its foundation. I will take it one step further and say that these mitzvoth were actually in force before they were ever written onto stone or papyrus. These Royal Mitzvoth were in force for Adam and Chavvah. They are part of our spiritual Bill of Rights; infused into our unalienable humanity. They are inherently woven into our relationship with the One who gave us the force of love.

As humans, we desire to both love and be loved. The first piece of legislation was to not eat of the tree in the center of the garden. You shall love your neighbor, and Me (God), and you shall demonstrate your love by not eating of this one tree (obeying), for that (disobeying) would ultimately affect our relationship and all your offspring. Let me further support this concept. If the instruction to love the Lord and our neighbor were not in force before Moses declared it, then all the people who were judged by the flood, were murdered by the Lord with no justification. After all, there were no rules to follow, right? Wrong! Look here:

I will multiply your descendants as the stars of heaven, and will give your descendants all these lands; and by your descendants all the nations of the earth shall be blessed; because Abraham obeyed Me and kept My charge, My commandments, My statutes and My laws. (Genesis 26:4 & 5)

Remember Paul taught us that we are also accountable to our conscience. Whether we have ever read the Scriptures or not, the Lord has placed a capacity within us to recognize the need for righteousness. Righteous<u>ness</u> is right doing and right standing. Although this is unquestionable, this verse regarding Abraham's obedience goes beyond conscience. Abraham received instruction from both the Lord Himself, and through the wisdom and basic precepts passed down from Adam, through to Noah and beyond.

Without defining love, and having practical instruction by which to express it, there will be chaos. Without defining love for our neighbor, a deranged version of "love" could be demonstrated by rape, or theft, or murder. Some pretty horrific things have been done in the names of gods, and as an expression of "love" for them. Without defining love for the

Destiny and Desire

Lord, "affection" could be demonstrated by child sacrifice, temple prostitution, gluttonous feasting and debauchery. And by the way, it was.

It is very easy to see that the concept of "law" being a crippling burden, or unnecessary, can only be applied to manufactured religion, and not to the moral and ethical standards given to us by the Lord. The first law was a do or die instruction. Was that unfair of the Lord to set such a demand before them? Would it have been more or less loving to have not told them at all about the off-limit tree? That law was just as much an expression of the Lord's love as all of His laws were/are. Love always requires boundaries, to establish a hedge of protection. Structure and boundaries are always necessary to uphold an environment capable of perpetuating goodness and peace.

Yet, there is always a perversion to guard against. This same need for law, if corrupt and outside the confines of holy love, can and will promote oppression and slavery. An overabundance of unnecessary law, or law that is written to crush the will and freedom of man, is indeed a burden and not true love. Law written by man to serve man is susceptible to being manipulated to the advantage of the legislator. Allow me to creatively illustrate, through a couple, angled examples.

A "big-boned" man (whose god was his stomach) that governed over a small village established a law that stated, "Due to the limited amount of agricultural resources available, all common citizens of our village will from this point forth be limited to diets totaling fifteen hundred calories. All harvests gathered will be brought to the storehouses on my estate, and I will distribute each day the portion appropriate for your size family. By doing this, we will insure the survival of our people."

Although this law, on the surface, could possibly make sense, it was actually and unknowingly created to ensure Mr. Big Bones would have first access to all the food. And since he did not consider himself "common," he could have all he wanted. This law, though on the surface appearing reasonable, was not motivated by nor did it contain loving intentions. Mr. Big Bones justified this law by its potential validity, not by its necessity. This analogy demonstrates that, like so many things, the true motivations behind legislation are often (though not always) factors in assessing whether they are truly "good".

Person #1 is traveling at 55 mph in a 55 mph zone and will never get a ticket for speeding. Person #2 is traveling 75 in a 55 mph zone, gets caught in a speed trap and not only pays a fine, but is at enmity with the law now. The legislator (God) wrote the law to save the lives of people; but the lawbreaker (Sinner) doesn't consider that until the officer (Spirit) expresses it. The law is both righteous and condemning at the same time. Might you even say that person #1 is blessed, and that the fact the law was written shows a gracious intent toward all who drove on that road?

The Laws of God are not evil. They are rules established to protect and preserve us from personal loss and pain. The very first command was given to establish God's authority over creation, and plainly state His desire for us (to not know evil). And it was *good*. It was intended to keep us close to Him, where He could commune openly with us, and reveal Himself to us. Any rules established thereafter were done so with the same intent. But this time, they were composed around the reality that perfection was outside our grasp, and that evil inclination (Adamic nature; known within Judaism as the *yetzer ha-ra*) was now inside our minds. Considering these laws were issued by God, how can we conceive of them having ill motivations? We cannot. He told the Hebrews to gather a certain amount of manna only, but was that because He wanted to horde the rest for Himself? I'll let you answer that.

Prior to beginning my final presentation of this chapter, I need to bind up any wounds that may have potentially been created through lack of understanding. Before you discard all possibility that God had anything to do with Adam and Chavvah's fall, you must be also willing to reject the truth of Deuteronomy chapter thirteen. It is there we discover that God intended to send false prophets into the camp, to test the Israelite's commitment and love. The Israelites followed suit and failed equally in their obedience, in several cases culminating in the loss of life. God knew that would happen in advance. How is that any different? He didn't desire them to fail! Jesus was slain before the foundations of the Earth were laid. Not for chance, but for planned necessity.

An Allegorical Reality

Here is my reasoning on an age-old question: It's both. The trees and their fruit were both real. The garden was real. The serpent was real. But, it was also an amazing and beyond genius, allegorical drama that was fully purposed to reveal the divine plan, and to teach us that things that happen on Earth are conceived in Heaven, and things that occur in Heaven are reflected on Earth. The Garden scene laid a foundation for life, for every generation thereafter.

The Tree of Life represents perfection (as righteousness, demonstrated by Jesus). The Tree of the Knowledge of Good and Evil represents the mixing of what is good with disobedience. They initially had unrestricted access to the Tree of Life. They could eat of it whenever they wanted, and were encouraged to do so. Prior to the fall, they were immortal. As perfect beings, maintaining perfect obedience to His instruction, they would have lived forever. We, if capable of perfect obedience, would be immortal too. But we are born into sinfulness and therefore cannot, and are not. That option no longer remains.

Destiny and Desire

After the fall, perfect obedience was no longer possible. So immortality was blocked from us—colorfully illustrated by the guard of the two Cherubim with flaming swords, appointed after the banning. Have you ever noticed that we were not blocked from the other tree, the one that caused all our grief? That's because we still have full access to it. We still have the "free will" to eat of it upon our choosing. We "became like them, knowing good and evil," and that was never revoked. Our recognition of (and contention with) both righteousness and all things less than was imparted to us. But there was no way we were going to be allowed to maintain immortality with our fallen state. Don't misunderstand me. God is not fallen because we are "like Him." Familiarity with evil does not make one evil, but that knowledge in the hands of fallen man is too volatile to be left unchecked.

Where else do we see such a sword? It proceeds from the mouth of the Righteous Judge upon His return. It is a two-edged sword, powerful enough to separate soul and spirit. It is His instruction. There is no way to avoid it, especially if attempting to sneak past the Cherubim.

John 10:9, "I am the door; if anyone enters through Me, he will be saved, and will go in and out and find pasture."

His Word swings to and fro, and so will judge us all. Some get back into Paradise, and some will undergo everlasting destruction.

We, as believers, will have unguarded access to the Tree of Life again...eventually. Actually, we can taste of it now, but we are not allowed to have our fill. We just have a sampling. We are caught in a paradox, whereby we are allowed to know spiritual satiation, yet we continue to hunger and thirst for righteousness.

Here lies the allegorical reality: He is the Bread of Life. He is the River of Life. He is the Tree of Life. He is our Righteousness. He is *The Life!* Just like the way Jesus is also "The Word" now, He was "The Word" then. Jesus represented the Father on Earth. The Tree of Life represented His will in the garden. In clear contrast is HaSatan, cloaking himself so as to disguise what and who he really is...a hideous liar. He had to borrow a garment of scaled flesh, and has spent his existence seducing man into believing that good is better when mixed with evil. Suggesting God's commandments are negotiable is also quite seductive.

In Eden, we had perfect intimacy with Him. We *yada* "knew" Him. We "partook" of Him. By eating of the 'other tree', we were unfaithful to Him. We *knew* of something else because we succumbed to its temptation. That *other* tree's sole purpose was to prove our love and devotion to the first tree. It represented the mingling of the profane with the holy. I'll even go so far as to say, it's quite possible that the knowledge they obtained from the off-limits tree was little more than that the first tree was so much better. Like in our human marriages, just one taste of the forbidden is all it takes to put separation and death into motion. "Sin *tastes* good for a season." For all we know, any other knowledge they gained that day, besides sin and shame, was available to come to them eventually. But it was supposed to be distributed on His terms, by His timing and for His purposes. Their increase of knowledge was not their biggest problem.

A special people were given a special land, and were given a special law to obey. They broke the law, got scattered from their land, and lost the fullness of blessing. Sacrifices were required to cover their transgressions. They had to toil throughout their lives. They lost intimacy with the Gardener. Does any of this ring a bell? What happens to the fathers, happens to the children. Selah.

Before the throne of God and the Lamb, there is "a tree of life whose leaves are for the healing of the nations (Revelation 22)." Can you think of what it is that's going to cause this healing to happen? It is the will of the Lord finally being universally adhered to. It is the instruction into all righteousness being perfectly obeyed. Were you able to catch the fact that this time though, it's the leaves and not the fruit that is mentioned as having the power? Maybe it's as simple as the leaves represent shade or protection. Or, perhaps, it's as fantastic as the allegorical reality that though leaves were once used to cover shame, being the restorative kind of God He is, it will now be leaves that heal our shame.

The fruit that this tree bears every single month, faithfully, with no regards to season, we will have our fill of it. We will live forever gathering it. I'll bet that one of those twelve fruits it bears is a fig. Maybe, it just might be that simple.

Destiny and Desire

3

Conduct Becoming

A long time ago, there was a visionary who formed a corporation, which up until that day was unlike any business structure previously conceived. One of the truly unique characteristics of its development was seen in the way he set out to find employees. He didn't advertise job postings in the traditional sense, but started out looking for them on his own, by simply observing the world around him. If someone caught his attention, he would get theirs.

Even after a good, long go of it, the company continually struggled to grow and the prospect pool seemed to evaporate away. For a while, the boss only had a handful of faithful employees. Because of their history, and his commitment to them, he decided to keep them on board as he made the tough decision to dissolve the company and reorganize.

Over time, the new company slowly grew out of its former slump. Once it reached a certain size, he developed a human resources team to do the recruiting for him. The boss found a couple of nobodies, stuck in a dead end job somewhere and raised them up to head the division. I don't know what the boss was thinking, but he got the idea that going to a local labor pool would be a great place to get the help he needed to kick off the next phase of growth. It was the strangest thing though. You'd think a labor pool would be a good place to go, but the operator of that company just gave them the hardest time, and wouldn't give their laborers up. After a pretty persuasive argument, that company relented, and thus the boss had a huge resource of people to draw from.

Conduct Becoming

Up until this point, few had ever really gotten to know the boss. So, he felt it was time to reveal himself, and in so doing, finish up his part in the interview process. He gathered all the candidates together in the basement of a huge convention center and declared to them who he was, what his intentions were, and what it would mean to accept a position in this company. If you read the minutes from that meeting, you'd surely think that nobody would have rejected the offer, so profound was it. On paper, it seems that the majority of them did verbally accept; but over the next 38 years or so, time proved otherwise.

It seems that the boss had given to the HR team an employee handbook to distribute to everyone interested. At first, he tried to teach it himself, but the people thought it less intimidating to get it from HR instead. Unfortunately, it appears that they thought the book was not mandatory reading, and that somehow they would be able to figure out on their own how to function, and get promoted within the organization. The result of that attempt was they all ended up tragically dying before they ever saw their retirement packages kick in.

HR was told that as they were to look for employees who might be interested, to never cherry-pick based on someone's background, education or experience, and that they must be equal-opportunity employers. The boss was very specific about this, and became quite upset when he heard of potential candidates who had been passed over for one of these reasons.

The company was about to go into another expansion mode, and so the boss sent his HR team to further clarify some parts of the procedural guidelines that were written in the handbook. He gathered everyone together again and made it crystal clear that what they were hearing then, as well as all the rest of the handbook, was to be read and followed exactly. He even went so far as to share the designs for the new corporate office. That way, the employees would be inspired, the company would run smoothly, everyone would prosper, and other companies would observe their success and hopefully desire to merge. He then further expanded the HR team to be able to handle the imminent influx that would soon occur from any further expansion.

(Actually, the boss had instituted several major agreements with the employee unions over the years, and they all continued to require the same level of commitment to the boss's orders as any previous one did. He didn't change the handbook at all, for he had said all that needed to be said. He was pleased with his design, and now it was up to the employees to decide where they wanted to go with the company.) Yet, when you leave critical areas of a company in amateur hands, problems inevitably arise. So the company ended up splitting in half. One covered the Northern region; the other…the Southern.

The success of the company ebbed and flowed over time, until one day, the company's key ambassador ended up dying. This of course left a power vacuum, and although most of the employees knew what their duties were at that point, the company was vulnerable to hostile takeover. At times, many read the book and the company did well. At other times, they forgot the regulations and the company struggled. Over the years, as times changed and societal influences weighed heavily upon the company's policies, people concluded that the handbook had become outdated, and in some areas, obsolete. Many concluded the boss's first edition wasn't modern enough.

Now, unlike a traditional corporation, the HR department was the largest and most powerful division, because turnover was unfortunately a bit higher than it should have been. HR was also the first area everyone promoted in the company found themselves going. A new entrant into this division was given a quick rundown on operations.

Once a potential candidate was approached and found to be interested, they would then be given an appointment to go through a very unusual interviewing process; although the candidate would not know it had actually already previously begun. What dumbfounded the candidates the most was as they began their actual interview, as is customary, they were asked for their resume. But as soon as it was grasped by the hand of the interviewer, it was crumpled into a ball and tossed right into the can.

The interviewer was then required to explain that the company was not interested in anything related to what the candidate thought they could bring to the table. They were then told that it was a ground-floor opportunity, into an entry-level position, and that is exactly how everybody starts out. Nobody comes in at middle management, or executive level positions. The benefits were "out of this world". Yet, being an internship, there will be no salary. In many cases, that was enough to get people to rise up and walk away.

Here and there, someone would at least stick around and hear more about the opportunity. The HR person would then explain (if they were doing their job appropriately) that once they came on board, their life and future would never be the same. They would have to sell everything they had, and in order to remain with the company they would have to dedicate their whole life along the way. This was typically the point in the interview where candidates started to become fidgety.

After the ambassador died, it seems like many thought it was a good time for everyone to do things their own way. They could explain things about the company and the boss from their own perspective. After all, if they weren't against it, they were for it. He never desired them to stop following the manual, but he couldn't really force them. At the beginning, at least in most cases, they didn't stray too far. Sometimes their

Conduct Becoming

description of the employment experience was far from reality. But then tragedy struck, corporate headquarters burned down, and from that point on, people just worked out of their homes and/or opened regional offices all over the known world.

Candidates who decided to accept the job had to first shadow another employee. They often arrived their first day with a wagon or pick-up full of junk, supplies, and equipment from their previous employment. It was a very emotional and personally challenging experience to watch their 'stuff' be taken from them and brought to the landfill. Some people downright refused to let the past go, and jumped back into the driver's seat and sped off. Others just wept and beat their chest. Everybody was forced to start with nothing, but was given a nice, new, white uniform to start work in. Now here's where the story gets simply odd.

Once you got started, you were free to do whatever you wanted. You could attend the employee meetings, or not. You could punch out at the time of your own choosing. At least, that's what some proclaimed. You could read the manual you were handed, or you could read somebody else's Cliff Notes. People would regularly stand on the entry steps of their very impressive edifice and shout their interpretation of the manual. Crowds would gather and confusion would ensue. Some manager types had commentaries for sale they had written, that looked pretty extensive. It was rather chaotic really.

More and more as the days went on, the original intent of the manual's text was heavily debated. In some cases, context was downright rejected. Some shouted, "Loving the boss and the employees is all that matters!" Others saw it as a corporation whose success rested solely on adherence to rules and regulatory bylaws. If you were sensitive enough, you could really pick up the bitterness, jealousy and confusion in the staff. There was so much debate. New recruits would show up to training and see a heated argument and that was enough to turn some people away. Others listened to the arguments, and figured if the people who had been around a while are still not sure what they're doing, what hope did they themselves have? It was very discouraging at times, and the Boss would look down at the crowds from his lofty vantage point, and just shake his head.

If people chose to stay on, and they had obtained their security clearance and started to inquire about, they'd discover that there were about a dozen, big, regional offices. Although they were all decorated a little bit differently, they all had some things in common. They all had strange architecture with multiple halls and confusing doors. But they all had a big sign on the main foyer wall, just above the reception counter that read: Welcome to the Kingdom! Here you will find some 33,000 ~~Directions, Persuasions, Opinions,~~ Diversions to get to the Boss's Desk.

Only One Easy Way - Have a Blessed Day! Next to the big sign always stood a quiet and cute little girl holding a sign of her own. It read, "You can follow me." If you approached her and asked her for specifics, she was trained to just look at you, giggle and reply, "Do what *His* manual says, silly!" From what I understand, they are still standing there today, and they look incredible for their age.

So what was one to do? What door would one take? What hall walked down? Whose interpretation of the manual accepted? I often wonder why the crowds were not dispersed by security. That would have made things very much nicer. So many possibilities. So much freedom to choose.

Let's think back to Mr. Big Bones. Whoever controls the food (knowledge of the law) controls the behavior (adherence to the law). Whoever translates the law (HR), or removes the law (Handbook), is the one who dictates the level of submission by those they have influence over. But the original law itself, and its original intent, in its original context, is not annulled by ignorance or misunderstanding. This is such an important concept to grasp, because if the Sinai-given Law, or intent and will of God (through Moses) has been altered or distorted, we need to work diligently to find out what the Boss still wants.

The Demandments

The sum of Your word is truth, and **every one** of Your righteous ordinances is **everlasting.** (Psalm 119:160)

For truly I say to you, until heaven and earth pass away, **not the smallest letter or stroke shall pass** from the Law until all is accomplished. (Matthew 5:18)

<u>Whoever then annuls</u> one of the **least** of these commandments, and teaches others *to do* the same, shall be called least in the kingdom of heaven; but <u>whoever keeps and teaches</u> them, he shall be called **great** in the kingdom of heaven. (Matthew 5:19)

Look very closely at this last verse for a second. Take your time. Read it again. What is Jesus saying? What "commandments" is He talking about? Is He saying we should not eat of the tree; that the tree still remains somewhere and to leave it alone? Well, we covered that concept. Plus, I think the two, flaming-sword-bearing Cherubim will take care of that. You know...the ones who went from guarding a Tree, to guarding the Mercy Seat. How absolutely fitting that abundant life found through obedience in the garden, would then become abundant life found through obedience in the desert.

Is He referring only to the two greatest commands, as previously cited? Well, if the two are inseparable, which one is the least? If you

Conduct Becoming

choose the "loving your neighbor" portion, because it appears *lesser* than the "loving God" portion, you are missing the clear impossibility of being able to love Him without action. Remember, you can't love God and hate your neighbor/brother. What about this verse disputably understood as pertaining to *only* the 'two Greatest'?

John 14:15, "If you love Me, you will keep My commandments."

Wouldn't Jesus be a bit redundant in saying, "If you love me... you will love me."

Perhaps He is referring only to the first, "formal" commandments, the ten written on tablets of stone. Well, that seems reasonable. So let's follow that line. The first five of the ten laws are summed up by the first of the two greatest. The second five of the ten laws are summed up by the second of the two greatest. Which one is okay to annul then? Which group of five of the 'ten in stone' is no longer to be complied with? If, as some say, we are only currently accountable to the two greatest, are they the only two that when not obeyed, qualify as sin? Now there is a recipe for disaster. Talk about a perpetual sin condition! What kind of loving God would tell His children to obey His commandments or die, but not tell us how?

What's interesting is that in one breath, some spiritual leaders teach we are not under the weight of the "old" law, but in another, they tell us we are to follow the "spirit" of it. That sounds spiritual enough, but is that what Jesus said? No, it's not even close to anything He said. But He certainly should have if that's our requirement. That becomes like undecipherable double talk when held against the Ten Commandments. How does one "not kill" only in spirit, but not by the letter?

If you, reader, consider yourself a Christian, how do you view the Ten Commandments? Are they bondage for you? Are you accountable to them at all? Or, are they just the original articles read sometimes for nostalgia, a.k.a. the ten suggestions? Maybe they are like the liberal American's view of the Constitution—it being a living, evolving document that changes its meaning through the moral climate and interpretation of culture. As I look upon the list of ten, I struggle to figure out what parameters *we* should set, to help us assess which ones to obey, and not to obey. Why? Because there is no exclusively "cultural" or "socio-economical" or "traditional" or "Levitical" or "ceremonial" or "sacrificial" or "oral" aspect, to any of them. They transcend them all. Yes, they are also our moral constitution; but they stand strong, and are not to be taken ala carte! One obvious clue as to why that is, is found within Scripture's terminology. Notice the difference between the start of the 20th and 21st chapters of Exodus.

20:1, "Then God spoke all these <u>words</u> (devarim), saying…" (Then follows the ten.)

21:1, "Now these are the <u>ordinances</u> (mishpatim) which you are to set before them…" (Then follows the rest.)

Classical Judaism has always given recognition to the difference, right from the beginning:

> Then Moses came and recounted to the people all <u>the words</u> of the LORD and all <u>the ordinances</u>; and all the people answered with one voice and said, "All the <u>words</u> which the LORD has spoken we will do!" (Exodus 24:3)

The last agreement they made is almost a prophetic faux pas, but that's off point. The Ten 'Devarim', (Hebrew for 'words'; usually translated 'commandments'; also the Hebrew name for the book of Deuteronomy) are believed to *not* have been originally titled commandments, or ordinances, or precepts, or mitzvoth, because these are the basic and fundamental requirements of existence. They are "above the Law." It could be said, that if one was to seriously *believe* the Ten Words, *obedience* to the rest of the laws would come naturally.

Here's the problem. Theologians have mistakenly deduced from the difference, a distinction leading to separation. From that silly and misguided…"Well, God personally wrote only "the Ten" with His finger, and man wrote down the rest. So we only have to adhere to the Ten…" viewpoint stems a whole slew of theological ramifications. For example, many sins aren't mentioned within the Ten that aren't mentioned by Jesus either. The reason God didn't write all of them down had nothing to do with the "inferiority" of the other 603. (Traditional Judaism recognizes 613 specific commandments in the Torah.) God only needed the *etched* Ten to create a *testimony*, or *witness*, which would be placed into the Ark by the same name. Those tablets were supposed to stand witness to the authenticity of the Sinai experience, as well as to the authority of all Moses would adjoin to them, in addition to their symbolism of permanence. They were never supposed to be an end-all! Plus, for Moses to walk down the mountain with enough stone tablature to fit the rest, he would have ended up dropping them due to weight, instead of anger, and that would clearly have made Charlton Heston's performance much less dramatic.

Okay. So far I have been a little soft on you. Are you ready for a twenty-five thousand dollar question? When Jesus died on the cross, did He take the Ten Commandments down to the grave with Him, along with many of the others that are presumed annulled? Or, are the Ten Commandments still in force? Remember line upon line, precept upon precept. You'd better think carefully before you answer. Because if He didn't, is it possible that there are more that are still in force? Are the Ten Commandments what are being spoken of, when Sha'ul the Pharisee (Paul of Tarsus) says in Romans 2:13, "For *it is* not the hearers of the Law *who* are just before God, but the doers of the Law will be justified." And in Romans 2:18, "...and know *His* will and approve the things that are <u>essential</u>, being instructed out of the Law," or not?

Could Paul be referring to more than just the "big" ten? If not, again I ask which mitzvoth are being spoken of? It certainly appears that there is some kind of law we are to obey, doesn't it? Contrary to consensus and unexamined opinion, the Ten are actually not an independent covenant within the greater "Law" (Deuteronomy 29:1). And if that's the case, isn't it possible that in the event we are not obeying these commands, that there could be negative consequences?

"Your iniquities have turned these away, and your sins have withheld good from you." (Jeremiah 5:25)

And following that thought pattern, what could those consequences be? Does disobedience cost us anything? Considering none of us have full-privilege access to the Garden in this life (thanks to disobedience), besides legal consequences, perhaps it effects what that entails: reduced intimacy in our relationship, and its fringe benefits.

You may have noticed that I bounce back and forth in my 'law' terminology (as I will do with other terms and names as well, for the sake of developing familiarity.) I have done that, in this case, because I want to express a point. Did the way I titled this section "Demandments" provoke a response from you? If God had called them that, would you feel more pressure to be accountable to them? Or, contrariwise, does your flesh resist adherence to those principles primarily because they have been labeled "commandments"? Nowhere in the Scriptures are those "Words" on stone labeled as the Ten Commandments. Reason being, it flows with the whole concept of...if you believe "He <u>is</u>" (the first 'Word'), you will believe His principles are "true" and His truth never changes.

The meanings, or in many cases, 'perceived' meanings of words, have a lot of influence on our interpretation, and therefore response, to everything from everyday dialogue, to more importantly, the Scriptures.

Many of us have, from the beginning of our walks, been taught to perceive the Law negatively. We have been taught that *grace* is the opposite of Law, and that grace is the better of the two. Because of this, the term 'Law' has a strong, negative connotation. That's very sad, because if more people were law-abiding, the world would be a much better place! Let's do a little re-educating, and start with a fresh definition of terms.

Torah

The word 'Law', as seen in traditional, English Old Testaments, is predominantly the word used to replace the Hebrew word 'torah', which I have already made mention of previously. Torah (toe-raw'), according to Strong's Hebrew Dictionary (#H3451) means: Precept or Statute, Law. Although James Strong has done a great service in producing concordances, he is only moderately acclaimed by the majority of linguistics scholars for his Greek and Hebrew exegetical skills. Let's try another authoritative source; in this case, the Bible's context itself.

Now the LORD said to Moses, "Come up to Me on the mountain and remain there, and I will give you the stone tablets with the law (torah) and the commandment (mitzvah) which I have written for their instruction (yarah). (Exodus 24:12)

Please receive instruction (torah) from His mouth and establish His words in your heart. (Job 22:22)

My son, do not forget my teaching (torah), But let your heart keep my commandments (mitzvoth). (Proverbs 3:1)

What I want you to see here, are the obvious multiple usages of the word torah, and how at different times translators choose which definition they feel best suits the context. Torah carries all three meanings and more. It is instruction, it is teaching, it contains precepts. It is law. It is found in the entirety of the Scriptures, but predominantly and traditionally it is understood to encompass the five books of Moses. It's the employee's guide to the kingdom corporation. However, even as defined as 'law', it is not exactly synonymous with the idea of a legislated rule, or dictatorial command, as it is construed today. Traditionally, the Hebraic definition of the word *torah* is 'teaching' or 'instruction'.

I want you to take special note of the word 'yarah' seen there in Exodus 24:12, which was translated into *instruction*. That is the root word for *torah*. It essentially means: To hit the mark, like an arrow hitting its target. Related to it, is the word 'chatah' (an important word we will further reckon with), which has essentially the opposite meaning of, "missing the mark." Torah then, is God's system for "hitting the mark". It is easy then to see how we "all have sinned and <u>fall short</u> of His glory." We are all like arrows falling short, and missing the target of perfection.

The form of government which presided over Israel, until the time of the judges, was called a theocracy; although, even during the time of the judges, they made their rulings based on theocratic principles. Because this theocracy was created, written, and enforced by God, there was no law that was free from its function being derived from a moral, ethical, or spiritual principle. For example, "you shall not murder" is not just a law in a legislative sense, but it has also been etched into the conscience of man by his Creator, as exampled by Cain's response to God's inquiry of Abel's whereabouts, as being, simply wrong!

If that law (to not murder) was never written in stone, it would make no difference, for it would be inherently wrong and worthy of just and divine retribution. Cain murdered Abel long before the stone tablets came down from Mt. Sinai, and it was appropriately deemed an unrighteous act. Although, "you shall not murder" is a mitzvah punishable by death, it is also a moral principle, an instruction to maintain civility, and a teaching to encourage the recognition of the value of life. (Note: Cain was not given a death sentence, though he was worthy, because there was no written law and consequence. This establishes the principle that God intended the rule of law to be instituted upon His words, as equally as what was written on the heart.) Cain was shown mercy (spared death), but he was nonetheless guilty.

Romans 5:13, "...for until the Law sin was in the world, but sin is not imputed when there is no law."

Would it be appropriate to determine that the "new covenant" does not consider it necessary to abide by the law, instruction or teaching, "thou shalt not kill"? No, of course not! Therefore, when considering the whole law of Moses (further articles and subsections to the original) as being valid or invalid for today (which is different than, in force versus not in force), we must take into consideration the function of the law itself. What so many people just don't seem to realize is that even though the "ten" are "above the law," they are also inextricably interwoven.

If Moses had declared from the Mishkan (Tent of Meeting /Tabernacle): "You shall not remove your neighbor's tree from his yard, though its limbs over-shade your garden, without his permission. If you do, and your neighbor complains about it, he shall take up his cause with the heads of his tribe, and if you are found at fault, guilty of this unlawful deed, you shall not only replace the tree, but you shall plant for him another as well," would you now say that this "law" would be void solely *because* Jesus died on the cross?

Just Olde Laws

The reality is that many of the so-called "old laws" are very much like that last example. Some are simply a compilation of principled teachings that instruct us, in the event we do harm to our neighbor, to make sure they are appropriately compensated and we pay appropriate restitution. These would be an example of what are considered the

"Societal Property Right Laws" of the Israelites. Here is a full list of different kinds of laws we find in the Torah. There are laws regarding:

1. YHVH, His Name, and His dealings
2. His Torah itself; it's appropriation
3. Sign and Symbols of the Israelites
4. Prayer and Blessings
5. Love and Brotherhood
6. The Poor and Unfortunate
7. The Treatment of Gentiles (Both Foreigners and Sojourners)
8. Marriage, Divorce, and Family
9. Forbidden Sexual Relations
10. Times and the Seasons
11. Dietary Laws
12. Business Practices
13. Employees, Servants and Slaves
14. Sabbatical and Jubilee Years
15. The Court and Judicial Procedure
16. Injuries and Damages
17. Property and Property Rights
18. Criminal Laws
19. Punishment and Restitution
20. Prophecy
21. Idolatry, Idolaters, and Idolatrous Practices
22. Agriculture and Animal Husbandry
23. Clothing
24. Firstborn
25. Kohanim (Priesthood) and Levites
26. T'rumah (Wave/Heave Offerings), Tithes, and Taxes
27. The Temple, the Sanctuary and Sacred Objects
28. Sacrifices and Offerings
29. Ritual Impurity and Purity
30. Lepers and Leprosy
31. The King
32. Nazarites, and...
33. Wars

Many of you have never seen it presented in this light. These mitzvoth have obvious implications beyond your basic, "Thou shalt not steal"-like principles. And all are worthy of consideration for..."All Scripture is inspired by God and profitable for teaching, for reproof, for correction, for training in righteousness; so that the man of God may be adequate, equipped for every good work (2nd Timothy 3:16 & 17)."

Conduct Becoming

In the Torah, we are told not to have sexual relations with our parents. It is a transgression of the Law to do so. Is this still a valid law, or is it merely a democratically derived morality? Should we still consider this law right and just, even though it was first described as abhorrent behavior in the "Olde Law," or was it crucified too? It is not one of the Ten. Look back at those last verses again. Did you see the part about being "trained in righteousness"; how about the phrase, "all Scripture"? What was the Scripture during the time of the Apostle Paul's writings? You guessed it… the Torah (Moses), the Prophets and the Books of Wisdom; the very *teachings* we commonly find tuned-out today because of their "antiquity" and location. Apparently, Paul found more value in Moses than just historical reference.

Leviticus 18:5, "So you shall keep My statutes and My judgments, by which a man may live if he does them; I am the LORD."

If God tells people they can live through obedience to the statutes and judgments found within the Law, but the message we always hear preached is that we can't, what does that lead us to conclude? What kind of mixed message does that bring? Who are we to believe? There has to be different functions of the Law of God, than just to damn us into needing a savior.

As far as being "trained in righteousness" goes, doesn't our righteousness only come from Jesus? Aren't we incapable of any righteousness on our own? In a way, yes; only because our carnal nature left unrestrained would naturally rebel against His instruction. In a regenerated state though, empowered by the Holy Spirit, we desire to obey the Lord. Being declared righteous, in relation to status before the Lord, is different than doing righteousness (right deeds/good works). We can do righteousness! And how do we know we are obeying? We study Torah! Otherwise, as many unwittingly suggest, we wing it based on feelings and circumstances. Considering that the human heart is "more deceitful than all else, and is desperately sick" (Jeremiah 17:9), I would call that a risky venture. But trusting the Torah is like light unto our paths, because…

Your righteousness is an everlasting righteousness, and Your law (torah) is **truth.** (Psalm 119:142)

Jesus said to him (Thomas), "I am the way, and the **truth,** and the life; no one comes to the Father but through Me." (John 14:6)

The **law** of **truth** hath been in his (Levi) mouth, and perverseness hath not been found in his lips. In peace and in uprightness he walked with Me, and many he brought back from iniquity. (Malachi 2:6)

I would like to pull out a few specific verses out of the book of Leviticus, for you to examine and see whether you can conclude that these laws are no longer for us—as a modern, civilized, New Testament people.

18:18, "You shall not marry a woman in addition to her sister as a rival while she is alive, to uncover her nakedness."

18:22, "You shall not lie with a male as one lies with a female; it is an abomination."

18:23, "Also you shall not have intercourse with any animal to be defiled with it, nor shall any woman stand before an animal to mate with it; it is a perversion."

19:4, "Do not turn to idols or make for yourselves molten gods; I am the LORD your God."

19:10, "Nor shall you glean your vineyard, nor shall you gather the fallen fruit of your vineyard; you shall leave them for the needy and for the stranger. I am the LORD your God."

19:13a, "You shall not oppress your neighbor, nor rob *him*."

19:17, "You shall not hate your fellow countryman in your heart. You may surely reprove your neighbor, but shall not incur sin because of him."

19:26, "You shall not eat *anything* with the blood, nor practice divination or soothsaying."

19:31, "Do not turn to mediums or spiritists; do not seek them out to be defiled by them. I am the LORD your God."

19:32, "You shall rise up before the gray headed and honor the aged, and you shall revere your God; I am the LORD."

19:33, "When a stranger resides with you in your land, you shall not do him wrong."

Can anyone really believe these are just old laws? Here is another critical principle to accept: Jesus is the Torah personified! That's what He was telling Thomas when He declared to Him, "I am the Truth," and that's exactly what I'm telling you. If there is any more important revelation to grasp at some point in your walk, beyond accepting His Messiahship, I do not know what it is. Did Jesus keep Torah? Well, if He didn't, He transgressed God's Law, which by definition is sin.

1st John 3:4, "Everyone who practices sin also practices lawlessness; and sin is lawlessness."

That would make Him the ultimate personification of hypocrisy. After all, He wrote it! If keeping torah perfectly is what rendered Him perfect, and qualified Him as our acceptable sacrifice, and being that He is the "greatest" in the kingdom, what should be our aspiration for *doing* righteousness? It should be emulation of what He did. That is what "exceeds the righteousness of the Pharisees." It's not just about doing, it's about doing (obeying) with a heart of love. That's what disciples do. They strive to live like their Master.

I Double Dare You!

I've heard some pretty weak arguments against keeping commandments, but none could be shallower than saying we don't have to live like Jesus. Apples shouldn't fall far from their tree. I challenge anyone on this planet to show me any empirical evidence that Jesus didn't agree with, or follow Moses's instruction. If you can, I will throw my faith away and end my life because all will be lost. If Jesus was God's vessel of flesh, and He couldn't keep His own Law, then let's eat, drink, and be merry because we have nothing better to do with our meaningless lives. Not only that, but Jesus would have died on the cross **in vain**, and did it to atone for Himself as well, but failed! Selah.

Let's ponder something together. The Lord gave us teachings to learn from and obey. Anyone who understood them for what they were, praised them throughout Scripture. But let's say they were wrong and misguided. God's Word (including torah) comes and inhabits flesh and dwells among us. He then came to abolish the Law (Himself being the Lawgiver), so in order to do that He perfectly obeys it; yet while doing so, teaches His disciples not to because it's flawed. They ask Jesus,

"Why are you living hypocritically?"

He answers, "Well, it wouldn't be right for me to have made everyone before my coming live one way, and I live another."

They respond, "But shouldn't you live the way you want us to live, so we can see your example?"

"Do as I say, not as I do!"

"But you have not told us how to live differently than You!" one states.

He follows, "You have a point. Maybe I should have thought this thing out better before I came."

Perhaps He did not come "to abolish the Law or the Prophets...but to fulfill" them, after all (Matthew 5:17). What would that mean to us? Well, the first thing we should do is believe Him. Then, we should figure out what 'fulfill' means. According to Thayer's Greek Definitions, fulfill (*pleroo*, G4137) means to:

1) to make full, to fill up, I.e. to fill to the full; 1a) to cause to abound, to furnish or supply liberally; 1a1) I abound, I am liberally supplied; 2) to render full, I.e. to complete; 2a) to fill to the top: so that nothing shall be wanting to full measure, fill to the brim; 2b) to consummate: a number; 2b1) to make complete in every particular, to render perfect; 2b2) to carry through to the end, to

accomplish, carry out, (some undertaking); 2c) to carry into effect, bring to realization, realize; 2c1) of matters of duty: to perform, execute; 2c2) of sayings, promises, prophecies, to bring to pass, ratify, accomplish; **2c3) to fulfill, I.e. to cause God's will (as made known in the law) to be obeyed as it should be, and God's promises (given through the prophets) to receive fulfillment; Part of Speech: verb**

It *could*, in a really roundabout way mean 'end', although that word is strangely avoided in its isolated and narrowest form. Actually, the word 'end' is used somewhere else in relation to this, and it is the word 'telos'. Romans 10:4, "For Christ is the end (telos) of the law for righteousness to everyone who believes." But that word actually can mean goal, aim, or purpose. You'd never know that, if you read the Good News Bible's rendition…"For Christ has brought the Law to an end, so that everyone who believes is put right with God." Wow that's bad. I'm uncomfortable even displaying that here.

I'll pick out a couple other options. Since it cannot mean 'abolish' or a synonym thereof, nor can it mean 'terminate' because He did live it out, it must mean something more like: render perfect, or ratify, or fill to the fullest, or carry out, or to cause to abound. I'll take any of those really. But the most accurate definition would be the one that best reflects His actions in relation to the Torah.

I have another challenge for any takers. Show me one instance where Jesus directed anyone, at any time, to disobey original, scriptural torah. Surely, if He "had" to live it, but didn't want anyone else to have to anymore, He would have focused a lot of His energy on teaching against Moses. Yet, that's not what we see at all! Even after He healed people, He instructed them to go show themselves to the priest. That little, almost insignificant detail was a Torah instruction (Mark 1:41-44; cf. Leviticus 14)! The only times He ever taught against abidance to "laws" was when the law in question was an extraneous, enslaving example of the man-made variety. The only time it "appears" He was breaking torah, was when He was not yielding to the leaven of the Pharisees, or when He used a loophole to teach a lesson in torah misappropriation.[1] Go ahead; prove me wrong. I am generally open to the possibility, but in this case, I will not be found as such.

Here is a great example: A woman was caught in the act of adultery. She was brought before Jesus by some local leaders to set a trap for Him, in hopes to ensnare Him by His own words and prove Him to be the false prophet they so desperately desired Him to be. Torah teaches that someone caught in adultery is to be put to death, so they tested Jesus to see if He would condone the punishment. If He said no, He would be teaching against Torah, and would be declared a false prophet and condemned. If He said yes, they would have twisted Him into an enemy of the state, because it was against civil Roman law for Jewish citizens to impose the death penalty upon themselves.

So what does Jesus do? Since He knows the Law perfectly, being its author and all, He set them up to make it impossible for her to be *convicted* according to Torah, and never even had to answer to them. The Law requires that two or three witnesses be present in regards to a capital offense. It also requires a fair trial. Not only are there those stipulations, but it is the witnesses themselves that are required to throw the first stones; hopefully assuring that false testimony wouldn't take place. It's one thing to lie, it's certainly another to kill. So, Jesus simply has to get one of the accusers to back out and the case is closed for lack of evidence. Violà! Our Savior has always been pro-life! He is not out to get us! But He is a "Go and sin no more!" kind of Teacher. The wage for sin is death—as much today as it was one, three hundred, or six thousand years ago. He just happens to know when mercy is warranted and how to bestow it.

I pray that the Spirit would open your eyes to see this truth now, so that the rest of this book will be a true blessing to you. If you choose not to see this, you will continue to struggle in properly interpreting the Apostolic Scriptures (especially Paul's writings) in light of the earlier Hebrew Scriptures. Our God has not and will never contradict Himself, nor can He lie...

For I, the LORD, do not change; therefore you, O sons of Jacob, are not consumed. (Malachi 3:6)
Also the Glory of Israel will not lie or change His mind; for He is not a man that He should change His mind. (1 Samuel 15:29)

...nor will the original intent of the Scriptures change, considering Whom they're about. The Old will never contradict the New, and vice-versa, because the Word is the Word, all throughout the Scriptures! Whatever apparent conflicts are in the Scriptures are man's problem, not His. We need to work it out. We need to find resolution to the conflict. We must always build upon that foundational prerequisite.

Now He said to them, "these are My words which I spoke to you while I was still with you, that all things which are written about Me in the Law of Moses and the Prophets and the Psalms must be fulfilled." (Luke 24:44)
Philip found Nathanael and said to him, "We have found Him of whom Moses in the Law and *also* the Prophets wrote—Jesus of Nazareth, the son of Joseph." (John 1:45)
And the Word became flesh, and dwelt among us, and we saw His glory, glory as of the only begotten from the Father, full of **grace** and truth. (John 1:14)

In the Apostolic Scriptures, the Greek word for law is obviously different from in the Hebrew, although 'mitzvah' would have been the word Jesus used personally, since Hebrew/Aramaic was His native language. The earliest scribes/translators, when penning the word 'mitzvah', would have looked for its closest equivalent in Greek. They would most often have used the word, 'nomos'.

G3551; "nomos" Thayer Definition:
1) anything established, anything received by usage, a custom, a law, a command 1a) of any law whatsoever; 1a1) a law or rule producing a state approved of God; 1a1a) by the observance of which is approved of God; 1a2) a precept or injunction; 1a3) the rule of action prescribed by reason; 1b) of the Mosaic law, and referring, acc. to the context. Either to the volume of the law or to its contents; 1c) the Christian religion: the law demanding faith, the moral instruction given by Christ, especially the precept concerning love; 1d) the name of the more important part (the Pentateuch), is put for the entire collection of the sacred books of the OT. Part of Speech: noun masculine.

The difficulty here is that this word is used variably to represent the Laws of the Land (government), the Law of Moses (Torah), and the Religious or Oral Law. This needs to be kept in mind when reading the Apostolic Scriptures, otherwise there are times when the original intent of the author will be easily misunderstood. *Context is critical!*

The Dual Functionality of Grace

Grace is undoubtedly a most precious offering from our Abba. It is given high regards, and many a song has been written about it. Like the term 'law', let's see what the standard definition of it is.

The common word used in the Hebrew text, which is translated as 'grace', is "khane".

From H2603; *graciousness*, that is, subjectively (*kindness, favor*) or objectively (*beauty*): - favour, grace (-ious), pleasant, precious, [well-] favoured. (Strong's #2580)

Strong's corresponds fine with all other relevant lexicographers. Although there are better Lexicons than Strong's, when it works appropriately, I will use it for the sake of its popularity and the ability of people to quickly test or confirm my commentary.

Popularly, it is defined as: "unmerited favor". Its first 'written' appearance in Scripture is in (depending on the translation of course) Genesis 6:5-8:

Then the LORD saw that the wickedness of man was great on the earth, and that every intent of the thoughts of his heart was only evil continually. The LORD was sorry that He had made man on the earth, and He was grieved in His heart. The LORD said, 'I will blot out man whom I have created from the face of the land, from man to animals to creeping things and to birds of the sky; for I am sorry that I have made them.' But Noah found **favor** in the eyes of the LORD.

'Grace' has been translated here into its dominant, defining word. In the art and science of scriptural interpretation (Hermeneutics), there is a principle called "the Law of First Appearances". It is not the kind of scientific law that is firm and unwavering. It leans more to the 'art' side. But it is a very helpful interpreting tool. It essentially tells us that when a concept or word first appears in Scripture, its context can often times give us its truest meaning or intent, and that meaning or intent should be considered first, when it is continued to be used additionally throughout Scripture.

In this case, though, it is barely necessary to use this principle, because the only potential confusion comes when someone won't read the Scriptures for what they plainly say. However, reading these verses with this principle in mind, what do you see? Noah was a special man in the Lord's eyes. And do you know why he was? Genesis 6:9b, "Noah was a righteous man, blameless in his time; Noah walked with God." See that word 'righteous' right there? Guess what? That's also a first usage word. In the Hebrew, that word is tsadiyq (tsad-eek), and it means: lawful! It also means: just. There is no such concept as just/justice without lawfulness supporting it. This is simply more evidence that the Law is more than just some archaic concept, since in Noah's day there was not yet a codified, Mosaic-level, covenantal law. At that time, it was predominantly moral and ethical values at work.

Let's get back to grace. I want you to take a deep breath, relax, and say to yourself, this is good stuff! Trust me. You are going to enjoy exploring this *new* grace thing with me as well. I already gave you the original, Hebrew word and definition. Now here is the Greek equivalent:

G5485 charis; Thayer Definition: 1) grace (1a) that which affords joy, pleasure, delight, sweetness, harm, loveliness: grace of speech 2) good will, loving-kindness, favour (2a) of the merciful kindness by which God, exerting his holy influence upon souls, turns them to Christ, keeps, strengthens, increases them in Christian faith, knowledge, affection, and kindles them to the exercise of the Christian virtues 3) what is due to grace (3a) the spiritual condition of one governed by the power of divine grace (3b) the token or proof of grace, benefit (3b1) a gift of grace (3b2) benefit, bounty 4) thanks, (for benefits, services, favours), recompense, reward. Part of Speech: noun feminine.

Before we go further, I have to ask you to do something. Please look back at the definition of Law/Torah (page 61), then come back and read this definition of Grace again. Go ahead. Really do it. Don't cheat now. BACK HERE! Okay. Tell me how grace has come to be considered the opposite of law. Jeopardy music is playing in the background. Hear that buzz again? Alex, what is: "It's not!" I'm sorry. That was your daily double take. I don't want you to miss these concepts. Please don't rush through this book as if you *have* to read it to please someone else. This book will not self-destruct anytime soon. So, if you're sleepy or need a snack, go ahead. I'll be waiting right here when you get back. If not, let's get down to some very significant stuff.

Let's go back in time—way back. I just showed you where the first usage of the word 'grace' came up in the Book of Beginnings (Genesis), but can you think of another character that was shown grace? Although I have showed it to you in the life of Adam, and really, the concept of grace was already at work before the world was created. (After all, He did end up making it, didn't He?) How about Jacob?

Talk about a man who got a lot of things wrong! Initially, his only significance was found in his relation to Isaac. He was the fortunate heir to a promise that was made to his forefathers. That promise was later fulfilled in the form of a nation of peoples, ratified by his name change to Israel. His sons were a motley bunch to say the least, but they were the progenitors of the chosen people. This leads me to the obvious grace factor. Why were they chosen? What did they do to deserve being called out and separated from all other peoples? Who were they that they should have "a god so near to them as YHVH, whenever they call on Him," or "statutes and judgments as righteous as the Law they were given (Deuteronomy 4)"? Nothing! As a matter of fact, a few chapters later God reminds them that they were of no worthy significance, but that He did these for them because He loved them, and because He keeps His promises.

The reality is that in every case where a man has been appointed unto salvation, he has been given a gift of life. Anytime a boundary was established to protect and therefore bless, it was an act of grace. Now let's move ahead to a New Testament example of the word 'grace' being used. In the Greek, there is but only a slight variation in meaning. It expands a little on the Hebrew, and adds a bit of personal effect on our hearts; creating a response from us to want to reciprocate with like virtue. Look at this well-known passage of Scripture:

> But God, being rich in mercy, because of His great love with which He loved us, even when we were dead in our transgressions, made us alive together with Christ (by grace you have been saved), and raised us up with Him, and seated us with Him in the heavenly *places* in Christ Jesus, so that in the ages to

Conduct Becoming

come He might show the surpassing riches of His <u>grace in kindness</u> toward us in Christ Jesus. For by <u>grace</u> you have been saved through faith; and that not of yourselves, *it is* <u>the gift</u> of God; not as a result of works, so that no one may boast. (Ephesians 2:4-9)

Ancient Grace

Notice that the faith that saves us comes as a result of the gift of grace which is given to us. Grace, as demonstrated here, is the utmost example of the Lord's showing us favor. And when we receive grace, our hearts are stirred to reciprocate. So what do we do? We...

Therefore, laying aside falsehood, speak truth each one *of you* with his neighbor, for we are members of one another. Be angry, and yet do not sin; do not let the sun go down on your anger, and do not give the devil an opportunity. He who steals must steal no longer; but rather he must labor, performing with his own hands what is good, so that he will have *something* to share with one who has need. Let no unwholesome word proceed from your mouth, but only such *a word* as is good for edification according to the need *of the moment*, so that it will <u>give grace</u> to those who hear. (Ephesians 4:25-29)

What is this telling us to do? It is clearly telling us to show kindness and favor (by doing good works, the heart of Torah) to people, in a way that will cause them to see the Messiah in you, and encourage their faith. So again I ask you, how does this gift of grace cause the laws found in Torah to have no validity, especially since it is through the laws of Torah we learn what God considers good works to be?

Let me build upon this with you. Let's travel back again to the days of the Temple service. We know the act of performing sacrifices had already been in the works long before the lengthy and more complex procedures had come down from Mt. Sinai, and later additions. We have examples such as Cain, Abel, Abraham, Isaac, and Noah to show us this. If you have not spent any significant time studying the sacrificial procedures, you could quickly fall prey to much of the false assumption perpetuated by those who teach and have done likewise.

The first thing I want to reveal to you, and this might come as a surprise, is that there are no specific sacrifices prescribed to cover the breaking (transgressing) of any of the Ten Commandments. You may look all you like through the latter part of Exodus, throughout the books of Leviticus and Deuteronomy, and wherever else you desire; you will discover this to be true.

The very same can be said for the "two greatest". Nowhere is a sacrifice mentioned, that is prescribed to cover anyone for not loving the Lord their God with all their heart, or our neighbors as our self. That would seem obvious, wouldn't it? Let's get more practical. If you (man) found yourself one day looking over at your neighbor's wife and thinking, "Wow that's a mighty fine woman, I'll bet she...," you would find yourself in a bit of a practical dilemma. First, because depending on what you think next, you are either coveting or lusting. And second, because there is apparently no hope for you, because there are again no specific sacrifices to get you out of this trouble. For, if you look around in the Scriptures, you will find that Torah does not have a specific "fix" for the sins (transgressions) of lust or covetousness. Let me give you another scenario. Please allow me creative license.

Your neighbor has really irked you lately with her flaunted, but actual beauty (covet). You really despise her (hate). You (woman) know she is especially fond of a horse she has had since she was a little girl. So, you concoct (premeditate evil) an idea to "show her a thing or two (malice)." You ask to borrow her horse and take it for a real, long run and somehow "forget" to water it. You bring it back near dead and declare you have no idea what's wrong with it (lie). The next morning it passes away (horse-slaughter). What in the world do you do to find forgiveness, once you realize how really bad you were, and want release from guilt? I mean, you never really meant to kill it; you just wanted to hurt her.

Would you go about looking through Torah for the required sacrifice for each of the individual sins? Well, you could certainly try, but there is not a given sacrifice for any one of those listed offenses for you to make. That's right, not one! However, Torah does teach us how to make restitution for the dead horse.

Here's another scenario: There is a neighbor who bothers you immensely. He has a small goatherd that seems to keep traveling over onto part of your property. They tend to eat up your crops, and plant putrid land mines all over. You've asked him countless times to control his herd, but he seems to shun you. So, every time one comes onto your property, you kill that one and three more as well. You know that the value of the sheep are 4 shekels of silver each, so you hand him nineteen (value plus one-fifth) and berate him.

The owner obviously gets the point and begs you not to do that anymore. He tells you he is poor, and can't put a fence up yet, but that he hopes to soon. You then say to him, "The Torah tells me that if I do wrong to you regarding your animals, I am to make restitution and add one-fifth. I am a rich man, so the next time your goats cross over I will kill them all and pay you their worth." So one did, and that's exactly what you do.

Is that okay? Is the law satisfied here? What if the covetous woman above, instead of animal slaughter, chose to just cut her face and rob her of her beauty? How much would she have to pay the woman to make that wicked deed go away? Could we be looking at what may be part of the problem of the Law, as discussed in Romans 8:3?

For what the Law could not do, weak as it was <u>through the flesh</u>, God *did:* sending His own Son in the likeness of sinful flesh and *as an offering* for sin, He condemned sin in the flesh.

The Law is powerless in itself to make the citizen who is subject to it, not twist it or abuse it, or to affect the person's heart. The Law in itself cannot make anyone righteous. The Law was unable to get Moses into the Promised Land. And doubtfully, anyone besides the Messiah was more obedient than he was. It's a curious predicament for us to contemplate, considering the fact that there were no specific sacrifices mentioned for many sins. I'm sure the Torah-conscious out there are chomping at the bit for me to bring up the 'once-per-year' ultimate, all-encompassing sacrifice which occurred on Yom Kippur; the one that was to cover the iniquities of the Israelites. But nope! Not even the Yom Kippur sacrificial program had an effect on those who were not contrite and unrepentant. It had no capacity to change man's heart, or cause anyone to love Him.

The Law itself, according to the letter (particulars) of it, was not capable of 'forgiving' sin. Just like baptism doesn't make a new creation. Contrary to popular belief, it never was, and was never supposed to. Forgiveness could be obtained *through* it though. Sacrifices are *Korban* in Hebrew. They "drew us near (Strong's #7133/7126)" to His presence. They certainly were not designed to appease the just wrath of God for repetitive and malicious transgression, for nearly all the teachings on sacrificial procedure began like this:

Then the LORD spoke to Moses, saying, "speak to the sons of Israel," saying, "If a person sins **unintentionally** in any of the things which the LORD has commanded not to be done, and commits any of them…" (Leviticus 4:1 & 2)

God summed up this great prequalification with this reasoning:

But the person who does *anything* <u>defiantly</u>, whether he is native or an alien, that one is blaspheming the LORD; and that person shall be cut off from among his people. Because he has despised the word of the LORD and has broken His commandment, that person shall be completely cut off; his guilt *will be* on him. (Numbers 15:30 & 31)

Certainly none of my given examples would qualify as malicious, right? There are also no sacrifices specified for personally failing to make sacrifices. There are no specific sacrifices for evil intent that was not acted upon. Can you see how that would make all of us damned by the Law, if we were to rely on the letter of it to save us? Examine these verses and see how they clearly support the original understanding that grace awakens faith to save.

Hebrews 10:4, "For it is impossible for the blood of bulls and goats to take away sins."

Psalm 20:3, "May He remember all your meal offerings and find your burnt offering acceptable! Selah." (He apparently didn't have to!)

Psalm 40:6, "Sacrifice and meal offering You have not desired; My ears You have opened; Burnt offering and sin offering You have not required."

Psalm 51:16, "For You do not delight in sacrifice, otherwise I would give it; You are not pleased with burnt offering." (He'd rather it not be necessary.)

Psalm 86:5, "For You, Lord, are good, and ready to forgive, and abundant in loving-kindness (another word for 'grace') to all who *call* (not sacrifice) upon You."

Psalm 25:18, "Look upon my affliction and my trouble, and forgive all my sins." (Cried from the heart.)

Psalm 84:11, "For the LORD God is a sun and shield; The LORD **gives grace** and glory; No good thing does He withhold from those who walk uprightly." (It's not earned through works of sacrifice.)

Psalm 51:17, "The sacrifices of God are a broken spirit; a broken and a contrite heart. O God, You will not despise."

Habakkuk 2:4, "Behold, as for the proud one, His soul is not right within him; but the righteous will live **by his <u>faith</u>**."

That's right! Faith is the *olde* way too! Sin and Guilt sacrifices were really for us, not for Him. Restitution is for us, not for Him. They were designed to cost us something, and hopefully deter us from sinning. The Red Heifer sacrifice (Numbers 19) was for national sin, as well as for personal sin; but its greater purpose was to point us to the Messiah, who would personally remove our contamination of death. Yom Kippur (Day of Atonement; Leviticus 16) only occurred once per year, so what if someone came in contact with death, and then personally died before the next time it came around?

The reason there was no designated sacrifice for so many sins is that animal sacrifices, by their own intrinsic merit, don't forgive sins! Can you imagine if they did? Sacrifices would then have been constantly abused by those who will to do harm. They provided a means to obtain forgiveness, by faith in their substitutionary quality. Because Christianity has chosen to separate itself from Judaism, and has condescendingly presumed to understand Temple ritual better than Judaism does, and due to the fact that it is two thousand years distant, it is unable to rightly

Conduct Becoming

deduce these truths. Our theology has gone so far off course; it completely ignores the fact that Judaism never understood the sacrifice as causing the forgiveness. This naïveté has even found its way into biblical translation.

The Hebrew word *Chatah*, generally translated as sin (when used in relation to sacrifice) is better understood in the sense of impurity. "Sin offerings" are more accurately purification *korbanoth* (offerings; derived from *qarab*, meaning: to approach). The animal's blood, poured or splattered by the priests, made atonement and sanctified our flesh (Hebrews 9:13) so that we could again "draw near" to God. (If you search this phrase out in the NT, and regard it as referring to the concept of sacrifice, the text will richen deeply.)

Sacrifices restored the breach in accessibility to God that sin creates. Do you think that guilt and shame just vanished upon the simple shedding of blood? If you think that, you are very mistaken. In fact, improper bloodshed, even of animals, is constituted as murder. If animal blood has that kind of power, certainly a human sacrifice would accomplish more than a goat! But we know how God feels about throwing children into the fire for Molech (Jeremiah 32:35). So it required the applied blood of a higher order of human, a substitutionary korban, from a uniquely qualified priest (of the Melchizedekian order; Hebrews 5:6) to enable perpetual absolution with adjoining, soul-felt restoration. Jesus's death made it possible for us to again draw near to God, and find forgiveness. Yes, it did more than that as well.

Deceived was (and is) the Israelite who only followed the Law for the intent to, or thought that sacrifices were sufficient to, get he or she declared righteous enough to enter the Olam Ha-ba (World to Come). If they did, they missed the whole point and died in their trespasses. "Sin unintentionally" is the dominant thought in at least fifteen portions of Scripture pertaining to this. It is the running theme of the sacrificial system.

Repentance

Let's go for a quick walk together. I really could use your support because this is going to be very difficult for me. I did something very wrong, and I knew I shouldn't have, but I did it anyway. I have become overwhelmed with shame, and I can sense the Lord's disapproval (the work of the Spirit). I am going up to Jerusalem to take my prize ram and offer it as a guilt offering to the Lord.

On the way, the journey is full of emotion. I can't stop thinking about what I did and how it hurt my neighbor. I get so frustrated with myself sometimes for how stupid I can be.

I see the Temple at the top of the hill now. I just don't have a strong stomach for this. Just thinking about what I'm about to do makes me nauseous. It is such a long ascent. As we finally approach the western court area, I am confronted…

"Are you here to offer a sacrifice?" the kohen (priest) asks me.

"Yes, I am." I reply.

"Do you understand what is about to take place?" he asks.

"I do."

"Then let us not delay."

Looking into the eyes of the ram I have cared for, for years, I place my hands upon its head.

The kohen asks, "What is it that you have done that this animal should die on your behalf?"

"In a fit of rage, I filled my neighbor's well with rocks. I was mad at him because he would not allow me to draw from his well, to tend to my animals. My well has run dry. He said he feared his would as well, but I thought he was just being selfish."

"Does your neighbor know you did this to him?" the kohen inquired.

"No. He doesn't." I answer.

"Then you know that in addition to this sacrifice, you must confess this sin to your neighbor. You must seek his forgiveness by digging him a new well. If you do not do these things, this sacrifice will not be acceptable."

"I know." I whisper.

"Here is the knife." the kohen states abruptly.

I take the knife in my hands, and place it against the throat of my animal; an animal that has done nothing wrong. My heart is pounding as the drops of sweat are flowing from my brow. I'd give anything to take back what I did.

"This should be me!" I acknowledge and mumble through my tears as I begin to apply pressure to the blade. "Oh God, forgive my iniquity, and accept this ram in my stead. I promise to make it right with my neighbor. Please show me mercy, and return to me Your Spirit, that I might not do this kind of thing again."

Then I lift hard on the knife and slide it as quickly as I can across its neck. If it has to die, it should at least die painlessly. I watch its nephesh vanish like a vapor, and I acknowledge it is I who is left standing as it keels over onto the ground. Not for long though, because the reality of what just happened is so heavy I collapse to my knees. The kohen allows my show of contrition to go on for a bit before he reaches down and helps restore me to my feet.

"Now, go and sin no more!" is the last thing I hear as I walk away.

Conduct Becoming

What you just experienced with me is a somewhat scriptural illustration of repentance. It was touching, but there are a few little flaws in what you just read. Test time. Did you recognize them?

First, Torah required me to go set things right with my neighbor first, and then bring my sacrifice. That's exactly what Jesus repeated at the Sermon on the Mount.

> Therefore if you are presenting your offering at the altar, and there remember that your brother has something against you, leave your offering there before the altar and go; first be reconciled to your brother, and then come and present your offering. (Matthew 5:23 & 24)

So exactly in fact, it may as well been taken straight from Moses's instruction:

> …he shall make restitution for it in full and add to it one-fifth more. He shall give it to the one to whom it belongs on the day *he presents* his guilt offering. Then he shall bring to the priest his guilt offering to the LORD, a ram without defect from the flock, according to your valuation, for a guilt offering, and the priest shall make atonement for him before the LORD, and he will be forgiven for any one of the things which he may have done to incur guilt. (Leviticus 6:5b-7)

And you thought Jesus came to discard Moses? Does the way Jesus taught that sound to you like a command that was intended to last for round about two years? Wasn't obeying the command of recompensing multiple times the amount stolen, the way Zaccheus the tax collector reacted upon conviction of his sin (Luke 19:8; based on Exodus 22)? I don't remember Him telling Zaccheus that repayment was unnecessary, since it was part of the *olde* system. Actually, this act of repentance brought salvation to his home! Really, what would have been the point of this teaching if sacrifices had no future meaning? There wouldn't have been one! The sacrificial system was far more than just about dealing with sin. It was a system of worship. It was a system of good-will. It was a means of sustenance for the Levites and the poor. It enabled Israel to come into His presence. The book of the Acts of the Apostles, no matter what level of creativity people come up with to explain it away, shows us this truth clearly.

Another misrepresentation is seen in the fact that the guilty man did the slaughtering himself. During the temple periods, people did not perform their own sacrifices. The Levites got that job, as a continuing reminder of that little incident with Dinah.

Here's the real kicker though: Another misrepresentation is found in the fact that the guilty man brought an offering for something he did with full recognition of its sinfulness. That would not have been acceptable. In modern terms, we see motive, intent and possible premeditation. And that, my friends, is a real problem, because sins committed under these conditions have no stated, ceremonial white-wash. A detailed examination of the various sacrifices and their corresponding transgressions show no solution for purposeful sins. As a matter of fact, the resultant penalty is seen in Numbers 15:30, "But the person who does *anything* <u>defiantly</u>, whether he is native or an alien, that one is blaspheming the LORD; and that person **shall be cut off** from among his people."

Sin is never-ever okay, but when it is blatant disregard for God's laws, its result is a more severe danger. Sin is deadly serious business, and Jesus's crucifixion did not change that. It is my belief that the sacrificial system was Master-fully orchestrated in its design, so that personal salvation would be equally dependent on faith, and not solely the mechanics of ritual slaughter.

Allow me another moment of creative liberty. Many ancient Hebrews will cry in that day, "Did we not ascend Mt. Zion, and bring you our tithes, and perform the necessary sacrifices in your name?" But He will respond, "Depart from me! I never smelled a pleasing aroma on your behalf. I don't know you."

So, where does that leave us? Well, no matter when one lived, be it pre or post incarnation, our only access to the World to Come is provided through faith in, and love for, the Lord. Since true love desires to not sin against its lover, the result should be great regard for the rules of relationship. All of us, though, have sinned. All of us, though, have done so intentionally. And because of that, we were "cut off," so to speak.

What then was I to do in that previous example? Well, grace understood that a one-time transgression was not to be considered "defiant". There were clearly sins that no mercy was to be shown for, like murder. Other sins didn't carry the same weight and were to be dealt with differently, because they are separated and listed as such. I could find forgiveness through faith and ritual. But I assure you, if I kept treating my neighbor like that, over and over again, I'm pretty sure my contrition would be disingenuous. And the Kohenim (priest, pl.) would eventually catch on to that. And God would know all the better. And I might very well be sent away from my community. And if I didn't get my act together, I might very well have no legal defense when I am judged.

All sin requires forgiveness, regardless of its weightiness. But not all sin could be dealt with through animal blood. Obviously, that too, has not changed. Metaphorically, people often turn the knife on its side and smack it against the animal's hind-quarters, sending it running off until they sin again, and have to re-gather it for use another time. That doesn't put any blood on the altar! Lip service, and going through the motions,

Conduct Becoming

were not and still are not enough. People who really are repenting should spiritually and symbolically lay their hands upon the head of Jesus as they confess. Perhaps if they did, they might reconsider the seriousness of their sinful behavior, (the throbbing punctures in their palms from his thorny crown would aid in reminding), and actually get victory over it.

If anyone sees his brother committing a sin *not leading* to death, he shall ask and *God* will for him give life to those who commit sin not leading to death. There is a sin *leading* to death; I do not say that he should make request for this. (1st John 5:16)

There is somewhat of an unspoken, three (or so) strike rule. It is not unlike the three steps to the archetypal excommunication we see Jesus teaching in Matthew 18:16. Forgiveness is found where repentance is found. Perpetual sinning (by definition) is not repentance. Jesus also taught we should always be willing to forgive seventy times seven, but who can really repent four hundred and ninety times for the same sin?

For if we sin willfully after that we have received the knowledge of the truth, there remaineth no more sacrifice for sins, but a certain fearful looking for of judgment and fiery indignation, which shall devour the adversaries. He that despised Moses's law **died** without mercy under two or three witnesses: Of how much sorer punishment, suppose ye, shall he be thought worthy, who hath trodden underfoot the Son of God, and hath counted the blood of the covenant, wherewith he was sanctified, an unholy thing, and hath done despite unto the Spirit of grace? (Hebrews 10:26-29, KJV; extrapolated from Deuteronomy 17:6.)

How do we insult the Spirit of grace? We cheapen grace. We make it "sloppy". We smear the blood of Jesus to hide our sin addiction. Church: Do you really think the cross relaxed His need, or desire, for our holiness? So I ask you…how is holiness defined, and Who is the Definer?

Ninety-five percent of the KJV translation of that last portion of Scripture is "spot-on". There is just one, teensy, weensy issue we need to deal with. It's a verb tense—barely worthy of note. "Anyone who has set aside the Law of Moses **dies** without mercy on *the testimony of* two or three witnesses (NASU). The ALT, ASV, ESV, Geneva, GNB, ISV, OJB, RYLT, WNT & YLT all agree. Where is this portion from? The New Testament—many years after the ascension of Jesus. That almost sounds like there were people who still upheld the requirements of Torah, or at least recognized its continuing authority. Allow me to paraphrase what the author of Hebrews is really saying:

For if we purposefully continue to break the commandments, even after we are made aware of them, and have understanding regarding them, there is no sacrifice that you can give, or have applied on your behalf, that will be capable of compensating for your lawlessness. You will have, however, good reason to expect severe judgment; because that behavior equates you among His adversaries.

Even now, if you are caught in rebellion, rejecting the LORD's commands given through Moses, if two or three witnesses can be found against you, you are worthy of a death sentence.

Let's think about this. How much more serious a punishment do you deserve, if you behave rebelliously, now that the blood of the Son of God has been shed on your behalf? Your incessant sinning is no less than standing at the base of the cross during His death, and stomping around on the blood which has puddled on the ground, making it into red mud for swine to bathe in. You would obviously consider His covenants to be trash, and equate the Spirit of Grace to be worthy of equal treatment.

SELAH! In the sacrificial program, sin always had to be dealt with (in the form of a chatah'at; sin/purification offering) before any other offerings were acceptable. Atonement was made first by the priest, and then we were able to find our personal relief (Leviticus 4 & 5). Are you yet seeing the picture here? We have always needed an intercessor to deal with our transgressions. We have no way to do it alone! It started in the Garden. "He is forever in intercession on our behalf." How is it then possible for us to think the sacrificial system was throw out, due to some conflict it has with what Jesus did? They are not exact parallels, and mostly were quite different. What the *earthly* sacrificial system certainly couldn't do was produce a priest that had the ability to perform a one-time Chatah'at (purification offering), that had the power to change the heart of mankind. Jesus came to deal with our sin nature problem, not to withhold us from sacrificial blood offerings! (Although we cannot, nor should, perform them now!)

Grace buys us time to set things straight. Mercy protected the Israelites when there was no temple. Grace intended to drive the Israelites to obey Torah 'out of a Love' for the Lord (the intended response). The function of grace has not changed! Who wouldn't find themselves less likely to repeat their sinful behavior after going through a costly ritual like the one I just took you along? Moreover, shouldn't we who are the recipients of His expiatory gift, all the more fervently resist temptation? How much more so should the price Jesus paid deter us? Without grace being bestowed upon us, we would soon think we have earned blessings through our <u>dis</u>obedience. Stay with me now.

Conduct Becoming

The Paradox of Grace

Too much grace…What? Certainly, we want grace, and must appreciate it; but to seek grace as a replacement for obedience is not possible! They are never mutually exclusive. Furthermore, the greatest need for grace comes to those who have not yet died to their sin. Where sin abounds, so all the more does grace.

Romans 6:1 & 2, "What shall we say then? Are we to continue in sin so that grace may increase? May it never be! How shall we who died to sin still live in it?"

In reality then, the desire for more grace (when seen in contrast to the Law) is to desire freedom to transgress, for that is where grace is most found. Grace does not say, "You don't need to bring an offering," or "You don't need to make amends." Please listen to the Spirit here, because if I lose you now, you will lose much more.

One of the greatest deceptions of HaSatan, which has been and is still being perpetrated on the church, is in its understanding of grace, or lack thereof. If you, like me, were raised under typical evangelical doctrine, you were taught that grace shows patience when we sin. You were taught that because of Jesus's sacrifice, we are no longer under law, but under grace; which means He can more easily overlook our sin.[2] I'm not saying verses that say things sounding like that do not exist, but their proper interpretation can only be found with true understanding of what those terms mean, and in context. If patience with sin was any kind of option, Jesus paid far too high a price. The abuse of grace is likened to the same as disbelief, which is the ultimate reason that first generation had to die off in the wilderness.

Jude 1:5, "Now I desire to remind you, though you know all things, once for all that the Lord, after saving a people out of the land of Egypt, subsequently destroyed those who did not believe."

Ouch! A bit of sarcasm there Jude? Most think it was because they grumbled. Jude goes on to further describe the abuse of grace as ungodliness, demonstrated as lasciviousness, and that those who do so are headed for destruction (1:4).

The only thing that cleanses us permanently is The Lamb's cleansing blood. That ultimate, free gift causes the believer to *want* to be obedient in response. Listen to me carefully. The sacrificial system often left people of weak-faith concerned about whether or not their offerings were accepted. Only God knew for sure. Jesus's offering of Himself was most definitely accepted by the Father; but that in no way abrogates your personal concern over sin. You can't just splash His blood around when you feel like it. You should have *more* distain for your sin now, than when you first laid your hands on His head. (I am again speaking symbolically here.) However, often it is the exact opposite that takes place—thanks in part to these prevalent, destructive, paradoxical and twisted teachings..."There is no good in you" and yet "we can no longer sin as Christians." A problem now comes when we ask the question, "Obedient to what?" To our conscience, we surmise. Well, maybe.

Romans 2:13, "For the hearers of the Law [are] not righteous before God, _but_ the doers of the Law will be justified," [or, declared righteous].
Romans 2:15, "...who show the work of the Law written in their hearts, their conscience also bearing witness with [them], and among themselves their thoughts accusing or even defending [them]..." (ALT)

Apparently, the only way you can trust your conscience is if it's been written over with god's law (torah). Did you know your knowledge of Torah will either accuse you, or defend you on the Day of Judgment? If you are new to studying torah, as regards seeking relevant applications for modern living, I bet you never heard that before. Guess we better study Torah after all, eh? However, if you think a lack of studying (ignorance) is your ticket out—nice try. Romans 2:13 tells us that it is the 'doers' of nomos (law), not the 'hearers' that will be declared righteous.

Before you jump further into the Apostles' Scriptures to test this teaching (which I truly hope you do), I am going to give you a head-start, and bring up to the front a passage that is most often used to defend the "No need for any Law anymore" argument, and expose its true meaning.

John 1:17, "For the Law was given through Moses; grace and truth were realized through Jesus Christ" (NASU).
"For the Torah was given through Moshe. Grace and truth came through Yeshua the Messiah" (HNV). (*Moshe* is pronounced as Moe-shay.)
"For the law was given by Moses, *but* grace and truth came by Jesus Christ" (KJV).

Not much difference between them really, but I present you these three different versions to show you a couple, slight word variances. The primary word difference is the one in respect to how "grace and truth" came via Jesus. "Realized through," "came through," and "came by" are the phrases here used. 'Realized' is the closest to the original meaning. I'm not proposing that this statement is untrue in any way. The Torah came *through* Moses, and Grace and Truth were *realized* through Jesus. These are independently true, and should not be interpreted as opposing one another. Actually, that "but" added in the KJV, isn't in the actual Greek.

Understanding the meaning of the word 'realized' is one clue. 'Realized', in the Greek, is 'ginomai'. According to Thayer, it means:

1.) to become, I.e. to come into existence, begin to be, receive being; 2) to become, I.e. to come to pass, happen; 2a) of events; 3) to arise, appear in history, come upon the stage; 3a) of men appearing in public; 4) to be made, finished; 4a) of miracles, to be performed, wrought; 5) to become, be made.

Since we have already established that grace existed in the olde covenant Scriptures (other clue), in this verse it cannot be the first or second meanings. The third and beyond is where we see the picture more clearly. Jesus came to put grace on the stage, to be the embodiment of this characteristic of the Father, and to perform its function perfectly. And that He did. Grace surely existed amidst the old covenants, but was a gift given on a more selective basis (due to the fact that Jesus had not yet shed His blood for the world), and was often expressed through types and symbols. But now, Grace has been poured out on all who believe, being available to the entire world, and fully realized in the person and deeds of Jesus the Christ.

Grace truly is a gift; one which you are to greatly appreciate, each time you open it. We must cautiously make the decision to draw on it, acknowledging that the fallen state of this existence doesn't naturally take God's commandments into consideration, and that His perfect will often collides with earthly and human requirements in this present, unregenerate world. Resolve to use it sparingly, and with fear and trembling. It is the gift of drawing us closer to Him, through obedience wrought by love. Grace calls upon all mankind to accept Jesus as their Savior, by whispering to our conscience when it is seen in action. Still, grace need not exist without law. And grace need not be shown to the perishing. Neither grace, nor the Law, is appreciable or has real value to any but the redeemed of the Lord.

Then when he (Simon Peter) arrived and witnessed the grace (gifts) of God, he rejoiced and *began* to encourage them all with resolute heart to remain *true* to the Lord. (Acts 11:23)

That's always been its function, and still is today.

Getting Testy

Then the LORD said to Moses, 'Behold, I will rain bread from heaven for you; and the people shall go out and gather a day's portion every day, that I may test them, whether or not they will walk in My instruction' (Exodus 16:4).

There was a creative and illuminating test given back when I was an elementary school student. I don't know if it's still given, but this is how it worked. You were given a single sheet of paper with about 30 questions on it. The teacher handed them out and gave specific instructions to read the written directions on the exam, prior to beginning it. There was some time limit involved which I can't remember. The teacher told the class when to begin, and we raced to finish it.

If you did the correct thing, and read the opening instructions carefully (which ninety-five percent of the class did not), you would have read the primary instruction that directed us to read all the questions in advance, before beginning to answer them. If you had, you would have seen that question number thirty directed us to write our name on the upper right corner; then to turn the paper over, and that was all. But of course, that is not what the vast majority of us did. We were under time pressure and that seemed like a wasted effort. By the time we had gotten to question number thirty, there was no way to erase/hide the fact that we had already written twenty-nine answers first, and therefore failed. That was a brilliantly designed and valuable illustration on following instructions for a child.

What I am about to say is not going to be a good enough answer for many of you. But I believe there are commandments in Torah that are just like that test. We can sit around and debate the rationality and purposes of His regulations numbered one through twenty-nine 'til we are blue in the face (Greek thinking), but there may or may not be a correct answer. Obedience may be the only exam you don't need to have the answers to, to pass. Sometimes, it may not even be about protecting us, or blessing us, or anything but "will you?" Do you trust Him enough, and love Him enough, to do what He says, even if it makes absolutely no logical sense? Even if you think you'll look silly, or be misunderstood or ridiculed? And yes, even if few support your decisions (Hebrew thinking). The Boss is looking for employees who will follow His procedural manual, and love Him in the process. He is looking for people who will help to get others promoted before themselves. He recognizes our commitment to the Kingdom Corporation by our abidance to His policies. If we don't like them, we are all free to resign.

The Boss is like any parent, who begins with a loving request of their child. When their child immediately and joyfully obeys, the parent

Conduct Becoming

delights in that and often rewards. If the child resists, or is slow to respond to their authority, the loving request becomes a firm, but still loving order. If the child scoffs at the order, the parent becomes frustrated and the order intensifies into a strict command, to a level where even if obeyed eventually, there will be no reward. If the child outright refuses to obey, discipline is sure and strong until obedience is obtained; but then something else is likely to be affected, or even taken away. At this point, the child suffers loss.

The thing you need to recognize here is that neither the parent's goal, nor their love has changed in any way; just both parties' attitude toward the request, and the end result. In a nut-shell, that is Torah as depicted in the life of ancient (and I believe should still be for modern) Israel. That is the "tutor" role of Torah (Galatians 3:24 or 25; varies pending publisher.)

If we all agree that life is a testing ground, why wouldn't parts of the manual on life be a test as well? Perhaps the test is, "Will you read my primary instruction, get to question number thirty (persevere to the end) and pass the test (be saved)? Or, must you answer the other twenty-nine first, which I never asked you to answer, before you do the very simple things I have definitely asked of you?" Perhaps the highest score is given to the one who bucks the system least. Sometimes, and I know this is not scientific analysis, I think that God means exactly what He says. When He says, "Don't kill!" we proudly say, "Yes Sir!" Yet, when He says, "Don't be like the nations!" we ask, "For how many centuries?" and "To exactly what extent?" I really hope, for all our sakes, that God grades on a slide or curve. This is the very essence of the difference between law-exalted and law-diminished thinking.

I would like to begin closing this chapter and forge into the next, with a positional closing. My intention is not to write a dry book on law vs. grace. (Although I struggle to think of a more critical and misunderstood concept). I know I have not yet answered many questions I hope you are asking, but the rest of this book will continue to support this concept and intermittently, through various topics, explain 'how' to let grace perform its function, and demonstrate lawfulness without bondage. The Law never justifies, and never did. Works alone do not justify now, and never did. Grace does not make the Law go away, and never will!

You could, in theory, obey the ceremonial, civil, and sacrificial laws perfectly, and still not be saved.[3] Jesus came and taught that transgression begins in the heart, and for such, the blood of livestock was not adequate. If one did not approach the altar with offerings mixed with faith in the permanence of God's covenants (symbolized by salt), and in His loving-kindness, with a contrite heart, the sacrifice was also not acceptable. Please keep this in mind the next time you read the letters to the Galatians, the Romans, and everywhere else torah (law) is mentioned. And keep in mind as well that there are different kinds of sacrifices, and differing purposes of 'law', and not all of it applied to everybody. There is neither reason nor right to assume that His crucifixion cancelled them all. It filled them full!

We weren't capable then of judging the acceptance of the sacrifice, living or slain. We could only perform (work) it correctly, and believe. Only the Lord knew if the sacrifice was acceptable, and only He knows now if our faith is a saving faith. Salvation is currently an ongoing work, just as daily sacrifices were continually needed "…for our very survival… (Deuteronomy 6:24)." But our redemption price was paid one final time for all, and the curse of the tree removed our (believers) curse of the Law. You can't pay it, so you have to let Him pay it for you, and accept that payment on your behalf.

Jesus was more than just a perfect sin offering, and the Torah is far more than just about blood. The misunderstanding of grace, this "cheap" grace message that we now salt our theology with, is the new opiate for the church masses. Instead of "myriads and myriads of people who are all zealous for the Torah (Acts 21:21)," we now have innumerable masses of churchgoers who feel no obligation to commandment-based sanctification at all!

Obedience is not always the "to be determined how" subjective, personal mystery it often is considered; therefore, neither does the will of the Lord have to be. As a matter of fact, it is reasonable to wonder why, when there is so much pre-established instruction to living obediently that we don't follow first, we bother to spend so much time asking to know His will? He has already told us what to do. "Delight in His ordinances (Isaiah 58:2)." Likewise, we desire to see visions, but we don't even know, nor understand the ones already given to us, through the eyes of His prophets. If Divine law existed before Moses, if it established the heavens, why shouldn't it exist forever? Jesus was, and is, and is to come—the manifest Law. The Universe operates by laws He has written. Nothing was made except through Him, right? Let me give you some brick and mortar Scripture. Please consider these verses carefully.

It will be righteousness for us if we are careful to observe all this commandment before the LORD our God, just as He commanded us. (Deuteronomy 6:25; similar to Abraham's behavior.)

Then it shall come about, because you listen to these judgments and keep and do them, that the LORD your God will keep with you His covenant and His loving-kindness which He swore to your forefathers. (Deuteronomy 7:12)

Conduct Becoming

As you have also seen here, Laws and Covenants are independent, different, yet harmoniously intertwined things. There has not been one covenant made by God that has ever ended. Every covenant from His perspective is perpetual in its construction. An earlier covenant is not cancelled by a later. They build upon and strengthen each other. If it was any other way, we would have no genuine security in our future. For one, when He says "perpetual" or "everlasting," we couldn't trust Him. And two, He could cancel a covenant at any time, and the Covenant of Peace we are all awaiting full participation in, may never come.

The reason we need not fear that, is best illustrated through the Tabernacle. The instructions given to Moses were to enable Israel to make something on Earth, which reflected the true Temple in Heaven. The furnishings were picturesque of the person and work of the Messiah to come. The Law, likewise, reflected an already existing set of Divine principles and precepts. We are told to not lie, because He is not a liar. We are told not to steal, because He is not a thief. Just because Yeshua came, and "fulfilled" the picture of the Tabernacle, doesn't mean the Temple in Heaven ceased to exist. And just because people shun the Written Law, because they imagine their heart is more trustworthy than what God etched into Stone Tablets, that doesn't make the Heavenly and eternal principles become inferior. The Torah is to Messiah, as the Tabernacle is to Heaven.

In continued consideration of the grace/law misunderstanding (that being they cannot coexist in a symbiotic relationship), and in closing, there is another misnomer I need to also expose. A long time ago, a man by the name of Clement of Alexandria played a key role in popularizing a phrase we use today; one that never even entered the thoughts of the disciples. This phrase is none other than "The Old Testament".

He, of course, is not the only early church father to use and promote this concept; and likewise, it is hard to say who the first was or when it occurred. But for the sake of this discussion, it is the fact that it began at all I wish to bring your attention to. Jesus never used the phrase, nor did any of the Apostles or Prophets for that matter.

The totality of Scripture was written beginning several thousand years before the coming of the Christ, to about one hundred years following. In between, there is a gap of about four hundred years. Christianity often calls them the "Silent Years," for the lack of written material by God's prophets. Considering that the most recent Scripture we have was written near two thousand years ago, I would suggest that all of it is rather "old" at this point. In actuality, there is more ancient Scripture, and more recent.

In the Apostolic Scriptures, the word *testament* (Grk: diatheke) is often used as a synonymous replacement for the word *covenant* (Hebrew:

b'rit). 'Testament' also carries the meaning of a written proof or testimony. Therefore, by the way it was and still is currently used, it seems apparent that the intent behind developing the phrase "Old Testament" was to create a line of demarcation between what some considered an old covenant (singular; apparently grouping them all together), and the new covenant. That is not so easily justified.

In the entirety of the Bible, there is only one instance where the phrase "old covenant" has been used, and it is found in the second letter to the Corinthians. In the next chapter, we will explore this concept in more detail. Nevertheless, it is not in regards to the overall compilation! Likewise, the 'new' covenant of Jeremiah 31 has absolutely no meaning, or standing, without the earlier covenants being in force. My friends, that page that separates the first three-quarters from the last quarter of the pages of the Protestant canon is the page with the fewest words, and yet it is arguably one of the most impacting (and divisive) pages the Bible contains. That imaginary line parallels the other imaginary line that has been created between the Law (Torah) and righteousness in the minds of many believers. When Paul told Timothy to "rightly divide the Word of Truth," he wasn't suggesting he segregate it. What did the Lord tell Moses was the reason for the Law?

Leviticus 19:2, "Speak to all the congregation of the sons of Israel and say to them, 'You shall be holy, for I the LORD your God am holy.'"
Leviticus 20:7, "You shall consecrate yourselves therefore and be holy, for I am the LORD your God."

When Jesus commended His spirit, the temple veil was torn in two, under the cloak of unnatural darkness. The Father rent His garments in anguish over the suffering of the Son. It was not meant to suggest a dividing rift between people groups, faiths, the applicability of portions of Scripture, or that just anyone can now waltz right into the Most Holy Place (as emotionally charging as that is.)

4

Signed in Blood

After Paul arrived, the Jews who had come down from Jerusalem stood around him, bringing many and serious charges against him which <u>they could not prove</u>, while Paul said in his own defense, "<u>I have committed no offense </u>either against the <u>Law of the Jews</u>, or against <u>the temple</u>, or against Caesar." (Acts 25:7 & 8)

Then they <u>secretly induced</u> men to say, "We have heard him (Stephen) speak blasphemous words against Moses and *against* God." They put forward <u>false witnesses</u> who said, "This man incessantly speaks against this holy place and the Law." (Acts 6:11 & 13)

It all made such good sense. I was very comfortable with my pattern of life, my perspective on God, and the way I would throw Him bones. I knew there was supposed to be more, and that here and there people seemed to have ascended to significance within the kingdom, but how close is the average Joe(anne) supposed to get to Him really? He is too holy. After all, He did end the life of a man for simply trying to stop the tipping Ark from falling over during transport.

On the other hand, the message that had been drilled into me from childhood was one of great simplicity, "Call upon the Lord and be saved!" (Yet another Hebrew Scripture passage.) It was a message of liberty for sure, but it was a program without a schedule. I had developed a "God does not get angry anymore because Jesus died" mentality; along with a "He loves you unconditionally to a fault" perspective. That, of course, culminates in a "His grace sees no sin" understanding. Actually, that is often the popular message. What a great religion! My God was a great, big, volleyball that never stops smiling, and makes no specific requests of me other than to love Him and my neighbors. As long as I seek the kingdom first, whatever that means, He'll take care of the rest. Deep inside I knew He couldn't be that much of a push over, but I lived as if I sure hoped He was a Wilson.

As I look back at the times that I read certain portions of Scripture in the past, even multiple times, I really have to wonder how it is I missed so much. How could I have seen the words that were right in front of me, but not understood their meaning? But then, I just have to think back to when I was not walking the road that leads to life, even though I knew better, and that's even more amazing. Paul the Pharisee said that we see things sometimes as if we are looking through a dark glass dimly. I'd say that's a pretty good analogy, considering that even though it's dark, when held up to bright enough light it may still reveal a beautiful color. I deduce there to be different sources of that dimness. One source might simply be our mental capacity to understand. We are all born with varying degrees of intellectual capacity, and that plays a role in our ability to comprehend complex matters clearly. (However, only God can judge this justly.) That is not to suggest intellect diminishes overall effectiveness within the Kingdom.

Then there's the education factor. We may have a perfectly capable intellect, but we don't exercise the muscle of our mind and therefore limit ourselves. Yet with Paul, something like scales had to fall from his eyes in order for him to be able to see more clearly, as he was very highly educated. That darkness was more like blinders on a horse, put there by the owner to limit available sight. This is an example of Spirit controlled enlightenment. We can exercise the muscle of our mind, which we should, but the other two factors are out of our control. One may never change much. But the latter, the one that is Spirit governed, that's what we want to consider here.

When it comes to reading the Scriptures, if you should decide to read in a cursory, survey/scan sort of style, as though it was a high-school textbook, most likely you will familiarize yourself with the passages, but not gain much understanding. If you were to read it multiple times, you would likely do more than familiarize yourself, and move into the realm of memorization. However, mortal man must need something more than that to gain enlightenment, for many a man has read the Scriptures and yet heaped destruction upon themselves and humanity, through extreme misinterpretation. Heinous and evil crimes of demonic proportion have been executed by people quoting Scripture to support their actions.

For the word of the cross is foolishness to those who are perishing, but to us who are being saved it is the power of God. (1st Corinthians 1:18)

And even if our gospel is veiled, it is veiled to those who are perishing, in whose case the god of this world has blinded the minds of the unbelieving so that they might not see the light of the gospel of the glory of Christ, who is the image of God. (2nd Corinthians 4:3 & 4)

That's pretty easy to understand, being that some of Scripture can be challenging enough to interpret, even as a believer indwelt by the Holy Spirit, being so far removed from its context. An unbeliever has no chance, outside of the Spirit. But how then does the Spirit affect our understanding? Is He just your "gut feeling or instinct"? Can your gut be completely different than someone else's, and you both be right? Remember, I am speaking in regards to Scripture's meaning.

Is it possible that comprehending the Scriptures is not as hard as it is often made out to be, at least to the level that directly affects the quality of your life? Is it possible that the seeds of doubt and discouragement, over our ability to apply it, had been planted in us from early on, and have now grown into a fruitful tree of complacency? How theologically savvy do you think the crowd was, that originally received it? Allow me to contemplate with you.

I am not proposing to think exactly like our Savior, but if I was to use the spiritual insight He has given me, and knowing He wants all men to be saved, I might deduce that the means by which He guides all His children into Truth, would not be way over our heads. Don't get me wrong. I am well aware of the complexities inherent in exegetical research, and various apologetics. But doesn't it stand to reason that if He made us, knowing quite well our human (in)capacities and all, that He would not only give us the road map for life, but a key to understanding it as well? And not only a map for Mensa members, but one that is decipherable by us common folk. Hey, keep this truth just between you and me. We don't want the priests to lose all their power.

Haven't you ever had a moment or two when you had read something in a passage that seemed fairly clear, and then a teacher twisted it all around to mean something completely different? Sometimes it was with good result—sometimes disturbing. Let's think about this again. To whom was the Torah originally given? A nation of scholars, or a mob of simple slaves? As difficult as some study is, some part of it has to be comprehendible by the everyday reader. Knowing something of God, albeit a teensy bit, I would venture to guess it would be the parts that really matter the most. Also remember how it was given. It was just told to them. They didn't all get a copy to read over and over. It really just needed to make plain sense. Even if some things are questionable, wouldn't it also stand to reason that it would be better for us to err on the

Signed in Blood

side of caution, in an attempt to do the right thing, than to overlook/ignore what the Word says; which would surely result in our doing the wrong? Yet, that's exactly what we see happening all around us.

Isn't it, yet again, a bit paradoxical that we can come to faith in Jesus with the simplicity and trust of a child, but then from that point on we require professorial, rabbinical, and institutional think tanks, assembled to autopsy the Scriptures, to conclude for us the real meanings of 'do' and 'don't do?' Do we need them? Yes. But can they walk our walk for us? No! Is the fullness of the Scriptures beyond our individual understanding? Yes, because they reflect an omniscient God. Yet understanding has to be attainable, or the Bible becomes a prejudiced, exclusive and elitist manual. It has even been suggested that a very complicated, logarithmic software program is required to deduce its hidden treasures. To that I holler, "GARBAGE!" For that would pretty much put anyone but Einstein and Stephen Hawking-types out of contention for salvation.

I believe that all believers can learn, by the Spirt, to comprehend Scripture enough to be empowered to live uprightly, and to reflect our Redeemer; and yet it doesn't have to be the grueling discipline many of us think that it is. God's words are not only for the PhD's and for ThD's among us, to read and regurgitate back to us in a "dumbed down" format. The same Spirit that endued Solomon with great wisdom is the same one that indwells us. He never had a Pentium® processor at his disposal, or even a *Strong's Concordance*. Some of that gift must be accessible to us also.

The first thing we have to do is change our attitudes toward this Book of Books.

You Can Do It!

For this commandment which I command you today is <u>not too difficult</u> for you, <u>nor is it out of reach</u>. It is not in heaven, that you should say, 'Who will go up to heaven for us to get it for us and make us hear it, that we may observe it?' Nor is it beyond the sea, that you should say, 'Who will cross the sea for us to get it for us and make us hear it, that we may observe it?' But <u>the word is very near you</u>, in your mouth and in your heart, that <u>you may observe it</u>. (Deuteronomy 30:11-14)

He (Moses) said to them, "Take to your heart all the words with which I am warning you today, which you shall command your sons to observe carefully, *even* all the words of this law. For it is <u>not an idle word</u> for you; indeed <u>it is your life</u>. And by this word you will prolong your days in the land, which you are about to cross the Jordan to possess." (Deuteronomy 32:46 & 47)

Somewhere along the line we went from, "You can understand and do!" to "You must have a highly trained graduate, of a most prestigious university, interpret the imbedded coding and reduce it to mush, so that you can sip it through a straw." Even worse, the more common message is now, "You can't do!" Oh really! Tell that to God! Who's lying here? What can't you do...not murder, rape, or steal? What then? You can't avoid yeast for a week, or help your enemy's donkey out of a pit? What a lovely message the enemy is preaching today: "You can't do it, so don't bother trying." Talk about ear tickling. He either set before us that day a blessing and a curse, or a curse and a curse (Deut. 11:26). He either gave us the choice between life and death, or death and death. Which is it? Oh, that's right. That message wasn't for us.

Children of the Father, you most certainly CAN do it, and it would behoove you to endeavor diligently to do so. You CAN live holy lives, pleasing and acceptable to the Lord. It is the *how* and *what* questions, not the *whether* variety, that we need to be answering first. We can obey, because we should obey, because we want to obey, because we love Him—because if we don't, we'll die. "The soul that sins...dies!" Loving God with everything within you is not only a principle, but also obedience to a command. Will we blow it? Of course we will. Will we fall short of perfection? That had already been considered from the beginning of time. We can do it. We just can't do it perfectly. Just because we make a mistake does not mean we should throw our hands into the air and declare, "Forget it! I can't do it. I quit trying!"

That kind of attitude won't get you very far in this physical world, and it won't get you far in the Kingdom either. It is an ignoble, immature, and pseudo-spiritual cop-out at best. Yes, we must depend fully upon our Lord for our salvation, as well as the strength, and wisdom, and power to overcome our circumstances. If we surrender ourselves to our own incompetence, we are in actuality attributing incompetence to Him, to work in us and through us. That is why we can't give up.

Compounded with the "You can't *do*" message, has been the "You can't *understand*" message. Together, they are a recipe for disaster. What really bothers me is that similar to the government's educational system, much of today's topical preaching is getting more and more watered down—creeping along the ground in an effort to find a low, common denominator in which to pool. It lies to us about our ability to maturity instead of keeping the bar high, in order to cause us to have to reach. What if we treated Olympic events that way? If the committee noticed there were fewer who could qualify that given year, should they drop the high jump about a foot and see how things go?

After listening to probably thousands of assorted messages, by various ministers from differing backgrounds, and having spoken to several that have confirmed this fact, I know that many are strategically teaching on a third grade level—for fear the average blocked ear won't be able to handle the loftiness of the wisdom of Scripture (as they interpret it), causing the ear to leave. I know first-hand that a commonly taught principle in Bible School is, "As soon as you say something in Greek or Hebrew, you'll lose them."

If I were you, I wouldn't consider any lone statement, enough to stake a claim on either, so look at the living evidences. Look at the overall maturity and quality of the fruit being harvested by the modern church growers. People are getting picked before they're ripe…and then they rot. Fruit needs nourishment, and water. Would it be that much of a shame if someone didn't instantly and fully understand a pastor's teaching, requiring them to ask for further explanation? Didn't we learn to do that in kindergarten? They might have to find someone to elaborate for them, or struggle a bit to get it figured out. So what! Once they do, I'll bet the meal would stick to their ribs better than if it was day old, spoon-fed, gruel.

Pastors and teachers, you need to start demanding (expecting) more of His (not your) little lambs. This may sound insensitive, but if they don't want to learn, and you can't encourage them to, that is not on you! Let them go find a non-teaching church to play "spiritual" in. You leave the flock to recover a sheep, not retain a sheep to sacrifice the flock.

When your physical offspring come to you as children struggling to grasp a concept, do you look at them with sad eyes and tell them, "Sorry, you're just not up to my caliber," then neglect them for their ignorance. Of course not! You carefully teach just a bit beyond their understanding, and if you do it right, they learn how to learn, and ask even more questions. A significant reason the average congregant does not know the Word is because its treasures are often kept buried by the very ones they anticipate receiving help digging from. How is it kept buried? When you teach your people that they need you to intellectually intercede on their behalf, and when you teach them not to obey what they do learn, because they can't! By your doing so, it results in their concluding on their own that they are not competent, so why bother?

A Call to Shepherds
If the Staff Fits…

Orators of the gospel, let not these verses be speaking of you:

As I live, saith the Lord GOD, surely forasmuch as My sheep became a prey, and My sheep became food to all the beasts of the field, because there was no shepherd, neither did My shepherds search for My sheep, but the shepherds fed themselves, and fed not My sheep. (Ezekiel 34:8)

Wail, ye shepherds, and cry; and wallow yourselves in the dust, ye leaders of the flock; for the days of your slaughter are fully come, and I will break you in pieces, and ye shall fall like a precious vessel. (Jeremiah 25:34)

You teacher/preachers need to stop leafing through your old collegiate notes and looking for what you think the little people can handle, and keeping the rest for yourselves. The only reason you know anything at all is because you were privileged enough to have *learned* it from someone who *learned* it before you! You weren't born with it. So give it back. Unless of course, your notes were wrong, or you've run your course. It's not as if you have anything truly new.

That which has been is that which will be, and that which has been done is that which will be done. So there is nothing new under the sun. (Ecclesiastes 1:9)

Son of man, prophesy against the shepherds of Israel. Prophesy and say to those shepherds, thus says the Lord GOD, Woe, shepherds of Israel who have been feeding themselves! Should not the shepherds feed the flock? You eat the fat and clothe yourselves with the wool, you slaughter the fat *sheep* without feeding the flock. Those who are sickly you have not strengthened, the diseased you have not healed, the broken you have not bound up, the scattered you have not brought back, nor have you sought for the lost; but with force and with severity you have dominated them. They were scattered for lack of a shepherd, and they became food for every beast of the field and were scattered. (Ezekiel 34:2-5)

Are you afraid that if you preach at a level respecting your flock's ability, they might learn what you know and you won't be needed anymore? Have you run out of material because you are too busy doing 'stuff' that you were not called to do, and have no real time to "study thy *own* self" approved anymore? Are you afraid people will mature so much, that they won't need your council? If you are responsible for spiritually nurturing adults, stop teaching them like they're learning disabled. They can take it!

Jeremiah 3:15, "…and I will give you shepherds according to My heart, who shall feed you with knowledge and understanding."

This is what is needed! If you do not have His heart, and/or you are not capable of feeding His sheep, lay down your staff. That's honorable. You're holding back the fullness of His Word, and/or your lack of humility is dumbing down and sickening the flock. You are fulfilling the Great Omission. If this staff doesn't fit you, bless the Lord! But if it does, let Jeremiah's warning to you strike at your hearts and potentially spare you from painful correction. Your job is to bring *His* flock into green pastures…SO THEY CAN EAT! If your *Purpose Driven* Churches are doing something other than spreading the <u>entire</u> gospel, which includes teaching submission to His voice, then you'd better

Signed in Blood

revising your mission statement.

ɔr though by this time you ought to be teachers, you have need again ᵤₒᵣ someone to teach you the elementary principles of the oracles of God, and you have come to need milk and not solid food. But solid food is for the mature, who because of practice have their senses trained to discern good and evil. (Hebrews 5:12 & 14)

Discernment is exactly what we all need, now more than ever. Don't you want your people to have this capability? Then wean your people off your breast and feed them meat so they can develop it! It is not the instructions of God spoken to man that are overly complicated and require systematic theology to comprehend. It is the words spoken by man, on behalf of God, which are so confusing. God says, "Don't steal from your neighbor!" We come along and ask, "What exactly can't be stolen? Who is my neighbor? What exactly is the punishment for that? Will I lose my salvation if I do? Must I confess what I've done? Who is qualified to hear my confession? Do I need a priest? How much time do I have before a confession is invalid? How many times can I expect to be forgiven before I run out of mercy?" The words God spoke are pretty easy to understand. His voice is the one we need to clearly hear and obey, not Wesley's or Calvin's. I believe they have something to offer, but I am not in a covenant relationship with either of them.

I was speaking with a close friend, a contemporary pastor, and he shared with me his acknowledgement that, "the weak area of his church was in its Bible teaching." That struck a chord with me that forever resonates. Churches may have all the "cutting edge" technologies, modern looks and feel, even great numbers and programs, but until the church prioritizes teaching the fullness of His Word as primary, it will forever fall dearly short of His plan. Do you really prefer favoring the attendance numbers, over fearing the potential churn rate?

Pastors/teachers, help your people believe in their capacity to learn, hear (obey), by teaching solid (deeper) truths that are co-witnessed by Scripture and the Spirit, and stop instilling in them that they can't understand (or obey), by not. Of course you should have a new believer's class...a long one. That only stands to reason. Just stop preaching to your whole congregation as if it's one, big "hold on to the faith" pep rally, week after week. The real reason you feel you have to is because the faith you're professing is shaky, which means the faith you're possessing is also.

Your new believer's class is truly where you have the opportunity to improve the next church generation. Teach them the basics, like: how to use a lexicon, how to properly study and interpret Scripture, who they are in the Kingdom, what discipleship is, what sin is, our obligations as children of the Most High, how to actually carry a cross versus just wearing one, etc. Maybe with true understanding, we will reduce relapsing into the world.

A Warning to Sheep

A popular catch phrase within the church is, "I am not getting fed." That may be true, but it may also be your own fault. Sheep can be led to green pasture, but they can't be made to eat! Your pastor/teacher's duty is to serve you a healthy portion, it is not to force feed you.

If you are fellowshipping in a local body of believers, no matter how impressive the edifice, excellent the child-care, or good the pot-luck food, and they are not teaching you God's Word, all of it, at a challenging and enriching level (taking you out to pasture), you seriously need to consider finding a new family and shepherd/s. First, though, for the sake of a clear conscience, you should seek to know why there is this problem.

If they tell you it's because in their experience, people don't want to hear it, or that much of it is not "relevant", then you do need to run. That kind of thinking doesn't come from a competent leader who knows what people need (not want), and probably has nothing left to give. If the teacher's heart is in the right place, and realizes the weakness, and has tried previously to elevate the content with some resistance, then maybe you should help. Maybe you should start a home study group or mid-week class and stoke the flames.

The Human Factor

Have you ever wondered why it appears that sometimes the Bible seems to be saying something so clearly, but yet it's not something your leaders believe? Or, vice-versa; it says something different about how to handle something, than the way it's done? Do you ever think to yourself that you seem to understand the text just fine, but you scratch your head and second-guess yourself because of the contradictory nature of your interpretation, when held against mainstream practices? "But...but...oh well. I guess I just must be missing something, and who am I to argue with the status quo."

What is discernment for anyway, if not also to help *you* and *I* understand His instructions? There is not a past or present citizen of God's kingdom who has not had to rely on the Spirit for guidance. That doesn't mean we always do though. People will lay claim to having been led by the Spirit, and then say or teach something that is completely wrong. We are often far too quick to give credit to our personal interpretation as being "Spirit led". None of us are above that possibility. Torah does teach that we need at least two or three who agree to establish

Signed in Blood

a matter (Exodus 23:7). So what are we to do? If highly intelligent and studied people see vastly different things within the same Scriptures, and have debated them since their inception, is it reasonable to believe that we, as average laity, have any hope of getting to the Truth?

Well, the answer is…maybe; and in many cases…sometimes. Here's why though:

1.) We are either too busy or too lazy to study. I'm assuming most readers of this book will be American, so that says a lot. We like to have our coffee weak. We need the air temperature in our churches to be seventy-four degrees, plus or minus two. We think everyone should bathe, dress, and drive as we do. All this is true (ha-ha), but the biggest thing we have against us is our belief that everyone should <u>think</u> as we do. The problem is nobody who wrote any of the Scriptures did any of those things, especially the think part.

2.) We are creatures of habit. That's more than a procedural issue. We just don't like to rock the boat much when it comes to traditional thinking. Claiming the world was round, could once have gotten you killed.

3.) We are intellectually proud and spiritually arrogant. It's our way or the highway from a denominational perspective.

4.) God is Spirit. We are flesh that wants to be like God.

5.) We like to please that flesh, so we interpret Scripture through lenses with pleasing and accommodating color tones.

6.) Every translated Bible, and definitely every commentary we read is influenced by someone's opinion.

7.) Did I mention we are humans? That's clearly our biggest problem.

Unfortunately, that gives us a fairly narrow window of opportunity to get things right. Yet we must work with what we have, mustn't we? So, the logical solution is to purpose in ourselves the willful intent to compensate for these problems. Here are some ways to do that:

1.) Get off our high horse! Learn how other people think, and how they used to think. What was/is the Hebrew mindset? What was/is the Greek? Learn some basic Bible language comprehension. Or, at least familiarize yourself with, and become comfortable using, linguistic aids such as lexicons and dictionaries.

2.) *Practical:* Create new habits. Be willing to try new things. Volunteer for different ministry positions. *Analytical:* Ask questions regarding your church's history and faith practices. Don't accept being a spiritual simpleton. Generate unfamiliar thought by reading material outside your normal scope. Leave behind your *Left Behind* and try works that are more educational.

3.) There will be no denomination in the Kingdom of God. It's one thing to find a group of believers that think the way you do; it's another thing to be in a group who tells you what to think. Find a helpful study group. And feel free to question. Be no man's mental slave.

4.) Be humble enough to always be teachable, and possibly wrong.

5.) Desire Truth at any and all cost—even if that results in something challenging and superseding a previous understanding. Sometimes the truth is stinging and scary; but only at first, and never forever.

6.) Go Literal! As best as you can, learn to study the Scriptures by referring to the original languages as much as possible. The further you drift from them, as easy as some translations may be to read, what you are reading becomes more influenced by some other group's opinion. Perform a little background study on translations. Get several and compare them. Observe the discrepancies and variances, and work to explain them. Discover who wrote them, when, using what original manuscripts, and for what purpose? As far as commentaries go, sure they help. Just keep in mind that a commentary is an educated persuasion. What is the background of this thinker? Do they have an agenda? To be blatant, if you won't do word studies, you will not mature in your understanding.

7.) We have the Spirit, whose current obligation and delight is to council, comfort, teach, and write God's Word on our hearts. Beg Him, plead with Him to guide you into all Truth. Then, when He does, don't ignore (reject) Him by preferring only interpretations that please your flesh.

8.) Identify and embrace the difference between doctrine (tradition) and actual Scripture. Many would like to think they're one in the same, but they're not. Often times, doctrine is a well-stated argument for why we should not take the Scriptures at face value. Remember, there was one point in history that the doctrine of men was responsible for blocking our access to the Scriptures of God.

What you do with what you know is important. But what's more important is knowing that what you do is right. Discipleship has no room for complacency! Ignorance is not bliss! A man can grab a shovel, with hopes to dig a well to rescue his drought-plagued village. He may relentlessly and ambitiously dig with great aspiration, but if He does so right next to yesterday's dry hole, he is but a valiant fool.

Signed in Blood

Blindness is Not a Virtue!

I hope you do see things clearly. If you go to a church, Synagogue, or fellowship and you think it's operating perfectly, I would love for you to send me the address because I'll publish a list called, "Heaven is Here: _____!" Who really goes to the First Church of Utopia? That's not what I'm telling you to search for.

"But Love covers a multitude of sins, right? No place is perfect." True, but the "sins" that should be being overlooked are: the wrong chord struck by the pianist, or the papers falling off the podium, or Miss Billwulweaver's heel breaking off as she's dancing in praise, or the temperature being a little too warm or a little too cold. Not the fact that while the minister is speaking, the worship leader is simultaneously "speaking in tongues", through the loudspeaker, without interpretation. Or, that excessive amounts of your offerings are being sent all over the world for foreign missions (and being spent on local materialism), while there are sick people who can't afford their medications right in your own congregations. Or the bishop, who is secretly seeing a local parish's secretary, who knows what her priest is doing with little Johnny, and keeps quiet. Let's not forget the denominations that embrace homosexuality into the anti-ministry. These sins are not meant to be covered up. Some are meant to be exposed, rejected, and corrected! There *is* therefore condemnation for those things which are *not* done in Christ! The adverse must also be true. (Rom 8:1)

If we are not willing to acknowledge these blatant errors, how can we expect to fix the little, doctrinal differences we have? Maybe, if we could get our churches in order, we could alleviate the bottle-neck of extraneous issues that clog our souls up, and don't allow us to flourish in the Word. Since it is hardly going to get better until His return (come quickly!), and since we will not be able to blame our life's actions on anyone else at our Judicial Assessment, we are just going to have to get spiritually fit however we can.

It's one thing to read the Bible; it's another to pay attention to it. Did you recognize the true sins listed in that prior paragraph? Do you know that's because you were hearing the Witness of Truth's voice, echoing off the mountain, resonating into the future and onto the pages of your heart? Actually, you have probably heard it plenty of times, for a variety of concerns; but maybe you didn't have the wherewithal to answer, "Yes, my Lord. I hear!"

Instead, we go to see the prophet and prophetess teams that arrive into town—the ones that have no accountability for what they say—who can just pop into our lives, mesmerize us, and take off as quick. We go to "miracle" crusades because we need some man to tell us what the Bible says on healing (the man with no professionally documented cases of a miraculous healing), and how big a sacrifice offering we need to give, instead of just reading it for ourselves. How about the revival that's coming next month, from the twelfth to the nineteenth? I'll bet that if you fast that week, and attend every service, you'll hear His voice for sure! But seriously, do you really expect Him to tell you something differing from what He's already been saying for the past six thousand years?

As I imagine you're aware, much of Paul's writings can be easily twisted to one's desired effect. Sadly, this reality is largely responsible for many of our intra-church, factional problems. Unfortunately, those complications are not isolated to intra-church, as they have done their share of damage to the Israel/Christian relationship. After having just taken you through an excursive admonishment on the seriousness of the teaching ministry, we are ready to move forward into even weightier matters, and into the heart of this chapter.

In the letter to the Hebrews, the author spends some time reflecting on the new covenant, as prophesied by Jeremiah, but most have read this through a dark glass because of traditional oversight and bias. I implore you...pay very close attention to this next section. It is complex, and the devil is very much in the details. If you need to read it several times before you are secure in it, do so. To just acquiesce to confusion will be problematic, and a shame. If you can conquer this, prepare to soar.

The New and Improved Covenant

But now He has obtained a more excellent ministry, by as much as He is also the mediator of a **better** covenant, which has been enacted on better promises. (7) For if that first *covenant* had been faultless, **there would have been no occasion sought for a second.** (8) For finding fault **with them**, He says, 'BEHOLD, DAYS ARE COMING, SAYS THE LORD, WHEN I WILL EFFECT A NEW COVENANT WITH THE HOUSE OF ISRAEL AND WITH THE HOUSE OF JUDAH; (9) **NOT LIKE THE COVENANT** WHICH I MADE WITH THEIR FATHERS ON THE DAY WHEN I TOOK THEM BY THE HAND TO LEAD THEM OUT OF THE LAND OF EGYPT; **FOR THEY DID NOT CONTINUE** IN MY COVENANT, AND I DID NOT CARE FOR THEM, SAYS THE LORD. (10) FOR THIS IS THE COVENANT THAT I WILL MAKE WITH THE HOUSE OF ISRAEL AFTER THOSE DAYS, SAYS THE LORD: I WILL PUT MY LAWS INTO THEIR MINDS, AND I WILL WRITE THEM ON THEIR HEARTS. AND I WILL BE THEIR GOD, AND THEY SHALL BE MY PEOPLE. (11) AND THEY SHALL NOT TEACH EVERYONE HIS FELLOW CITIZEN, AND EVERYONE HIS BROTHER, SAYING, 'KNOW THE LORD,' FOR ALL WILL KNOW ME, FROM THE LEAST TO THE GREATEST OF THEM. (12) FOR I WILL BE MERCIFUL TO THEIR INIQUITIES, AND I WILL REMEMBER THEIR SINS NO MORE.' (13) When He said, 'A new covenant,'

Signed in Blood

He has made the first obsolete. But whatever is **becoming** obsolete and **growing** old is **ready** to disappear. (Hebrews 8:6)

Did you just read that right? Hold on. The first covenant could have possibly been adequate? And this new covenant, the one we are apparently participants in, "is *becoming* obsolete and is *ready* to disappear"? That can't be right! It must mean the *Old* one is "becoming obsolete". But that can't be right either, because that would mean the old covenant had/has not yet fully disappeared. But that can't be right, because that would mean there are two covenants operating simultaneously. What a covenundrum!

And I will establish My covenant between Me and thee and thy seed after thee **throughout** their generations for an **everlasting** covenant, to be a God unto thee and to thy seed after thee. And God said: Nay, but Sarah thy wife shall bear thee a son; and thou shalt call his name Isaac; and I will establish My covenant with him for an **everlasting** covenant for his seed after him. (Genesis 17:7 & 9)
And He <u>established</u> it unto Jacob for a statute, to Israel for an **everlasting** covenant. (1st Chronicles 16:17)

I let that sound a bit confusing on purpose, so I can show you how easy it is to take some Scripture and send it in two different directions. This is especially capable of happening when it is taken out of context, or when the interpretation conflicts with Scripture given elsewhere. Most of us have all read this and been told, or assumed, Paul was reminding us the old covenant was history, and not in the sense of time.

First of all, no one knows who wrote the book of Hebrews, and it was very likely not Paul. Most scholars agree that the writing style and Greek construction does not reflect his. But even if it was Paul, he sure knew how to confuse an issue (as he was already renowned for, even in his own day; e.g. 2nd Peter 3:16). And second, it seems that one minute a covenant is everlasting, and the next, in Hebrews, it's obsolete. What singular, "first" covenant is being spoken of anyway? There are several covenants in Scripture, and the first was made with Adam. You obviously have to read this a little more carefully to get to what's really being said.

Jesus is the mediator of the, "…better covenant built on better promises." I have absolutely no problem with that. However, "better" does not necessitate *entirely different*. When I read this, being the slightly inquisitive person that I am, I am inclined to ask myself, "What though, exactly are the terms of this better covenant?" Every covenant in Scripture given previously laid out some terms. They were either, "If you do this, I'll do that." Or they were, "If you don't do this, I'll do that." Or the covenant was simply, "This is what I AM going to do."

The covenants with Noah, Abraham, Isaac, Jacob, and David are clearly stated, and as they continue to develop from generation to generation, more and more revelation as to the details of the redemptive plan are discovered. There are other covenants as well; covenants of salt and of peace. We'll not go into those, as they are off-topic for now, but I brought them up for the purpose of further establishing that we can't lump the entirety of the Hebrew Scriptures into a singular, contiguous covenant package.

Then, following Jacob, comes the Lord and Moses together, who declare the continuing covenants with even more detail regarding both the stipulations and the promises. As Moses re-teaches Torah again in Deuteronomy to that next generation, even more detail is given. Was it this proclamation that remained intact, until Jesus came along and trashed it; or was it all of them, including the Ten Words, that were cancelled? Did Jesus, in all His actual, infinite wisdom forget to tell us, and left this most crucial detail up to an anonymous author to do it? Strangely, the first time we hear the phrase "new covenant" from Jesus Himself is at His last Passover meal, and all He says about it is that it exists, and that His body is what will be the 'b'rit' (the cutting), and that His blood will be poured out for the remission of sin. How can there be such silence over such an incredibly weighty topic?

Looking throughout the transcribed teachings of the Master's direct words, we find any number of allusions and referrals to events that correspond with aspects of the new covenant, as seen in Jeremiah. Yet, He personally is curiously silent about the particulars of how His forthcoming death was going to affect the system of *worship* Israel had always known. We are able to gather that He would be the first and only atonement offering that was eternally acceptable, with both retroactive and perpetual qualities, more from external commentary than from Jesus Himself. Have you ever noticed that? To me, that just seems odd. Why would Jesus not plainly come out and say, "I am replacing the entire sacrificial system" or, "I am terminating the Levitical system as the new High Priest"? Jesus's atonement is most definitely a very great work, but where and what are the other aspects of this *new* covenant? Let's begin by examining the phrase itself.

Any lawyer will tell you that a covenant is an agreement between two or more parties, and that the terms of the agreement must be clearly specified in advance. Really, what kind of incredibly important, life-altering contract would you sign without reading the stipulations? Another thing any lawyer would tell you is that any time the slightest adjustment is made to an existing contract, a new draft should be drawn up; or, at the

Signed in Blood

least, adjustments need to be signed off by both parties. A contract with an amendment would be considered a revision. Also, no single party can make an adjustment after the document has been signed, without the other's acknowledgment and/or consent, depending on how it's written. That means that an enhanced version of a previous covenant can retain any given amount of the original and be called "New" or "Better".

In the Hebrew, the word for 'new' is: Chadash (H2319). This word has some controversy associated with it in relation to this very topic, because of the implications inherent with Strong's secondary meaning of: repaired, renewed or restored (H2318). Although it would be advantageous for me to claim that alternate definition, I am going to take the more critical approach and build this exposition on the primary, which is simply: "a new, fresh thing".

What I am saying is this: the Law, which came four hundred and thirty years later, **does not invalidate a covenant** previously ratified by God, so as to nullify the promise. (Galatians 3:17)

Yet we are mighty quick to presume a future one does? God's covenants are never anything less than eternal. Not one has He ever reneged on. We're the ones who do!

Let's look at the details of this new covenant. What are the obvious differences? There are, depending on your perspective, about seven major components. For the sake of this current discussion, we will be focusing on five. Let's start with the first three:

1. We have a new mediator; a Great High Priest, in Jesus.
2. The Law (Torah) will be 'perfectly' put into our hearts and minds, more than just being written into stone, and further taught and encouraged by the priesthood. I say 'perfectly', because our obedience to it currently is far from automatic and instinctive. (Psalm 40:8, "I delight to do Your will, O my God; Your Law is within my heart.")
3. The Torah will be fully known by all, and there will be no more need to be taught it. The Spirit Himself will teach us.

It appears then that the "law-oriented" covenants are still active. The latest covenant is happening and will continue to progress until, "all has been fulfilled." The fullness of it is far from accomplished. The work of redemption was what was being referred to in the words, "It is finished!" not our need for Torah. It then also only stands to reason that a whole lot of the original terms of *the* covenant are still active (e.g. "You shall not lay with the wife of your neighbor." Leviticus 18:20), and therefore are independent of the Temple's or priesthood's state. I want you to note that this law is located outside the list of Ten in Exodus 20—the reason being that there is no scripturally supportable teaching that the Ten Words are the stipulations of a separate (and depending who you talk to…eternal or temporary covenant) while all the other laws have been abolished.

The First Covenant

…not like the covenant which I made with their fathers <u>in the day I took them by the hand</u> to bring them out of the land of Egypt, My covenant which they broke, although I was a husband to them, declares the LORD. (Jeremiah 31:32)

One of the aspects noted here is that it will not be *like* the one made upon exiting Egypt. Technically, there is a separation with distinction between the covenant made at the departure ("the day He took them by the hand") and the three made at Sinai (about three months later; Exodus 19:1). That difference is seen in the overall quantity and specifics of the information given. It is noteworthy because it is rarely considered, and does create a possible variance in how we could understand this portion of Hebrews.

When this difference is considered, it separates the Passover/Unleavened bread instruction found in Exodus 12, from all the rest of what is asked of us later. The main subject of Exodus 12 is the means of redemption through which the Hebrews would be rescued. The Passover Seder, which acts as the memorial meal for this event, was supposed to be perpetually observed by all generations. The instruction to *remember* the Passover was given at the same time as the instruction to *perform* it was; that first time it was done. It could then be understood that when they agreed to be rescued from slavery, via the blood of the Paschal lamb, they simultaneously agreed to perpetually require the blood of a future one for the same, exact thing.

Obviously, due to the importance of this matter, after that first generation of Israelites died off in the desert, the next generation was reminded of their obligation to this event (Deuteronomy 29), and all the rest of the "Ways of the LORD" (Jeremiah 5:4), by renewing the previous covenants (albeit with some additional commentary) just prior to their entering the Promised Land. Eventually, they reneged on this obligation and symbolically this was, in God's eyes, from them taking their eyes off their need for a redeemer. Is there a bigger mistake than that?

If this is the context from which the author of Hebrews has chosen to derive his teaching, then the need for a new covenant is more specifically related to Jesus coming and being our Passover Lamb, whose blood is perpetually applied to the doorposts of our hearts. And if that is true, it would even more clearly support the idea that the new covenant was not instituted to destroy the other, larger areas of instruction later given at Sinai.

If the "first" covenant with the Hebrews is not that isolated in content, and "the day He brought them out" is a figurative phrase encompassing the first couple months of their freedom, then what is being spoken of is found outlined in the book of Exodus, in chapters 20-24, and includes all the instructions that came down from the mountain. When carefully examined, you will find that this contract with the Hebrews was agreed to, both before and after the terms were given. It was originally agreed to without all the details (by faith), and later confirmed with complete, albeit at times progressive disclosure. This is exactly how we still come to faith today! We hear a little bit of the promise. We like what we hear. We accept Jesus as our Savior. We come as we are, and then as time goes on we learn more about our responsibilities (sanctification) as believers. If you put the cart before the horse, the Law would eventually kill you through a works-based salvation attempt.

(Before) Exodus 19:8, "All the people answered together and said, 'All that the LORD has spoken we will do!' And Moses brought back the words of the people to the LORD."

(After) Exodus 24:7, "Then he took the book of the covenant and read *it* in the hearing of the people; and they said, 'All that the LORD has spoken we will do, and we will be obedient!'"

After their agreement to the terms, came the ratification in blood:

So Moses took the blood and sprinkled *it* on the people, and said, 'Behold the blood of the covenant, which the LORD has made with you in accordance with all these words. (Exodus 24:8)

Sound familiar? Jesus revealed to us the meaning of the blood symbolism seen through the wine, during the Final Seder (Last Supper).

And when He had taken a cup and given thanks, He gave *it* to them, saying, "Drink from it, all of you; for this is My blood of the covenant, which is poured out for many for forgiveness of sins." (Matthew 26:27 & 28)

We must go back to look at something though. It all didn't go down quite that smoothly. Moses did read the book of the covenant to them; the same one they had agreed to in advance to obey, and re-agreed to. Moses then went back up the mountain for a forty day revelation, and upon completion received an honorary degree in Tabernacle engineering. What happened while He was up there? Certain people, assisted by the future High Priest himself, Aaron, had already broken the covenant they made by breaking the second commandment.

The result was a severe chastisement. The merciful Elohiym that had just delivered them gave them an accelerated education on taking Him and His words seriously. The Lord then called Moses back up the mountain, and did something that is rarely recognized. He renewed the covenant. He re-inscribed the stone tablets and sent Moses back down to institute the new theocracy and society of Israel. God didn't change the stipulations of this second chance, *renewed* covenant at all. The people broke the covenant, by disobeying the covenant terms. Keeping this in mind, we are ready to look back at Jeremiah's new covenant, as mirrored in Hebrews, looking for the part where it tells us what the problem with the earlier instructions in righteousness were.

8:7, "For if that first *covenant* had been faultless, there would have been no occasion sought for a second."

8:8, "For finding fault with *them...*"

Huh, that's strange. I've always been taught the Law was the problem. Actually, it *appears* to be the 'covenant' that had a problem. And what's even stranger is that God would make a faulty covenant. I want you to think very carefully here because if that's true, God really did rescue the Hebrews, to create a nation of them, to damn them in the desert. I told you this wasn't going to be your average book.

What is the fault mentioned here then? One clue is seen in the fact that the word 'covenant' in verses seven and thirteen is in italics. Why? Because there is no 'diatheke' in the original text, following the word *first*. It could easily be assumed, which is the point of the *italics*, that the covenant is what's being considered here. Maybe there is another possibility. And if so, what *first* is in question?

Hebrews 7:28a, "For the Law appoints <u>men</u> as high priests <u>who are weak</u>..."

Hebrews 8:1, "Now the <u>main point</u> in what has been said *is this:* we have such a <u>high priest</u>."

Perhaps it is the priesthood being discussed here, and the *first* priesthood was inadequate to affect the heart of man.

We have a constitution and a government, but they are both powerless to make us love America, or its leaders. It goes on to say that the fault was, "found *in* <u>them</u>!" Have you ever noticed that? Is the *"them"*

Signed in Blood

speaking in reference to the House of Israel and the House of Judah? The "them" mentioned could be either the priesthood or the Israelites, but it is clearly not the covenant. The reason Jesus had to cut a new covenant was not because the perfect Law failed! It couldn't fail at something it was never intended to do:

Hebrews 7:19a, "for the Law made nothing perfect..."

What was weak in the Law was our flesh! Paul understood this, and agreed with it in Romans 8:3:

"For what the Law could not do, weak as it was through the flesh, God did: sending His own Son in the likeness of sinful flesh and as an offering for sin, He condemned sin in the flesh..."

Neither the Torah nor His covenants are capable of failing! The LORD's instructions for His people to live righteously are not faulty. We are! We are the fault! Contrary to modern, traditional thought:

Psalms 19:7, "The law of the LORD is perfect, restoring the soul; the testimony of the LORD is sure, making wise the simple."

So then, how can something He made perfect be "growing old"? Isn't *growing* a present, continuous tense verb? Considering the letter to the Hebrews was written after the atoning blood of Yeshua was poured out, and since we as believers are participants in the new covenant now, how could the author be saying that the new covenant is growing old, or *becoming* obsolete? This text is truly a challenging one to understand, and can't be if read without focused intent.

The letter to the Hebrews has always been understood to contain difficult material, which is ultimately the reason it was one of the last books to get into various canons. There are some who propose it should never have gotten in at all, due to some of these very issues. I'll not make that call, but I will confess there are problematic issues that, although great strides have been made to clarify them, most expositors are not on the same page. But if it is to be reconciled, it must be done in light of all the rest of Scripture, both Hebrew and Greek. Perhaps we don't always know the original intent of the author. Perhaps we can only come real close. In order to attempt to, we may have to think outside the dogmatic box. It's a lot easier to just pretend things are not what they are, and not deal with them, but I'm not going to let you get away with that here.

For something that was made perfect by God, to then become obsolescent, requires a little contemplation to get a handle on. It can only be understood with accurate interpretation and context. It is not without precedent, however. Can you think of any examples of things God originally made perfect, that did not remain as such? Sure you can. And aren't we expecting those things to one day be restored again? Keep this line of reasoning in mind as we consider the "better" covenant. If we are going to endeavor to reconcile this passage with other areas of Scripture, we are first going to have to accept the fact that if we can't, then it is not true. So let's try hard, shall we?

Now, what if this text is actually speaking of the *first* covenant, and not the *first* priesthood? Although they are different, because they are so intertwined, thematically, in the end, we will obtain the same result.

Let's imagine you are a homebuyer. You find a house that you desperately want, but you can't quite afford it. You go to your bank and negotiate a hybrid promissory note that requires interest only payments for a ten year timeframe. You accept the terms of the mortgage, sign on the fifty or so dotted lines, and voila!—you are the owner of a new home. Nine years go by, and you start coming to the end of that term of your mortgage agreement. Let's say for the sake of argument, from about the ninth year on, a part of your contract is beginning to expire. But it is actually a fully in force, perfectly legal contract, up until the clock strikes twelve at the end of the thirtieth year. Let's try another angle.

You are part of a property investment group. There are ten of you. All of you pooled an equal amount of money together and purchased a speculative parcel of land, in hopes of it becoming a commercially desired plot someday. Amongst your group, you have an agreement which you all accepted, and drew into a contract, which states that every year on such and such a date you will all come together to discuss your investment, and the options that are currently available. The property is owned by the entire group, and that cannot change without a majority vote to sell. Your business agreement states that each and every year a vote to hold or sell must be taken. That is a term that expires and must be annually renewed. Those are examples of perfectly good and active, legal contracts between participants, which still have "growing old" characteristics. Let's call an agreement like that, "The Time of the Gentiles".

There is neither evidence, nor prophecy, anywhere else in all Scripture that suggests any of God's eternal covenants are not just that...eternal. That does not mean that certain terms cannot expire, or that adjustments can't be made; or, and this is where much of the confusion comes from, conditions need to be met. This would not be true however, without disclosure. If that's true (and I believe with absolute confidence that it is), none of the previous covenants were ever cancelled by a following one. The Noahic covenant was not cancelled by the

Signed in Blood

Abrahamic. The Abrahamic covenant was not cancelled by the Mosaic, and so forth (Galatians 3:17). So, a condition not being met by man, as set forth in the Mosaic covenant (the only conditional covenant given in Scripture), only invokes the "if you/then I" stipulations. It clearly does not cancel the entire covenant, because "they (Israel) did, and therefore He…" quite often happened, with apparent covenant retention.

Whether or not this new covenant is truly brand new, or simply another renewed and improved version, there is absolutely not one comment made by Jesus, or the Father, a prophet or apostle, that instructs us to consider any one of the previous covenants cancelled. To prove this, simply pick any one covenant, cancel it and consider the consequences. It would be nothing less than catastrophic. It would disrupt the whole flow of Scripture—hence our denominational nightmare, and doctrinal incongruence. I personally believe Jesus did "cut" a brand new covenant, through His death, framed around the one Israel had been party to for the previous fifteen hundred years. A fantastic, "praise the Lord" aspect of this new covenant, is found in its similarly unconditional nature.

So, why are we so quick to believe the Mosaic covenant has been put through the proverbial shredder? Why does it grate many of our nerves to think He still wants to guard our lives from pain and sorrow? Pure ignorance. We simply do not understand that the old covenant is only old when the reader cannot read Moses with eyes unveiled. It is old, when Yeshua is not seen in the Torah. It is old, when we have no desire to understand it, or submit ourselves to it, with a heart of love. It is old, when our hearts are hardened towards it. What is done away with in the new covenant is not Moses, it is the veil! Read it again:

> But their minds were hardened; for until this very day at the reading of the old covenant the same veil remains unlifted, because it is removed in Christ (16)…but whenever a person turns to the Lord, the veil is taken away. (2nd Corinthians 3:14 & 16)

So, in fact, what makes this old covenant, "…not like the one made with Israel, when they came out of Egypt," is that Israel could break that one; and the new one, once fully engaged, they cannot. The first was conditional, the second is not. Which means that it is not fully engaged until the millennial reign is underway; and even then, it's only for the glorified. The same "ministry of death and condemnation," (to the lost), switches modes and becomes a "ministry of righteousness, and transforms us from glory to glory." Again, let me remind you of the better promises we are considering:

1) The full capacity to be naturally obedient because the Torah is etched by His finger on our hearts of flesh, instead of on tablets of stone, which can be shattered (Ezekiel 11:19).

2) The ritual sacrifices would no longer be necessary because the Perfect Lamb would eventually be slain.

3) We would have a greater High Priest, who is in continual intercession for us at the throne of the Father.

4) The restoration of the land to Israel (Northern and Southern Tribes).

There is something else to see here; something of great significance. This covenant that is *growing* old (because not everyone is in perfect submission to it, or believes in Yeshua) was made with the House of Judah and the House of Israel (Hebrews 8:8). Notice now, this new covenant results with only a House of Israel (8:10). There is no church or religion mentioned. What is that all about?

Say to them, thus says the Lord GOD, Behold, I will take the stick of Joseph, which is in the hand of Ephraim, and the tribes of Israel, his companions; and I will put them with it, with the stick of Judah, and make them one stick, and they will be one in My hand. (Ezekiel 37:19)

5.) The fulfillment of this new covenant will also be seen in the joining of the two houses of Israel. Physical Israel and their fellow sojourners (metaphorically: believing Jews and believing non-Jews), will no longer function as two separate halves of the Kingdom.[1]

So, we have ourselves a little issue here, don't we? The details of this new covenant don't appear to line up with our current spiritual state, religious ideology or national identity. And there is another discrepancy. Did you catch it? I planted it. Promise #2 is actually not mentioned at all, but it is often presumed. Actually, contrarily, just a little past the new covenant portion of Jeremiah 31 is the "Davidic line will always sit on the throne" portion of chapter thirty-three. Congruent with that prophecy is the "Levitical priesthood will offer sacrifices continually" portion. We say that Jesus will sit on the throne of David as King of Israel, but what about the sacrifices? Are they actually separable? You should go read it. The prophecy is sworn with the same faithfulness as night and day's continuance. Jesus's sacrifice certainly accomplished something; but apparently sacrifices are about more than just sin. Don't fret; we'll get into that too.

None of these "better promises" appear to demonstrate a complete eradication of any previous promises either. It is a troubling paradox that the book of Hebrews is both a large foundation stone for the church's theology (which happens to be somewhat antinomian), and it is also very squarely built on traditional, Pharisaical thought. The way Hebrews was written shows us a primary intent of the author was to verify the preeminence of Christ—and rightfully so, when contrasted with an earthly high priest and earthly temple. But it should not be understood as doing so, at the expense of what else this same Christ said when acting as the Word of God, before His incarnation.

The book of Hebrews has other contextual issues which we will not discuss here. Studied individuals are very aware of them. I have no desire to pet that tiger. This is not the time or place for such an exposition. What I have chosen to do instead is draw optimistic conclusions about the writer's intentions, in order to explain certain inconsistencies which have been used to promote the cancelled covenant heresy. So let's move forward.

This portion of Jeremiah is the only reference in the Hebrew Scriptures to the new covenant. There is a portion of Ezekiel regarding the "heart of stone becoming a heart of flesh" which is definitely related, but it is not in the same covenantal structure, nor does it use the label. If this is all we have to go on, it is likewise what we have to base our doctrine on. There is then no doubt that the new covenant has only partially been fulfilled. Are you now beginning to contemplate the ramifications for this fact? Let me remind you again.

What I am saying is this: the Law, which came four hundred and thirty years later, **does not invalidate a covenant** previously ratified by God, so as to nullify the promise. (Galatians 3:17)

The earlier and the latter covenants are still functioning; therefore, the "Old" cannot be so quickly shunned or disregarded. Remember, covenant and law are two different things, but the Mosaic covenant would not be a covenant without the Law to define its terms. The covenant is "We will do!" The Law is "what to do". And just like how *some* of that Law is not currently applicable, *some* of the new covenant is not yet visible. This makes perfect sense when you understand that we are continually, and have been from the very beginning, *entering* into it. We are just not there. This is the truest expression of progressive covenant theology!

Likewise, *covenant* and *testament* are also different things. They can both be contracts, but one is in force during the lives of the parties, while the other doesn't become active until a party dies. This latter type of contract is commonly known as a will. In the Greek, the word for covenant is the same one used for testament. This is why in differing

Bible translations the words 'covenant' and 'testament' are used interchangeably, in Hebrews chapter nine. However, their meanings are not so easily interchangeable. Here is a perfect example of our problem:

Hebrews 9:18, "Whereupon neither the first *testament* was dedicated without blood (KJV)."

Everybody knows blood doesn't need to be shed for a will to be written. A closer examination of this ninth chapter of Hebrews shows a shift in topics right in mid-stream, from covenant to will, and back to covenant again. If you're not careful, you'll miss it. We know this because the author verifies his return to topic in vs. 20, which is being drawn from its original location in Exodus 24:8:

"saying, 'THIS IS THE BLOOD OF THE COVENANT WHICH GOD COMMANDED YOU.'"

Moses was not talking about a will there in Exodus. But clearly, the writer is here:

For where a covenant is, there must of necessity be the death of the one who made it. For a covenant is valid *only* when men are dead, for it is never in force while the one who made it lives. (Hebrews 9:16 & 17, NASU)

The NASU, staying true to its desired literary accuracy and consistency, inserts the word covenant. Obviously, in context, it makes no sense. Nowhere in Scripture has a man had to die to *create* a contract. Keeping all this in mind, we can now see how to make sense of this verse:

For this reason He is the mediator of a new covenant, so that, <u>since a death has taken place</u> for the redemption of the transgressions <u>that **were** *committed* under the first</u> covenant, those who have been called may receive the promise of the eternal inheritance. (Hebrews 9:15)

It appears that the author understood that Jesus's death enabled a will to go into effect, where the inheritance is eternal life, for those who sinned prior to His death. The author is speaking of sins committed in the past tense. Then, as is clear by the rest of the chapter, he understands that this inheritance becomes available to all, as the new covenant has been instituted. A new covenant, yes; but not a new testament! Jesus is not going to have to die again, and we are already full heirs. The only semblance that can be made from this author's wording comes if he is understood to be speaking with a degree of poetic license, because none of the previous covenants given to us are spoken of, or should be

Signed in Blood

understood as having been intended to be, wills becoming active upon death. If they were, an awful lot of people have received their inheritances inappropriately, and still are. And what happens when that happens? People go prodigal!

What really disturbs me is the fact that the greater part of the church has allowed a very significant portion of its theology and ideology to be built upon this creative analogy, found in an obscure verse, in a very Hebraic letter. THERE IS NO "NEW" TESTAMENT, when understood in today's contractual vernacular! Hence my use of the preferred terms: *Apostolic Scriptures* or *Greek Scriptures*. And yet, that's what nearly every single Bible publisher has titled the latter quarter of its textual content. Some may consider this to be insignificant, but when considered in combination with the doctrinal errors associated with "New Testament" era, replacement theology, it is a very big deal. The Bible is one continuous story of redemption and revelation. The Gospels are *testimony* that Jesus is in fact the awaited Messiah. As much as some wish it to be true, it is not two books (one being "archaic") inside one cover!

The book of Ephesians is often touted by Christian educators as being the book which expresses the new covenant, because it speaks in terms, and is arranged in a format, that allows for this suggestion. But you really have to stretch the intent of the letter. Regardless, if any Apostolic Scripture contradicts Moses, it would have been written by a false prophet and it must be rejected. Therefore, how we go about interpreting and understanding the Letter to the Ephesians must be done in consideration of that fact as well. Whatever the book, whoever the author, no humanly derived, covenantal teaching supersedes this:

When you are in distress and all these things have come upon you, **in the latter days** you will return to the LORD your God and listen to His voice. For the LORD your God is a compassionate God; He will not fail you nor destroy you **nor forget the covenant** with **your fathers** which He swore to them. (Deuteronomy 4:30 & 31)

I hope you read that verse and let it sink in. What is the point of remembering a dead covenant?

<u>We</u> are commanded by Scripture to consider ourselves as having been with the Hebrews as they were delivered from Egypt.

When your son asks you <u>in time to come</u>, saying, 'What *do* the testimonies and the statutes and the judgments *mean* which the LORD our God commanded you? Then you shall say to your son: We were slaves to Pharaoh in Egypt, and the LORD brought us from Egypt with a mighty hand.' (Deuteronomy 6:20 & 21)

You shall remember that you were a slave in the land of Egypt, and the LORD your God brought you out of there by a mighty hand and by an outstretched arm; therefore the LORD your God commanded you to observe the Sabbath day. (Deuteronomy 5:15)

Understanding that these verses were spoken to a mixed crowd of people, the majority of whom were born in the desert, or were just children upon leaving Egypt, let us do that!

We were rescued from slavery and given the hope of a "Promised Land" to look forward to. We (you and I), at some point, stood at the base of Mt. Sinai/Horeb and listened to the thundering of God's voice as He began to declare the terms of *a* covenant. After receiving the Ten Words, we couldn't handle His voice anymore and requested that Moses receive and deliver all other instruction to them himself. Eventually, they all heard them. And as shown previously, they accepted them. Therefore, by proxy, so did we. But what did we accept, and what was its purpose? You did know it was made with you too, didn't you?

Now not with you alone am I making this covenant and this oath, but both with those who stand here with us today in the presence of the LORD our God, **and with those who are not with us here today**. (Deuteronomy 29:14 & 15)

Just Believe?

Here is its purpose and what we agreed to: Our Covenant.

See, I (Moses) have taught you statutes and judgments just as the LORD my God commanded me, that you should do thus in the land where you are entering to possess it. So **keep and do** *them*, for that is **your wisdom** and **your understanding** in the sight of the **peoples who will hear** all these statutes and say, 'surely this great nation is a wise and understanding people.' For what great nation is there that has a **god so near** to it as is the LORD our God whenever we call on Him? Or what great nation is there that **has statutes and judgments as righteous** as this **whole law** which I am setting before you today? (Deuteronomy 4:5-8) (Original, life-style evangelism.)

But from there (the Promised Land) you will seek the LORD your God, **and you will find** *Him* if you search for Him with all your heart and all your soul. (Deuteronomy 4:29)

So you shall **keep** His **statutes** and His **commandments** which I am giving you today, **that it may go well with you and with your children after you**, and that **you may live long** on the land which the LORD your God is giving you for all time. (Deuteronomy 4:40)

You shall not add to the word which I am commanding you, nor take away from it, that you may keep the commandments of the LORD your God which I command you. (Deuteronomy 4:2)

Signed in Blood

Notice, this is not soteriological (salvation-oriented) rhetoric here! The Hebrews agreed to do whatever God says, and that's exactly the same thing we agreed to do (or should have done) when we made our confession of faith and accepted the covenant of Love. This leads me to something else that has to be said.

The Fire Insurance Fallacy

You shepherds out there, whose desire it is to bring in the lost sheep, would you do those same lost sheep a big favor, and determine to tell them what they are actually doing when they walk up to your altars to "accept Jesus!" There are far too many, who are inadequately informed as they, "Call upon the name of the LORD to be saved"; as if that's all there is to it.

You need to teach people that they are entering in to a prenuptial agreement ("For they will be my people, and I will be their God."), and that there are some stipulations (like submission and faithfulness). I'm not suggesting you teach them every commandment there is before they pray the "wretched man that I am" prayer. That would be the undoing of the Acts Fifteen council's verdict, and would be counterproductive to the gospel. But don't lead them on into thinking there is no responsibility upon them, but to "believe". At least tell them they will need to "take up a cross and follow Him." (Do what He did.)

A sneaky, 'get-em-in', raise your numbers gospel is a disservice at the least. It's a future abortion at its worst. His people quickly need to learn that disobedience is as rotten fruit. People need to count the cost, so when they make the decision to invest, they'll not make an early withdrawal and have to pay the penalty. Where in the Scriptures is it taught that we are to make converts? What we should intend to do with those coming to faith is make disciples. One does come before the other, but how long should one remain under the title 'convert'... a week, maybe a month? I see no reason why there should ever be an instance where one coming to faith has not been informed of their essential obligations, prior to their confession of faith, with the exception of death bed ministry. (Which is generally a last ditch effort for hope's sake anyway.)

Oh that there were one among you who would shut the gates, that you might not uselessly kindle *fire on* My altar! I am not pleased with you, says the LORD of hosts, nor will I accept an offering from you. (Malachi 1:10)

Apparently, going through the motions is just not good enough! "But I thought that there were no more requirements to our faith but love? After all, love is the heart of the Torah, isn't it?" Uh huh...but how exactly do you express it? Who is the grand, exalted Pooh-Bah in each local fellowship that gets to dictate the definition of love for that group? Doesn't love also require discipline? Who gets to decide the appropriate action? With God, it's possible to love everyone, granted it might be hard. So why don't we let adult people marry as many children as they want? Jesus never taught we couldn't. What if someone defined love as exterminating abortion doctors? After all, they are murderers, and love would want all those little children to have a chance? Why can't we have sex with animals? Don't we *love* them? Sure, it *seems* wrong, but the Apostolic Scriptures don't specifically say not to! Maybe someone *thinks* it would be an expression of love to the Creator, to adorn His creation (a tree) with ribbons, and bake little cakes to put in their branches, and burn incense as a sweet smell to His nostrils. How much sarcasm must I use before I effectively make my point?

A scripturally undefined system of loving, yields an 'all emotions allowed' religion. A partially undefined system yields denominations. A homosexual person is capable of love, isn't he or she? So let's give them a collar and a pulpit shall we? Why not let pedophiles work in your nurseries? I'm sure they *feel* something they define as love for children. A fundamentalist, polygamist Mormon loves all of his wives. Some people really love the person they are living with, but are not married to. But is that the agape variety, or the eros? Left up to our own devices, we would never create our own Torah of Truth (Malachi 2:6). We would destroy each other in an unbridled game of survival of the fittest and best *feeling* religion.

Thankfully, God, in His providential care, has deemed it wise to give us, in written form, His prescribed way to love Him and to serve Him. It must be found though, from cover to cover. We don't need the Bible to tell us there is a God. We need a Bible to tell us what He's like, and what He expects of us personally. He has also given us His program to run a society in the best way possible, whilst under the curse of the fall. So, let's get back to the requirements.

If Jesus's personal sacrifice has done what other sin offerings couldn't, and through His death has taken upon Himself the sentence due all humanity, for our various forms of rebellion, we can consider those "Due upon Receipt" provisions, "Paid in Full!" But what are the other requirements of our spiritual constitution? How can we know what we are still obligated to? Well, I guess that takes us back to an earlier question. How hard is it to comprehend (obey) the Bible? And I will now add, are we as 21st Century believers, scattered abroad the world, capable of it?

Signed in Blood

Is it Worthy?

So the LORD commanded us to observe all these statutes, to fear the LORD our God <u>for our good</u> **always** and <u>for our survival</u>, as *it is* today. <u>It will be righteousness for us</u> if we are careful to observe all this commandment before the LORD our God, just as He commanded us. (Deuteronomy 6:24 & 25)

Now there's a verse that could use to be preached on more often. Do you know why you don't hear that? Because it will mess with Joe preacher's cookie-cutter theology in a way that he's not prepared to deal with. Observing Torah is **good**, **always**, and will help us **survive**, and be accounted as **righteousness**. There are <u>not</u> two separate categories of *doing* righteousness: an old one for Jews and a new one for Christians. Neither is this suggesting that before Jesus's death, there was a works-based salvation program, as it is generally understood.

Finally, brethren, whatever is true, whatever is honorable, whatever is right, whatever is pure, whatever is lovely, whatever is of good repute, if there is any excellence and if anything worthy of praise, dwell on these things. (Philemon 4:8)

Running Torah through these filters it becomes a lot easier to conclude what is of value to us…all of Torah! Yes, there are things we are not to do, but from all of it is derived priceless knowledge and life-protecting wisdom. In some cases, Torah cannot be obeyed because there is no temple structure. In other cases, Torah cannot be obeyed because the Levitical priesthood is not presiding. You may be thinking, "But we are the new priesthood!" I am speaking in the literal, Aaronic, lineage-based sense that Moses was speaking of. Even though Israel was a "kingdom of priests (Exodus 19:6)," not everyone was a Levite. Sometimes, the Torah cannot be fully obeyed because Israel has been scattered. Not all are residing in geographic Israel, and not all men are capable of going there at least three times a year.

So do we throw out the baby with the bathwater and say forget the rest if we can't keep some? Are we believers that the Lord could not foresee these problems? If we are to believe that, we should also ignore the fact that a Mercy Seat perpetually covered over the Law-containing ark.

Haven't you ever noticed that when a situation arose amongst the Israelites, for which protocol wasn't already clearly established in the Law, Moses would bring it before God, in the Tent of Meeting, and He would give instruction as to how to attend to it? An inheritance issue would arise—He would solve it (Numbers 27:1-11). A person couldn't attend Passover for some reason—God would set an alternate date for them

(Numbers 9:6-11). It's not just about the details of the letter. It's about our attitude towards it, and desire to follow it to the best of our ability. That should be our attitude as well. If we can do it, and we don't break Torah in an effort to follow Torah, then we should, especially if its teachings are: true, honorable, right, pure, lovely, of good report, excellent, and worthy of praise. Now I'm going to pull out the big guns. Theologians out there...Are you ready? Remember how I recently mentioned that we also accepted the covenant?

> ...that you may **enter into** the covenant with the LORD your God, and into His oath which the LORD your God is making with you today, in order that He may establish you today as His people and that He may be your God, just as He spoke to you and as He swore to **your fathers**, to Abraham, Isaac, and Jacob. Now **not with you alone** am I making this covenant and this oath, but both with those who stand here with us today in the presence of the LORD our God and with **those who are not with us** here today. (Deuteronomy 29:12-15)

Okay. What we have here is a portion of Scripture that anyone can clearly see is being given to both the current audience and to all of future Israel, as far into an indeterminable future as can be seen. Before you jump to the conclusion that when Moses said, "Those who are not with us," he was talking about the kids, and the women and such...

> You stand today, all of you, before the LORD your God: your chiefs, your tribes, your elders and your officers, *even* all the men of Israel, your little ones, your wives, and the alien who is within your camps, from the one who chops your wood to the one who draws your water. (Deuteronomy 29:10 & 11)

...apparently, he was not. Having clearly established that, let us now consider the fact that the following proclamation he was about to make was to be received by both the House of Jacob and those who attached themselves with it. Consider the weight of that reality as you contemplate further the legitimacy of Torah observance today, and as you read this:

> So it shall be when (not if) all of these things have come upon you, the blessing and the curse which I have set before you, and you call *them* to mind in all nations (not just Babylon) where the LORD your God has banished you, (2) and you return to the LORD your God and obey Him with all your heart and soul according to all that I command you today, you and your sons, (3) then the LORD your God will restore you from captivity, and have compassion on you, and will gather you again from all the peoples where the LORD your God has scattered you. (4) If your outcasts are at the ends of the earth, from there the LORD your God will gather you, and from there He will bring you back. (5) The LORD your God will bring you into the land which your fathers possessed, and you shall possess it; and He will prosper you and multiply you more than your

Signed in Blood

fathers. (6) Moreover, the LORD your God will <u>circumcise your heart</u> and the heart of your descendants, to love the LORD your God with all your heart and with all your soul, so that you may live. (7) The LORD your God will inflict all these curses on your enemies and on those who hate you, who persecuted you. (8) And you <u>shall again obey the LORD</u>, and observe <u>all His commandments</u> which I command you **today.** (Deuteronomy 30:1-8)

Let's break this down. Moses knew in advance, and declared to all present and future hearers, that at some time in the future they were going to break their obligations to the covenant they were **entering** into (29:14). This covenant then is renewed with every generation that hears it, and accepts the terms. We enter into this covenant when we come to faith!

When God's long-suffering had been adequately tested, scattering is exactly what happened. Whether you realize it or not, most all believers still are scattered. Even though we are not lost but are found, we still are not home yet. Now read verses two and three again. Remember, Moses is speaking to a future generation. This future people group, in the midst of their scattering (a curse), according to verse five, was going to be a multiple of the current one (which was more than a couple million—a blessing). I would feel comfortable in calculating the current body of believers as a multiple of that crowd. And they were expected to obey, even while in exile.

What did God have Moses declare was going to happen when that crowd found its way back to the land (yet unfulfilled)? God would circumcise their hearts (vs. 6). Isn't that "new covenant" terminology? Jeremiah spoke the same way in chapter four. So, after their hearts have become circumcised, what will happen because of this act? Verse eight tells us, "And you shall again obey the LORD, and observe **all** His commandments which I command you **today**." Looks like we've come full circle, doesn't it? Obedience is required both before and after circumcision! The commandments that were declared that day went far beyond the Ten only, confirming my position there is more we are accountable to. This future group, we of the new covenant, was prophesied here by Moses to begin returning to compliance just prior to the ingathering (vs. 2). Ezekiel is also in complete support of this concept, as seen in chapter 37:21-24.

Before your head starts spinning too fast, I feel that I must reiterate a critical point. Which of you were redeemed by a particular work you did? None of you were! (Ephesians 2:8 & 9) Therefore, it stands to reason that you are not un-redeemed by any particular work either. Non-redemption comes from non-faith. This is no different than it was/is for the Israelites. There was no *single* sacrifice that redeemed them (yet). Likewise, if they missed one, it didn't damn them either; for the annual sacrifice of the Red Heifer (Numbers 19) covered unacknowledged disobedience for the year. But any Israelite, who thought they could transgress the Torah as much as they wanted, because the next Red Heifer would cover them was a fool and a lost soul. Any Christian who thinks they can transgress Torah all they want because of Jesus's once-for-all sacrifice is no less a fool. Let's take this a step further.

If the Israelites were delivered from Egypt and placed under a salvation-by-works based religious program, they were all damned from the moment they stepped off Egyptian soil. "For the righteous shall live by faith." If they were "saved by works" when the temple was not in operation, it sure would stink to be a firstborn male Israelite, since you were clearly damned at birth. For where was your half-shekel of redemption supposed to go now? Or, who could make the appropriate sacrifices on your behalf? What about the scattered Jews who lived after the Temple's destruction in 70 AD, but never heard the message of Messiah's coming? Just to illustrate how off our thinking has become, can you name one person in the Hebrew Scriptures who is described as having been given eternal life based on their obedience? I assure you; you cannot! No respected sage has ever taught a works-based redemptive program. They may have taught that access to the "world to come" was available through birthright, but never through obedience alone.

The reason that no one can judge your soul is because no one can judge your motivations. Likewise, your "good deeds" don't always prove your heart. No one knows how much Torah you can get away with disobeying, before you cross over to becoming a "Lawless" one. It should be safe to say though, that no son or daughter of the Lord would ever want to find out. It should be safe to say, except it's not true. Many Christian sects, even including Evangelical Protestants, have at times gone to great lengths to see how far they can veer from the written Torah, and still be grafted into the Torah Giver. Not only have they refused to accept much of Torah as relevant, but they have substituted God-spoken Torah with man-designed traditions, and sanctified them instead.

I believe that one's understanding of Torah will play a role in one's ramifications for disobedience (grace abounds), but consider these facts: We have far less excuse for disobedience than any other people group in history. We have more ancient manuscripts and linguistic knowledge than ever before. We have the written accounts of His disciplinary measures. We have the written descriptions of the blessings that are promised to the obedient. We have our Christ's teachings that elevated the requirements of Torah to even greater levels than what most Israelites ever knew (Matthew 5). And, we have modern history to give us valuable hind-sight into the atrocities of misinterpretation. So here is the big question. Do you study Torah and thereby become accountable to it, with the reward of doing so being greater levels of maturity, intimacy, and

Signed in Blood

perhaps the experience of:

1st John 3:22, "**Whatever we ask we receive** from Him, **because we keep** His commandments and do the things that are pleasing in His sight."

...and be considered this:

Now therefore, if ye will hearken unto My voice indeed, and keep My covenant, then ye shall be **Mine own treasure** from among all peoples; for all the earth is Mine. (Exodus 19:5)

...or, do we play the fool and live an ignorant life, while basking in cheap grace; not considering that, "Everyone who does sin also does lawlessness; and sin is lawlessness (1st John 3:4)."

And if any one sin, and do any of the things which the LORD hath commanded not to be done, <u>though he know it not</u>, yet is he guilty, and shall bear his iniquity. (Leviticus 5:17)

May it never be!

Take heed to yourselves, lest your heart be deceived, and ye turn aside, and serve other gods, and worship them; and the anger of the LORD be kindled against you, and He shut up the heaven, so that there shall be no rain, and the ground shall not yield her fruit; and ye perish quickly from off the good land which the LORD giveth you. (Deuteronomy 11:16 & 17)

Does only the "Old God" of the Bible get angry? Some preach yes! The heresy of Marcion still appeals to us. If so, did He love Israel differently than He loves us now? I'm not suggesting there is no forgiveness, but the LORD does discipline those He loves. Why? Because He is looking for a spotless bride; the one spoken of in the book of Revelation.

And the dragon was enraged against the woman, and he went off to make war with the rest of her seed *[fig., offspring]*, the ones **keeping the commandments of God** and having the **testimony** of Jesus (12:17).

And in like context...

But if you are without discipline, of which all have become partakers, then you are illegitimate children and not sons. All discipline for the moment seems not to be joyful, but sorrowful; yet to those who have been trained by it, afterwards it yields the peaceful fruit of righteousness. (Hebrews 12:8 & 11)

Discipline before established boundaries is abuse! The whole point of Torah is to keep us on the narrow path that leads to life. You know…the one that few find. It will keep you from turning to the right or left, and from going off and worshiping other gods. Tell me then, what is the flaw in that? I know if you are reading this book as a believer, your heart is being challenged. I know, because I already believe this, and every time I think about it, I still am stirred as well. We want to be considered obedient children. The Spirit encourages that. If there is a chance I am walking around in willful disobedience without knowing it (paradoxical, but true), I want to seek out this possibility and take it to whatever conclusion I am led to. That is all I am asking you to do.

Here is another means to know how to determine accurate interpretation. When the Lord says something, and anyone else seems to say something that contradicts, the Lord always wins. Keep in mind though, just because the Lord justified the annihilation of a pagan people four thousand years ago, does not mean we are still under Joshua's leadership to do it today. All interpretive teaching must be held up against the light of context. When this is remembered, the difficult passages of the Apostolic Scriptures also become much clearer. It is when we have to jump through hurdles to make them *not* line up with Torah, that we are likely going off into error.

What is left then of the Torah for us to obey? Much! And considering the wonderful promises for obedience, I would get excited about the new possibilities. Wouldn't you like to have new found confidence that you are walking in obedience? If I can show you where to begin, and have it not be a yolk you cannot bear, wouldn't you want all you can get? I am going to answer for you by faith, and give that a resounding, yes! After all, you don't really think intimacy and sanctification comes without some personal sacrifice.

In case you have begun to panic, and have reverted to thinking that the Law requires perfection, slow down and begin to think with a renewed mind. The Laws of Moses are not just a bunch of "don'ts", with death breathing down your neck at every turn. I realize most of us have been made to believe like that. Whether it's the blood of bulls and goats, or the blood of Jesus, blood is always necessary for the propitiation of sin. Nothing new there! What needs to be new though is a clearer understanding within the believing community, that neither sanctification nor atonement is the same as forgiveness.

You have to look past the rust colored patina of the iron rod, to see His loving discipline. The Law never expected your perfect abidance in this life. It just demands it, and anticipates it in the next. Several of those many different sacrifices were the back-up plan, (not in the sense of afterthought), instituted to ceremonially cleanse the flesh, to give you

Signed in Blood

access to the House of God, where you would there seek your true forgiveness. If you think you have any more license to transgress now, than you did back then, you have completely misunderstood the cross/grace relationship. Haven't you ever wondered why there will be altar service again, and during the Millennial Reign no less.

I will also take some of them for priests *and* for Levites, says the LORD. (Isaiah 66:21)

In that day there will be inscribed on the bells of the horses, 'HOLY TO THE LORD.' And the cooking pots in the LORD's house will be like the bowls before the altar. Every cooking pot in Jerusalem and in Judah will be holy to the LORD of hosts; and all who sacrifice will come and take of them and boil in them. And there will no longer be a Canaanite in the house of the LORD of hosts in that day. (Zechariah 14:20 & 21)

Even those I will bring to My holy mountain and make them joyful in My house of prayer. Their burnt offerings and their sacrifices will be acceptable on My altar; For My house will be called a house of prayer for all the peoples. The Lord GOD, who gathers the dispersed of Israel, declares, 'Yet *others* I will gather to them, to those *already* gathered.' (Isaiah 56:7 & 8)

Maybe you don't believe that. That's not hard to understand; because to most, the idea of further sacrifices seems irrational and purposeless. Well, of course it does, when we don't fully grasp the program. However, they will no longer be about transgression. Why do you think the book of Acts clearly shows the Apostles continuing in Temple worship long after Jesus's ascension? Why did Paul still speak positively of the Temple service, as a benefit of being a Jew? (Romans 9:4). There is such a lack of understanding. It has been prohibiting accurate doctrinal construction for far too long now. This is an elementary thing, as the writer of Hebrews would call it. And just as the believers in that day were challenged for not going beyond the basics, so do we (two thousand years later) need to heed the same, corrective voice.

Remember my referral to the similarity between Adam's and Jesus's tests in chapter two? When Jesus was "reminded" of His power to transform a rock into bread, what was His response? It was, "Man cannot live on bread alone, but by every word that proceeds from God's mouth." Then He demonstrated for us this truth, by countering the subsequent tests with more statements found in the Hebrew Scriptures. I have a few fundamental questions for you. Where were God's words found at that time? Were they written down somewhere? Was Jesus using sloppy grammar when He chose the word "every" regarding how much we should listen to? Wasn't the benefit of obeying God's *every* word: life, blessing, and protection?

Answering some earlier questions, the reason Jesus didn't tell us He cancelled all the sacrifices and priesthood, is simply because…He didn't! Remember, He is a priest in the heavenly tabernacle, in the order of Melchizedek. If He was a priest on Earth, He would not be a Kohen (Hebrews 8:4). Why? Because He was not a Levite. If He cancelled the entire priesthood model forever, it would mean He also cancelled the kingdom of priests (Revelation 1:6), and He lied through Ezekiel, in chapter forty-eight.

Jesus is our Pesach/Paschal Lamb (technically, a type of zeva shelamim) peace offering. His *sacrifice* did not happen to put an end to Grain, Peace, Drink, First-Fruit, or Wave *offerings*. Jesus didn't cancel these! He just could be foreseen in them. Only one of those listed even has to do with sin. Even the topic of sin (Chata) itself is often misunderstood. A good example of this would be that a sin offering was required after a mother gave birth (Leviticus 12). Did the mom do something wrong?

It was our appalling corruption of the temple on earth—the one no longer acting as the image of the heavenly one (Psalm 11:4 & Hebrews 8:5) that caused our loss of it and its operators. (Can't use it right, He'll take it away!) And now, currently, these offerings cannot be properly performed. Even if they could, they would likely be misappropriated by many, just as they were in the past. They would also be condemned by well-meaning believers, in their assumption that Jesus would be offended. When the altar does get rebuilt, I would strongly suggest that believers be very careful not to blaspheme it, out of ignorance.

His Table

The altar is also God's fellowship meal table. Haven't you ever noticed that on it was continually served bread, wine and meat? Look carefully at this portion from Numbers:

Command the children of Israel, and say unto them: My food which is presented unto Me for offerings made by fire, of a sweet savour unto Me, shall ye observe to offer unto Me in its due season. And thou shalt say unto them: This is the offering made by fire which ye shall bring unto the LORD: he-lambs of the first year without blemish, two day by day, for a continual burnt-offering. The one lamb shalt thou offer in the morning, and the other lamb shalt thou offer at dusk; and the tenth part of an ephah of fine flour for a meal-offering, mingled with the fourth part of a hin of beaten oil. It is a continual burnt-offering, which was offered in Mount Sinai, for a sweet savour, an offering made by fire unto the LORD. And the drink-offering thereof shall be the fourth part of a hin for the one lamb; in the holy place shalt thou pour out a drink-offering of strong drink unto the LORD. And the other lamb shalt thou present at dusk; as the meal-

Signed in Blood

offering of the morning, and as the drink-offering thereof, thou shalt present it, an offering made by fire, of a sweet savour unto the LORD. (28:2-8; JPS)

These offerings have nothing to do with covering personal transgression. These were the perpetual, *tamid* (daily) offerings the Lord delighted in. No, I'm not suggesting He has nostrils like a man, or an appetite. I realize that this might be very confusing to some of you, so let's journey down the road a ways.

In the beginning, man walked around with a physical expression of God in Eden. Then, sin came and made our 'togetherness' less physical, and less frequent. For a select few, He came and showed Himself. But that is because few walked uprightly enough, or were directly involved in His plan of redemption enough, to warrant otherwise. God then shows up in even more amazing array. He delivers the Hebrews from slavery, with clear intentions to make a mighty nation out of them. Not only were they to be a great nation, but they were going to be given the land that was promised to Abraham and his children—a land flowing with milk and honey. Further reading into the Scriptures shows us that they were going to be given a very large parcel of land; "whatever place the sole of their feet treaded (Deuteronomy 11:24)." This land would forever be Israel's to inhabit, as long as they remained faithful to the covenants.

Additionally, God wanted to restore the state of our relationship with Him. He wanted to pour His Spirit into the hearts of His people. But due to sinful circumstances, He needed a transportable, external dwelling place. So He gives plans to Moses, and special talents (via the Spirit, by the way) to others, to build a Tabernacle for His presence to be in the midst of His chosen people. The Tabernacle was supposed to be a representative illustration of what He wanted to do in their hearts, and how it was to be done. That lesson is equally valuable for us today. Moses puts out the call for the people to bring the needed materials, "as each man's heart desires," and the supplies were so abundant that Moses has to order the people to stop bringing stuff. During this desert wandering, God was at first as an angel, and pillars of fire and smoke, but then His Shechinah sat between the Cherubim, and remained there.

For a long time, God remained manifest in the midst of His people. Initially, He was traveling along with them—going before them and revealing His presence often, as they moved into the Promised Land and beyond. God was their General, Husband, Father and King. But sadly, in keeping with their pattern, they rejected His voice at the mountain first, and then later, His personally administered authority. So, God gave them a series of judges, followed by a series of kings, beginning with Saul and then David, and then Solomon. When the people obeyed, they were successful and prospered. When they didn't; well, you know.

God gave the vision to David, but permission to Solomon, to build a temple for a more permanent dwelling place. God obviously still wanted to be with His people, and showed up in style at the conclusion of the dedication. As time went on though, Solomon began to do business with, buy horses from, and obtain women from nations he was specifically ordered not to. Being the leader, the people would follow, and so their hearts went astray as well. Subsequent kings would come and go. Some were good and some bad. All throughout those tumultuous days, He was still right there with them. Prophets needed to be sent to bring people back to His ways, but generations rejected them and so they fell far short. Judgments came. The first temple was destroyed, and the physical expression of God's dwelling place went with it. Sinfulness always results in separation from His presence, but not necessarily His affection.

A second temple was built. God indwelt it again, but the people are short in their faithfulness. Each time the nation was judged, the manifest presence of God became less apparent. At best, man and God came into each other's manifest presence once a year, on the Day of Atonement, and even that eventually ended. More time passes, more judgments come, more temple damage, more dispersion…even less of His presence is evident.

Jesus comes onto the scene, and everything is in shambles. The Temple is filthy. The High Priestly office is now bought and sold. Caiaphas wasn't even a Levite! The Sanhedrin is running the Temple show, but their puppet strings were being pulled by the weighty hand of the Romans. The Law of Moses is not being followed. Behind the veils of the Temple are replacement furnishings now, as everything had been destroyed previously. The Ark was gone, and nobody even knew where it was. (We do! Revelation 11:19.) There really hadn't been a manifest presence in the midst of His people for hundreds of years.[2] There weren't even notable prophets speaking on His behalf (with the exception of John the Baptizer). The religious ritual of Israel was mostly a façade, and a transparent one at that.

God, in a tabernacle of flesh, comes back into the midst of His people. This time, however, it is not due to our obedience at all, or because He heard our cries from oppression. It was because of the hopeless state of our religion and national soul. We literally couldn't have rescued ourselves if we wanted to, just like in our beginning. There was nobody qualified nor sanctified enough to perform the new covenant's High-Priestly office. So, He places Himself up on the altar and simultaneously became our atonement offering and new High Priest. Then, upon His final breath, The Father tears the veil (His garments) from top to bottom, to express His anguish.

Signed in Blood

HE DID NOT DO THAT BECAUSE HE OPPOSED THE TEMPLE SERVICE ITSELF! It was, after all, His House. To suggest that is to say He hated being in our midst, being our General, and being our King. Neither did He scourge the merchants who set up shop there because they were charging too high prices. He did it because we perpetually refused His best. We didn't want to hear His voice. We wouldn't obey Him with a loving heart. And quite simply, He couldn't stand being away from us anymore! Remember, it is something desecrating the next temple that is called "the abomination that causes desolation," not the temple itself!

All throughout history, the presence of God has shown to have decreased as His children's sin increased; right up to the point where He was virtually silent. Jesus came and stirred the pot of Israel. But overall, there were few who actually "tasted to see His goodness." About thirty-five years later, the current acting High Priest, Hananiah ben Hananiah (Ananias) had banned all "believing" Jews from Temple access, had murdered the Apostle James, and God had had enough. So He then sends Titus to destroy the Temple one last time. What else could be done? We are the temple now, so He's back in our midst. Our lives are the sacrifices, and our prayers are the incense.

I hope you enjoyed my Stephen-like synopsis. It was a necessary excursus, to give you perhaps a different perspective on how we got here. By chance, did this verse come into your mind during it?

Hebrews 7:12, "For when the priesthood is changed, of necessity there takes place a change of law also."

If so, quick thinking! But a change in regards to a specific portion of the law, the laws pertaining to the High Priest, or even the ceremonial, is not a blanket cancellation of a covenant! Remember, adjustments can be made to an agreement without complete dissolution. In the event you felt my little lawyer/contract analogy was creative, and my history lesson educational but not persuasive—back to the Greek we go.

'Metathesis' is the word which has been translated 'change'. Thayer defines it as: to transfer or change. It is the same word used later in Hebrews 11:5 to describe what happened to Enoch when he 'changed' and went up to Heaven. Enoch was not eradicated in the process, nor was the first priesthood, nor was the law. It was adjusted and altered. Even set aside perhaps. The verse, in context, in no way establishes an abrogation of all the Torah. Let me summarize in undisputable terms: When there is no Sinai Covenant in force, there is no more legality. And where there is no Law (where we find God's definition of sin), there can be no transgression. "But if we say we have no sin, we are deceiving ourselves, and the truth is not in us (1st John 1:8)." Not only that, but where there is no altar, there is no more propitiation.

Those people who suggest that the Temple is somehow in opposition to the Church, or that they've swapped places and that is why we no longer have one, have a detrimental flaw in their theology. Why do you think that when He comes to dwell in our midst, He will be ruling from a Temple again, after this world is cleansed and not before? I'll tell you why. It's because this time, He intends to never have to withdraw His presence again! I'm sorry, but I can't wait for God's presence to be manifest in the Temple again, and if you don't feel that way, you may need to examine yourselves to see if you are indeed in the faith. The Lord praised David for having the desire for a Temple in his heart (1st Kings 8:18). We should all desire any further manifestation and expression of God we can get! This is what God had to say at the time of the dedication of Solomon's temple:

Then the LORD appeared to Solomon at night and said to him, 'I have heard your prayer and have chosen this place for Myself as a house of sacrifice. (2nd Chronicles 7:12)

For now I have chosen and consecrated this house that My name may be there <u>forever</u>, and My eyes and My heart will be there <u>perpetually</u>. (17) As for you, <u>if you walk before Me</u> as your father David walked, even to <u>do according to all that I have commanded you, and will keep My statutes and My ordinances</u>, (18) then I will establish your royal throne as I covenanted with your father David, saying, "You shall not lack a man *to be* ruler in Israel." (19) <u>But if you turn away</u> and forsake My statutes and My commandments which I have set before you, and go and serve other gods and worship them, (20) then I will uproot you from My land which I have given you, <u>and this house</u> which I have consecrated for My name <u>I will cast out of My sight</u> and I will make it a proverb and a byword among all peoples. (21) As for this house, which was exalted, everyone who passes by it will be astonished and say, "Why has the LORD done thus to this land <u>and to this house</u>?" (22) And they will say, "<u>Because they forsook the LORD</u>, the God of their fathers who brought them from the land of Egypt, and <u>they adopted other gods</u> and worshiped them and served them; therefore He has brought all this adversity on them." (2nd Chronicles 7:16-22)

But, as the infamous, isolated, in-between verse (which is often inappropriately expounded upon because it gets stripped from its context) goes:

...and My people who are called by My name humble themselves and pray and seek My face and turn from their wicked ways, then I will hear from heaven, will forgive their sin and will heal their land. (2nd Chronicles 7:14)

Signed in Blood

That Christians can claim this verse as a necessary component and requirement for healing each their own lands, without also acknowledging that "My people" is actually Israel, and that obedience to the Torah is also a necessary component, just goes to show how corrupted our biblical faith has become. If you, Christian, want to lay claim to that verse's validity, then you must also take blame for your nation's spiritual deterioration, caused by your responsibility to vs.19.

Everyone should be aware that the Temple is going to be restored in the last days and that initially, during the Great Tribulation, from it the anti-Messiah will rule. Yes, we are metaphorically the temple now, but if we are the true Temple, then it will be through us believers that the anti-Messiah will reign, and we will house the Abomination of Desolation. I personally have a problem with that, unless the abomination is metaphoric for Lawlessness? Additionally, the Temple with its altar will be God's ownership symbol of Earth. Just like now and just like before, there will be both followers and rejecters of Messiah, even during the Millennial reign (Zechariah 14). The Temple will stand as a witness against rejecters. Reason this out for yourself: If future sacrifices would be such an abomination, why would the anti-Christ cease the service? Wouldn't it make more sense for him to throw more fuel on the fire?

...who opposes and exalts himself above every so-called god or object of worship, so that he takes his seat in the temple of God, displaying himself as being God. (2nd Thessalonians 2:4)

The Lord still considers it to be His house! In the book of Daniel, in the ninth chapter and twenty-fourth verse, the future Temple is called the "Most Holy Place". The reason the Temple is now gone, and His manifest presence (Shechinah) is still cloaked, is the same reason there is war in the land, and Israel (the people) is still scattered abroad. It is because, "we adopted other gods and worshiped them and served them!"

Closing Thoughts

If Adam and Chavvah hadn't sinned, they and their offspring would have eternally lived in paradise, and in the very presence of the Lord. That was His perfect will.

If Israel hadn't gone on to sin on a national level, The Lord would have remained present in their midst, and they would have lived in the Promised Land forever. It is conceived by the sages that had they not made the golden calves, God would have dwelled in their hearts in the way He dwelled in the Tabernacle. The Temple then, was actually His next, 'next-best' perfect will. This last arrangement though, was Israel's last opportunity to have it so good. Unfortunately, they blew it. So from that point on, what you see is God's plan to compensate for our incessant, disobedient behavior. Yes, the Law was given because of sin, but not to punish it! It was given to assist in overcoming it! Please forgive me for how simply put that was.

If He wanted to make life truly impossible for us, by giving us 'Words' we were hopeless to abide by, He would never have given us a means to make restitution and asked us to be perfect (Matthew 5:8; Genesis 17:1). And remember, the law made nothing perfect (Hebrews 7:19). What you really have to understand is that it was never meant to. But if it was never meant to, why are we so afraid of it? Why is it nearly universally assumed within modern Christendom that any adherence to it is demanding perfection from it, imposing legalism, and thereby intruding on grace's rightful place? It's quite bizarre.

It is blasphemous to think He gets a kick out of our failure. Unless you were a murderer, sexual deviant, kidnapper or rebellious hater of God, you really had little to worry about, as far as your physical life goes. Scripturally supported capital punishment served as a physical representation of a potentially lethal, spiritual condition. The Torah only spiritually condemns us when we have unrepentant hearts. Even if someone did receive the death sentence, that didn't mean he or she had no chance for forgiveness. The same is true today. "There is therefore no condemnation for those who are in Christ." What makes us "perfect" as Jesus requested, is not just found through our righteous works, but also how we respond when we commit unrighteous works.

We, as the Body, need a "Chadash" understanding.

Signed in Blood

5

Yea, Hath God Said?

Deuteronomy 6:3a, "O Israel, you should listen and be careful to do *it*."

The instruction He gave, that we must first listen to and come to terms with is:

I am the LORD your God, who brought you out of the land of Egypt, out of the house of slavery. You shall have no other gods before Me. (Exodus 20:2 & 3)

Is this understood by you? I don't mean to sound condescending, but is this an established thing in your soul? If it is, you have already won half of the battle. It is really no different from when...

He said to them, "But who do you say that I am?"

And you answered as Peter did...

"You are the Christ, the Son of the living God."

For to acknowledge Jesus for who He is, is to accept His teachings with the same regard and authority as the Words etched into stone. In the Hebraic understanding, the First Commandment is actually,

"I am the LORD your God." Therefore, if you don't sh'ma (hear and obey) this one, the rest are of no significance. As believers in the Messiah of Israel, we understand who He is as regards deity; well, at least somewhat. Lesser than angels—one minute. At the right hand of the Father—another. It can seem confusing sometimes. But we can all agree that if He is the Word made flesh, He didn't stop being the Word in either scenario.

Jesus didn't waste His breath on meaningless analogies and ear-tickling illustrations. Everything He said had purpose. In reality, like I mentioned earlier, sometimes His instructions initially seemed to make no logical sense…"You shall mix the ashes with the hyssop and the cedar wood and the scarlet wool…" to basic logic and reason. Often, He was quite clear. "But when you give to the poor, do not let your left hand know what your right hand is doing." Though His instructions may sometimes be hard to wrap our minds around, I can assure you at no time was complete understanding a prerequisite for obedience even in Solomon's mind (Proverbs 20:24).

Reasoning out whether or not something is to be obeyed today, and how to go about doing it can be and often is controversial. This is especially true when dealing with people who have no compulsion to go past the outer courts, or disregard the Mosaic covenant in general. The common, opposing concerns with the Torah observant lifestyle are typically: 1.) "How can you obey one thing and not another?" and 2.) "But if you obey a part of it, you become accountable to all of it." Then there's always this sarcastic assumption: 3.) "So I guess we are just supposed to start stoning people again, huh?" When you can properly answer these questions, you have the ammo for winning the other half.

Let me shed some light on the conflict. As has already been alluded to, the first question could be answered with, "I do not obey whatever I cannot obey." If you think about it, shouldn't that be the litmus test for every believer, and equally applied to all of Scripture? And likewise, shouldn't it be our response to the attempted manipulations of HaSatan? It swings both ways. If someone came up to you and told you that the Holy Spirit was telling them to direct you to quit your job, ditch your spouse and family and become a missionary to the Ukraine, why wouldn't you do it? Because that would be wrong! That would be a false word of knowledge. How do you know? Because…

…if anyone does not provide for his own, and especially for those of his household, he has denied the faith and is worse than an unbeliever. (1st Timothy 5:8)

Because the Bible tells you so! If someone suggests you are to sacrifice a goat in your backyard because that's what the Torah says to do, the appropriate response would be, "Not true! No one can make sacrifices outside of the sanctuary (Deuteronomy 12:14), and they are to be made only by the Levites (Numbers 3); and I am not one, therefore I can't." You respond in no different way than if someone tells you to handle poisonous snakes because we have authority over them. You tell them that we are not to test God, just as Jesus taught us in the desert (Matthew 4:7). You use The Word to validate The Word.

Then, to answer the second question, we are all already accountable to all of Torah. We are just as required to Love God as we are to not bear false witness, as we are to care for the widows. If all the Law and the Prophets hang on the two love commands, then all the commands are expressions of love. If the Royal Commandment to love God is found within the Torah first (Deuteronomy 6:5), when you choose to obey that, you choose to obey all applicable others that are associated with it as well. The third, usually sarcastic remark, I will answer a little later.

You judge truth by The Truth. You interpret a verse by comparing it with the rest of the chapter, and with the rest of the book, and with the entirety of the Bible; along with the patterns and principles God has established throughout it. The Torah observant lifestyle is unbelievably rewarding, but it requires study and prayerful contemplation. We must always be on our guard against the yolk of extraneous laws (burdensome rules beyond Scripture's intent, as well as rules that break other rules). Likewise, we must always watch out for Judaizers (those who would suggest that redemption is found in obedience, or falsified adoption papers, a.k.a. circumcision). This is the very same "bewitchment" Sha'ul the Pharisee exposed within the fellowship at Galatia.

Keeping this in mind, let's start with the very basics, and perhaps a little more testing. Can the clay tell the Potter what to form it into? Would you agree that we were made by the Potter? Excellent! Then we have also established that as our Creator, He has the right to tell us how to maintain His own creation. He has ordained that every creature would reproduce after its own kind, and that we should not crossbreed differing families of animals (Leviticus 19). He has told us how to manage our fields and vineyards (Deuteronomy 22). He gave us the authority to subdue the earth and to name the different creatures (Genesis 2:20), but He established that certain animals were appropriate for sacrifice, and eventually food (beginning in Genesis 3:21, though not fully revealed yet).

The world soon rejected God (minus one family) and fell under cataclysmic judgment. An ark was built in which to save the human race,

Yea, Hath God Said

as well as whatever other creatures God deemed worth saving. In that fortunate lot were designated two kinds of flesh: clean and unclean. The unclean animals came to Noah in one breeding pair. The clean animals came to him in seven pairs. That only makes sense, for if there was only one pair of each clean animal, Noah's sacrificial offerings, upon coming out of the Ark, would have caused the immediate extinction of that species. It was after the flood that God gave *permission* to His people to eat flesh; though it is believed that heathen man had already partaken.

It would be keen of you to take note that this establishment of classification for animals took place long before any formal laws were given, such as those found in Leviticus chapter eleven. Let's jump forward though, to see what God offered as the reason for this division.

Leviticus 11:43, "<u>Do not render yourselves detestable</u> through any of the swarming things that swarm; and you shall not make yourselves unclean with them so that you become unclean.

11:44, For I am the LORD your God. <u>Consecrate yourselves</u> therefore, and be holy, for I am holy. And you shall not make yourselves unclean with any of the swarming things that swarm on the earth.

11:45, For I am the LORD who brought you up from the land of Egypt to be your God; thus <u>you shall be holy, for I am holy</u>."

And then, just before Moses is about to repeat the original laws of kashrut (kash-root; kosher) to the next generation, he states:

Deuteronomy 14:2, "For you are a holy people to the LORD your God, and the LORD has chosen you to be a people <u>for His own possession</u> out of all the peoples who are on the face of the earth."

Apparently, touching certain things renders us unclean, but eating certain things renders us detestable. There is a significant difference.

To be unclean (Hebrew: *tamei*) according to Torah, should not be broad-stroke painted as synonymous with being in a spiritually depraved condition. Neither Moses nor the Lord ever referred to the state of 'unclean' in such a way. Being tamei only required a mikveh bath (a topic I cover in chapter nine) and/or the sun to go down. However, doing things that rendered people as "detestable" was considered sinful, did require sacrifice, and in the worst-case scenario, got them kicked out of the land (Leviticus 20:22). To be unclean put someone in a state of physical inapproachability toward the Tent. It didn't necessarily affect their relationship with God. To do detestable things had more severe consequences, and certainly thwarted the blessings available through covenantal adherence. Doing detestable things is frequently equated with participating in the ways of the heathen nations.

Do we not consider ourselves to be His possession? Are we not supposed to be a set-apart people, consecrated for the Lord's use? Is there no shame in having our Mighty One look down upon us and think to Himself, that's disgusting? Please note that tamei doesn't render *rejection*. These regulations were not to torture the Hebrews, nor were they meant to starve them. They were to make them different from the surrounding and pagan peoples! I ask you…why would that have changed?

God's adherent people never had any reason or desire to understand this differently. The laws related to food consumption were followed by His people until they no longer could be identified as such, by going off into idolatry, and after being scattered and assimilated into the nations by Assyrian conquest. Let me put it another way. Believers left their original faith and freedom and went back into slavery.

Hosea 9:3, "They will not remain in the LORD's land, but Ephraim will return to Egypt, and in Assyria they will eat unclean *food*."

Why did this happen? Hosea 9:1 tells us it was because of spiritual harlotry. Here is a strong teaching: Spiritual harlotry, by demonstration, is the disregarding of God's commandments for the sake of another's, or one's own. It is unfaithfulness to the vows we make.

Six Yummy Volts

I am now going to tell you the same story I told my daughter, when first teaching her this basic concept. Obviously, it will seem juvenile, so please don't be insulted. I hold no copyright on it, so feel free to use it with yours if it so suits you.

"Do you see that doll over there?" I asked.
"Yes Dad."
"It's not a real person, right?"
"Right." she answered.
"So what makes it work?"
"I don't know." she answered.
"Batteries…Right?" I offered.
"Right!" she exclaimed.
"It takes a special kind of battery, huh?"
"Yes, a little one." she recognized.
"Actually it takes four little ones." I specified.
"Okay." she acknowledged.
Then I inquired, "Do you think it would work if I put really big ones in it?"

Yea, Hath God Said

"I don't think so." she presumed.

"Right! And do you know why they won't work?" I asked.

"No." she responded.

"Because the person who created it made it a special way."

I then asked, "Do you think the toy told the toy-maker how to make it?"

"Of course not Daddy, toys don't talk." she retorted.

"That's true," I responded, trying to not chuckle at the obvious recognition of absurdity in her face. "Do you think you could put rocks in there and the toy would work?" I asked illogically.

"No." she acknowledged, with a look of curiosity.

"Why not?" I asked.

"Because rocks aren't like batteries." she recognized.

"That's right! Batteries are *like* food for toys."

Moving the conversation along I asked, "Can you eat rocks?"

"No Daddy, rocks aren't food," was her obvious response.

So then, I asked, "Are batteries food for you?"

And she replied, "No daddy, that's silly."

So I followed with, "Yes it is. So we only eat food right?"

"Right!" she declared.

"When *you* play with Play-Doh, does the Play-Doh tell you what to make it into?" I continued.

"No." she said confidently, but baffled.

"You make the Play-Doh into whatever you want, right?" I provoked.

"Uh-huh." she stated, needing to know where this was heading.

"Well sweetheart, we are like the Play-Doh, and God made us exactly how He wanted us to be. We can't tell Him how to make us, right?" I furthered.

"Right." she concurred.

"He made us to eat only certain things, okay? Just like how the toy only works with the right batteries, we only work with the right food. We are different from toys, and can't eat what they eat. But we are the same in that we only eat what makes us work, right? Does that make sense?" I hoped.

"Yes Daddy, it does!" And then I proceeded to teach her what qualifies.

Now, to conserve space I am not going to paste the affiliated scriptural text here. Perhaps you are familiar with the passages. I would still like you to break now, and read Leviticus chapter eleven. It is also repeated (reinforced) again in Deuteronomy chapter fourteen. I'd like for you to refresh your memory as we continue down this road. At the end of this book, I will also reference a few sources that will further your ability to study this topic.

If you were not raised by a Jewish family, or spent time in advanced academia, it is unlikely that you ever invested much time in Leviticus, due to its stigmas of boring and useless. I was born and raised in the Protesting Catholic church, and have overall spent much more time in it than out; but I do not remember a single message on this subject that wasn't a cursory glossing over, "not for us anymore" kind of teaching. If you can, you are fortunate. That is, if what was taught to you was true. What if I declared to you that this is the Potter's list of ingredients for His set-apart clay? Would that add an angle of perspective you had not considered? And if that's truly what it is, which I firmly believe it is, how is it that Jesus's execution empowered us to look at the Potter and reject His design? This is truly one of those subjects I feel so silly about not seeing long ago. I simply accepted someone's confused teaching on "all things are permissible" and figured this food thing fell under that category. If you are running your finger along the band of your collar, that's okay. He knows you didn't know. I am aware of how much the perverted version of "all things are permissible" message tickles our ears, but let's be reasonably wise here, "all things"—really? Would you need for me to list a *gazillion* things that are not permissible as children of the Most High, to validate my point? I'm sure that it isn't necessary.

The animals and plants that are listed in Scripture as "clean" or *not* "unclean," and "good for food" verses "abominable" or "detestable," are what is considered by the Lord to be food; all other creature forms are not considered food. We all teach our children this concept: "Just because you can put it in your mouth, does not make it food!" Enough seasonings and you could make just about anything taste good, but that doesn't make it healthy, or deemed appropriate for consumption. If you don't accept this fact, you will, in no uncertain terms, be incapable of accurately interpreting the food related passages found throughout the Apostolic Scriptures as well.

I am a Yankee-Doodle-Dandy, born on the shores of Cape Cod, Massachusetts. I was raised to be (and didn't argue) a devout and full-spectrum seafood lover. If you could catch it, I would eat it. (Except eel. I never caught a taste for that.) But Lobster and shellfish, and shrimp on the barbie; I could never get enough of. I'd eat 'em raw, steamed, broiled, fried, however and whenever possible. I have been known to devour several pounds of crab legs at one sitting, with drawn, garlic butter, of course. When I watched the advertisements of popular restaurants, and saw the shimmering shrimp as they pirouetted to the choreographed lights and sounds, it really spoke to my heart. I almost shed tears in delight. But today, the idea of eating that stuff really disturbs me. Not just because of

Yea, Hath God Said

what my research has taught me regarding the function of those animals in nature, (being the Lord's garbage disposal and sewage filtration system for the ocean; a.k.a. cockroaches of the sea), but because the 'scales' have fallen from my eyes in this area. And now, eating those non-food creatures is to me the equivalent of eating dirty diapers, or batteries.

To be honest, when my eyes were finally opened to this truth, I initially wasn't thrilled. A friend of mine had brought this truth to my attention a couple years previously, and I about laughed at him. My mind went right back to the great feasts I had previously participated in. Worse than that, I travel back to the Cape once in a while, as much of my family is still there. I knew the temptation would be unbearable. But as soon as I had spoken these words in prayer, "I will surrender this part of my life to You, if that's what you want." I kid you not, all my cravings to eat that family of animal evaporated. I think He knew how much I would need His help, and He just came through for me. I shouldn't have been surprised though, as He did the same exact thing for me with illicit drugs and smoking.

Now I'm not saying it is that easy for everyone, because it's not. But I have heard a number of testimonies like that, and so I know I'm not alone. And that's not the only category with which He helped me. For, if you notice on that list, swine/pork is not on the menu. Yes, swine. One of nature's filthiest, visually unappealing, bacteria-ridden animals, that man has chosen to push through its GI tract. I don't want to get scientific here. I will leave other's works for that. But rest assured, when you do begin to look further into this, you will probably (hopefully) never want to touch that non-food, consumable ever again. Granted, we can pump them full of antibiotics, and make sure we cook them at a high enough temperature to disinfect them, but that alone should tell you something. The most challenging thing about pork is that it's literally everywhere!

Bacon, draped over your burgers. Bits, sprinkled on your salad. They're in your baked beans and on your potatoes. You can get it pulled, or have it barbequed, as ribs, roasts, sausage links and patties, strips, chops, fried, as pepperoni, and all the other 'onies'. It's put in soups. It's honey baked, spiral sliced, hocked, pickled, kippered, smoked, and on and on. How many yummy things have lard in it? The next time you go to Denny's, just for fun, look at the menu and see how many items *don't* come with some type of pork product. It will be a lot easier to count that way.

Listen to that! Can you hear the searing of the succulent ribs that are basking in their own natural juices, and the sauces being tenderly twice-brushed upon them? There has been an inundation of marketing to get us to eat "the other white meat". America is truly saturated with the stuff, and it's hard to see just how difficult it is to stay away from, until you try. The United States is the world's third largest producer and second largest consumer, exporter, and importer of pork and pork products. Pork accounts for about a fourth of domestic meat consumption (USDA.org). I might be mad, and I am not a scientist, but combine these statistics with the Dept. of Health statistics on our national obesity and heart disease rates in relation to the rest of the world, and there *might* be a connection.

The Scriptures provide no instruction regarding eating human flesh, but we don't eat that, even though we could just *"give thanks."* The reason we don't though, is not solely ethical. There is/has been cannibalism in the world for us to examine and see that by it there comes serious ill-effects. Science has discovered these effects to be related to the ingestion of genetically similar material. Likened to mad cow, a cannibal's brain deteriorates. Genetic material is found in all life forms. God knows what genetic material and flesh types are best suited for human consumption. It just so happens that pigs have a higher degree of similar coding to humans, than other animals we consume. Perhaps His command not to eat it is just a coincidence.

Like all things tempting, strength and steadfastness is required to overcome. And just as He has overcome the world, so can we. This book is about saying it like it is. So, as much as it will seem uncomfortable to accept, and easy to reject, eating creatures that are not on the list of Leviticus chapter eleven, is a transgression of God's Law. Is there mercy bestowed upon you if you accidentally eat them, or if you are starving? Sure. Until your personal conviction is established, I also believe there is a measure of grace. Eventually, you do become accountable for what you know, and I was just used to put you "in the know". For that, I do not apologize. Your obedience will be recognized, I assure you. However, like all the laws of Scripture, they do not *become* a law upon "conviction"; they stand on their own merit. There is no such principle in Scripture as that of only being required to do what we *feel* convicted of.

At this point, I must interject a couple quick things. I do not believe the installation of a pig valve into a human heart, to save a life, is the equivalent to unnecessary ingestion. I also do not believe that the consumption of pork, either purposely or accidentally, damns the spirit; although it may hurt the soul. Therefore, as may be the case in both situations, for the effort of saving life, I believe there is abundant grace. To those who abuse His grace, you need more mercy.

That now said, as within our own justice system, ignorance doesn't cancel out guilt. Just as a human judge can, God takes into consideration our understanding of the Law as the penalty is being weighed. He administers mercy on our behalf all the time. We may be guilty, but there is plenty of amercement money in God's blood bank. We now need to leave the days of the Torah's establishments, jump into the

Yea, Hath God Said

future a bit, and see how the topic of food is handled by our first century, leadership team.

The Jerusalem Council

Most of you, I am sure, are familiar with the Jerusalem council event that is documented in the book of Acts, in chapter fifteen. I will use this portion of Scripture simultaneously as more supportive material for our last topic, and as a springboard into others; as I wrap the food discussion up.

Background Check: Jesus is no longer physically with us. Actually, it's about 49 AD, and as with all good endeavors, challenges must arise. Judaizers (but believers) were coming into synagogues, as well as fledgling assemblies, and bringing with them a bit of controversial, and in this case, heretical doctrine (though they could not know that.) The erroneous teaching was that converts to Judaism, but more specifically Messianic Judaism, must undergo ritual circumcision (official conversion to Judaism), and take upon themselves the Law—to not only come into fellowship, but to maintain a place in the world to come.

But some of the sect of the Pharisees who had believed stood up, saying, 'It is necessary to circumcise them and to direct them to observe the Law of Moses. (Acts 15:5)

Neither the overwhelming majority of leaders in the Hebrew-Christian community then, today, nor I, believe this to be true.

This teaching (assured salvation through circumcision, or Abrahamic lineage) was so erroneous and contrary to what Paul had come to understand, as well as the issue of the inclusion of gentiles into the faith, needed to be officially debated with a formal resolution. So, Paul the Benjamite, James the brother of Jesus, Barnabas, and several other key figures presided over a council that concluded with a statement of belief, culminating in a letter written and hand carried to Antioch. Here is the doctrinal statement from the edict:

Therefore, it is my judgment that we do not trouble those who are turning to God from among the Gentiles, but that we write to them that they abstain from things contaminated by idols and from fornication and from what is strangled and from blood. For Moses, from ancient generations, has in every city those who preach him, since he is read in the synagogues every Sabbath. (Acts 15:19-21)

Except to Accept

I'm sure you won't be surprised at this point, when I tell you that this portion of Scripture is commonly misunderstood, and is a triangular cornerstone upon which a round building has been erected. If you inspect this carefully with me, you will hear the traditional walls cracking even as you read.

If we set aside the verse 21 for now, we have two verses that speak of certain basic principles that anyone coming to faith in Messiah, specifically from the outside nations, would initially have to adhere to. These requirements were the bare minimum necessary for table and synagogue fellowship with the Jews. They are actually an elemental outline of the moral and ethical Torah teachings found within the Pentateuch. They were not an entirely new teaching by any means. They were likely influenced by the Noachide Laws, but definitely supported by Leviticus chapters seventeen and eighteen. These chapters are found in the very center of the Torah, and are known within Judaism as the "Heart of the Torah".

1.) Abstain from **things contaminated by idols** (Defilement; Paganism: Exodus 20:3, Leviticus18).

2.) Abstain from **fornication** (Sexual Morality: Exodus 20:14, Leviticus 18 & 20:10-21, Deuteronomy 5:18).

3.) Abstain from **what is strangled** (Kosher eating laws: Deuteronomy 14:2-20, Leviticus 17).

4.) Abstain from **eating blood** (Abominable acts/Kosher: Genesis 9:4 (Going back to Noah), Deuteronomy 12:15-32, Leviticus 17).

Remember, we are talking about a council's edict that took place about eighteen years *after* Jesus ascended. If Jesus crucified the Law, how could the Apostolic Fathers assume the authority to illegitimately pull these sections back out of the grave, build these instructions on them, and force them on converts from the nations? Well, some fairly creative answers have been offered to explain it away. But I'm not interested in propagating anti-Torah thinking, so you can research that if you desire. If obeying the Torah separated the gentiles from the world then, how does not obeying Torah today do the same? I stated earlier that you are capable of interpreting and understanding Scripture. This is one of those times I am going to allow you and the Spirit to discuss amongst yourselves this pretty obvious truth, and answer the above, underlined question. Ultimately, the point of these essential rules was to counter opposition to the allowance of gentiles, into the places where they would further their learning. These rules were able

Yea, Hath God Said

to do that, by keeping traditionally pagan people from associating with, and/or falling back into their historical, temple-ritual practices. We have to remember that the mythology of today was the theology of yesterday. This list was never meant to be an exhaustive, all-inclusive, *new* Torah for gentiles. It was a reasonable and light, initial burden. Obviously, they were not allowed to do many other things as well, which is no different for us today (e.g., lie, steal, etc.). Without the Mosaic code still in force, there would be no condemnation for many other such things.

Predictably, we have another opportunity to see the need for comparative textual analysis, within this portion as well. Many have strengthened their doctrinal viewpoints on a verse which is very misleading. I hate to do this to you "King James only" subscribers, but many of you have read Acts 15:24 like this:

> "Forasmuch as we have heard, that certain which went out from us have troubled you with words, subverting your souls, saying, *Ye must* be circumcised, and keep the law: to whom we gave no *such* commandment."

The problem with this verse is that the key words that drastically influence the theme of this text have actually been added to it over the years. In the Greek, *Textus Receptus* manuscript, the phrase: "be circumcised, and keep the Law" is found. This manuscript is the source text for the King James Bible, as well as several other older versions. However, this phrase in not found in our oldest manuscripts.[1] The NIV renders it more accurately: "We have heard that some went out from us without our authorization and disturbed you, troubling your minds by what they said."

Pretty significant difference, eh? I didn't realize that adding to the Scriptures was only wrong for the first century believers. Might you be willing to concede there is perhaps a theological slant associated with the wording? Like the way we should not impose additional meaning to Peter's dream, (as you shall soon see). Likewise, here, we should be careful to avoid doing the same. Obviously, that is what some have attempted to do. The Jerusalem Council was called to order, to handle the issue of formal conversion of gentiles, not the entire spectrum of lifelong sanctification.

So now, let's go ahead and add that third rail, third verse into the equation. What does it say, and what does it tell us?

Acts 15:21, "For Moses from ancient generations has in every city those who preach him, since he is read in the synagogues every Sabbath."

Well a couple things seem to stand out right away. The first is that it is clear the goal was to get them into fellowship, for that's where they would continue to learn *Moses* on "every Sabbath". 'Moses' is basically a synonym for Torah, and any Jewish believer of that day would have understood that. This ultimately means that the Council recognized that burdening those investigating and converting to the faith, with the whole of Torah, would be too overwhelming and more likely a deterrent. We were all first (starting with the Hebrews): delivered (redeemed from bondage), baptized second (Red Sea), and then sanctified (the Law). This order is what the council's heart was seeking to maintain. 'Moses' was not to be a prerequisite for salvation.

The second thing that should pop out at you would be the fact that they were still meeting in synagogues. Jews, believing Jews, and Christians were still capable of being in fellowship with each other. The debate over the authenticity of Jesus as the Christ was undoubtedly continuing and ever-present; but His first and second century disciples were much more like their Jewish contemporaries than most modern Christians have an acknowledgment of. Otherwise, they never would have been able to co-exist for as long as they had, and continued to do for quite some time. The third jaw-dropper would be the fact that believers were still meeting on the Sabbath. The Sabbath, or *Shabbat*, is and was at that time the Seventh Day of the week. It begins at sundown on the 6th day, and ended at sundown on the 7th. The reason 'days' began at night is because of the pattern and order of creation, as seen in the first chapter of Genesis:

1:5, "God called the light day, and the darkness He called night. And there was evening and there was morning, one day."
1:8, "God called the expanse heaven. And there was evening and there was morning, a second day."

This is reinforced by this command regarding the Sabbath, which occurs on the Day of Atonement (Yom Kippur),

It is to be a sabbath of complete rest to you, and you shall humble your souls; on the ninth of the month at evening, from evening until evening you shall keep your sabbath. (Leviticus 23:32)

Although not commonly acknowledged, Jews and believers in the Messiah Yeshua, would have met together on Shabbat as they did during His days on Earth, and continued to regularly do for hundreds of years afterwards. We will talk more about this in just a bit. Keeping things in context is critical to a proper interpretation of a passage. Have I said that before?

Yea, Hath God Said

Total Freedom?

When Sha'ul said, "...all things are Lawful, but not all things are profitable. All things are lawful, but not all things edify," do you really think he thought that he could eat anything he wanted, or can have immoral sexual encounters, or worship idols? I guess he could, if there was one single piece of supportive evidence, anywhere in Scripture, that exposed anyone else in Christ, eating unclean things with "thanksgiving". There is another place, where a terribly misunderstood story in Acts has been used to prop-up this building, on its sandy foundation. I am going to kick that stilt out now, and let that house fall. It is the well-known story of Peter's vision, as found in chapters ten and eleven.

After reading this for the umpteenth time, having finally gotten the point, I find myself again amazed at how something so obvious could have been so elusive. I don't think I'm alone here when it comes to having believed the typical, mainstream interpretation that this story somehow had a two-fold meaning. The first being Peter should accept gentiles into the sheepfold (greater). The second being we can now eat anything we want (lesser). Let's examine this text in context, and see if we can still digest that teaching.

Peter's Vision

Peter, up until this point, after having spent 3 years under His direct tutelage and many years after Jesus ascended, had not yet let any unclean food cross his lips.

Acts 10:14, "But Peter said, "By no means, Lord, for I have <u>never eaten</u> anything <u>unholy</u> and <u>unclean</u>.""

I should ask you to stop here and honestly ponder this reality. Assuming there are no other additional evidences, by this fact alone you must conclude that Peter should have certainly, by then, eaten unholy and unclean items if he had the clearance to do so. Don't you think at some point, if the Master Rabbi had told Peter and His other disciples that as soon as He left, they could go about snacking on fried rinds, they would have? Even if Peter was only avoiding it for the sake of not offending other Jews, I'm sure there was a time he could have indulged with a nice ham steak via gentile hospitality. The smell of swine flesh roasting and tantalizing the nostrils of someone who had not yet tasted it, but was finally free to do so, would be very tempting. But since people usually need more than one piece of evidence to cast a verdict, here's more.

He also still continued to call the animals unholy and unclean. Could Kepha (Peter; Aramaic) use any more a persuasive adjective than *unholy*? Surely he would have been told that was going to end, and the terminology would have changed. If this dream had an additional, "secondary benefit" of showing Peter he was to embrace converting gentiles, because Peter had already known that "non-food" was going to transform into "food" through some amazing and unexplainable organic transformation, the dream would have not had the same shock value or view-changing impact.

Peter had a dream that involved three individual occurrences of "something like a sheet" coming down from heaven. Coincidentally,

While Peter was reflecting on the vision, the Spirit said to him, "Behold, **three** men are looking for you." (Acts 10:19)

Three visions—three men. Could this be a confirmation, instead of a coincidence? Peter, when explaining the vision to Cornelius said,

I most certainly understand *now* that God is not one to show partiality, but in every nation the man who fears Him and does what is right is welcome to Him. (Acts 10:34 & 35)

When Peter had his opportunity to retell and explain the dream to circumcised brethren in Jerusalem, for they had heard he had "eaten" with gentiles (11:2), he shared with them the details and interpreted the dream.

When they heard this, they quieted down and glorified God, saying, "Well then, God has granted to the Gentiles also the repentance *that leads* to life." (Acts 11:18)

Why do you think that in either one of these cases, Peter didn't share the other, quite important, alternate meaning of the dream? Really, if this was the Lord's way of changing the terms of the covenant, and transforming the entire, future dietary program for all mankind, forgive me but He was rather ambiguous don't you think? It is quite clear that this story has nothing to do with food at all, and to suggest otherwise is terribly irresponsible interpretation.

The fact that Peter had eaten with gentiles, (though some would suggest), is not evidence he ate unclean food. Actually, the offense that this was initially causing was based on twisted, rabbinical, oral tradition, not Moshe's (Moses) or Jesus's Torah. "If you eat with a non-Jew, it is the same as eating with a dog (TALMUD: Tosapoth, Jebamoth 94b)."

Yea, Hath God Said

I believe any reasonable effort you put into confirming and furthering your investigation of the dietary laws, from a balanced perspective, will support this teaching and expose a doctrinal error ignorantly perpetuated by mainstream teachers. To consume unclean things, according to the listing of Leviticus 11, is to mock the Creator's authority, and makes your stomach and appetite a god. I pray your freedom to eat whatever you want is curtailed and governed by your desire to love the Lord.

Yea, Buts...

But when you read the story of Noah, you distinctly remember God saying, "Every moving thing that is alive shall be food for you." O.k., and He also said, "The end of all flesh has come before Me (Genesis 6:13);" and that's not exactly what took place, is it? Get your Bible.

"All-s" and "every-s," in biblical Hebrew, are often not concrete terms. You'll quickly find that to be true once you begin to look around, such as exampled in the wording of 9:2. (That verse needs to be understood as being in reference to dominion and responsibility being given to man, not food permission.) It would have been very easy to just say that all moving creatures are now food, eat what you desire, and left it at that. However, there appears to be a couple caveats.

First, flesh was given to eat "as was the green plants." Actually, the fact we are told to eat *green* plants that bear seed and fruit "after their kind" has scientific merit. The Creator obviously knew that green was the clue to photosynthetic activity. The fruits and seeds themselves did not need to be green, but the source for them needed to be. But this then raises the question: Are all green plants food? Go lick an Amorphophallus titanum plant and then try arguing the protagonist cause. And second, the moving creatures also needed to be "living creatures".

The description of *living* and *moving* creatures seems to be a redundant overstatement of the obvious, but Scripture doesn't waste words. Mankind then receiving permission to eat meat also needed the understanding that it was to be living before becoming food. In other words, if you happened upon a dead animal and had no knowledge of how or why it died, it was not to be considered food. Later on, this instruction is developed further in Scripture. Properly, the nephesh (soul) of the animal leaves through the blood, and therefore the blood was to be handled with respect and returned to the earth. A dead animal that could not be bled would therefore not be edible. (I personally think pre-deluge man was horribly disrespectful of life-blood principles, and by that, a poisoning of man's soul occurred, contributing to its condition. Judaism incorporated this notion into its Noahic law code by stating that gentiles who seek to be righteous must not eat flesh removed from living animals.)

To properly understand what's really being said to Noah, you need to better understand the scene. All the animals had just exited that ark. Noah and his family immediately followed. All humanity was present and appreciating their feet standing on the earth. It was the proper time for the Creator to present details regarding the new state of creation. Up until that point, flesh was not a permitted food source. Also, up to that point, the man-to-animal as well as animal-to-animal relationships were still in a higher order of harmony; but much was about to change.

Contrary to a popular thought, Scripture nowhere teaches that animals ceased being vegetarians when Adam and Eve were cast from the garden. Nor should we assume that man had lost all his authority over the animal kingdom. Actually, the curse was on the ground, and dealt with the way it was going to need to be worked, by man...for man. Also, it affected the serpent, and how it would live, as compared to other creatures. It intensified human childbirth, but animals still enjoy a less demanding experience. Animals have never needed to "sow nor reap". Even now, they just catch or take. The Lord provides for them differently. It is also customarily assumed that it was at this time when man lost his ability to commune with the animals. But in fact, there is nothing written to suggest a change in relationship, until the flood. And these facts are major clues as to what's really taking place in this narrative.

It's not just that mankind is being given permission to eat meat, it's at this point that all of creation that is being "turned into food" for all the rest of creation. Noah was the audience to God's declaration that major, creational alterations were taking place, and one of them was that the appetites of all His creatures were about to change. It was a good idea for man to have this knowledge before discovering it for himself. Understandably, it would have been terrifying to just see them start mauling each other, if you hadn't seen that before.

Another modification was the fear of man being instilled into creation. More importantly, had the fear not come, Noah and his family would have quickly become a main dish. Prior to this, Noah, according to Genesis chapters six and seven, had the capacity to select and control all the animals, get them onto the ark, and deal with them accordingly while on the ark. Once off the ark, then yet another change took place. Although we cannot know for sure all that this entailed, it appears that the more balanced relationship Noah (and mankind) previously had with the Lord as regards husbandry, morphed into one whereby we carried a higher responsibility. Really, get your Bible!

To further develop this, the pronoun "you" found in 9:3 is customarily assumed to be speaking directly to, and only to man. However, it is equally possible that under these unique circumstances,

Yea, Hath God Said

"you" represents both man and animal, and it certainly extended for the benefit of future generations as well. (9:10 & 12 validate this, as well as the subsequent command given specifically to humanity in 9:7.) These facts, as well as my belief in unchanging Kingdom principles, form my contention that the category of food known as "living, moving creatures" that pertained to man would have been understood by Noah as those "fit for sacrifice" or "clean". This was also further validated at the very end of Leviticus chapter eleven. Regardless, when all is said and done, even if Noah was allowed to eat anything he wanted, it was only for a limited time, as God later restricted His set-apart people.

What about when Paul said that, *everything* is clean?

I know and am convinced in the Lord Jesus that nothing is **unclean** in itself; but to him <u>who thinks</u> anything to be unclean, to him it is unclean. (Romans 14:14)

This is another great example as to why you should always read the surrounding chapter, get the context, look up word meanings, and not just yank one verse out; thinking you can interpret it in isolation.

This chapter opens with Paul asserting that while some are convicted about eating any kind of meat, and prefer to be a vegetarian, others do not carry this conviction. He then brings up the topic of some days having different values to some than others (vs.5). (Notice, these are generic days, not God's appointed times. They are most likely in reference to added special days and/or fast days that were commonly observed, but not mandated.) Then the chapter closes with the summary point of the discussion; that being to not allow personal convictions to undo the work of God, as seen in other's convictions. We are all His servants, and therefore accountable directly to Him. But what actually qualifies as food, is not the issue of this verse. Besides the fact that Paul clearly acknowledged that there still is such a thing as unclean, unclean is a designation. As you will better see illustrated in the next paragraph, something isn't unclean because of its composition, and isn't a permanently transferable condition.

The Greek word *unclean*, seen here in the NT (koinos), is not the opposite of the word *clean* in the OT (tahor), when used in relation to acceptable foods, according to Leviticus ch.11. The actual opposite of the Greek word for *clean* (katharos) is akathartos. Koinos simply means: common. This word is a differentiator, which is conceptually analogous to the idea of what a certain someone today, who has a snooty palate, might consider acceptable, as compared to Joe Citizen's everyday grub.

Certain people of the upper religious echelon would not eat foods that were prepared to a perceived lower standard. It may have been found on the acceptable list, but didn't *meat* the criteria of those who are not 'commoners'. It may have been butchered appropriately, but was being sold in a gentile marketplace, by a gentile who surely touched it. McDonald's may provide something deemed clean by the list, but because they simply have bacon on the premises, some may not even enter. Paul was simply expressing the fact that these kind of debatable issues were not worthy of bringing judgment, condemnation, or division in the Body. No *food* is "common," except in our minds. "To him who thinks" is not a phase associated with actual Torah commands.

If the idea of bringing your body into submission to rules of dietary conduct seems bothersome and unnecessary, because the body is temporal and it is only the spiritual that matters, you have eaten from the devil's tree of asceticism, and gone back for more.

But didn't Jesus Himself declare all *foods* clean?

And He said to them, "Are you so lacking in understanding also? Do you not understand that whatever goes into the man from outside cannot defile (koinoo) him, because it does not go into his heart, but into his stomach, and is eliminated?" *(Thus He declared all foods clean.)* (Mark 7:18 & 19)

See those words in parentheses? They are in parentheses for the fact they are not in the original text. They are a later inserted, opinionated redaction as to the meaning of Jesus's comments, perpetuated by several translators. It was obviously added by a gentile, because a Hebrew would never have written it. It is nonsensical. To be considered food in the first place, it would have to be clean.

The word rendered 'defile' in this verse is of the same root as the 'common' we just discussed. Eating common food doesn't make a person 'common', or polluted, or a sinner. The actual phrase from the Greek is: "purging all the foods," and that's exactly what happens once they're digested. Again, removing this verse from the context, we can get lost. Jesus's teaching here is in response to an inquiry made by some Pharisees. Therefore, it is an answer to a specific challenge, and here is what it was:

...and *(the Pharisees)* had seen that some of His disciples were <u>eating their bread</u> with impure (koinos) hands, that is, <u>unwashed</u>. (For the Pharisees and all the Jews do not eat unless they carefully wash their hands, *thus* observing the <u>traditions of the elders</u>. (Mark 7:2 & 3)

There is that word again, and there is your reason for Jesus's answer. Common, dirty, unwashed, everyday hands do not transfer

Yea, Hath God Said

defilement to a man's spirit. To jump to the assessment that Jesus is saying it's okay to eat lizards is atrocious exegesis. If there be any doubt, all one has to do is read the parallel passage in Matthew chapter fifteen. The dirty little secret is that any pastor with a modicum of Bible education knows this; they just disregard it for the obvious reason.

But you thought Paul said Jesus nailed the Law to the cross, and wouldn't that include the laws of kashrut? Actually, that's not at all what he said. In Colossians 2:14, Paul tells us He nailed the *debt* of the Law, not the Law itself to the cross. Some of that debt perhaps being incurred…

…through philosophy and empty deception, according to the tradition of men (not God), according to the elementary principles of the world (not Heaven), rather than according to Christ. (Colossians 2:8)

But you thought Paul said Jesus abolished the law in His flesh?

Yeah, I know; it's a popular thought. But again, it's not what he said. Jesus abolished the *enmity* of the law. Okay. *But* what law? In this case, the clue to answering that question is found within the verse itself.

…by abolishing in His flesh the enmity, *which is* the Law of commandments *contained* in ordinances, so that in Himself He might make the two into <u>one new man</u>, *thus* establishing peace. (Ephesians 2:15)

Reading this verse like this really steams me, because I cannot help but consider all the people who have readily accepted the wording as it is (as I likewise did) and have allowed it to negatively influence their attitude towards the Law. The translators of the NASU have chosen to determine the "enmity" to be "the Law" itself. You can see this through the insertion of the italicized words, "*which is* the Law." Truth be known, "*of* the Law" is an equally viable rendering, and when used, the verse's structure would be subtly but significantly changed. In fact, the enmity is not the Torah itself. It comes *via* the law. We just saw that expressed through a different avenue, in Colossians. There is more.

Notice that they have chosen to capitalize the 'L' in the word 'law' there, to more specifically associate it with the Law of Moses, as opposed to the various other possible connections. The word rendered 'ordinance' here is the Greek word *dogma*. This is the only time the word 'dogma' is rendered *ordinance* in the entirety of the Apostolic Scriptures. It is normally rendered 'decree', and is a word used for civil as well as ecclesiastical law. This verse could just as well be talking about the same kind of partition-thickening "law" written by man, as was the issue occurring in Colossae. And actually, this man-made law is discussed in much of Paul's writings. Any open-eared Israelite would know the phrase "one new man" is a direct reference to the breach between the two houses of Israel being repaired and closed, as prophesied by Ezekiel. So what is Paul saying really? The laws (and/or misrepresentations of Mosaic Law) that were created by man, that resulted in division, prejudice, and those of the nations (where the scattered Tribes could be found) being thought of as filthy dogs, unworthy of redemption, were rendered powerless through the cross. He died for all alike. How can we feel more confident about this interpretation?

Do not handle, do not taste, do not touch!" (which all *refer to* things destined to perish with use)—in accordance with the commandments and teachings of men? (Colossians 2:21 & 22)

Because the only laws Paul has a problem with; the only laws he would dare discredit; the only laws he'd ever encourage breaking, are those! All right, you almost agree with me, *but* he also said…

If one of the unbelievers invites you and you want to go, eat anything that is set before you without asking questions for conscience' sake. (1st Corinthians 10:27)

It's just that it was only seven verses earlier when he ordered us to not become sharers with demons, by eating animals sacrificed to them. Then, only one verse later, he further explains the liberty he is presenting, by qualifying it as best suited alongside ignorance. If you don't know, then don't ask. Meat is meat, and idols are deaf, blind and mute objects. The opportunity to save a soul outweighs the value of a meal. If though, you do know, you shouldn't eat it. If others know you know, definitely don't eat it—for the sake of both your consciences. Yet again, when Paul is speaking of meat here, he is assuming it is actually food qualified for consumption. He is not condoning unclean food in any way. Eating food dedicated to idols was condemned at the Jerusalem council, as well as by Jesus, amidst His admonishing the churches of Pergamum and Thyatira, in the book of the Revelation.

Okay, you're really close to accepting this teaching, *but* Paul also said,

To the Jews I became as a Jew, so that I might win Jews; to those who are under the Law, as under the Law, though not being myself under the Law, so that I might win those who are under the Law. To them that are without law, as without law, (being not without law to God, but under the law to Christ,) that I might gain them that are without law. (1st Corinthians 9:20 & 21)

Yea, Hath God Said

…and you've always understood that to mean…When with the Jews, eat like the Jews, and when with the gentiles, eat whatever they eat.

Well, sure you did! That's what most want it to say, because then it is interpreted in agreement with a pre-existing and desired belief. The only problem is that it's an entirely errant interpretation. The surrounding verses wrap this text into a perfectly appropriate practice in homiletics. To go outside this meaning is a terribly bad practice in hermeneutics. Knowing your audience, in order to best reach them, is not a new idea. What Paul is saying is that when preaching to the Greeks, he uses philosophical platforms to make his points. And when he is preaching to those "under the law," he derives his apologetic stands from Torah. "And this I do for the gospel's sake (vs. 23)." Paul was not being a hypocrite, or a *righteous* misrepresentative, as could be derived if this was interpreted otherwise.

But what about missionaries, or people who are starving?

Ah! Now there's a great example of the need for and proper usage of grace. Do you really think He'd rather have you die, or for someone to end up in hell, all over food? Just be careful to not abuse the grace available to you, by *really* looking forward to smackin' on some ribs at your "heathen" friend's house, all in the name of evangelism. I doubt that would deem you a missionary. In actual foreign lands, you must do your very best. I'd argue that torah observance, when properly explained (seasoned with salt) is, in fact, very evangelistic. As I said, there are plenty of available and comprehensive works on this subject, so I will not go on much further. I just want to leave this topic with a detail, which is debatable amongst Messianic believers, but worthy of mention. To my Jewish brethren out there, I mean you no disrespect or offense.

Due to modern vernacular, there is a difference between eating biblically versus eating kosher. Kosher food will always be clean, but clean may not always be kosher. Some people insist that everything eaten must be koshered. For those of you who don't know what that means, food gets koshered by a certification that comes from rabbinic oversight and approval. There are various protocols that are necessary to be observed, for different foods to qualify as Kosher, or Parve (no meat or dairy).

As far as meat is concerned, I have no problem with people who choose to commit to kosher only. It ensures the meat to be as bloodless and humanely slaughtered as possible. It's a bit more expensive, but appreciably worth it. My personal conviction on kosher deviates more in regards to the non-meat related items. There are plenty of foods which are perfectly fine, and qualify as eatable, that are not certified kosher.

Again, I respect those who do keep the added kosher regulations, but my studies have led me to lean towards avoiding *certain* regulations that add unnecessary weight to the Torah's light yolk. I am also not an obligated Jew. I believe fear of extraneous and overwhelming regulation has played a significant role in hindering Christianity from this biblical observance. The Sola-Scriptura (Scripture only) laws of Kashrut are what I accept full obligation to. I accept Oral Tradition's views on a case by case basis. A good example of this would be the chicken. It is not mentioned in Scripture as eatable, or uneatable. They actually have some characteristics of other birds that are off-limits. I trust that because Judaism permits chicken, I am fine.

I'm sure I will receive ridicule for this from somebody. You will ultimately have to pray, study, and make these kinds of decisions for yourself. I choose to eat clean. I don't eat blood-based foods, and I don't eat meat sacrificed to Idols. Other Sola-Scriptura types paradoxically prefer man's teachings on this subject, and reject the 'Scriptura' part.

That's it! I'm done with this topic. Congratulations, you weathered that storm. But I'm not done making waves. Believe it or not, I have waited to pull out the heavy artillery until now. I must have you see Paul's perspective on the Law as clearly as possible. If you don't, you will find yourselves too easily tossed to and fro, being blown by winds of man-made doctrine. So, that is where we will now go. You'll have to jump awfully high to clear these hurdles:

> But this I admit to you, that according to the Way (which they call a sect) I do serve the God of our fathers, **believing everything that is in accordance with the Law** and that is written in the <u>Prophets</u>. (Acts 24:14)
> After Paul arrived, the Jews who had come down from Jerusalem stood around him, bringing many and serious charges against him which <u>they could not prove</u>, while Paul said in his own defense, "<u>I have committed no offense either against the Law of the Jews</u>, or against the temple, or against Caesar." (Acts 25:7 & 8)

These comments were made during a latter year of Paul's ministry. They were not made *about* him, but *by* him. This is his testimony. To a Jew, "believing" is not just a cognitive exercise. If you *believe* without response, it means nothing. The fact that Paul was not a Law-breaker, as much of the church deems him to be, is further established by these verses which tell us what Paul was actually on trial for:

> Brethren, I am a Pharisee, a son of Pharisees; I am on trial <u>for the hope and resurrection of the dead!</u> ...We find nothing wrong with this man; suppose a spirit or an angel has spoken to him? (Acts 23:6b & 9b)

Yea, Hath God Said

And now I am standing trial <u>for the hope of the promise</u> made by God to our fathers. (Acts 26:6)

...and when they had gone aside, they *began* talking to one another, saying, "This man is not doing anything worthy of death or imprisonment." And Agrippa said to Festus, "This man might have been set free if he had not appealed to Caesar." (Acts 26:31 & 32)

There was no substantiating evidence brought by any credible witnesses that proved Paul had broken neither the Laws of God, or even of man (of the Jews). Neither was it provable he was teaching others to do so. Do you remember who came and prayed over Paul, to return his sight and instruct him as to his calling? It was Ananias. Do you remember how Paul described him, when he was giving an account to the leaders in Jerusalem?

Acts 22:12, "A certain Ananias, a man who was <u>devout by the standard of the Law</u>, *and* well-spoken of by all the Jews who lived there."

The Spirit sent a mature, believing, Torah-abiding man, to bring Truth and healing to a devout, Torah-abiding, newly-believing man. The man of works needed a man of faith to cause the scales to fall from his eyes, so that he might see clearly. Selah. I could fill this book with this kind of banter, but we must move forward.

Libation or Liberation?

So, When Paul declared...

Therefore, stop letting anyone judge you in eating or in drinking, or with regard to a feast or of a new moon *[festival]*, or of Sabbaths, which are a shadow of the coming *[things]*, but the body *[is]* of Christ. (Colossians 2:16 & 17, ALT)

...what did he mean? Who doesn't love a good feast? Here is the common viewpoint: The feasts of YHVH are generally thought to be curious but obsolete times found throughout the Hebrew year, through which certain occurrences of the past are brought to a Jew's remembrance. Since the church isn't "Jewish," and Jesus came to do away with any obligation to Laws, there is no reason to actively continue fulfilling the requirements associated with these "memorials". While studying them is interesting, and seeing the prophecies contained in them regarding the coming Messiah is profitable, that is what they were all about anyway.

He will speak out against the Most High and wear down the saints of the Highest One, and he will <u>intend to make **alterations** in times and in law</u>; and they will be given into his hand for a time, times, and half a time. But the court will sit *for judgment,* and his dominion will be taken away, annihilated and destroyed forever. (Daniel 7:25 & 26)

Now, does that really sound like commentary on a person with whose actions the Lord is pleased?

Speak to the sons of Israel and say to them, "the LORD's appointed times which you shall proclaim as holy convocations—**My** appointed times are these:" (Leviticus 23:2)

I'll bet you can hear that buzzer going off again. It is true that there are fulfilled foreshadows. What is not often considered is that there are also unfulfilled foreshadows, a progressive salvation story, and the words like 'perpetual' and 'forever' that are associated with them. For those of you who jump at the opportunity to proclaim how the words 'everlasting' and 'perpetual' can, in Hebrew [olam], also mean 'indefinite' (as if to say they can end), you will hopefully see as we go on that your enthusiasm to do so is only founded on your faulty misconception of the Law. Here is a textual example regarding Passover or 'Pesach':

Now, this day will be a memorial to you, and you shall celebrate it *as* a feast to the LORD; throughout your generations you are to celebrate it *as* a **permanent** (olam) ordinance. (Exodus 12:14)

Looking down through history, to establish their continuation, here are but a fraction of the available examples of their being observed:

King David called for their observance.

Psalm 81:3, "Blow the trumpet at the new moon, at the full moon, on our feast day."

King Solomon continued the burnt offerings…

…and *did so* according to the daily rule, offering *them* up according to the commandment of Moses, for the Sabbaths, the new moons and the three annual feasts--the Feast of Unleavened Bread, the Feast of Weeks and the Feast of Booths. (2nd Chronicles 8:13)

Yea, Hath God Said

Jesus continued to keep the Appointed Times.

And His parents were traveling yearly to Jerusalem to the feast of the Passover. (Luke 2:41)

But the feast of the Jews was near, the Feast of Tabernacles. But now in the middle of the feast Jesus went up into the temple and began teaching. (John 7:2 & 14)

As did Paul, here seen keeping Pentecost or Shavuot:

But took leave of them, saying, "It behoveth me by all means the coming <u>feast</u> to keep at Jerusalem, and again I will return unto you—God willing." And he sailed from Ephesus. (Acts 18:21)

Although these are significant examples, I believe that these prophecies of their being attended to, in the future Millennial Kingdom, are to be examined with the utmost consideration:

And it shall be from new moon to new moon and from sabbath to sabbath, all mankind will come to bow down before Me, says the LORD. (Isaiah 66:23)

Moreover, they (priests) shall teach My people *the difference* between the holy and the profane, and cause them to discern between the unclean and the clean. In a dispute, they shall take their stand to judge; they shall judge it according to My ordinances. They shall also keep My laws and My statutes in all My appointed feasts and sanctify My sabbaths. (Ezekiel 44:23 & 24)

I realize that there are many of you who believe that even if these verses are prophetic of the future, that the future is not yet here and therefore are not for today. This is rather unfounded reasoning. To believe this would be to acknowledge that recalling: the creation (Shabbat), the beautiful story of redemption from slavery (Passover), acknowledgment of sinfulness and need of cleansing (Unleavened Bread) new life/rebirth/promise of resurrection (First-Fruits), the giving of the Torah and Spirit, to induce sanctification and to seal (Shavuot), assembling of the camp of the righteous, tribulation/war and resurrection (Trumpets), Judgment (Yom Kippur), and through to the 'future' coming kingdom (The Last Great Day), has no modern day value. By chance, did you notice that not all of these appointed times have been "filled-full"? So then, how could they be cancelled? The story of appointed time begins in Genesis 1:14:

Then God said, "Let there be lights in the expanse of the heavens to separate the day from the night, and let them be for signs and for seasons and for days and years."

From the dawn of creation (before Moses), there was a plan to observe a schedule, and to identify their times of observance by the actions of astral bodies. To understand the holy-days on God's religious calendar, and their details, an examination of Leviticus 23 and Numbers 28 & 29 is necessary. If you've never really read them, you should do so before continuing here. The first seven are the most renown of the scripturally mandated. This is a summary list.

The Mo'adim (Appointed Times) of YHVH are These:

#1, Abib (Spring Harvest) Nisan 14, "Pesach" or "Passover" Lamb, Bitter Herbs, Unleavened Bread (Exodus 12; Leviticus 23:5)

#2, Nisan 14-21, "Hag HaMatzot" or "Unleavened Bread" From the start of the Pesach meal, thru seven full days. Sabbath on first and last day. "There shall be no leaven found among you." (Leviticus 23:8; Numbers 28:25

#3 "Bikkurim" or "First Fruits" or "Feast of Harvest" (Day originally varied based on harvest.) "On the day after the sabbath" Disputed interpretation. Waving offering of the 1st sheaf. (Leviticus 23:10; Exodus 23:16)

#4, Sivan 6-7, "Shavu'ot" or "Feast of Weeks" (Day varies due to First Fruits calculation) Seven-weeks plus 1 day, fifty days from the offering of the 1st sheaf waving (having counted the Omer), upon which a grain offering is due. Now coordinated with "Pentecost" (Leviticus 23:15-16, 23:21; Numbers 28:26)

#5, Tishrei 1, "Yom Teruah" or "Feast of Trumpets" On the 1st day of the 7th month. "You shall blow trumpets." Coincides with *Rosh HaShanah.* Meaning: Head or beginning of the New Year. Marks the beginning of the non-religious civil year. (Leviticus 23:24; Numbers 29:1)

#6, Tishrei 10, "Yom Kippur" or "Day of Atonement" On the 10th day of the 7th month. Highest holy day. A sabbath. Only Mo'ed with a scripturally *mandated* fast! (Leviticus 23:26-27 & 32; Numbers 29:7)

#7, Tishrei 15-22, "Sukkot" or "Feast of Tabernacles" On the 15th day of the 7th month: "You shall dwell in booths." First and last days are sabbaths, with holy convocations. (Leviticus 23:34, 23:39; Numbers 29:12)

#8, Tishrei 23, "Last Great Day" On the 23rd day of the 7th month: 'the Assembly of the Eighth Day' or Great Day of the Feast. (John 7:37; Leviticus 23:36, 23:39; Numbers 29:35)

Yea, Hath God Said

Non-Mandated, but Scripturally Recognized:

#9 Purim: Deliverance of Jews from annihilation. Book of Esther **#10 Chanukah** or "Festival of Lights" or "Feast of Dedication" Memorializes the Maccabean revolt and Rededication of Temple. (Books of Maccabees and John 10:22)

#11 Rosh Chodesh: The New Moon recognition. The beginning of the Month; lit. Head of the Month. Celebrated with a festival and the sounding of the shofar. (Exodus 12:1,2; Numbers 10:10)

The Mo'adim are not, as you may have concluded, in a random order either. They are perfectly arranged to remind us from where we came, right through the stages of redemption and deliverance, to where we are going (Promised Land). This happens in an annual, cyclical, and perpetual program. Not that humanity could use any reminding or anything. There are many thorough teachings which go into great detail as to the meanings behind the Feasts, as well as the traditions and requirements associated with attending them. My purpose in bringing this topic up is to show that Scripture doesn't let us ignore them, and so neither should we. As is usual, I will refer you to some quality teachings on them at the end of the book, in the resources section.

"Luney" Israelites

Now for the third item in the list of things "not to be judged for"—the New Moons. At first, this might sound like it was concocted by Andy Worhal. That's only because in this day and age, HaSatan has successfully duped most modern day believers into thinking that the calendar was always 365¼ days long, being based only on Earth's length of time to orbit around the sun.

Actually, that was only part of the original plan. Although the length of time the sun shone down would tell us what agricultural season we were in, and its position in the sky would tell us what point in the day we were in, it was not until 46 AD, when the Roman emperor Julius Caesar asserted his calendar that the modern system of calendar calculation was based solely on the sun. Solely...get it? Previous to that, the Mayans, the Egyptians, and the Indians (Eastern) were the only predominant people groups who did. And with a cursory consideration as to what kind of religious peoples these were, you should surmise a problem.

From the most ancient of times, pagan people groups considered the sun and celestial bodies to be either gods themselves, or emanations of them. Unfortunately, the ancient Israelites were not innocent in this regard.

They will spread them out to the sun, the moon and to all the host of heaven, which they have loved and which they have served, and which they have gone after and which they have sought, and which they have worshiped. They will not be gathered or buried; they will be as dung on the face of the ground. (Jeremiah 8:2)

You have all heard the name Ra, the highest god of the Egyptians. This is the very same one that God dispelled when he smote the land with darkness, in His plan to free the Hebrews. You've read of Moloch, Sun god of the Canaanites, and Apollo, the Greek god of the Sun; the son of Zeus. Even the modern Roman Catholic Church still uses the Monstrance, or Ostensorium, a representative symbol of a sunburst.[2] Sun worshipers still exist today, and I'm not talking about skin-tanners. For example, there is the Indian sun god, Bhaskara. The Sun has been in some way revered in every society, and somewhat rightly so. For if the Sun was to no longer give its light, all life would cease; hence the adoration and fear of the power of the Sun. The problem is that we have a clear mandate by the Lord to not worship the creation, only the Creator.

Exodus 20:3, "You shall have no other gods before Me."
Exodus 20:4, "You shall not make for yourself an idol, or any likeness of what is in heaven above or on the earth beneath or in the water under the earth."
Exodus 20:5a, "You shall not worship them or serve them."

You may have noticed, when reading the Scriptures related to the Mo'adim (Appointed Times), that their scheduling is mostly dictated by the New Moon. From Passover to the Last Great Day, a solar year is not fully realized. We can't deny that there is practical value in a solar year. So neither an entirely lunar, nor entirely solar calendar is adequate to attend to both the Mo'adim, and the scheduling of specific, future, secular appointed events. So wouldn't you just guess, God planned for that also.

God said, "Let there be lights in the dome of the sky to divide the day from the night; let them be for **signs**, seasons, days and years." (Genesis 1:14)

You see that word 'seasons' in this last verse? That's not the most appropriate rendering. The only popular translation I know of that actually renders it accurately is the *Good News Bible*, oddly enough. The word in the Hebrew is mo'ed; the singular root of the word 'Mo'adim. If you didn't know before, you now know what the verse should say. Mo'ed is the word also typically translated as festival or feast. Here we see intent

Yea, Hath God Said

by the Creator, to have us use the sky for calculating the Appointed Times, long before Israel was ever formally instructed in them. That makes Divine scheduling transcend the typical 'Law' affiliation, and helps us to understand how Abraham was described as obedient to such things, prior to the giving of the Law at Sinai (Genesis 26:5). Granted, we don't know specifically what he observed. They were probably prototypical.

God's lunar month, the biblical month, begins at the sighting of the New Moon, by the naked eyes of the men whose duty it was to observe, and is either 29 or 30 days long. This is due to the fact that the time it takes for the Moon to orbit the Earth is approximately 29.5 days. Interestingly, it coincides with the typical menstrual, life-cycle of humans.

Israel's religious year begins in their spring, just before Passover, and continues around to the following "Abib". Although it became the name of the first month, originally abib was not actually a month, but the time of year when the barley grain has reached full growth. The name of the month that corresponds with this time of year is now known as Nisan. Israel's civil year begins at Yom Teruah (a.k.a. Rosh HaShanah), on the 1st of Tishri, corresponding with our Sept./Oct.

> And the LORD spake unto Moses and Aaron in the land of Egypt, saying, "this month shall be unto you the beginning of months: it shall be the first month of the year to you." (Exodus 12:1)
> On this day in the month of Abib, you are about to go forth. (Exodus 13:4)

I would like for you to read this excerpt, regarding our current calendar:

> The Gregorian calendar takes its name from Pope Gregory XIII, who reformed the Roman calendar in the year 1582. Before that, the civil calendar was called the Julian calendar, after the Roman Emperor Julius Caesar, who had also altered the calendar in the year 46 BCE. One of Caesar's amendments was TO PATTERN THE CIVIL CALENDAR ON THE CALENDAR OF ANCIENT EGYPT, which was at that time the only calendar in which the lengths of the months and years were fixed by definite rules. In other words, the civil calendar, which hangs upon your wall in your home or office, is similar in parts of its structure to the calendar that was used in ancient Egypt. Like its Egyptian ancestor, the sun alone governs the civil calendar, and its months (January to December) are in no way influenced by the moon. In the civil calendar of today, a new moon can occur on any day in the month; days begin in the middle of the night, and years in the northern hemisphere begin in the middle of winter, on the 1st of January." [3]

Keeping this in mind, I would now like to have you consider some other interesting facts regarding our modern Gregorian calendar.

Remember, Genesis does not give us names for the days of the week; they are just numbered.

1st Day, Sun-day: is the day appointed to honor the Sun god "Sol Invictis".

2nd Day, Monday: is named after the Moon. Affiliated Roman goddess name Luna.

3rd Day, Tuesday: is named after Tiu, an ancient Teutonic deity.

4th Day, Wednesday: is named after Woden, a god in Norse mythology, associated with the Roman god (and planet) Mercury.

5th Day, Thursday: is named after Thor, the supreme god in Norse mythology, associated with the Roman god (and planet) Jupiter.

6th Day, Friday: is named after Friga, wife of the god Odin, or Wodin, another god in Norse mythology.

7th Day, Saturday: is named after the god Saturn, for whom the planet is named after.

Well, I suppose we have to name them something, right? Now consider this. From where did the names of our months come?

JANUARY: Named for Janus, the Roman mighty one of portals and patron of beginnings and endings, to whom this month was sacred. He is shown as having two faces, one in front, the other at the back of his head, supposedly to symbolize his powers.

FEBRUARY: This name is derived from Februa, a Roman festival of purification. It was originally the month of expiation.

MARCH: It is named for Mars, the Roman mighty one of war.

APRIL: This name comes from the Latin APRILIS, indicating a time of Fertility. It was believed that this month is the month when the earth was supposed to open up for the plants to grow.

MAY: This month was named for Maia, the Roman female deity of growth or increase.

JUNE: This name is sometimes attributed to Juno, the goddess of the marriage, the wife of Jupiter in Roman mythology. She was also called the "Queen of heaven" and "Queen of mighty ones". The name of this month is also attributed to Junius Brutus, but originally it most probably referred to the month in which crops grow to ripeness.

JULY: Named for the Roman emperor Julius Caesar, this is the seventh month of the Gregorian year.

AUGUST: Named for Octavius Augustus Caesar, emperor of Rome. The name was originally from *augure*, which means, "to increase".

SEPTEMBER: This name is derived from the Latin septem, meaning "seven".

Yea, Hath God Said

OCTOBER: This name comes from the Latin root octo, meaning "eight," and was the eighth month of the Roman calendar.

NOVEMBER: This name is derived from Latin novem, meaning "ninth," and was the ninth month of the Roman calendar.

DECEMBER: This name is derived from the Latin decem, meaning "ten," and was the tenth month of the Roman calendar.

This list of facts is verifiable in practically any dictionary or encyclopedia available. At this point you may still be saying to yourself, "Yeah, so what?" or, "I knew that, but that's the world we live in though! Why does it matter?" I'm glad you asked. Because the one who controls our calendar is the one who dictates our cyclical (perpetual) pattern of living, and what we memorialize. If HaSatan had reason to believe that all the anti-Semitic propaganda he has thrown at us from the first century on was not enough to get us to forget the Mo'adim, then the next angle of attack would be to covertly bury God's calendar over with the adherence to a new, alternative one. Not only that, but read these verses of Scripture:

Now concerning everything which I have said to you, be on your guard; and do <u>not mention the name</u> of other gods, nor let *them* be heard from your mouth. (Exodus 23:13)

You shall tear down their altars and smash their *sacred* pillars and burn their Asherim (Ishtar/Eostre worship trees) with fire, and you shall cut down the engraved images of their gods and <u>obliterate their name</u> from that place. (Deuteronomy 12:3; parenthetic addition is mine.)

The sorrows of those who have bartered for another *god* will be multiplied; I shall not pour out their drink offerings of blood, <u>nor will I take their names</u> upon my lips. (Psalm 16:4)

We can choose to take these commands literally or figuratively, and either way we lose. Either we really should never even speak them, and yet constantly do with every day—and most months we mention; or figuratively, we should not give them honor with our lips, and unknowingly we resurrect them daily from the destruction they were supposed to have come under, when we accepted YHVH as our God. Take your pick! You may see thing differently, but I believe HaSatan has had a field day with getting us believers to unknowingly break commands; and he delights in just hearing their names roll off our tongues. After all, he is the source of their invention.

So what are we to do? After all, the majority of the modern civilized world uses the Gregorian, or sun-based calendar. We can't just go walking around calling Wednesday the "Fourth Day," can we? I'm not so sure we can't, at least a lot of the time. If people have to use their fingers and sound out the days of the week, to figure out which day you are speaking of, is that so bad? If they can't count from one to seven, that's the least of their problems. When you are writing the months down, write the (numerical) equivalent first, and then after a slash, write the corresponding Gregorian name abbreviated.

I realize you may not always get away with that. But I believe that if in your heart you understand the error of the names, and seek the mercies of the Lord as you adjust, or seem to have no choice, you will certainly receive them. When you are writing a letter, you can get away with it easy enough. Do it when you can. Say the numbers when you can, and when people ask you why you are doing that simply tell them, "I prefer to pay the least respect possible to the false gods that are associated with them." It may seem spiritually obnoxious, but in the end, it may be an evangelistic tool. After all, one of the benefits of *proper* Torah obedience is its inherent shining of light to the nations.

I also realize there are some of you, who at this point are thinking I have just gone over the top. Those among you, who are fond of your adapting "WWJD" filtered thinking into your lives, do you really believe He followed the "Do what the Romans do" ideology? Would He have supported the memorializing of pagan gods, by attributing His creation to them, so as to not ruffle any feathers? Selah.

The major point of this discussion was and is the perpetual aspect to the "Feasts of God". HaSatan has been trying to erase the appointments (as if they're written in pencil) so we won't attend. If we don't attend, we primarily miss out on a huge blessing; and secondly, we disobey. They are His feasts, not ours! (My appointed times are these...Leviticus 23:2.) And most Torah teachers would agree that the reasons He chose to word it this way is so that we would attend, and because He wants to be with us more than we want to be with Him. How many of us, if given a formal invitation to attend a most-benevolent king's banquet, would simply turn it down because we'd never been to one before. It's never too late to start attending His Majesty's fine affairs, so please attend the next one if at all possible.

Just in case you still don't want to attend, here is one of those verses that commonly plays a role in influencing others to feel the same way. It, like so many others, needs to have correct understanding brought to it.

Bring your worthless offerings no longer. Incense is an abomination to Me. New moon and sabbath, the calling of assemblies-- I cannot endure iniquity and the solemn assembly (NASB).

The incense you bring me is a stench in my nostrils! Your celebrations of the new moon and the Sabbath day, and your special days for fasting–even your most pious meetings–are all sinful and false. I want nothing more to do with them (NLT).

Yea, Hath God Said

Here are two translations of Isaiah 1:13, with two completely different ways of saying *almost* the same thing. The subtle variance, however, is significant. I'm not insinuating that the *New Living Translation* is the enemy's propaganda tool. However, when I see these kinds of interpretive influences, I am greatly troubled. On the surface, it looks like God just cancelled His holy-day program. The only redeeming value to that interpretation is the usage of "your," which generally gets lost in the tone. All we have to do is but read one more version, to get the clearest expression of His heart in this rebuke.

Stop bringing worthless grain offerings! They are like disgusting incense to me! Rosh-Hodesh, Shabbat, calling convocations—I can't stand <u>evil together with</u> your assemblies! (Complete Jewish Bible)

Isn't it amazing how much of a difference a translation makes? When you decide to begin your journey into the Mo'adim, Passover is really the best place to start familiarizing yourself with them. It is not only the most widely recognized of the Mo'adim, which might make it easier to find a fellowship or family to celebrate it with, but it is also the beginning of the cycle. You can also obtain a Passover guide, called a Haggadah, and learn about it that way. Or, although it's not the first in order, you could also attend a fellowship that participates in Succoth (the Feast of Tabernacles). It may just be the first of the Mo'adim that we all participate in, at the start of the millennial reign.

Then it will come about that any who are left of all the nations that went against Jerusalem will go up from year to year to worship the King, the LORD of hosts, and to celebrate the <u>Feast of Booths</u>. (Zechariah 14:16)

Add this bit of related symbolism:

For this reason, they are before the throne of God; and they serve Him day and night in His temple; and He who sits on the throne will spread His tabernacle over them. (Revelation 7:15)

It's really somewhat ironic...

Even the stork in the sky knows her seasons; and the turtledove, and the swift, and the thrush observe the time of their migration; but My people do not know The ordinance of the LORD. (Jeremiah 8:7)

He Wants to Meet with You!

God has picked out specific, appointed times each year for you to meet with Him. How's that for an opportunity to know Him better? He looks forward to significantly revealing Himself to you at least eight times per year. If you haven't been attending, where have you been? Have you been missing Him on behalf of work, or the Late Night Show, or maybe because a very popular, modern version of the Bible says not to bother, like this:

> Therefore do not let anyone judge you by what you eat or drink, or with regard to a religious festival, a New Moon celebration or a Sabbath day. These are a shadow of the things that <u>were to come</u>; the reality, however, is found in Christ. (Colossians 2:16 & 17; NIV)

Or the disappointing way the NASU slides an extraneous adjective in verse 17: "...things which are a _mere_ shadow of what is to come; but the substance belongs to Christ." when there are other versions that say it more like this:

> So don't let anyone pass judgment on you in connection with eating and drinking, or in regard to a Jewish festival or Rosh Chodesh or Shabbat. These are a shadow of things to come, but the body is of the Messiah (JNT).
> Therefore, stop letting anyone judge you* in eating or in drinking or with regard to a feast or of a new moon _[festival]_ or of Sabbaths, which are a shadow of the coming _[things]_, but the body _[is]_ of Christ (ALT).
> ...which are a shadow of <u>the coming things</u>, and the body _is_ of the Christ (YLT).

Are you able to discern the difference? Look carefully. If you can, you are hearing His voice just fine, all by yourself. Part of hearing His voice accurately, requires looking deeper into the Scriptures than what is on the surface. In case you have some doubt, look at the verb tense differences between "were to come" and "of the coming". This is no minor detail folks! It is so significant actually, and compared to a dozen other correctly translated versions, one has to wonder how the NIV came up with such an impacting change. It's actually a lot like this variance, found in Hebrews 9:11.

> So Christ has now become the High Priest over all the good things that **have come**. He has entered that great, perfect sanctuary in heaven, not made by human hands and not part of this created world (NLT).
> But when Christ appeared _as_ a high priest of the good things **to come**, _He entered_ through the greater and more perfect tabernacle, not made with hands, that is to say, not of this creation (NASU).

Yea, Hath God Said

Of course, there is no way these are motivated by an ideology, because that would mean they "added to, or took away from" the Scriptures. Big things come in small variances.

You may have heard Colossians 2:16 & 17 exposited in one sermon or another. There are two polar extremes, leading to three popular variances in its potential meaning. Most translate it incorrectly, so therefore it's also interpreted wrong. Obviously, you will have to pray and study to verify this for yourself; although I will be assisting you in the next chapter. This is a good example, of a time you need to ask yourself to whom this letter is being written, to get the correct answer. The Colossians…sure, but more specifically, to a fellowship of 'gentile' converts in Asia, who lived near Laodicea.

So like many of the epistles, this letter was likewise written to bring loving correction to a heresy, or doctrinal controversy, that was unique to a specific, regional fellowship. The Colossians were Phrygian *gentiles*, and were mostly a mystical people group steeped in philosophies and mythologies. According to Colossians 2:18 & 23, they probably practiced self-humiliation and chastisement, angel worship (angels being thought to be the intermediaries between the Lord and man), and sexual indulgence. Having these practices in their background, their re-mingling (syncretism) of indigenous paganism with the pure faith was inevitable. The social pressures to revert back to their previous practices, especially by those they love, would be great. This is at the heart of the admonition in verses sixteen and seventeen.

One possible interpretation is that they are not being told *not* to observe the listed items, they are being told not to let anyone tell them how to do them, "except for the body (is) of Christ." Take the added *is* out of where it has been added in several versions and the Greek text literally reads, "ho deh soma Christos," or simply: "but the Body Christ." So a possible rendering is, "stop letting anyone judge you in (these miscellaneous things), but the body *of* Christ."

"Body," as seen here, *could* be a well-acknowledged, scriptural idiom for 'members of God's family'—the only appropriate people to wield spiritual authority for these believers. If you remove the hurdle *'is'* out of the way, the gauntlet becomes more negotiable. I know many of you will take issue with this interpretation, for various reasons, and that's fine. I personally like that rendering, but must confess it to be unsubstantiatable. So, even if we were to drop that detail out of this exposition, it really detracts nothing as you will see. This verse has often been debated; and yes, the substance/body of the "shadows" is the Christ. Therefore, if the Christ is their point of origin, and ultimate culmination, I would say that's serious grounds for our involvement.

It is obvious, if you read the entire second chapter at once, without isolating this verse from its proper textual context, that Paul does not want syncretizing or legalistic people, who have their own opinion on how things should be done, to come in and alter the prescribed ways of the Torah. Make no mistake, this was a weighty issue then and it still is today. If only the people who had the capacity and gifting to teach would do so, we would have a far more correct walk of faith and much stronger believers. And just how do we know who is correct, and what our walks of faith should look like? That is at least partly answered by knowing what the actual heresy being dealt with here in this letter to the Colossians was.

On top of the defense over the question of the deity of Jesus, and a warning to avoid mysticism, this portion of Scripture is speaking specifically about the Lord's pattern for our lives. His design including: the feast days (Mo'adim, or "Appointed Times"), the observance of new moons (calendar calculation), our diet (clean versus unclean), and the observance of Shabbats (Sabbaths and High Sabbaths).

I'd like you to contemplate something. This verse has been used to support the cancellation of all the Lord's perpetual, annual events. It is commonly interpreted to be telling us not to let anyone tell us we *should* observe them. Many others and I take extreme issue with this interpretation, and believe that to accept that errant belief one would ultimately be putting their self into a perpetual state of disobedience. Albeit, ignorance of this fact may cause grace to abound more, but it still robs believers of a depth of their maturity and understanding that they really need to have.)

If these "shadows" are of things "*yet* to come," should we not still be looking forward through them, as some are yet unfulfilled? Never mind the fact we can still look back through them with thanksgiving. That's what the Apostles did.

I want to expose another grammatical "oops!" You really must see how important it is to study with comparison, and how small variances can change meanings substantially. These variations can lead us to blatantly false interpretations of verses; e.g., Paul telling the Colossians to reject God's calendar of events. These variations, understandably, are often the foundation for the false teachings that have arisen from most of today's Protestant and Catholic denominations.

Don't you think if Paul believed in such a radical and extreme change in Israel's M.O., he would have gone to far greater lengths to support and spread the word? A passing mention in a letter to gentile converts just falls short. Peter and James surely would have had to be called to give supportive testimony, and themselves written of such to the Jewish community. No such validation is seen anywhere. This next example, the (NASU) even bungled, (hence their needing to use a small

Yea, Hath God Said

"l" instead of a capital, which denotes Torah, to attempt to reconcile it.)

…realizing the fact that **law** is not [made] for a righteous person, but for those who are lawless and rebellious, for the ungodly and sinners, for the unholy and profane, for those who kill their fathers or mothers, for murderers… (1st Timothy 1:9)

The word *made*, seen in the brackets is 'keimai'. It is the very same word used in this also popular verse:

Luke 3:9, "Indeed the axe is already laid at the root of the trees; so every tree that does not bear good fruit is cut down and thrown into the fire."

Might you guess what it is? It carries the metaphoric meaning of being applied against, as in a judgment! Here, the axe is being *applied* to the bottom of the tree, so as to kill it. *Keimai* has been rendered here as *laid*. Let's try that verse in Timothy again rendered without that bias.

…realizing the fact that Law is not [laid down] for a righteous person, but for those who are lawless and rebellious, for the ungodly and sinners, for the unholy and profane, for those who kill their fathers or mothers, for murderers…

There are several versions (including the RSV and ALT) that have translated it this last way. It is not my invention. The uncorrected translation doesn't even make sense if you will think about it. It is the Law that keeps us from being those things! Of course, the Law is for righteous people! If transgression of the Law is sin, adherence to the Law is sinlessness! Oh, I see the problem. I also took this verse out of context; for yet another illustration for you. The previous verse says this:

1st Timothy 1:8, "But we know that the Law is good, if one uses it lawfully…"

By using it lawfully, Paul means that good works (adherence) is <u>never</u> to be used as a means to redemption. This always has to be on the forefront of your mind as you read Paul's writings, or you will quickly misunderstand him, as so many have. And finally, the last thing we should not be judged for:

Therefore, no one is to act as your judge in regard to food or drink or in respect to a festival or a new moon or a **Sabbath** day. (Colossians 2:16)

Well, Shabbat Shalom!

We have already seen that the Mo'adim are, or have within them, sabbath regulations. Even if they do not fall on the Seventh Day, they are considered 'set-apart' and have some stipulations associated with them. But what we are talking about here specifically is the Great Sabbath, the weekly, perpetual memorial of His work of Creation and the deliverance from Egypt; the day the Creator wants His creation to gather around Him and receive blessings.

So the sons of Israel shall observe the sabbath, to celebrate the sabbath throughout their generations <u>as a perpetual</u> **covenant**. It is a **sign** between Me and the **sons** of Israel forever; for in six days the LORD made heaven and earth, but on the seventh day He ceased *from labor,* and was refreshed. (Exodus 31:16 & 17)
You shall remember that you were a slave in the land of Egypt, and the LORD your God brought you out of there by a mighty hand and by an outstretched arm; therefore the LORD your God commanded you to observe the sabbath day. (Deuteronomy 5:15)

But the Sabbath is for Jews, and Sunday is for Christians, right? No more than the Hebrew Scriptures are for the Jews, and the Apostolic are for Christians. Only if you wish to not be considered His sons and daughters. Due to the controversial nature and sensitivity of this topic, we cannot fly through this. Strap yourself in, because we are about to go for a bumpy ride.

Let not <u>the foreigner</u> who has <u>joined himself</u> to the LORD say, "the LORD will surely separate me from His people." Nor let the eunuch say, "Behold, I am a dry tree." To them I will give in My house and within My walls a memorial, and <u>a name better than that of **sons** and daughters</u>. I will give them an everlasting name which will not be cut off. Also, <u>the aliens that join themselves</u> to the LORD, to minister unto Him, and to love the name of the LORD, to be His servants, every one that keepeth the sabbath from profaning it, and holdeth fast by <u>My covenant.</u> (Isaiah 56:3, 5 & 6)

But aren't the Sabbath and Sun-day the same thing? Well, are the Seventh day and Sun-day the same thing? For many, it apparently is. What's curiously overlooked, as this verse (Colossians 2:16) is used to support the change of the Sabbath, is that at this time in the early church's history, Sunday was not even considered a Sabbath day option. It is anachronistic to impute that intent into the verse!
Imagine if half the believing community of ancient Israel decided that Passover should take place on the 23rd day of Shevat/November, instead of its appointed time, would it have been intolerant of God to

Yea, Hath God Said

consider that disobedient? Is God's kingdom a democracy? Although this is a worthy contemplation, it's not even the heart of the matter.

The Sabbath, though existing within time, is not a day, a date, or even a commanded break, in its rawest form. It is the method by which the Creator has established a means for us to acknowledge Him as such, and take upon ourselves the 'sign' of a covenant. *But* isn't circumcision the sign of the covenant? For one of the covenants it is. So also is the rainbow. Although the homosexual community has hijacked it, it belongs to everyone. The Sabbath is representative of the Mosaic; but unrecognized by many, the Sabbath is also a stand-alone covenant that works in conjunction with all the others. Also often overlooked is the fact that Shabbat is actually a pre-Law concept!

There are multiple covenants in the passages of Holy Scripture. And although they are progressive, and sometimes unique, not one of them can operate in total independence. In this case, I think more specifically than in the other covenants, this pledge has the most to do with the future coming bride/bridegroom relationship we will be enjoying in our future marriage. Yes, He is our Creator, but for what did He create us? He created us to be a partner in an eternal romance; to completely love and be loved. The deliverance and its adjoining Mt. Sinai covenant are more expressive of the Father/Child relationship (Exodus 4:22). Circumcision is the "I will acknowledge my Abrahamic lineage and its promises" sign. The Sabbath is more the "I will love and be faithful" sign of our betrothal. Let's compare some of the aspects to see the differences.

The general, compliance promises/benefits of the Mosaic/Mt. Sinai covenant are:

...so that you may prolong *your* days on the land which the LORD swore to your fathers to give to them and to their descendants, a land flowing with milk and honey. (Deuteronomy 11:9)

...that He will give the rain for your land in its season, the early and late rain; that you may gather in your grain and your new wine and your oil. He will give grass in your fields for your cattle, and you will eat and be satisfied. (Deuteronomy 11:14 & 15)

"...to give you, great and splendid cities which you did not build. and houses full of all good things which you did not fill, and hewn cisterns which you did not dig, vineyards and olive trees which you did not plant, and you eat and are satisfied. Deuteronomy 6:10b, 11)

And He said, "If you will give earnest heed to the voice of the LORD your God, and do what is right in His sight, and give ear to His commandments, and keep all His statutes, I will put none of the diseases on you which I have put on the Egyptians; for I, the LORD, am your healer." (Exodus 15:26)

Of course, there are many more. But they are summed up in these words: "...that it may go well with you and your children." Examining them, you find a common theme. He promises to take care of His people. God did express Himself as a Husband to them (Jeremiah 31:32). By their actions, it would appear they did not acknowledge Him as such. I think that experience was more specifically like a betrothal; one which is still waiting to be consummated. A promise to marry back then was contractual. But they were unfaithful, and therefore He had to portray more of the strong Father role, who one day intends to express the role of Bridegroom. (Of course, this is all picturesque, as He really is all these roles and more, all the time.)

Now, here are the benefits of Shabbat observance as promised through Isaiah:

If because of the sabbath, you turn your foot from doing your *own* pleasure on My holy day, and call the sabbath a delight, the holy *day* of the LORD honorable, and honor it, desisting from your *own* ways, From seeking your *own* pleasure and speaking *your own* word. Then you will **take delight in the LORD**, and I will make you **ride on the heights** of the earth; and I will **feed you *with* the heritage of Jacob** your father, for the mouth of the LORD has spoken. (Isaiah 58:13 & 14)

What's different? These are not so much physical things we are talking about anymore. These are about relationship and emotive things. Think about it. The 'terms' of the Shabbat covenant are if you...

1. Don't Create or Labor (Rest in and Trust each other)

2. Surrender your Will (Submission; Keep our Vows)

3. Keep the Sabbath a Delight (Encourage Peace and Joy)

4. Focus on His Pleasure, (Which results in our Pleasure)

5. Acknowledge Him as Creator (Remain Faithful)

...then you will take delight in God, ride high, and be blessed! Kind of looks like a healthy marriage doesn't it?

All He really is saying is, "I'll give you six days a week to toil, create and seek your own pleasure. If we are to someday be wed, we are going to need to spend some quality time together, at least once a week, to demonstrate your commitment to me, and to prove/improve our relationship, until that great and glorious day comes. Six thousand years you can do your own thing. But in the Seventh, I will come and set up my kingdom."

Yea, Hath God Said

He, the Bridegroom, has asked that we do this on the Seventh Day of every week. And not just for a couple hours in a church building, but for the whole day. Many tend to think of the Shabbat as our holy engagement ring. Likewise being a sign, you can remain engaged without wearing it, but how would that make your fiancé feel?

There are those who typically ask or say things like: "*But* the Spirit shows up on Sunday." "How do we know that our current Seventh Day is the real Shabbat?" "*But* I have to work on the Seventh day." And, "He doesn't care when we worship Him. After all, we should be worshiping Him all the time." or any one of a thousand stumbling blocks you can place before yourself to resist the obvious. Rest assured, every one of these kinds of statements can be rebutted, and quite easily. It's not the Lord's fault we don't live in a community of Torah observant people. If everyone else in church was doing it, then so would you…Right?

Since I realize you may not be satisfied with my allegorical evidence, I will provide you with a few more substantive supports, answering more questions and objections along the way, beginning with: How do we know our modern Seventh Day is the Shabbat, and that the calendar has not been altered somewhere along the line? If you presume that the Shabbat may have been lost, or incurred a variance between Creation and the Exodus, then we can presume Jesus, the Lord of the Sabbath, fixed that discrepancy (if there was one) upon His coming. I'm comfortable believing He would know when it was supposed to be.

Could it have been lost between the early church and today? The Jews who were and are Torah observant, who entered the Diaspora (dispersion), regardless of where they went or what calendar they were under, would no doubt have been able to continue to count to seven wherever they went. The Shabbat is held in such high regard within Judaism, that if one or two rabbis got confused, there would still be hundreds, then thousands of independent leaders and groups to set the record straight.

If the civil calendar itself was bungled up, the religious calendar continued to operate independently. A bungling of sorts did occur during an adjustment made to the Julian calendar, by Pope Gregory XIII, in October of 1582. He added ten days between the 5th day and the 6th day, making the calendar jump from Thursday the fourth to Friday the fifteenth. However, note that by adding a quantity of days he did not alter the sequence of day's names. Therefore, Shabbat remained on the 7th day that week as usual.[4] What is interesting to note is that the motivation behind this adjustment was to enable the observance of Easter to take place on the original date established at the council of Nicaea, in 325 AD.

But what makes Shabbat observance different than going to church on Sunday, besides when (Sunday) and where (synagogue)? As it should be understood, it is a twenty-four, sometimes twenty-five hour period, which begins at the *erev* (meaning: evening) of the 6th day, through to sundown the next day—otherwise understood to be Fri. through Sat. night. But that's really just the beginning.

Sadly, much of where it goes from there is why Shabbat is commonly rejected and misunderstood by the modern, autonomous from Israel, church. Our dominant, currently identifiable representation of physical Israel (the Jews) have, in an effort to build fences around the Sabbath and keep it protected, added an awful lot of additional regulation to yet another set of God's beautiful instructions. Actually, what Torah dictates is very reasonable, and is in all cases. What our big brother has done has made it, with all due respect, alienating and burdensome. My dear Judah, can you not see that you have made keeping the Sabbath so difficult, there is little opportunity for the goyim to see the delight, as you struggle to *work* to observe it? You believe the Messianic age will begin if everyone keeps it perfectly, but you sabotage the possibility. The Lord's original directives logically assist us in making Shabbat a success and a blessing. Your traditions make it near impossible for that to be true. The honey has turned sour and the flies taste not. Do you purposely ignore Elohiym, for the sake of Moshe? Have you forgotten the governor these commands were instituted with?

You shall not add to the word which I am commanding you, nor take away from it, that you may keep the commandments of the LORD your God which I command you. (Deuteronomy 4:2)

Whatever I command you, you shall be careful to do; you shall not add to nor take away from it. (Deuteronomy 12:32)

I recognize the need for some guidance in adherence, but I literally would double this book's thickness with all the stipulations I would have to find room for—all sixteen hundred plus of them. (See additional note, under "End Notes" p.473.) You can knead that puffy dough if you want to, but I am just going to give you the Matzoh Mitzvoth. Notice here, that the actual Shabbat-related instruction, within the Decalogue itself, happens to be the most textually voluminous of them all:

Exodus 20:8, "Remember the sabbath day, to keep it holy.
Exodus 20:9, "Six days you shall labor and do all your work.
Exodus 20:10, "But the seventh day is a sabbath of the LORD your God; *in it* you shall not do any work, you or your son or your daughter, your male or your female servant or your cattle or your sojourner who stays with you.
Exodus 20:11, "For in six days the LORD made the heavens and the earth, the sea and all that is in them, and rested on the seventh day; therefore the

LORD blessed the sabbath day and made it holy."

Out of the sixteen verses which comprise the Ten Commandments, four of them (twenty-five percent) relate to the Sabbath. When God was handing Moses the two tablets back for the second time, as He was doing so He audibly reminded Moses of two of the Ten Words (Exodus 34): Don't make forged gods, and keep the Sabbath. He then follows this in later passages with at least six more commands to "keep My Sabbaths." Here is some more detail regarding the application of it, as depicted in this portion from Nehemiah:

In those days I saw in Judah some who were treading wine presses on the sabbath, and bringing in sacks of grain and loading *them* on donkeys, as well as wine, grapes, figs and all kinds of loads, and they brought *them* into Jerusalem on the sabbath day. So I admonished *them* on the day they sold food. (16) Also men of Tyre were living there *who* imported fish and all kinds of merchandise, and sold *them* to the sons of Judah on the sabbath, even in Jerusalem. (17) Then I reprimanded the nobles of Judah and said to them, "What is this evil thing you are doing, by profaning the sabbath day? (18) Did not your fathers do the same, so that our God brought on us and on this city all this trouble? Yet you are adding to the wrath on Israel by profaning the sabbath." (19) It came about that just as it grew dark at the gates of Jerusalem before the sabbath, I commanded that the doors should be shut and that they should not open them until after the sabbath. Then I stationed some of my servants at the gates *so that* no load would enter on the sabbath day. (20) Once or twice the traders and merchants of every kind of merchandise spent the night outside Jerusalem. (21) Then I warned them and said to them, "Why do you spend the night in front of the wall? If you do so again, I will use force against you." From that time on they did not come on the sabbath. (13:15-21)

As for the peoples of the land who bring wares or any grain on the sabbath day to sell, we will not buy from them on the sabbath or a holy day; and we will forego *the crops* the seventh year and the exaction of every debt. (vs. 31)

This is a major area from which the customary practice of not conducting business on the Shabbat is derived. We finish our work, do our banking, make our purchases, and cease our employee/employer obligations by the Sixth Day's eve. If we don't get it all done, we wait. The world seemed to stop spinning only once before (Joshua 10:13), and it wasn't because of this. Usually in order to buy something, there must be a seller. If the seller is a hireling, e.g. a retail clerk, your purchase has caused them to have to work; and in a way, you have hired them to serve you. This is the weightier matter, as it is now in direct issue with the fourth commandment. Now, passages from other areas of Scripture:

Acts 1:12, "Then they returned to Jerusalem from the mount called Olivet, which is near Jerusalem, a Sabbath day's journey away." (What came to be understood as 2000 cubits; a little over ½ mile. Derived from Numbers ch.35)

Jeremiah 17:24, "And it shall come to pass, if ye diligently hearken unto me, saith the LORD, to bring in no burden through the gates of this city on the sabbath day, but hallow the sabbath day, to do no work therein."

Matthew 24:20, "But be praying that your flight shall not be in winter nor on a Sabbath." (Was he talking about way in the future?)

Mark 2:27, "And He said to them, 'the Sabbath came to be for the sake of humanity, not humanity for the sake of the Sabbath.'" (So it's a gift? God gives a gift that we don't want?)

Mark 16:1, "And the Sabbath having past, Mary the Magdalene and Mary {the} [mother] of James and Salome bought spices, so that having come they should anoint Him." (She waited until sundown to make a purchase, even for the Messiah's burial. Jesus even forgot to tell them.)

Exodus 16:23, "Then he said to them, 'this is what the LORD meant: Tomorrow is a sabbath observance, a holy sabbath to the LORD. Bake what you will bake and boil what you will boil, and all that is left over put aside to be kept until morning.'" (We are not to cook on Shabbat (a daily work), but some consider it okay to reheat (not work). There is debate even amongst the branches of Judah as to how exacting this instruction is.)

Exodus 16:29, "See, the LORD has given you the sabbath; therefore He gives you bread for two days on the sixth day. Remain every man in his place; let no man go out of his place on the seventh day." (The word *place* [maqom] here, can be defined as narrow as "where you now stand," to as broad as vicinity, town or locality. It is vague, but *home* would be the ultra-conservative definition. 'Hometown' would be the more liberal interpretation. Considering the creation of a "Sabbath Day's journey" was done so early on, it is reasonable to deduce that the heart of the command is not to 'labor' in your traveling, and do all you can to not travel far. One key reason is being available to attend a fellowship.)

Now, let's discuss two of the most popular verses of contention; the first being Exodus 35:3, "You shall not kindle a fire in any of your dwellings on the sabbath day."

Even though this pertains to fire, we need to take off our dark, safety glasses again. In context, this commandment was given in relation to the commandments/instructions regarding the construction of the Tabernacle. Out of context, God promised to meet all these people's needs if they were obedient. That would include anything conceivable: climate, food, clothing, health etcetera. In other words, there may not have been any reason to "kindle" (start) a fire at all. To start one would be pure disobedience, rebellion, and blatant distrust. But certainly, if it did get cold during the desert night, this command was not to force them to freeze.

Stemming from that thought, the command does say "kindle". Consider the fact that most people were not required to regularly work

Yea, Hath God Said

long, hard days. Gathering extra wood throughout the week to prepare for Shabbat would have been quite reasonable, especially if wood was collected predominantly for cooking. Observe carefully that it was actually for "gathering" that the man was stoned, not for stoking (Numbers 15:38). He was working (disobeying, as defined by their setting) for no good reason. The fact that the word *kindle* (baar) is used, verses add 'fuel' (ma'akoleth; as seen in Isaiah 9:5), could allow for the idea that He would preserve the coals through the night, and it was okay for them to lay a few, *already gathered* logs on them throughout the day.

Also, we are told not to cook. Most modern practice allows for reheating; but again, Scripture does not specifically deal with that. It is reasonable to assume that was allowed, or that a pot of stew made prior to Shabbat could be kept over a fire, throughout Shabbat. Some ultra-orthodox Jews go so far as to shut off electricity on Shabbat, to keep bulbs from "burning" and to prevent cooking. This reasoning naturally extends to living in close proximity to synagogues, so they won't have to start fires in their automobile engines, but can walk.

I have no problem looking at it like this: The whole desert experience, as well as Shabbat, was one great, miraculous environment. Anything was possible. We just don't know everything for sure. Some think otherwise, but I'm not convinced. Most conservative Torah observers simply don't cook (create food from *not* ready-to-eat items). It's something we can feel pretty confident about, and we'll just have to trust in His mercies regarding other areas of application.

Another aspect of fire is that it was the source of energy required for many forms of work (another potential use of electricity). Metal-smithing is a good example. Again, something which is of great import that has to be recognized is that these Sabbath regulations were strongly and initially expressed around the work of the Tabernacle. By not creating a fire, the temptation to work (even though it was affiliated with ministry) would not have been there. Even during the construction of God's special dwelling place, the craftsmen were to cease from their labors on Sabbath. I'm pretty sure that truth is rarely if ever considered by most church building projects, or functions. I think the fact that the two places the fire-oriented commands are given are in context with the Tabernacle's construction (generally male work), and with cooking (generally female work), should not be overlooked. For the record, our household does not reject electricity usage.

So a third question gives rise. Does this mean we have to work for six days, and not five, or four or even none at all? The commandment does not say "must" work. In the Hebrew text, it just says, "six days labor." There are six days available to work. For this commandment to be taken in such a strict sense, as you *must* work six days a week, one would also have to assume that no consideration was made for retirement, age, health, travel, education, recreation etc. Historically, the vast majority of rabbinical consensus has been not to interpret it in that imperative sense. If it was intended that way, we truly would have a cruel taskmaster for a god. Why even bother rescuing us from Pharaoh?

The Capital Offensive

The second contentious verse is:

> For six days work may be done, but on the seventh day you shall have a holy day, a sabbath of complete rest to the LORD; whoever does any work on it shall be put to death. (Exodus 35:2)

Yes, it's the ugly "D" word again. In our modern and reprobate society, the idea of putting someone to death for something like this seems preposterous. But this was not today, and the Lord is never preposterous! Again, we have to remember that this entire society was under the same Torah, and under the direct protection, care, and instruction of the manifest presence of the God of the universe. Therefore, there was absolutely no reason for this blatant disregard for God's instruction. (And by the way, that kind of blatant misbehavior will kill all of us, even if only the flesh.)

There is another picture found in Shabbat that may shed more light on the strictness of the punishment for breaking the terms of the covenant. To work for six days and relinquish the seventh, regardless of your preparedness for it, your incomplete projects, your undone laundry, need for more money, or whatever excuse you may have to do as *you* will, not only demonstrates your submission to His authority, but it also pictures the end of days.

There is coming a day when such an event is going to happen to the entire human race. One day, on an individual basis, our lamp is going to go out—our personal "end of days," if you will. No matter to what level we have accomplished our goals, no matter what our spiritual maturity or state we find ourselves in, our time will be up. Our decisions and pursuits will have run their course. It will then be too late to repent, confess, or make amends for anything. Our sun will set.

The same is true on the corporate, human level; when the Son of Man is seen coming on the clouds. The sun is going to go down on all who are not prepared to be with Him. They will have run out of time. We all need to live as though our lives are the first six days of the week, recognizing along the way that it is appointed that every person has a seventh coming. That is how we are to run this race. Not too busy, that

Yea, Hath God Said

we pay no attention to the times, but busy enough so that the reign of peace will be all the more sweet. When the prophetic seventh day comes, wherever you are, whatever you're doing, a dramatic change is coming.

Had this Sabbath violator been deaf and not heard the rule, or had he been cognitively impaired, I firmly believe that he would have been spared. I don't know everything about the Lord, but I think I know Him well enough to believe in His ever-renewing mercies. This man, for whatever reason, had wickedness in his heart that would have proven to be a rotten apple in an Israelite bushel, and he needed removal. If I have to read between the lines to support the Lord's decisions, I will put Him first, trust Him and do it. The believing community is quick to express their aversion to this Law in general, due to its death clause. But it is slow to see (because it doesn't even look) just how few examples there are of the sentence's administration. If you don't like the "D" word very much, then you probably very much dislike Paul's list of its applicability. It goes something like this:

> …unrighteousness, wickedness, covetousness, maliciousness; full of envy, murder, strife, deceit, malignity; whisperers, backbiters, hateful to God, insolent, haughty, boastful, inventors of evil things, disobedient to parents, without understanding, covenant-breakers, without natural affection, unmerciful. (Romans 1:29-31, ASV)

In the very next verse he says, "…they that practice such things are worthy of death." I would say those verses covered all of us at some point.

Let's be rational thinkers here. It is because of the death sentence associated with disregarding Sabbath stipulations, that Judaism has so many rules established for proper observance. Not that they are all justified. The severity of punishment is also another assurance for Sabbath's historically accurate placement in the week. Would you want your life resting on the whimsical calculation of a jury comprised of mathematically incompetent peers? Sabbath rules both convicted and protected Israelites. Defining "work" was clearly essential.

Those who are Sabbath observing people must follow Torah as it is best understood, as is applicable, and by the inspiration of the Spirit. We had all been given a death sentence already, and it has already been paid for. Oh, and by the way, the threat of a death sentence for unrepentant and belligerently lawless behavior, "so that all would hear and fear," may be just what The Physician ordered. If that possibility was on our minds growing up, I guarantee you many of us would have walked a different, and more smoothly paved road. And whether we liked it or not, it would have done us good. God is good, and so are His commandments.

So rejecting Sabbath observance because it places us under "bondage" is simply more nonsense, and the ideological workings of the Adversary. Our Christ died for the smallest of infractions, as much as for the big ones. As a matter of fact, He died for sins you don't even know you committed, as well as for the ones you knew better regarding and committed anyway. But, we don't "work" to gain access to "rest". We work up until, and because we already have access to rest...through Christ. We should prayerfully conclude how the Shabbat should be handled within our communities and homes, and grow for it!

"The Lord's Day"

But isn't the Lord's Day, Sunday? Actually, there is not one piece of scriptural evidence to support this notion. Contrary to what most Christians have been encouraged to believe, via again taking verses out of context, the phrase "The Lord's Day" is not connected to the 1st Day of the week at all.

I was in the Spirit on the Lord's Day, and I heard behind me a loud voice like *the sound* of a trumpet. (Revelation 1:10)
The sun shall be turned into darkness, and the moon into blood, before the day of the Lord come, that great and notable *day*. (Acts 2:20)

These verses are speaking of the same exact day, and for anyone to declare otherwise, context must be completely ignored and the Greek text abused. Another verse often promoted as evidence Jesus changed the day is found in this text:

On the first day of the week, when we were gathered together to break bread, Paul *began* talking to them, intending to leave the next day, and he prolonged his message until midnight. There were many lamps in the upper room where we were gathered together. (Acts 20:7 & 8)

Seriously, if people are going to take a verse like this and use it to destroy a covenant prepared at the very beginning of creation, what else has been done to His Word? Even isolated from its context, reality can easily be derived through its plain language. Here is the explanation of this interpretation: It was the common practice of then, as it is still today, to come together for a holy convocation on Shabbat. After whatever formal service of teaching and song they would have, as the Sun set, fellowship time would begin. Gatherings often included what is now called 'Oneg', a fellowship meal. This night though, because Paul was planning to leave the next day (avoiding travel on Shabbat), he used all the time available to him, to squeeze in every precious word he was inspired to give them, and

Yea, Hath God Said

spoke throughout the meal. The reason there were "many lamps" in the room with them is that a late night was anticipated, and nearly everyone there had brought one to help illuminate the room, and then later guide them home.

This "first day of the week" arrived while they were gathered together, because the Sun had fallen on Shabbat! It says, "...when we <u>were</u> gathered." It doesn't say "when we eventually gathered" or "started gathering". They were already together. Now, to frustrate things further, I could take this in a different direction. To do so, we must revert to older manuscripts, like the Latin Vulgate and Textus Receptus, to find the original wording of Acts 20:7.

> Latin: "in una autem <u>sabbati</u> cum convenissemus..."
> Greek: "εν δε τη μια των <u>σαββατων</u> συνηγμενων..."

I have underlined the word which can mean either Sabbath or week in both of the languages, and yet Sabbath seems to be strangely missing from nearly every English translation. They both translate roughly to: "Now (And) on this one Sabbath we gathered." To their credit, the Good News Bible renders it accurately. It is a fact that the word sabbaton can be used to mean a 'seven day period', but in this context, it would not be the most appropriate usage, as it wouldn't even make logical sense. In either case, using either translation, there is no support for the altered Sabbath view.

"I was in the Spirit on the Day belonging to the Lord." (Revelation 1:10).

I realize that's not likely how you've ever read it, but that is what's actually being said. John is not saying, "I was having a vision on Sunday." There is no honest student or scholar, who can refute this absolutely. They can only want it to be otherwise. I discuss the actual concept of "the Lord's Day" more fully in my commentary on the end times, in chapter twelve, because that's actually what this phrase is in regards to.

For those of you who want to tout the "unique" rendering in the Greek as your evidence I am wrong, you are clearly missing the bigger picture. From the most ancient of days, and up through the first century and beyond, Israelites never named the days, as we have. There was the Sabbath, and six other days leading up to it. First century Jews would have felt no compulsion to name the first day "the Lord's Day". It wasn't until later, when the "venerable Sun-day" began competing with Sabbath rejecting Christianity, that this term became popularized. Would you like a proof text? Paul, prior to visiting Corinth, sent this instruction:

On the <u>first day</u> of every week, each one of you is to put aside and save, as he may prosper, so that no collections be made when I come. (1ˢᵗ Corinthians 16:2)

Shouldn't Paul have said "the Lord's Day" here? I elaborate further on this verse in ch.12, under the subheading "Out of Your Increase." Paul didn't even want collections for him being taken in on Shabbat. Additionally, it was the practice to not even carry money on the Sabbath, to avoid the temptation to spend it.

For those of you whose hearts have been stirred to investigate this, and ultimately obey the Lord through it, just begin to pray about it. If you are currently required to work on the Seventh day, He will be patient with you and help you find a way. After all, He did bring you into His family under your current circumstances; an example of His grace in action. There is an exemption. It is understood throughout Judaism that if your occupation is involved in life-saving and protecting fields; i.e., police, fire, medical, etc., you should not bear any guilt. To preserve life is the highest order of service and the thread that runs through all Torah.

There are many great testimonies from those who have received this teaching, sought the Lord's will, adjusted their lives, and ended up blessed for it. Do what you can and lean on His mercy. He knows the secular society we live in, and how it hates Him and works against Him. Desire in your heart, ask in His name, put legs on your intentions and He will provide a way.

So much depends on the answer to this question. Are the Ten Commandments for non-Jews too? But these secondary questions need also be answered: Is the Bible the final authority on defining what the Sabbath is, or is it found somewhere between you and the church? And, if Sunday is the new Sabbath, do you still work on it or hire people to work for you? It's funny how we want to be bondservants of the Lord, and love Him and obey Him, right up until it encroaches on our personal liberties. The ironic thing is that's what people think it's doing. Yet, the Sabbath was made for man, and was/is a gift given to already free men.

I will now offer a few quotes and positions, written by some of our historical church pillars, who themselves had to grapple with this subject. Since I am a man of limited repute, perhaps you'll receive what they have to say.

To Shabbat or Not?

Christians must not Judaize by resting on the Sabbath, but must work on that day, rather honouring the Lord's Day; and, if they can, resting then as Christians. But if any shall be found to be judaizers, let them be anathema from Christ.

Yea, Hath God Said

Here, <u>the Fathers order</u> that no one of the faithful shall stop work on the Sabbath as do the Jews, but that they should honour the Lord's Day, on account of the Lord's resurrection, and that on that day they should abstain from manual labour and go to church. But thus abstaining from work on Sunday, they do not lay down as a necessity, but they add, "if they can." For if through need or any other necessity, any one worked on the Lord's Day, this was not reckoned against him. (Canon XXIX, of the Council of Laodicea, 363-364 AD.)

The Sabbath was binding in Eden, and it has been in force ever since. This Fourth Commandment begins with the word 'remember', showing that the Sabbath already existed when God wrote the Law on the tablets of stone at Sinai. How can men claim that this one commandment has been done away with when they will admit that the other nine are still binding? (Dwight L. Moody, *Weighed and Wanting*, pp. 7, 48)

But, the Moral Law contained in the Ten Commandments, and enforced by the prophets, He [Christ] did not take away. It was not the design of His coming to revoke any part of this. This is a law which can never be broken...Every part of this law must remain in force upon all mankind, and in all ages; as not depending on time or place, or any other circumstances liable to change, but on the nature of God and the nature of man, and their unchangeable relationship to each other. (John Wesley, *The Works of the Reverend John Wesley, A.M.*, John Emory, ed. (New York: Eaton and Mains), Sermon 25, vol. 1, p. 221)

And where are we told in the Scriptures that we are to keep the first day at all? We are commanded to keep the seventh; but we are nowhere commanded to keep the first day...The reason we keep the first day of the week holy instead of the seventh is for the same reason that we observe many other things, not because the Bible, but because the church has enjoined it. (Isaac Williams, *Plain Sermons on the Catechism*, vol.1, pp. 334, 336)

We have made the change from the seventh day to the first day, from Saturday to Sunday, on the authority of the one holy Catholic Church. (Bishop Seymour, *Why We Keep Sunday*)

They [Roman Catholics] refer to the Sabbath day, as having been changed into the Lord's Day, contrary to the Decalogue, as it seems. Neither is there any example whereof they make more than concerning the changing of the Sabbath day. Great, say they, is the power of the Church, since it has dispensed with one of the Ten Commandments. (*Augsburg Confession of Faith*, art. 28; written by Melanchthon, approved by Martin Luther, 1530; as published in *The Book of Concord of the Evangelical Lutheran Church*, Henry Jacobs, ed. (1911), p. 63)

And one more for effect:

But they err in teaching that Sunday has taken the place of the Old Testament Sabbath and therefore must be kept as the seventh day had to be kept by the children of Israel…These churches err in their teaching, for Scripture has in no way ordained the first day of the week in place of the Sabbath. There is simply no law in the New Testament to that effect. (John Theodore Mueller, *Sabbath or Sunday*)

Worshiping on the First Day is not wrong, nor is it the "Mark of the Beast," as some assert. We should and can worship every day. It is just not the Sabbath of the Scriptures. That is why He still shows up and blesses His people. Two or more are gathering in His name, and He is in the midst. He appreciates the effort for what it is, but an hour or two a week does not constitute the covenantal Shabbat, any more than a husband and wife spending that same amount of time together constitutes a rich and fulfilling marriage. The First Day and the Seventh Day will continue in this life to be next door to each other; existing independently and serving similar but differing purposes. There is obviously a lot more to Shabbat, than just going to church.

I apologize for how lengthy this teaching has been, but the volume of material is not just for persuading you. It is also to help those of you who already hear the call to Shabbat, but are challenged in your ability to explain it to others, or further justify it for yourself. This is a very dicey topic at the least; but with what I included, you can usually bring naysayers to the point where they can't really refute you anymore, and have to resort back to their *feelings* about it. For you in the latter, I have just a little bit more ammo to fire.

Now after the Sabbath, as it began to dawn toward the first *day* of the week, Mary Magdalene and the other Mary came to look at the grave. And behold, a severe earthquake had occurred, for an angel of the Lord descended from heaven and came and rolled away the stone and sat upon it. (Matthew 28:1 & 2)

Even right up to His death, Jesus forgot to tell His closest friends there was no Sabbath anymore. He did have one of the authors of Scripture tell us that we should keep all the Appointed Times "all the more as we see 'the day' approaching (Hebrews 10:25)." Jesus even told His followers to pray that their flight out of Jerusalem would not occur on a Sabbath; the flight that would take place during what they thought would be the "end times". How awkwardly irrelevant a thing for our Master to say, when in that future day, there would be no more Sabbath.

So there remains a Sabbath rest (keeping)[4] for the people of God. (11) Therefore let us be diligent (make every effort/work) to enter that rest, so that no one will fall, through following the same example of disobedience (non-observance). (Hebrews 4:9 & 11; parenthetical additions are mine.)

Yea, Hath God Said

Because it *still is* a picture, of a day *yet* to come! Note also that we do play a working role in our walk of salvation. We just have nothing to boast about. So, when Jesus said:

> Do not think that I came to abolish <u>the Law</u> **or** <u>the Prophets</u>; I did not come to abolish but to fulfill. For truly I say to you, until heaven and earth pass away, not the smallest letter or stroke shall pass from the Law until all is accomplished. Whoever then annuls one of the least of these commandments, and teaches others *to do* the same, shall be called least in the kingdom of heaven; but whoever <u>keeps</u> and teaches *them,* he shall be called great in the kingdom of heaven. (Matthew 5:17-19)

...He actually meant exactly what He said! I realize how difficult that is for some of you out there. Many have worked so diligently at avoiding or corrupting the meaning of these words. But as crazy as it sounds, this instruction is not a parable, an allegory, an idiom, hyperbole, a metaphor, or an analogy. Anyone who believes any differently may as well also believe that the great fish that swallowed Jonah was actually a scouting submarine from Atlantis. The word 'keeps' used there does not mean, "appreciates from a distance." *Poieo* means: to do, or perform. Jesus knew to include the 'Prophets' with the 'Law' in this statement, so that people two thousand years later should be unable to say He was talking about some *new* Law invented during the Sermon on the Mount. And yet, that's exactly what people say and believe.

People also believe that since we can't obey Torah perfectly, because we are not in the land, or capable of performing sacrifices, that then negates our responsibility to any of it. Imagine that. A Christian suggesting a "do it perfectly, or discard the faith entirely" ideology. It sure is a good thing that thinking wasn't in the minds of the prophets sent to Israel, while in their captivities. That could be akin to crying, "Peace! Peace!" when there is no peace.

> And it shall be from new moon to new moon, and from sabbath to sabbath, all mankind (including gentiles) will come to bow down before Me, says the LORD. (Isaiah 66:23)

This future looking verse is rather difficult to ignore. It is even clearer than that verse in Colossians, where Paul tells us how all these "shadows" teach us about our future coming King. If we see Messiah in them all, how do we discount them? If their "body" is Messiah, then they have substance. Why have we divorced ourselves from our rightful inheritance? You see, the festivals take us beyond the cross, and the Sabbath was made for man. They are not to enslave us. Like all the topics I bring up, do your own research and pray about it. Ask yourself if there is any evidence that either Jesus, or the Father, ever personally stated intent to, had prophesied through His prophets regarding intent, or actually did set-apart (sanctify) the First Day and its change. Again, does God cancel His covenants, especially without telling us?

Everyone must ask themselves, what must I go through to make the Sun-day day of worship align with what the Scriptures portray? If the Israelites were sent into captivity because they wouldn't let the *land* rest on the sabbatical year, how much more seriously does He take His *children's* resting on the Shabbat today, considering He had to receive our punishment because we broke that also? The church may have appointed itself the authority to move the Sabbath, and assumed the position of "Creator and Deliverer", but they apparently forgot to move a few of its appointed details alongside it. I know that sounds rough, but I am just presenting to you the severity. Everyone must choose his or her own covenant participation level.

Keeping the Sabbath never assured salvation for anyone. Avoiding the consumption of pig is not a ticket out of eternal damnation. They simply set us apart. They align with holiness. They are *doing* righteousness.

Ecclesiastes 12:13, Let us hear the conclusion of the whole matter: Fear God, and keep his commandments: for this *is* the whole *duty* of man. (KJV)

6

Divided We Stand

Due to the fact that those who lived in the Apostolic Era had no other Scriptures besides the "Old Testament," to them, there was no such thing. Any letters written by the Apostles would not, at that time, have been considered 'Scripture', especially by the authors themselves. They may have felt "inspired," but it is doubtful they knew the scope of their work. They certainly never imagined themselves as superseding Moses.

As we just finished examining, there really wasn't much brand new stuff at all. Even the teachings of Jesus weren't totally new; they were just the buried and hidden heart of the Torah, resurrected. Dissect carefully the Sermon on the Mount (Beatitudes), and you'll see it is the heart of the teaching at Mt Sinai. Even Jesus's "new" commandment "to love each other" wasn't completely new. Building on this reality, I would like to talk to you about other matters of the heart of faith. In case I haven't stepped on your toes enough, put on your steel tipped shoes. I figure if I've held your attention this long there is probably a good chance you're either ready for more to chew on, or you're gathering more evidence to send me out of the camp.

I truly believe there is a new day dawning, when the Body of the Messiah is going to shake off the fog, and will begin to aggressively prepare itself to be the Bride. By the look of things, it needs to happen soon. We are so far from unity it's embarrassing. The church is as blinded to the truth regarding Torah as the Jews are to the Truth called Jesus! Christianity sits around feeling pity for (and wondering why) the Jews won't receive their gospel message, while it simultaneously presents its Christ in such a way as to actually disqualify Him from being their Messiah. Jews don't bother trying to evangelize Christians (anymore), because they see us as well-intentioned people, but impossibly disobedient, spiritually arrogant, and ignorant in all matters covenantal. Both groups have thick scales over their eyes. We are not exactly meeting halfway. If there is supposed to be "one new man," what is his name? Is it Baptist, Lutheran, Hasidic, Episcopalian, Catholic, Moravian or Amish? What does he look like? Is he wearing sackcloth, or adorned in fine white linen? Is he institutional, or is he home-based? Are our fellowships being Spirit-led, or led by the visions (vain imaginations) of a counterfeit? How did we get to the place where a "prophet's" single, out-of-context verse interpretation is grounds to file the articles to become an independent 501c3 anyway? It had to start somewhere.

True North

If you and ninety-nine other people were dropped into a forest, given a map, a compass, and all the necessary provisions to make the journey to a distant pick-up point, the odds are exceptionally good every one of you would make it there just fine. Take half of the compasses away, and half the maps and the odds would likely still remain the same, because people would just pair up into a long line. Overall, there would be enough people heading in the same direction to play the averages fairly safely.

But what happens when you take ninety percent of the maps and compasses away? You begin to develop some sociological problems. Now we have people debating, maybe fighting over who gets to carry them, and who's qualified to use them. There might be some *key* deciphering concerns, because there are less people from which to draw a consensus. Groups of ten, maybe more—maybe less would probably form. And due to the lack of elbow room, the decision to spread out would probably take place. But what if there were only three maps and compasses? Whom do you follow? Who is going to make the best leader? Which group do you join?

In one case, you might join the leader with certain life experiences that would seem to best suit the situation you find yourself in (the *practical* choice). In another case, the one who seems to have the best persuasion power might be your choice (the *inspirational* choice). You might look for the older-looking group because they will have the most wisdom. Or, if you're young, you might join the younger looking group because they might be the fastest, and maybe more interesting to hang around with (*demographic* choices). A woman might stand up in the crowd and shout that she has an acute sense of which way to go; call it 'intuition'. Do you follow her? She doesn't even need a map (*intuitive* choice).

Then you are told of another complication. Only one of the maps is the original map. The other two are hand-drawn copies, and by two very different people no less. Can you trust all three maps? Picking your leader is pretty important, but wouldn't you rather be sure the map is accurate and your compass is working. Your leader may fail you.

How can you say, 'We are wise, and the law of the LORD is with us'? But behold, the lying pen of the scribes has made *it* into a lie. (Jeremiah 8:8)

Ultimately, the question now being, do you follow the leader or the map (*analytical* choice)? I could always throw in the *philosophical* choice, but I would have to contemplate that for a while.

Now, take all the compasses away and leave one, undecipherable map. Welcome to the Dark Ages. After countless persecutions of early believers, the first and second Jewish revolts, and the Diaspora sending the 'keepers of the oracles of the Lord' all over the known world, what was left was an opportunity for a powerful, highly-financed religious organization to come along and partner with the most powerful governments in the world, and ultimately come between (block the way, as compared to intercede) the Lord and man.

I'm not going to write another church history book here. There are more than enough versions of those. What you need to see is when people are stripped of the ability to read and understand Scripture, abuses of the highest proportion are sure to follow. (Sorry RCC, I'm going to use you as an example.) The only way a religion could ever have gotten away with:

1. Selling indulgences: Psalm 49:7, "No man can by any means redeem *his* brother or give to God a ransom for him."
2. Transubstantiation: Genesis 9:4, "Only you shall not eat flesh with its life, *that is*, its blood."
3. Absolution of sins: 1st John 1:9, "If we confess our sins, He is faithful and righteous to forgive us our sins and to cleanse us from all unrighteousness."
4. Sprinkling instead of Baptism (Mikveh): Colossians 2:12, "having been buried with Him in baptism, in which you were also raised up with Him through faith in the working of God, who raised Him from the dead."
5. Praying to saints: Isaiah 8:19, "When they say to you, 'Consult the mediums and the spiritists who whisper and mutter,' should not a people consult their God? *Should they consult* the dead on behalf of the

Divided We Stand

living?"

6. Mary, Queen of Heaven worship: Jeremiah 7:18, "The children gather wood, and the fathers kindle the fire, and the women knead dough to make cakes for the queen of heaven; and *they* pour out drink offerings to other gods in order to spite Me."

7. Making Latin the official prayer and Bible language: 1st Corinthians 14:9, "So also you, unless you utter by the tongue speech that is clear, how will it be known what is spoken? For you will be speaking into the air." And, "You shall write on the stones all the words of this law very distinctly (Deuteronomy 7:8)."

8. Keeping the Scriptures away from all but the priesthood: 2nd Timothy 3:15 & 16, "...and that from childhood you have known the sacred writings which are able to give you the wisdom that leads to salvation through faith which is in Christ Jesus. All Scripture is inspired by God and profitable for teaching, for reproof, for correction, for training in righteousness."

...is if people did not know the truth. And I could go on and on regarding the sacraments, angelic veneration, the doctrine of celibacy, icons and statues, priestly garment coloring and design, the Pope as Vicar, Purgatory, Rosary beads, etc. The sad fact is that there is little of The Universal Faith that does pass the test of Scripture. Yet, they have remained the dominant wavelength within the religious spectrum of Christianity.[1] The three largest world religions are:

1. Christianity; originating at 30 CE, Main teaching text: the Bible; 2.39 billion members; 32% of world population (dropping)
2. Islam, originating at 622 CE, Main teaching text: Qur'an & Hadith; 1.226 billion members; 19% of world population (growing)
3. Hinduism originating at 1,500 BCE, Main teaching text: The Veda; 828 million members; 13% of world population (stable) [2] [3]

"The 2001 edition of *Barrett's World Christian Encyclopedia,* successor to his 1983 first edition, which took a decade to compile, identifies 10,000 distinct religions; of which 150 have 1 million or more followers. Within Christianity, he counts 33,830 denominations. The biggest Christian shift since the encyclopedia's first edition is the emergence of the 386 million "independents" as the second biggest category, after the 1 billion Roman Catholics."

Today, there are probably more Bibles in the world than there are people. The reason those errant practices are not accepted within all Christendom is primarily because the Bible has been read by so many. If more Catholics (as well as Protestants) were to actually read, and study their own Bibles for themselves—as opposed to blind reliance on being told what they say by their priests/pastors—the remaining vestiges of those and other ignorant teachings would also fade away. How's that for hopeful thinking?

I don't care if there are ten denominations. There are too many! We are without excuse anymore. I have no problem with different fellowship groups, with perhaps differing affinities,

> After these things I looked, and behold, a great multitude which no one could count, from every nation and *all* tribes and peoples and tongues, standing before the throne and before the Lamb, clothed in white robes, and palm branches *were* in their hands. (Revelation 7:9)

...for tribes and tongues and ethnicity can be legitimate divisions, unless they become exclusive. But for all, there is only one Way. All our self-drawn maps to gain access to the throne are tattered, and I believe the territorial boundary lines have practically become indistinguishable. This is nothing less than displeasing to our Father.

> Bring your worthless offerings no longer; incense is an abomination to Me. New moon and Sabbath, the calling of assemblies-- I cannot endure iniquity and the solemn assembly. (Isaiah 1:13)
> Thus says the LORD to this people, 'Even so they have loved to wander; they have not kept their feet in check. Therefore the LORD does not accept them; now He will remember their iniquity and call their sins to account.' (Jeremiah 14:10)

In context, these verses show the result of doing religious practices that are meaningless or wayward. God has made it abundantly clear that we should not mix: hedonism, occultism, immorality, superstition, paganism, sorcery, pantheism, polytheism, or deviant behaviors with the pure faith. But now, we go to our own great lengths to justify the allowance of various aspects of them into our religious practices. If there is a *pure* faith, then it should stand to reason that much of what creates denominations would be the allowance of these man-made additions/subtractions into that faith; as well as our overall ignorance of the Scriptures. I understand your feeling if this bothers you. I don't like it either, but we can't escape its truth. "Not my church!" I can hear it now. Here's the problem: a false interpretation of Scripture's teaching, and I'm not talking about historical facts or figures, or date sequencing, or character studies per say, but real doctrinal error is from no other source than the evil one. In addition to doctrinal error, the allowance of false religious practices into the church is encouraged by the same source. What fellowship does darkness have with light?

Divided We Stand

Think back to the statistic of three hundred and eighty-six million independents; from what are they independent? Do they see error in other denominations and can't effect appropriate change, so they start their own? Thirty-plus thousand denominations—come on people! What have we let the enemy of our souls do to us? I guess Jesus knew exactly what our biggest problem would be when He prayed "that we would be one, as He and the Father are One." Are we so blinded and proud, that analyzing our situation openly and honestly is also wishful thinking? Wouldn't it appear to be obvious (considering the empirical evidence of overwhelming segregation), whatever the cause of this is would be the work of HaSatan—and it's happening right beneath our noses. And if that's the case, we should aggressively and relentlessly war in the Spirit against it.

Stemming from this pretext of division, we need to examine an event that occurred in Israel's past, which continues to have a ripple effect today. This one occurred between the North and the South as well, which seems to be a trend.

Jeroboam's Curse

Found in the First book of Kings, in chapters twelve and thirteen, we see a by-product of this split. What was the given reason for this division?

> So the LORD said to Solomon, 'Because you have done this, and you have not kept My covenant and My statutes, which I have commanded you, I will surely tear the kingdom from you, and will give it to your servant.' (1st Kings 11:11)

The Northern tribes of Israel, under the leadership of Jeroboam, revolted from the high taxes that were being imposed by Rehoboam (Solomon's other son, and king of the Southern kingdom of Judah.) That may be understandable, but it's what else took place that I'm in pursuit of.

In an effort to thwart the possibility that some of his people might make pilgrimage to Jerusalem (in the Southern kingdom) for the Mo'adim, and end up staying, Jeroboam concocted the idea of setting up formal, alternate places of worship, as well as creating alternate coinciding holidays, so that there would be no need to travel. The problem is, neither the places the altars were set up, nor the feasts, nor was the priesthood authorized by God. So He sent an un-identified (of no reputation) prophet to declare it as such. God then split their altar in half, for effect, and all the ashes poured out upon the ground. What is the lesson here? We cannot approach (worship) God any old way we want! That will forge a golden calf. That is unacceptable! When we do, we become a fractured house. Granted, Judah was no innocent party, for they had gone off into idolatry as well. Ultimately, both houses of Israel would end up in judgment. What I want you to see here is a prophetic picture. One house splits into two houses. Now there are two systems of worship. One authorized but in rebellion; the other unauthorized and in rebellion. They both incorporated symbols of idolatry into their religious programs. Judah was sculpting Asherah trees, and Israel was worshiping golden calves.

Both times golden calves show up on the scene in Scripture, it is resultant of Israel's departing from the covenant stipulations. Each time, it was due to weak leadership; and in every case, God made Himself abundantly clear about how He feels regarding such matters. I don't believe that as much has changed, as we would like to believe. Asherahs only came down when the king of the period was obedient to the covenant.

The sins of Jeroboam are frequently (at least eighteen times) brought up as the defining failure found amongst the kings of both sides of Jacob's house. Just type the words 'sin' and 'Jeroboam' in a Bible search engine, and you will quickly see the prominence. The Lord went way out of His way (which is pretty hard to do considering who He is) to express His abhorrence of Jeroboam's deeds.

Pastors so and so, "Because you have done well in executing what is right in My eyes, *and* have done to the house of Ahab according to all that *was* in My heart, your sons of the fourth generation shall sit on the throne of Israel. But you were not careful to walk in the **law** of the Lord, the God of Israel, with all his (your) heart; he (you) did not depart from the sins of Jeroboam, which he made Israel sin. And as for all the other acts of pastors so and so, are they not written in the Book of the Chronicles of the Pastors of the Church" (with a wee bit of paraphrasing). You can do "well", but still not walk in His ways.

Even Jehu, one of the best kings Israel had, still didn't get this completely right. He "thus destroyed Ba'al out of Israel (2nd Kings 10:28)." But what did he fail to do? Keep Israel from sinning. How did he do that? By failing to do what we all must do. He didn't remove the golden calves from the land (church house), which were found both in and outside of the temple (Body). His greatest downfall was the acceptance of blending both pagan and Judaic systems of worship. The summary: "But Jehu took no heed to walk in the law of Jehovah, the God of Israel, with all his heart (10:31a)."

There still are two houses today. One is ethnically identifiable; the other is not. They are both Diaspora, dwelling among the nations. Some have been returning home; many are yet to follow. I speak of *our* dispersion, from the standpoint of our common citizenship being in a

Divided We Stand

land we do not currently occupy, under a King from David's line, we do not currently see.

There are those from the Southern House that may not appreciate this idea, because the other house has not been persecuted in the way that would redeem it in their eyes, nor have they held on to their Hebraic/Judaic identity. I can understand that. However, as you have read (and will be further explored later), I believe the Prophets tell of a time when that is going to change.

In addition, both of these houses are also in another kind of exile. We also have each been kept out of the Garden; out of our original, perfect condition and full intimacy with the Creator. We all want to be gathered up again "the way a hen gathers her chicks under her wings." If it was disobedience that brought division, I wonder what will reunite us. Perhaps, removing the symbols and acts of idolatry from our churches is a start? We need some pastor Josiahs and Asas to rise up and tear down our annual asherahs, but that will finish strong as well.

Consider the parable of the wayward (prodigal) son. I'm going to give you a very different perspective. Remember, a parable is a physical story representing a spiritual truth. Although it has predominantly been applied to (and kind of works for) a backslidden individual, that is not its highest meaning. It is an elaboration on Yeshua's other comment regarding His "sheep that are not of this sheepfold." Though the church does not normally empathize with the concept of national salvation, and focuses on the individual, to Judah, salvation was something anticipated for Israel at large. Keep this in mind as we re-examine this classic parable.

Judah, the wayward son's big brother, has always stayed home and remained committed to the kingdom of his father. He has not wandered away from, though not fully grasped, the policies of the estate. The younger son, Ephraim, got the idea that there were better ways to do things than what the father required. So he claimed the blessings that were due him as an heir, but wanted little to do with the covenantal responsibilities that came with them. So he departed, and proceeded to do things his own way.

Some time goes by, and he eventually comes to his senses. He realizes that his decisions hadn't paid off as he anticipated, and eventually returns to his father's estate. Judah, who remained nearby, sees the father's excitement about his little brother coming home, and is covetous of the attention Ephraim receives. The father reminds Judah that the entire kingdom has been available to him, but that Ephraim (and all who have joined his house) has come back, and that is worth celebrating!

But I say, surely Israel did not know, did they? First Moses says, 'I WILL MAKE YOU JEALOUS BY THAT WHICH IS NOT A NATION, BY

A NATION WITHOUT UNDERSTANDING WILL I ANGER YOU.'
(Romans 10:19)

The meaning behind the analogy of eating with the pigs is nothing less than going the way of the gentiles. It represents the departure from Torah! Here's something for a little added perspective: Often when you encounter an X+Y=Z style prophecy, parable, or even certain portrayals, X and Y are often representing the House of Judah and the House of Joseph (Ephraim), and Z = the Divine plan. Try it next time and see how much it can shed new light on many illustrations and situations. Let me give you some examples:

'X' was hired early. 'Y' was hired later. They both receive the same pay, so Z = access to the kingdom. See what I mean?

Martha 'X' was the worshiper (Ephraim). Mary 'Y' was the worker (Judah). Neither was rejected. Z= Salvation by faith followed by works, instead of the other way around.

X = Caleb (representing the tribe of Judah). Y = Joshua (representing the tribe of Ephraim) Z = the two dominant tribes in the Kingdom.

Or: X = old wine-skin (Judah/Moses), Y = new wine-skin (Ephraim/Yeshua), Z = Covenant Revelation. Sometimes, it's not as obvious.

For instance: X = Jesus, Y = the crucifixion (great price), Z = the Pearl (The whole House of Israel). It's all very telling. Jesus wasn't an algebra teacher; so why do we tend to make His equations so complicated?

I mentioned earlier what our war is. It's the war of Truth verses deception. We must diligently pursue and defend Truth. When we see deception, we must not bow down or succumb to it, but defeat it. Do you know why you do not see that happening in many churches today? Because in the deepest recesses of the hearts of many of our leaders, they fear they are not confident themselves about the altars they have erected, and whether or not they are qualified to operate them.

Take Me to Your Leader

What I'm about to proclaim may very well be one of the most provocative and challenging things I have thus far. The comforting thing for me is that I was not the first to say it. And He who said it first said it best, so I will let Him. Through Moses, the Lord declared:

If a prophet or a dreamer of dreams arises among you and gives you a sign or a wonder, (2) and the sign or the wonder comes true, concerning which he spoke to you, saying, 'Let us go after other gods (whom you have not known)

Divided We Stand

and let us serve them,' (3) you shall not listen to the words of that prophet or that dreamer of dreams; for the LORD your God is testing you to find out if you love the LORD your God with all your heart and with all your soul. (4) You shall follow the LORD your God and fear Him; and you shall keep His commandments, listen to His voice, serve Him, and cling to Him. (5) But that prophet or that dreamer of dreams shall be put to death, because he has counseled rebellion against the LORD your God who brought you from the land of Egypt and redeemed you from the house of slavery, to seduce you from the way in which the LORD your God commanded you to walk. So you shall purge the evil from among you. (Deuteronomy 13:1-5)

What does this say to a modern, cross-bearing people? The first consideration is that a prophet of God does not necessitate an Elijah or Elisha. A prophet is (should be) one who is gifted by the Spirit, to declare the Word, and to bring correction and exhortation to His people.

The second is that a prophet is not 'required' to show signs and wonders to be legitimate. What is required is that what he or she says does not contradict known Scripture, and comes to fruition. Abraham is a great example, as he was called a prophet in Genesis 20:7, but did not perform 'signs and wonders' in the supernatural sense.

The third, located in 13:2a, is added to say that prophets may have the capacity to perform supernatural acts, and that if they do, that alone is not enough to substantiate them as legitimate. 13:2b tells us that they may bring a message suggesting to serve foreign gods. How does one do that exactly? Obviously, there are varying ways, but you can rest assured they will all encourage breaking the laws of Torah when they do; hence vs. 13:4. The word *follow* here has a special meaning to the original hearers of this mitzvah (command). They had spent the last thirty-eight years *following* a pillar of fire, and a pillar of smoke, throughout their desert wanderings. It means: to go where He's leading or instructing, by keeping your eyes on Him—nothing less than, "keeping His commandments, listening to His voice, serving Him, and clinging to Him."

So what's so provocative about that? God is telling us, through Moses, to not follow anyone who teaches us to disobey His commandments. That's no big deal, until you realize that if Jesus came performing signs and wonders, but taught against the keeping of His Father's commandments, He automatically is to be deemed a false prophet. And, even worse, based on the things He said and did, He would have made Himself out to be a false god. Let that sink in, because even worse than that, if you believe that Jesus did come teaching a different Torah, and that He did away with Moses, you are worshipping a false god. And if you, pastor or priest, are promoting that version of Jesus, evil will be purged.

Considering we no longer condemn people to death, due to civil law, and the religious court (the Sanhedrin) not being "in session," we can rule out having to put people to death for these reasons. We can still purge without capital punishment. That would be done by another program.

1st Timothy 5:20, "Those who continue in sin, rebuke in the presence of all, so that the rest also will be fearful *of sinning.*"

And in a worst case scenario,

"…deliver such a one to Satan for the destruction of his flesh, so that his spirit may be saved in the day of the Lord Jesus (1st Corinthians 5:5)." (Although it could mean more, it is believed this means to cast out of fellowship and back into the world—HaSatan's domain.) Now watch this! This is pretty enlightening.

Not everyone who says to Me, 'Lord, Lord,' will enter the kingdom of heaven, but he who does the will of My Father who is in heaven *will enter.* Many will say to Me on that day, 'Lord, Lord, did we not prophesy in Your name, and in Your name cast out demons, and in Your name perform many miracles?' And then I will declare to them, 'I never knew you; DEPART FROM ME, YOU WHO PRACTICE LAWLESSNESS.' (Matthew 7:21)

Sound peculiarly familiar? Didn't Moses just basically say the same thing? For me, if people present themselves as believers, I can learn things from, associate with, and even be close to those who do not promote the obeying of all His commandments (Torah). I certainly do not condemn them (for they are in Christ). I just cannot wholly accept them as my spiritual authority, and I must be careful to not let them convince me to follow after other gods. Nor am I to fear them.

How does the Bible define following other gods? This would be demonstrated through the following of instructions that contradict Torah, either from the "old" or "new" sources. This is figuratively known within Judaism as "eating things sacrificed to idols." Reason being is that false teachings come from the false teacher, and the false teacher is the father of false gods. And people ingest those lies. It would appear that works (fruit or miracle) may not be enough to assess one's spiritual state. Love, without fruit, is tantamount to faith without works. So at a bare minimum, we need to see both fruit and love.

There may be controversy as to how to be obedient to the commandments today, but that is far better to deal with than the outright rejection of the authority and influence of Torah in a believer's life. If someone is being obedient to what they understand, and they bear both

Divided We Stand

love and fruit, then they are my brother. However, the idea that we have no obligation to the Mosaic covenant is a doctrine of demons, and if they are not seeking to be obedient to it, how can they possibly lead someone who is? The master would automatically default to a student. The Greater in the Kingdom of Heaven, would then be following the lesser (Matthew 5:19).

Consider this. I could take a typical, smooth-talking, non-believing actor, put a nice suit on him, give him a Bible, tell him to read dramatically some portion word-for-word and follow it up with a dramatic script I've given him, and it's quite possible someone could be healed, or even come to repentance (sign and wonder). After all, every word said could be true, and the recipient carried his or her own faith. It's a statistical fact that in a large group setting like that, some people will leave feeling better than when they came. The "healer" might just get credit for that. How much more mischief can someone familiar with Scripture achieve?

Would Balaam qualify as a leader in God's kingdom? After all, he spoke genuine blessings didn't he? He also, though, cursed the Israelites. And how did he do that, if not in verse? He mingled the lawless lifestyle of the nations into Israel's camp. That caused the Israelites to curse themselves!

But I have a few things against you, because you have there some who hold the teaching of Balaam, who kept teaching Balak to <u>put a stumbling block</u> before the sons of Israel, to eat things sacrificed to idols and to commit *acts of* immorality. (To the <u>church</u> at Pergamum! Revelation 2:14)

The litmus test for a potential leader should be one who does not reject Moses, or our Torah-observant Master. "For if you had believed Moses, you would have believed Me... (John 5:46)." And a true leader keeps Balaam from teaching his strategies to God's people. And a true leader watches out for people setting up altars to demons and inventing replacement days for God's Appointed Times! Sadly, that leaves some of us with a lot fewer options. For you, it may be a different story. You are accountable to what you know to be true. If your pastors/teachers teach/preach in agreement with what you believe, obviously you don't have the same problem. As time goes on, and you become more aware of our need for sanctification, things may change. You want a leader who is going before you in the direction you are being called to go. If you have to drag your leader along, or constantly overlook doctrinal conflict, then they are by all rights no longer your leader; even if that leader has had extraordinary historical influence, or graduate degrees.

From the time of Paul, there have only been a handful of thinkers who significantly influenced large segments of the believing world. They have written their commentaries, and we refer to them often. Their sermons have been preserved, and we still preach from them. Here is the crux of the matter: They are all differing in their opinions. How many Wesleys, and Edwards, and Calvins, and Henrys have there been, or are? How many have started their own movements? Sure, they were brilliant, and their thoughts should be considered. But they don't always agree with each other, and therefore somebody's theology has to be wrong. Otherwise, their works should be part of our canon.

I am thankful for their efforts and insight, and we certainly have needed pioneers, and some did get the reforming ball rolling. But for that, I will not elevate them to equal with or above the Scriptures, or universally submit to them. Yet there are many that did and do. They additionally did not have access to the same historical and biblical information we have available today (e.g., Dead Sea Scrolls). Since they are not God, we must acquiesce to the reality that not everything they said was inspired. If someone is teaching disobedience to God's commandments, then they most certainly are not.

On the other hand, there are teachers and prophets today, who in various ways perform great signs; maybe even heading up renowned, charitable ministries "In His Name," whom I must not submit to at all. There are "quote-unquote" healers, prophets and prophetesses, authors, and even mega-church pastors that…

As we have said before, so I say again now, if any man is preaching to you a gospel contrary to what you received, he is to be accursed! (Galatians 1:9 is really Paul's administration of Deuteronomy 13.)

I'm not following a 'should-be *cursed*' (*anathema*; excommunicated) person around for leadership, just because the mainstream church world doesn't see it, or they do many 'good' works before men. Remember, the recorded gospel message is, "Repent! For the Kingdom of God is upon us!" It is not, "Come, get saved, and be rich!" But it is also, "I have come for the lost sheep of Israel!" And it is also, "Turn back to Torah, and do not continue in the sins of your fathers!" And it is also, "I intend to rebuild the tent of David." And it is also that all ethnicities can engraft into Israel (the "mystery" of Ephesians 6:16). It is not just "Jesus saves!" as true as that is. Many do not understand what the original concept of repentance was, and still is. It is not a feeling. Sorrow and guilt are feelings that should be associated with repentance, but repentance is a turning away from being an active transgressor of the Law (a sinner), and turning toward a life of right doing according to the Law (what is righteous and holy).

Divided We Stand

I don't expect most of you to agree with me on everything, and this is certainly one of those areas that require a lot of consideration, but whose feet you sit at is an absolutely crucial decision. Submitting to the authority of a torah phobic is perilous to one who is pursuing a walk that imitates our Christ. (Although to be fair, Christians in general abide by a lot more Torah than they realize or admit.) This is why people who are being led by the Spirit to return to a covenantal-compliant faith are squirming in their seats, as they are learning the Truth outside the church walls, but fellowshipping inside them.

First and foremost, our Rabbi/Teacher should be Jesus, by His Spirit, through His Word. The Father wanted to be all we need, but we rejected that notion at Sinai first, and later preferred a human intercessor/king instead. It's true that a matter is confirmed by two or three witnesses, so we shouldn't run around like a bunch of maverick disciples. But anyone can find a few false witnesses. It might only cost you a few shekels. What we need to see in our earthly leadership are the same things Jesus required of the Pharisees. They should be people who "don't neglect the weightier matters of the Law: justice, mercy, and faithfulness; **without neglecting the other areas of the Torah** (Matthew 23:23)."

There are many people who don't know what to do with the feelings they are having as mainstream Christendom is failing them more and more; but it is all they've ever known. If you are one of those people, I would give anything to be able to tell you exactly what to do. Just know you are not alone. Sometimes it's the lone voice crying out in the wilderness that is the one you have to trust. Pray hard and seek out kindred souls. Sometimes you need to make subtle, probing inquiries to see how people respond. You might be quite surprised. You may just happen to have someone nearby who's been just as unsure what to do, and has remained quiet for the same reasons. Maybe you will just have to walk it alone for a while. Maybe you'll have to nail your own thesis to a cathedral door—so to speak.

Ultimately, you are accountable to what you know to be true, so make the right decision. Maybe *you'll* actually be the lone voice for a while; though I believe, not for long.

Waxed Love

Many false prophets will arise and will mislead many. Because lawlessness is increased, most people's love will grow cold. But the one who endures to the end, he will be saved. (Matthew 24:11-13)

Or, according to a conceptualized, modern, universalistic translation: "…because of the non-loving (only commandment being "to love") of the people, people's love will cease loving."

One of the significant by-products of lawlessness (torahlessness) is the loss of love of man. That only makes sense when we take into consideration that love is defined by Torah. The entirety of Torah (the Law and the Prophets) hangs on these two greatest commandments—to love God fully, and your neighbor as yourself. And just as it has already been discussed, how you do that is defined in the subsections, in the very things we must 'endure'.

Who cannot see that in the current state of our culture, love hasn't become a very subjective thing? Our congregations, coincidentally, are in one of their more torahless (grace alone—without works) points in history, and also in their most liberal (from a doctrinal perspective.) Is that also a coincidence? Love is being redefined before our very eyes.

Fathers and Mothers alike are "in love" with their careers, so that they can afford to have other people raise their children. Parents are "loving" their precious little girls by letting them walk around with their pierced tongues and midriffs showing, making them more appealing to sexual predators and hormone-saturated, teenage boys. The church is *fabulously* accepting gay ministers; and if not ordaining them, they'll at least gather them together in unholy matrimony. Speaking of marriages, half or more of marriages are failing whether they are believers or not. So it seems love is a disobedient breaker of blood covenants (Malachi 2:14). No surprise there really. If we are not going to be faithful to God's covenants, why should we think we are capable of fulfilling our own? The hate and violence filled music genres, games, and cinematic experiences seem to be irrelevant to loving parents. Tell me how it is that we can reconcile letting our children do what they want, dress like thugs and whores, be with who they want, watch and listen to what they want, be pharmaceutically controlled because we have no patience or parenting skills, and not be "too sheltered," for fear of "social adjustment" issues, with raising our children in the ways of the Lord, "so they will not depart from them"? You can't! And they are the future congregation! Hold on...I need to catch my breath.

Many parents of this current teen generation actually think they don't have to worry because they came through their own rebellious years all right. If you think your little cigarette and rock-and-roll rebellion is the same as what's going on in the world today, perhaps parenting was a bad choice for you. HaSatan is dancing the Lambada with your children and you think it's cute and harmless. Might I suggest you stop disciplining your children like your shaking a twig at a rabid Rottweiler?

You do know that love is more than a feeling, don't you? It is demonstrable. It must be! The clearest demonstration of love you can make to God can be done by simply following His instructions. If your

Divided We Stand

marriage and enlarged families were wrapped around the observance of the Feasts, and the Shabbat, and Torah study, how much closer do you think you might get? Substitute the secular, materialistic, man-made replacement holidays with the original Appointed Times (Mo'adim), and obtain the blessings you have been being robbed of. Torah encompasses every aspect of daily living when instituted, and so will the rewards. Including Shabbats, Torah observant believers have around sixty "holy-days," so we really don't feel like we're missing out on much.

Even our churches have played a role in redefining love for us. They marry straight couples who should not be together yet. They turn a blind eye to abuse and misconduct. They won't correct their members because they might lose their tithe. It used to be that premarital sex or pregnancy was an embarrassment to the entire nation of Israel (Genesis 34; Deuteronomy 22). Today, churches proceed to throw celebratory shower parties for their pregnant, unwed mothers-to-be, thanks to 'grace' overlooking such behavior. Love even keeps pastors in their posts while their   families are in shambles (1st Timothy 3:4). Love for God's Word is an idea brought up during membership class, but then sound doctrine is swept under the carpets of the elevated platforms on which the pulpit sits. The places of honor at the potluck dinner go to the members with the highest salaries. Corruption and love *cannot* make good bed-fellows. **Love teaches Truth** no matter how confrontational it may seem. There is little if any real disapproval of sinful behavior shown anymore.

If I'm not talking to you, that's great! But there are those of you out there who know exactly about what I'm talking about. It is to you this warning goes out. You think the story of Jesus turning the tables of the merchants over was bad? You just wait. It would behoove you to turn your own tables over first—now! You think you're teaching His will, by selling your books and cd's, even your messages immediately following service, and you don't even realize you're doing the very same thing the money changers were. After all, Sunday is the new Sabbath, right?

What about all these differing denominations? How does love fit into that equation? Apparently it has become taboo to "speak ill" of other brothers and sisters of the faith, by exposing doctrinal errors for what they are. It's okay for pastor so-and-so over there to tell their congregation such-and-such, knowing full-well that it's wrong, and ignore it because "It's not *our* church!" I thought the church was the Body of our Christ, and that every one of His sheep is precious in His sight. I realize that there will always be some difference of *opinion,* but correcting *error* is every community leader's responsibility. Three thousand people died for worshipping the golden calf, but everyone else experienced a plague for not stopping them.

So, how can we have thirty-three thousand different belief systems? How can there possibly be thirty-three thousand different, valid opinions? To put it succinctly, there is not! The reason we are now so divided is because when a group of people are stripped of their guiding constitution, chaos and anarchy are the inevitable bi-products. I want to be transparent and tell you that the reason I bring all this up is to further support our need for Torah, in case you didn't already figure that. But I also want it to show you that "tolerance" is not necessarily the great virtue it's being presented to be, when in its secularized form. And it's finding its way into our fellowships!

Sitting around and tolerating everything that comes down the pike, because we think that is the sensitive and politically correct thing to do (due to its church affiliation or origin), is a concept that stinks of brimstone. There was a day when our spiritual leaders would tell us when we were wrong, or preaching error, or breaking God's law—in ignorance or otherwise. If we wouldn't receive the correction, two or three more respected individuals would be brought into the picture. And if that didn't work, the whole community would get involved. If that didn't work, we were removed from fellowship (lost our citizenship). I guess those days are over for now. Yet, **love doesn't demand tolerance of error!**

In Jewish culture, the rabbi is certainly highly respected, but he is not so far above his peers that he is unquestionable. Judaism is devoted to asking questions. A midrash (Bible study) would be nothing without hammering out truth through debate. A rabbi's wisdom is received as a gift from above, like all the other gifts that the Body may have; but that does not absolve him from consensus opinion. A rabbi who has been confronted for teaching error, and will not receive correction, is not going to last long. One of the reasons for this is that unlike the thirty-three thousand-plus different places a Christian pastor has available to go, the Jewish rabbi has about three different main categories, with only a couple different sub-groups for each. I'm not suggesting that's perfect, but it is definitely an improvement. There's just not nearly that many different ways to be Jewish.

In an imperfect analogy, both Christianity and Judaism independently could be likened to the Republican, Democratic and the Libertarian parties, with their varying ultra, moderate, and liberal variants. They would all like to attain the most political power, but it can't happen. They all exist because of a central constitution. But they do not all interpret the constitution the same way. Christianity in turn creates a party for every little variance, while Judaism is far more unified and seeking of solidarity. Christianity accepts the Bill of Rights through Grace, picks a few articles of the Constitution it is willing to live with, and tries to overturn certain subsections it doesn't like. Judaism more readily accepts

Divided We Stand

the whole Constitution, but applies the articles differently. Judaism could accept the newest version of the Constitution, (because it is not in opposition to the previous), if it weren't for their failure to see the legitimacy of Jesus as Messiah, who penned its beginning in blood. After all, the newest covenant is described in the Hebrew Scriptures, by Hebrew prophets. Christianity does not embrace their participation in the entirety of Moses's Torah, because it interprets Moses's teaching as contradicting what Jesus taught. **Love seeks after unity**, **not compromise**. They are not the same thing. But it isn't afraid to divide when needed. God separates and divides all the time. It's called "making holy".

I am not advocating converting to Judaism by any means, primarily because in order to do that one must reject Jesus as the Messiah. But I am impressed with the majority of Jewry's devotion to keeping Torah in high regard. Christianity has allowed itself to fracture so far, that there is practically no continuity left. A house divided cannot stand. Behind the scenes of major Christian denominations, unity is often far from us. We begin at the cross together, but then we think it's a signpost heading in four directions. What we fail to acknowledge before we head off is that one point leads up, one point leads down, and the other two eventually take us full circle, right back to where we started. The irony of tolerance is that it is praised for its virtue and power to unite; but in the end, it cuts us to pieces.

Christians, Christians Everywhere

When you look at just about any chart showing the percentages of religions, and their prospective sizes in proportion to the world population, a very interesting phenomenon seems to occur. Somehow, Christianity is comprised of every religion, cult, or sect that in any way has the name of Jesus associated with it. Jehovah's Witnesses, Coptics, Anglicans, Latter Day Saints, Eastern Orthodox—heck, even Christian Science, are all examples of Christianity. They are considered by statisticians to be similar enough to lump them all together. In actuality, there are serious and significant differences throughout.

The Body's fractured state has made us impotent, because there are such obvious differences between us. "Christians" (Protesting Catholics) will not deem themselves Catholics; but Catholics, on the other hand, are Christians. Who does that make sense to? Perhaps all the varying denominations feel that if they'll just embrace tightly as "Brothers and Sisters" and sing *Kumbaya*, all will be made well. Maybe, Jesus, from high above, won't be able to tell the wheat from the tares. Simply because the name Jesus is associated with a religion, does not mean we have much, if anything, in common. Calling yourself a "Christian" today sadly means very little. "Let the faith with the most Truth win!" sounds so insensitive and intolerant, but **love operates independent of religion,** regardless.

Error is not going to be corrected if it is not exposed. And you who call yourselves pastor/teachers, it's primarily your job to do. But we laypersons who have neighbors and family who are in error; it is also our job as well. We have to have a new breed of leaders who will actually defend the sheep from wolves and lions and bears—leaders who will sling stones at HaSatan's entourage. We need teachers teaching Truth, and leaving political correctness to those running for office. **Love is not politically correct.**

So why are we even in the 'New Testament' era at all? It is because we have gone from three types of believers in God: Jew, Messianic Jew, and God-Fearers, to multiple thousands of types, believing in whatever they want to believe. Without Torah as our compass, everyone will go off course. Torah does not only exist amidst the older covenants; it has also been re-given to us in the newest, through the Apostles. Due to fact that the Apostle's torah does not contradict Moses's torah (when properly and contextually understood in their original, Hebraic perspective), and Moses's torah is considered obsolete, we should not be surprised to see the Apostles' neglected and misunderstood the same way. That is exactly what I am contributing the primary source of our problems to.

Now that we are three thousand, four hundred and fifty years into the future, from the giving of the Torah on Mt. Sinai, quite obviously we live in a vastly different world. Adding this to our biblical language barrier, we have a real challenge on our hands. But no matter how enlightened our age, how sophisticated our technology, or vain our intellect has become, the Lord's Word will always transcend human reasoning. It has never been outdated by anything we can create or conceive. To think that the Lord didn't foresee our current government, society, or philosophical viewpoints as twenty-first century man is simply ludicrous.

A primary reason that Jesus came and died was because we wouldn't keep our part of the covenant. Two thousand years later, you'd think we should have learned that lesson. Not only are we now not keeping our part again, but even the "new" covenant teachings, which are supposedly so much more lenient and graceful, cannot seem to be kept.

Our degree of division is indicative of the obvious need to re-examine our theological perspective of Torah. I do not propose that Judaism, in its current Jesus-rejecting form, has the answers to our problem. But since they have carried the written Torah of the Father since about 1445 BCE, I'm pretty sure that qualifies them to teach us a thing or two about something. They are not all "blind guides". I believe there is

Divided We Stand

one true faith walk, and I believe that it is the style closest to the one walked by our Messiah, no matter how 'Jewish' it may prove out to be.

So where do we begin? The enormity of the project of undoing the "new" church, after nearly eighteen hundred years of combative resistance to the Truth of Torah, is overwhelming. Fortunately, because no human could possibly do it, we can rely on the One who wrote the Book on it. His Word does not lie. I am writing this book knowing fully-well that I have no idea if it will get into enough hands to make a large scale difference. But it's in yours now, and you are as significant as anyone is.

Everyone I ever talk to about church matters is willing to confess that the church world has problems. We all agree that anything that is composed of human beings is going to have flaws. But of all our institutions, the church is the one place we should be exceedingly concerned with its unified character. There is a time and a place for debate, dissention and even division, but having our nakedness exposed to the 6:00 news is just shameful.

With a blood thirsty media always looking to make a joke of us, must we just keep handing them an over-flowing cup of controversy, extra sweetened? The world watches us and keeps looking for the living evidence that supports this personal, singular, all-Sufficient God we declare to be out there; but sees little other than the negative and controversial aspects of organized religion. That we are flawed will not suffice as an excuse for them on the Day of Judgment, but that does not negate our responsibility to reflect a less broken family. Granted, the liberal media will never be our proponent, but we can certainly do our part to make their bias look blatant. The best way to do that is to demonstrate His love through an upright and unified front; one wrapped around Torah. What would be really great, is when a "church" gets caught with its hands in HaSatan's cookie jar, it would be recognized as having been done by a "religious organization" instead of by "the Body".

I believe in most cases, there is no way for *us* to change the greater status quo. We can only change ourselves. *He* must open our eyes before we can see. Then, when He does, we need to spend some time in the mirror. When enough of us do that, the image of Jesus's body (as demonstrated by and acknowledged as the church) will begin to appear fit. To put it more creatively: We can wash our own clothes, or He can toss us into the washer. It is, however, the latter option whereby we *may* drown.

Now that some shifting sands have been packed down a bit, and we have poured a new foundation as well, we can be confident our framing will be square and true. We must now spend a little time talking about our God, our Messiah, and His Body as manifest on this earth.

Hopefully, we can now begin to see what it takes to construct a strong building, one whose cornerstone is the true Christ, that the righteous can run into and be safe. Before we go there, I want to take a second and clarify something that could have been misconstrued at this point—one of many, I'm sure.

Firstly, I am not anti-church. For if I was, I would be an anti-Body, while within His Body. I am simply tired of passive and hyper-tolerant leadership. I am tired of our divisions. Secondly, I believe in the same concepts Yeshua understood as regards the Two Houses. I do not, however, believe in engaging in genealogical arguments, or British Israelism. I believe in people from the nations remaining citizens of their respective countries, and Christian Jews remaining Jewish. I believe in the inevitable, One New, Torah observant Man. I realize that there will always be differences in our opinions regarding interpretation. But if they are at least based on solid exegetical study, that is far more acceptable. It is my firm belief that Torah can and ultimately will unite us.

There is no way for me to talk about what I am next about to, without rubbing someone the wrong way. For that reason, I will have to continue to use a lot of scriptural evidences, as well as outside references. So, as we begin the dissecting part of our next investigation, we will begin with a closer look at the very 'God' all of this pertains to. Then, of course, we will need to look closer at ourselves.

7

Who is this G-d?

And what is He God of? Well that certainly depends on from what religious group you come, right? Wrong! Adamantly, unrelentingly, and decidedly wrong! Who in the world do we think we are; deciding who God is per our own imaginations? The only trustable sources of information we have about God are: what He has revealed to us through His actions, as recorded in His Word (synonymous with and reflected by His Begotten Son), His manifest creation, and the conscience of man (as is consistent with concepts in His Word—we being made in His image.)

Anything more than that is pure speculation. Even what He has revealed can only be understood as being limited by our finite minds. All the "definites" of what we conceive are more likely inferior shadows to the reality of the source of their expression. That being the case, it stands to reason that whenever we diminish anything He has graciously chosen to reveal to us, we further limit our understanding of Him. If we go too far, we reconstruct His revelation into a man-made image, with potentially idolatrous ramifications.

Therefore, being offspring of God, we ought not to be thinking the Divine Nature to be similar to gold or silver or stone, an image *[shaped by]* humanity's skill and imagination. (Acts 17:29)

We often pray that God would show Himself to us, usually disregarding a lot that He already has made available to us, much of which we don't already know. We beg for a glimpse of His glory, when all the while smoke and fire is erupting from a trembling mountain, right before our eyes. We just have to open them. The first key to unlocking the mysteries of His revelation is so simple that it seems foolish to mention. Read His-tory.

Enter the Word

It will revolutionize your ability to learn and grow if you will simply become a character, or an extra in His story. Go to the garden and take a look around. Smell the fragrances of the vibrant flowers and freshly birthed life all around. Everything is new. Everything is exciting. Whatever your eyes fall upon, you know was thought-crafted by the One who walks beside you in the mist.

Watch Cane strike Abel and shed the first innocent blood. See his shifty eyes and the sweat on his brow, as he contemplates the gravity of what he just did. He knows it was wrong, but how? What will come of it? Observe the blood sinking into the ground, and staining the place with a mark that could not be hidden. It cried out to be known.

Pick up a hammer and start helping out your old friend Noah. Take upon yourself some persecution. Every day, mockers, teasers, and brutally cruel pagans with reprobate hearts work their mental witchcraft in an attempt to get the last righteous man, and his family, to forfeit the cause and thus end the human race. Carry some of that weight. Walk around inside the mighty vessel as you ponder what the future really holds. Is this big box really going to protect me? Do you have the faith?

Don't forget to also be the bad guy once in a while. Hastily you help forge the beast, for perhaps the leader of these people may actually come back soon; and if so, he may reestablish the fact that you can't worship in the heathen ways you've become accustomed to.

As you dance around the golden steer you helped create from the fires of hell, you swallow hard, for here he comes now. Who does he think he is anyway, trying to tell us what to do?

"Don't look at me," you think to yourself. "I'm not the only one who thought you were dead."

"Silence!" is heard echoing off the mountain ledge, as Moses looks down upon the frenzied dance and cultic debauchery.

"I go away for such a short while, and you have already forgotten that it is the LORD your God who rescued you from Egyptian bondage, and He allows no sculpted images of Himself?" Do you sometimes forget?

Can you hear Moses almost cursing under his breath? I probably would, wouldn't you? So instead of words he reacts aggressively and tosses the tablets etched by the finger of God. They crack and sink into the ground below, breaking the covenant with an earth-trembling thud, as a deafening silence spontaneously sweeps the crowd.

"What's he doing now?" you think to yourself as he pounds and pounds the calf into crushed powder. "Why is he mixing it into that water? Huh, I'm not going to drink any such thing."

"Oh yes, you will!" he shouts, as something forces the cup to my lips with a strength I cannot withstand. "You broke the covenant!" echoes across the rippling waters. I choke on the silted potion, as an overwhelming nausea grinds at my gut, from which I find no relief. I am taken back, in my mind's eye, to the horrible sounds of the weeping Egyptian families of those who lost their precious children that night.

"The LORD did that, didn't He? Oh please LORD, don't take my life too with this potion of judgment! I don't want to die. Forgive me. I was a fool to think anything I made is worthy of worship. All I can do now is wait. If I die, it will be a just reward by a just God."

By entering this story more fully, you will see things you might have overlooked, like the fact that these people actually thought they were worshiping YHVH, and avoid making that same kind of mistake.

Exodus 32:5, "When Aaron saw this, he built an altar in front of the calf and announced, "Tomorrow there will be a festival to the LORD."

By entering into His story, you are then able to experience the feelings associated with mankind's encounters with Elohiym, thereby bringing you closer to Him vicariously through others. If you believe the events depicted in the Scriptures actually took place (a huge hurdle for many), you have no need to have a *physical* encounter with Him, in order to "build your faith," or deepen your relationship with Him.

Ask yourself as you read the Scriptures: Who am I with? Where am I? When is this taking place? What's going on around me? Why is this situation occurring? What can I experience through the lives of these characters, and therefore learn? A thousand lessons are lost when we disassociate ourselves from the historical accounts of these seemingly unlikely events and near-legendary people. For all those "I don't think I could do thats!" and "How could they be so dumbs?" are not there to instruct the "I got it all figured outs". They are there because there are no such people.

There is no randomly recorded or meaningless information given to us in Scripture. It is thought by some that even single letters, in their original, pictorial Aleph-Bet, have a lesson within them. Maybe so, but each person, trial, judgment, blessing, dilemma, occurrence, etc. has a

Who is this G-d?

purpose for being woven into the passages of Holy Writ. Always try to figure out what it might be, and your rewards will be handsome.

If you are willing to believe that, and I hope that you are, ask yourself these questions: Why would something appear over six thousand times throughout Scripture, yet be paid little to no attention to? Why would such an obviously significant occurrence be involved in a conspiracy? Before I tell you what it is, let me tell you why you might not be aware of it. It's hidden. And not only hidden, but has been in some cases removed altogether. Care to offer a guess what it might be? You might find this hard to imagine, but it is the personal, "memorial" name of the Mighty One commonly known as…God.

The Missing Key

It is true that ultimately our relationship with Him is what's going to cause Him to welcome us, for He *knows* us. However, the subjective and sometimes esoteric means by which we strive to 'be known', are what often get us into a lot of our trouble.

"All who call upon the name of 'the Lord' shall be saved (Romans 10:13)." It's a great and powerful verse, isn't it? But what is it saying? Where is its historical foundation? Does it agree with or is it paradoxical to the verse which tells us that "many have done great things 'in His name' and He will tell them to depart; He never *knew* them"? Calling upon 'the Name' of the Lord will save us, but does it say His name is "the Lord"? What about these verses: "The name of 'the Lord' is a strong tower" and He has "The Name above all Names" or "Blessed be 'the Name' of the Lord" and "Blessed is He who comes in 'the Name' of the Lord"? Do you see a pattern here? I'm sure you do, but it might not be what you think. In the original Scriptures, a lot of those "Lords" did not say that. And when you're reading the 'old' part of your Bibles and you see the word LORD in all caps, do you ever wonder why, being that the Hebrew language has no capital letters?

We are about to embark on a highly sensitive mission. I am pretty passionate about this topic, as you will soon see. I really did not write this book to appease a particular group, or advocate a "branch" of any specific movement. Those of you who belong to such things will have varying responses to this teaching, as is to be expected. Title me an "advocate" or whatever you like, but I've analyzed much of the available rhetoric, and now I'm contributing mine. If you are Jewish and are offended by the use of His Name, please just struggle your way through this section. You will at least gain more insight into this sojourners' perspective. This will be different from what your forefathers handed you, but you just might find it reasonable.

Which Way Did He Go?

There are multiple thousands of places where the Name above all Names has been methodically removed from most all Scripture versions. Let us all pause and give thanks to the translators who took it upon themselves to endeavor in this great accomplishment; although they were never asked to! That fact is really the height of my argument. If His name (second key) has no practical value, or usable quality, why did He bother to tell us? Moreover, why after telling us did He follow it with:

God, furthermore, said to Moses, "Thus you shall say to the sons of Israel, The LORD [YHVH], the God of your fathers, the God of Abraham, the God of Isaac, and the God of Jacob, has sent me to you. This is My name **forever**, and this is My **memorial-name** to **all generations**." (Exodus 3:15)

Why did He alter Avram and Sarai's name, when He brought them into covenant relationship? Names matter. Why was part of His Name included in the name of the tribe with the Scepter, the Yahudim (Jews)? Why is it mixed with, in some form or another, most every prophet's name? Yirmeh Yahu (Jeremiah; Yah will Rise); Yesha Yahu (Isaiah; Salvation of Yah); Eliyyah (Elijah; Yah is El (the Mighty); Nechemyah (Nehemiah; Consolation of Yah); Zekaryahu (Zechariah; Yah has Remembered), and on and on. Perhaps it was just a coincidence. We must not forget about David's best friend, Yehonathan (Yah has Given). And who was it that came to show us the Lord? Why, it's our own Messiah Yehoshua (Yah is Salvation).

What if there is plenty of evidence to show that He *wants* to be known by His name and not only by a title? Would it then not matter if we don't use it? What if the term 'God' is so generic and diluted of its capacity to identify the Elohiym of Abraham that it has been rendered near powerless? Remember, 90% of Americans are "Christian". Everyone but atheists believe in a 'god' (or so they claim; as they idolize themselves.) Some believe in many of them. What separates our God from all the other false gods of this world (besides the capital G) is the fact that our Elohiym tangibly manifested and personally revealed Himself to us, in character *and* by name. Every other god is man-made and man-named!

"My people will know me by My name (Isaiah 52:6 and Ezekiel 39:7)." Also, "I have revealed Your name to the men (disciples) You gave Me from the world. They were Yours, You gave them to Me, and they have kept Your word (John 17:6; *Yehoshua's words*)." These speak nothing of titles. If you want to do something amazing, go to your concordance, look up 'name' and just quickly survey the texts. You will quickly and undoubtedly discover His Name, and names in general, do matter to him.

Who is this G-d?

He placed His Name in the tabernacle and temple (1st Kings 8:16). Do you really think if 'God' was His preferred name, the concern of: "Do not treat my holy name as common and ordinary. I must be treated as holy by the people of Israel (Leviticus 22:32)," could even be relevant at all?

Exodus 34:5, "The LORD descended in the cloud and stood there with him as he called upon the name of the LORD."

Moses beheld His descent and called Him by the Name He had revealed Himself to have. Although the phrase "the name of" can carry the connotation of being an ambassador for, or having to do with the characteristics of, there are times like this one where it carries its simplest and literal meaning. Translators often attribute the figurative meaning: "character," to the phrase "the Name," even during the times where there is no grammatical or contextual substantiation, or need for it.

A Name Game

Let's say your name is Robert—sorry ladies. You take a trip to China. There, somebody asks your name and you courteously tell him or her. They try to say it back to you but it comes back as Wobert. So you try and try to help them annunciate it correctly, but they really struggle to get it right. They can't seem to get that 'R' sound worked out. There are different things that can take place at this point. My apologies to Chinese readers. This is not in jest.

You could change your name and simply introduce yourself as Wobert from now on. Problem is, every time you do that people erupt in laughter towards you, because thanks to an English-speaking native, you discover 'Wob' means 'loser' and 'ert' means 'boy'. You're most likely not going to take this route. You know your name happens to mean "bright fame". So, you ask your English-speaking friend how you say "bright fame" in Chinese. He tells you some goofy sounding words that make a horrible sounding name. So you ditch that as an idea. What now?

All you can do really to preserve your name as much as possible, would be to find the Chinese characters with the closest corresponding sounds to your English letters, and arrange them to produce: Robert. Three things could result. You could end up matching a pre-existing letter sequence that has another meaning altogether (good or bad). Or, you would end up breaking certain language rules and create a nonsensical word in Chinese that would have to be adjusted, rendering the sound of the word further from the original. Or, you would end up accomplishing the goal of transliterating the word, but lose the original meaning of the word altogether.

Let me reverse this a bit for some more perspective. A foreign exchange student comes to your house for a couple months. She tells you her name is Anastasia. You have a hard time saying it the way she does, so you call her Stacey. She doesn't really care for that because her name has a special meaning to her. She asks you to try to say it the right way, and after much practice, you get it figured out. She is delighted. But for some reason you still feel like Stacey is a better name for her, and so that's what you call her. She is a guest in your house and she's not leaving for a while. So, she decides to put up with it. She doesn't want to cause more stress to the situation than necessary.

Imagine you were invited to a royal feast where you were going to be introduced to the sovereign king of a nation. The protocol for the event included a passing before the king, a proper bow, and a particular blessing which required you to say his name. His name is a little difficult to say, but He is an understanding king who takes joy in the effort people make. Do you not bother going? Or, do you take the appropriate measures to learn how, and practice it until you get it right? I suppose you could just call him Mr. King Guy.

Do you get mad when little children say your name imperfectly? When your friends call you on the phone, do you answer, "Hi Consort"? Would you call your cousin 'sir', if he or she was not in the military? How about calling your wife, *spouse* or *ma'am*? Would you call your Dad, *sire*? Then why do we primarily substitute the name our Elohiym told us to know Him by with the (as of late) neutral and insufficient title 'God'?

Similarly, why do we call the name of our Savior something other than what the Lord sent an angel to declare His name to be? Why send an angel at all? Why not just not let Miriam and Yoseph make something up? Actually, to add to the confusion, we not only keep calling Him something that has little lingual meaning, we follow it up with the title 'Christ', in a way that suggests it's His last name. Did we really feel that just because it is a modern tradition to have a last name, He who is without beginning or end, must?

But when he had considered this, behold, an angel of the Lord appeared to him in a dream, saying, 'Joseph, son of David, do not be afraid to take Mary as your wife; for the Child who has been conceived in her is of the Holy Spirit. She will bear a Son; and you shall call His name Jesus, [for He will save] His people from their sins.' (Matthew 1:20 & 21)

Notice that the name He was to be called is followed by a definition: "...*for* He will save." That tells us that His name has to have that meaning at least somewhere in its construction. The word 'Jesus', popular as it may be, does not carry that meaning within it anywhere. A further and sure tip-off to seeing the inaccuracy of 'Jesus' is the fact that

Who is this G-d?

the letter 'J' did not even appear, in any language, until around the 14th century. It wasn't until 1630 AD that it was generally adopted in England, the motherland of our language.

So where did 'Jesus' come from? The American Heritage Dictionary has the following etymology of the name: Middle English [Jesus], from Late Latin Iesus, from Greek Iesous, from Hebrew yeshûa', from yehôshûa', (Joshua). Even a secular dictionary can recognize this. Any decent Bible will have a footnote that adds clarity to the fact that His name (as declared by the angel in Matthew 1:21) has to mean something related to the work of salvation, e.g., "Yah will save."

The common, Aramaic form 'Yeshua' is quite fine, as it still carries the recognizable meaning "salvation" within its construct. As far as His last name is concerned…there just isn't one! The Greek term 'Christ' is cognate with Chrism, meaning "perfumed oil". In fact, 'Christ', in classical Greek usage, could mean *covered in oil* and is therefore a literal and accurate translation of Mashiach/Messiah (*anointed one*).

So, is this all really one big, *semetical* argument with a fruitless end? Not even close! I do not believe that calling Yeshua 'Jesus' is even remotely close to a sin. Many people, including myself, have found their redemption through that name, and other foreign variations. I'm just telling you certain facts and hopefully drawing you closer to Him through understanding. But, as you will see, the same cannot be said regarding 'God'.

There has been a recent development regarding the Son's name, which you may have already heard about. What appeared to be the ossuary of James His brother surfaced in early November of 2002. It has not been proven authentic, but it does appear to be of the period. Inscribed on the box are these transliterated words in Aramaic: Ya'akov bar Yosef akhui diYeshua"—that is, "Jacob [English: James], son of Yosef [Joseph], brother of Yeshua [Jesus]. What we can derive from this is a confidence in how His name was spelled. You will find in some literature, Y'shua as the English script. In Aramaic, the Master's name is contracted from yehôshûa, seen as ישוע. Without the later added vowel markers, there are some minor variances to many words in Scripture, but that is not the issue, nor of consequence.

There are those out there who profess the name Jesus is pagan because it means: 'Son of Zeus'. There is no substantiating etymological evidence to support that whatsoever. It does tickle the ears of someone newly entering into a 'rebelling against the mother church' mentality. Many teachings that are intended to discredit modern Christianity can tickle, but don't hold up under scrutiny.

My argument, though, is much simpler than that. If He (Messiah) has an original name, and we know what it is, and we can at least closely pronounce it, I see little reason not to. If you introduced yourself to me with a name I could pronounce (Anastasia), it would simply be rude and discourteous for me not to; especially if I knew that by changing your name I would be stripping it of its heavenly ordained meaning. It's one thing to say something in ignorance. It's another to ignore what you know. Do with that what you will.

Forget Me Not!

Now, what about the Father's name? Ask an average Christian and they will tell you it's 'God'. Or, if they're a little studious they might give you a Jehovah, or even add a Jirah. Adonai (The Lord) and HaShem (The Name) are Jewish preferences, but those are not His name either. Adonai (pl. form of Adon; master) is a majestic title, but this was also used by the Phoenicians for the pagan god Tammuz and is the origin of the Greek name Adonis. It is still not His name.

Like Adon, another ancient, Semitic word for master (and lord) is ba'al. Adonai, although it represents essentially the same thing, for the sake of association, is definitely better. Abraham was called 'Adon' by his head servant in Genesis 24:12. 'Lord', in the King's English vernacular, is a word denoting a landowner or a territorial magnate. This definition is very similar in root to the meaning behind the Hebrew term 'ba'al'. The baals of the Bible were 'master deities' of their particular region, as shown by the name of the land immediately following the title. An example of this would be ba'al Peor (master of the land of Peor, Numbers 25:3). Ba'al also was the title given to a master of a particular skill. Ba'al was a title given to teachers who were thought of as particularly knowledgeable in an area of study. The title was used in Scripture for the Lord, believe it or not (NASB; Isa 54:5, rendered in the plural as *Husband*). But it ceased being used around the time of the Israelites entry into Canaan, for obvious reasons. Calling Yeshua or the Lord "Ba'al," just doesn't seem appropriate anymore.

It will come about in that day, declares the LORD, that you will call Me Ishi and will no longer call Me Ba'al. For I will remove the names of the Ba'als from her mouth, So that they will be mentioned by their names no more. (Hosea 2:16 & 17) Interestingly, the word 'Ishi' here means 'male person'. Is this a reference to Yeshua? Of course it is!")

Since everyone is a "Christian" (regardless of what their theological bend is), when one person speaks of God, you do not have the ability to discern accurately from that alone, from what viewpoint they come. Most famous psychics attribute their perverted gift as coming from God. You know a Muslim, because the name of their god is Allah. You

Who is this G-d?

know one is an Aborigine, if his god is called Bunjil Binbeal. A Hawaiian's creator-god is Kane. He is an Indian if his gods are Brahma, Krishna, and Vishnu. But believers, all being members of the commonwealth of Israel, are known by their god being called 'God'. Why?

Look back for a second at what "God" said Himself about His name in Exodus 3:15. "This is My name **forever**, and this is My **memorial-name** to **all generations**." This statement was made to Moses shortly after he heard it spoken by the Adonai Himself, but additionally with His affiliation with Avraham, Yitzchak (Isaac), and Ya'akov (Jacob). This Name was to be carried to the enslaved Hebrews and delivered as an announcement as to who would be the one to save them. Thirteen chapters later, at the giving of the Ten Commandments, the God (Elohiym) that rescued these Hebrews, brings up His name again and puts a stipulation upon it, giving it the highest level of importance.

You shall not take the name of the LORD your God in vain, for the LORD will not leave him unpunished who takes His name in vain. (Exodus 20:7)

What is He really saying though? Let's go back to the Hebrew. The word translated as 'vain' is the word 'shav'. It actually means 'desolation or ruin'. It has been most commonly taught that through this commandment, 'God' is telling us to not use His name as a swear word. That worked back in children's church, I suppose. But what actually is being said falls right in line with His declaration in Exodus chapter three. He is telling us to not allow His name to be desolated, and therefore ruined and made powerless. To further support this interpretation, since it appears the word 'take' does not now flow in context, we should also examine this word. 'Take' in Hebrew is 'nasa', and it has a wide variety of applications. A few of the meanings of the word are: to lift away, accept, or advance.

It shall be on Aaron's forehead, and Aaron shall <u>take</u> (nasa) away the iniquity of the holy things which the sons of Israel consecrate, with regard to all their holy gifts," (Exodus 28:38a)

Can you see it now? We are not to let His Name be 'taken' and discarded, like what Aaron did to those iniquities. As far as I'm concerned, that's exponentially more significant than the simple misuse of it; not that we shouldn't prevent that as well. Who wants their name to be disrespected or forgotten anyway? It makes perfect sense to me that He would not want us to forget His name. Wouldn't that be a stone's throw from forgetting His existence? But there is yet more to this than meets the eye.

There is yet another component to traditional interpretation of this command. It is connected to the cultural practice of attaching the names of gods to oaths. I guess that's really not hard to understand, as it is still readily practiced today. "I swear to God" is a commonplace phrase, used by believers and non-believers alike, which denotes a strong emphasis of commitment and intent. Understandably, the Lord does not want His reputation and character besmirched by attaching His name to an oath not kept. Even with the best of intentions, our promises are often not kept. This is the very reason for Jesus's teaching on oaths (Matthew 5:37). But that's not true when it comes to the words of our Lord. I have no doubt that this is a genuine concern, and a valid application of the command, but it still is rooted in something bigger. Let's look at some other concepts associated with this.

When the Israelites were scattered into the nations, the people of those nations often either mocked His name to them, or didn't pronounce it correctly. In addition to this concern, His name was held in such high regard that it was thought if someone, anyone, invoked His name accurately, the very act of its utterance would invoke a mystical power to perform the miraculous. (For evil or for good).[1] In order to reduce this blasphemous act, they instituted a policy to stop using His sacred memorial name and circumlocuted it with a fabricated name. The most common replacement name is the one I mentioned earlier, HaShem. Translated, it simply means: The Name. If 'HaShem' was read from a scroll or literary work and mispronounced or mocked, it would ultimately be of no concern.

Because the Name was so closely guarded, and due to other man-fabricated regulations regarding the appropriate use of the Name, over the centuries the Name became nearly unknown and its pronunciation became debatable. It was so guarded, that eventually only the High Priest would utter the Name one day a year, on Yom Kippur. Each time it was spoken, the people would bow low and declare His name to be kadosh (holy). This practice began prior to the appearance of Yeshua during the second temple period, but long after the original Name was given to us. As time went on, the temple was destroyed, the Levitical priesthood ceased, and the result ended in even more obscurity.

With the original paleo-Hebrew language becoming ever more archaic, and as the Babylonian form morphed into Aramaic, phonetic exacts were lost. However, the Masoretic text preserved the Hebrew's vowel sounds, and archaeology has enabled a high quality of etymology, so we can say His name with some degree of certainty. The difference being likely compared to that between Peter and Petre.

Wouldn't you like to know your God by His Name? I thought so. In the same way you're okay with someone doing their best to say your

Who is this G-d?

name, I believe, so is He.

What's in a Name?

You may be familiar with the term 'tetragrammaton'. If not, it is the Greek term given to represent the four-letter name of the Father; the letters being the yod, then hey, then vav, and then hey again. His Name is found nearly seven thousand times throughout the Scriptures, but here is where He cuts to the chase and just declares in no uncertain terms:

Isaiah 42:8, "I am the LORD (YHVH), that is My name; I will not give My glory to another, nor My praise to graven images."

Notice the indicative use of "all caps," in the letters constructing LORD. Everywhere you see that, in most Bible translations, we know that His Name is being hidden again. In the Hebrew, clear as day, hwhy or YHVH appears there. It's definitely more than just a *Shem* that His Name is being methodically brought to desolation. What's also a *Shem* is that His name has been primarily replaced with the title 'God'. Shortly, I will expose a profound ramification. In some translations, where once was written the actual Name, 'He' is now the replacement. As always, do your own research. But here are just a few sources of definition for your examining:

Encyclopaedia Britannica: God

GOD is the common Teutonic word for a personal object of religious worship, applied to all the superhuman beings of the heathen mythologies. The word "god" on the conversion of the Teutonic races to Christianity was adopted as the name of the One Supreme Being.

A Critical Lexicon and Concordance to the English and Greek New Testament, E.W. Bullinger; pp. 331:

'God' originally came from the worship of heathen idols, before it was accepted by man, for the TITLE OF THE FAMILY OF HEAVEN. This word 'God', also is connected to SUN WORSHIP, to Zeus, Deuts, Dios, Theos, Diva, Diu-piter (Jupiter) etc. 'God(s)' a name reclaimed from the Heathen, and used in the New Testament for the True Mighty One. Various derivations have been proposed, but it is nearly certain that its origin is from the East and comes from the Sanskrit root, Dius, which means: 1. masc. fire - The Sun 2. fem. - a ray of light or day, 3. neut _ Divs - the sky, or heaven.

Random House Webster's College Dictionary 2000 Second Revised and Updated Random House Edition:

God (god) n. 1. The creator and ruler of the universe; Supreme being. 2 (l.c.) a. One of several immortal powers, esp. one with male attributes, presiding over some portion of worldly affairs; deity. b. The image of such a deity; idol. 3. (l.c.) Any deified person or object. 4. Christian Science. The Supreme Being considered with reference to the sum of His attributes – interj. 5. (used to express disappointment, disbelief, frustration, or the like.)

Wikipedia Encyclopedia: Etymology – God

The word God comes from the Old English/German/Norse (Teutonic) language family and is equivalent to the derivatives of the Latin word *Deus*. The meaning and etymology behind the Germanic/Indo-European word God as used in English and its cognates (such as Gott in modern German) have been hotly disputed, though most agree in a reconstructed Proto-Indo-European form 'ghuton', which means something like "possession" or "inspiration," and could be related to everything from the old Germanic divinity Wotan/Odin to the Greek word "khute," meaning "libation".

Well, how do you like them apples? Either way, 'God' is not His proper name, even if we capitalize the first letter, or replace the 'o' with a hyphen. At the most, it's not even the most complimentary of titles. A good analogy would be like casting a good, long gaze at Michelangelo's Statue of David, and then finally responding with, "Nice rock!"

The word and concept of 'god' existed before the *name* 'God' ever did. The two most generic words which are translated as god in the original languages are: El (Hebrew for 'the Mighty One'; also meaning 'strength') which is found in a variety of forms, and conjoined with other attributes. It is also the name of a Canaanite god. The second is Theos (Greek: A deity of any origin, Divinity). Even with these scriptural terms, the reason we know that they are being used to represent Adonai is in their context, or as stated before, by their conjunction. Examples being: El'Elyon, El'shaddai, etc. 'God', even when in conjunction with adjectives and attributes, can still represent any deity, depending on one's perspective of that deity. For instance, 'Mighty God' could be Zeus, Allah or Krishna to their respective worshipers. In contrast, the names/titles: Yah, Elohe-Echad, or YHVH, are unmistakably connected to the El of the Hebrews alone.

Because there is some legitimate debate over the pronouncement of His actual name, I am not going to take a firm stand. The grammatical rules of today's Hebrew are certainly not exactly the same as thousands of years ago, but there has been fairly little change overall. The characters look different, yet this Semitic language has preserved itself quite nicely.

Who is this G-d?

One major reason being, it is the language of Scripture, so He preserved it. The most common sounding form of His memorial name is the one usually written as Yahweh (Yäh-way). Some say Yäh-vay, or yäh-hō-vay, or Yäh-hō-väh. The way I conclude and prefer to pronounce it is more like (Yeh-hoo-wäh). From a linguistic and grammatical standpoint, it is pretty much impossible that Yah-way is the way it originally sounded. But, If I want to speak the name (depending who I'm with), I say Yahweh more often for its more common recognition. It is likely itself a contracted form of the Name. It is mostly in the vowel sounds where we find our debate.

The letter Vav was originally pronounced as a 'W'; similar to the changed sound to the same letters, in classic Latin. Without any vowel markers to assure the sounds between the letters, one can only make an educated guess. But let me substantiate my choice. The similarity of the names YHVH and Judah, I believe, is not coincidental. Actually, in Hebrew, the only difference is the added dalet, which creates the 'd' sound. (Phonetically, in Hebrew, the name Judah is actually pronounced, "Ye-hoo-dah" as there is no 'j' sound in Hebrew.) Visually compared, they appear as hwhy and hdwhy respectively. If you just remove the 'd' sound from Yehudah, you get Yehuwah, basically speaking.

The familiar name Jehovah, as supported by the same name's "Witnesses," as well as many popular translations of Scripture, is merely JHVH with speculative vowels drawn from the title 'Adonai'. As thoughtful an attempt as that is, considering the history of the letter 'J', it can't possibly be right; even if it is close. In our endeavors to remain authentic and accurate, we should at least stay in the realm of possible. All this is easy to confirm.

The only reason any name's accurate pronunciation would have such debate over it, especially ones that belong to our Maker, would be if it was once known but had been lost or hidden. The exact way to pronounce YHVH will be debatable until it is spoken again by the King Himself (and it will be), and that's really okay.

I'm going to ask you to *feel* a little bit now. Let me reason with your heart. Do you introduce yourself as "Person" when meeting someone new? Aren't you impressed when someone, whom you have not seen in a while, remembers your name? Your name is a major part of your identity; and sometimes, in correspondence, just one letter change makes a difference. Yet, depending on the body of the letter, you can know for sure if it's for you. We are unique in creation in that we name ourselves. I believe that to be divinely intended, and part of our being made in His image. Practically every name in Hebrew has a particular meaning, unlike the meanings that are often concocted in name books. Therefore, being that the ancient peoples of Scripture did not have the practice of last names, if you change the first name, one becomes further less identifiable. That is, until their name is attached to their lineage. Being that our Elohiym has no lineage, it is His attributes that act on that behalf, and attributes are infused into His Name.

Is the Mormon god the same as the Elohiym of Abraham, Isaac and Jacob? Is the god of the Universalists the same G-d as the "One" of the Hebrews? Is the 'Jesus' of the Christadelphians the same one as the Rabbi of the Apostles? Yes, a name does matter. Call it Semitic semantics if you want, but I've never had a closer relationship with someone whose name I did not know, than with someone who I could call by their name. Let me say this: If you consider the title of 'God' hard to use with a stranger, or when bearing witness, try using Adonai or Yeshua instead. Jesus is a cuss word to much of the populace. Although it certainly shows a complete lack of respect and decency when used this way, perhaps you can take some comfort in the fact they have no idea who He is, or that it's not even His accurate name. It's not what His mother called Him. It's not what His disciples called him. He never even heard that word during His lifetime.

Obviously, you can see that in this, I differ from many of my contemporaries. I can understand the original motivation. I can appreciate the concern with holiness. But in so doing, protecting the Name became desolating the Name. Here is a case where attempting to follow a law too extremely, ended up yielding the opposite result of the intent of the same said law…a breaking of His commandment. Ironically, it is with pseudo-sacred, meaningless names that we commonly replace the meaningful name—that is not to be made desolate.

Whatever the exact pronunciation is, it is the intent and desire that at this point will honor Him. It will even put you on a first name basis with the Creator of the universe. But most of all, it will assure no confusion as to which god is being spoken of when dealing with those who call themselves 'believers'. If you absolutely cannot allow yourself to speak it due to concerns with pronunciation, you can just speak the letters: Yod-Hey-V(W)av-Hey. Some of you may have just been introduced to your Elohiym for the very first time. Trust me, your prayer time will really change as you go from talking to "It," to your Abba with a name.

I will say this: There is a risk of going to the extreme and over using the memorial name. This would have the opposite effect of desolation and bring about a disrespectful "commonness". This would greatly offend our Jewish brethren and thicken the wall of partition we have both rewoven. There are "Sacred Name" advocates out there who will go so far as to say that one cannot be saved unless His actual name is called upon. It is not the prevailing thought, and you may never encounter

Who is this G-d?

this teaching. I only bring it to your attention because if this book influences you the way I hope it will, as you're doing your own research it could show up. I do not subscribe to this nonsense. Please use caution when contending with unorthodox orthodoxy.[4]

On the other hand, as mentioned earlier, there are those who say The Name should never be spoken. I consider that position to be on the opposite extreme, for all the aforementioned reasons and sixty-eight hundred-plus verse texts. If the non-use of the name is obviously an evolution of man's doctrine, how can anyone say it is YHVH's intended delight? There is not one verse in all of Scripture that suggests His Name is not to be said. He is not a generic god. Likewise, there is not one prophecy which predicts His Name should disappear. Prophecy actually states we would forget who *we* are—as Israel! I expound on this in the upcoming subsection titled *Identity Crisis*. There are some teaching contemporaries I greatly respect, whose opinions are that if Yeshua and His disciples didn't say it, neither should we. On the surface, that seems a strong argument (their viable argument), being that Yeshua is our example to be duplicated. I would like to respectfully appeal to them and you a different position.

First, the Apostolic Scriptures cover maybe five percent of the "there are not enough volumes in the earth" worth of material that could have been written about Him. Because the sparse snapshots of His life don't portray Him saying it openly, doesn't mean He didn't.

Second, even if Yeshua did use the name, it is perfectly reasonable to assume that due to the era-current tradition to not, it would have been circumlocuted on paper, or just left out of the narratives. The writers of Scripture would have been within reasonable license to avoid writing what may have been spoken. Just as Paul was Greek-mannered with the Greeks, so would Yeshua have been Pharisaic with the elders. (PS, knowing that the pronunciation of "Yahweh" is almost certainly not the original way it was said, by definition, the use of it is in itself is already a type of circumlocution.)

Because it was an era-current tradition to not even pen The Name (for fear the material it was written on would not be respectfully disposed of), and considering those who were writing the Apostolic Scriptures at the time didn't consider their writings to be future, canonical material, they would have thought their letters would eventually perish—taking The Name with them (another potential validation of the alternate interpretation of the third command.) Again, although it is still a current practice, we do know for sure it wasn't always this way.

Thirdly, even if Yeshua didn't use it, it was likely for the same reason He preferred to go by the prophesied Messianic title: "Son of Man," for most of His ministry. If He used The Name too often, too soon, it may very well have gotten Him killed ahead of schedule, for what would have been considered blasphemy. This would be all the more true if Yeshua flagrantly attributed it to Himself.

Fourthly, I believe if He did use it openly and often, it would have very likely caused deeper and horrible divisions within the Judaisms, with tragic ramifications. Certain devout Jews would have avoided fellowshipping with the Hebrew believers immediately. The Hebrew believers would have been excommunicated from the Temple service even sooner. New proselytes, without an understanding of the issues behind The Name yet, would have abused it; profaning it in other's eyes. In the end, The Name would have found itself in the midst of even more controversy than what they were trying to avoid in the first place.

Fifthly, we just don't know that He, or they, didn't. Just because it appears at times He respectfully circumlocuted the name when in the presence of certain officials, and sometimes actually did, does not mean He did not use it ever, or in private. I'll bet anything Yeshua taught His disciples the true, corrected meaning of any questionable commandments (oral or scriptural) during their many, late night campfire chats. And sixthly, there is no way to write the name Yod-Hay-Vav-Hay in Greek! Real respect for the Name would keep one from inadequately transliterating it, possibly causing it to lose its richness and meaning.

As far as the second through fourth arguments I just made go, they are based on a presupposition that the tradition to not say His name was well-established and widespread among the laity at that time. Any written record of such laws did not come onto the scene until at least two hundred years after that period. Such laws would have been self-imposed by the religious leadership, and that mostly within the confines of the Temple city, and neither Yeshua nor His talmudim (disciples/students) would have considered themselves that, nor spent all their time there. Didn't He come to point the way to the Father by removing the yeast of the Pharisees, and all man-made obstacles? Aren't we moderns, who are attempting to be Torah observant doing the same thing, or should be? Man removed His name. He didn't! Why do we choose to succumb to this tradition, when it actually does appear to be conflicting with the original intent of the command? Is it because we don't want to ruffle religious feathers? Like that's something Yeshua never did.

Any faithful, open-eyed Jew of the time was fully aware of the corruption of the Temple authority, and any unscriptural laws created by them would have been disregarded behind their backs anyway. Do you really think that if the U.S. government legislated that Christians could not say the name Jesus, we would abide by that rule, at least in private?

"No-Name" advocates quickly tout that Yeshua taught us to obey the Pharisees, "for they sit in the seat of Moses" and the Pharisees

Who is this G-d?

wouldn't say His name. What they fail to recognize or simply ignore is that in this context the seat of Moses is a reference to presiding over judicial matters. He was not instructing us to do exactly as they do. That should be apparent to all. Are you who tout this also taking upon yourself the whole yolk of the Oral Law? I highly doubt it. And I ask you this: Why do you prefer to obey the traditions of man, than to obey the commandment of YHVH? How anyone can even begin to think He wanted His name silenced or forgotten is just bizarre. By supporting the "No Name" ideology, you are strengthening the same walls Yeshua came to break down! Why don't you build one around Yeshua's name? Is His name so much more inferior, or can that name not be blasphemed?

So, now we get to what I think is the bigger point of this issue. It is well-understood that in Scripture, the phrase "The Name" is often synonymous with representing His divine character or reputation. The Hebrew word *shem* (name), is the root from where HaShem (The Name) is derived. The only way we can determine whether or not that usage is to be applied in Scripture is solely by context, and is quite subjective. Is it possible for this alternative meaning to be the correct one, for the third commandment as well? "You shall not allow the shem (character) of your God to be desolated, ruined or destroyed." I'm not suggesting that is how it should be interpreted definitively; but as you can see, it does work. It works quite well in fact. And, it even supports the avoidance of attaching it to oaths. It is my contention that this is the higher imperative, but that it does not negate the other.

"HaShem" is the preferred circumlocution within the majority of Judaism. In common usage, it parallels Christianity's usage of God, as a generalized replacement. I have no problem with it as a substitution for the title "God". As a matter of fact, based on the definitions previously shown for "god," I greatly prefer it. My problem lies squarely on its primary usage as a replacement for His memorial name.

I believe desolation can be done a number of ways, only one of which, although extremely significant, is keeping it unspoken. As a matter of fact, there are very interesting narratives in Scripture where it appears quite likely Yeshua did use the Name, or at least its less formal variant, and pertaining to Himself no less. Notably, the incidences take place toward the very end of His ministry. Here is one reason why, as seen through this reaction:

Then the high priest tore his robes and said, 'He has blasphemed! What further need do we have of witnesses? Behold, you have now heard the blasphemy.' (Matthew 26:25)

Why is this such a big deal? After all, it seems like people rent their garments all the time.

The priest who is the highest among his brothers, on whose head the anointing oil has been poured and who has been consecrated to wear the garments, <u>shall not</u> uncover his head nor <u>tear his clothes</u>. (Leviticus 21:10)

Ordinary priests and people did, but not the High Priest! It came about later on (Oral Law) that the Kohen ha'Gadol could only tear his garments upon hearing blasphemy. Let's now look at the "blasphemy".

But He kept silent and did not answer. Again, the high priest was questioning Him, and saying to Him, 'Are You the Christ, the Son of the Blessed One?' And Jesus said, '**I am**; and you shall see THE SON OF MAN SITTING AT THE RIGHT HAND OF POWER, and COMING WITH THE CLOUDS OF HEAVEN.' (Mark 14:61 & 62)

When you look at the words "I am," on the surface, it appears to just be an answer to the High Priest's question; but there may be more here. The Scriptures we have are in Greek. So, based on linguistics alone, it would not be appropriate to definitively state that Yeshua actually said, "Hayah" (Hebrew for: I am). However, He could have simply answered, '*yes*', which would have been rendered in the Greek, 'nai'. But He didn't. He answered, "I am," which in the Greek is 'eimi'. It would, however, be appropriate to assume Yeshua was speaking either Aramaic or Hebrew, to a Hebrew priesthood/court. It's actually a bit silly to argue they were speaking Greek. So, 'hayah' (subtly meaning: the Yah) is more likely what He responded with. Then, He followed it up with an attributed comment, found in the book of Daniel.

It is also interesting to note that this same answer dropped soldiers to the ground, as if dead, when they went to arrest Him at Gethsemane. It took Yeshua's resuscitating touch to restore them to upright. People can think what they will, but I believe in both of these circumstances the "I AM" form of the Name was used, and it obviously caused a real ruckus. You'll see why in just a bit. Since Yeshua was by no means the only person to ever claim to be the Messiah (as there were false leaders back then as often as there are today), there must be more to Yeshua's declaration that riled the religious leaders. After all, they didn't go killing every false messiah that came around, as expressed in Acts chapter five, by Gamaliel's consideration on the Apostles' activities. To the Jew, the Messiah was going to be a king...not the Mighty One Himself. So it was not a capital offense to call oneself a king. There is no doubt in my mind that whatever "blasphemy" Yeshua said here, was more than a "Messianic" claim. And there is yet another possible time.

Who is this G-d?

David prophesied of the coming Messiah, and in several profound ways, foreshadowed Him. One of David's writings gave a declaration that He would "come in the name of the LORD." (Psalm 118:26) Curiously, it is this very declaration that was made as Yeshua rode into Jerusalem on a colt, for the Passover:

The crowds going ahead of Him, and those who followed, were shouting, 'Hosanna to the Son of David; BLESSED IS HE WHO COMES IN THE NAME OF THE LORD; Hosanna in the highest!' (Matthew 21:9)

I am about to share something profound to you (at least I think so), so pay close attention. When David wrote that passage down, he used the name YHVH, not the title 'kurios', as it reads from the Greek. I am pretty confident that when the Jewish followers of Yeshua were praising and acknowledging Him upon His famous entry, they were not using the word *kurios*. If they truly thought Yeshua was the Messiah, it would have been perfectly appropriate to use The Name there. That's not the profound part though.

When Yeshua was weeping over Jerusalem, He made this statement:

For I say to you, from now on you will not see Me until you say, 'BLESSED IS HE WHO COMES IN THE NAME OF THE LORD!' (Matthew 23:39)

What do you think His word choice for 'LORD' was there? Was it a Greek word? I highly doubt it. He was reverting back to and quoting directly from David's statement again. And most anyone who heard either one of these declarations knew exactly from where that saying came; and that David, in the original language, uses the name YHVH. (I wonder why it was all right for him to use, being a man after His own heart.) But that's still not the really profound thing.

Yeshua's statement in Matthew 23:39 is actually a prophecy. It is a forward looking statement from the mouth of Israel's Messiah. This statement was a direct reference to when Yeshua would finally be known as who He is, by the Jewish community. It turns out, that just like at that acknowledgment made during that previous Passover, it will be at a future Tabernacles—when the ingathering of all Israel finally is accomplished—that they truly recognize the One they pierced. Now that's profound! Oh those silly, archaic, *Jewish* holidays.

And now there's yet another possibility. This one nobody can dispute, because nobody was there to witness it. We have to assume Yeshua, at a later date, described this happening to His disciples, and it was written into the gospels because of its significance.

When Yeshua was being tested in the desert, He responded to HaSatan's third challenge with these words: "It is said, 'YOU SHALL NOT PUT THE LORD YOUR GOD TO THE TEST.'" This is a direct reference to Deuteronomy 6:16. That verse clearly says, "Do not test YHVH your Elohiym!" Do you really think Yeshua spoke Greek to HaSatan, or 'circumlocuted' The Name by the use of 'HaShem'? Do you really? For those of you who do, nothing I use for evidences will be sufficient, and the last fifteen pages have been a waste of paper. I have made as strong a case as can be made for not cowering to false religious doctrine (which is what I believe it comes down to.) So I will now move to speaking to those of you, who do not.

I believe that using His name in your personal prayer life is empowering. I do believe it should be written minimally, and with discretion, as to give it life, but not to make it common—like on bumper stickers. Small groups that are on the same page may use it respectfully within their settings. We should avoid flippantly using it in mixed company that is not educated in this regard, as they may presumptuously take up the Name and abuse it, or the name may be shunned and ridiculed. Let me be frank, if you know you are in Jewish company, you would be insensitive and rude to use The Name without first hearing them say it, which you likely won't. Likewise, there are overly sensitive people to this issue that must be contended with. And please, whatever you do, don't argue about pronunciation.

I would be remiss if I didn't acknowledge that those six previous arguments are just as much not provable, as their counter arguments are not. It would also be unbalanced of me to not express clearly the fact that the Tetragrammaton is not the only name He has declared. He has several names: Holy, Jealous, Redeemer, Savior, Good Shepherd etc. It is more than acceptable to use a different one, if it is most appropriate at the time. I realize the word "God" isn't going anywhere soon. The majority of time, it is understood Who is being spoken of, amongst close-knit communities. But everyone has a god. There is only one YHVH!

Even if there was once a day when the name 'God' struck fear in man, it doesn't anymore. I just don't see its overall benefit. These disregarded truths make the Jewish practice of writing the title 'God' as 'G-D', out of respect, seem a little bit hyper-reverent. Don't be afraid of His Name, just *fear* it. Now that we know *of* Him, let us turn to contemplating *about* Him, by looking a little more closely at this *Hayah* declaration.

Who is this G-d?

To Be or Not to Be

Our Elohiym, although far above our understanding, has not left us with nothing from which to draw some firm-ish conclusions regarding His being. Through the analysis of scriptural detail, we have surmised such things as His Omniscience (all knowing), His Omnipresence (all places at all times) and His Omnipotence (all-powerful). Through His interaction with humanity, we know He is: Loving (Romans 5:5), Kind (Psalm 18:25), Gracious (Exodus 33:19), Patient (2nd Peter 3:9), Merciful (Psalm 86:15), Just (Psalm 89:14), Holy (Revelation 15:4), Creative (Genesis 1 & 2) and it continues on indefinitely. For all these listed reasons, as well as His direct command, we are not to attempt to reproduce Him with any type of man-made construct, for what image is 'Patient'? (Images are discussed further in chapter nine.)

Not only is He all these things, but He represents them in their perfect form. All these things in human form, when held up to His standard, fall short. We most easily confirm this through the recognition that we, being the creation, can never become greater than our Creator. HaSatan found this out in a hurry when he attempted to disprove this fact. We will fall under the same judgment if we attempt the same. If He is always exponentially greater than we, and we cannot surpass our Master (or we then become the master), it would be a wise discernment to accept that knowing the most we can about Him still leaves us terribly simple.

How you perceive Him directly affects every part of your life. It governs from how you treat others, to how to treat yourself. It influences the way you think, act and reason. But most of all, it controls how you interact with, fear, revere, and respond to the words of Adonai Himself. It is much like how these very same effects are shaped, by your assessment of, and relationship with your earthly father. How much you respect (or fear), is how much you obey. As wise as you think His council is, is how much you listen. To the degree you enjoy his person, will you spend your limited, available time with him. The biggest factor in the quality of your relationship will ultimately be how much you know him.

How much have we spent of our prayer times making these requests: We want to know you more. Reveal yourself to us. We want to see your face. Show us your glory. Show us your power. Come be with us. Inhabit our praise, and so forth. All these pleadings are just various ways of saying the same thing. We want to better comprehend the incomprehensible, and why wouldn't we? If He is our all-in-all, then it stands to reason that the more we can know and understand Him, the more we can know and understand ourselves. This is both true and positive. But here lies the problem: When looking at ourselves to try to understand Him, we are capable of drawing conclusions that are very different from an appropriate equivalent. This, unfortunately, is when many people allow their imaginations to rule their reasoning. Then… ta-dah! We have conceived an idol. This is false and negative.

When contemplating our Mighty One, there are some key things that need to be considered at all times:

The heart is deceitful above all things, and it is exceedingly corrupt: who can know it? (Jeremiah 17:9)
And He was saying to them, 'To you has been given the mystery of the kingdom of God, but those who are outside get everything in parables.' (Mark 4:11)
And in the greatness of Your excellence You overthrow those who rise up against You; You send forth Your burning anger, *and* it consumes them as chaff. (Exodus 15:7)
For the LORD your God is the God of gods and the Lord of lords, the great, the mighty, and the awesome God who does not show partiality nor take a bribe. (Deuteronomy 10:17)
Out of the north cometh golden splendour, about God is terrible majesty. (Job 37:22)
The Almighty, whom we cannot find out, is excellent in power, yet to judgment and plenteous justice He doeth no violence. (Job 37:23)
Your way, O God, is holy; what god is great like our God? (Psalm 77:13)
For My thoughts are not your thoughts; nor are your ways My ways, declares the LORD. (Isaiah 55:8)
Such knowledge is too wonderful for me; too high, I cannot attain unto it. (Psalm 139:6)

It's the top and bottom verses that really hold together this textual sandwich. As yummy as the meat in-between is, these verses must be consumed within these two slices of Bread. Granted, as we mature in our faith, we gain better control over our carnal nature. Yet we must remain vigilant in our fight to not let pride cause us to forget that these verses will always remain true; or we'll get toasted.

There are some things that He has said about Himself that are quite telling and allow for some great meditation and conversation. Let's explore the self-description/identification He gave to Moshe when he inquired of Him as to who he should say has sent him?

God said to Moses, 'I AM WHO I AM'; and He said, 'Thus you shall say to the sons of Israel, I AM has sent me to you.' (Exodus 3:14)

This very popular verse is unbelievably deep in its theological and philosophical richness. I would venture to guess, that a whole book could probably be written, dwelling solely on what's contained in these few,

Who is this G-d?

short words. Here is the text as it appears in modern, Hebrew translations:

ויאמר אלהים אל־משה [אהיה אשר אהיה] ויאמ
כה תאמר לבני ישראל אהיה שלחני אליכם:

Although the original paleo-Hebrew would look a lot different, this is what has been passed down to us, and we have no reason to believe there is any flaw within this text. If there was ever a sequence of letters that the scribes of all generations would have taken the utmost care to keep accurate, this would be it.

I have placed brackets around the words that are translated traditionally as, "I AM THAT I AM." The Hebrew transliteration into English is Ehyeh-Asher-Ehyeh. No one but our Elohiym Himself could have come up with a phrase that on the surface seems to say so little, and yet actually says so much. The root verb in 'Ehyeh' is 'yah', meaning 'be'. Yeh is the present (perfect) tense of yah, from where we get the 'am/is'. As an aside, in the Hebrew language the word 'yeh' (am) is thought sacred enough to warrant being left out of every day, conversational language. An example of this would be instead of saying, "I am hungry," what is actually said is, "I hungry."

The reason for this is really the heart of this section. There is nothing that can make this claim of 'being', in its sense of existing under its own power, other than He. For something to 'be', in the truest sense of the word, suggests it always 'has been' and has 'no end' in sight. YHVH simply 'IS'! Thus the construct of His Memorial Name! "Who was, and is, and is to come" is potentially a fuller expression of the verb in its past, present and future tenses. Anybody recognize that from somewhere else? Yeshua was declaring Himself the "I Am". Yeshua cannot be just another good prophet then, can He? This is supported by the sometimes translated, more accurate variance of the verse: "I WILL BE THAT WHICH I WILL BE." (Those three tense terms don't actually exist in the Hebrew language. I am imputing modern English grammatical variants to the verse text.) Ideologically, it is both arrogant and inaccurate to call ourselves 'human beings'. We 'be' only because He says so; and we only 'be' because He 'IS' has brought us into existence. It may be more humble and revering to refer to ourselves by the term, human-creatures. For we do not 'be', we be-gan; and as creations! And someday, if for but a vapor's momentary life, we end.

Psalm 147:1, "Praise the LORD (Yah)! For it is good to sing praises to our God (Elohiym); for it is pleasant *and* praise is becoming."

Our Yah, from that revelation on, did exactly that. He revealed Himself as a: Being, Artist, Romantic, Architect, Gardener, Care-Taker, Ark, Covenant Partner, Teacher, Consuming Fire, Shepherd, Staff, Healer, Rock, Well-Spring, Commander, Guide through the Night, Guide through the Day, Thunder and Lightning, a Smoking Fire Pot and Flaming Torch, Earth Quaker and Opener, Jealous Bridegroom, Warrior, Poet, Time-Traveler, Carpenter, Peace-Maker, Miracle-Worker, Storm Maker and Calmer, Fisherman, Friend, Sacrificial Lover, Spelunker (a little grave humor), High Priest, Intercessor, Savior, soon to be Judge and things yet to be known—any of which are enough to stagger our minds.

What does all this mean to you? Every different part of who He is, by itself, is an aspect to be considered when you are communing with Him. What do you want to relate to at this moment in your life? What do you need from Him? What part helps you in your fellowship with Him? What are you dealing with? We must be careful not to dwell so much on one particular part of Him, for that would inadvertently shrink Him into something much less than He is. But being able to see the fact that He can be somewhat divided into somewhat comprehendible parts, makes Him the only Elohiym that has even come close to letting us know Him, never-minding the fact that He is the only Living Elohiym there is! Call Him what you may. Know Him as He *be*.

For what great nation is there that has a god so near to it as is the LORD (YHVH) our God (Elohiym) whenever we call on Him? (Deuteronomy 4:7)
Has *any* people heard the voice of Elohiym speaking from the midst of the fire, as you have heard *it,* and survived? Or has a elohiym tried to go to take for himself a nation from within *another* nation by trials, by signs and wonders and by war and by a mighty hand and by an outstretched arm and by great terrors, as YHVH your Elohiym did for you in Egypt before your eyes? To you it was shown that you might know that YHVH, He is Elohiym; there is no other besides Him. (Deuteronomy 4:33-35, Restored)

These words are as unique to religious literature as any could be. Obviously, the Holy Scriptures are unique in many ways, but one of the most significant is that unlike the false prophets of false gods who have walked among men (living as warriors or sorcerers), our text is the only one that dares claim to have the directly recorded words of its Elohiym, as having been audibly spoken to millions of witnesses; not just translated through a self-promoted, human channel that *supposedly* heard them.

For any unbelievers out there, have you ever wondered why, for the thousands of years' worth of history the Tanakh [Acronym for the three dominant writing forms found in the Hebrew Scriptures: Torah, Nevi'im (prophets), Ketuvim (writings)] spans, for every "impossible"

Who is this G-d?

thing that is recorded, there is no mass-written opposition to its authenticity, by period historians or 'concerned citizens' who were around at the supposed event's non-occurrence? Surely, when the "fables" began to spread, someone who knew it didn't happen would have refuted it on papyrus, to be found by later generations. And not just by someone, but by many. Yet, any refutation is done long afterward, by non-witnesses.

Either the Sinai event did take place, or the entire story is the most historically influential, amazing, and unverifiable yet believed and passed down for a thousand generations, load of garbage the planet has ever seen and undoubtedly ever will. When I consider that Judaism, being based fundamentally upon these very events, has stood the test of time as no other religion has, combined with there being no legitimate refutation, it leaves me no place to go but to believe that equates to authenticity. That even more so helps to demonstrate that our Elohiym is the one and only True Elohiym. The one and only to show Himself to His people!

Know therefore today, and take it to your heart, that the LORD, He is God in heaven above and on the earth below; there is no other. (Deuteronomy 4:39)

But He is not the Elohiym of everybody is He?

For this reason You are great, O Lord GOD; for there is none like You, and there is no God besides You, according to all that we have heard with our ears. And what one nation on the earth is like Your people Israel, whom God went to redeem for Himself as a people and to make a name for Himself, and to do a great thing for You and awesome things for Your land, before Your people whom You have redeemed for Yourself from Egypt, *from* nations and their gods? For You have established for Yourself <u>Your people Israel</u> as Your own people **forever**, and You, O LORD, have become their God. (2nd Samuel 7:22-24)

Identity Crisis

The stranger who resides with you <u>shall be to you as the native</u> among you, and you shall love him as yourself, for you were aliens in the land of Egypt; I am the LORD your God. (Leviticus 19:34)

The <u>same law shall apply to the native</u> as to the stranger who sojourns among you. (Exodus 12:49)

In every book of the Tanakh, as in every book of the Apostolic Scriptures, He has revealed Himself primarily not through manifestations, but through spiritual characteristics. The study of the attributes of Yah is well beyond the scope of this work, but is well worth the effort. However, what is an attribute of sorts, which is rarely considered through to its honest conclusion, is that the Elohiym that we deem ours, the One of all the Hebrew Scriptures, is not and never has been known by the title: "El of the Gentiles" (third key). Before you blow a gasket, let me explain this thoroughly.

The word 'gentile' has shifted in its meaning over the centuries, as have the Hebrew terms: 'ger' (resident alien) and 'goy' (foreigner), to now be construed as anyone who is not a Jew, whether a Christian or otherwise. But clearing this up is not that simple. In the Apostolic Scriptures, the word 'gentile' has been used in place of several different, specific words, and here is a list of them and their individual meanings:

akrobustia; *the prepuce, foreskin,* hence *uncircumcision:* - uncircumcised (10), uncircumcised man (1), uncircumcision (8), without being circumcised (1). ethnos; prob. from a prim. root; *a race, a nation,* pl. *the nations* (as distinct from Israel.): - Gentiles (93), nation (30), nations (37), pagans (1), people (2). Hellen; from *G1671; a Greek,* usually a name for a Gentile: - Greek (9), Greeks (17).

So as you see here, the word 'gentile' has been used to replace the words: uncircumcised, nation, pagan, people and Greek. The term is too broad to simply say He is the Elohiym or Theos (Grk.) of the Gentiles. And moreover, not only is it too broad, but upon looking at these specific terms in their context, there are but a few uses that even suggest an affiliation with the "House of El". Here is an example of 'gentile' being used to represent one who is an unbeliever, a.k.a. lost. It comes at the end of Yeshua's teaching on kingdom policy:

If he refuses to listen to them, tell it to the church; and if he refuses to listen even to the church, let him be to you as a Gentile (ethnikos) and a tax collector. (Matthew 18:17)

"The nations," when seen in an *accepted,* or *blessed* scriptural context, is predominantly due to the term being applied in reference to the dispersion of Abraham's offspring into them. The people of various races are only seen in a positive light, when they've accepted the grace that has been given to them by Adonai, to come into the family of faith. Yet, the way they enter is by being branches grafted into the Olive Tree (Romans 11).

"The Uncircumcision," in its narrowest meaning, is a reference to those who have not participated in the sign of that particular Abrahamic covenant. In the broader meaning, this term includes those believers who simply have not yet undergone the procedure (God-fearers; e.g. Cornelius), and pagan citizens of foreign lands.

"The Circumcision" is a term generally applied to Israelites who were initiated into the covenant via circumcision on the eighth day, or proselytes to Judaism who had undergone the procedure and were practicing members of the Judaic religious system. (Acts 10 & 11 show examples of this term used.) There are of course, circumcised males who are not active participants in the Judeo-Christian faith, and therefore their circumcision is meaningless (Romans 2:25). This is fairly equivalent to babies christened at birth, who never embrace the faith of their parents.

It should be noted, that the practice of circumcision was not unique to the Israelites. It was practiced by several other people groups as well. It is actually the eighth day (trauma free), and non-sexual aspects of the Abrahamic sign, that distinguishes it from the others. What is so marvelous about this sign is that Yah's desire for it to be done on the eighth day is a clear indication of how widespread His salvation is intended to be available. An eight-day old child has no capacity to reject the covenant. He wants to place his mark on us at that age, so that we have every opportunity to receive the blessing available to us. What love this is! Also worthy of note, is that the command regarding circumcision was given to Avraham, and "everyone in his household" and all future additions to the family, including "foreigners and slaves". Meaning that circumcision, and its adjoining covenantal values, was available to non-Jews from the very beginning.

What is even more amazing is that even though there is an aggressive move to make circumcision illegal, and the church often teaches that it is an antiquated and unnecessary act (due to a lack of understanding early church religious practice), the vast majority of parents still have the procedure done. You can guise it with a medical excuse if you want, but I think there is a spiritual force that compels us toward it. You probably could guess that I also believe it should still be done on the eighth day, even if it's "inconvenient".

The term "Greek" is generally applied to a native of the land of Greece, but is also a figurative term for all who are outside Israel. There are several verses where it is possible that the usage of this term is being applied to 'foreigners to the covenant'. But in context, the term's usage does not do harm to the intent of the passage in either case. Example:

For I am not ashamed of the gospel, for it is the power of God for salvation to everyone who believes, to the Jew first and also to the Greek. (Romans 1:16)

Before I continue, and you surmise that I'm saying something I'm not, YHVH is the Elohiym of all that is as big as the universe, to what is as small as any man who calls upon His Name. He is the Theos of *some* gentiles, as He is the El of *some* Hebrews (Romans 3:29). In the truest sense, being that He made all of us, He is the "Lord" of all. He will be the

King of anyone who will serve Him. Yet, He will be the Destroyer of all His enemies. I know you are not one of those who reject His authority, so fear not; but what this Scripture is about to state has a lot to say about who is considered His family.

The word of the LORD came again to me (Ezekiel) saying, (16) "And you, son of man, take for yourself one stick and write on it, for Judah and for the sons of Israel, his companions"; then take another stick and write on it, "For Joseph, the stick of Ephraim and all the house of Israel, his companions." (17) Then join them for yourself one to another into one stick, that they may become one in your hand. (18) When the sons of your people speak to you saying, "Will you not declare to us what you mean by these?" (19) say to them, "thus says the Lord GOD, Behold, I will take the stick of Joseph, which is in the hand of Ephraim, and the tribes of Israel, his companions; and I will put them with it, with the stick of Judah, and make them one stick, and they will be one in My hand. (20) The sticks on which you write will be in your hand before their eyes." (21) Say to them, "thus says the Lord GOD, Behold, I will take the sons of Israel from among the nations where they have gone, and I will gather them from every side and bring them into their own land; (22) and I will make them one nation in the land, on the mountains of Israel; and one king will be king for all of them; and they will no longer be two nations and no longer be divided into two kingdoms. (23) They will no longer defile themselves with their idols, or with their detestable things, or with any of their transgressions; but I will deliver them from all their dwelling places in which they have sinned, and will cleanse them. And they will be My people, and I will be their God. (24) My servant David will be king over them, and they will all have one shepherd; and they will walk in My ordinances and keep My statutes and observe them." (Ezekiel 37:15-24)

We are able to know who His family is, by knowing Him. If YHVH is our Elohiym, and being that He has never made a covenant with any other nation besides Israel, where do gentiles fit in? He is the "Elohiym of Israel". He is never, not one single time, called the Elohiym of any other specific nation; e.g. El of Zoar. He is the Elohiym of Jacob, the father of the twelve tribes, all patriarchs in the House of Israel. He never made a covenant with "the church". He never made a follow-up covenant with another race, and every prophecy of the end is in relation to the restoration of the Northern and Southern kingdoms of Israel. So, of which kingdom are you part? Is it Judah and the sons of Israel, his companions? Or, is it Joseph, the stick of Ephraim and all the house of Israel, his companions? Either way, it's Israel!

There are twelve gates which the redeemed can travel through in the New City Jerusalem. They are named after the twelve tribes. There is no gate called "Church". There is no gate called "Lutheran," or even "Protestant". Which gate will you be going through? "My people" always refers to Israel, whether native born, or the companions who sojourn with

Who is this G-d?

her. I'm sure you would like to consider yourself at least a companion, if you are not a direct descendant. So would I. But how do we qualify to be sojourners with them, when we seem to be heading in such different directions? Well, the same and only way we always have. We must be participants in the covenants with Israel!

> *Remember* that you were at that time separate from Christ, excluded from the commonwealth of Israel, and strangers to the covenants of promise, having no hope and without God in the world. (Ephesians 2:12)

If the gentile Ephesians were at one point "separate, excluded and without hope," and as the next verse says are now "brought in by the blood," what are they/we now? We are Citizens in the Commonwealth of Israel, participants in the covenants, and familiar with Elohiym!" You don't get to YHVH except through Messiah, and you don't get the blessings of the covenantal promises, except through the covenants.

Yeshua (as the Word made flesh) is as much the Author of the covenants, as is the Father. You may think you have access to everything as a Christian, but if as a Christian you have embraced the idea that you have replaced Israel as the partner of the covenants, you have access to a lot less than you think. Spiritualizing and allegorizing the literal Israel of Scripture, in order to avoid the theological ramifications, is no less than undermining the will of, and subverting the eternal plans of Adonai. Thinking that your practice of "Christianity" guarantees you'll receive all of the covenant benefits available in this life, is about as foolish as thinking that being circumcised guarantees you eternal life.

> I prayed to the LORD my God and confessed: 'O Lord, you are a great and awesome God! You always fulfill your promises of unfailing love to those who love you and keep your commands.' (Daniel 9:4)
>
> I said, 'I beseech You, O LORD God of heaven, the great and awesome God, who preserves the covenant and loving-kindness for those who love Him and keep His commandments.' (Nehemiah 1:5)

You will never know Him as much as He can be known, unless you embrace the fact that there is no such thing as a citizen of the church, and that the church is not autonomous outside of Israel. Judah is Ephraim's big brother, not the other way around. It is my belief that according to the original scriptural perspective, when one becomes a believer in the Elohiym of Yisrael, one is no longer simply a gentile. One may well be a non-Jew (physically *ethnikos*), but an Israelite...for sure.

Perhaps you are a little uncomfortable with this affiliation, so let's try another angle on this. Father Abraham has many sons. Many sons has father Abraham. I am one of them, and so are you, so...what does that make you? As a matter of fact, what was Abraham? Now that you're thinking of it, what is a Hebrew? First of all, it is not a nationality. Abraham was from Ur. That would make him a Chaldean. There are a couple of theories as to the origin and meaning of the term Hebrew. But the more readily accepted meaning of *evrit* (not quite accurately pronounced: ee-vreet) is "from over there" or, "one who has crossed over." Have you, as a born-again believer, crossed over from anything?

Yacov (Jacob), Avraham's grandson, had a name change. A name change in Scripture is often associated with a life-changing experience with YHVH. He became known as "Yisrael"—yet another word with various opinions on meaning. The two major beliefs are "striven with El" and "prince of El". Regardless, you can't be a child of Abraham, and not be a child of Isaac, the son of promise. If your god is YHVH, you have "crossed over" from death unto life, accepted the promise of the Messiah, and are walking a journey by faith. Yisrael is far more than a piece of land. It is a spiritual ideal. It is an identity. It is composed of Kingdom people. You, my friend, are not only a Hebrew, but are an Israelite; and not just in some ethereal sense. Most don't know that. Many don't accept that. Do you know why? Because it was prophesied to be that way.

The prophet Hosea was told to marry a harlot (representing Yisrael being unfaithful to YHVH). Together they had three sons. The first was called Yizre'el. His name's meaning prophesied the Lord's intention to "scatter" Israel, and dismantle the kingdom. Hosea's second son was named Lo-ruhamah. His name's meaning prophesied the Lord removing His compassion from them. The third son's name was Lo-ammi. His name's meaning prophesied that during their scattering, they would stop being His people, and they would lose their identity. That is exactly what happened. And just so that you don't think this is not related to you, the first chapter ends with a prophecy that this lost group of people would become innumerable, accept YHVH as their El, and join with Judah in the last days, under the authority of one King. It's not much of a challenge deducing who those people might be.

If you want to know Adonai, you also need to discover who you are in relationship to Him. It should come as no surprise that if His standards for holy living have not changed, then the requirements for citizenship in His chosen nation have not either. And, if you think your citizenship has been obtained, then you have become part of the nation; the same nation where He placed His name, where He dwelt, is always watching, and from where He will reside again, reigning over this Earth. So, when in Rome…

You do know that Israel is where we will all be going right? You do realize that Hebrew is the foundational language of the Scriptures, derived from the earliest tongues of the Human race (possibly Akkadian).

Who is this G-d?

There is a very good chance that during the future Messianic era, while residing in Israel, we will all be able to speak it.

For then will I turn to the peoples a pure language, that they may all call upon the name of the LORD, to serve Him with one consent. (Zephaniah 3:9, JPS)

Please note that I am in no way suggesting the Greek Scriptures are to be rejected, or are not inspired. This just undoes the curse of Babel.

I have actually heard people say, "I'm not a citizen of Israel; I'm a citizen of Heaven!" I've also heard, "I'm not grafted into Israel; I'm grafted into Jesus." As witty as those statements sound, where pray-tell is your Heaven going to be? Are you unaware that Heaven is coming down to us, at least for a thousand years? Where is Heaven going to be centered? You got it! Israel, a.k.a. the Promised Land. And New Jerusalem will become the capital of the Universe.

Ezekiel 36:24, "For I will take you (His people) from the nations, gather you from all the lands and bring you into your own land."

Israel is the homeland of all believers. It is your land, as a rightful heir of Abraham. I hope you want to go. It's not going to be America. It won't be reminiscent of Europe, or China, or the Outback. Perhaps familiarizing yourself with your future 'home away from home' is not such a bad idea. It is this land Yehoshua wept over, because of His deep love for it and its people. It is the land that we have been asked to pray for. It is the land Solomon told us to face when we pray nationalistic prayers (1st Kings 8); a concept stolen by Islam. It is the land that if we bless it, He will bless us.

If I forget you, O Jerusalem, May my right hand forget *her skill.* May my tongue cling to the roof of my mouth if I do not remember you; if I do not exalt Jerusalem above my chief joy. (Psalm 137:5 & 6)

I fear there is a great loss suffered when we think of YHVH being a "Christian" God. He is not a Baptist, nor Episcopalian, nor Swedish or Czech. He is YHVH, the Deliverer of the Hebrews, the Elohiym of Abraham, Isaac and Jacob. He is the future coming Judge and King, who will reign from Jerusalem. This is the One you all want to know better, and all this should be kept in mind when you're wondering whom your Elohiym is. "I say then, God has not rejected His people, has He? May it never be!" Remember, you do not support the root, it supports you. Am I saying YHVH is a Hebrew? No. Of course not! (Although He did cross over from deity to humanity.) But He chose them to be the target of His affection, to be the carriers of His oracles, and to be the "Light to the Nations". If they are the 'Chosen', and you have been chosen, you have been chosen with them and through them.

Let me give you one more heads-up. A 'Christian', in the very early ekklesia, was nothing other than a synagogue attending Jew, or proselyte, who had accepted Yeshua as the Messiah that they were already looking forward to. (They had begun to be *called* "Christians," but they did not *practice* "Christianity".) Contrary to the allusion, Christianity is technically not the religion of the Bible. Actually, regardless of popular opinion, relationship has always been the key factor. The Lord never called anyone to join a religion. He expected us to become a citizen. He asks us to trust in Him and accept His kingship, and His Anointed One. That is all! Followers of "The Way" were just part of a sect within greater Judaism, as there were several Judaisms. Christians did not become 'non-Israelites', until Jews began to be persecuted by HaSatan's "Christian" fronts.

As for the assembly, there shall be **one statute** for you and for the alien who sojourns *with you,* a <u>perpetual statute throughout your generations</u>; as you are, so shall the alien be before the LORD. There is to be **one law** and **one ordinance** for you and for the alien who sojourns with you. (Numbers 15:15 & 16)

There is one body and one Spirit, just as also you were called in one hope of your calling; one Lord, **one faith**, one baptism, one God and Father of all who is over all and through all and in all. (Ephesians 4:4-6)

For there is <u>no distinction</u> between Jew and Greek; for the same *Lord* is Lord of all, abounding in riches for **all who call on Him**. (Romans 10:12)

There is <u>neither Jew nor Greek</u>, there is neither slave nor free man, there is neither male nor female; for you are all one in Christ Jesus. And if you belong to Christ, then <u>you are Abraham's descendants, heirs according to promise</u>. (Galatians 3:28 & 29)

These verses say nothing of the termination or divorcing of the covenant people. They have everything to do with the inclusion and qualification of all, for salvation! These are only true in the spiritual realm. Any other interpretation is from the Evil One.

Being an Israelite is not like being a citizen of a communist country. The Kingdom's borders are always open. The Lord is not a ruthless dictator, who'd sooner kill you than let you leave. If you hate America, or our governing system, you can emigrate to some other country you think is more blessed. You can go feed the pigs. If you don't like YHVH's rules of conduct for citizenship, you are free to cross His borders of protection. But you'd be unwise.

Who is this G-d?

Two thousand years ago and beyond, if you didn't want to live under the yolk of possibly being stoned for sinning, you could have moved to the surrounding nations. Nobody put a chain leash on you to remain in the Land. Jews, other tribal members, and the foreigner who joined themselves with them (all summed up as citizens of Israel) subjected themselves to Torah because they loved their King and trusted His ability to rule justly, or they figured the risk/reward ratio was worth remaining, or both. What has so easily ensnared us into thinking we can be citizens of Yah's kingdom, yet be free to break His laws of conduct, or legislate our own replacing alternates?

We all want to know our Abba better. But quite honestly, we want to do it on our own terms, under conditions we approve of, and through the methods we select. We want to be part of His family, but we don't want to be related to our siblings. We want to receive our inheritance, but we don't know the name of the executor. We think Israel is no longer a covenanted nation, but we still have males and females. We all preach, "Live holy!" but we won't let Torah tell us how to be set-apart. We want to be citizens of Heaven, but we don't often concern ourselves with where exactly that will be. Someday you may get a call from someone asking, "How's the weather over there in Paradise?" And to answer, all you'll have to do is look out your window. But instead of floating on clouds with angels, the backdrop may very well be where the Gaza Strip is now.

The Church

Please remember that I'm here to provoke thought, not attack. Some of you will easily understand why I included this, and some may not. Often, it's the most obscure piece of evidence that sways the jury most. Sometimes, it's the motive.

Throughout the Apostolic Scriptures, the English word 'church' is used to replace the Greek word 'ekklesia'. Ekklesia is the word the translators/scribes of the Septuagint felt most closely represented the Hebrew word 'qahal'. A qahal is essentially a "called-out assembly," and it is the description often used for the children of Israel. It is the term used by Stephen to describe all who stood at the base of Sinai (Acts 7:38). It is used all throughout the Tanakh.

The word 'church' is most often accepted as being derived from the Old English word 'cirice', which itself is thought to have evolved from the Greek word 'kuriokos' (minus a step or two), which literally means "of the Lord (Kurios)." Still other dictionaries and commentaries suggest that the word *church* is derived from the Teutonic *kirk or kirche* (Scottish and German respectively, from the ancient Greek 'Kuriakon', which still are in current use.)

However, there is also evidence for a differing etymology. The word *kirke* is more ancient than Christianity's influence on the English language, and was possibly derived from the name of the ancient Greek sun-goddess Circe, daughter of Helios (the Sun), whose priests and priestesses gathered in a "circle" to worship her. (Her name being a possible origin of the word circle.) Interesting, but too far removed from today's meaning of church to be significant in that regard.

When Tyndale produced the first English translation of the Bible, he correctly translated the word *ekklesia* as "assembly". However, when King James commissioned the 1611 translation, he deemed it more appropriate to translate the word using the term common within the Roman religion. That tradition has continued to be followed by modern translators, without regard to the actual meaning of the word *ekklesia*.

The synagogue was the place both believing (Messianic) and non-believing Israelites and proselytes met for worship, study and societal business. A synagogue is simply an "assembling of people". In modern terms, it most closely represents the words: congregation, and/or fellowship. It was originally a neutral Greek term, until the need for Christians to distance themselves from all things Jewish was too strong a force, and they needed a differentiation through classification. Interestingly, Christianity has chosen to retain using the Greek in the derived term "Pentecostals," instead of using the phrase "Fiftieth Day People".

We are all familiar with the phrase, "The church is not a building. It is the people!" The "people" (both Jew and otherwise) are the "called out assembly," a.k.a. the "Body," and the "Olive Tree" (with Yeshua as the root). Eventually, the church became the building non-Jews meet in. Messianic Jews are often careful to designate their locations as synagogues, to help differentiate themselves from Christian churches. Also ironically, though many believe the church began "in the upper room" and was a new institution, it is the exact opposite! Nowhere in all of Scripture does Jesus create or promote a separate group of followers called "the Church" that was intended to exist as an island outside of Israel. He acknowledged there were "....other sheep, not of the same fold" but they were supposed to be "brought in" and made into "one fold" (John 10:16). In many churches, you can be *ethnically* Jewish (can't undo that) as long as it doesn't promote being *culturally* Jewish. There's little patience for that.

At the Shavuot/Pentecost gathering of Acts 2, three thousand souls were *added* that day. Added to what? A new institution? The qahal, or ekklesia, or church did not 'begin' on that day. Upon Peter's profession, "He would <u>re</u>-build (oikodomeo) His Qahal/Synagogue

Who is this G-d?

(Matthew 16:18)." Check the Greek.

The Messianic "Movement"

There is another area we need to discuss before we move away from this topic. The formal, sectarian title that is recognized to describe those of us who live a life of Torah observance, and believe that Yeshua is the Messiah, is "Messianic Judaism." But like the phrase "New Testament," Messianic Judaism is not a fully descriptive or accurate categorization.

All who believe in Jesus are in some form or another Messianic; but not all are Judaic. Messianic Judaism, in its purest form, is best understood as ethnically Jewish believers in Jesus Christ as the Messiah, who have not rejected Moses' nor departed from their historical, cultural and religious expression or background found within Judaism. In other words, they did not deem it necessary to embrace modern church culture, to authenticate their faith. They are Christians, but not in the religious context of Christianity.

Non-Jewish "Messianics," contrary to what a superficial examination might project, are not Jew "wannabees." (Granted, some may be.) Those who are not very familiar with the messianic expression of faith, when looking from the outside, are understandably confused in this regard. It is true that there are some practitioners that go to varying degrees of extremity, and take upon themselves the broader cultural aspects of Jewry and orthopraxy. Then there are also some who sway far from that, and attempt to disassociate themselves as far from the culture as they can, while endeavoring to maintain a more torah-centric approach. This "one new man" is still a developing adolescent, and its two heads make it a mutation.

A Jew, today, is generally understood to be someone of Israeli descent, possibly from the area of Judea; with direct, genealogical lineage. Initially, biblically, a "Jew" was specifically a tribal member of Yehudah (a Yehudite, if you will). The allotted area of Judah is the commonly understood, physical origin of the Yehudim (pl.); yet, the tribes of Simeon and Benjamin were predominantly absorbed into Judah, and together they spread throughout greater Judea. The other regional tribes went off into dispersion (diaspora) and had, until somewhat recently, been considered indistinguishable. Still, fundamentally, a Jew is a Jew and a non-Jew is a goy (anyone not a Jew). Although naïve, this is also seen as circumcised vs. uncircumcised. Likewise naïve, from a religious perspective, a Jew is someone who practices Judaism, whether through familial inheritance or formal conversion.

The "Hebrew Roots" movement is also a commonly ascribed label. This is perhaps more accurate in some aspects, for a 'Hebrew' (as was just discussed) is not a true, tribal association, but a descriptive term that depicts a person who has "crossed over" from another place. It's the 'movement' part that may be a little shallow, for a 'movement' by definition ceases to be one at every pause, and it assumes a pause. For example: The Protestant Movement is no longer really moving. It is just adapting. In many ways, it isn't even protesting anymore. Actually, it is frequently conforming. I prefer to think of the Messianic proliferation as more a "return", because the end of it will not come until the end of all religion—*religion* being man's manufactured attempts to access YHVH.

What is implicated by being "Messianic" is that a certain someone is identifying with, and is living their life in accordance with (at least some of), both Old and New (a.k.a. Mosaic and Pauline; a.k.a. Hebrew and Greek) sources of instruction, for their expression of faith. Being one myself, by that definition, I seek to blur the devil's demarcation between Judaic and Christian theology. Technically, the only people who qualify to be Messianic Jews are actually...Jews. They have at times, by some, been called "Completed Jews" (a term they don't always appreciate.)We who are non-Jews are all identifiable and known in Scripture as followers of The Way, or God-Fearers. And yet again, Paul says something that makes it not quite that straightforward either.

...but a Jew *is* he who is *so* inwardly, and circumcision *is* of the heart, in spirit, not in letter, of which the praise is not of men, but of God. (Romans 2:29)

This statement has caused a certain sense of justification for non-Jewish followers of The Way, to label themselves "spiritual" Jews. Look, it doesn't really matter. If you want to think of yourself as spiritually Jew*ish*, fine. That is acceptable within boundaries. It is generally understood that the meaning for the word Yehudah (Judah*)* is "praiser of Yah". The term *Jew* is just derived from Yehudi (Judean). Since we all should be "praisers" of Him, the viewpoint is understandable. Just do everyone a favor and don't usurp what rightfully belongs to others, at their expense. The belief that spiritual Jews have replaced covenanted Israel is abominable.

In proper context, Paul was stating that one's Jewish ethnicity and heritage, in and of itself, is not enough to stand on in regards to personal justification; nor is simple outward observance to laws. That's pretty clear. So, for instance, if you see someone in your church wearing a prayer shawl or tzitzioth, (the four tassels (fringes) composed traditionally of white cords, sometimes with a thread of blue), who is not *physically* Jewish, they may not necessarily be trying to be Jewish at all. They may be "spiritual" Israelites/Hebrews/Jews making an effort to obey this

Who is this G-d?

commandment for <u>all</u> Israel:

> The LORD also spoke to Moses, saying, 'Speak to the sons of Israel, and tell them that they shall make for themselves tassels (tzitzioth) on the corners of their garments <u>throughout their generations</u>, and that they shall put on the tassel of each corner a cord of blue. It shall be a tassel for you to look at and remember all the commandments of the LORD, so as to do them and not follow after your own heart and your own eyes, after which you played the harlot, <u>so that you may remember to do all My commandments and be holy</u> to your God.' (Numbers 15:37-40)

Externals

I'm really going to step into it now. Those in my corner of the camp aren't really going to appreciate my coming into their tent—if you know what I mean. I guess I'm kind of an equal opportunity offender. My mishpocha, know that I love you. Just let me get this out.

The sometimes valid argument for "wannabee" status gains more credence when a non-Jew takes further steps to honor certain commandments (some written; some oral) through Jewish or cultural methods (i.e., the wearing of a tallit, or prayer shawl) than is required.

The **tallit** (tah-leet) is an ornate, traditional, Jewish, religious garment which was designed to enable the continuing observance of wearing **tzitzioth** (tzit-tzee-ote) within cultures whose clothing does not regularly involve four corners. It is not required through the specific wording of the written commandments, but it is certainly interwoven with plenty of religious meaning. Originally, they were simply added to the bottom four corners of the common garment of the day, which was very similar to a tunic.

If you're not Jewish, and it's your persuasion to don them during worship, you should not be judged by anyone for that. Just as long as you understand, it is an ethnic and religious *tradition*. Does that make it wrong for non-Jews to wear? Well, not exactly. But, just like the challenges that pigment-enhanced people marrying pigment-deficient people face, even in this modern day, those who take upon themselves ethnic associations have to be willing to contend with the prejudices that may come with them. To some, that heat is deemed persecution for the Name. That notion is of course, rather speculative. A traditional church setting may not be the best place for them, and may actually do harm.

The commandment to wear tzitzioth was a gracious institution by Adonai, not coincidentally given directly after the Israelite community had to stone to death a man who rejected Sabbath observance. Apparently, God wanted this to be a one-time offense. The little representation of tekhelet (blue) in the tassel was intended to connect each Israelite to the priesthood, who wore more tekhelet in their garments also, that tied the priesthood to the Tabernacle that had a lot of tekhelet in its curtains, and kept them accountable to the high standards of holiness affiliated with being a "kingdom of priests".

The tzitzioth could be likened to the Hebraic version of a WWJD bracelet. By being worn on the four corners, no matter which way they turned or traveled, the Torah went before them to keep straight their paths. In this case, however, one might say it's more of a WDJD. Yes, He wore them! He was, after all, a Torah observant Jew. Some Hebrew-roots Christians, in an effort to be like Yeshua, are again wearing tzitzioth.

According to the original commandment given through Moses, the tassels must contain at least one thread of blue. Certainly, garment styles have changed over the centuries. The period common garment was something akin to a tunic, which already had four corners; so adding tzitzioth was a simple modification. From the wording of the commandment, the sages have implied that 4 corners should always be involved. Once tunics were no longer vogue, to be able to fulfill the commandment on a daily basis, a garment called a tallit katan was created. It is essentially an unornate, thin rectangle with a cut-out for passing over the head. Judaism later developed certain tassel regulations regarding their length, design, strand count and knot patterns, and use gematria (numerical values) to weave certain meanings (and His Name) into them.

Today, most non-orthodox Jews have opted (due to their own inclinations) to generally neglect the commandment of tzitzioth. If they are fairly religious, they may wear a tallit while they are in the synagogue. Although that's pious, (and to be fair, the Lord didn't specify how often they must be worn), I am forced to question how that helps remind them to keep the commandments throughout the week. I liken that to Christians wearing WWJD bracelets on Sundays only, and only in church. After all, temptation is overwhelming there? And by the way, it was very likely the tzitzit (tzit-tzit; sing.) of Jesus's garment that the woman with the issue of blood reached out and touched to receive her healing (Luke 8:44; hem; kraspedon; G2899, fringe/tassel).

To non-Jews who wear tzitzioth daily, outside a congregational setting, you should attempt to not make a spectacle of yourself, lest you be ensnared into the religious pride of the Pharisees. Or even worse, think of yourself more highly than gentile Christians. Don't try to make Judah jealous, all the while making yourself look silly. It is my *opinion* that you should wear a tallit katan, and preferably tucked in. I also *opine* that your thread of blue should be authentic tekhelet, avoiding multi-colored, fashionable varieties (as per the commandment.) Just ask yourself whether you are still connecting a bridge, or further distancing yourself?

Who is this G-d?

So here's a challenge: Which covenant is the command to wear tzitzioth part of? Hint: It wasn't spoken from the mountain. Answer: None! It was given separately, for the purpose of directing Israel's thoughts to their covenantal obligation. Might we still have some "obligations", even if we don't like to associate them with Laws? Do Christians not wear them (anymore) because one day they discovered Moses declared the rule? Maybe it's because we don't need any reminding. Perhaps it's because it's now a "Jewish" thing (albeit only 10% or so of those who received the commandment were Yehudim.)

A **kippah/yarmulke** (yamaka; the small, round head-covering) is of the same nature, but carries a tad more controversy. In this case, however, there is actually no scriptural commandment for it. It is derived predominantly from talmudic teaching (Shabbat 156b and Kiddushin 32a). According to the popular *Jewish Book of Why*, the yarmulke "serves a more parochial need: to remind the Jew of his Jewishness."[2] Most observing Jews wear them for the sake of *yirat Shama'yim* (reverence of Heaven /God); for He is always "above". Many Messianic non-Jews who wear them are courteously trying to blend into Jewish culture. For others, it is an attempt to make Judah jealous (Romans 10:19). Again, if a non-Jew has a personal compulsion to wear them, they are free to do so without condemnation. They should just be fully aware of their own reasoning.

The kippah is seen as a symbol of Jewish national identity, as well as a statement of submission to God and His commandments. If an ethnic Jew wants to identify him or herself as such, by this means, who can argue? But for a non-Jew, or as a religious practice, it is of little value as far as the Lord is concerned. He didn't ask us to put anything religious on our heads (except for the Levites during service), so it's completely of manmade origin. He did command all the sons of Israel to wear tzitzioth! Why many Jews seem to prefer this tradition to the Lord's instruction, is a question with no good answer. (Disagreements over the exact shade of 'tekhelet' (blue) or the precise, original dye process is not a valid excuse.)

A kippah is technically not a veil, so it is not contrary to the natural order. It is, in essence, a barrier from God's direct radiance; I suppose. The current, messianic practice of women covering their head with a scarf or wrap, as supported by Paul, is not inappropriate; for it is just a continuing demonstration of their recognition of propriety. He taught that it was only required during times of prayer and religious instruction, but in many communities it has developed into a lifestyle. In Hebrew culture, as well as in middle-eastern societies, a woman's hair was/is her seductive lure. Long, let down hair was a sign of a loose or defiled woman (Numbers 5:18). Binding and/or covering differentiated observant and/or married Hebrew women from worldly women; for again, they both have a natural covering (long hair). Obviously, during religious gatherings, it would be appropriate for women to avoid bringing attention to themselves. It was really no different from women avoiding wearing mini-skirts, or low-cut shirts to church today.

The **head-covering** practice is not exclusively Jewish, and is found in various other religious circles as well. The size, color, material and shape of them may also represent specific religious affiliations— ranging from the Muslim 'doppa', to the kabalistic 'kufi'. Traditionally, kippot (pl.) they were only worn by men. Women, as of late, have begun to wear them, in keeping with the movement towards equality and liberation. As a female non-Jew, wearing a kippah is a big stretch, and possibly well on its way to impropriety. It is arguable that this is inappropriate within a Torah observant society, for it is commanded that women are not to dress like men and vice-versa (Deuteronomy 22:5)— which is a good lead into the next controversial item in question.

Paul taught as though, in his day, it was understood that a head covering was a symbol of submission. For this reason, men *were not* to grow their hair long (except during a Nazarite vow), for it is not "natural" and may be a "disgrace" (1st Corinthians 11:15). Women *were* to grow out their hair for this reason, for they should "have a symbol of authority on their head (11:10)." He also taught that men should *not* veil (katakalupto; as to hide under) their head (11:7), which has a different meaning than the word used for 'covering' in 11:15:

"But if a woman has long hair, it is a glory to her. For her hair is given to her for a covering (peribolaion; as a protecting cloak)."

Head covering was (and is) both a sociological and spiritual act. In ancient times, it was also very practical, and still is in many desert regions. Today, women who choose to wear some form of head covering while congregated, generally do so for noble reasons. It may not be culturally American or overly practical anymore, but it still demonstrates a few things. First and foremost, it shows a high reverence for Adonai's word, even if it is deemed to be culturally unnecessary, and at the risk of mockery. Allow me to further support that statement before your post-modern defenses get built too strongly.

Paul was not teaching in reference to abusive submission (unlike the satanic extremism seen elsewhere); he was teaching congregational administration. Most of the entire first letter to the Corinthians, especially from chapters six to fifteen, was about conduct regarding the believers. It was a letter intended to help immature fellowships consisting of many gentile converts, and not just gentile converts but even orthodox Jews who had accepted Jesus and were partakers in the Spirit's new dispensation. The teachings ranged from: spiritual gift etiquette, to a

Who is this G-d?

woman's speaking liberties, to valuation of people, to defilement issues, marriage, dispute settlement and other topics. Taking that into consideration, head-covering properly falls into a category of conduct.

At the risk of sounding derogative towards the male gender, the practice keeps men's minds off female eligibility, by symbolizing her "covered" status by a man, or her devotedness to the Lord. A woman's hair is the glory of her head, and can be a very attracting part of her. Today, most head-coverings worn by messianic or conservative women, are mostly symbolic and often do not even fully cover their hair. Today, if long, flowing hair was the only temptation men had to contend with, life would be a cake-walk. I think the plunging necklines and short skirts which are the trend today are exponentially worse. Apparently, though, some women are capable of not allowing our current, cultural norms to control their behavior and dress quite modestly. Kudos to them!

So, apparently culture is a negotiable influence after all, and not a dictator. Just because fish is generally not an item on the modern American breakfast menu, doesn't mean we don't have to try and feed the hungry masses anymore. I'm pretty confident that when God's children adopt the standards of their surrounding culture, much of our decline in propriety begins.

Most modern, messianic congregations are fairly small and are composed of people who know each other very well; therefore they know fairly well who is "covered" and who is not. Yet, according to a rather curious verse, there may be certain visitors who do not take that into consideration:

1st Corinthians 11:10, "Therefore the woman ought to have *a symbol of* authority on her head, because of the angels."

The difficulty with this verse is obviously found in the word *angels*. Aggelos is the Greek word used here, and it is definitely related to the spiritual beings we know as angels. Haggios is the word most commonly rendered as saints. Some believe this is a throw-back reference to the idea that angels can be attracted to humans. This idea stems from the folkloric interpretation of the Nephelim mentioned in Genesis chapter six, and embellished in the apocryphal book of Enoch; being the result of fallen angels procreating with humans. It should be noted, there is an available Greek word for demons (fallen angels), but it was not used here.

There are clearly huge, theological ramifications to such a concept, but it is a well-recognized belief within certain Judaisms and other various groups. I personally have not subscribed to it; though it's an entertaining debate. But I also recognize that someone's stated persuasion, or allowance for someone else's persuasion, even if it's in the Bible, doesn't make it condoned by God. Paul was a highly educated Pharisee, and had knowledge of things that go well outside the written Word. So, whether or not such a concern is legitimate, it was worth the cautionary statement. Angels clearly take us beyond basic custom.

The other possible explanation for the angelic concern may lie in the scriptural representation of angels covering themselves in the presence of the Lord (note: Isaiah 6:2). "If angels show their submission with a covering, then so should the ladies," may well be the thought. In addition, since angels are not omniscient nor omnipresent, it may be a symbol for them to readily identify those they should keep a watchful eye on, and minister to, as their purpose is.

For those who regard hair itself as being the adequate covering spoken of here (due to the wording in verse fifteen), you have to overlook the fact that verse six could not then make any sense: "For if a woman does not cover her head, let her also have her hair cut off." You don't cover hair with hair. It was preferable for the women to cut their hair, than to force the man to "pluck out his eye!"

Lastly, but highly worth mentioning, is the fact that Paul closes this conduct-related instruction with: "But if one is inclined to be contentious, we have no other practice, nor have the churches of God (vs. 16)." At this point, it would have been good for Paul to go ahead and offer liberties on this matter, as he is so often championed for in other areas. To Paul, a woman covering their head during prayer and prophecy was as natural as the hair on her head. He apparently foresaw no reason for that practice to cease, and likewise the Spirit did not give him utterance to effect that change.

Again, if you are not Jewish and want to embrace this custom, you are free to do so. I do think they should be worn by non-Jews, when in a Jewish setting that respectfully calls for them. Just realize, when Jewish people see questionably non-Jewish people wearing their tribal affiliations, outside of services, it can potentially create friction and friction is an effective fire-starter. If you think it's a neat opportunity to make Judah jealous, it's not the way. So you might avoid the Judaic symbol printed fabrics for daily wear. I'm sure that debate will continue on.

So what am I really saying here? What's my point? I am simply defending the choice of women who practice this. I likewise considered this practice as "religious" and "old-fashioned" before bothering to actually look into it. Do you, if a woman, have to cover your head? Not for salvation, and obviously not even for acceptance. This is not about oppression. It is not about "keeping the woman down." It is about elevating holiness. It is about restoring the sanctity of marriage, and etiquette in fellowship. At worst, it errs on the side of caution. Ironically, I

Who is this G-d?

find my wife highly attractive when she honors the Lord, and me, with this simple act.

Beards are another common, outward expression of religious affiliation, and not just of Judaism, as current events in the Middle East have made us all too aware. The commonly held application of the instruction found in Leviticus 19 is to have either a complete one or nothing at all. The beard is the glory of a man's face, as the hair is the glory of a woman's head. It is apparently part of the male design, and we who wear them for "religious" reasons, more do so to honor our Creator. Some feel this instruction commands all men to have a beard. Others, like me, interpret the Scripture to be only regulating its shape if one chooses to have one.

The shaping of a beard into certain styles was indicative of certain pagan and tribal affiliations that the Israelites were not to be related with. Separation between the upper corners (side-burns) and bottom creates what we now call a goatee. The goat head with beard have long been considered both satanic and cultic symbols (Leviticus 17:7), and the command to not look like one may be part of the issue; as is much of the context of these instructions (Leviticus 20:23). I'll not go so far as to tell people they cannot have them, because goat idols are not a real problem today, and there is a lack of surety as to the exact meaning of the instruction. But personally, I choose not to take the chance. The long, side-burn tendrils (payoth) that the Hasidic Jews are readily recognized by come as a result of their over-application of this instruction. The squaring off of the bottom of a beard is a style often portrayed on Greco-Roman god figures, and was often done by humans who thought that highly of themselves.

I hope the reason I am bringing these topics up is becoming obvious to you. It is an attempt to break down the false presumption, and possible deterrence, the lack of understanding these things create. When a proper identity is established, the second chapter of Romans can then, and only then, be properly negotiated. Otherwise, it is read with prejudice. The same is exceptionally true for chapters nine, ten and eleven.

Messianic types are often lumped into a generalized, pseudo-Jew pile of "weaker brethren", by the disassociated church community. However, that is far from the truth. The caliber of apologists and their associated scholarly material, respectability of persons, and former denominational leaders who are coming to terms with the truths associated with Messianic theology is impressive; and only continues to gain momentum. The majority are not trying to be Jewish; they are trying to be scriptural!

Our El is a "rewarder of those who diligently seek Him." How does one seek Him? In His Word! What's in His Word? What would be the reward? Yes, *He* is our very Great Reward, but so are the covenant promises. You can't have the promises though, without the covenants. Study the covenants. Honor them. Secret revealed.

A healthy relationship with earthly parents comes through fear (reverence) and obedience. A healthy relationship with your heavenly Parent comes through the same channels. Studying to show yourself approved takes work. It is no different from the same work and time required to make any relationship work. Now, to return from my detour.

The Blessing of Affiliation

I would now like to bless you in the way the priests were to bless the Israelites, as found in Numbers 6:24-26:

וִישְׁמְרֶךָ יְהוָה יְשְׁמְרֶךָ

Yivarekhe-kha YHVH v'yeesh-m'rekha.

May YHVH bless you and keep you.

יָאֵר יְהוָה פָּנָיו אֵלֶיךָ וִיחֻנֶּךָ

Ya'er YHVH panav āy-lekha vee-khu-neka.

May YHVH make His face shine upon you and show His favor.

יִשָּׂא יְהוָה פָּנָיו אֵלֶיךָ וְיָשֵׂם לְךָ שָׁלוֹם

Yeesa YHVH panav āy-lekha v'ya-sem l'kha Shalōm.

May YHVH lift up His face toward you and give you peace.

Numbers 6:27, "So they shall <u>invoke **My name**</u> on the sons of Israel, and <u>I *then* will bless them</u>."

Okay, I can't let it go. There it is again, in the original text and in no uncertain terms. Yet, although this blessing is still spoken constantly within the Jewish community, they remove His name from it, substitute it with HaShem, and therefore remove His name from the sons of Israel. This verse is not suggesting His *character* be "invoked". Nowhere does it say the Aaronic blessing should be done only once per year. It's really a shame. But in case there is still doubt in your heart as to whether it is appropriate to use His name, I offer you this:

Who is this G-d?

Behold, *the* days are coming, declares the LORD, When I will raise up for David a righteous Branch; and He will reign as king and act wisely, and do justice and righteousness in the land. In His days Judah will be saved, And Israel will dwell securely; and this is His name by which He will be called, 'The LORD (YHVH) our righteousness.' (Jeremiah 23:5 & 6)

No one in his or her right mind would argue this text is not speaking of the Messiah. So, along with our ingathering, and along with our perfecting, all mankind will finally acknowledge Yeshua as who He really is and call upon Him accordingly. And of course, yet again, the "He" in that verse is not there in the original text, but was an assumed addition, by scribes. The "He," however, is traditionally understood to be referring to the land itself. Well, they had to come up with something to avoid the deifying implications. Funny thing is, when Jeremiah declared this again, he apparently confused his genders and called *it* a *she*:

In those days and at that time I will cause a righteous Branch of David to spring forth; and He shall execute justice and righteousness on the earth. In those days, Judah will be saved and Jerusalem will dwell in safety, and this is *the name* by which <u>she</u> will be called: the LORD is our righteousness. (Jeremiah 33:15 & 16)

Shockingly, the gender specific 'she' is not in the original text either. So is it Israel that will be called, or Jerusalem that will be called "YHVH our Righteousness"? It is clearly neither, as these verses are most definitely referring to the Messiah. How sad.

So, as we end this chapter, and more specifically this subject, I need you to consider a fundamental concept. It is very likely you have never even thought about this before, seen in this light. Are you a Christian? Are you a citizen of the greater Israel? Or, are you perhaps both? How you answer these will have wide-ranging ramifications. Is that promise in Jeremiah for you?

Subjectively, there is no wrong answer; because you are what *you see* yourself as. But I believe there is only one right answer, and that a whole lot more is depending on what *He sees* you as.

Psalm 8:1, "O YHVH, our Adonai, how majestic is Your name in all the earth, who have displayed Your splendor above the heavens!"

The next chapter's subject is also of great importance. I ask that you would be careful to not take things beyond their intended meaning, or misconstrue the intent. The difficulty with dealing with subject matters such as these, is that you will probably never hear it taught from a pulpit (all of it anyway), and that inevitably carries with it a conception that it must be wrong. You will discover the reason for its silence is quite apparent. It is not a very self-serving teaching.

This surgery can prove very effective, but the instruments to perform it can also be used abusively. Even if something is found to be true, we need to be sensitive and merciful when we contemplate how to apply the science. I believe the skills must be self-discovered and instituted for them to be effective. When the Spirit touches the hearts of His leaders in these areas, the results can have a truly beautiful side-effect. But when the understanding is shaped into a 2" x 4", and swung around indiscriminately, it makes for a terrible operation.

I believe these subjects are necessary to be examined, but no one individual should appoint himself or herself to Chief of Medicine, or demand the immediate resignation of their interns. Once the 'whys' are understood, the 'hows' must be prayerfully considered.

Like much of what you will read as this book goes on, not everything pertains to everybody directly; but it may very well do so indirectly. Some words are for the laity, and some are more poignant for the leadership. Remember how I told you in the very beginning I will be administering at times "strong medicine"? Well, down the hatch!

Who is this G-d?

8

Body Parts

I really am compelled to see the Body of Messiah in peak physical condition. To enable that, we must train (discipline) the spiritual strengths inside of us. An unhealthy focus on certain muscle groups will deform us. Inadequate use will cause atrophy. Like all new exercise routines, we should seek proper medical advice before we begin. In this case, we will consult the Great Physician's Journal.

One of His most promising interns was Sha'ul the Pharisee, MD. He became a very articulate and detail-oriented surgeon, with a pretty good bedside manner. As a graduate of Professor Gamaliel's School of Advanced Internal Medicine, he was exceptionally versed in O-R protocols, and in administrative procedure. Because of his credentials, he was asked to do some traveling, and set up satellite practices. Taking all his knowledge with him, he did not forget the gift that his insight was, and offered free lectures wherever he went. There were times when his reputation was challenged, but his wisdom supported his skill level.

As an expert anatomist, when he heard of a cough or a sneeze coming from one of his patients, he was quick to write the necessary prescription. If the patient followed the doctor's orders, the sickness would soon subside. But if they just held on to the prescription, and ignored the recommendations, the sickness would remain and maybe develop even more complications.

Today, we can still go back to those journals of First Century medicine, to glean knowledge as to how to deal with 21st Century maladies. An apple a day then, was as good as one today. In the church, there are no new diseases (Ecclesiastes 1:9). All we are dealing with are new strains of the same old, same old. And though the signs and symptoms are everywhere, either we often refuse to go see the Doctor at all, or we quit taking our meds before the prescription is completed.

We need to go back to biology 101. It would be demeaning of me to make the assumption that you don't understand that a body's systems will fail if its parts are in the wrong place, or are performing the wrong function; so I won't. I am going to, however, state that there are practitioners that know this, and either haven't studied enough to assess certain problems accurately, or simply don't care. In either case, they need someone to MRI their ministries and establish a course of treatment.

For the body is not one member, but many. If the foot says, 'Because I am not a hand, I am not *a part* of the body,' it is not for this reason any the less *a part* of the body. And if the ear says, 'Because I am not an eye, I am not *a part* of the body,' it is not for this reason any the less *a part* of the body. If the whole body were an eye, where would the hearing be? If the whole were hearing, where would the sense of smell be? But now God has placed the members, each one of them, in the body, just as He desired. If they were all one member, where would the body be? (1st Corinthians 12:14-19)

I am going to probe around a bit now, by better defining the roles of the individual members of the Body, as defined by Sha'ul—popularly known as the "Five-Fold" ministry.

I have strong beliefs regarding this topic, as you will soon come to know. In most cases, the teaching will be based on Scriptures that cannot be any clearer. In some instances, Scripture is quieter, and I draw from my own and other's experiences. If you are in the ministry and find yourself taking offense to something, or sense a "check" in your spirit, don't be too quick to go with your gut. It's gotten you into trouble before, and it can do it again (e.g. Inappropriate Bias Syndrome). Take the necessary time, and pray the needed prayers, to see if what is said here is true. It may very well be the diagnosis you didn't want to hear; but, in the end, the prognosis is good.

The Five Medicines

Ephesians 4:11, "And He gave some *as* apostles, and some *as* prophets, and some *as* evangelists, and some *as* pastors and teachers."

There are those out there who will teach that this listing is in a divinely instituted, descending order. I am not sure I fully subscribe to that notion, although the concept is appreciable. In my mind, I see them all as equally valuable and without any one of them, the Body would be severely handicapped.

As far as the Gifts of the Spirit are concerned (1 Corinthians 12), I will concede to there being differing degrees of importance, or perhaps it would be better to look at it as impact, but we still need them all for good health. For those of you who do accept the idea of a divine order, notice how far down the list the pastor is found, in contradiction to how highly they are exalted inside our fellowships. It is grouped together with the teacher, at the end of the list. Are our pastors submitting to the hierarchal order of authority (assuming there is an appropriate one within their denomination), or have evangelists over them to which they are accountable? Are our evangelists submitting to prophets? Enough said for now.

The Apostle

The Apostolic gift is given less specific prerequisite than others are. But in depiction, it is not lacking.

There are those who say that there were only 'The Twelve' well-recognized. There are others, who along with them may allow for a handful of others. And then there are others still, who build their ministries upon their often, self-proclaimed office. Perhaps there is a healthy middle. It has been suggested, that to qualify as an apostle one would have had to, at some point, been either in direct contact with the Master, or under the direct tutelage of one of the original twelve. These guidelines are difficult to support from purely a 'scriptural evidence only' standpoint, although they are portrayed as a dominant factor.

When Judas was being replaced, the protocol for which this was to be done was:

Therefore it is necessary that of the men who have accompanied us all the time that the Lord Jesus went in and out among us—beginning with the baptism of John until the day that He was taken up from us—one of these *must* become a witness with us of His resurrection. (Acts 1:21 & 22)

When Paul was being deliberated over, as to whether he should be accepted into fellowship…

Barnabas took hold of him and brought him to the apostles and described to them how he had seen the Lord on the road, and that He had talked to him, and how at Damascus he had spoken out boldly in the name of Jesus. (Acts 9:27)

In these verses, we see the *essential,* personal interaction with the Master. Saul saw Him, and they spoke to each other.

It has also been suggested that to be considered an apostle, one would have had to have written a canonized epistle. That clearly doesn't work, unless you subscribe to the idea that there has never been another apostle since Jesus's day. This would then become the support for the first twelve and no more ideology. One of the problems that arise with this is in the area of canonization. Barnabas, for instance, is listed among the apostles (Acts 14:14). Yet though he is considered one of the probable writers of the book of Hebrews, it's not confirmed. The earliest epistle which bears his name is also in dispute. Besides him, Paul lists Andronicus and Junias (Romans 16:7) among the apostles, and we have no canonized epistles from them.

Worthy of note is the fact that Matthias (the replacement for Judas), once elected, was never heard from again. He was chosen by lot, and quite possibly not by the Spirit. It was prophesied that Judas should be replaced (Psalm 109:8), but Peter may have ultimately jumped the gun, as Paul may have actually been the one who was to do the replacing.

Another consideration is the New City, whose foundation is *twelve* layers deep, and each layer is representative of one of the twelve. But even that description does not name them individually. It is my personal *opinion* that Paul was Heaven's appointed replacement for Judas. Why there is no thirteenth layer representing all future apostles is obviously because it's only symbolic of the first twelve, and I don't think Judas' name is on one. Therefore, it doesn't help us down the road of surety.

The root of the Greek word *apostolos* means: delegate or ambassador. Since we really should all be considering ourselves active in these roles, it also doesn't give the fullest description. What we know of the apostolic calling, can only be gleaned through the apostolic expression. Here is what Scripture portrays: It appears to be fellowship founding. It seems to act as if it is under its own authority, although it clearly is directed by Adonai. There are signs, wonders and dreams associated with it; and to be frank, it appears to be the only office besides the prophet, through which the power gifts are exampled. Luke 11:49 & Revelation 18:20 actually place them closely together. Not only that, but Scripture words it in such a way as that signs and wonders are validation of the authentic office (2nd Corinthians 12:12). It ministers the gospel. It can bring strong medicine to the Body. It is divinely appointed, and doesn't seem to require a PhD. All summed up, it appears that the apostle carries the other four ministry types within it (1st Timothy 2:7). Because of that, it would seem that this would make it the higher of the group. But like all great things, they come with great sacrifices (1st Corinthians 4:9). All of the original apostles, except for John, died at the hands of an executioner. And since Paul also ended up dying a martyr, we should be slow in declaring how exalted this ministry is. I can almost guarantee that if you want to be an apostle, you are not one. You might want to stop handing out your cards.

The Prophet

I had earlier already mentioned a bit about the role of a prophet in our discussion of false teachers. In Scripture, the dominant characters that carried this calling were the extreme examples of the ministry. The reason they had to be of this nature was due to their critical roles, acting as the mouthpieces and engineers of the divine plan. Adonai was always the architect, but the humans through whom He spoke, rescued, corrected, rebuked, illustrated lessons and encouraged the children of promise, were His prophets. They counseled kings and generals, and they interceded on behalf of nations. Ultimately, the Greatest Prophet would come, and both His words and the words of the preceding oracles would be recorded for future generations to draw from.

Now, having those prophet's words available to search, the office of the prophet has been drastically redesigned. Now, there are two kinds of prophets among us; the one which Adonai sends out to test our hearts to see if we will still obey Him (Deuteronomy 13), and the one who sees the true plan of Adonai and works to keep us on course. Although there is evidence of a 'school of the prophets' seen in the Hebrew Scriptures, we do not see any examples of the graduates becoming part of the story of redemption. It is my opinion that genuine prophets are far and few between, just as in Scripture, because we already have plenty enough direction in the passages of His Holy Word.

There is a gift of prophecy at work in the Body, but it is a gift of admonition and exhortation far more than it is a future-telling gift. This is clearly exposed in Scripture, but not so in the church. Anyone who makes a ministry of traveling around and telling people their future is not to be quickly trusted, if at all. A person who does this must have a history of accuracy (which is hard to verify in most cases), or they are to be rejected. A true prophet is recognized by bringing an encouraging word, or an opportunity to escape judgment, following any correction. Even then, if their words do not line up with what is already known to be true from Scripture, they are to be rejected. Not only should they be rejected, but I also believe a notice should go out to all who may succumb to receiving them into their local fellowships, warning them to avoid their ministry. Wouldn't that just make most "prophet's" careers less "profitable"?

You husband and wife prophelying ministries had better heed Scripture's warnings. YHVH has little patience for people claiming to

Body Parts

speak in His name, but are spewing lies for personal gain. If you do not know, that you know, that you know whether or not what you are about to declare is directly from Him, and going to come to pass, the Body would be much better served if you'd bite off your tongue, walk off the stage and repent. Maybe He will show you mercy (Romans 9:15).

The Evangelist

Then there is the Evangelist. This ministry is considered the 'soul-winning' member of the Body. I don't particularly like that definition very much, because I think it gives the false impression that soul winning is a special calling, and belongs to a certain *kind* of person. Actually, the gifting that the evangelist carries with them is the Spirit-led ability, to perceive the particular message necessary to break through the strong-holds that either an individual or a group may have, that are causing a resistance to repentance.

An evangelist engages in holy warfare over the spirit of man. He speaks life to death, and truth to lies. He recognizes demonic theologies, and tears them apart with deeply felt compassion (as does the teacher.) But make no mistake; it is done with surgical precision. No lost person encountering the evangelist's gift will walk away not having heard a convicting message on the Truth. The blood of the sinner will not be on the evangelist's hands.

But if you think it is *their* job to save a lost and dying world, you are very mistaken. It is each and every one of us, whose responsibility it is, to shine the light of Truth. We should all be ready, in and out of season, to give testimony to the validity and power of the blood of Yehoshua. By definition, I have a very difficult time justifying in my head, how there should be such a thing as a full-time, paid evangelist inside a single church fellowship. If an evangelist receives the call to deliver testimony to a group somewhere, and some group wants to make a financial contribution to that person, to cover the travel expenses and be a blessing to them, then that is more than reasonable.

If an evangelist wants to minister full-time, because they are not tied to a family, and are not worried about finances so much, great for them. But if you have a family to support and lead (no matter what special gift you are endued with), that's your first and most important ministry. So what are you doing running around, being gone for days, leaving your spouse and children home while you're out selling your gospel? It is an unacceptable sacrifice! You go home where you belong and leave the traveling to the freely capable. When you are released to do so, take your spouse with you and go together…with Him.

I realize that many of us think what we have is extraordinary, and that if we don't use it, who will? I know that the money can be as good as, if not much better than, working out in the real world. But those are not reasons to leech onto the financial arteries of fellowships that can barely meet the needs of their local communities. Freely give what you have been freely given (Matt 10:8). Isn't the joy of seeing your ministry save lives reward enough. I'd hate for you to find out that you've already been receiving your eternal rewards all along.

If you are a gifted evangelist who has taken up your call, and are doing so appropriately, thank you for your contribution to the Kingdom. We desperately need more of you.

The Teacher

Nearly every single verse that speaks of this ministry does so in the light of being a tutor of the Torah or Laws of Adonai. This should be obvious, for again there were no other Scriptures to teach from at the time the title came into context. It is this office that has the equivalent Hebrew title 'Rabbi', throughout Scripture. 'Didaskalos' is the Greek word for teacher, instructor, or master (in the expert sense). Someone who was called Rabbi, or Teacher, was paid that honor because of the depth of their knowledge and worthiness of being paid attention to. Here are a few interesting examples of this gift, as given in Scripture:

But a Pharisee named Gamaliel, a teacher of the Law, respected by all the people, stood up in the Council and gave orders to put the men outside for a short time. (Acts 5:34)

…A corrector of the foolish, a teacher of the immature, having in the Law the embodiment of knowledge and of the truth. (Romans 2:20)

…Then teach them the statutes and the laws, and make known to them the way in which they are to walk and the work they are to do. (Exodus 18:20)

For though by this time you ought to be teachers, you have need again for someone to teach you the elementary principles of the oracles of God, and you have come to need milk and not solid food. (Hebrews 5:12)

Let not many *of you* become teachers, my brethren, knowing that as such we will incur a stricter judgment. (James 3:1)

This gift is the one which is most recognized as being delivered from the pulpit, podium, or pedestal; or at least, it should be. But it also is the gift that moves throughout the congregation, *subtly* listening for error and *discreetly* brings correction, without haughtiness or pride of knowledge. It seems quite apparent to me, that for one to be qualified to be a teacher, one must know about what is being taught; and more than just know

Body Parts

about, but have a rich depth of understanding while walking it out. A teacher is also someone who by nature, does not live in a grayish toned world of wisdom, especially when it comes to scriptural things. They demand accuracy. They want proof. And when they get it, they want others to know it. Newly obtained insight is exciting to them. Fresh revelation drives them to study more, but their thirst is never quite quenched. The teacher wants the truth exposed, at any cost (hopefully).

To a teacher, knowledge truly is power. It is the power to overcome the evil one. It is the power to shatter deceptive bindings. It opposes lies, ignorance, and naiveté. A teacher's dream is to be forced into early retirement, because all of their students have learned all they have to teach. For this reason, this verse is very insightful:

Matthew 10:24, "A disciple is not above his teacher, nor a slave above his master."

This is exactly why no single person is qualified to teach an entire congregation. Typically, the senior pastor will respond to this by agreeing and touting that this is the reason for assistant and associate pastors. On the surface, this would seem a valid argument. But it is really not the point. How learned is the person behind the pulpit? Not considering their jokes, anecdotal evidences, speaking skills, private interpretations, plans and visions etc., how much knowledge do they carry? These things are certainly helpful in the delivery process, but they do not qualify them as scholarly.

You may have a very knowledgeable pastor; if so, that is great. But if you are being "taught" by a spiritual adolescent, or someone who only appears well-versed in the NT—no matter how entertaining the delivery—you cannot, through them, grow in your understanding any more than them. Keep in mind the fact that someone who doesn't know the Hebrew Scriptures cannot possibly properly interpret the Apostolic. Granted, you should certainly not be relying on any one person alone to train you anyhow. Even if you are not personally, there is still the whole church to consider.

Let's move forward a couple thousand years. Fellowship groups have become non-profit organizations. The pastor title has been given to ministry CEO's. Why does one whose gifting is found in the application of the Balm of Gilead, now Chair corporations? Times have really changed. So far, we really haven't seen an office that acts as the spiritual authority, on the local level. The average pastor of today's church is not the modern equivalent of the pastor in the early ekklesia. The reason for this is that Scripture speaks of another office, not included in the famous five, which in many ways more closely describes the person behind the pulpit today. Actually, it speaks of two other offices. Let us examine them and then return to that famous fifth.

The Overseer

The first is commonly recognized in the KJV by the title 'Bishop'; a title which has had resurgence in use within the western church as of late. It has been alternately translated by the title 'Overseer'.

Paul and Timothy, bond-servants of Christ Jesus, to all the saints in Christ Jesus who are in Philippi, including the overseers and deacons… (Philippians 1:1)

Let me show you how Scripture defines the office of the Overseer:

So Joseph found favor in his sight and became his personal servant; and he made him overseer over his house, and all that he owned he put in his charge. (Genesis 39:4)

The LORD has made you priest instead of Jehoiada the priest, to be the overseer in the house of the LORD, over every madman who prophesies, to put him in the stocks and in the iron collar." (Jeremiah 29:26; I'm sorry. I couldn't help but put that one in.)

…Not addicted to wine or pugnacious, but gentle, peaceable, free from the love of money. *He must be* one who manages his own household well, keeping his children under control with all dignity but if a man does not know how to manage his own household, how will he take care of the church of God, *and* not a new convert, so that he will not become conceited and fall into the condemnation incurred by the devil. And he must have a good reputation with those outside *the church,* so that he will not fall into reproach and the snare of the devil. (1st Timothy 3:3-7)

For the overseer must be above reproach as God's steward, not self-willed, not quick-tempered, not addicted to wine, not pugnacious, not fond of sordid gain. (Titus 1:7)

The Greek word for this office is 'episkopos'.
Thayer Definition:

1) an overseer
1a) a man charged with the duty of seeing that things to be done by others are done rightly, any curator, guardian or superintendent
1b) the superintendent, elder, or overseer of a Christian church

Body Parts

The Deacon

The second office is that of the Deacon. It has been alternately translated into the terms: servant, minister and attendant. Here is how Paul explained to Timothy what kind of person this office is to be filled by:

Deacons likewise *must be* men of dignity, not double-tongued, or addicted to much wine or fond of sordid gain. (1st Timothy 3:8)
...*But* holding to the mystery of the faith with a clear conscience. (3:9)
These men must also first be tested; then let them serve as deacons if they are beyond reproach. (3:10)
Deacons must be husbands of *only* one wife, *and* good managers of *their* children and their own households. (3:12)
For those who have served well as deacons obtain for themselves a high standing and great confidence in the faith that is in Christ Jesus. (3:13)

The Greek word for Deacon is 'diakonos'.
Thayer Definition:

1) one who executes the commands of another, especially of a master, a servant, attendant, minister
(1a) the servant of a king
(1b) a deacon, one who, by virtue of the office assigned to him by the church, cares for the poor and has charge of and distributes the money collected for their use
(1c) a waiter, one who serves food and drink

Of these two offices, both noble as they are, there is only one which commands the authority to act as the superintendent of YHVH's house. But more than that, it is not the pastor.

The "elder" concept is rooted in Torah. Without studying its function and usage there, it cannot be understood in a First Century context. The zekenim (Hebrew for: elders) were the respected, and older (as the root of the word, *zeken* indicates) members of the community, who were responsible for speaking on behalf of their families and clans. They were internally appointed from among their own communities. They were also frequently involved with judging civil matters, and determining courses of action in their regard. Although they were not technically judges, "Righteousness! Righteousness! They were to pursue."

Let's return to the most represented office in the Body. Paradoxically, it is also among the least described. But before I scrutinize this ministry gift, I need to say a couple things. As you will see, the pendulum has swung far from center in many areas of spiritual life. The

Yah-ordained positions within the kingdom are not immune to cross contamination. Please understand that my intention here, just as it is throughout much of this book, is to get the pendulum to swing back. But it's very heavy, and will undoubtedly swing beyond center before it returns. So, if you are a pastor, and the shoe fits, wear it. If it doesn't, you are a rare commodity and may you be richly blessed.

The Pastor

Well, what one was, as compared to what one is now, is quite a bit different. In the early church, a pastor was synonymous with a shepherd, as the etymology of the word suggests. Someone who was called a pastor received that title not by a commission from man, or obtained from an ad in the back of some magazine. It came by the recognition of one's attitude towards people. One did not aspire to be a pastor; you just were one. They might recognize a calling on their life, to love and nurture people. The gift was performed as being done unto the Divine. One would want to be excellent at what they were doing, but not for personal gain or notoriety. There was no school from which you would graduate with such an office designation.

Many probably held the office without even knowing they were. Because of their special love gift, they were regarded worthy of esteem. They were a servant of YHVH. Not because they were expected to be, but because if they were cut, they would bleed compassion. It's really not a "special education required" part of the Body; but it could be enhanced by schooling, and nurtured by discipleship. Its complexity is found in the inherent, emotional struggles that love brings with it.

Every good Father is a pastor to his family. A believing boss should be a pastor to their employees. The reward for pastoring is found in the strength and maturation found in those shepherded. An early church pastor never knew the concept of being paid for leading someone to green pasture. He might entertain enjoying a nice meal with some sheep who welcomed him into their home. But if someone ever offered them money for visiting them because they were sick, not only would it be the furthest thing from their mind, it would have been offensive. Similarly, if someone offered to pay them to go minister to some person in need, it would have been flat rejected. During the time of the disciples, this was a title of recognition, not a career objective. That's not a poke; it's just a fact.

Body Parts

Posturing vs. Pasturing

Here is where this is all ultimately going. The person who 'teaches' you is not necessarily the person who 'pastors' you. The gifts'/offices' paths may certainly cross in various ways and at times, but it is not the "must-be" protocol of the Bible we often presume. The senior pastor, if there ever was such a thing, should actually be someone placed in charge of the ministries of compassion (helps), which is more closely related to the title, 'Deacon'. They should make sure people are being visited, counseling is taking place as necessary, benevolence is making it to where it is needed, and the sick are being cared for and prayed over.

The person at the pulpit on Shabbat, or whenever, should be one of several qualified people—none of which are expected to do any more than what their gifting requires. Even Moses, the greatest, human-only prophet/Torah teacher to walk the planet, needed a well-organized group of volunteers to accomplish what he could not. There are several significant benefits to organizing the church, and its leadership model, after scriptural examples and descriptions.

If the people in our pulpits were truly gifted teachers/expositors of the Word, our congregations would rarely have to split due to the foolish indiscretions of *one* man. Another of the groomed and ready-to-go teachers would just step right up to the plate if one was to fall, and a being-groomed teacher would fill their void. People in the fellowship would not have to sit there, trying to suppress all their judgmental thoughts regarding the apparent imperfections and inadequacies of the person as a "pastor", while they try to learn and grow (which is the point of putting someone up there anyway.) There are other people appointed for the other needs of the flock.

Another benefit to the church being used to having various teachers share the responsibility is that the congregants get a more rounded array of material. And those teachers, if called to other fellowships, though missed, could move on with our blessing instead of with such controversy. The Scripture is the Scripture, and if it's true…it's true! I'm not discounting the need for quality character in the teacher, but pastors and teachers are judged by the public with differing standards. (Whether or not that's right is its own debate.) "Blah Blah… I didn't get invited to the pastor's house party, and so and so did!" Along with all that, "He must tithe more than me. Look at all the time they spend together." kind of nonsense. The reputation of a church should not ebb and tide on the shoulders of any one man's but Yehoshua's.

If we didn't insist upon calling the man at the pulpit 'pastor', who he rarely is except to maybe a few higher ups in the organization, we would not expect nor demand the impossible from him; for no one man can *pastor* a thousand. If we had an accurate understanding as to the role of pastors, we would be able to identify them more accurately. The Mosaic example broke the community down to leaders over groups of ten, and Yehoshua's example is that of twelve. There should be plenty of pastors, who work voluntarily, ready to be a help in time of need.

If the person behind the pulpit was one of many available teachers, we also would not have to draw out of the storehouse, sometimes hundreds of thousands of dollars a year, to subsidize the lifestyles of some of these church's CEOs. The reason they are demanding so much compensation is not for their preaching skills, it's for all the other 'stuff' they fill their schedules with—stuff that others should and could be doing instead. If they are being paid predominantly for their inspiring rhetoric, then they are in actuality motivational speakers. Certainly, teachers don't get that kind of salary. This extra 'stuff' is what assorted volunteers, and committees, and minimally paid helpers could be doing, and would be doing if the big church cheeses would step out of the way. We sure know how to swing the pendulum wide and away from a healthy self-denial.

The one in charge of the church should not be the dominant teacher. It's a natural conflict of interest. He could teach and preach according to *his* motivations and not just for the raw Truth of the Word. The one in charge should be an Overseer; the one with a clear calling and gifting to put into motion the ideas and purposes of Adonai. He should be someone with little to gain personally from his decisions. His heart should have been proved over many years of service and sacrifice. He cannot be power hungry. He must be pure of heart (as far as is humanly possible). He is the one the prophet would go to with the word, rarely the teacher or pastor, and practically never a common layperson. If the word of the prophet was good, then the overseer would send it down the appropriate channels. The apostle would go to the overseer, and inform him of what needs to be done administratively, and regarding maturation, within his and the larger congregation abroad.

The Minister

The word 'minister' (Latin for servant) is another common title used within the church. A minister is one who administers. Technically, there is no gift, or Five-Fold-like ministry called *ministering*. However, it is commonly understood to represent the preacher.

Is it possible, a reason this umbrella-like title functions within religion's framework, being more a political role and descriptive verb, is to legitimize a sixth, invented medicine? This title allows for someone to come along and assume the position of any role, or combination of roles

Body Parts

they like, and be legitimized by the generic, non-specific description that it denotes. Under this title, one can do just about anything that seems useful, along with preaching, and justify a lofty position in the church.

Often, as has already been discussed previously, people will combine various functions within the Body. Ministers: marry, preach, do visitation, council, author, do conferences and workshops, work soup lines, landscape, prophecy, cook, teach, evangelize, clean toilets, pastor, etc. Therefore, a title such as 'Minister' is universally ideal. When it comes down to it, there is no believer who should not also be a minister of something.

Subject to, does **NOT** mean, Object to

This is also why female pastors are fine, when they are *pastors*. Women need pastoring as much as men; but men in no way should be being "pastured" by a woman who is not their wife. A woman may be gifted to teach, but she should not be the spiritual, overseeing authority for a man. They may be gifted to preach, but on spiritual matters they (as men also) have nothing new under the sun; hence, they shouldn't preach to men whatever a man can just as easily preach. I know women have much wisdom and insight (I'm married to such a one), but they should offer it to their husbands privately, and then they (men) can share it with others appropriately—where it will be appreciably received and hopefully implemented.

But I want you to understand that Christ is the head of every man, and the man is the head of a woman, and God is the head of Christ. (1st Corinthians 11:3)

Don't like it? Take it up with Adonai. Truth is Truth, and Truth from a woman's mouth is as much truth as if from a man's mouth. She may instruct other woman freely, but she should not publicly tutor men on spiritual matters, for that would be improper conduct. That is why Sha'ul taught this protocol for the ekklesia:

The women are to keep silent in the churches; for they are not permitted to speak, but are to subject themselves, just as the Law (nomos, not culture; Genesis 3:16) also says. If they desire to learn anything, let them ask their own husbands at home; for it is improper for a woman to speak in church. (1st Corinthians 14:34 & 35)

How is it possible for a woman who is appropriately quiet in church, to simultaneously be preaching? The word used for 'speak' in the

Greek is 'laleo'. It is a word that carries the meaning of speaking, but it is also used for preaching. The word implies more than just making a comment though; it's more about protocol than that. It is not saying all women must sit with their lips tightly pursed as though they should be seen and not heard. It means they should not 'control the floor', so to speak.[1] Oh, I can hear it now. But contrary to the "cultural" relevance that is often attributed to this principle, it is still as valid today as it ever was. If you don't agree, that is as much your prerogative as is your acceptance of everything in this book. Have there been occasions in Scripture when a woman did the man's job? Yes—and there were special circumstances for each of them. Then, when men became available, it reverted back to the ordained structure. Would you like me to hammer this nail home? Here is the seemingly overlooked (ignored) passage that immediately follows:

Was it from you that the word of God *first* went forth? Or has it come to you only? If anyone thinks he is a prophet or spiritual, let him recognize that **the things** which I write to you **are the Lord's commandment.** (1st Corinthians 14:36 & 37)

This past subject of teaching is about what the final verse of this chapter in Corinthians states: "Things are to be done in an orderly manner." If we are going to deem this "Lord's commandment" instruction by Sha'ul regarding women "culturally irrelevant" for today, then we must also apply the same litmus test to the rest of this chapter as well. Perhaps we should begin with the opening line, "Pursue love". While we're at it, we might as well go ahead and apply it to every single teaching of the Apostolic Scriptures, as well as what came straight from Yeshua's mouth. Heck, we already do it to Moshe's! This is, after all, a "New Testament" instruction. You want to go down a slippery road? There's one for you.

You must answer whether or not it is pure coincidence that the increased percentage of female preachers appears to have begun showing up predominantly during the feminist movement. And also, why there are more often than not, odd and disturbing "charismatic" manifestations that accompany their ministries/revivals/movements, etc.? One must wonder why their persona seems awkwardly strong, approaching masculine—never minding the trendy reception of lesbianism into leadership roles within certain church groups. "Well, until men step up to the plate!" carries little merit anymore. There are more than enough men. I ask the women who stand in the pulpit every week to prayerfully consider your situation, humble yourselves, step down and make room for the man Adonai has lined up to take your place. You really must reflect

Body Parts

upon why you would even want to bear that weight. Forget about one judge, a few prophetesses, and first-century congregational start-ups. They're not the same thing. I should end here for the sake of preserving female readership, but look at the other interesting detail of this mitzvah by Sha'ul. He is supporting the Law again, in regards to being "subject". I thought Paul vehemently preached against subjection to the Law?

Please understand. I am not opposed to woman teaching or even preaching, under the right circumstances and within boundaries. I truly have great respect for any articulate witness. No one who knows me would ever deem me a chauvinist. I am, however, opposed to the Scriptures being ignored and sloughed off by its teachers; teachers who negate instructions from the Lord for mankind's declared "higher" purposes. What higher calling is there than to love and obey our Mighty One? There is a forum for women and a forum for men. Within our fellowships, they are not exactly the same, regardless what secular ideology has infiltrated them.

Getting back on topic now, there is a clear difference between the preacher/teacher and the pastor/deacon. If that's the case, then we are harming our fellowships by imposing pastoral requirements and presbyterial responsibilities onto the man who's teaching on stage. If the church was taught this Truth, if we could turn this Titanic around, we would undoubtedly reap great rewards within our fellowships. It would have to start though, with many pastors dropping their generally, inaccurate titles. A license to preach within a certain denomination does not automatically make a pastor. Yes, another silly, semantical argument I'm sure.

Warning: the commentary you are about to read is bold, corrective and purposely matter-of-fact. I really am not thrilled about being the deliverer of this message, but I believe I have been called to do it. I write it with righteous trepidation and a love for the Body. This corrective instruction must be understood in light of this previous teaching on the offices. Hopefully, it's not for you and the shoe won't fit. It delivers the opposite of John's scroll. It is bitter upon ingestion, but becomes sweet in the finish. I will begin by quoting the Lord first.

Be All You *Should* Be

Because if you don't:

Son of man, prophesy against the shepherds of Israel. Prophesy and say to those shepherds, 'Thus says the Lord GOD, Woe, shepherds of Israel who have been feeding themselves! Should not the shepherds feed the flock? (Ezekiel 34:2)

As I live, declares the Lord GOD, surely because My flock has become a prey, My flock has even become food for all the beasts of the field for lack of a shepherd, and My shepherds did not search for My flock, but *rather* the shepherds fed themselves and did not feed My flock. (Ezekiel 34:8)

You eat the fat and clothe yourselves with the wool; you slaughter the fat *sheep* without feeding the flock. (Ezekiel 34:3)

Those who are sickly you have not strengthened, the diseased you have not healed, the broken you have not bound up, the scattered you have not brought back, nor have you sought for the lost; but with force and with severity you have dominated them.' (Ezekiel 34:4)

Therefore, you shepherds, hear the word of the LORD. (Ezekiel 34:7)

Thus says the Lord GOD, 'Behold, I am against the shepherds, and I will demand My sheep from them and make them cease from feeding sheep. So the shepherds will not feed themselves anymore, but I will deliver My flock from their mouth, so that they will not be food for them.' (Ezekiel 34:10)

What strong and challenging words these are! If you are not shepherding appropriately, He has given His warning. The weight of integrity He has placed on the shoulders of His leaders is very great. Though He may allow you to get away with some things, for a season, it is purely to accomplish a greater good. His patience is long, but apparently it is tempered by our conduct.

Please, if you are shepherding sheep, and you are not feeding them, protecting them, or guiding them as you know you should be, it is the noble thing to do to hand over your staff. That doesn't mean you are not called. That doesn't mean your value is gone, or that it's permanent. It is purely a love thing, and it would seem wise. No one is saying that as a pastor, you can't also be a teacher, or vice-versa; but there is a clear distinction that needs recognition.

Don't think that just because you happen to be a vice-versa yourself, you are justified to "receive the double portion" (another misapplied verse). Rare is the pastor who should be paid much if anything, just based on the office's characteristics. If you want to come clean and be a teacher, as I said earlier…how about a teacher's salary, based on however many hours you teach in a week? I know you *feel* you should be paid more because you have been to school (maybe), and that cost you time and resources, or because you do such a needed job. Again though, I must point out the error in that being a valid justification.

First, all knowledge is acquired from three prominent sources: media, educators, and experience. Books can be bought anywhere, anytime and read at our leisure. It's commendable when someone chooses to consume literature at an accelerated rate, but that does not in itself demand a reward. Especially since, like in any educational program, we only retain a small percentage of it anyway. Don't preachers typically have

Body Parts

to refer to new source materials, along with their prior notes, for their next sermon?

Secondly, educators are being paid for offering a service that is contracted. They obtained their knowledge basically the same way, and if there are people willing to pay them to distribute it to them, it is their right to collect. You could become a professor someday as well. The question is: Are you a pastor or an educator? If an educator, are you supposed to be selling Bible knowledge at church, to make a living? A few hours of prep, and an hour or so on preaching day, is worth how much exactly? If you're only working once or twice a month, because you share that role with others, how much is your service worth now?

Then thirdly, what did you go to school for? If you went to become a counselor, then sell your talents and skills to those who need it. Or, you could give them away. If you went to learn administrative skills, sell them and administrate. Or, you could give them away. If you went to learn the Scriptures, great! You've matured in your walk. But I ask you to please analyze honestly your scriptural knowledge. Did you basically just survey the Scriptures in school? Or, did you become an expert on something to the point people should pay to learn from you? Are you in fact redistributing that knowledge? If your answer is no to either, well then I'm sorry, but your being a nice person doesn't translate to big dollar signs, does it? Perhaps you are a motivational speaker?

How much is your sharing the gospel worth? Please do not say "priceless". Do you have something others cannot possibly obtain through their own studying? If you have rationalized, in essence, that the church members who are paying your salary are, in actuality, hiring you to divulge knowledge to them that they can't get for themselves, then you darn well better start giving them something besides church-house humor and shouted out clichés. It is possible to put on a show of hating idols, but still rob from temples.

A challenge for you (the modern day pastor) to accept is that the other roles you play (besides preacher) are not as unique and autonomous as they are considered to be. The apostle is the closest to being gifted as a jack-of-all-trades and unless you are one, which you're probably not, quit trying to be. I doubt you want to be one anyway. The price is often far too high. Many of the things that often keep a pastor busy are things that should be done by volunteers, or are done outside normal business hours. If you want to perform menial tasks to "keep yourself humble" that's fine. How much is mopping the floor worth?

Another challenge is two-fold. Pastors have been indoctrinated to believe they are to earn a good living at pasturing, and congregants have been nursed-up to believe the same way. What a great day it would be, if a preacher educated their fellowship into understanding these things, and then personally refused an inappropriate salary. What leadership!

Are you, if a pastor, assuming that the high salary you're receiving for your ministry is justified because the First Day's (Sunday) morning service you perform, for most people, is all the spiritual input they will get that week? If so, that demonstrates another by-product of the liberal, welfare mentality that so permeates our secular institutions. Teach your disciples (students) to teach themselves, and stop making them dependent on you and your personal interpretations. Get them dependent on the Lord! Then you will have truly done something significant, and the Body will have strength and the capacity to duplicate, as opposed to just multiply. Don't you want to see your people become healers, instead of them sitting around and licking their perpetually open wounds?

We have to stop misappropriating Kingdom resources! Pastors or any other office/gift shouldn't be receiving more than a small token of love from their congregations. If that's not enough, or they do other tasks, I revert to my previous comments. They should make supplemental money somehow. If you lead a church where you are the only gifted teacher, then it is definitely too small a church to be paying out a full-time salary to you. There are times when a part-time salary may be warranted, but you better earn it by doing an awful lot more (than pastoring) and just speaking for a couple hours a week, and only because there are literally no other people capable, and only for a season. A good leader will find and encourage others to do what you've been doing extra. And, if you can't after a good go of it, maybe your church is a work of the flesh. The idea that there are people out there with pastor titles, receiving high, six-figure incomes drawn from storehouse money, is absolutely absurd and bankrupt of justification. Paul was boastful in his declarations of "not being a burden". So should you be.

Pastoring, in the modern vernacular, should not be a default job taken by freshly graduated believers who simply have no other job skills. Teach the word when your turn comes around, and leave the business matters of the church to business people. As a teacher, if you run out of material, your job is done. As a pastor, if you don't have the time, or run out of steam, your job is equally done. Leave the administration to administrators. Leave the counseling to trained counselors. Leave the pastor title to those who have the time to justify the title. Leave the building plans to the building committee, etc., etc. It will be okay.

I know that many of you are saying to yourselves, "Maybe in a perfect world, where humans aren't required." If church leaders want to be well-staffed with quality volunteers, they are going to have to end the cycle of self-abuse. They must stop the enabling of the masses who give so little, by doing it all themselves. Twenty percent of the church does eighty percent of the work, largely because we allow it to be that way. It seems so unnecessary that we have to tell capable people to make a contribution besides money. But that's exactly what needs to be done. It's not about what the people want; it's more about what they need!

If that means you can't build your new, super sanctuary as fast as you'd like, then that's what it means. If that means some pruning needs to be done, then that's what it means. If I was the overseer of a church, I would much rather have a group of two hundred, with a high involvement level from many, than a church of two thousand pew warmers. If you disciple people appropriately, they will become people who are compelled to serve. If you just try to gain in numbers, you will have to coerce them.

Too often, our churches from above look like a big nest full of squawking, adult birds—fully capable of flying, but don't, because nobody has ever pushed them out of the nest. Haven't you heard them, with their mouths wide open crying, "Feed me! Feed me!" There is a difference between giving food to the genuinely hungry, and shoveling food into the spiritually lazy and obese. If you're letting yourself be paid off by people, to do the job of studying Scripture so they don't have to, what does that make you? Didn't Yeshua say something about not having that kind of hunger anymore, if we eat of the right bread? What are you feeding them that keep them so insatiable? Parents demand more from their children than the children themselves think they're capable of. Don't you know why?

The Common Folk

For the rest, who don't seem to have a clear call to one of these Fab-Five (or seven really), you are not out of the woods. In order for the Body to function right, you cannot be a wart or polyp just hanging off like a parasite; not that you are of course. You have something positive to contribute. I'd hate to see anyone have to get lanced.

Faith without works is (and still is) dead! Upon your coming to a saving faith, and receiving the indwelling of the Spirit, what you were made to do becomes possible. Your gifting is not to be opened and stuck on a shelf. You have the kind of gift that no matter how much you give away, there is more waiting. Sometimes you don't know exactly what it is, especially in the beginning. Sure, there are questionnaires out there to help you figure it out. But most often it takes time, confirmation, and third-party recognition to accurately acknowledge them.

Wherever you are, if you have the time and/or the resources to take some of the burden off the leadership of your fellowship, and there is nothing stopping you from doing it besides motivation, you are being disobedient to the same Spirit who gave you the ability, and you are handicapping the Body. You are a key component to the efficiency of its metabolism. Need-meeting is not limited to any one kind of member. If you see a problem, that you have the capacity to solve…do it. If you know someone is struggling in an area, and have a solution…give it. If someone is lying wounded on the side of the road, bind their injuries. You may never get a badge, plaque, or applause, but do you really need them? (After this book, I'll likely not.) If that is what you need, take some time off to mature, and then you can go from being a civilian, to being an army recruit.

If you have been given the pastoral calling by the Spirit, you have been given a most excellent thing. You don't have to seek a "job" as a pastor to be one. What is going to make you most effective in your gift is to work mostly within its confines. The ironic thing is that 'pastor' is the title most commonly given in the church, and yet it is the very thing the Body of Messiah needs and is lacking the most. You are the hug and kiss of Messiah upon the Earth. You are the living bandages He is wrapping around His wounded children. You are the mud that is applied to blind eyes. If you see that, and you embrace your purpose, you will truly change the face of a sorely misrepresented institution. If you are mature and competent, nothing or nobody can or should stop you, when you fully embrace your purpose and position.

My next commentary is truly a "if the shoe fits" sort of piece. It is a warning to the guilty, and a checklist to the associated. But to the rest, it is a release.

Ten Thous in Mega-whats?

We all know the church is not a building; it's the people that join together inside it. And for that reason, I'm a proponent of gathering anywhere that is appropriate. Three couples in a home, or five hundred in a school (depending on your circumstances), one may be just what you need, for the season of life you are in.

I appreciate aesthetic beauty and recognize the value in acoustical design. Yet, I can't help but think that the only one truly impressed with our magnificent edifices is we ourselves. I cannot conceive of how many multiple billions of Adonai's dollars have been spent on trying to stir our emotions, with our architecture and sophistication. I know, "He's worthy!" I realize that the Temple Solomon built was expensive and extravagant, but it was also the place that He manifested Himself in a way not since paralleled. It is also the last place He gave specific instructions for construction, and it was located in the only city He said He, "placed His Name."

Each church has to be prettier than the one down the street, to attract new members. The sound system has to be upgraded frequently to

Body Parts

keep the cutting-edge technologies working their magic. Trendy bands perform the worship. Laser lights and smoke effects give a kickin' show to compete with the world. My questions are these: Are we trying to cover something up? Are we afraid that if the visitor found out that all we do inside our walls is simply love, worship, fellowship, and grow in the knowledge and grace of our Messiah, that they would not be impressed enough to stay? Or, is it possible that the meat being distributed for the weekly portions is so lean, gristly, and cooked-up, that nobody wants to come back for second helpings?

The Body should never have to have a stage show to grow. In the same way Moshe had to stop the people from bringing in the treasure to build the Tabernacle, I believe that the intent of Messiah, as related to congregations, is to put people together and prosper them until they have all they need. Which may not be much. That may take a while, and there is some subjectivity to what that equates to in size. But I would rather fellowship within a size that is conducive to the intimacy and development that is essential for me, than be swallowed up by the enormity of a faith-based populous, for bragging rights. That's just my opinion.

Of course, that's why large churches have affinity groups, cell-groups, and multiple service times are engineered. Small groups certainly have their purpose. We have to be careful that these divisions, when used to facilitate large numbers, don't inhibit the value of cross-generational exposure and education. They certainly can be a great place and opportunity for relationship and leadership development. As far as multiple services go, your attempt to solve a growth problem, is creating a growth problem. Leaders, if your congregation size is too big for your building, maybe instead of adding services, you should start another fellowship. If you're not willing to do that, perhaps that is a control mechanism for something else?

Somewhere along the line, the 501c3 CEO/pastor not only started to do other's jobs, but also stopped encouraging their middle management to go forth and "expand their borders" (unless, it's out of state, or overseas). All growth must be done "in-house". We'll often add more chairs, build a balcony, add a story, do more services; whatever it takes to keep the people who should be venturing out and pioneering from doing so. Instead of encouraging more leaders (although they have classes that say otherwise), they take on a big-bully role and pull little, covert, hostile takeovers of embryonic, mom and pop fellowships. Maybe someday we'll have Wal-Churches across America.

Why is this done? Is it for prestige, reputation, money? What is the need? These giant churches cost far more to operate than a number of smaller, mostly volunteer ones. Big Red® does eventually lose its flavor. I wonder how many pastors equate head-count with tithes, and tithes with salary. Just a thought. Mega-fellowships can get so *powerful*, that when someone within is ready to go off on their own and help plant a fellowship, they know full-well that they cannot compare, and it will be nearly impossible for them to compete. So they don't. These mega-minded CEO/pastors may also consider "branching off" to be a personal threat to the solidarity of their empires.

Nobody owns any part of the Body, and there are other places people can go if you can't house them. "If you love them, let them leave. If they come back…" You know the saying. Too many pastors take ownership of their flocks, and forget the sheep actually belong to the Great Shepherd. It clouds their judgment, when they have to make the tough decisions which could result either in preserving their position, or in protecting the flock. They may not be able to both be accomplished. You do not want a hireling for a shepherd (John 10:12 & 13).

I have no idea why looking around and seeing all the new fellowships that have been planted, through their ministry, is not substantially more rewarding than looking inward at all the stunted and burned-out, wish-they-weres they've managed to accumulate over the years. Enough already! If you represent an already monolithic church, I realize it's highly unlikely you will accept some of this message. It's also likely you're not even reading this line because you've just thrown this book in the trash. But if you're still here, or if you have your hopes set on becoming one, I beg you to at least reconsider your next growth project. Where will it stop? How big is big enough? How much debt, or kingdom funds, do you need to toss onto the shoulders of your congregants, to pay for *your* vision? It's never too late to do the right thing. I know that you as the leader could never fall, but what if you did? What would happen to *your* empire? How many people would find themselves homeless, or disillusioned, or ultimately…lost?

As smaller fellowships, you can still network together, draw from each other's resources, and celebrate each other's victories. From the earlier 'Moshe-Tabernacle' analogy, I draw another conclusion as well. If you have to go into enormous debt to build up His kingdom, you are building for the wrong king. The amount of interest money that is thrown away into the word's economy is staggering. I can't help but think someday there will be a *Schindler's List* like epiphany, when board members will have to contend with how much more good they could have done, and lives they could have rescued, if they had only managed to do with less.

Just because He owns the cattle on a thousand hills, doesn't mean we can go ahead and just slaughter them all. Imagine the amount of money that a fledgling fellowship could save up, if there was a voluntary

Body Parts

leadership team? Wouldn't that be odd and impressive? If your fellowship is the will of Adonai, the resources will come. There is no record of anything Adonai did through man, in the Scriptures, that ever required a loan. Think about that! The only way a mega-church can even begin to be justified, is if it is debt free. Everyone is quick to agree that we are not supposed to be "of this world". But then we go out and do spiritual work according to the world's economy and philosophy. Who can understand this?

I wish that things could be ideal. I really do. And I know that there are plenty of excuses why these principles just won't work. I even hear the rebuttals in my own head, and sometimes they are pretty persuasive. I just can't help but think though, that if these principles are found in His Word, that they are not there for hypothetical theory. We need to run our churches as if they are accountable, "for-profit" businesses, without seeking the profit. Yehoshua reacted rather strongly when He saw that kind of stuff going on around His Father's House.

I believe there are a few churches who have amassed greatness in both size and health. (Note: One roof not required!) It is a chemistry that can only be created in the lab of the Creator, and they are very rare. But they are also very volatile. I believe we need to be extremely careful that we don't look at great size as a meter for success, nor even a goal to aspire to. It is no more indicative of His will being perfectly manifest, than a secular company who has successfully strategized its own growth, but sells questionable goods. If He chooses to work that way through your ministry, then He will. By looking at His MO in Scripture, it will likely be out of your hands to determine.

We need to get back to a place where righteous men lead righteous women, and the gospel message is followed by signs and wonders; not signs and wonders created by smoke and mirrors. We need to get to the place where church leaders aren't trying to win popularity contests, or build the biggest building, or sponsor the next, coolest seminar trend. We need to have a system, where the ones preaching about money aren't the one's receiving the majority of it, and where the song service is not elevated above the teaching of the Word.

Why can't we lead the world by example, instead of the world leading us by the nose? It is a vain and futile work to try to outdo the world's fantasy lifestyle. So let's be different, revolutionary, and operate our congregations with humility and modesty.

The Timothy Complex

It should stand to reason, that there is little knowledge given through the rapid-fire system of institutional learning, which is not available to be received, over the long span of our lives, as a disciple. I appreciate the value in university study. Honestly, I do. I've spent some time there. It very well may, and often does, enhance one's capacity to articulate their faith and wield one's gifts. It is just not adequate to *validate* or *justify* a person's calling, and granting it that power may potentially create an unwittingly detrimental division in the Body.

Somehow, the Five-Fold-like ministry positions have generally become reserved for graduates only, especially when denominational biases exist. There are many people in the Body who have a calling to perform one of these roles, who are cut off at the knees because they are not 'licensed' to do so, through an institution of higher recognition. Along with all our incapacitated brethren, we have been inundated with a fairly new phenomenon of overly young ministers. There seems to be some kind of 'timothy complex' in the church, which encourages its leadership to be young, high-energy and "cutting edge". The irony is that the wisdom, experience, and street smarts the Body needs, are rarely even found there.

They can't be blamed, because many of them are graduates of schools with the very same complex, as well as their being employed by ministry leaders who support the ideology. I am not challenging their calling! I'm certainly not going to discount that. It's just that there is absolutely no reason why they cannot build tents, while they serve the Body and mature in life. I realize the modern perks of ministry can be very compelling, but they cannot be a motivating factor for circumnavigating around the value of seasoning.

Timothy is the poster boy for young ministers, because the book of Acts tells us he was just that—young. The fact is that Timothy was a rare gem among men. Timotheus was a half-Greek, half-Jew who was the spiritually adopted son of Paul. He accompanied Paul on several of his journeys and because of their closeness, was able to learn and mature at a much-accelerated rate. So would you, if you were one of Paul's companions and confidants. This really is a special circumstance, and should not have set a precedent for age being hurried past scrutiny in the qualification process, for a "professional" pastor.

We are warned in the first book of Timothy that someone given a ministry without enough maturity can find themself puffed up, and fall under condemnation. That seems a fitting warning to a young person, coming from a caring friend, who may know a thing or two about the pride that comes with position. Maturity is a primary qualification.

If the Body was healthy, and functioning according to the scriptural plan, there would be plenty of volunteers to compensate for not having such the mass of full-time pastors. Young adults are herded through religious universities, where they are indoctrinated into a system

Body Parts

of questionable beliefs, with expectations of graduating into their ministerial opportunity machine and all its grandeur. However, if you, being early in life, have the ability to support yourself, Scripture demonstrates you should. If you, when older, have the ability to write books, sell videos and DVDs, or CDs, do seminars, guest speak, or whatever to supplement your income; you should do that as well. If this won't work for you because you are of no reputation; then again, the storehouse should not pay for you to develop one. To live completely on the charity of others, when it is not necessary, is like living on Kingdom welfare, when you already have a well-paying job.

The Body should not have to pay for fledglings to mature, any more than the coiffures of the Kingdom should be drained for me to read when I come home from work. If our future leaders would just absorb the teaching available to them, via life experience, being discipled, and diligent study throughout their lives, their calling would not be repealed as this takes place. After building their families and adding to their own personal storehouses, the time would come where their call and opportunity would unite, and their dependency upon tapping into the King's storehouse would diminish. If you simply must serve while you are in your youth, then you should give your service away, as much has been freely given to you. When we remove the vain obstacles in our life that rob us of our limited time and resources, all of our ability to serve can be greatly increased.

To be a youth pastor, it would seem fitting that one should be "young," although there are plenty of examples of successful "old" youth pastors. Youthfulness really does lend itself to be valuable to this ministry. It has energy. It has demographic familiarity. It has edge. But it is also state of mind and attitude. What it just doesn't have is experience. Not just experience in general, like more different job types, or travel. I'm talking about faith-testing kinds of experiences. And they definitely shouldn't be babes in the faith, having recently had their own spiritual awakening. For someone to lead someone else, the guide really should have a depth of wisdom that exceeds the follower. Is it possible that a twenty-two-year-old has what it takes? I would have to say, rarely.

Being a youth leader is a highly influential position, for an extremely influential age group. The almost blind should not be leading those who can barely see. If you are responsible for obtaining or approving leaders for your fellowship, please don't be too quick to hire a youth pastor on the basis of high energy levels, or even on education. Actually, in the ideal scenario, you really wouldn't 'hire' at all. You should open a door of opportunity, for a selected *group* of individuals, to gain experience and be discipled in the skills required for whatever future ministry they feel called to. Which leads me to another concern.

Commonly, the youth pastor's intent is to go on to adult ministerial work. Youth ministry is often a stepping-stone, if you will. Let's think about that for a minute. We now have a program where we take young adults, pull them out of the environment most conducive to growth, give them an isolated from the world job, where they start learning the art and science of church, and then anticipate their natural progression into adult ministry. It is a disturbing cycle. Many would suggest that wealth makes people lose touch with the common man. How much more disadvantaged then might a blossoming leader be, who never really leaves the shelter of the occupational church nest.

It is my *opinion* that in most cases, a wanna-be pastor, fresh out of school, who one day hopes to become a pastor to adults, should be encouraged to first become a well-rounded adult themselves. This would be accomplished by their having regular employment—tackling the world and its relationships, for their individually appropriate amount of time. Am I saying there is an age limit to ministry? By no means! All I am suggesting is that we should be slow to heap on young people, eternity-weighted, spiritual responsibility.

Kingdom Order

As we end this chapter, I feel it necessary to clearly confront an underlying issue which many of you may have reflected upon, throughout this last teaching. History repeats itself. And even if certain happenings are deemed old, they are not quickly forgotten.

About forty years ago, a very serious and damaging movement took place within the charismatic, Pentecostal church. It took on the various titles of: "Shepherding", "Discipleship Movement" and "Covenant". Authoritarian abuses of the highest order were rampant throughout Christendom. Lives and ministries alike were left destroyed in its path. When the divine order of authority is disregarded in the Nicolaitan manner, there is no limit to the potential damage. Christ is the Head of the church—period! He ordered that Apostles and Prophets act on His behalf whilst He is away. People (and that includes you) need to be very careful to not let those who have *appointed themselves* into positions of leadership control your spiritual life. All heavenly authority is given by Adonai alone. If what mankind orders is not in line with what He says in His Word, you are not to subject yourselves to its demonic doctrines. For those of you who have come out from that ecclesiastical disaster, you know exactly what I mean. For the rest of you...take heed!

Evaluation

Everyone in the Body of Messiah has a purpose.

Now in a large house there are not only gold and silver vessels, but also vessels of wood and of earthenware, and some to honor and some to dishonor... (2nd Timothy 2:20)

This verse is not talking about value folks. It's talking about function! As will our eternal rewards be different, but not because of valuation.

There are also heavenly bodies and earthly bodies, but the glory of the heavenly is one, and the *glory* of the earthly is another. There is one glory of the sun, and another glory of the moon, and another glory of the stars; for star differs from star in glory. (1st Corinthians 15:40 & 41)

We have our fine china for special events, and our Styrofoam for picnics. Everything/everyone has a purpose. Though some are less gifted, in the Lord's china cabinet they are to be displayed and put on the same shelf. If you look out into your respective, little flocks the same way Jesse looked upon his, you may very well overlook the one with the anointing.

...and those *members* of the body which we deem less honorable, on these we bestow more abundant honor, and our less presentable members become much more presentable. (1st Corinthians 12:23)

It is this latter verse, which is far too often not applied by those who have become "professional" ministers. I'm talking about it being applied—to them, by them. Do you, pastor, deem yourself of no more value than someone else? It is conducive to esteeming others more highly than yourself. Why is this honoring of everyone so critical?

...so that there may be no division in the body, but *that* the members may have the same care for one another. And if one member suffers, all the members suffer with it; if *one* member is honored, all the members rejoice with it. (1st Corinthians 12:25 & 26)

Is this really the model we now follow, or was this also a "cultural" thing that was for another time?

9

Sacredligiosity

One of the most challenging areas of personal discipline we have to contend with is that of keeping an ever-sweeping eye on our surroundings, for the relentless invasion of the profane. The secular and humanistic societies mankind lives within have never, nor will ever work with us as disciples of Yeshua, to accomplish righteous living. The desires and passions of our carnal nature, combined with the pressures exuded via our "advancing" culture, create a continuingly more hostile environment—within which we are commanded to remain kadosh (holy).

It sure would be nice if those pressures would just stay outside our church buildings, and selectively leave us believers alone; but they don't. They mingle into our crowds and into our individual lives, ultimately finding their way into our homes. It would be one thing to contend only with ourselves. Like Paul, we can deal with that through the buffeting of our flesh and a daily dying ritual. But how does one take on a society? Most of us, even with the fifteen minutes of fame we are allotted, will never impact more than the small social ring that encircles us.

What the pressures bring with them is an almost irresistible force. If your home was like a levy, society is like a flood. Remember the classic children's story, *The Little Dutch Boy*? Hans saw a leak developing in the city wall and realized it was his responsibility to save the town. So he stuck his fingers into the hole, all throughout the night, until help came the next morning. Can you relate to that? There are always holes developing in our defenses. Our walls are always being tested. As parents, it often seems as though we have both our hands and feet stuck into the walls of our homes, and we are forced to watch over our shoulders as we helplessly observe holes and cracks forming, that we cannot shore up. Single parents only have four plugs. At least married couples have eight. Extended family may provide more plugs (as well as more leaks), but there never seems to be enough plugs.

Societal pressures, when mingled into our array of religions, have manifested themselves in various forms throughout history. The most common resulting manifestations seem to present through symbolism, festivals, icons and practices. Some of these subjects are very serious. Some are a bit on the lighter side. I pray you receive them accordingly.

Idolatry

Earlier, we discussed a desire of YHVH related to preservation. What else did He ask of us regarding Himself? He warned us to protect his Name from desolation and misuse, and He also asked us to protect His image from corruption.

You shall not make for yourself an idol, or any likeness of what is in heaven above or on the earth beneath or in the water under the earth. Thou shalt not bow down unto them, nor serve them. (Exodus 20:4 & 5)

Cursed is the man who makes an idol or a molten image, an abomination to the LORD, the work of the hands of the craftsman, and sets *it* up in secret. And all the people shall answer and say, 'Amen.' (Deuteronomy 27:15)

Anytime we try to reproduce the image of YHVH (which nobody has a copy of anyway), we effectively limit, reduce, or misrepresent His image in the world. Not all idolatry is done in an attempt to represent YHVH. Most is not. I'm going to assume that you, the reader, are not an idolater, in the pagan understanding; but I would like to talk to you about what could be considered "Christian idolatry".

Temunah is the Hebrew word for likeness. In addition to likeness, it also means: *Something portioned* (that is, *fashioned*) out, as a *shape*, that is, (indefinitely) *phantom*, or (specifically) *embodiment*, or (figuratively) *manifestation* (of favor): image, likeness, similitude. (Strong's #8544). Likeness, as well as these other added particulars, combine to portray a very broad-sweeping directive disallowing any reproduction of His image or character.

Have you ever wondered why there are no period-authentic etchings or carvings of the Messiah? Surely, considering His popularity and fame (to some) during His earthly life, someone would have recognized the value of immortalizing His image for future adoration. But because He has all knowledge, He knew that any image of Him considered genuine would have quickly become an object of worship. Just look at what happens when a pathetic resemblance of a woman's face shows up on the side of a turnip. It's Mary, Mother of God! Even as I am writing this, a report of Jesus's face being seen in the fins of the tail of a cocktail shrimp came over the radio waves—a cocktail shrimp of all places!

Let's consider the images we have in our midst today. We have statues of saints, Mary "Mother of God" and "Queen of the Universe". There are statues of Grecian and Roman gods and demi-gods, statues of Buddha, Confucius, Shiva and Vishnu, as well as the statues of the African tribal deities with which many ignorantly decorate their homes. Considering the fact that there are literally thousands of different gods, who can really count?

It's easy to recognize a "foreign" god/idol isn't it? But why is that? Is it because it's clearly not our god? How is it so clear, when we have no idea what our god looks like? The reason we are confident that no sculpture or statue represents YHVH, is because we know He transcends time and space, and we are forced to work within those confines. What people seem to be quick to forget is that so does Yehoshua. Simply because The Word spent thirty-three years here, in a tabernacle of flesh, does not necessitate that whatever He looked like here is what He looked like before His coming, or what He is going to look like when He comes again. He even apparently had two different looks during his residence here, considering His lack of being recognized following His resurrection. Any picture of Him that *falsely represents* Him is definitely wrong, and if it's definitely wrong then what is the point?

If painting an image of Him with gentle and comely eyes, soft and long, flowing, light-brown hair, a well-groomed beard, a miniature heart necklace wrapped by a ring of thorns, along with a solar disk around His head is supposed to help us adore Him, then we are *adoring an image.* Therefore, to some extent, that is idolatrous. Since we know He did not look like that because He was not praised as a handsome physical specimen (Isaiah 53:2), because he was a drifter (Matthew 8:20) and a Semite (medium dark-skinned), by making Him look otherwise for the purpose of adoration is also potentially, albeit ignorantly, committing a type of idolatry. I'm really perturbing people now, aren't I?

I believe, based on scriptural instruction and currently exampled shrine and image adoration, that any sculpture of Jesus, as well-meaning as it may be, is a type of idol. It is a "fashioned by human hand" image of something that "is in Heaven". Understand this though. Since there is only one true Elohiym, this creates a unique situation and problem. I believe it's possible that in this case alone, it *may* not be idol-atry to have

Sacreligiousity

this image. That sure sounded like double-talk to me also, so let's sift through this.

A picture that contains a likeness of Him, but does not focus on representing His image to assist our worship, may not be idolatry. For instance, if a poster had a rendition of Golgotha, and off in the distance there are three crosses with human forms upon them, that would not qualify as idolatry. A solely artistic, abstract, impressionist or other stylistic work that focuses on an event that occurred (e.g. daVinci's Last Supper) would be hard to qualify as idolatry. Historically, stained glass has done the work of evangelizing the illiterate, by telling stories of Messiah's work. Pending the details, in most cases, this too would scarcely qualify. As you can see, it can be difficult to define what is—not unlike the sometimes fine lines drawn between nude sculpture, sensual art and pornography. You might not be able to clearly define the difference with words; you just know it when you see it. And even that is subjective, according to the convicting eye of the beholder.

I do believe it is possible to idolize an image of Him. Otherwise, why the warning? I believe we primarily attempt to reproduce Him into an image to assist our worship, or to invoke emotional response. We adapt Him into something we are comfortable with; into our imagination. All these, though logically appreciable, are dangerous ground. Consider the fact that there are no images, in either painted or sculpted form, that attempt to represent the Father, found anywhere in Judaic centers of worship. The notion of such an idea is preposterous, working towards abomination. I'm not exactly sure why the idea of doing that to the Son has so much more liberty. Do we not, as believers in the Messiah, maintain high regards for Him, similar if not as unto the Father? If not, we most certainly should!

Is a picture of Jesus as abominable as false-god manufacturing? I would think not. His grace overlooks our ignorance often times. But then again, how much should we push it? The humanity of His incarnation is to be appreciated, but it is not to be worshipped. And, if you're not going to adore the image, why have the image? It is an unnecessary risk. Don't you think you will get to know Him better by studying His Word? If an image comforts you until He comes, then you're asking an image for something, and that's idolatry too. I know how silly this seems to some, but try to consider it wisely. I can guarantee you the disciples wouldn't have had a statue of Jesus in their homes. In their minds, He was to be just as esteemed as the Father was, and to try to make an image of the Father could have gotten them killed.

Because of the subjectivity in the identification of Christian idolatry, I will not conclude nor define for you, all that does qualify in your homes and places of worship. It is something you need to prayerfully assess and do for yourself. How far do you have to bow down? How much do you have to adore your images for it to be constituted idolatry, is hard to say. I can only suggest that as you examine your religious art you must, with open eyes, look and see whether or not the art brings you comfort, or a sense of security, or another inappropriate response that seems dependent upon the art itself. I pray that you will be able to recognize those pollutants, and clean your houses effectively.

Crux-Contamination

Speaking of what the disciples wouldn't have had brings a good lead-in for our next icon of choice: the crucifix, or cross.

The crucifix has found its way onto jewelry, t-shirts, plaques, steeples and sanctuary backdrops, gravestones, rear-view mirror air fresheners, stickers, Bible covers, greeting cards and more. Take a walk down magazine lane at your local bookstore and you'll see glittery, diamond-crusted crosses hanging from the necks of society's most popular urban icons; from heavy-metal rock stars to Oprah, Madonna and Cher. From the monk to the mayor, the cross knows no prejudice.

Although that's true for redemption, it has become a grossly over-glamorized symbol. In case you were not aware, the crux, stake or tree, as stated in Deuteronomy 21:23, is a potential curse. This Carthaginian/Roman death instrument was considered an extremely horrific way to be executed. It was a determent of crime and visual offense like no other.

Josephus tells stories (*War* 6 & 7) of the Romans crucifying people, along the walls of Jerusalem. Slightly paraphrased, he also said that the Roman soldiers would "amuse themselves by crucifying criminals in different positions. In Roman style crucifixion, the victim took days to die—slowly from suffocation. The dead body is not removed from the cross, but is left there for vultures and other birds to consume. The goal of Roman crucifixion was not just to kill the criminal, but also to *wreck* and dishonor the body of the condemned. In ancient tradition, an honorable death requires burial. So to wreck the body and not permit them to be buried, but to leave them hanging on a cross to decay is a serious dishonour on the person."

To make matters worse, there are stories that tell of the nails that were used to hang the victims on these trees, being gathered afterwards and used as healing amulets. Similarly, folklore ascribed magical powers to things related to the gallows in feudal times. Hmm, don't we have cross and spike jewelry now?

Because crucifixion continued into the fourth century, up until it was outlawed by Constantine, many of those who died upon this torture device were Jews as well. The Japanese killed Christians by crucifixion in the 16ᵗʰ Century. Hitler thought it would be humorous to restore the procedure and execute Jews this way, at the Dachau concentration camp. Considering all this, it is not hard to see another reason why Jews don't run to the Christian religion. Believers seem to adore the cross as much as they do the sufferer. To non-believers, the cross has literally become a meaningless symbol to the world. That shouldn't seem strange, because the cross is very familiar to it.

In various forms, the cross, or crux, has either been incorporated into, or is the main symbol representing various world religions, since at least as early as 2000 BCE. It has been seen on objects and writings from Ninevan, Egyptian, Grecian, Indian, Thessalian, Phoenician, American Indian, Luciferian, Mexican, Aztec, Etruscan and Celtic sources, as well as many more. There is nothing uniquely Christian about the cross.

Shouldn't the symbol (not the image) of Yehoshua, if there has to be one, be a menorah, or a Kiddush cup, or maybe a loaf of bread? Better yet, it would seem to me that the open and empty grave should be more what we focus on. Wearing a big-ol' cross around your neck in the early church period would have gotten you thrown out of the synagogue in a Brooklyn, New York minute. They would have probably considered you a necromancer, or at least someone infatuated with death. It would be comparable to adorning yourself with a glittery, golden guillotine or a stunning, electric-chair charm today. Have we forgotten how many Jews were killed in front of that symbol during the Crusades and Inquisitions?

This icon, when supporting an image of the dead body of Messiah, is as truly offensive as one can get. It is the quintessential example of idolatry! He is not dead! He is risen! Those of you with churches that bare an image of a dead Savior, tear down your idols! What a ridiculous notion it is to think Yehoshua is somehow blessed by such a scene. It's grotesque. Regardless of your feelings, is Yeshua in Heaven? Is it a crafted-by-man image? Is the image being bowed down to? If your answers are yes, I refer you directly to the second Commandment! He is our reflected image of the Father!

As far as I'm concerned, the mere fact that practically the whole world adores the cross shape (which likely isn't the actual instrument's shape; being that the two, common styles were more like a single pole, and a capital 'T'), would really cause me to second guess its value as an icon. Christians who wear them around your neck, I ask you to reconsider it as not the 'beautiful' reminder you think it is. If you are living the life of a disciple, you do not need a homicidal torture device hanging around your neck, to remind you of the cost. You should be carrying one on your shoulders instead. Anyway, it's not the cross that's precious, it's His blood. (Now don't go hanging a vial of that around your neck either!)

People of "the faith," go through your homes and remove the images and icons that seek to propose an image of Him. The gain you think you obtain from their presence is far outweighed by the injury of breaking the first couple of commandments. Prefer the feeling of obedience vs. nostalgia and image adoration. The symbol of the plain and simple wooden cross, somewhere *not* the focal point, inside the church or home is not horrible. I know many of you will still want one on a necklace. So if you must wear one, wear a humble one, under your clothes, in secret. Otherwise, it's no different than when the Pharisees wore their tzitzit (tassels) long and phylacteries wide, for all to see. Remember, Jesus rebuked them for that.

Some of you set out to collect various shapes and sizes as if it's an addiction, and have one on every wall. Just think about it. The world is celebrating His death with that symbol (even if unwittingly)—certainly not His life. And the churches that erect three, forty foot telephone pole crosses on your property, or mount one at the top of your high-place spires, or make money off it being a cell phone tower, have obviously no idea of its insensitivity and atrociousness, to the ones (Jews) you supposedly want to reach. The same is true with your images. Until we clean our church buildings out of their idols, you can pretty much forget about effectively reaching them. Although that is significant, it pales in comparison with the effect it has on the Spirit's desire to visit your places of worship. It's really rather creepy, and all the more so with a bloody body hanging off it.

There are those out there who want to be able to say this, but can't for various fears. I pray you discover the strength to lead your people in this truth. For those of you who don the plain fish symbol on your car, or something along that line, in that there is no harm. A symbol which represents you, or a group, is quite different from an image of adoration that represents Yeshua; unless of course, you are worshiping yourself. The exception to this though, is seen when the fish, which originally represented the "fishers of men," then develops teeth, (representing Yeshua), which is eating a fish with feet (representing evolution). As humorous as it may seem, Yeshua is not a fish. And having him represented that way, pretty clearly conflicts with Exodus 20:4.

Today, wearing a cross does not make a Christian, any more than an "I Voted" sticker makes you a patriot. The America one voter is hoping develops may be far different (Socialist) than the one many of you have fought for (Representative Republic). Just as the person of the Christ, many are proclaiming is Lord, may be far different from the One for which the Apostles died.

Sacreligiousity

Bust or Busted

What about statues? Well, in general, the rule of thumb would appear to be that any image created to receive adoration, or for the purpose of veneration, would be unauthorized. I do not believe that stuffed animals, or busts of Beethoven, are inherently wrong. But if you (as adults) were to draw upon them for strength, make requests of them, or habitually gaze at and/or touch them, then you've moved into the realm of idolatry; as anything that acts as a go-between (besides the Son) or substitute for the Father, is. In the case of human-figure statues such as the 'saints' of church history, or Greco-Roman gods, or images of foreign gods from other nations, or (and I know this is going to bother many of you) angels; I am confident there is no good to be found in them.

As far as the apostolic saints are concerned…once again, we don't really know what they looked like; but that's the lowest issue on the long, problematic list. Over the centuries, albeit sculptural masterpieces, many statues of those the Catholic and Anglican churches consider saints have been made and adored by the masses. First of all, The Holy Scriptures do not condone this behavior. As a matter of fact, the disciples were quick to make sure inappropriate adoration of them was abruptly stopped, and that it was redirected to the Messiah (Acts 14:12).

Next, the word rendered 'saint' in some translations of the Tanakh, in the Hebrew is: 'kadosh'. It is often used to identify an angel. The word itself means "to be set-apart" and is the origin of our term 'consecrated'. The term was applied to Aaron as the high priest as well, which identified him as a distinctly, holy person. Kadosh is from where the variant Kodesh comes from, which when combined with the word for Spirit 'Ruach', we get the Hebrew phrase for The Holy Spirit, Ruach HaKodesh. (Set-Apart Spirit)

Psalm 106:16, "When they became envious of Moses in the camp, And of Aaron, the holy one (kadosh) of the LORD…"

Another Hebrew word for saint is 'chasiyd', and it is used to represent people who live a pious and righteous life; in other words, encompassing all who were Torah observant lovers of Adonai. In the Greek, the word is 'hagios', and it has basically the same meaning as the Hebrew word 'chasiyd'. Because of this, we can see that 'saint' is not a special achievement term, but simply a term that all who are devout followers of Adonai can be labeled with. For simply being one of these, do you feel it is appropriate to have a statue made of you? I hope your answer was no. To live holy (set-apart) and devoted is the call of every child of the Most High. Many of the "saints" of the various religions previously mentioned have been given (attributed) particular powers or authorities, which can supposedly be called upon by mortals through prayers and rituals, to provoke change or blessings. According to Catholic online (catholic.org), there are over ten thousand different, named saints. Upon one visit there, I discovered Saint Isidore of Seville Sanctus Isidorus Hispalensis. He is the "Proposed Patron Saint of Internet Users." There is a prayer *with* him "before logging on".

But just so there is no misunderstanding about their relationship with these saints, I will give you a direct quote from their FAQ page.

Do Catholics pray *to* saints?

We pray with saints, not to them. Have you ever asked anyone to pray for you when you were having a hard time? Why did you choose to ask that person? You may have chosen someone you could trust, or someone who understood your problem, or someone who was close to God. Those are all reasons we ask saints to pray for us in times of trouble. (Sounds innocent enough, eh?)

Since saints led holy lives and are close to God in heaven (as compared to…?), we feel ("feelings, nothing more than…") that their prayers are particularly effective. Often we ask particular saints to pray for us if we feel they have a particular interest in our problem. (As if they have a clue.) For example, many people ask Saint Monica to pray for them if they have trouble with unanswered prayers, because Monica prayed for twenty years for her son to be converted. (Like that's never been done before.) Finally, her prayers were answered in a way she never dreamed of. Her son, Augustine, became a canonized saint and a Doctor of the Church. (Parenthetical sarcasm is mine.)

Question: Is this deemed okay by the Scriptures? You know—our authoritative resource for Truth?

But you, when you pray, go into your inner room, close your door and pray **to your Father who is in secret**, and your Father who sees *what is done* in secret will reward you. (Matthew 6:6; Yehoshua's words)

Question: If I have access to go straight to the Father, and He hears me, will he not answer my prayer because it came from me and not from someone else?

Question: If any given saint is not omniscient, and 8,397 Catholics are praying to him/her at any given time, will all the prayers be heard? Or, how many will be heard, and what aspect of the prayer got it through? Perhaps it is the one who prays the most, or the loudest, that gets the answer. Maybe if they say a prayer over and over again, it will push its way to the top. Perhaps, except…

Sacreligiousity

...when you are praying, do not use meaningless repetition as the Gentiles do, for they suppose that they will be heard for their many words. (Matthew 6:7, Yehoshua's words)

Keep this verse in mind, as you contemplate the Catholic pattern for penitence for sin, through repetitious prayers and the ritual of the Rosary Beads.

Hosting the Host

Another resurgence of an age-old, errant practice is that of invoking angelic interaction. Next time you take a trip to one of your local bookstore chains, take a wandering through the Religion/New-Age areas and see how many books exist regarding angels. There are books on getting to know your own guardian, learning to see them and call upon them, and learning the names of them and yours. There are books on the mythical escapades of their wars and their interactions with man. There are even books on how to communicate with them.

These creatures are little known and little understood. As mysterious as they are, there is no scriptural support for much, if any, of what these books teach about them. I'm certainly not going to embark on a journey of heading down their same road. I will only say a few things that are actually scripturally expressed. They war against demonic principalities. They are messengers. They bring judgment. They declare the Word of Yah. They refuse worship. They come in various forms and serve in various ways, around the Throne and in the Cosmos. One thing we know for sure...

Let no one keep defrauding you of your prize by delighting in self-abasement and the worship of the angels, taking his stand on *visions* he has seen, inflated without cause by his fleshly mind... (Colossians 2:18)

What is the only "prize" spoken of in Scripture that this verse could be talking about? Philippians 3:4 calls it the "upward call of God in Christ Jesus." Whatever that involves, I want it! And I'm not going to have any inappropriate affection towards a creature that the Scriptures specifically mention not to, especially if it can "defraud me."

Infatuation with the unknown is genuinely problematic when it comes to spiritual things. We have a bad habit of isolating a verse or two, and taking them out of context. Then, we'll create a doctrine, or even a whole religion from them, and that's a huge issue. If you have that habit, here are a couple verses to build your religion on:

1st Peter 1:12, "Unto whom it was revealed, that not unto themselves, but unto us they did minister the things, which are now reported unto you by them that have preached the gospel unto you with the Holy Ghost sent down from heaven; which things the angels desire to look into." (Angels are not omniscient, making them disqualified for worship.)

Matthew 13:49, "So it will be at the consummation of the age; the angels shall come out and separate the wicked from among the righteous…" (This may possibly happen to you if you treat angels inappropriately!)

The manufacturing and collecting of man-made, imagined images of these creatures, for the sake of promoting a greater intimacy with them, is idolatrous and mystical. Let me remind you again: Are angels from heaven above? Are we supposed to not make images of things from the heavens? You out there with angel fetishes—not smart. There is no teaching in Torah, or any Scripture, which allows for or encourages the attempt to develop relationships with these creatures. There is no scriptural evidence that we each have a full-time, appointed guardian angel to get to know. There is no scriptural evidence to support the idea that babies become little angels (cherubs), unless you believe that at some point babies are going to be judged.

1st Corinthians 6:3a, "Do you not know that we will judge angels?"

You would think the notion of keeping idols out of the house of a believer would be "a given". Apparently, that is not the case. Over the past fifteen years, my employment has taken me into the homes of more than three thousand customers. I, being an avid observer of people in general, always make a habit of looking for the evidences that would lead me to conclude from what religious flavor they come. I have been to homes with whole rooms dedicated to various gods, with miniature temples, twenty-plus idols, incense burning, libation, food and coin offerings, odd posters on the walls and so forth. As much as I hate seeing that, I have an easier time laughing at its foolishness, than dealing with another type of scenario.

I know this is a bit anecdotal as well, but I have been in an amazing amount of homes with all the typical, tell-tale signs of a believer, such as: Bibles, Jesus pictures, libraries with various Christian literature, *Footprints in the Sand* plaques, crosses on the wall, and copies of *The Purpose Driven Life* and *The Prayer of Jabez* on the nightstand. Yet, simultaneously, their house is adorned with Dream Catchers, Totem Poles and Celtic symbols, along with Brazilian, African, American-Indian, Mexican and Aboriginal statues and masks of the foreign gods of their land.

Unknown by most, I'm sure, many of those 'decorations' are masks and objects that were originally intended to invoke/provoke spirits to interact with man. They were used during rituals intended to control the weather. They were used to enhance fertility. They were used to entertain their gods and to appease them. They were/are used to increase luck and prosperity. They were also used to imbue individuals with demonic powers and the ability to perform witchcraft. I know the stuff can be aesthetically beautiful, artistic and curious, but I've not been able to find the verse that says, "I, YHVH your Elohiym, am a jealous Elohiym, who does not want you to love the things of this world, and do as it does. But, it's cool with me if you bring the world, with its gods, into your home to 'appreciate' them."

How many idols does it take to upset a Holy Elohiym? Sounds like the intro to a joke doesn't it? But I really don't think He's laughing. I have actually discussed these subjects with people who justify their appreciation, by labeling it a "heart issue". These same people, and I'm sure many others, would also find themselves capable of judging right or wrong by how they *feel* in other areas as well. But I'll warn you again...

Jeremiah 17:9, "The heart is more deceitful than all else and is desperately sick; who can understand it?"

If we were so good at judging things by our heart feelings, we wouldn't be in this depraved world to begin with. If we can trust our hearts so well, surely a king appointed by YHVH would be given a special gift of built-in discernment.

Now it shall come about when he sits on the throne of his kingdom, he shall write for himself a copy of this law on a scroll in the presence of the Levitical priests. It shall be with him and he shall read it all the days of his life, that he may <u>learn to fear the LORD</u> his God, by carefully observing all the words of this law and these statutes, that his heart may not be lifted up above his countrymen and that he may not turn aside from the commandment, to the right or the left, so that he and his sons may continue long in his kingdom in the midst of Israel. (Deuteronomy 17:18-20)

Guess not! If Yah's anointed king must study His Torah to practice it, and *learn* to fear Him, how much must we?

I would like for you to now read an excerpt from an article entitled, "*Idols and Icons: The Misrepresentation of Hinduism in the Press*" by David Frawley (Vamadeva Shastri). It was supposedly distributed to a Hindu student council at North Eastern University, date: Jan. 20th, 1994. I hope you find it as revealing as I did.

All the religions of the world - with the general exception of Protestant Christians, Muslims and Jews - use some sort of images or statues in their religious worship. Roman Catholic and Greek Orthodox churches abound with statues, paintings and pictures of various types. Hindu, Buddhist, Taoist and Shinto groups use them as well. Native American, African and Asian religions abound with them. The ancient religions of the entire world from Mexico to Greece, Egypt, Babylonia, Persia, India and China used images, as archeology so clearly reveals. The use of images appears as an integral part of human religious practices and no universal religion could be regarded as complete without them. Even many Protestant Christians have pictures of Jesus in their house or church, and Muslims often have pictures of their religious or political leaders, occasionally even depictions of Mohammed.

However, there is a strange dichotomy in how such religious images are judged. When they are part of the Christian tradition, they are called icons, and classified as works of art and regarded as sacred in nature. When they are part of non-Christian or pagan traditions, they are called "idols," which is a derogatory term that indicates not the sacred but mere superstition. In the case of Native American and African images, even when done by a culture as advanced as the Mayas of Central America which built great pyramids and had many great cities— they are lumped along with so-called primitive art. An image of Christ as the good shepherd is called an icon and viewed with respect. An image of Krishna as the good cow herder—which is a similar image of the Divine as watching over the souls of men—is called an idol, which encourages one to look down on it.

This is prejudice and negative stereotyping in language of the worst order. What Christian would accept calling a depiction of Christ an idol? To call such images as idols implies that those who worship them practice idolatry or take the image itself as a God. This adds yet more prejudice and error to this judgment. The use of an image—whether we call it an icon or an idol—does not imply belief in the reality of the image. That we keep a photograph of our wife and children, at our work desk, does not mean that we think our wife and children *are* the photograph. It is a reminder, not a false reality.

Well there you have it! I hope you are able to understand why I included that. Where is he wrong? Where is he right?

If you want to look at idols for some reason, go to a museum. But don't bring them into your home. Yes, that means when your decorator suggests a wonderfully coordinating fertility mask for your tropical room, you are going to have to 'just say no'. Seize the opportunity to share your beliefs if you can. I just cannot see why this is not so obvious; but apparently, it's not. If you want the Ruach to be comfortable in your home, why not make it a little less competitive for His attention. He is a Jealous Elohiym.

No matter how long we have been believers, or mature we think we are, we must take the time to examine our lives, and seek to know how

Sacreligiousity

idols find their way in. That is why He knew to give His children an annual Feast called "Unleavened Bread," where we are told to go throughout our dwellings, and search out the inevitable invasion of sin and idolatry, and "not let it be found among them." From a spiritual standpoint, it's hard enough to prevent these things from entering into our minds. Let us at least control what we can see, from entering into our homes.

Passover the Truth

Bede's *Historia ekklesiastica gentis Anglorum* ("Ekklesiastic History of the English People") contains a letter from Pope Gregory I, to Saint Mellitus, who was then on his way to England to conduct missionary work among the heathen Anglo-Saxons. In it, the Pope suggests that converting heathens is easier, if they are allowed to retain the outward forms of their traditional pagan practices and traditions, while recasting those traditions spiritually towards the one true God, instead of to their pagan gods (whom the Pope refers to as "devils").

…to the end that, whilst some gratifications are outwardly permitted them, they may the more easily consent to the inward consolations of the grace of God.

In the letter, the Pope sanctions such conversion tactics as biblically acceptable, pointing out that God did much the same thing with the ancient Israelites and their "pagan" sacrifices. Oh, I'm not so sure about that.

Another seemingly innocent gift from Catholicism is the replacement of YHVH's commanded, annual Passover Meal, with the invented weekly/monthly serving of the sacraments (Holy Communion). The wafer and the wine have become an ordinance of the church, and sadly, many have been duped into thinking it is a scripturally based liturgy.

Before you blow a gasket, the first and most obvious evidence for the connection is in the use of 'unleavened bread' within the ceremony. Unleavened bread is not part of any other laity-participating feast or ritual besides Pesach, and its adjoining week of 'Unleavened Bread'. Let us again go to the Scriptures, to look past our feelings and get back to the Truth.

In the first month, on the fourteenth day of the month at twilight is the LORD's Passover. Then on the fifteenth day of the same month there is the Feast of Unleavened Bread to the LORD; for seven days you shall eat unleavened bread. (Leviticus 23:5 & 6)

In the second month on the fourteenth day at twilight, they shall observe it (the Passover lamb); they shall eat it with unleavened bread and bitter herbs. (Numbers 9:11; This being the back-up date, for those who couldn't make the first.)

You shall remember that you were a slave in Egypt, and you shall be careful to observe these statutes. (Deuteronomy 16:12)

Now on the first *day* of Unleavened Bread the disciples came to Jesus and asked, "Where do You want us to prepare for You to eat the Passover?" (19) The disciples did as Jesus had directed them; and they prepared the Passover. (Matthew 26:17 & 19)

And when He had given thanks, He broke it and said, "this is My body, which is for you; do this in remembrance of Me." In the same way *He took* the cup also after supper, saying, "this cup is the new covenant in My blood; do this, as often as you drink *it*, in remembrance of Me." (1st Corinthians 11:24 & 25)

No matter how you roast and slice it, Yehoshua was continuing to be obedient to the Torah's mitzvoth regarding Pesach, and Paul promoted the continuation of Passover after His death (1st Corinthians 11). I freely challenge anyone to show me the text where Yehoshua instructs anyone to be disobedient to, or teaches contradictory to, the Torah of Moses. You can't! So then, specifically relating to this case, where did He tell them to attend the Passover more than when it was supposed to be done? If you assume, as apparently many others do, that the words "as often as you drink it" implies an unrestricted amount, you are inserting more into the text than what is actually there.

What *is* actually being said in the original text, is no more than and no different than the slightly less poetic, "When you do it, remember me." ('When' and 'whenever' can have the same exact meaning.) If you were going to impute something into the text, it could be the well understood (at the time) tradition of four, different glasses being on the table (*m. Pesah.* 10:1; *t. Pesah.* 10:1). These four cups being the cups of: Sanctification, Deliverance (a.k.a. Judgment), Redemption and Hope (a.k.a. Kingdom). It is possible that He was saying, "When you drink this cup ("Redemption") during this ceremony, understand that I will now be fulfilling this symbol." I will admit that this is at best an implication, but it is a far more likely interpretation than the one that says: The 'church' (once it arrives), from now on will not have any obligation to Passover. Just take two symbols out of the many, and use them whenever and however you want.

When was the last time you were reminded during Communion, that we were slaves in Egypt? When were you last instructed to begin the feast of Unleavened Bread (the 14th through 21st of Nisan), directly following Communion? What about the bitter herbs? The gospels' depictions of Yehoshua's participation in the Abib (springtime/early

Sacreligiousity

barley harvest) festivals <u>contain no reference to their being eradicated</u>.

The majority of the visible church teaches that Yehoshua fulfilled all the prophetic shadows of these things, and that they have replaced Israel, so they instituted another fabricated 'remembrance' in the form of the communion, to remember the 'remembrance' (new covenant institution) Yehoshua added to the 'remembrance' of the Egyptian deliverance, which is Pesach. You see, many celebrate a third generation, knock-off. Who authorized this? Surely, if He intended for the Egyptian deliverance to be forgotten, He would have been clearer about that to His disciples. His Final Passover (last supper), would have been the perfect time to *abolish* the shadow; but it is quite clear that did not happen.

As I just mentioned, it is likely that "this cup," the one Yehoshua was holding at the time He made His declaration of institution, was the third cup of the traditional group of four. The word used for cup in every occurrence in the narrative is the same; 'poterion', which means "a drinking vessel," so that is not where we find the clue. He took the cup and blessed it, just before He broke the bread. Following the pattern of the traditional Seder format, the cup that is drank from, just prior to the breaking of the Afikoman (the special dessert matzoh), after the meal, is that of 'Redemption'. The Torah *sanctifies* us (cup 1). We had been and will be again, *delivered* (cup 2). Our *hope* has always had to be placed in the Elohiym of Israel, and on His future Kingdom (cup 4). But we were about to see the full redemptive strategy for the first time. The new covenant has a New Redeemer/Priest (cup 3)!

"*But* why wouldn't He appreciate our desire to remember Him more often than once per year?" There we go again, assuming He thinks as we do. If we are living out a walk of faith that presumes our reasoning supersedes Adonai's authority, as in controlling our calendar, we can plan on a lot more divine disciplining in our lives. Of that, you can be assured. There is a cup that remains to be drunk from, and it is the same one Yeshua said He would wait to drink anew, in His Father's Kingdom.

Again, I refer to you the concept of the Mo'adim being HIS, not ours. They are His appointed festivals, and we are invited to them. Sure you don't have to go, but is that really what you want? Try following Adonai's calendar for a while, and I assure you, it lacks no good thing. The Holy Sacraments, as well-meaning as they may be to many of us, when misused, trick the Body of Messiah into being partly disobedient, while thinking they are doing just the opposite.

Communion, also known as the Eucharist, once involved the belief that upon the "Consecration" of the elements, the "Presence of Christ" would dwell within the elements, and then upon ingestion into your body, are transfigured into the actual flesh and blood of the Messiah. This is called the doctrine of transubstantiation. The "Adoration" of the elements takes place prior to their consumption. This adoration of the bread and wine is nothing less than idolatrous, for it worships the 'presence' within the elements.

Leviticus 7:26, "Moreover ye shall eat no manner of blood, whether it be of fowl or of beast, in any of your dwellings (KJV)."

Genesis 9:4, "But flesh with the life thereof, which is the blood thereof, shall ye not eat (KJV)."

Deuteronomy 12:23, "Only be sure that thou eat not the blood: for the blood is the life; and thou mayest not eat the life with the flesh (KJV)."

Leviticus 3:17, "It shall be a perpetual statute for your generations throughout all your dwellings, that ye eat neither fat nor blood (KJV)."

Though not all practitioners of the Eucharist believe in the transubstantiation of the elements, the Adoration of them is commonplace in the RCC (Roman Catholic Church), and they do so because of the supposed 'presence' of Christ surrounding them (transignification). Taking an object, stone or bronze, bread or wine, and worshiping His proposed presence indwelling or surrounding it, is idol worship as far as He has defined it in His Word. These verses now become much more disconcerting:

Therefore, whoever eats the bread or drinks the cup of the Lord in an unworthy manner, shall be guilty of the body and the blood of the Lord. (1st Corinthians 11:27)

For he who eats and drinks, eats and drinks judgment to himself if he does not judge the body rightly. (1st Corinthians 11:29)

For this reason many among you are weak and sick, and a number sleep. (1st Corinthians 11:30)

Why is this level of importance and judgment placed on such a 'common' observance? Think about it. How many times have you heard these verses read during the communion ceremony, and as hard as the preacher tried to make an impression with these words, it never seemed to really click as to who these words were really speaking to, or how they related to us? Here's the thing: For those of you out there who think that the Tanakh is useful for history, but contains little obligatory instruction, you cannot also say this "New Testament" mitzvah is not for you as well. I suppose you can say it, but if you believe it, masks on your wall are the least of your concerns.

If you understand that this commentary by Paul is in relation to Pesach, (or at least a "gentilized" variant of it, e.g, Jude 1:12), it becomes much clearer. The rules regarding its observance are clear. Strangers to the covenant are not allowed to participate. Men, to eat the lamb, must be

Sacreligiousity

circumcised. Pesach must be performed on the 14th day of Nisan, etc. If these rules are not being met, we are mocking the Deliverer of both our flesh and our spirits, and also His appointed remembrance.

So then, my brethren, when you come together to eat (Passover), wait for one another. If anyone is hungry, let him eat at home, so that you will not come together for judgment. The remaining matters I will arrange when I come. (1st Corinthians 11:33 & 34)

With these closing words of this chapter, it is apparent that this feast/rite was a notorious event for those who did not fully understand it, (new "gentile" converts) to think they were invited to a 'shindig' for a chow-down. Firstly, what the church does for communion now is incapable of being perverted into a chow-down. And secondly, this was a post-ascension scenario being discussed by an Apostle of the early church. Therefore, the ramifications of abuse, weakness, sickness and death, should still be considered as potential, current effects. Allow me to really challenge you now. Could these results of disobedience be remedied by medicine? Can a doctor look at a sickness and diagnose it as an effect of sin? "Ah yes, Mr. Smith. It appears that you are suffering from acute Passover abuse. I'm sorry. There is nothing more we can do." Is it possible that the apparent lack of blessings promised in accordance with the covenants (much of which is health-related) the church seems to have, is related to this simple, errant practice we think is so holy?

Then thirdly, we have the "remaining matters" to be dealt with. We know of several issues the Corinthians had to do deal with; but in context, this comment is related to Pesach. We can only speculate that there were other abuses and misappropriations regarding this feast, but the mere suggestion that there were issues, should call us to further guard ourselves from such things occurring within our fellowships.

Therefore, **let us celebrate the feast** (Passover), not with old leaven, nor with the leaven of malice and wickedness, but with the unleavened bread of sincerity and truth. (1st Corinthians 5:8)

Luke 22:16 & 18 tells us that the Passover, although originally ancient, evolved into something new in the Apostolic era. It is still yet going to evolve again, because Yeshua is waiting to eat it again. It therefore stands to reason we should continue to observe it for all three reasons.

You can strip away the transubstantiation, and withdraw any adoration of the elements, and what you'll have left is still a substitute for the truth. The modern form of Passover we call Communion is not His desire, obedient to Scripture, or authorized by the Apostles. Is it a sin? No, if it supplements and not replaces! My prayer is that someday the church will open its eyes to this deception, and restore the authentic for the imposter. There are some out there that are; and if you are part of one, you are blessed. Just try not to *play* Passover. Embrace it like the slave you once were.

Yochanon the Mikveh Man

Repent, for the kingdom of heaven is at hand. (Matthew 3:2)

...and they were being baptized by him in the Jordan River, as they <u>confessed their sins</u>. (Matthew 3:6)

As for me, I baptize you with water <u>for repentance</u>, but He who is coming after me is mightier than I, and I am not fit to remove His sandals; He will baptize you with the Holy Spirit and fire. (Matthew 3:11)

Then Jesus arrived from Galilee at the Jordan coming to John, to be baptized by him. But John tried to prevent Him, saying, "I have need to be baptized by You, and do You come to me?" But Jesus answering said to him, "Permit it at this time; for in this way it is fitting for us to <u>fulfill all righteousness</u>." Then he permitted Him. (Matthew 3:13-15)

Tell me you've never scratched your head over this passage. How in the world is Yehoshua "fulfilling all righteousness"; especially since others were confessing and repenting? What does that mean? If we keep in consideration that righteousness should be understood as right obedience, with a right heart, according to YHVH's instruction, it will quickly lose its mysteriousness.

Although the Scriptures do not tell us exactly what Yehoshua was doing just prior to this event, it is quite possible and probable that He was in a ritually unclean (tamei) state, and was undergoing a mikveh (immersion) before sundown, as is prescribed by Torah.

Furthermore, anything that the unclean *person* touches shall be unclean; and the person who touches *it* shall be unclean until evening. (Numbers 19:22)

For this reason, it was pretty much a given that if you were going to go into the synagogue, but most definitely when entering into the temple area, you would undergo a ritual bath; even as a *just in case* you were unclean and didn't know it. Appropriately, it was quite common that some people, especially priests, would be "baptized" on a daily basis. Although there were differing regulations for the Levites and High Priest than for a common citizen, Yehoshua knew who He was in the Spirit, although others had not yet discovered.

He shall bathe his body with water in a holy place and put on his clothes, and come forth and offer his burnt offering and the burnt offering of the people and make atonement for himself and for the people. (Leviticus 16:24)

This verse is speaking of Aaron, and all following High Priests, regarding the procedure immediately following the release of the scapegoat (azazel) into the wilderness, and just prior to the fat of the sin offering being burnt upon the altar. This ritual *may* be understood as a foreshadowing. Whereas when Yeshua was to undergo His mikveh, HaSatan would be released into the desert, in preparation for Yeshua's proving. Though His pop quiz began and ended in the desert, His exam really continued up until the day of His becoming the Passover Lamb for all mankind.

Speaking of the scapegoat, there are those who have interpreted it to be a picture of the Messiah. A quick glance at the ritual could bring that conclusion, but I would like to present another possibility. The azazel was one of two goats. One bore the guilt of the Israelite's forever, by being brought into exile, by a special man. The other became a sin offering, whose blood was sprinkled upon the east side of the Mercy Seat. Michael the archangel will be leading HaSatan away, for eternal banishment and suffering, and will carry with him the guilt; as though they are the spoils of his achievements. Yehoshua became the one who shed His blood for atonement. It would seem that Yehoshua is actually best represented by the "goat for YHVH," and not the azazel. (Note: Azazel is the name of HaSatan, in the apocryphal book of Enoch.)

I do not want to be dogmatic on this issue of the symbolism, but the reason for the baptism I am quite sure of. The practice of a ritual bath is both well-documented and archaeologically supported, by the multiple pools which have been uncovered, surrounding the temple sight. Also, it is still practiced all over the world, for various reasons, such as: purification after a woman's niddah (menstrual separation), after childbirth, for the koshering of utensils, before weddings, in preparation for Yom Kippur and more.

John was a prophet, whose ministry was to assist those undergoing this ritual, to see the bigger picture in it, and to call people to repentance (always the heart of Torah). A rule of mikveh is that the immersion itself must take place in 'mayim chayim' (living water) for 'teshuvah' (repentance), so what better place than the ever-renewing Jordan River; (where all of Israel symbolically underwent a mikveh, upon entering Canaan.) He pointed people to the coming Messiah, who would soon come and be the true, living water for Israel. He saw the temporal nature to the mikveh, as it was something that required reapplication continually within the Israelite community.

What is not generally understood about this scriptural story regarding Yehoshua's famous mikveh is that this was by no means the first time he had undergone this, and it was certainly not the last. Up until the day He died, in order to "fulfill all righteousness," He would have had to undergo this ritual every time He touched a dead person, or a leprous person, after the healing of the woman with the issue of blood, and whenever He visited the house of a tamei (unclean) woman. And not just Him alone, but any Torah abiding citizen of Israel would find themselves undergoing the mikveh quite often. Another significant use, which is also represented in Scripture, is the mikveh that was done as part of the conversion process of becoming a 'Jew'. As a proselyte to Judaism, one would go under the water as a gentile, and arise as a new creation—a Jew. This is still practiced today.

Since Yehoshua clearly didn't need to repent of anything, that leaves the conversion bath to consider. He certainly wasn't converting to anything (becoming a Christian), so this specially noted mikveh should not be thought of as one. The only reason it has any significance at all, is due to all of the extraneous events associated with it, and because it demonstrates His commitment to obeying even the seemingly unnecessary laws.

One of the many ramifications of the "no OT rules for me" theological perspective is the idea of baptism being a 'one-time' special ceremony that is part of the conversion process to Christianity. Catholicism and other religions have chosen of their own accord, to forgo the scripturally supported submersion, and substitute it with a 'christening' or 'sprinkling'. As precious as that moment may seem, it has no spiritual meaning or value whatsoever; considering the required 'repentance' that was always adjoining the original process. I would like to meet the two-month old who is concerned with ritual purity before entering the sanctuary, or is converting to the faith of anything for that matter. Baptism/mikveh is only of consequence, with a full understanding of its purpose. Early Christians did adopt the sprinkling practice (for conversion) when no mayim chayim was available. (Didache ch.7)

Due to the church's historical rejection of most all things Jewish, there has been a great loss of understanding regarding this ritual, hence the misuse. "Go ye therefore, make disciples, and baptize (mikveh) them" never meant or alluded to this being a one-time act. When they made converts, they underwent a mikveh as part of that process, as was the custom. But instead of just participating in the 'shadow', they were baptized with the fullness of understanding. A funny thing about the Jewish perspective is that they consider the mitzvah of mikveh to be one of the laws that fall under the category called 'chukkim'. This basically means it is a requirement of Adonai that has unspecified rationale, or

Sacreligiousity

there must be a meaning that goes beyond human understanding. I can understand that, if I think too analytically. I don't look at it like that, for it seems to me a beautiful picture of the need for purity in His Bride. But that's just my opinion. Much understanding is lost without Messiah.

These mitzvoth are found in Leviticus 15. When examined, we recognize that without a temple, some of the details become inapplicable. But that does not invalidate the heart of its purpose. Again, a full study on the laws of Niddah is beyond the scope of this book, but it is also a worthwhile endeavor in one's pursuit of personal holiness (i.e., avoiding intercourse during menstruation).

I, in my desire to be Torah observant, conclude the mitzvoth related to Niddah and Mikveh are still valid and to be considered; and I'm not alone. Repentance and purity are not issues that ceased relevance, upon the crux. However, due to the work of Messiah on that crux, there have definitely been some changes. As just mentioned, we no longer have a temple edifice. But there is a living temple, of which we are the stones. With Living Water now flowing from Yeshua's side, we are spiritually cleansed by that (Ephesians 5:26). Though these are true, there is still a physical principle at work.

Therefore, COME OUT FROM THEIR MIDST AND BE SEPARATE, says the Lord. AND DO NOT TOUCH WHAT IS UNCLEAN; and I will welcome you. (2nd Corinthians 6:17)

Physical things teach us spiritual principles. The mikveh is a physical action designed to focus our attention on spiritual contamination. Yeshua is perpetually cleansing us spiritually, but like how we dealt with sin and grace before, we should not abuse this fact by disregarding contaminants. Remember, we are talking about ritual contamination here, so without ritual it seems moot. But our life is now a continuous rehearsal for perpetual holiness later. Again, you won't lose your salvation necessarily, but how much contamination do you think you can take, without some kind of detriment? During the thousand-year reign of Messiah, when the temple is again physical, even though there will be spiritual perfection, there can still be physical contamination. What do you think was the issue at hand, in John 20:17, when Yeshua told Mary not to touch Him? Is it starting to come together for you now?

The choice of believers who mikveh today, is not to diminish the work of Messiah. It is to more appreciate and reflect upon Him. It is also forward-looking. As the tzitzioth (tassels) relate to sin, a mikveh is a reminder to avoid the unclean. Uncleanness and holiness are spiritually contrary.

But the man who is unclean and dos not purify himself from uncleanness, that person shall be cut off from the midst of the assembly, because he has defiled the sanctuary of the LORD; the water for impurity has not been sprinkled on him, he is unclean. (Numbers 19:20)

Your study in these matters will also lead you to conclude that baptism is full submersion (#G908, Baptisma; to dip, or sink. Ceremonially wash). Sprinkling is altogether different. That verse is a prop used to support the practice of sprinkling as a form of baptism. However, the act of sprinkling water, as detailed in Numbers 19, was reserved specifically for dealing with uncleanness from contact with human death; not new life! And since it is unlawful to manufacture the specific mixture required to make this water, it's a moot point for now. Either way, baptism is not the once-forever act that many think it is. Since we dare not suppose Yehoshua was converting to anything, what else could He have been doing?

So what is modern, infant sprinkling then? In reality, it is nothing. Not a single thing is either accomplished, or set in motion to be accomplished, by the dribbling of water on an infant's head. It is purely a religious ceremony. Submersion is required to represent a death and resurrection. Sprinkling could be performed on ritual utensils (to make them ceremonially clean) because they were non-living. Sprinkling for ceremonial cleansing and baptism (mikveh) are two different acts entirely.

My fear is that, as well as with the Protestant version of 'Dedication', parents can *potentially* feel that this act sets the destiny of the child in motion, and that they can relax their duties in regards to actively promoting the spiritual welfare of their children. The acts of christening or dedicating your children, in themselves, have no divine power to assure accomplishing anything whatsoever. Such is the same for adult water baptism. If you've never heard the Adversary laugh with glee, just say aloud, "That's not what I believe!"

Before the Heavenly throne, there is a great river of living water. I wonder what that represents. Perhaps, Jeremiah 17:13 will shed some light on it.

O LORD, the <u>hope</u> of Israel, All who forsake You will be put to shame. Those who turn away on earth will be written down, because they have forsaken the fountain of living water, even the LORD.

In the Hebrew text, the word seen translated here as *hope*, is actually *mikveh*! I trust that you will pursue a deeper understanding of this topic, and apply the principles to your own life. Thereby fulfilling the commandments (all righteousness) and receiving Torah's promised accompanying blessings.

Altar or Motives

Deuteronomy 12:13 & 14, "Take heed to thyself that thou offer not thy burnt-offerings in every place that thou seest; (14) but in the place which the LORD shall choose in one of thy tribes, there thou shalt offer thy burnt-offerings, and there thou shalt do all that I command thee (KJV)."

A popular trend, in most all traditional churches, is to have what are called 'altars' down at the front of the sanctuary. Sometimes they are tables on which the sacraments are placed. Sometimes they are called 'kneeling altars', as they are spots appointed for prayer and meditation. It is generally understood that the area down front, below the pulpit, where responders to a call to repentance or for prayer go, is considered the altar; hence the phrase "altar call".

I realize the purpose of these places is to create an emotional tie with the One who was our sacrifice, so I want to be sensitive to the innocent intent. Being one who has spent some time down at them myself, either for me or for others, I have an affiliation with them as well. But I am not immune to misunderstanding, and have had to have my mind regenerated as much as the next person does.

Having an "Altar of Remembrance" display the holy sacraments is built on the transubstantiation concept. That stomach turning notion is entirely unbiblical, and therefore unsupportive of a need for such an item. The place where the "Bread of the Presence" was displayed in the Tent of Meeting was called a table, and so should it be in our places of meeting.

From the time of the Second Temple's destruction, there has been no authorized place to continue the offerings, as prescribed in Torah. This is the entire reason that Israelite communities do not have altars set up in their larger regions around the world; i.e., there is no 'Baltimore' altar. For the same reason, no synagogues have one in their courtyard. It has always been understood that without 'thee' altar, there are no sacrifices. This is the reason many Jews struggle internally to cope with the possible ramifications, and hope upon hope that all will be well for them, as they die without tangible atonement. The absence of a real altar is why we have "remembrance" altars; but is there inappropriateness we should be cognizant of?

We have been called to be living sacrifices, holy and acceptable. We are shown the concept of being "poured out like a *drink* offering" by Paul the Pharisee. Do we have an example of anyone suggesting we literally give our lives as a *sin offering*? No, of course not; as that would be false-doctrine. We cannot be our own sin offering, and even if we could, we have no authorized location for such. Going down to an 'altar' inside our churches is considered spiritual symbolism, but it is an emotionally driven practice in principle. Furthermore, there has never been an indoor altar for sacrifice described or authorized in Scripture, and the only place that type of altar may be found, is in cultic expressions of false religions.

My real problem with indoor, traditional church "altars" is that they are often dramatically *offered* in a way as to give the false sense that you can toss yourself onto some imaginary fire, and let yourself be consumed, as if that would please Adonai. Human sacrifices are not allowable and are again, only seen occurring within cultic expressions of false religions. You never would have been invited to toss yourself onto an imaginary altar in the early church, as you are not an acceptable burnt-offering. The whole notion would have seemed quite inappropriate and absurd. Yes, our sin deserves death; but stoning was the prescribed method. The imagery is therefore built on a rather detestable premise. We are not Phoenixes rising up from the ashes! I realize this seems like a silly argument, but that is only because of our loss of a Hebraic mindset, and because we are unfamiliar with Temple life.

The only sacrifice we are to be is a living one. There is no material altar needed for this to take place. I'm not saying making public confessions of faith, or praying and being prayed for down front, is necessarily a bad thing (although it's actually a recently developed practice in church history). I just think we should avoid calling them altars. The "old man" dies there sometimes, but not as a sacrifice. The only place a "spiritual" altar now exists is within your soul, where you willfully surrender your carnal desires.

The next time you are in a service where you are asked to "go to the altar," I hope you will think about the concept a little more accurately. Obviously, if it were a viable option, surely people would all leave the altar wholly consumed. There simply is no such thing as an indoor altar in Scripture. Stairs are prohibited for use in approaching the altar, and the only place authorized to have an altar is the place where "He placed His Name"; that place being Jerusalem. And, if that's not enough, "consuming fire" is also symbolic of judgment. The Refiner's fire is altogether different.

Now, if you want to think of yourself as a: member, citizen, vessel, heir, son or daughter, bond-servant or whatnot, then feel free. You can go up and down the *aisle*. I believe ministering to people down front is fine. It just shouldn't happen at a place made for sacrifice—made for humans.

Exodus 20:26, "And you shall not go up by steps to My altar, so that your nakedness will not be exposed on it."

Sacreligiousity

In many churches, the platform, under which the officiating of the service is done, is wrapped around the front by steps used to "go up" onto it. It is also this very same area that is often strewn with people who have responded to an altar call. Again, seems silly I know. But this is in direct violation of His prescribed means to perform sacrifices. There is no other purpose to an altar than to burn offerings, or splatter blood against, no matter what we 'feel' otherwise. So, by hanging out on steps crying out, "Consume me!" we are really stretching ourselves past the point of proper symbolism, even if that is our only intent. Does this mean there should be no steps up to the platform? Not at all! As long as it's considered a platform. There is one more related, 'silly' thing I would like for you to think about—this time, with an actually humorous aspect.

Looking closely at the previous verse, you will notice that the command is regarding our 'nakedness' not being exposed. I figure you might have already been thinking to yourself that this is not something to be worried about. But when you read that either this time, or in the past, did you ask yourself anything like: How would that happen? Although it is true that certain garments may have allowed for 'easy viewing' if you were directly under them; in this case, that is not the entirety of what is being considered.

Holy Fruits of the...Loom

The Levitical priesthood was required to wear undergarments (Exodus 28:42) as part of their uniform, rendering Exodus 20:26 rather pointless on the surface. And since the priests would be the ones performing the service, why even mention it? The word rendered 'nakedness' in the Hebrew is 'ervah'. Although this word is related to the exposure of one's private parts, it is also affiliated with the shame and uncleanness associated with that exposure. Based on the prescribed covering of these areas, and the simple fact that Adonai has x-ray vision anyway, it would seem that there has to be, in addition to the literal/physical meaning, a symbolic/spiritual one as well.

What was the very first occurrence of nakedness we encounter in Scripture? And what had to happen in response to its appearance? A covering and a sacrifice. Sin creates shame. Sin initiated the knowledge of nakedness. The shame of nakedness is a remembrance of original sin. Sin requires sacrifice. Each time a priest put on his undergarments; he was reminded that the whole purpose his office existed was to help counter the effects of sin. There is another religion in our world that is familiar with 'holy' undergarments. Among many other errors, their wearing of them is based on the false predication that they can become Koheins (priests of the lineage of Aaron) known as 'saints', upon completing their secret temple rites. It is hard for me not to laugh, as sad as it is, when I think about how they can concern themselves with such obscure and whispered details, and yet miss the much more critical and thunderous calls from the mountain.

Please, at least take this opportunity to see how even with the best of intentions, we are capable of allowing our feelings to rule our behaviors; instead of allowing Scripture to rule our reasoning. In regards to spiritual things, we should be over-cautious. Everything we practice and teach has a consequence, and not always obviously. Envisioning yourself offered as a sacrifice is appealing to your emotions, but you will utterly be placing your trust in a vain imagination. But then again, maybe because of grace, we don't need to concern ourselves with all these old details. Except for one little thing: The entire sacrificial program was an institution designed to illustrate grace. I hope you are soon, if not already, readily able to see this.

Anointing for Appointing

I really want to apologize if it just seems like I'm beating up on everything that seems so innocent and sacred. It is very difficult to tackle ancient traditions, and even more so, ancient principalities. I'm not saying that everything we do wrong is necessarily due to demonic influences, but they are a strong source of confusion. They are, in a sense, the agents' provocateur of the Father of Lies.

This next area of study, I believe, is truly one of the more innocent but misappropriated practices commonly engaged in.

Then Jacob awoke from his sleep and said, "Surely the LORD is in this place, and I did not know it." He was afraid and said, "How awesome is this place! This is none other than the house of God, and this is the gate of heaven." So Jacob rose early in the morning, and took the stone that he had put under his head and set it up as a pillar and poured oil on its top. (Genesis 28:16-18)

This is the first instance of oil being used in the Scriptures as an 'anointing' tool. At best, we can only speculate how the concept of anointing with oil came about. Prior to this usage, there does not seem to be any instruction to do so, through either inspired man or recorded unction. Logically, it wouldn't make sense that someone, after having the experience Jacob just had, would react by looking around, setting up a stone marker, and then grabbing some spare olive oil and dumping it on top of a stone. Really, how long was the oil residue going to last anyway? But that's not the oddest part. What in the world was Jacob doing, carrying around some oil on his person anyway? Who carries oil around?

Well, someone who lived several thousand years ago most certainly would. Having to bake a fresh loaf of roadside bread was a given, if you were journeying far, and oil was a key ingredient to doing so. Not only was olive oil a food related need, but it was also a skin-healer/protector for minor injuries one might incur. Olive oil is also used in the making of castile soaps, although no one can say how far back exactly this particular use goes. But there is another use that is significant; that use being the main fuel of ancient (and modern alike) oil lamps. Oil was more than the juice of pressed olives; it was a staple of life. Although it could be considered plentiful, like anything of quality back then, a good amount of work was required to press and filter olives into fine, clear oil. One may go so far as to say it was near precious.

Haven't you asked yourself when reading this story in the past, "How could anyone sleep on a rock pillow?" It's easy, when you understand a certain aspect of the story. The answer: Jacob was really, really tired. But seriously…the Rock has at numerous times in Scripture been an allegorical symbol of the Messiah. "…and all drank the same spiritual drink, for they were drinking from a spiritual rock which followed them, and the rock was Christ (1st Corinthians 10:4)." When you lean upon this Rock, you will always be comforted!

So Jacob awoke, realized he had been with the Almighty in some form or another, and felt the need to memorialize the event. Turning the pillow vertical, a marker was created; and then to top it off, he 'set-apart' the rock, by taking some of his precious oil and pouring it directly onto it. Having then been 'anointed', even if that rock was to topple, it would still remain set-apart in the mind of Jacob.

The next place oil shows up on the scene is in Exodus 25, and here it is shown to be the fuel for the Lampstand of the Tabernacle. As you know, the Tabernacle was the first 'House of YHVH', and as all the furnishings of its composition did, the Lampstand symbolized Yehoshua; this one being He as the 'Light of the World". The Oil in this lamp was to never run out (Exodus 27:20). I wonder why that is? Right away, after this appearance, in the same context, oil is found being mixed with fine flour to produce the three different, ceremonial breads. This bread, another picture of Messiah, was to be perpetually fresh and displayed on the special table set aside to do that. Now watch what happens in 29:7,

"Then you shall take the anointing oil and pour it on his head and anoint him."

Here we see it again, being poured out as a marker of sorts. This time, on a person. Not just any person either, but Aaron, who was about to become the first Kohen ha'Gadol (the High Priest). Then it was sprinkled on his garments and on his son's garments, setting him and them apart for their special purposes.

Then Samuel took the horn of oil and anointed him in the midst of his brothers; and the Spirit of the LORD came mightily upon David from that day forward. And Samuel arose and went to Ramah. (1st Samuel 16:13)

This kind of anointing is known by the Hebrew word 'mashach'. It is a mark of consecration. It is from where we get the word Mashiach, or Messiah (Anointed One). And if you haven't already guessed, the Greek equivalent 'chrio' is from where we get the word Christos, or Christ (Anointed One). This is how oil initially came to be connected with, and representative of, the Spirit.

Are you seeing the obvious? Oil being placed upon someone in the Scriptures is often a means of appointing someone to Elohiym's specified role. Quite clearly, a simple examination of all the references to the anointing by oil in the Hebrew Scriptures, shows it is mostly synonymous with the appointing of either a position in the priesthood or kingship, or into a significant place of authority, such as a prophet. Oil was used in the dedication process of setting-apart the furnishings and vessels for use in the Mishkan (tabernacle) and temple. The other references to anointing with oil relate to its cosmetic value of brightening the countenance, generally for those who are fasting or mourning. Now let's examine the Apostolic Scriptures and see how they portray this application.

But a certain Samaritan, being on a journey, came by him, and having seen him, he was moved with compassion. And having approached, he bandaged his wounds, pouring on oil and wine. Then having placed him on his own beast [of burden], he brought him to an inn and took care of him. (Luke 10:33 & 34)

This story portrays the act of what the other references to the application of 'anointing' are also expressing. When you see people 'anointing with oil' the sick, this is what is going on. For example:

Mark 6:13, "And they were casting out many demons and were anointing with oil many sick people and healing them."
James 5:14, "Is anyone among you sick? Then he must call for the elders of the church and they are to pray over him, anointing him with oil in the name of the Lord."

The Greek word for anoint that is used here is *aleipho*. This word is used when the idea of applying something like a balm or make-up is being portrayed. Although it fits into our modern mold of understanding,

Sacreligiousity

a dab of oil being placed on someone's forehead, in the shape of a cross, is not what's being alluded to. And it is certainly not, what a first century reader would have understood this to mean. What is being presented is that the appropriate application of soothing oil to wounds and skin diseases is to be done while praying under the authority of Adonai. It is synonymous with the modern administration of medicine and prayer over the infirmed. There are just no specific references to the act of applying oil and instant healings taking place upon oil contact.

The word for 'healing' in the Greek is *therapeuo*, and it is from where we get our modern words *therapy* and *therapeutic*. It means to cure, to wait upon, and to relieve. Something to take note of is that the portrayed, instantaneous, miraculous healings that occurred through Messiah and His disciples did so without the recorded application of any oil at all. But even if they had applied oil, it would still have been a situation where someone was being prayed for, cared for, and 'nursed' back to health.

Psalm 23:5, "You prepare a table for me, even as my enemies watch; you anoint my head with oil from an overflowing cup."

In this portion of the Psalms, the Lord is being referred to as a shepherd. David, having been a shepherd himself, was analogously referring to a common preventative and healing practice performed on sheep. Sheep can get an infirmity called Myasis. Flies lay their eggs down in the crevices of the sheep's wool, often around their head, ears and tail. The larvae grow and eat down into the moist, warm skin.

By pouring oil over the affected areas, a barrier is created which helps to allow for healing to take place. Olive oil also contains anesthetic properties which helped to reduce any discomfort or itch, myasis or human skin conditions, might have associated with them. In ancient times, and still even today, other agents were also infused into the oil for their additional properties, including pain killing and de-fouling.

I do fully believe that people in the early ekklesia were healing at rapid rates and in significant quantities. I believe these were notable healings and that they were demonstrations which confirmed the authority of those who were preaching the gospel message. Let's state the obvious here. Medicine was pretty primitive, and there was not much more to do than love, pray for, and lift up the sick person's countenance, in hopes that they would eventually recover. Many common-day sicknesses that can easily be treated today, would take the lives of even the strong back then. Having a disciple or group of elders come by and participate in the caring of the sick, and see them come back to health, in itself was pretty significant considering the circumstances.

Yehoshua recognized and mentioned an appropriate function of anointing, since He was not sick in this passage:

You gave Me no kiss; but she, since the time I came in, has not ceased to kiss My feet. You did not anoint My head with oil, but she anointed My feet with perfume. (Luke 7:45 & 46)

Yeshua's comments here are double-edged. He was not being recognized and treated how He should be, if it was understood as to who He was. It would have been appropriate for someone (a prophet) to have anointed Him with oil, in recognition of His identity as King of the Jews. Likewise, oil was often applied to the scalp and hair as a smoothing and moisturizing agent and therefore would have been, at the least, a hospitable gesture for someone having traveled a distance through dusty territory. Somewhere between then and today, through various influences and practices, the use of anointing with oil has taken quite a turn. Today, people will line up in a row and be 'anointed' by a pastor, with a cross-shaped dab of oil, and assumedly there is supposed to be some kind of supernatural response.

Catholicism has complex liturgical processes called the "Extreme Unction" and "Last Rites," in which olive oil is applied as part of an elaborate ritual for those with terminally ill conditions. The <u>Dictionary of the Greek Language, 2004</u>, by George D. Babiniotis, states that this sacrament (anointing with oil) in the Greek Orthodox Church, "is customary in cases of sickness or when someone thinks he is having ill luck." Ill luck? What exactly does that mean? In the Eastern Church, oil seems to have even more capability; as this statement usually made during the anointing process expresses: "Through this holy anointing, may the Lord pardon you whatever sins you have committed." That's some powerful oil! Leave it to religion to take a perfectly reasonable practice in context, and turn it into the watered down liturgical act that it is. Oil and water have an obvious mixing problem.

Among Eastern Orthodox Churches, the only one having the privilege to prepare *Myron* (Μύρον, Holy Oil) for anointment is the Church of Constantinople. The Myron is made out of olive oil and a secret recipe of aromatics (*myra*) that are infused, and is under the care of the Archontes Myrepsoi, lay officials of the Patriarchate. The Oil is consecrated once a year on Holy Wednesday and distributed to Orthodox Churches throughout the world.[2] I'm sorry, but secret scented potions belong either in witchcraft, or under suspension of production. It too closely parallels the forbidden manufacturing for use outside Temple rites, which YHVH placed on His recipe for anointing oil.

Sacreligiousity

And thou shalt speak unto the children of Israel, saying, this shall be an holy anointing oil unto me throughout your generations. Upon man's flesh shall it not be poured, neither shall ye make *any other* like it, after the composition of it: it *is* holy, *and* it shall be holy unto you. (Exodus 30:31 & 32, KJV)

An ironic fact about healing oil is that we actually see it being used to mark the *already complete* healing of people with skin diseases, <u>after</u> they were healed (Leviticus 14). I'd like to end this topic with a bit of personal, albeit anecdotal commentary.

Minus several years of teen rebellion, I have spent my whole life either directly or indirectly affiliated with several large churches, very open to charismatic expressions of implemented faith. I have also visited countless others. I have never seen nor heard of anyone being instantaneously healed upon the anointing of oil. Neither have I read of examples in any "healer's" biography, or credible documentary piece. I really do not desire to be involved in any degree of diminishing one's faith in healing, so let me say it like this: If you are putting your faith in oil, you should invest in rigs. If you want to find healing, take care of your body; eat clean food; seek wise medical council; get prayed for by mature leaders, and trust in your Creator. If you are still called home, I feel very comfortable in declaring that the oil couldn't have changed a thing. But at that point, bless Adonai. You're healed anyway! I speak more comprehensively on the topic of healing, in chapter eleven.

Balder-ash

Warning: If you are Catholic and you have made it to this point in the book, I beg you to continue pushing through. Please understand that I was raised Protestant, inherently having made me religiously prejudice, and you know by now that I have strong convictions about error.

As I stood in line in the midst of many of my schoolmates, I watched as each one approached our teacher, and upon an unseen movement of her hand, each fellow student would proceed to turn around and head back to their seat, with a dark smudge on what was once their clean palate of a forehead.

As I made my way to the front of the line, I was a bit apprehensive, and had only paid enough attention to my teacher's explanation to realize it was a religious thing; but not one that I, or my religion had ever taken part of, as far as could be remembered.

It was my turn now, and I remember not feeling comfortable, but having no capacity to verbalize why, or justification to resist. So there I stood, as my teacher pushed her thumb into a small bowl of burnt something and raised it to my head, where she proceeded to 'anoint' me for some unknown purpose.

Finding my way back into my seat, I was a little anxious. The realization that I could not see what I looked like, and could only guess based on the fairly silly looks my fellow classmates had, really bugged me. I concluded to myself that knowing for sure would not occur until my next bathroom trip, so suddenly the need to relieve myself came on strong. With my teacher's additional blessing, I made my way there.

Approaching the mirror as if I was seeing myself for the first time, post-op of plastic surgery, I stood there as if in a daze; until another boy arrived shortly and snapped me out of it. Watching him wash the smudge off his forehead, I couldn't help but think that he was a bad kid expressing his rebellious nature. "Surely he must not go to church" was my thinking, as I ashamedly contemplated doing the very same thing. "Is that wrong? Can it just be washed off? How long does it have to stay on? Would that in any way be disobedient to God? I did not know the answer to any of those questions, and I had no intention of asking my teacher either.

As the day went on, I noticed that other students outside my class had also received this mark of sorts; many of them actually. But there were clearly many who didn't as well; and to be honest, I really wanted to be one of those. At some point later in the day, I got the guts to make another potty run and did the un-dirty deed, becoming again the common child I remembered being so fond of at the start of the day. What couldn't be ascertained for sure was whether or not there was some kind of residue remaining on my soul.

You may think this a ridiculous embellishment of my childhood experience, but I really did think this way. (As if you can't believe that.) I wanted to know what exactly had just happened to me.

As the years of my life continued forward, Ash Wednesday would be a day that would pop up once in a while in writings, or be mentioned by the media, or on the foreheads of walking reminders, but for the most part it remained a rather obscure event to me. I was not a Catholic, nor had ever attended Mass, so why would it have been otherwise? The only accumulated knowledge of Catholicism I had, was that it seemed boring and overly religious; there was a risk when alone with the priests; that its committed adherents resided in homes decorated like little shrines, but many of them lived as if they were adorned with beer signs and license plates.

Of course, I now know that not all Catholics live carnal lives, just as not all protesting Catholics live holy lives. But I guess it was a conception developed through what I heard via the grapevine, and from the little bit I observed. The one thing I did know was that something seemed wrong with the religion. I just wasn't sure exactly what that was.

Sacreligiousity

That also stood to reason, because my church told me that ours was the right one. I knew Catholics believed in Jesus, but they also believed in holy water, and that Mary was far more than just Jesus's "blessed *among* women" mom. It always bothered me that they showed Him either as dead, or as a baby. Overall, I just wasn't a Catholic, and I was fine with that.

After leaving childhood, and my fairly dark but classic falling away, He compellingly wooed me back again. It was a radical transformation if there ever was one. After the post-operative recovery, I needed to embrace and understand the faith that belonged to me now, as the faith of my parents was no longer adequate. As I matured, and started to feed my newly developed appetite for Biblical knowledge, I began to identify things that I had been raised to believe, that didn't seem to line up with what Scripture was saying. Things like practices, doctrines, and teachings from various denominational sources, were really getting my attention; as I was reading material from a variety of them.

It seems to me, that a big part of the influence that evoked my attentiveness came from within my own denomination. There, as well as the fact that within Protestantism abroad, there seemed to be so much debate and disagreement. The tribulation over when it's coming; the needs further reforming theology, charismania, dispensable theology and everything else in-between, were enough to cause my head to spin. But I knew that there had to be Truth out there somewhere, and I wasn't so sure I had it myself.

Something we are trained to do when evangelizing is to explain to the intended, that it is possible they believe what they do, because it's what their parents believed, and that their parents weren't going to have any negotiating power at their judgment. Imagine that! And one thing I had come to observe during various evangelistic encounters was that even those who had no active religion, still labeled themselves as whatever their parents were. I'm a 'this', or, I was raised a 'that'. Why is that? Why won't people just say, "I'm a nothing"? There may be several answers to that. But a fairly consistent pattern most had, seemed to be a sense of confidence and family pride in a religion they personally were not even faithful to.

I obviously encountered just about everything on the streets during my times in outreach evangelism. Many of whom I was able to engage in discussion, upon my asking, would freely tell me from what religious background they were. "I am a Buddhist." "I am Agnostic."

Sometimes they would even go so far as to tell me about the positive things their religion boasted, often to convince me they were *good* people. But other times, I'd get the impression they were drawing from their own training in reverse proselytizing, and would have liked to have seen me seriously consider their religion as an option for myself. It was very educational, and if you've ever done it yourself, you know it can also be somewhat entertaining.

I had personal knowledge, and heard stories within my faith of people being rejected by their families and friends for accepting Jesus, but I had really never heard of that happening within Catholicism (not that it hasn't.) I had never had a Catholic try to witness to me; not that they don't. Of all the other witnessing teams I crossed paths with, not a one was Catholic, nor had I ever heard of Catholics doing any evangelistic crusades besides the ones that ended in massacre. Not that they don't.

Now, I will freely admit that this is all anecdotal evidence, from which it would not be fair to draw any conclusions regarding their religion. But they did catch my attention, along with other things previously observed, and that caused me to further consider other aspects of the Catholic faith. Things such as, "good little Catholic girls" being a code phrase for risqué girls in plaid skirts, didn't help. The Pope was supposed to be the holiest person in the world—even the Christ personified—but never seemed to perform supernatural miracles. Catholics married outside the faith quite often. They had different holidays than what I grew up celebrating. Mary seemed to show up on potatoes and large flakes of people, and *Wheaties*. It really seemed that as monolithic as this religion was, it was near 'universally impotentate'. Mother Theresa was about the only positive thing I could see from the outside, and she has since passed on.

But that couldn't be. The churches are so impressive, and the priestly wardrobe looks so pious. The Latin sounds so rich and meaningful. All the gold, stained glass, and religious utensils have got to be very impressive to Jesus, right? Or, is it possible that neither these things, nor having ash rubbed on your head, are what He's really interested in? Could it be that much of what *I did* seemed pretty significant *to me*, but my heart was far from Him? Was I spiritually impotent too—emanating a religiosity, but more like a man travailing in labor, only to give birth to wind?

Symbols and signs are all very intriguing and mysterious, but what good are they if you don't know what they mean? We'll talk about several more in the next chapter. But let's finish this chapter exposing the truth behind the shadow of Lent, or at least that's what its mark looks like anyhow.

All Lent Up and Twisted

The Code of Canon Law states: "All Fridays through the year and during the time of Lent are penitential days and time throughout the

Sacreligiousity

universal Church" (CIC 1250). (This being predicated on the fact that Friday is crucifixion day, of course.)

Lent is the 40-day period (Sundays excluded) prior to Easter, which the church observes as a penitential season. It begins on Ash Wednesday (which can occur any time between February 4 and March 11, depending upon the date of Easter), and it concludes with the Passiontide; the two-week period during which the church's liturgy follows Christ's activity closely, through the final stages of his life on earth. These two weeks are called Passion Week and Holy Week. It was once claimed that the Lenten practice was of apostolic origin, but historians fix its establishment at a later date, probably the 5th century. Catholics are required to fast and are urged to adopt other penitential modes during the season.[1]

Lent is kind of like a Catholic, forty days of purpose–ing, to remember. Ash Wednesday was established as the first day of Lent by St. Gregory the Great (Pope from 590 to 604 AD). During Lent, there are special masses for each day except Sunday, as there are no feasts held on Sundays (except Easter), according to the Catholic Encyclopedia. (I guess that's regardless of whether YHVH's appointed times fall on the 1st Day or not?) The forty-day idea is derived from the forty days of fasting Yehoshua underwent during His desert trial. At this point, a quick note stating that the Scriptures nowhere ask for such an event to take place, would I'm sure be unnecessary.

"Ash Wednesday" is always forty-six days before Easter. The *dies cinerum* (Day of Ashes) likely began around the eighth century, and is the starting ritual to begin Lent. The ashes used in this ceremony are made by burning the remains of the palms that were blessed on the Palm Sunday of the previous year. For the blessing of the ashes, four prayers are used; all of them are ancient in origin. The ashes are sprinkled with holy water and fumigated with incense. The Bishop or Cardinal then places his thumb into the bowl and applies the ashes to the recipient's forehead, in the sign of a cross. He then says these words, "Remember man that thou art dust, and unto dust thou shalt return."

The Catholic Encyclopedia tells us that the origin of the ashes is based on the scriptural concept of Jewish repentance, being represented by the tossing of ashes on the head, and putting on sackcloth for clothes. That's fine I suppose, except that I find it interesting they would save this relic of Judaism, but dispose of Passover, by replacing it with Easter. Throwing ashes on your head in humble grieving is an act far removed from this modern act. Fasting is fine. A contrite spirit is good. So obviously, that's not my problem. I'll bet, at this point, you can figure out what it is.

Let me sum it up this way. A man-made institution that thinks it is the habitation of the Christ,[3] has at times assumed the roles of Israel's leadership and replacement, and exterminator. Yet:

> Thus says the LORD, Who gives the sun for light by day and the fixed order of the moon and the stars for light by night, Who stirs up the sea so that its waves roar; The LORD of hosts is His name: 'If this fixed order departs from before Me' declares the LORD, 'Then the offspring of Israel also will cease from being a nation before Me forever.' Thus says the LORD, 'If the heavens above can be measured and the foundations of the earth searched out below, then I will also cast off all the offspring of Israel for all that they have done,' declares the LORD. (Jeremiah 31:35-37)

But, it can go ahead and cancel one of the Mo'adim, and replace it with a man-made holiday. Then it prepares for the man-made holiday with a man-made fasting period, and launches it with the application of a type of holy ash (by a self-appointed, non-Levite, wearing purple instead of white). And this ash's only scriptural precedent demands it be used for ritual purification, for coming in contact with the dead. If none of that was a problem, I offer you this:

In Scripture, a mark on the forehead is a sign of ownership. Cain received a mark that designated him as Elohiym's property, and gave him a 'hands-off' status. Ezekiel saw a vision in which an angel marked the foreheads of Elohiym's remnant, and it put them under a hand's-off status to the angel of judgment. Upon the High Priest's forehead was written, "Holy to the Lord". In the apocalyptic writing of John, Revelation speaks of two marks of ownership: one will mark Yeshua's remnant, the other is demanded by the Beast and received by his followers. Those who take this mark are identified as belonging to HaSatan.

Since this ash-mark is never attributed to be a replacement for the anointing to a position, and it certainly doesn't lift one's countenance, then either it's an 'identifier of ownership', or it's an unauthorized act of liturgical nonsense and disobedience. If it's an identifier, it only affiliates one with Catholicism, because nothing like this is found within the Covenants, which compose the scriptural religion. Throwing dust/ashes on one's head is clearly not the same thing. I don't expect Catholics to stop doing this because in general, Catholicism does not concern itself with a lot of Torah-based specificities. But as a Protestant or Jew, I would strongly recommend not marking yourself with anything but your obedience and love. Yeshua came down pretty hard on those who made a point to be *obviously* engaged in religious ritual; i.e., the fasting man. In case marking yourself seems of no consequence, perhaps this will bother you:

Sacreligiousity

Shaivaites, those of their branch of Hinduism that worship Siva, paint their foreheads with a holy ash. This 'Vibhuti' (Vibhooti) is applied by many devotees in India. The 'Konkanis' worship Lord Shiva, as well as Vishnu. They believe the holy ash has very good medicinal value, and that it destroys sin. They believe it can prevent/cure 81 diseases that are air-born (*vata*), and sixty-four diseases caused by bile (*pittam*), and two hundred and fifteen through phlegm (*kapham*). This sacred ash is used during meditation, and the practice involves putting it on other areas of the body as well.

Vibhuti is created under *careful preparation* according to Siva Baba's standards. They believe it is a tool that comes from "the Divine" to assist spiritual seekers in opening the *third eye*, and absorbing spiritual realization at an accelerated pace. (Now where was that other ash mark put again?) They claim the sacred ash has properties for both erasing karma, and for helping you with "authentic desire" (whatever that means).

Vibhuti also refers to the paranormal powers that Sage Patanjali claims that one can develop by the practices described in his book (I'll not advertise it here if you don't mind), which is part of the body of Hindu philosophy. Oops, it looks like I forgot to tell you how Vibhuti is made.

The dung is obtained from cows that are fed sixteen varieties of medicinal leaves. The collected dung is then formed into flat cakes and dried in the sun. 108 types of herbs, and twigs (Samithi) of high medicinal value are used in the (homa) into which the dried dung cakes are added. Six added types of medicinal leaves are burnt along with these.

You can learn more about Vibhuti with a simple web-search. I hope that I can trust you to make the right decision, when the temptation comes upon you to roll around in a pile of Vibhuti.

Fat Tuesday

What does this have to do with anything? Did you know "Shrove Tuesday" or "Fat Tuesday" (a.k.a. Mardi Gras) was originally intended to prepare for the season of fasting at Lent?

The Lenten season is a time of fasting, so Shrove Tuesday was a day to eat lots of food, with the idea of storing up fat for Lent (as well as "fellowship" with other believers). The origin of the name Shrove lies in the archaic English verb "to shrive," which means to absolve people of their sins. It was common in the middle ages for "shriveners" (priests) to hear people's confessions at this time, to get them spiritually ready for Lent.

Warning! My final comment on this event is going to be stinging, and a bit sarcastic. I say it this way because, in this case, I really want it to shock those of you who may need a little shrove over the fence of indifference.

Perhaps, before you celebrate Lent the next time it comes around, you could get ready by indulging in this hedonistic festival as well. Then, when your hang-over is no longer chastising you, you can wear your beads into church the next day, as you get your mark identifying you with the lord of Mardi Gras!

You can only have one master. You can only be marked one way. Whom do you serve? The church, or the Cornerstone it's built on? Yeshua is looking for a bride who will concern herself with who she fellowships with, and how she behaves. Things can seem so innocent; so devoted to spiritual things. It's not always about being "spiritual". It's about being virtuous. This holiday is a white-washed tomb. I'm sorry. I realize many of you out there are greatly offended by that comment. This book hasn't cut corners yet. It's not going to start now.

If people would just be committed to what Scripture has already laid out for us, there would be no need to invent these pseudo-holy religious practices and procedures. Mankind has always found itself more religion-oriented than relationship-oriented, when it comes to its various forms of worship and orthodoxy.

How much more the true, when the worship is directed towards man-made gods. He asked us to worship Him first at a mountain, then in Spirit and Truth; wherever we are, and until we're back at another mountain. We rejected His way then, and I guess we still are. The Spirit leads us into Truth, which is found in His Word.

When you are examining "religious" things, don't blindly trust what your eyes see. Judge them against what you read in His GPS (in this case meaning, all His Word). What you'll find there are not just points of interest. It's your only hope for not getting lost.

And the Fourth Cup

When we were talking about the four cups of the Seder meal, I brought up the fact that Yeshua drank the third cup of Redemption, when instituting the new covenant. There is a wonderful, but hidden message within this story. Yeshua, after drinking this cup, also promised to not drink wine anymore until He "drinks it anew," in His Father's kingdom. Some have said they believed He was taking a Nazarite vow at this point. Perhaps—but I believe there is something richer.

I think the reason He is *waiting* to drink with us again, is found in the meaning of the fourth cup. The cup of Hope is looking forward to the future world. It is looking forward to our resurrection, and the reign of peace. He is the First Fruits of the resurrection, but that came about after the meal. He is now sitting and waiting for His enemies to be made His footstool. He is awaiting the future kingdom, even more than we are. But, we are waiting together.

At the end of the age, when the redeemed are gathered together by the Bridegroom, to celebrate the Wedding Supper of the Lamb (the new Pesach), the glass we will all be toasting L'Chaim to, will be the fourth cup we are all waiting to drink together, when all our hopes have come to fruition.

Baruch atah Adonai Eloheinu melekh ha-olam, borei p'riy hagafen. Blessed are you, LORD our God, King of the Universe, who creates the fruit of the vine. Amein.

10

Cleaning House

Speak to the sons of Israel and say to them, 'I am the LORD your God. You shall not do what is done in the land of Egypt where you lived, nor are you to do what is done in the land of Canaan where I am bringing you; you shall not walk in their statutes.' (Leviticus 18:2 & 3)

...and so as to make a distinction between the holy and the profane, and between the unclean and the clean... (Leviticus 10:10)

Thus saith the LORD, 'Learn not the way of the nations, and be not dismayed at the signs of heaven; for the nations are dismayed at them.' (Jeremiah 10:2)

It's never been okay to do what the heathens do. YHVH has never been interested in being treated, worshipped, or understood to be like the gods of the nations. He's also never been interested in having His people be like those who are from them. The ordained, and sometimes complete annihilation of many of those nations (as well as certain Israelites who joined in their practices), along with the six hundred-plus boundaries found amidst the Tanakh and Apostolic Scriptures, that have been designed to protect and keep us, are evidence of that.

...and when the LORD your God delivers them before you and you defeat them, then you shall utterly destroy them. You shall make no covenant with them and show no favor to them. (5) But thus you shall do to them: you shall tear down their altars, and smash their *sacred* pillars, and hew down their

Asherim, and burn their graven images with fire. (Deuteronomy 7:2 & 5)

As I continue to grow and learn more of the Scriptures, it becomes all the more apparent to me that we…"are A CHOSEN RACE, a royal PRIESTHOOD, A HOLY NATION, A PEOPLE FOR *God's* OWN POSSESSION, so that you may proclaim the excellencies of Him who has called you out of darkness into His marvelous light (1ˢᵗ Peter 2:9)." By no means is this accomplishable by being like the world. But in reality, that is very much what we have become.

Another by-product of the Torah resistant lifestyle choice is our inability to clearly recognize the difference between the holy/clean/tahor, and the profane/unclean/tamei. If you are not persuaded to acknowledge it; if it is not a part of your daily thought processes, you may actively look all you want, but you will not be able to recognize it as clearly. It is there we learn to identify the sources and strategies of our adversary and his strongholds.

Being that sin is the transgression of the Law (1ˢᵗ John 3:4), Torah is also how we learn to avoid sin. I'm not talking about turning carnal music to a lower volume, or abstaining from improper sexual conduct, or even saying no to drugs (*Results*). I'm talking about the age-old roots of mysticism, superstition, pagan cultural influences and the like (*Causes*). I'm talking about the things we do and have no idea why, outside of the fact that they're what everyone else does, without guilt of conscience.

I need to say in advance that there is a plethora (you have to use this word somewhere) of material on the topics we are about to cover, and they come from every perspective: supportive, non-supportive and afraid to take a stand. A common denominator of many of these practices is found in their predating Christian affiliation, and accommodating modification. I am not proposing that all these expositions are definitive. Some are simply "more than likely" derivations. Like an uncomfortable amount of things that the church now embraces as orthopractic, the origins of them are not internally devised, but are external adaptations of pre-existent, often foolish, sometimes idolatrous practices.

The reasons for celebrating **our** major feasts when we do are many and varied. In general, however, it is true that many of them have at least an indirect connection with the pre-Christian [pagan] feasts celebrated about the same time of year—feasts centering around the harvest, the rebirth of the sun at the winter solstice (now Dec. 21, but Dec. 25 in the old Julian calendar), the renewal of nature in spring, and so on. (Source: *The New Question Box - Catholic Life for the Nineties*, copyright 1988 by John J. Dietzen, M.A., S.T.L., ISBN 0-940518-01-5 (paperback), published by Guildhall Publishers, Peoria Illinois, 61651., page 554.)

I followed this last quote immediately with the source text because I didn't want you to overlook it. (Please note whose feasts they admit they are, as contrasted by YHVH's written possessive, "My".)

For some reason, we as believers in Messiah Yeshua have allowed our culture and our leadership to dictate our behavior. And many have turned the blind-eye, full-well knowing that they will not be able to use these influences as justifications for their behavior, before the throne. We want to live righteous and set-apart lives, but not at the expense of our rationalized pleasures. What a lot of this behavior really boils down to is summed up in the answers to these questions: "Does how I feel about something, supersede the commandments of Adonai?" and, "Is my ignorance, my ticket out?"

It is my contention that Torah will be the standard of all our judgment, both for the just and unjust. Whatever the lost try to excuse themselves of, Yehoshua will open the Scriptures and point to a text and say, "Its right here! I told you right here. What made you think you could do otherwise?" For the redeemed, it will be a more complex reckoning than that. He is going to write His Laws directly on our hearts, and we are going to have a powerful awakening to the reality of our transgressions. But is that only something we are looking forward to? Or, should we go ahead and open the Scriptures now, and stop ignoring what it says regardless of the fact that, "everybody else is doing it!"

One of the great challenges that have to be overcome in regards to dealing with traditions is that they're just so darn traditional. Yehoshua even gave us these warnings, which should have given us a nice heads-up:

And He answered and said to them, 'Why do you yourselves transgress the commandment of God for the sake of your tradition?' (Matthew 15:3)

But in vain they do worship me, teaching as doctrines the precepts of men. (Matthew 15:9, pp: Isaiah 29:13, LXX)

He was also saying to them, 'You are experts at setting aside the commandment of God in order to keep your tradition.' (Mark 7:9)

With the same heart of not being anti-church, I am also not anti-tradition. What I am is anti, anti-commandment. If a tradition doesn't negate a commandment in the process of being practiced, then it is at least worthy of consideration. As soon as ANY man (or enemy) of YHVH creates traditions that cause us to neglect YHVH's Appointed Times, or instruction regarding His worship, we have a real problem. Some might say that much of our tradition is in an effort to honor Him. On the surface, that may seem justifying to our human reasoning; but as this chapter goes on, I will hopefully bring that into question, and then answer it.

We live in a world that is philosophically opposed to the Will and Word of Messiah, in nearly every aspect. And yet, we often find ourselves going to it for answers to questions of morality, spirituality, goodness and pleasure. Let's face it, the world knows how to throw a great party, and the Scriptures are a bit vague on the subject.

Selective Submission

Man has defined murder by segmenting it into three degrees, and punishes it in numerous ways. Torah tells us there is either accidental, or willful. Then it gives us two options: willful demands stoning; accidental requires refuge and restitution. Some people's immediate reaction to this would be, "Boy am I glad we don't live back then." May I ask why? Are you plotting murder? How much less murder do you think there was, considering if you were found guilty, you were going to be killed yourself, and quickly? How much less prison space was required then? How many less billions of tax dollars were spent on caring for each of them, during their sixteen year, all-expenses-paid, incarcervacation from society?

Or, do you want to commit adultery, and are concerned about the possibility of being caught? How much less infidelity was there, when being caught would be your death? I'll bet the church today would figure out how to solve their marriage problems with a bit more zeal. We might even have less divorce. Nah! We'd do the same thing unrighteous Israel did…make divorce easy. Then you could hop from spouse to spouse without calling it adultery. Adultery stones our souls anyway, even if mercy lets us live. Even when Scripture does say much, we still don't pay it attention and prefer man's reasoning.

There is no genuine believer who will state that the Ten Commandments are not a valid, bar setting for righteousness. But as I've clearly shown already, we won't allow Scripture to define for us what "keeping the Sabbath holy" means. Scripture does tell us. It is, therefore, clear that we ignore some Scripture, for the sake of our good intentions. Mankind, even when it accepts YHVH as its Elohiym, continues to perform a delicate balancing act, over what it *wants to do*, and what the Scripture tells us *how to do*.

There is hardly any area this is truer, in regards to this tightrope walk, than in the observance of holidays. Our human reasoning tells us that during our efforts to worship Adonai, to memorialize Him or an outstanding event of His interaction with us, that we should have no worry of unbridled celebration being problematic. We tend to think with a, "our loving Him is the only thing that matters" line of reasoning, and we cannot possibly conceive of Him caring less about how we go about it. Scriptural evidence however, strongly suggests otherwise.

Let me begin by reminding you that Israel's first encounter with the Living Elohiym was chock-full of regulations regarding how to approach Him. Does it seem that odd to you that the Sovereign King of the Universe would regulate humanity's approach? "Wash your clothes, abstain from sex, prepare yourselves and come to the mountain; but do not touch it," etc., etc. So what was with all the particulars? He was preparing them to "know" Him. He was about to reveal Himself and His instructions to His people. Then, the next means of approach was also full of regulations—the carefully designed tabernacle, with its adjoining ritual sacrificing program and priestly requirements.

Now, you may be thinking to yourself, "Well, that's all fine and good; but this is not relevant when it comes to holidays. After all, we are not asking Him to reveal Himself. We just want to honor Him." Well now, that's the problem! There is no scriptural holiday that He has asked us to honor, that is not an event through which He wants to reveal Himself to us; hence, the reason they *all* make some kind of request of us. We will deal with the concept of non-mandated holidays soon. You have to take pause and question, what would ever cause us to want to substitute an opportunity to encounter Adonai, for something we orchestrate to please ourselves. We have <u>never</u> been able to know, or approach Him, through our own devices!

I realize that it appears Yeshua was a lot more accessible during His earthly ministry, which would lead us to believe that the Father had relaxed His regulations. Let me propose a couple scenarios to you, and see how flexible our "new" Adonai is. Do you think that if someone was to have brought Him a sacred, pagan object, which represented the power of fertility in nature, to seek a fertility blessing in their life, He would have accepted it appreciably and followed up the gift by saying, "Your faith has brought your request"? What about if someone made a golden image of the Sun, put it on a chain and placed it around His neck to pay Him homage? How long do you think that He would have continued to wear it, so as not to hurt the giver's feelings? Do you suppose that if some naïve believers wanted to create an alternative to the Festival of Bacchus, to recognize Yehoshua for being the true giver of the "fruit of the vine," He would condone the event and join in the festivities?

If you think so, then I am afraid we worship two different elohiym, and thus the issue at hand. Our different elohiym may have the same name, but clearly not the same persona. The party-tolerant god described above is one many believers worship. It's the god created in the minds of some of His creatures. It's the god represented by golden calves; but it's not the One revealed throughout history.

There are many mainstream leaders who strongly disagree with the majority of what's in this book. This chapter will be a major

Cleaning House

contributor to that opinion. It may very likely be the chapter you most reject as well. I wouldn't expect a complete reversal of your opinion from a single chapter out of any author's book. I certainly don't expect all mankind to come out of its slumber and salute, until of course He comes and sets straight the course, as the Torah goes forth from Zion. Still, there is a need for this to be declared. It is seventeen hundred years long past due. The information composing this section was compiled, dissected, and reconstructed from quite a few, readily available sources. I really want to encourage you to do your own research and verification. I will tell you, a lot of it is paraphrased from *The Jewish Encyclopedia.*

One of the problems we have is, there is a lot of varying opinion on much of this information, and quite frankly, I'm not adamantly supporting anything but what is found in the Scriptures. If you don't want to agree with it, or don't like what you've read, then prove it wrong enough to be laughable and reject it. I assure you, I didn't make this stuff up; and mostly, it is not someone's original thought. If it is original thought, I will give it credit. Personally, it doesn't matter to me the exact date something began, or the exact reason a particular deity was worshiped. If Scripture rejects it, or it is senseless, or it is "extra-Biblical" and replaces YHVH's appointed times, that's good enough reason for me to dismiss them in my life.

I am very aware that tradition is the Titanic that doesn't turn easily. The ridicule, misunderstanding, and rejection that comes along with subscribing to, and modifying your lifestyle around the truths (that are) I am about to present, are really the biggest obstacles to most, as they consider their personal application. Some may even go so far as to consider this level of sanctification beyond heterodox, and more like spiritual treason.

I have come across very adamant and even hostile arguments against this kind of material. However, all throughout the opposition, I see the great hurdles that have to be leapt over to support, but not substantiate, their arguments. It is these same giant hurdles that have to be cleared, to reject the unambiguous instruction in Scripture. Leaping allows you to avoid having to read all the 'stuff' in between, until your feet come to rest. I've come to prefer the walking approach. It's much more likely you will enjoy the scenery along the way. So let's just walk right in, shall we?

Asherah and Ba'al Relation: A Brief Overview

Asherah (ăsh`ərə) or Asheroth (-rŏth), Canaanite fertility goddess, and the wooden cult symbol that represented her. She is the consort of El in the Ugaritic texts. Several passages in the Bible may refer to the planting of a tree as a symbol of Asherah, or the setting up of a wooden object as an asherah—the Hebrew words for "tree" and "wood" are the same.[1]

...and pl. Asherim, in Revised Version, instead of "grove" and "groves" of the Authorized Version. This was the name of a sensual Canaanitish goddess Astarte, the feminine of the Assyrian Ishtar. Its symbol was the stem of a tree deprived of its boughs, and rudely shaped into an image, and planted in the ground. Such religious symbols ("groves") are frequently alluded to in Scripture (Exodus 34:13; Judges 6:25; 2nd Kings 23:6; 1st Kings 16:33, etc.). These images were also sometimes made of silver or of carved stone (2 Kings 21:7; "the graven image of Asherah" R.V.). (See GROVE T0001556 [1].). Source: *Easton's 1897 Bible Dictionary.*

Although this last definition is also limited in scope, I place it here so that you can acknowledge the long-standing recognition of the practice, thoroughly encompassing all our lifetimes. (Note the source date.) I think the "sensual" part of Astarte/Ishtar is rather vague, so let's find out a little more about her.

To be forward, there is some confusion as to whether Asherah and Ashtoret(h) are synonymous. Astarte, or *Ashtoret* in Hebrew, was the principal goddess of the Phoenicians. She represented the productive power of nature. She was a lunar goddess that was adopted by the Egyptians as a daughter of Ra or Ptah. In Jewish mythology, she is referred to as *Ashtoreth*, supposedly interpreted as a female demon of lust. It isn't totally clear as to whether these were later mutations of the earlier Ashtart, but she was connected with fertility, sexuality, and war. Her symbols have been the lion, the horse, the sphinx, the dove, and a star within a circle, indicating the planet Venus. It is this goddess who is partly blamed for the downfall of the kingdom of Solomon:

...because they have forsaken Me, and have worshiped Ashtoreth the goddess of the Sidonians, Chemosh the god of Moab, and Milcom the god of the sons of Ammon, and they have not walked in My ways, doing what is right in My sight and *observing* My statutes and My ordinances, as his father David *did.* (1st Kings 11:33)

Ashtart was embraced by the Greeks under the name of Aphrodite. Both Ashtart and Aphrodite are essentially the same conception, and were both represented by the planet Venus. Even today, astronomy's official name for Venus' smaller northern continent is Ishtar Terra. The familiar symbol for the female, the circle with the cross underneath, is derived from Venus' hand mirror. But we need to go back further, to the origin of Ashtart, to see where she came from; for she already existed in the land of Canaan, when Adonai warned the Israelites regarding her, and compelled them to destroy all vestiges of her upon

Cleaning House

their entering into the land.

One possible theory relating to her origin stems from the fact that the inhabitants of each territory, or each wandering clan worshipped their own Ba'al. The Ba'al was chief deity of each; the source of all the gifts of nature. As their god of fertility, all the produce of the soil would be his, and so his followers would bring to him their tribute of first fruits. Since he was considered the patron of all growth and fertility, and through the use of analogy characteristic of early thought, their Ba'al would be the god of the productive element in its widest sense.

The concept of Ba'al's characteristics originated perhaps in the observation of the fertilizing effect of rains and streams upon the receptive and reproductive soil. This allowed for the smooth evolution of Ba'al worship to become synonymous with nature-worship. Joined with the Ba'als, there would naturally be corresponding female figures which might be called Ashtarts, these being the embodiments of Ashtart.

Through this same analogy, and through the belief that one can control or aid the powers of nature by the practice of magic, particularly sympathetic magic, sexuality might characterize part of the cult of the Ba'als and Ashtarts. Post-Exilic allusions to the cult of Ba'al Pe'or suggest that orgies prevailed. On the summits of hills and mountains flourished the cult of the givers of increase, and "under every green tree (Isaiah 57:5)" was practiced the licentiousness which was held to secure abundance of crops. Human sacrifice, the burning of incense, violent and ecstatic exercises, ceremonial acts of bowing and kissing and the preparing of sacred mystic cakes appear among the offences denounced by the post-exilic prophets. The cult of Ba'al (and Ashtart) included characteristic features of worship which recur in various parts of the Semitic (and non-Semitic) world, although attached to other names.

From Ishtar to Easter

Easter: "The day on which this feast is observed, the first Sunday following the full moon that occurs on or next after the vernal equinox." (Source: *The American Heritage® Dictionary of the English Language, Fourth Edition Copyright © 2000 by Houghton Mifflin Company. Published by Houghton Mifflin Company.*)

The Old-English name for April is Eosturmónaþ (Month of the Goddess Eostre). Who was Eostre (Easter)? She was a goddess of the Anglo-Saxons and was worshipped by neo-pagans. She has generally been attributed with life, spring and fertility. Due to her having no clear origin, and lack of historical evidence, Bebe, the famous "father of English history", has been accused of making her up. I'm sure there are many who wish that to be true. But if we look at the construct of her name, we can gain some insight.

Her name has the Old Teutonic root 'aew-s', which means 'to illuminate', especially in relation to 'daybreak', and is closely related to the "wes-ter-dawn servant" (the morning star Venus), and *austron*, meaning "dawn". That doesn't guarantee she has any relation at all, with the goddesses affiliated with Venus, but it sure is coincidental. Regardless of her name's origin, the practices associated with her are clearly detestable.

Aphrodite, the later evolution of Ashtart, is "coincidentally" the goddess of fertility. In Corinth, intercourse with her priestesses was considered a method of worshiping her. Hiding gifts in the forest is a "coincidental" activity in her worship. The highly fertile hare coincidentally happens to be the animal affiliation with Eostre. Eggs, the symbol of fertility to neo-pagans, Egyptians and Persians, happen to be the symbol of Easter. Coincidentally, eggs oddly enough don't come from hares, but have been combined symbolically to celebrate the holiday, and happen to have been being decorated to honor fertility long before our modern holiday. There are several varying legends and possible origins to the incorporation and decoration of eggs with the celebration of Easter, but all of them are pagan. Oh, and did you catch that earlier reference to making sacred mystic cakes for Ashtart? Why do you think hot-cross buns are affiliated with Easter? (Not unleavened by any means.)

Let me synopsize it like this: You can color-code eggs to tell a different "gospel" story (resurrection) than what they originally portrayed. You can make the bunny out of chocolate, so that it's just candy for kids to enjoy, instead of appreciating their reproductive propensity. You can fill eggs with jelly beans and hide them for the contest, instead of as a gift to Aphrodite. You can eat an unclean ham on Easter, instead of a Passover roast on Pesach. You can eat buns, instead of Matzoh. And to top it off, you can get up early on Sun-day morning to watch the sunrise (astrological, light-bringing body) during an Easter service, or you can watch the sun go down in preparation for Passover at twilight. But doesn't doing all that culminate into the epitome of syncretism? Easter certainly would not have been practiced by the apostles, nor should it be by worshipers of Yah.

There is no serious student of the Word that does not know beyond a shadow of a doubt that Easter predates Christianity, and that by all rights the secular aspects of it should be avoided. On that same note, that same student, should also know about (or at least of) the strenuous debate over its officially established date and affiliated practices. If you don't know of them, they are easy enough to find. Yet, although knowledge is easy to obtain, understanding must elude us. What teacher/preacher shouldn't be a serious student of the word? And yet,

Cleaning House

often they will be the first to lead their congregations in an egg hunt after service. I don't care how hard the church tries to justify mixing the pagan into the holy, "Easter" is an abomination unto the Lord, and when He comes, he will not be joining in this festivity, but decisively abolishing it.

The Resurrected Sun Day

There is another area of consideration I want to direct you toward regarding "Resurrection Sunday", as Easter is now cleverly disguised within. There has been ongoing debate over this subject for nearly ever. I have labored over this for what some would consider an obsessive amount of time, and I apparently am not the only one. I believe it is far more of an important issue than is normally recognized, and I would like to share with you the fruits of my labors.

Even if you mask it over with the resurrection, it still doesn't hide the fact it is not the correct date to remember the Passion event. Yehoshua's crucifixion took place mid-day, on the first day of Unleavened Bread, following the actual Pesach meal. Not only is that symbolically obvious, but it's accurate. So what? Who cares though, right? You should, and you'll see why. Although it's somewhat complicated, my intent is to present the most obvious answers (to questions you might have never asked) and stay as true as I can, to letting the Word do the work.

To begin with, it is frequently taught that the tradition of a mock/practice meal is what was taking place in the biblical narratives of "the Last Supper" (although, the phrase "Last Supper" does not occur in Scripture.) The main thrust for this teaching is to explain away some biblical narrative and depiction that doesn't correspond with certain perspectives. This meal is said to have normally taken place the evening prior to the actual event. These mock Passovers were apparently led by a rabbi, to instruct his disciples how to lead their own respective groups/families. This feast would not have included the actual Paschal lamb, but other representative elements. Factually, the historicity of such events is very vague. Is this what we are seeing here?

Now on the first *day* of Unleavened Bread the disciples came to Jesus and asked, 'Where do You want us to prepare for You to eat the Passover?' (Matthew 26:17)

On the <u>first day of Unleavened Bread</u>, when the Passover *lamb* was being sacrificed, His disciples said to Him, 'Where do You want us to go and prepare for You to eat the Passover?' (Mark 14:12)

Now it was the <u>day of preparation</u> for the Passover; it was about the sixth hour. And he said to the Jews, 'Behold, your King!' (John 19:14)

Then they led Jesus from Caiaphas into the Praetorium, and it was early; and they themselves did not enter into the Praetorium so that they would not be defiled, but might eat the Passover. (John 18:28)

Then the day of the *[Feast of]* Unleavened Bread came, in which it was necessary *[for]* the Passover *[or, Paschal Lamb]* to be sacrificed. And He (Yeshua) sent Peter and John, saying, 'Having gone, prepare the Passover for us, so that we shall eat.' (Luke 22:7 & 8, ALT)

Absolutely not! The usage of the actual word *Passover* occurs seven times in the synoptic gospels, in direct relation to what Yeshua and his disciples were celebrating. Matthew 26:20 goes so far as to tell us that they were "reclining" at the table, which is a direct reference to oral tradition associated with Passover. In no instance, does any terminology allow for or suggest a fake Passover was involved, and Luke specifically tells us the day to slaughter the Paschal had come—and Jesus was still here.

But we have ourselves a little consistency problem. Notice how John calls the day of Yeshua's death "Preparation Day," (which is normally the time before the event); while the others refer to Yeshua's death occurring <u>after</u> the meal. It may be answerable by some alternative tradition of celebration; but John was not alternative, which makes 19:14 a little more difficult to contend with. Luke seems to contradict himself in 23:54, by presenting Yeshua's death as occurring on "Preparation Day". Matthew does the same thing in 27:62. Mark states that the lambs were *being* sacrificed (Mark 14:12). There are likely answers for these seeming inconsistencies. There has to be, mustn't there?

Luke most likely got his source material from Mark, and verbal testimony from Paul. Paul was a Pharisee, and they believed in celebrating on the 14th, but in John's day, they were subject to the Sadducean control of the Temple. John, as well as the other talmudim (disciples), were Galileans, and strongly influenced by the Essenes and Nazarenes. Those groups were known to rebel against Sadducean regulation, when they felt it conflicted with scriptural Torah—and it just so happens that they did. They, in fact, did celebrate on the 15th, and that caused much conflict. In Yeshua's day, there were many people who chose to celebrate the Passover outside the city, and out from under religious control (Philo, Special Laws 2; p145-48),

The Sadducean observance later evolved to a "diasporal concern," and is still observed as such today. Because of these very issues, many observant Jews celebrate the meal for two days in a row; ensuring all their bases are covered. The Sadducees, whom John being himself a Jew, often conspicuously labeled "the Jews", would therefore have also required their own preparation day (John 19:31). YHVH actually added an

Cleaning House

observation day exactly one month later for the same reason, as well as for ritual uncleanness due to contact with death (Numbers 9:10 & 11). But John was not dispersed; neither is it recorded he had contact with death.

Passover/Pesach, according to Moses's instruction, is always to take place on a certain day: the fourteenth of Nisan. "Preparation Day" is normally understood to exist between the fourteenth day's morning, right up through just prior to the memorial meal. The meal itself technically begins at the point between days, at dusk, and finishes in the earliest part of the 15th. It is therefore my contention that we are dealing with the "preparation day" for the Sadducean observance; and the need for the Chief Priests and Pharisees to remain ritually clean (John 18:28; 2nd Chronicles 30:18-20) was because they would be eating their lambs in the Temple area. The evidence that there was an alternative practice is expressed in the apocryphal and highly esteemed Book of Jubilees.

Remember the commandment which the Lord commanded thee concerning the Passover, that thou shouldst celebrate it in its season on the fourteenth of the first month, that thou shouldst kill it **before it is evening**, and that they should eat it by night on the **evening of the fifteenth** from the time of the setting of the sun. For on this night—the beginning of the festival and the beginning of the joy—ye were eating the Passover in Egypt. (49:1-2)

This instruction stems from the understandably confusing phrase *ben ha-ʿarbayim*, found in Exodus 29:8, which literally means: "between the settings." This caused some to believe that the slaughter was to take place on the 14th, but that it was to be eaten the 15th.

Because John *was* an eye-witness, we should accept his words "as gospel". We have but limited options. Either he had mistaken memories when he penned his gospel (some forty to sixty years later—not an option!) or, he was describing it based on the official Temple program information I just presented. Luke, contrarily, borrowed text from Mark; *not* being an eye witness to the Passion. So, if Scripture be true and man be the liar, this has to be the solution; and John remains truthful. This is by far the better choice, and I will further establish this to be the case as we look at other important details I have compiled on this significant event.

Easter was artificially forced to fall on Sunday, and its calendar placement was based on the vernal equinox. If the "shadow" of the crucifixion day was on a specific date (not day), our "resurrection memorial" should be as well. Don't you think? It was after all, exactly three days later. Observant Israelites (especially those associating with Yeshua) would all acknowledge the following:

1. Passover is a mandatory event.

2. No one is allowed to do any regular work, from the meal forward through until the next evening, for that is the actual first day of Unleavened Bread (Leviticus 23), and is a Sabbath.

3. Leaving a corpse on a tree, overnight, is a transgression of Torah. He must be buried before nightfall (Deuteronomy 21:23). This is seen demonstrated by Joshua's dealings with the king of Ai.

These are the main thrust behind the desire to have Yeshua's body rapidly attended to upon His death. Obviously, the quicker a body was wrapped and spiced, the better. But there are two stories here as well. As I continue, remember that an observant Israelite's day began at sundown. Yeshua was betrayed and arrested early into the start of Unleavened Bread (night time following the supper), and passed between officials throughout the course of that evening, and following early morning. We know He was impaled before noontime.

Further Timeline Challenges

Now from the sixth hour (*noon*) darkness fell upon all the land until the ninth hour (*3:00pm*). (46) About the ninth hour cried out with a loud voice, saying, 'ELI, ELI, LAMA SABACHTHANI?' that is, 'MY GOD, MY GOD, WHY HAVE YOU FORSAKEN ME?' (Matthew 27:45 & 46)

And then very shortly from there, He died. It is commonly understood that His death was unusually quick (six hours). I concur, but want to add that I believe it was orchestrated to be that way, for two key reasons.

First, to continue fulfilling Torah, even after He died, His early death allowed Him to be taken down before nightfall. If he was still alive as nightfall was approaching, the Roman guard would have broken His legs, to induce faster suffocation. That would have been a problem, because He was prophesied to not have any broken bones (Psalm 34:20).

Second, because the execution took place initially in the daylight, it allowed for the miraculous darkening of the sky to get everyone's attention. It might have reminded the insightful of the ninth plague.

Leviticus 23:7 & 8 tells us that the first day of Unleavened Bread is a Sabbath, and that there is to be a holy convocation. This would be held the daytime following Passover. Can you imagine the tense environment and emotions that were present during that meeting? Imagine His disciples and loved ones sitting around and contemplating the Passover meal they last had, as they associated their Master having just been crucified, as well. Now those mysterious, previous teachings of

Yeshua were making much more sense.

According to one of those teachings, recorded in Matthew chapter twelve, His death would parallel the story of Jonah; in that He would spend three days <u>and</u> nights, *in the earth*. So the clock begins ticking sometime shortly after His death. Let's just say six-ish, for the sake of practicality, which would be the twelfth hour. This was the first day. Since from an analytical viewpoint a day can be counted if any portion of it is involved, being that a new "day" began at night. Now, let's take into consideration a few more details in the narrative. If we count from there three days and nights forward, an interesting thing occurs. If we begin our timing on a 5th Day/Thur., the 15th, from the time between days, we would then end up three days later, on a Sabbath/Sat. the 18th, at a similar time. So, in this scenario, technically, the resurrection did not even occur on a Sunday at all. Is this even a possibility?

But then there are the crucified on Thurs. (5th day), and the traditional "Good Fri." (6th day) scenarios. These are scenarios which have both been devised, with the end result of the resurrection occurring on a Sunday, and that would conveniently support the "Lord's Day", Sabbath replacement fallacy. Both of these require a non-literal interpretation of Yeshua's 'Jonah' analogy, as well as a lack of other facts, to work.

There were definitely two sabbath days involved in the story, and probably three. We know this because of the regulations and traditions regarding the feast days, and from the details surrounding the obtaining of the burial spices by the woman who were involved.

Luke, in 23:54-56, recorded that the women went home to prepare the spices *prior* to the Sabbath, and then they rested "according to the commandment." (This being written many years after the fact, it would have been a good time to use the word *custom*, if sabbath keeping ended with Yeshua. I'm just reinforcing.) Now, this would have been the Sabbath affiliated with Unleavened Bread, as none of the synoptic portrayals show any significant lapse of time, and it clearly wasn't the 7th Day. Notice also that it was simultaneously another "preparation day." Hmm? Ultimately, they never got the opportunity to apply the spices.

Nobody normally has the typical fifty to one hundred pounds of expensive spices required, just hanging around waiting for a death to occur. So, understandably, people would have to purchase them (or obtain it on credit.) Since it is scripturally unlawful to conduct business on a Sabbath, it would seem that the expensive quantity of spices would have needed to have been purchased two days after the crucifixion, or the 3rd day of Unleavened Bread, on Fri. Also, it is a commandment to not carry a load on Shabbat, and something approaching 100 lbs. would surely constitute that. Now it gets confusing.

Many merchants would have closed their businesses early, for their preparation of Passover; but all would have been closed the day after. Jerusalem ran on the Sadducean time table. Mark tells us the ladies *purchased* it "<u>after</u> the sabbath (16:1)," but Luke tells us they "prepared the spices and perfumes" <u>before</u> the Sabbath (23:56). I wish that timing was the only seemingly inconsistent fact John (or the Scriptures) gave us, but it isn't. According to his gospel, we are told that Nicodemus brought the spices, and that he and Joseph wrapped Jesus's body according to the *custom.*

Nicodemus, who had first come to Him by night, also came, bringing a mixture of myrrh and aloes, about a hundred pounds *weight.* So they took the body of Jesus and bound it in linen wrappings with the spices, as is the burial custom of the Jews. (John 19:39-40)

This seems to be in direct conflict with Luke's portrayal, because he states that, "on the <u>first day of the week</u>, at early dawn, they came to the tomb bringing the spices which they had prepared (24:1)." And why would the women come to do what Nicodemus and Joseph already took care of? We are going to have to make some educated assumptions to get all this to sequentially agree. Let's try to work this through.

Nicodemus brought myrrh and aloe, but due to the late hour of these events (Matthew 27:57), hastily wrapped and coated the body with a portion of them—perhaps enough to get the body through the holy-days. The ladies "who followed Him out of Galilee" saw this happen and "how He was laid", went home to gather together what they could contribute, (which further suggests the job wasn't done), but ran out of time to help, for the Sabbath had come upon them (Luke 23:55). Luke carefully and curiously goes on to tell us that when the 7th day Sabbath was complete, some ladies, specifically the two Marys, and Salome, went and *bought* (not just *brought*) their spices to contribute their part in the custom. These two sets of ladies had to be two different sets (Mark 15:41), having the same intentions separately, and that explains one discrepancy. In either case, it is hard to imagine that if Nicodemus was successful in performing a full burial, those ladies closest to Yeshua wouldn't have known that.

Now after the Sabbath, as it began to dawn **toward** the **first** *day* of the week, Mary Magdalene and the other Mary came to look at the grave. (This Sabbath is concerning the 7th day Sabbath. John confirms it was **still dark at the time**.) (2) And behold, a severe earthquake had occurred, <u>for</u> an angel of the Lord descended from heaven and came and rolled away the stone and sat upon it (Matthew 28:1 & 2).

Cleaning House

I realize Matthew is interpreted here as saying that they came to "look" at the grave, but Luke just told us their greater intent. If you look at the other synoptic narratives, (i.e. Mark 16:1) they don't use that wording either. I chose Matthew's rendering here, more to lead into the next issue at hand.

What is actually said here is not what is often extrapolated. As they were approaching the tomb, (1st Day's dawning; taking us into the light of what is actually the second-half of the 18th), an earthquake occurred as an angel rolled the stone away. The quake should not automatically be assumed to coordinate with the resurrection occurrence, as is often portrayed in passion plays. Yeshua could have been (and I tend to think was) resurrected between the eve of the 7th Day Sabbath, and start of the 1st Day. The quake was more likely related to the entrance of a great angel into our dimension (as suggests the wording of Matthew 28:2). Therefore, since He was already found resurrected as they approached the tomb, just at the start of the 1st Day's light, it only makes sense that He was actually resurrected on the Sabbath Day, which represents Shalom and restoration, on the verge of a new day, representing a new era.

So having gone through all this, what then is the issue with there being two or three Sabbaths? Well, since there were definitely two involved (first day of Unleavened and the 7th Day Shabbat), that means there were at least two full days between death and resurrection. Since not one of the respective Scripture authors mention the idea of a double Sabbath (which is significant in Judaism), and due to Luke's careful rendering, there was assuredly a day in-between. Depending on your religious persuasion, the second day following the crucifixion would have been a sabbath as well. That pretty much defeats the "Good Fri." afternoon thru Sun. morning (1½ day passion theory). Matthew 16:21 and Luke 9:22 both teach that Yeshua would rise on the third day. That phrasing does not mean it happened during daylight. It just as properly denotes a 24-hour period. Technically speaking, if Yeshua actually rose on Sun. morning, in this scenario, He would have risen on the fourth day following His crucifixion.

Can I say with one hundred percent assurance that how I have laid it out here is exactly how it went down? No, I can't. There are some who will take issue, due to their interpretation of things. But of all the scenarios that are out there, taking into account the fulfillment of prophetic foreshadowing, and grooming with Occam's razor, I am very comfortable with this sequence. It makes the most sense to me, and it follows the patterns. Yeshua left the grave right before the 7th became the 1st. Regardless, the prophecy of Jonah said He'd be "in the earth" for three days and nights. Unless He was buried alive, which He clearly wasn't, anything less cannot work. If Yeshua died on the 6th day's eve, it would have effected Passover observance for everyone in that day, and would have had Yeshua in the ground for only 2 days. Regardless of timeline challenges, it does not justify the church's current state of denial and disregard.

The biggest obstacle for me to overcome, to accept another scenario, would be that Yeshua didn't slay Himself on Passover. It just seems to me that the "Lamb that was slain before the foundations of the world" would have actually been slain on the day He had been symbolically preparing us for, for nearly fifteen hundred years prior. And, He would have done it on the correct day, resetting any calendar questions. To observe Easter, would also mean that the Sabbath-rest/resurrection picture that is given to us through "First Fruits" was irrelevant to the overall picture. In addition, because of the added premise that Passover is still to be observed, I just don't buy it. The fact that there are teachings suggesting the "Last Supper" not being a Passover meal, in an attempt to better justify the Sun-day Easter program, further adds to my conviction. It just isn't Biblical. Would Yeshua have so desired to eat an everyday meal, or chosen a mock meal, to institute the new covenant around? That really doesn't seem to fit the Lord's patterns.

There are those who will declare that knowing exactly when these events took place is insignificant in the overall scheme of things. There are others who will declare that it creates an unnecessary divide amongst believers. Although there is some truth to that, and it seems a pious notion, rejecting the obvious for the sake of a desire is what gets us into the kind of unnecessary trouble we find ourselves all too often in. If this is wrong, then I will go down having believed I sought after the Truth and lived by my convictions. You must conclude for yourself what Scripture teaches, and do likewise. At least be willing to look at the evidence though.

Truthfully, there is a lot more detail that can be added to this; some supportive and some not. It can get excruciatingly technical, with new moon issues and so-forth. Again, in Scripture, YHVH teaches in patterns and principles, far more than in mathematical equations. Should you have to be a genius to be able to see Yeshua as our Passover? No. The more technical the arguments get, the more variables get involved. The more variables, the more unsurety. The more unsurety, the less likely it's correct. I believe the more obvious is the most likely. Now, I'll try to tie up some loose ends.

There was another Lamb sacrificed on the first day of Unleavened Bread (the Sadducean preparation day). It was a ceremonial one, and it occurred on the 15th, at three o'clock in the afternoon. Ordinarily, it was part of the daily (tamiyd) sacrifice routine, which had been pointing to the passion event, every day of its happening. This lamb,

Cleaning House

a peace offering, not so coincidentally, happened to be being sacrificed at the temple around the same time Yeshua took His last breath! Also not coincidentally, another daily lamb offering took place at nine o'clock that morning. This corresponded with the time that Yeshua was placed upon the crux.

The desire to honor new life, and to remember the resurrection of our Messiah, is obviously not a bad thing. It's just that He has already given us the means through which to do it, within His Mo'adim. Passover is our remembrance of redemption from slavery, and deliverance from our enemies. It is also our remembrance of Messiah's new covenant institution. It is also, though, a looking forward to very similar and profound events, with likewise profound outcomes.

1st Corinthians 15:20, "But now Christ has been raised from the dead, the **First Fruits** of those who are asleep."

Remember how Shavuot is understood by the Jews as the 'giving of the Torah' on Sinai? Well, to believing Israel, First-Fruits (which occurred during the week of Unleavened Bread) is contributed with representing His resurrection.

Speak to the sons of Israel and say to them, 'When you enter the land which I am going to give to you and reap its harvest, then you shall bring in the sheaf of the **First Fruits** of your harvest to the priest. He shall **wave** the sheaf before the LORD for you to be accepted; on the day after the Sabbath the priest shall wave it.' (Leviticus 23:10 & 11)

Why do you think the High Priest lifted up the offerings during this festival? So we could get the attention of a near-sighted Elohiym? I think not. Yeshua was found harvested from the grave, on the same day. And the rest of the harvest couldn't be gathered in, until the first example was raised. Get it?

Masquerading as Mo'adim

See to it that no one takes you captive through philosophy and empty deception, according to the tradition of men, according to the elementary principles of the world, rather than according to Christ. (Colossians 2:8)

We just can't seem to get away from them. Prohibitions and warnings related to allowing our thinking to get in the way of Abba's purposes. It's the result of letting this happen, the being "taken captive", that strikes a chord with me. Being taken captive denotes becoming a slave, or possessed by someone else. I don't know about you, but I'm only interested in having one master, and I want to be His servant and His alone. "Empty deception" comes through the "tradition of men," and we are to "see to it" that this does not happen. Okay, fine. How do we do that? I would argue that we do it by thoroughly examining tradition before we embrace it.

One of the challenges we have in regards to this mandate, is in the fundamental identification of things that derive their origin or practice from tradition. This practice must be self-initiated and diligently maintained. For although there is nothing new under the sun, there are always evolutions and adaptations being instituted by the deceiver, for the sake of new and ignorant generations. There are many claims, which although sound possible, cannot be substantiated enough to confirm their truth, and that is what we're after. This is true for things both in and against our favor. For instance, people speak of all the ritual murders that take place on Halloween. However, no official government agency can substantiate this claim. So how do we get to the bottom of things?

First, we should begin by obtaining a lot of source material. Then we look for the common roots within them. Then we narrow them down to a couple sources which are the most reasonable and respectable, and assess their potential impact on our lives. It's not much different than the way we conclude the meanings and purposes of scriptural material as well. Always try to look past the agenda; to see beyond it and find the truth. Following, will be a compilation of some of the interesting traditions I've chosen to elaborate upon.

The farther away we get (in relation to time) from the origin of a tradition, the more difficult it is to ascertain its direct impact on modern culture. We grow more accustomed to things that in earlier generations, we would have quickly deemed heathen. Add to that the workings of revisionist historians, and numb...we more become.

Let me give you an example. Anyone who wanted to could do a rudimentary study on the jack-o-lantern. You know, that adorable squash with the funny smile and the candle-lit center. Harmless we think, but what do you know about it? Many of you know fully well, and respond accordingly. Some of you don't know, and now will. Some of you know, and don't really care; the very definition of lukewarm. For those of you who would like to know, or just need a booster shot, we'll start here:

Jack, the Irish say, grew up in a simple village where he earned a reputation for cleverness as well as laziness. He applied his fine intelligence to wiggling out of any work that was asked of him, preferring to lie under a solitary oak endlessly whittling. In order to earn money to spend at the local pub, he looked for an "easy shilling" from gambling, a pastime at which he excelled. In

Cleaning House

his whole life, he never made a single enemy, never made a single friend and never performed a selfless act for anyone.

One Halloween, as it happened, the time came for him to die. When the devil arrived to take his soul, Jack was lazily drinking at the pub and asked permission to finish his ale. The devil agreed, and Jack thought fast. "If you really have any power," he said slyly, "you could transform yourself into a shilling."

The devil snorted at such child's play and instantly changed himself into a shilling. Jack grabbed the coin. He held it tight in his hand, which bore a cross-shaped scar. The power of the cross kept the devil imprisoned there, for everyone knows the devil is powerless when faced with the cross. Jack would not let the devil free until he granted him another year of life. Jack figured that would be plenty of time to repent. The devil left Jack at the pub.

The year rolled around to the next Halloween, but Jack never got around to repenting. Again, the devil appeared to claim his soul, and again Jack bargained, this time challenging him to a game of dice, an offer Satan could never resist, but a game that Jack excelled at. The devil threw snake eyes—two ones—and was about to haul him off, but Jack used a pair of dice he himself had whittled. When they landed as two threes, forming the T-shape of a cross, once again the devil was powerless. Jack bargained for more time to repent.

He kept thinking he'd get around to repentance later, at the last possible minute. But the agreed-upon day arrived and death took him by surprise. The devil hadn't showed up and Jack soon found out why not. Before he knew it, Jack was in front of the pearly gates. St. Peter shook his head sadly and could not admit him, because in his whole life Jack had never performed a single selfless act. Then Jack presented himself before the gates of hell, but the devil was still seething. Satan refused to have anything to do with him.

"Where can I go?" cried Jack. "How can I see in the darkness?" The devil tossed a burning coal into a hollow pumpkin and ordered him to wander forever with only the pumpkin to light his path. From that day to this, he has been called "Jack o' the Lantern." Sometimes he appears on Halloween! (Source: the *Catholic Update*: "How Halloween Can Be Redeemed" by Page McKean Zyromski)

Have you ever heard such nonsense in your whole life? Why is it even necessary to "redeem" such foolishness? Granted, this is a retelling of what some sources of historical attributers to this practice say. Can't you smell the Adversary's stew in such a pot? Let's look past this entertaining façade and find out some truth.

Hallowmass

Halloween's origins date back to the ancient Celtic festival of Samhain (pronounced sow-in). During the celebration, the Celts wore costumes, typically consisting of animal heads and skins, and attempted to tell each other's fortunes.

By 43 AD, Romans had conquered the majority of Celtic territory. In the course of the four hundred years that they ruled the Celtic lands, two festivals of Roman origin were combined with the traditional Celtic celebration of Samhain.

The first was Feralia, a day in late October when the Romans traditionally commemorated the passing of the dead. The second was a day to honor Pomona, the Roman goddess of fruit and trees. The symbol of Pomona is the apple, and the incorporation of this celebration into Samhain probably explains the tradition of "bobbing" for apples that is still practiced today.

By the 800's, the influence of Christianity had spread into Celtic lands. In the seventh century, Pope Boniface IV designated November 1 All Saints' Day, a time to honor saints and martyrs. It is widely believed today that the pope was attempting to replace the Celtic festival of the dead, with a related but church-sanctioned holiday. The celebration was also called All-hallows, or All-hallowmas (from Middle English Alholowmesse; meaning All Saints' Day), and the night before it, the night of Samhain, began to be called All-hallows Eve and, eventually... Halloween.

A little later, in AD 1000, the church would make November 2 into "All Souls' Day"; a day to honor the dead. A later custom developed where people would go door-to-door requesting small cakes in exchange for the promise of saying prayers, for some of the dead relatives of each house. This arose out of the religious belief that the dead were in a state of limbo before they went to heaven or hell, and that the prayers of the living could influence the outcome. This may have been the precursor to Trick-or-Treat. It was celebrated similarly to Samhain, with big bonfires, parades, and dressing up in costumes as saints, angels, and devils.

Together, the three celebrations: the Eve of All Saints', All Saints', and All Souls', were called Hallowmass. Today, Americans spend an estimated 3.3 billion annually[3] on Halloween, the vestige of Hallowmass, making it the country's second largest commercial holiday. Hmm...what could we do with three-plus billion, more appropriately spent dollars? It is interesting to question whether or not candy, that has been purchased and distributed in honor of such an event, would qualify as food sacrificed to idols. It may seem like a stretch, but it cannot be far off. It's at least *dedicated* to them.

Cleaning House

Norse Elven Blót

In the old Norse religion and its modern revival Ásatrú, the day now known as Halloween was a blót, which involved sacrifices to the elves and the blessing of food.

A poem from around 1020, the *Austrfaravísur* ('Eastern-journey verses') of Sigvatr Þorðarson, mentions that, as a Christian, he was refused board in a heathen Swedish household, because an *álfablót* ("elves' sacrifice") was being conducted there. However, we have no further reliable information as to what an *álfablót* involved. But like other blóts, it probably included the offering of foods; and later Scandinavian folklore retained a tradition of sacrificing treats to the elves. From the time of year (close to the autumnal equinox), and the elves' association with fertility and the ancestors, we might assume that it had to do with the ancestor cult and the life force of the family (Source: Wikipedia).

Celtic Observation of Samhain

In the Druidic religion of the ancient Celts, the new year began with the winter season of Samhain on November 1. Just as shorter days signified the start of the new year, sundown also meant the start of a new day; therefore, the harvest festival began every year on the night of October 31. Druids in the British Isles would light fires and offer sacrifices of crops. And as they danced around the fires, the season of the sun would pass and the season of Samhain would begin.

When the morning of November 1 arrived, the Druids would give an ember from their fires to each family, who would then take it home to start a new cooking fire. These fires were intended to keep the homes warm and free from evil spirits, such as "Sidhe" (pronounced "shee"; most notable of which are the *beán sidhe* or banshees). At this time of year, it was believed that the invisible "gates" between this world and the spirit world were opened, and free movement between both worlds was possible. Bonfires played a large part in the festivities. Villagers cast the bones of the slaughtered cattle upon the flames. The word "bonfire" is thought to derive from these "bone fires". With the bonfire ablaze, the villagers extinguished all other fires. Each family then solemnly lit their hearth from the common flame, thus bonding the families of the village together. Hundreds of fires are still lit each year in Ireland on Halloween night.

Today, most people who do not want to *fully* participate in this pagan-rooted holiday choose to label it, and modify it into a "Fall Festival". Sometimes parents will dress their children as famous characters of the Scriptures, or other benign character types, so as to not rob them of the delights associated with the festival. Churches will throw "Harvest Festivals" to "redeem" the day, and often attempt to turn it into an evangelistic opportunity, to even more validate it. Isn't it interesting, how YHVH's fire was holy, and was not to be let to go out, or used for common purposes; yet this pagan party involves just the opposite?

Again, I feel compelled to remind you, He has already given us a "Fall Festival". It is also comprised of three holy-days, but the specific event related to the ingathering of crops happens to be Shavuot. I just can't seem to impress the fact enough, that although attending the Adversary's festivals is bad enough, the insidiousness of them is found in their 'replacing' the Appointed Times of our Elohiym.

Although the evangelism angle would seem to make great sense on the surface, I ask you this: What kind of Kingdom are you trying to bring them into? One that is afraid of being too unlike the world, or one that compromises its standards when holiness seems too hard to sustain. If you want to have a dress up day, how about Elul or Sept.12th (randomly selected)? Can't we do our own thing? Syncretism with the world's ways has never, nor will ever be the means to the end of unrighteousness. Rise up from your slumber, oh church!

Cristes mæsse

Debating Halloween rarely becomes a heated issue amongst believers. Differing opinions will usually result in each party thinking the other is silly, but that's about it. Ceasing to celebrate Christmas, on the other hand, will just about cost you your soul. I want to quickly state that Christmas and Halloween are definitely not in the same category. One really does have well-meaning intentions, while one has absolutely no redeeming value (no matter the attempt).

Unfortunately, good-intentioned opponents of Christmas have a lot of things going against them, even with the most persuasive arguments. For one, other main-stream cults are known for their eradication of the day and so if a cult does it, "it has to be wrong." Another negative is the stronghold of tradition. Although Christmas in its modern guise is a fairly young institution, it tapped its roots into us before we were old enough to say the word. Additionally, most opponents have been inappropriately antagonistic to proponents of the event. If honey attracts flies just as well as dung, why do we often prefer to use the latter to spread our understanding and convictions?

Christmas is part of our heritage. It is wrapped in warm, soft afghans around a crackling fire, while sipping on hot cider. It is beautiful, often worshipful music playing in the background, while lights dance upon the lovingly chosen tree that's emitting that sweet, forest scent.

Cleaning House

Norman Rockwell came close to capturing its enchanting character, but nothing could beat the arrival of the day of gifts, and family, and Grandma's home-made pecan pie. Trust me, I know! I've been there, and it was certainly a most memorable and delightful occasion. Not one part of this does any reasonable person, or I, have a problem with.

So how in the world could anyone have difficulty with such an event? By now, I hope you are able to see my heart as I delve into answering this question. I do not have an anti-Christ spirit, nor am I power-hungry enough to want to become him. For those of you who have no concern with this day, I intend to give you a clear enough analysis of the issues, that even if you do not end up in agreement, you will at least walk away with a non-hostile explanation. You may use this information to design your antithesis, or you may just end up appreciating the perspective—but still choosing not to modify your life.

Here is a compilation of various thoughts, regarding what most of us who struggle with the day want to say, but have a hard time expressing. A large portion of this next commentary is taken from an essay called, "The Untold Story of Christmas"—author unknown. Other portions are a blend of sourced material and my commentary.

Whose Mas?

The Son and the Sun—A Deliberate Mix: "If Christmas is not in the Bible, where did it ultimately come from? The answers to that question are found in nearly any encyclopedia, or in many newspapers or magazines appearing around December 25. What they have to say about the roots of Christmas, should shock every honest Bible believer into taking a hard, critical look at the annual observance. 'Christmas' is a contraction for 'Christ's Mass', a Roman Catholic observance. It was designed to compete with a heathen Roman feast of Saturnalia, in honor of the sun deity Mithras.

Mithras bore a remarkable similarity to the Biblical Messiah; and the Mithras feast, like Christmas, was to commemorate his birth. Notice the astounding parallels, as detailed by Joscelyn Godwin, professor at Colgate University. Mithras was 'the creator and orderer of the universe', hence a manifestation of the creative Logos or Word. Seeing mankind afflicted by Ahriman, the cosmic power of darkness, he incarnated on earth. His birth on 25 December was witnessed by shepherds. After many deeds, he held a last supper with his disciples and returned to heaven. At the end of the world he will come again to judge resurrected mankind and after the last battle, victorious over evil, he will lead the chosen ones through a river of fire to a blessed immortality" Source: *Mystery Religions in the Ancient World*, p.99.

Godwin remarks:

"No wonder the early Christians were disturbed by a deity who bore so close a resemblance to their own, and no wonder they considered him a mockery of [the Messiah] invented by Satan." These two popular movements were vying for the dominance in the Roman Empire—one pagan, the other Christian. Historian and archaeologist Ernest Renan once said, "If Christianity had been halted in its growth by some mortal illness, the world would have been Mithraist." (Marc Aurele, p. 597)

Caught in the middle were the Roman emperors, who wanted to unify and solidify their diverse empire. They didn't need divisive religious factions. Their motivation was political and not particularly religious; therefore, the Roman rulership saw great advantage in synchronizing and harmonizing these similar religious beliefs into one.

The Romans knew that religion was a powerful means for assimilating other peoples and cultures. If you respect a man's deities, you are halfway toward winning his friendship. They had been doing it for years. The Romans had Latinized the Greek Olympus, giving Latin names to Zeus (Jupiter), Hermes (Mercury), Poseidon (Neptune), and many others. The Syrian Ba'als all became Roman Jupiters, while cults of the Celts and Gauls were given Roman deities.

Although this syncretism or combining of diverse beliefs into one was never more than a political benefit for the Romans, it had a profound effect on Christianity. Even today, much of what is accepted as Bible-based is the direct result of compromising and mixing with heathen religion. Roman Emperor Constantine, a former pagan himself, was to give the most significant push to the Christian-pagan blending of teachings. Among other things, he would decree that worship for Christianity switch from the seventh day Sabbath to the first day of the week—Sun-day—the day the pagans worshiped the sun.

"This tendency on the part of the Christians to meet Paganism halfway was very early developed," says Alexander Hislop in *The Two Babylons;* p.93. Interestingly, Hislop notes that at the same time the pagans gave up precious little of their own beliefs and practices. "And we find Tertullian, even in his day, about the year 230 AD, bitterly lamenting the inconsistency of the disciples of [Messiah] in this respect, and contrasting it with the strict fidelity of the Pagans to their own superstition."

Hislop then quotes Tertullian, the most ancient of the Latin church fathers whose works are extant, as he decries the early church observances. "By us who are strangers to Sabbaths and new moons, and festivals, once acceptable to [Yahweh], the Saturnalia, the feasts of January, the Brumalia, and Matronalia are now frequented; gifts are carried to and fro, New Year's Day presents are made with din, and sports and banquets are celebrated with uproar."

Why a Death Celebration in Honor of a Birth? A 'mass' is a celebration of the Eucharist or the emblems of the death of the Savior. Yet, 'Christ-mass' is an observance supposedly in honor of His birth. Why? The answer is found with

Cleaning House

the secular ancients. Mithras was known as the Sun Deity. His birthday, "Natalis solis invicti" means: "birthday of the invincible sun." It came on December 25, at the time of the winter solstice when the sun began its journey northward again.

Pagan people were overly concerned with life and fertility. They saw life fading in the darkness of winter and so held festivals in honor of and to beckon back the sun to give life and light to earth once more.

Christmas was not observed for at least three centuries after the Savior's birth! *The Dictionary of the Middle Ages* explains how a mass came to be celebrated for the supposed birthday of the Savior.

"In patristic thought, [the Messiah] had traditionally been associated with light or the sun, and the cult of the "Sol invictus," sanctioned as it was by the Roman emperors since the late third century, presented a distinct threat to Christianity. Hence, to compete with this celebration the Roman church instituted a feast for the nativity of [the Messiah], who was called the "Sol iustitiae," (Latin for 'Justice of the Sun'). Usually when Christians celebrated the 'Natalis' (memorial day) of a saint or martyr, it was his death or heavenly nativity. But in this case, 'Natalis' was assigned to be the Messiah's earthly birth, in direct competition with the pagan *Natalis*."; pp.317-318. (That is, to compete with the birthday of Mithras.)

So confused were some about what or whom they were worshiping or celebrating at Christmas, that Pope Leo I (440-461) chastised Christians who were celebrating the birth of a sun deity! The sun cult was particularly strong in Rome, about the time Christmas entered the historical picture. According to the *New Catholic Encyclopedia*:

The Feast is first mentioned at the head of the Depositio Martyrum (Listing of Martyrs) in the Roman Chronograph of 354. Since the Depositio was composed in 336, Christmas in Rome can be dated that far at least. It is not found, however, in the lists of Feasts given by Tertullian and Origen, vol. 3, p.656.

Where did Mithraism come from? How did a Roman religion that venerated the sun deity influence Christianity so greatly? Kenneth Scott Latourette, in *A History of Christianity*, traces Mithraism to the mystery religions of Egypt, Syria, and Persia.

Almost all the mystery cults eventually made their way to Rome, he notes. They were secret in many of their ceremonies and their members were under oath not to reveal their esoteric rites. Numbers of them centered about a savior-god who had died and had risen again. As the cults spread within the Empire, they copied from one another in the easy-going syncretism which characterized much of the religious life of that realm and age, pp.24-25. *Nimrod:*

As we have seen, Christmas as the observance of the Savior's birth did not come into existence immediately. It was not observed for at least three centuries after the Savior's birth! But the secular/pagan characteristics of Christmas trace back thousands of years; all the way back to a man named Nimrod, the founder of ancient pagan Babylon. The ancient 'forefather' to Mithras, Nimrod began a counterfeit religion in the Book of Genesis that set out to compete with the True Faith of the Bible in every conceivable way through the centuries.

The Bible refers to it as the religion of Mystery Babylon. It is this ultimate false religion that will be destroyed when our Savior Yehoshua comes to set up His throne on earth, as seen in Revelation 18. From Babylon sprang up all forms of false worship, including: the Mystery Cults, Mithraism, the Greek and Roman mythologies, modern Eastern religions and today's New Age Movement. Babylon's false worship is found today in every nation and in some aspect in nearly all religions, including present Christianity.

The Madonna and child theme, which is universal and evident in hundreds of religions down through the centuries, had its origin in Babylon. Nimrod's wife was Semiramis, the first deified queen of Babylon. She is also known variously as Diana, Aphrodite, Astarte, Rhea, and Venus. Her son was Tammuz, also called Bacchus, Adonis, and Osiris. Supposedly, he was the reincarnated Nimrod. He came back to life when the dead yule log was cast into the fire and the Christmas tree appeared as the slain king-deity reborn at the winter solstice. (Source; *The Two Babylons*, p. 98).

My turn again. Adding all this to the fact that Dec. 25th was generally considered the birthday of many other false-gods (as though this was the time when the universe burped them into existence), as well as it not even being the correct time frame of the year for His birth, it would stand to reason that even if we were to want to celebrate His birth, this date should be purposely avoided. For the value of mental exercise, there is a rather neat way we *may* better calculate His arrival.

Examining Luke's historical record, we gather some useful information. We learn that John the Immerser's father is Zacharias. Zacharias was a priest from the order of Abijah (1:5). He had received the opportunity to burn the incense by the casting of lots, and went in to do so. While in the Holy Place, he encountered Gabriel, who informed him of a blessing the Lord was about to give him, a son...John.

Luke 1:26 & 36 tells us that Elizabeth, John's mother, was six months along in her pregnancy when Mary got word of her own pregnancy with Yehoshua. In plain math, that makes John six months older than Yeshua; or, for a different angle, Yeshua would be born six months after John. That enables us to calculate that Yeshua would be

Cleaning House

born fifteen months after John's conception, which is thought to have occurred during the Abijah rotation. Luke 1:57 gives us reason to believe Elizabeth's pregnancy was of normal duration; and undoubtedly, so was Mary's (Luke 2:6).

Abijah was the eighth course of twenty-four. Luke tells us Zacharias was working "in the order of his division," which offers another little detail. It tells us that when he received the vision, it was not during one of the three festivals that required all the priests present, those being Passover, Shavuot (Pentecost) and Sukkot (Tabernacles); (Mishna, Sukkah 55b). However, the week following the eighth course was the week of Shavuot. Which means Zacharias would have had to work back-to-back courses. Luke 1:23 tells us that as soon as his duty was completed he went back home.

The length of time the priests served was from the middle of one Shabbat to the middle of the next (2nd Chronicles 23:8). It was an eight-day cycle (1st Chronicles 9:25), and it was performed twice a year. Twenty-four courses, plus three weeks of mandatory Mo'adim, and then the twenty-four courses repeated, equates to fifty-one weeks. This is adequate to cover the lunar-based year. Because two of the three mandatory duties took place within the first nine weeks of the religious calendar year, the eighth course (Abijah) wouldn't actually serve their duty until the ninth or tenth week, depending on when the festival of Shavuot occurred.

What can be extracted from this information is the approximate month of both John and Yeshua's birth, because we can roughly calculate, from historical information, when the Abijah priestly course took place; as instituted by King David, in 1st Chronicles 24:10. We can then backwards calculate the coinciding Gregorian date with the Hebrew calendar. The ninth or tenth week of the Hebrew year falls in the middle of Sivan, which now corresponds to the middle of our May/June.

If John's conception occurred the next week sometime, (perhaps inspired by his reuniting with his wife after several weeks away), his birth could have taken place during the next Feast of Unleavened Bread. Mary became pregnant six months after Elizabeth. That would then have occurred between the end of Kislev and the beginning of Tevet; which is right during Chanukah. Nine months forward from Chanukah is Tabernacles. "And He came and tabernacled among us (John 1:14)."

There have been many, many attempts to prove and disprove this, for centuries. It can't be done. There are periods of history when the priestly courses were disrupted. There are gaps in historical documentation in regards to priestly schedule calculation. There have been calculations that ended up with December 25th (Saturnalia) being the day of His birth, or His conception (making modern "New Year's line up with His circumcision.) Also, Sept. 11th has been suggested. There have also been calculations that said the world was going to end in 1988. Sometimes, we have to settle with what seems most right. Doesn't it drive us nuts, not having solid answers for everything?

In most intellectually honest minds, Christmas is just a man-made event intended to honor the birth of the Savior. Most generally recognize that Dec. 25th is not likely the actual day of His arrival, nor is it a day He has asked us to remember. The Christmas tree wasn't found in America until 1821, brought by Pennsylvania Germans. Christmas wasn't officially recognized in America until 1836, when Alabama became the first state in America to make it a legal holiday. Actually, during Puritan America, it was illegal to celebrate, for its well-acknowledged (at the time) as having pagan affiliations. The day of someone's arrival on Earth, really only holds significance to the immediate family who was there to celebrate it. To Yehoshua, the day of His arrival was a fulfillment of prophecy and part of His plan; but certainly not something appropriate for creating all this materialism, stress, depression and debt.

I know that much of what has been sourced here will be discounted by the notion, "Who's to say that they are correct?" You are absolutely appropriate in your questioning. As I'm sure you see by now, I'm a strong supporter of questioning. There is overwhelming evidence that there is a lot of pre-messianic funny business connected with December 25th. So, when you're done reading this book, you should set about proving it either way, shouldn't you? The big question is: Are we only accountable to what we think, or to what is true? You can no longer plead ignorance, if you were so able to before. The next section will be a study on some of the various symbols of Christmas. But before I do that, I would like you to read a couple more quotes of interest.

A star cult, sun-worship, became (in the third century AD) the dominant official creed, paving the road for the ultimate triumph of Judaeo-Christian monotheism. So strong was the belief in the Invincible Sun (Sol Invictus) that for example, Constantine I (d. 337), himself at first a devotee of the sun cult, found it indeed perfectly compatible with his pro-Christian sympathies to authorize his own portrayal as Helios. And in 354, the ascendant Christian church in the reign of his pious but unsavory son, Constantius II, found it prudent to change the celebration of the birth of Jesus from the traditional date (January 6) to December 25, in order to combat the pagan Sun god's popularity—his 'birthday' being December 25. -*Frederick H. Cramer, Astrology in Roman Law and Politics, p. 4. Copyright 1954 by the American Philosophical Society, Philadelphia.*

Christmas: The supposed anniversary of the birth of Jesus Christ, occurring on Dec. 25. No sufficient data exist, for the determination of the month or the day of the event. There is no historical evidence that our Lord's

Cleaning House

birthday was celebrated during the Apostolic or early post-Apostolic times. The uncertainty that existed at the beginning of the third century in the minds of Hippolytus and others—Hippolytus earlier favored Jan. 2nd, Clement of Alexandria (Strom., I. 21) "the 25th day of Pachon" (May 20th), while others, according to Clement, fixed upon Apr. 18th or 19th and March 28th—proves that no Christmas festival had been established much before the middle of the century. Jan. 6th was earlier fixed upon as the date of the baptism or spiritual birth of Christ, and the feast of Epiphany was celebrated by the Basilidian Gnostics in the second century and by catholic Christians by about the beginning of the fourth century. The earliest record of the recognition of Dec. 25th as a church festival is in the Philocalian Calendar (copied 354, but representing Roman practice in 336). -*A. H. Newman, "Christmas," The New Schaff-Herzog Encyclopedia of Religious Knowledge, Vol. 3, p. 47. Copyright 1909 by Funk& Wagnalls Company, New York*

In the Scriptures, no one is recorded to have kept a feast or held a great banquet on his [Christ's] birthday. It is only sinners [like Pharaoh or Herod] who make great rejoicings over the day in which they were born into this world.-- *Catholic Encyclopedia*, 11th ed., art: "Natal Day."

Trees of Worship

Thus says the LORD, "Do not learn the way of the nations, and do not be terrified by the signs of the heavens, although the nations are terrified by them. For the customs of the peoples are delusion; because it is wood cut from the forest, the work of the hands man with a cutting tool. They decorate *it* with silver and with gold. They fasten it with nails and with hammers, so that it will not totter." (Jeremiah 10:2-4)

This warning/instruction was being delivered to the Israelites residing predominantly in the Northern Kingdom, who were going to be brought into captivity through the Assyrian invasion. This "House of Israel" or "House of Joseph," as it is also prophetically known by, was going to be stripped away from their inheritance for a limited but indeterminable amount of time. However, as prophecy tells us, the House of Judah (Southern Kingdom) and the House of Israel, will both be brought back into their land.

Just because they were about to undergo disciplinary action for rebellion against His commandments, did not give them absolution from adherence to the very same commandments afterward. His intent and plan is always restorative and merciful, so it falls right in line with His M.O. to send a prophet, to bring loving warnings to avoid the things that will become temptations and potential pitfalls. His discipline is always to bring correction and is rooted in perfect love. If our parents were to punish us without telling us why, and never instructed us as to how to avoid these problems in the future, that would not be love, but abuse.

Where the Israelites were heading, something they were going to encounter would be the foreign gods of the land (just like when they were first entering into Canaan), and the acts that were involved in their worship. Jeremiah, in this passage, is bringing up something that is also brought up and condemned by Ezekiel. Ezekiel, in 8:14-18, condemns ancient Israel for adopting the worship of Tammuz, which included both sun worship and the Asherah.

Then He brought me to the entrance of the gate of the LORD's house which *was* toward the north; and behold, women were sitting there weeping for Tammuz. He said to me, 'Do you see *this*, son of man? Yet you will see still greater abominations than these.' Then He brought me into the inner court of the LORD's house. And behold, at the entrance to the temple of the LORD, between the porch and the altar, *were* about twenty-five men with their backs to the temple of the LORD and their faces toward the east; and they were prostrating themselves eastward toward the sun. He said to me, 'Do you see *this*, son of man? Is it too light a thing for the house of Judah to commit the abominations which they have committed here, that they have filled the land with violence and provoked Me repeatedly? For behold, they are putting the twig to their nose. Therefore, I indeed will deal in wrath. My eye will have no pity nor will I spare; and though they cry in My ears with a loud voice, yet I will not listen to them.' (Ezekiel 8:14-18)

Here you see Tammuz being worshipped, by facing the sun and touching themselves with branches. Tammuz, Ishtar's consort, is another life-death-rebirth cycle representing deity. Tammuz was mourned, as you see here exampled by the weeping, which took place during the six day fast his worshipers participated in annually, as he 'died' when the summer solstice began. These branches are an affiliation with the Asherah, possibly the branches that are cut off in the process of making them. In the KJV, they were called *groves*. These groves were often found in the highland areas, where people would have to ascend up to them, in sort of a small version pilgrimage. Ritual sex would occur under these trees for their representative 'fertile' nature. Additionally, these trees were often decorated and offered gifts in the form of cakes, to bless them for their services. Why do we put gifts under the trees anyway?

These Asherah-groves were always under the order of Adonai to hew and burn down. Whenever they entered into a land to take it over, this was a straightway command. There was to be no trace remaining. You will clearly notice, as you travel through the books of the Kings and their Chronicles, that the overall quality of the legacies of the kings of Israel, were often synonymous with the way in which they treated the "high

Cleaning House

places". If they were sold out for Adonai, they would tear them down (usually). If they were lukewarm or wicked, they would leave them be. It was a prominent evaluator, and somewhat like a meter of the king's righteousness.

But the Asherah trees didn't just stay in the high places. They were often cut down, and in various ways brought into the home. And this, my friends, is where we find ourselves today. I'm familiar with what would be considered pro-Christian explanations of the symbolism of the holidays. I still cannot (and do not see how it will ever change) correlate the practice of chopping down a tree, bringing it into your home, propping it up and decorating it with gold, silver, and fruit, with worshiping Yeshua.

The "Christmas" tree, now so common among us, was equally common in Pagan Rome and Pagan Egypt. In Egypt, it was the palm tree; in Rome, it was the fir. The palm-tree denoted the pagan messiah known as Baal-Tamar; the fir tree referring to the one known as Baal-Berith. It may smell good, look pretty, and people can get pretty creative with their explanations for it; but no matter how you slice it down, this practice is condemned by the prophets. (Source; *The Two Babylons*, p. 78).

While working at one of my customer's homes recently, I observed something that really shored this up for me; not that I was actually shaky in any way. She had two conifer trees in her home. They were decorated perfectly, with leaves that had undergone the autumn change from green to orange, yellow, red and brown. Draped carefully from limb to limb was a lovely strand of jack-o-lantern lights. "Finally" I thought to myself, "a genuine expression". At least she portrayed a more accurate reason for bringing decorated trees into the home. I do have one more verse you need to see.

You shall not plant for yourself an Asherah of any kind of tree beside the altar of the LORD your God, which you shall make for yourself. (Deuteronomy 16:21)

Just in case you thought to yourself, "But I'm not worshiping the tree!" Doesn't matter! Not the point! It is an unlawful mixture. And by the way, don't churches call the front of their building, altars? And isn't that where we often find those "houses of worship" adorned with trees at Christmas? What about the "family altar?" Isn't church the people and not the building? Yes…I've pretty much got it all covered.

Even if two thousand years passed between the original practice and now, to think that HaSatan wouldn't resurrect the practice and cloak it behind a new façade, is a naive assumption. Nothing would delight him more than to trick the children of YHVH into committing an idolatrous act, all the while thinking they are performing a righteous offering. How quickly we will label the act of placing an evergreen on top of a high-rise during construction (for good luck) a superstition; and yet, we are awfully slow at recognizing the act of propping one up in our own homes as similarly irrational? But this is just one of the dominant, traditional symbols of Christmas. Let's take a closer look at some others.

More "Reasons for the Season"

What fall festivity is complete without a **cornucopia** displayed on your table, spilling over with the bounties of the harvest? The cornucopia (Latin *Cornu Copiae*), also known in English as the Horn of Plenty, is a symbol of prosperity and affluence. It dates back to the 5th century BCE. But what else is it? Here is the supposed oldest account of the origin of the Cornucopia:

Zeus (Jupiter) was committed by his mother Rhea to the care of the daughters of Melisseus, a Cretan king. They fed the infant deity with the milk of the goat. Jupiter broke off one of the horns of the goat and gave it to his nurses, and endowed it with the wonderful power of becoming filled with whatever the possessor might wish.

The original depictions were of the goat's horn filled with fruits and flowers. Deities, especially Fortuna, would be depicted with the horn of plenty. Modern images, such as those used in Thanksgiving murals, depict a horn-shaped wicker basket filled with fruits and vegetables. The horn of plenty was regarded as the symbol of inexhaustible riches and plenty. But where else might the horn come from?

Another story is about the "fifth labor" of Hercules. In which the Augean Stables were cleaned in one day, by diverting a river. Hercules fought the river-god Achelous, while they were delayed on their journey by the overflow of his waters. Hercules fought the river-god Achelous, who could take the form of either a snake or bull. Achelous failed to defeat Hercules as a snake, and took the form of a bull. Hercules ripped his horn off and diverted the river. This land was very fertile, and this is represented by the horn of plenty. Then, the Naiads took the horn, consecrated it, and filled it with fragrant flowers. (In the Roman version, it was the goddess Abundantia) who adopted the horn and made it her own, and called it "Cornucopia".

The **wreath** is simply a woven or bent grouping of typically evergreen plant/tree material, into a circular decoration. Whether the diadem (small head wreath) is the chicken or the egg, to its big brother wall wreath is unknown for sure; although it has been suggested that from the act of hanging up (displaying) the diadem (sometimes trophy), we get the practice of hanging the wreath.

What we do know is that the selection of evergreen plant material, due to its acknowledged longevity, is a custom derived from ancient German and Celtic solstice festivities, and their usage of such was to transcend the death which accompanies winter, and the future coming of Spring's new birth. It has currently come to be thought of as representing strength, as in what was necessary to endure the atonement sufferings, and the future coming King's arrival.

The circular shape is thought to represent eternity, as is seen in our traditional wearing of one on our ring finger, to represent our hope for our marriages. It is also a primitive shape symbolizing the Sun. Although points are not present, commonly, throughout ancient history, a ring with 4, 6, 8, or 16 points would have been found in its center representing different deities. "The 4 pointed cross inside a ring represented the Canaanite Ba'al storm god. The 6, 8, or 16 pointed star in the center of a wheel, represented the Akkadian Ishtar (Venus) connected to her triad consisting of herself, Shamash (Sun), and Sin (Moon). (*Encyclopaedia Brittanica* online, article: Ishtar)

I only quote this to ask you, "What else is the point?" Take a step back from your emotional connection to the beauty of the object. You think to yourself, "I want to celebrate Jesus's B-Day. I think I'll take some evergreen and form it into a circle, decorate it with silver and gold, then hang it on my door." Sounds reasonable to me—I guess.

The following items have a variety of explanations available. I list these with that reality out in the open, and not to necessarily personally substantiate their accuracy. I do, however, support their likelihood.

The **Yule Log** tradition comes to us from Scandinavia, where the pagan sex and fertility god Jul, or Jule (pronounced 'yule'), was honored in a twelve-day celebration in December. A large, single log (generally considered to have been a phallic idol) was kept with a fire against it for twelve days, a different sacrifice to Jul being offered in the fire on each of the twelve days. *Holidays and Holy Days, by Tom C. McKenney.*

This is where the Twelve Days of Christmas originated, which are now counted as the twelve days between Christmas and Epiphany (January 12th):

The Yule log was originally an entire tree, carefully chosen, and brought into the house with great ceremony. The butt end would be placed into the hearth while the rest of the tree stuck out into the room. The tree would be slowly fed into the fire and the entire process was carefully timed to last the entire Yule season. *-The History of Christmas*

Stocking hanging comes from an English legend:

Father Christmas once dropped some gold coins while coming down the chimney. The coins would have fallen through the ash grate, and been lost, if they hadn't landed in a stocking that had been hung out to dry. Since that time children have continued to hang out stockings in hopes of finding them filled with gifts. *-Ibid*

Mistletoe is a Druidic medicine that was thought to cure everything from epilepsy to infertility, the wax berries of this parasite are thought to be a sex stimulant. (The plant itself is highly toxic.) Among the pre-Christian Druidic superstitions, derived from ancient Babylon was the legend of the mistletoe. It was regarded as a divine branch which came down from heaven and grafted itself into an earthly tree. Thus the mistletoe became a token of reconciliation, the kiss being a symbol of pardon *-Ibid*

Holly's green leaves and red berries were respected in medieval times as protection against witchcraft and the evil eye; a good luck charm for men.

Ham is eaten because Tammuz (Adonis) was thought to have been killed by a boar. In his memory, pagans sacrificed and ate swine at the Saturnalia.

Christmas cookies may trace back to the cakes that were made to the Queen of Heaven or Semiramis (Jeremiah 44:19). Round ones were made for the Saturnalia and Brumalia to symbolize the returning sun. Ginger bread men may be the result of a precursor (human-shaped biscuit) which was eaten during Saturnalia.

HaSatan's goal is to get us to see him instead of seeing God. He wants to be like the Most High in any way he can. God receives praise when we follow Him. Satan receives praise when we follow him. His strategy is to get us to follow him, thinking that we're following God.

I can see him now, laughing at God every time he convinces some soul to replace God with himself. Celebrating may seem like a loving thing to do, but it is not reality based. Example: We celebrate Christmas and we say, "I know that Christ was born. It doesn't matter when. We choose Dec. 25th to represent his birth date." Then we follow the crowd, and sing and tell lies about a fat clown in a red suit. Then we take our children to the malls to see this perfect man who gives us gifts. As innocent as it all may seem, Satan is mocking God.

So let's not forget our buddy **Santa Claus**. I would now like to present you with a portion of an essay called, *"How Satan Mocks God (On Merchant's Day)"*; by Gary C. Michael. I personally think there are some things that are quite interesting, some things that seem questionable, and yet other pertinent things that are omitted. We could go on forever, but let's not. The truth is likely somewhere in the middle. Either way, it should at the very least, get you thinking.

Let's start with Santa's **hair and eyes**. Santa has white woolly hair; right? His eyes are said to have a twinkle in them. Rev. 1:14 says, talking about Christ, "His head and His hairs were white like wool, as white as snow; and His eyes were as a flame of fire." Fire twinkles, doesn't it? Are we talking about Jesus or Santa Claus?

Santa is from the **North** Pole; right? Why the North? Why not the South Pole? Well, God is from the North. We find in Isaiah 14:12-14 these words: "How art thou fallen from heaven, o Lucifer, son of the morning! How art thou cut down to the ground, which didst weaken the nations! For thou hast said in thine heart, I will ascend into heaven, I will exalt my throne above the stars of God: I will sit also upon the mount of the congregation, **in the sides of the North**: I will ascend above the heights of the clouds; I will be like the most high." I tell you, Santa is from the North because God is from the North.

Santa has **unlimited power**. Is there anything that Santa can't do? Ask a kid. There is no dispute about that. I don't need a text to tell you that only God has unlimited power.

Santa is **all-knowing**, huh? He knows when you are good or bad, so be good for goodness sake. "You'd better watch out..." You know the song. So we tell our children that Santa is omniscient (all knowing). Well, he would have to be in order to know about all the children in the world, wouldn't he? I don't need a text to tell you that only God is all knowing.

Santa is **immortal**. Have you ever heard of Santa being born? Oh, I know the story about Saint Nick. He was a generous man, but the legend of Santa Claus grew into the ridiculous tale that it is today. Only God is immortal.

Santa is **perfect**. To whom does he need to repent? Can Santa do any wrong? Ask a child. Who is Santa's boss? He has none. Does he ever say praise the Lord? Have you ever heard of Santa giving God glory or credit for anything? If he did, he wouldn't be Santa long. My-my-my.

Santa also **judges** us. I thought that was God's job. But according to Santa he's checking his list, checking it twice, gonna find out who's naughty or nice. Jesus Christ is coming to town. No; that's, "Santa Claus is coming to town." But I thought that Jesus was checking his list to see who has been naughty or nice and is coming to town to bring his rewards. Who's gonna do it, Santa or Jesus?

Santa **calls** the children to come unto him, **sits** them on his lap, and the children **repent to him** for the bad that they did during the year and promise to be good. I tell you, Jesus is the one we should teach our children to repent to.

Jesus often called the children to him and said forbid them not. Santa is fooling our children.

Santa is **omnipresent**, which means that he can be everywhere at the same time. How else can he visit every home on the same night? I don't need a text to tell you that only God can visit every home at once. I don't know about you, but I think that Santa is a clown; a big fat, jelly-belly, roly-poly, curly-headed clown. What about his red suit?

Why red? Revelation 19:13 tells us why. "And he was clothed with vesture dipped in blood: and his name is called the word of God." Need I say more? Santa, like Jesus, is the same in character today, yesterday, and forever.[2]

When does Santa come? On a **foggy** Christmas Eve, Santa asked Rudolph to lead his sleigh that night. There is no dispute that Jesus is coming in fog. What is fog? Clouds. The Bible tells us that the clouds are angels. Gabriel will probably lead the coming of my savior, not Rudolph.

Santa **lives in a shining ice palace**, like clear glass. Why? Rev. 21:18 tells us why. "And the building of the wall of it was of jasper: and the city was pure gold, like unto clear glass."

Santa is **tended by elves**, which are mysterious creatures; just as God is tended by mysterious angels. By the way, have you ever wondered why he has a female title? Santa is the feminine for saint. I guess that makes him a bit of a mysterious creature as well; doesn't it?

What is Santa's famous expression; **Ho, ho, ho**. Why ho, ho, ho? The word "ho" comes from the Hebrew "oiy" (meaning: woe, or alas); a word expressing a sense of warning. Why would HaSatan use such a word? In the book of Zechariah, chapter two, verses six and seven, we find the answer. Adonai is talking to his people. "Ho, ho, come forth, and flee from the land of the North, saith the Lord. Deliver thyself, O Zion, that dwellest with the daughter of Babylon." He is expressing anguish over the fact that His people are on the wrong road. This is the only thing that causes God pain. End of: *How Satan Mocks God*

If Christmas was really about Jesus, would nearly the entire world embrace it so readily? In some countries, Christmas is as big a binge-drinking event as is the global New Year debauchery. If Christmas was an authentic expression of worship to the Messiah, the world would reject it as openly as it does the Ten Commandments. And yet, the world has made it its largest, most costly holiday event! If the world loves it, it is probably not a good thing. You know, when it comes right down to it, if I had to lie to my kids, it wouldn't be about some fraud in a red suit.

Granted, those "attributes" of Santa did not come about through specific attempts by man to mock God; they're just the result of coincidental and progressive evolution. Surely, Satan had nothing to do with that.

Therefore shall ye keep mine ordinance, that ye commit not any one of these abominable customs, which were committed before you, and that ye defile not yourselves therein: I am the Lord your God. (Leviticus 18:30)

Well, alright! Let's get rid of all the pagan elements of Christmas, and just keep the "meaning" or "spirit" of it. What would we be left with? Perhaps a religion-neutral, winter festival, or maybe a nativity scene? Materialism will still remain strong. And let's not forget family gathering time and memory making. I know that you know, that these things can all be dissected and have a weak foundation. Additionally, there are other little details, like the fact the Magi arrived around two years after He was born. Or, that gifts were given to Him, not exchanged amongst the attendees. The shepherds would not have been out at night, in the dead of winter. Do your research and you will find these and other commonly held discrepancies to be true. PS, the likely reason there was "no room in the inn" is because Jerusalem was packed with attendees during Sukkot.

For believers, when all the nonsense and secularism is stripped away, there remains nothing but a desire to honor His birth, which is a nice gesture and all, but it's really His ministry and death that have the greater meaning. His virgin birth was just a sign. For non-believers, there is nothing left at all. If you really want to honor Him, do away the nonsense and secularism. Then, you can obey the requests He has made of us already. You see, we Torah-types really do mean well. Our issue with Christmas has nothing to do with an opposition toward adoration of the Messiah, or charitableness. It's really just the fact that Christmas doesn't hold a midnight candle to the fullness and legitimacy of all that the divinely appointed times have to offer. If we all observed them, families wouldn't miss a thing. Again, it's not His fault we don't. I end this topic with this simple thought:

Observe how the lilies of the field grow; they do not toil nor do they spin, yet I say to you that not even Solomon in all his glory clothed himself like one of these. (Matthew 6:28b & 29)

If the beauty of the simple lily is more wondrous than the magnificence of Solomon's garments, why do we feel the need to add more adornments to His already splendid creation? Do we feel His handiwork is not good enough? You may ask, "What if we stripped the tree of its ornaments then, and just propped it up plainly in respect to its Creator?" Now what you have is a tree that was once made alive by the Creator, dying in your home, being held up by artificial means and prolonging its demise with water, as if to say *we* are its givers of life now. "So let's just use fake trees instead." Now we really have something which, when it comes right down to it, is absolutely meaningless. Let's just stop the nonsense shall we?

In fact, there are far more, and far worse additional myths, legends, and or realities associated with the synthesized, pagan elements associated with this erroneous memorial (e.g. the gruesome human sacrifice that was done on the eighth day of Saturnalia; the marching of naked Jews around Rome, in 1466, under the homosexual Pope Paul II's watchful eye). All in all, we know one thing for sure. It's not His birthday!

I am now going to attempt to discuss three other topics briefly, and as neutrally as possible. The first two are related. There is a lot of debate over the first tradition, and due to the fact that other major religions, which most of us don't agree with, also remove this event from personal practice, there tends to be a thick wall of defense that intellectual reasoning cannot break down. I hesitate to even talk about them, for fear of their inclusion being interpreted as an evidence to not take me seriously. The reason I have decided to include the first two, is that there are many true believers who are re-examining this practice also. It is an issue on the horizon, so I figured it was worthy to bring up. The third illustrates the need to examine even the most common and seemingly innocent acts we engage in. Nonetheless, you've come this far, so I will not shrink back.

The Birthday Ritual

A birthday, by all rights, should within the construction of the name by which this holiday goes, be related to and memorialize births. The birth of a child is an unbelievably emotional and profoundly impacting event. To some, it's understood to be the divinely enabled event that it is. To others, it is but the final stage to the naturalistic mechanism of human reproduction. There are also some who believe it to be an event which was purposely caused to occur at a certain time within the astrological zodiac structure.

Wiccans and other pagan groups believe that this event, and the day it falls on, is the most important remembrance of the year in one's life. It is celebrated in various ways, and with very high regard. Don't believe me? Just go to your big-box book store under "spirituality," and look at all the material related to birthdays.

Another ancient belief is that on the day of one's birth, their personal, spiritual strength is at its weakest point, making it very susceptible to damage and infusion by dark spiritual forces. Therefore, a jubilant celebration by the surrounding of friends and family creates a protective field around the person. I suppose when you think about it, Wiccans may enjoy such a weakness and susceptibility to demonic influences (if that was true). But let's be honest, the majority of people think of it as a way to do something special for someone else, and not much more than that.

The thing that has to be considered when contemplating the appropriateness of the birth-day celebration is whether or not the 'birth' part of the day is really considered at all. For that to be true, the celebrators would have had to be attendees of the actual birthing event. In most cases, a couple at the most, at any given party, would qualify. One has to conclude that the actual 'birth' part of the birth-day event is an ever diminishing root of the purpose, as the years go by and we grow older. One could argue we appreciate the birth, in the sense of it being the means by which the celebrated arrived, and now blesses our lives.

In order to avoid giving any homage to the power of the astrological affiliation with the date itself, the focus would have to be placed firmly on something else like the birth-event (which we pretty much ruled out as being relevant, except for Mommy and her closest), or significant events and milestones. This would only be possible if the celebration does not occur every single year of our lives, and if our celebrations are more specifically related to those events and milestones; i.e., a graduation party. So often, we do what we do because it has been handed down to us from 'birth'. So, here is my perspective on it:

It is encouraging for children to be the cause of celebration. During the early years, I feel that the praise and kindness that accompanies these events have a clear and positive impact, but only when the event is governed appropriately. During the first ten or so years of a child's life, there are pretty significant changes, and it does keep their arrival memories fresh in our hearts. After that, we all have to grow up sometime.

As adults, if people just have to sing you happy birthday, choke back the gag and let them. Maybe someday, when they understand you better, and respect your devotion, they will ask you whether or not they can sing it, or if you want to receive gifts. You cannot control other people, you can only control yourself. You can, however, work to control the egocentric attention you receive, that accompanies an event based on a calendar date. We had no control over our coming, or when we came.

When it comes right down to it, how is that something to celebrate? Personally, I would prefer that significant parties only be thrown at the turning of each decade. I can see the significance in that. You want to throw an over-the-hill party for someone; I get it. That is my request to my family. I really don't need childish affirmation anymore. Come on—admit it! Don't you feel a little silly getting meaningless attention, and having "the song" sung to you anyway? To not make my own family a stumbling-block to my extended family, we simply desire for them to use moderation with our kids. It's not as if they are restricted from their graciousness all the rest of the year long. You can't stop people from wanting to bless you; so if they choose to get you something, it is appropriate to graciously accept it. And honestly, the statement "Happy Birthday" doesn't offend me. I just think the throwing of an annual party is a bit over the top.

One of the normal reasons/justifications for man-made holidays such as this is the benefit of getting family together, in an otherwise distant or distracted, relational world. I can sympathize with that. But if we are honest with ourselves, and this is what it takes to bring families together, we really have a more complex and deeper problem on our hands. It is in fact our compulsion towards celebrating ourselves that drives this day. And because we believe we think like the Lord, we are compelled to celebrating His coming as well. But He is not vain.

I am a reasonable man, for the most part, so I try to maintain a balance between walking out my convictions and being a living example, with trying hard to be non-judgmental of others. Inevitably, though, I'm sure you have found that living out your convictions is often automatically deemed judgmentalism. As I said before, we need to be gracious to those who don't understand our convictions. I know there are people out there who only see the birthday cake as a gift to the gods. Maybe it was once. I've contemplated it and come to the conclusion that in itself, it is just a fun food for our guests to eat. If you're going to have a party at all, I see no difference between cake, pie, cookies, ice-cream, pizza, or whatever else you provide. But there is an element to this birthday treat that I have agreed to conclude with others as problematic.

One of the things I work very hard to disallow in my home is superstition. I don't throw coins into fountains, (but I could if I wanted to). I purposely walk under ladders (unless they look like they are going to fall), and I've owned a black cat (prior to family allergy issues). So I had to come to terms with this popular practice, which now has no place in my home. You will ultimately have to decide whether or not it should be in yours.

Candles and Wishes

I know it seems silly. I really do. But the whole premise of making a "wish" is that by doing so, for no other reason than chance or by cosmic intervention, something good will happen, because it was asked for on this "special day". Believers don't make wishes. We pray. And when we pray, we ask for His will, not ours. And we ask Him, not the Four Elements.

There are some interesting theories about the origin of the involvement of candles. It is thought that they originally were put on round cakes to duplicate the sun, giving honor to Mithras for another year of life. It is also thought that the earliest forms of them were composed of wax produced from the fat of sacrificed children. Who can say for sure? Not I. But, everything has an origin except our Elohiym, and though I can't confirm the wax story, my gut deems the sun story plausible. Why? Because, here again is another practice with no *origin* in rhyme or reason. It exists outside the realm of logical rationalization. To even pretend that by not successfully extinguishing the candles, one forfeits their opportunity to receive their wish, is a silly game I'm just not going to let myself or my kids play.

I have a hard time believing candles started out representing years, and eventually they stop doing that anyway, because we run out of room. Plus, if you want to acknowledge the amount of years that have passed, you can just write it down with frosting. I'm perfectly comfortable with whatever mockery I receive for my belief in this matter. I'll just have to pray that my children survive this psychological abuse. This conviction of mine will certainly not be that of most others, but I am the overseer of my home, and I will let my conviction be my guide in there.

Okay. Here is that third topic. Remember, this is not a judgment call. I'm just making you aware for awareness sake.

Ah-choo…"God Bless You!"

It's such a nice thing to say to someone. But really, why do we say it? Here is another silly but curious act we perform without really knowing why. You may at least find this interesting.

On the surface, when we speak a blessing over people, its usual intent is to *increase* or *prosper* them in a particular area. If the blessing does not specify what for, i.e., "May the Lord bless you," then it would simply default to a basic increase in whatever area of need there may be. In this case, to ask Him to bless someone, in context with a sneeze, is to inadvertently ask for Him to give the recipient of the blessing, more sneezes. But this thought is based solely on the meaning of the phrase.

One does have to ask themself why this particular, involuntary physical activity requires a special recognition, whereas others do not. If you burp, you generally pardon yourself. When you "cut the cheese," in good humor, you project the blame on someone else. Nobody says "bless you" when you cough, or hiccup. Isn't that a bit curious? There are a variety of explanations for the origin of this expression. The four most common ones I will now share with you. Remember, even though there is likely a single origin (maybe one of these), that doesn't mean it wasn't used in various ways, at various times in history. Disclaimer: I do not claim that any one of these origins is "the one".

The first is that at the time of your sneeze, it was believed that your spirit would be expelled into the air. At that moment, it was vulnerable to being snatched by HaSatan. To prevent this from happening, somehow the announcement of the "blessing" would place a protective hedge around the spirit until it returned.

The second, which is kind of a converse version of the first, is that the act of a sneeze was an expulsion of a demon that was already inside the body. The "blessing" was what was required to trap the demon outside. Considering that they come back with a vengeance, and with seven friends, one could use all the "blessings" they could get. The third and fourth are affiliated, and not so spiritually oriented.

The third possible origin is claimed to be that sneeze-blessing started at the time of the Bubonic Plague, where sneezing was taken as a sure sign of the Black Death. The plague had a symptom of hard and repetitive sneezing. So, when a sneeze was heard, one would say "Bless you" to the sneezer, in acknowledgement of their impending demise, and in hopes of a better afterlife.

The fourth origin stems from the belief that when one sneezed, their heart would stop beating. A "bless you" was a verbal defribulator. The interesting thing is…the Black Death did kill many, and it did so by ending in cardiac arrest.[4]

Due to the blessing's affiliation with these stated possibilities and its meaningless connection to an involuntary physiological action, it is a validly questionable practice. Because of this, if you choose not to say it, you don't have to become an "insensitive jerk". There is a way out. Simply ask if they feel okay. After all, the sneeze is affiliated with allergies or a cold anyway. If they say, "Excuse me!" before you get the chance to show sympathy to their condition, return their courtesy in like kind; say, "No problem." When you sneeze, quickly follow it up with your own, "Excuse me!" Maybe they will feel it unnecessary to follow it with a 'blessing', and a "No problem" will follow it instead. It's pretty easy for me to deal with, because I am not a big fan of the name 'God' to begin with. And I'm certainly not going to mix His real name with such a silly situation.

By no means am I opposed to speaking blessings over people, so it has nothing to do with that. But I do think our 'blessings' should be given with some discrimination. Plus, you certainly don't have to use a sneeze as your opportunity to do so. Do you really think that by your habitual and insincere saying of the phrase "God bless you," something significant is going to happen to that person, that wasn't already coming in their future; especially if the person is living in rebellion? If not, then it is idol speech. Some of you may not say the word 'god' at the start of this pronouncement, and deliver the amended version, "Bless You!" Although it has a tinge more appropriateness, when 'God' is not involved in it, it remains a hollow and powerless statement.

Although I don't believe His name is, or should be rendered 'God', many out there do. Those very same people, without acknowledging it, would inadvertently be using His name "in vain" (by their own traditional interpretation of that commandment), by speaking it so often, and in such a trite way. Fortunately, they are technically not.

However, since the general affiliation with the word is the Judeo-Christian deity, it still has a diluting effect on His perceived holiness. I told you this might seem silly, and to many of you it still does. You have to admit though; this is a good example of how superstition can find its way into even the most rational and intelligent among us. When it comes right down to it, that's really the most significant issue at hand.

For a Little Introspection

Then you will remember your evil ways and your deeds that were not good, and you will loathe yourselves in your own sight for your iniquities and your abominations. (Ezekiel 36:31)

To whom is Ezekiel talking? Is it those about to fall into the pit of eternal damnation? Perhaps it is the personal reflections of the lost, just prior to repentance. Actually, it is another verse expressing our (believers) enlightening upon entering the Messianic age, and it happens right after this:

Ezekiel 36:27, "I will put My Spirit within you and cause you to walk in My statutes, and you will be careful to observe My ordinances."

To some extent and level, this will happen to us all. No matter how obedient to the statutes and ordinances we are able to become in this life; we will all fall short of perfection.

Personally, it is my hope and desire that I might stand before Him, requiring less correction than more. Again, the ironic thing about grace is that is calls out for us to require less of it. As wonderful as it is, it is not going to be necessary for us to receive in the age to come. We need grace now, because we are so disobedient now. When we come into perfect compliance with His Torah, and are "careful" in our "observance," it will no longer be needed as a tool driving us to righteousness.

Maybe we should endeavor to live our lives in such a way now, as to base our decisions regarding our traditions and practices, on how much grace is required to overlook them.

He who has My commandments and keeps them is the one who loves Me; and he who loves Me will be loved by My Father, and I will love him and **will disclose Myself to him**. (John 14:21)

Isn't that the point? In the end, it turns out to be that the Christmas tree, the Easter Bunny, and any number of other symbols related to other holidays with which the church seems to have no problem, come from Germanic and druidic origin. Perhaps you don't find that curiously disturbing. But I do. It is from the very land where the attempted destruction of Judah took place, in the name of "Christianity," that the influences which seek to diminish the Mo'adim of the Elohiym of Judah come from, and have intermingled with Christianity. You can have them!

I now speak to those of you who engage in, or attend churches that do, the selling of pumpkins and trees during the un-holy days. CEASE! Come out from among her! Your support and promotion of these abominations, without doubt, is putrid in the Lord's nostrils. Get Nimrod's influences out of your houses of prayer! Think what you want. *Feel* like I'm wrong. Take your chances. But your profiting off such things is prostitution of the faith, and not the faith, "…once for all delivered to the saints (Jude 3)."

I have no doubt that if Yeshua was to visit our houses of worship during these events, "smashing pumpkins" would no longer be affiliated with a rock group, and "chainsaw massacre" would no longer be a movie title. And no doubt, I would join Him. When I drive by your un-holy day markets, anger and disgust rises up within me. And I truly believe it is of His Spirit in me, and not of my own. If it doesn't bother you, I am confident you do not have the mind of Christ in this regard. You have allowed the complacency of the church to affect your sensibilities. Go ahead, laugh at me. I just plead with you to prayerfully consider all that you have read here. It is for these kinds of compromises that Israel got in such trouble. And it likewise plays a role in why the church is as well.

You don't need to replace the events on HaSatan's calendar with anything. Our children won't be "robbed" of anything by not attending his feast days. They will be taught to despise evil, and learn to recognize it in a world that apparently cannot, because holiness is foolishness to the perishing. They will learn that there are things that believers don't engage in, without having the need to apologize or excuse.

In case I haven't given you enough to consider, you should do your own research on Valentine's Day (or the Eve of the Feast of Lupercus; a.k.a. Lupercalia.) I don't want to be responsible for breaking couples up, so you'd better do it together. I would also strongly encourage you to study the ancient practices and severe degree of anti-Semitism associated with Saturnalia. It will offend you to the core. And maybe, when the next New Year's celebration takes place, you will consider your actions carefully, as the world works itself into a hedonistic lather, celebrating a day like any other, becoming the next day like any other, ending the cycle of the Earth's orbit around the Sun—but not the glorious schedule of appointments Adonai designed for His people.

11

Abuses of Power

But all things must be done properly and in an orderly manner (14:33a), for God is not *a God* of confusion but of peace... (1st Corinthians 14:40)

My dear engrafted family, I am really grieved over what we are going to consider now. One of the most discouraging aspects to the category at hand is that we really should be able to have a proper discipline about them, due to their fairly thorough coverage and instruction in Scripture. We don't though. If we would just believe what was written by the apostles, and trust the wisdom and instruction found elsewhere in His Word, this chapter would not have to be written at all. And to be frank, it has not been a pleasure to write. I have sat with my head in my hands, so many times, asking—pleading for Adonai to change us; to open our eyes to the truth that is right there before us. It just doesn't seem to happen...yet.

I am begging you, no matter what your persuasion, to give me a chance to speak to both your spirit and your mind. I realize you are going to come to this table with your personal experiences guiding your beliefs. You will also bring your educational, denominational, and intellectual biases. I can't ask you to ignore those, but I am asking you to take the chance that what you are about to learn is right, and to have ears to hear. You will hear Truth, because it will be the Word that does much of the speaking. I pray that this study will bless you, by helping you to see what so desperately needs to be seen. For I declare with complete confidence, it is in response to these portrayals of the Kingdom, that citizenship is quite often, not applied for.

According to the Word, we have gifts that have been given to us (the Body) by the Spirit, to exhort, encourage, and empower both each other and ourselves. Here is one list of these giftings, as described by Paul:

Now there are varieties of gifts, but the same Spirit. And there are varieties of ministries, and the same Lord. There are varieties of effects, but the same God who works all things in all *persons*. But to each one is given the manifestation of the Spirit for the common good. For to one is given the word of wisdom through the Spirit, and to another the word of knowledge according to the same Spirit; to another faith by the same Spirit, and to another gifts of healing by the one Spirit, and to another the effecting of miracles, and to another prophecy, and to another the distinguishing of spirits, to another *various* kinds of tongues, and to another the interpretation of tongues. But one and the same Spirit works all these things, distributing to each one individually just as He wills. (1st Corinthians 12:4-11)

This text includes what are commonly called the "Motivational Gifts of the Spirit". Wonderful gifts that they are; they are always trumped by the "more excellent way." Love is the first and most important thing to be considered when practicing these gifts, and it must not be disregarded during the assessment of their proper utilization. Since love causes us to esteem others more highly, it also regulates the manner through which we disperse these gifts unto others. Or at least, that's the way it should be.

Un-Motivating Gifts
Babyl-on

I would like to begin this examination with what is probably the most controversial of the gifts. Actually, the fact that something is itself a controversy within Scripture to begin with, lends creed to the necessity of its closer examination. Glossolalia is the technical, psychological, and theological term for speaking in *tongues*, and it is about this topic that we shall begin.

To set the stage, I think it would be valuable to give you a few different, dictionary definitions for the word 'glossolalia'.

1. "Fabricated and non-meaningful speech, especially such speech associated with a trance state or certain schizophrenic syndromes."
2. "See gift of tongues."

The American Heritage® Dictionary of the English Language, Fourth Edition Copyright © 2000 by Houghton Mifflin Company.

"Profuse and often emotionally charged speech that mimics coherent speech, but is usually unintelligible to the listener, and that is uttered in some states of religious ecstasy and in some schizophrenic states." *Merriam-Webster's Medical Dictionary, © 2002 Merriam-Webster, Inc.*

"Repetitive non-meaningful speech (especially that associated with a trance state or religious fervor." *WordNet ® 2.0, © 2003 Princeton University*

Granted these aren't religious publications, but it is illuminating to see what happens when outsiders examine what we do inside our religious circles. Do you think it's possible that there is something to be learned here? I most certainly do. To really deal with this subject effectively, we need to go back to another one of Scripture's first appearances and see what can be ascertained.

The LORD came down to see the city and the tower which the sons of men had built. The LORD said, "Behold, they are one people, and they all have the same language. And this is what they began to do, and now nothing which they purpose to do will be impossible for them. Come, let Us go down and there confuse their language, so that they will not understand one another's speech." So the LORD scattered them abroad from there over the face of the whole earth; and they stopped building the city. Therefore its name was called Babel, because there the LORD confused the language of the whole earth; and from there the LORD scattered them abroad over the face of the whole earth. (Genesis 11:5-9)

The very fact we have differing languages stems from the resulting judgment of man's rebellion. Nimrod and his followers likely either intended to ascend into the place it was supposed YHVH resided, to gain access to Heaven and conquer its Creator; or, to build a fortress that would be unconquerable from the outside, making them the most powerful people group on the planet. In either scenario, or in combination, the plan had evil intent and was being led by an evil man. It would seem by the Lord's response that it would have had a significantly negative effect on humankind, and required a decisive and severe response.

In the garden, man had access to life forever. Do you remember that conversation Elohiym had, once man had fallen? It was very similar to the one regarding the tower:

The LORD God made garments of skin for Adam and his wife, and clothed them. Then the LORD God said, "Behold, the man has become like one of Us, knowing good and evil; and now, he might stretch out his hand, and take also from the tree of life, and eat, and live forever"—therefore the LORD God sent him out from the garden of Eden, to cultivate the ground from which he was taken. (Genesis 3:21-23)

Abuses of Power

Now, here is the tower conversation again:

The LORD said, "Behold, they are one people, and they all have the same language. And this is what they began to do, and now nothing which they purpose to do will be impossible for them. Come, let Us go down and there confuse their language, so that they will not understand one another's speech." So the LORD scattered them abroad from there over the face of the whole earth and they stopped building the city. (Genesis 11:6-8)

Division, separation, and confusion are the consequences of sin. Mankind's extreme variety of languages is actually concrete evidence of this tower event, as the 'spreading out' part of this event alone, would not necessitate such variety. Skin varieties, and other minor physical variances currently associated with geographic affiliation, have always existed. The richness of the gene pool at man's earliest existence would have allowed for a wide variety of physical features, within the offspring of any given family. (So much for certain ideas foundational to racism.) And by the way, we all came out of Africa!

In essence, multiple languages are actually a curse, although it would appear it was for our own good. Understood properly, all of Adonai's curses are for our (mankind's) own good. One thing that should be pointed out here is that although everyone involved in this dispersion left Babylon babbling on and on, because what one person said was incoherent to another is no reason to assume he or she was speaking nonsense. If everyone that had been dispersed was unable to comprehend their own language, they would not have been able to carry their language beyond themselves or convert it to script. Due to this, it is also most likely the case that this city was broken down into fairly large groups (what would then have later subdivided into family tribes), to enable their languages to flourish. Now, we are going to travel forward through time to the next scenario; the one that takes place at Mt. Sinai. The subject matter here is drawn from both scriptural and Talmudic sources.

Let us consider the exodus. After a fairly lengthy series of dramatic, Earth-altering events, there were a lot more people than just Israelites who left Egypt that great day. Even Pharaoh's council was advising him to quit resisting the Elohiym of the Hebrews. The day of the exodus, anyone who wanted to walk away was able to; and if you had half a brain, you did. So there were many who "sojourned with them".

About three months later, upon coming to a range in the desert called Sinai, they parked their nomadic selves; and unawares to them, were soon to receive the Mitzvoth of Adonai, from His own mouth (so to speak). This time period is very close to what would come to be known as Shavuot, or the Feast of First Fruits. Today, the Jewish understanding and remembrance of this particular Mo'adim event, is about the giving of the

Torah. Moshe was told by YHVH to prepare the people for their first personal encounter with the living Elohiym of their fathers. They were told to "wash their clothes" and to, "abstain from sexual relations" and that on the third day, they were to be ready to hear from Him.

So it came about on the third day, when it was morning, that there were thunder and lightning flashes and a thick cloud upon the mountain and a very loud trumpet sound, so that all the people who *were* in the camp trembled. (Exodus 19:16)

So would we all have! The next couple of verses tell us that the mountain was quaking, and that the sounding of the shofars were growing louder and louder. That, mixed with the thick smoke, and the cracking of lightning and the rumblings of thunder, and you have the recipe for sheer terror. Moshe led the people from the camp to the base of the mountain, warning them sternly not to go up on their own, or to even touch it, "lest they die." Then they heard the voice of YHVH, coming from out of the fire, which declared the first series of commandments, beginning with: "I Am YHVH, your Elohiym…"

The sages have given us some insightful things to think about, that are not clearly expressed in the book of Exodus. These teachings are part of the Oral Traditions which were passed down as part of this story, which Moshe did not pen. These things are not verifiable beyond their originating source, but they are extremely interesting considering their likelihood and connectedness to future events. One interesting thing to consider, with regards to the validity of the Talmudic rendering, is that as you will soon see, it supports Early Church teaching. Had certain Jewish interests known that was going to happen, they would have quickly buried the story.

Consider the facts: At least six hundred thousand people were at the base of that mountain, if it were only the men. Something near three million is more likely the count, since everyone, men, women and children were accounted for. In that day, it is thought that men spoke in seventy different, dominant languages (not including dialects) based on the seventy significant nations that were recognized at the time.[1] If that's true, a majority, if not all of them, were present in this great congregation. Being that Egypt was the most powerful empire during that era, it had drawn people from everywhere and likely obtained slaves from everywhere as well.

Though the scriptural text does not explicitly say this, oral tradition tells us that every man heard the words of YHVH, each in his own language. In the Bible, there is no discussion of translators, and the law appears to have been given only once; therefore, it seems a reasonable likelihood. After all, at the time, all who stood there were playing on the

Abuses of Power

same field, as no man was preferred over another. Anyone willing to accept the covenantal terms was considered part of Israel, and how could you accept the call into covenant relationship, without understanding?

The next hidden detail is extraordinary. The sages concluded that during the giving of the commandments, the people were able to 'see' the sounds coming off the mountain. It almost appears like the world's introduction to a choreographed light show. In the Hebrew language, Exodus 20:15 reads like, "and the entire nation saw the voices and the thunder..." This is later confirmed by the text in vs.18, where YHVH says, "You have 'seen' that from Heaven I have spoken to you. The Hebrew language is not void of terms which clearly separate 'seen' from 'heard' or 'felt'. It could have been written differently, but it wasn't. There is something in the making here, and it gets even more interesting.

Tradition also speaks of something like fire coming down from the mountain and residing over the people.[2] Regardless of whether or not that happened down within the crowds, it happened upon the mountain—Fire and Truth dancing together in a most impressive spectacle of power. Knowledge of the Holy One's ways is being infused into each man's soul. An inducement of capability through understanding, to live a righteous life was taking place. Is this sparking any kind of remembrance, of a similar experience in your mind? Can you place this event anywhere else?

The Indoor Storm

The next example we are going to look at, related to a variety of languages, is that most famous experience of Acts chapter two. Fifty days after the first Sabbath following Passover (after Yehoshua's ascension), on Shavuot again, a group of people were celebrating and praying in a certain room, as was their custom every year at this time. In a fulfillment of Yehoshua's prophecy, the Comforter comes on to the scene with a rather grand entrance. Young's Literal Translation renders the "rushing mighty wind" like this, "and there came suddenly out of the heaven a sound as of a bearing, violent breath." How would you describe a spontaneous and intense presence of the Spirit of YHVH entering the room? Being that He is the personification of the "Breath of Life", in order to clearly identify Himself to a people, who might not recognize this manifestation, perhaps He emitted a sound that could be attributed to His reputation.

We should all know the story well enough that I may have the liberty to paraphrase. Then, something like tongues of fire begins to manifest itself over the heads of the individuals...right? Well, kind of. I want you to take note of something. In the Greek, there is a word that seems to disappear in many translations. There is a particular verb that is used, in regards to what this fire does. And with the knowledge of this word, you will get just a slightly different picture as to what's happening here. The fire 'diamarezo' (partitioned–divided) itself over them. In other words, it came into the room a mass of one shape, and then broke down into smaller pieces. At first, this might seem of little consequence, but wait.

The word for 'fire' is *pur*, in the Greek. Although there is a different word for lightning, the figurative use of the word *pur* is related to lightning, as in fire from the sky. I'm not suggesting it was actual lightning in the upper room by any means, so don't get caught up on that. But look at this:

Now Mount Sinai *was* all in smoke because the LORD descended upon it in fire; and its smoke ascended like the smoke of a furnace, and the whole mountain quaked violently. (Exodus 19:18)

Well, did you see it? The LORD (YHVH) first descended "in the fire," on Mt. Sinai, to give us His Torah to obey. Later, the Ruach (Spirit/Breath of Life) of YHVH is seen falling again, and distributing Himself over His people, to enable them to properly fulfill His Torah in Yeshua's absence. Although that is what was ultimately going on, as far as those in that room were concerned, they were having a miniature Mt. Sinai experience. If what the sages say happened at Sinai regarding the fire coming down and resting over them is true, that makes this an even more amazing story. This time, however, instead of the people rejecting His voice and standing at a distance, they were all having an intimate, one-on-one encounter with Him, and remaining with Him. Look again at this verse referring to Sinai:

Moses said to the people, 'Do not be afraid; for God has come in order to test you, and in order that the fear of Him may remain with you, so that you may not sin.' (Exodus 20:20)

I believe the Ruach was saying the same exact thing to the hearts of the people in that house, and for the same reason. Remember, only the people in the room actually 'saw' the experience, and the Spirit's purpose in indwelling the believer is to empower them to live a holy life. What was the evidence of this encounter? "They began to speak with other tongues, as the Spirit was giving them utterance." This was a transposition of Sinai, being that the first time it was Yah who was speaking in many languages. That, to me at least, confirms the idea that He wanted from the very beginning to indwell their hearts, even more than in the Tabernacle or Temple.

And when <u>this sound</u> occurred, the crowd came together, and was bewildered because each one of them was hearing them speak in his own language. They were amazed and astonished, saying, 'Why, are not all these who are speaking Galileans? And how is it that we each hear *them* in our own language to which we were born?' (Acts 2:6-8)

It's brass tacks time. All of this fun exposition leads us now here. There was fire and languages once, then fire and languages again. In both events, Elohiym came in the form of fire and spoke to and through us. The intensity of the first Sinai encounter was to experience something that would put the *"fear* of Him" in us, to cause us not to sin. The latter Shavuot experience put the fear back into us for the same reason, but also endued us with the capacity to do it. That is the individual's benefit from receiving the Spirit.

It is often thought that this 'upper room' event was to give us the gift of tongues. That is not the case at all. The by-product of encountering Adonai's Torah should always be the desire to live righteously, and the by-product of encountering the Ruach is the empowerment to do so. The gifts that we find coming from this, and following encounters, give us the ability to effect change in our and others lives. This leads to the corporate Body's, and the world's, benefit from the gifts.

Here we see the purpose of the gift of tongues perfectly presented. Being that it was Shavuot, Israelites from all over the region had journeyed to Jerusalem, as is commanded by Adonai, to celebrate the festival. This event was a perfect opportunity to influence a large amount of people. Knowing this, the Ruach chose this moment to begin fulfilling the prophecy Joel uttered, as retold by Peter, in this same chapter of The Acts. Parthians and Medes and Elamites, and residents of Mesopotamia, Judea and Cappadocia, Pontus and Asia, Phrygia and Pamphylia, Egypt and the districts of Libya around Cyrene, and visitors from Rome, both Jews and proselytes, Cretans and Arabs, all people of differing dialects and languages heard a miraculous event, and it bewildered them enough to get their attention.

The gift of languages was also the perfect way to demonstrably confirm the fact that the covenant relationship the Jews had with YHVH, was also accessible to non-Jews. That is exactly what we see taking place in Acts. The dispersion of mankind from Babel forced the population of the world. Pentecost forced the dispersion of the gospel into the world. How could a Jew tell an untrained Greek, who the Ruach suddenly and miraculously enabled to speak Hebrew, that he was not eligible for salvation?

Let me recap and evaluate. People, who spoke one language, were given a miraculous ability to speak another language they were not learned in, so that others who were, would recognize the miracle, acknowledge its source, be amazed, and turn to the Elohiym who made it all possible. Now let's look at what Sha'ul has to say about this particular gift, in one of his letters.

> For one who speaks in a tongue does not speak to men but to God; for no one understands, but in *his* spirit he speaks mysteries. (1st Corinthians 14:2)
> One who speaks in a tongue edifies himself; but one who prophesies edifies the church. (*ibid* 14:4)
> So also you, unless you utter by the tongue speech that is clear, how will it be known what is spoken? For you will be speaking into the air. (*ibid* 14:9)
> There are, perhaps, a great many kinds of languages in the world, and no kind is without meaning. (*ibid* 14:10)
> Therefore, let one who speaks in a tongue pray that he may interpret. (*ibid* 14:13)
> All do not have gifts of healings, do they? All do not speak with tongues, do they? All do not interpret, do they? (*ibid* 12:30)

Please play close attention to 14:10. There is no language without meaning! You might not understand what's coming out of your own mouth, or from another speaker, but if it has no meaning, it is not a language. You are capable of picking up a book written in a language you don't understand, and as long as you are familiar with the sounds of its letters/symbols, you could vocalize it reasonably well. You couldn't interpret what's written, but that doesn't render it meaningless. I'm about to preach now. The act (not gift) of tongues is capable of being meaningless, and when it comes right down to it, meaningless language is gobbledygook. I am convinced that a vast majority of what is being labeled 'tongues' in the church is just that, and for solid reasons.

> But now, brethren, if I come to you speaking in tongues, what will I profit you unless I speak to you either by way of revelation or of knowledge or of prophecy or of teaching? (*ibid* 14:6)

Words without meaning are pure nonsense. I hope we can agree on that. But even if the words have meaning, if we don't know what the meaning is, they may as well be nonsense. Of what profit are words with no meaning? What happens when someone hears words coming from our mouths that have no meaning?

> Even so, if unbelievers or people who don't understand these things come into your meeting and hear everyone talking in an unknown language, they will think you are crazy. (*ibid* 14:23, NLT)

Of course they will! And no matter how many times these verses are read, people refuse to consider this reality as they open their mouths in their respective congregations, and flail their nonsense out with no

Abuses of Power

capacity for control. I will openly admit, this is a huge pet-peeve for me, as I can't help but think of the folks who may be in our midst, who do not understand what's going on, and have nothing left but to judge the Body as a bunch of fruitcakes. Never-mind the fact it's disrespectful of the legitimate gift, the gift-giver, and is inappropriate behavior.

You pastors and worship leaders out there, who intermittently interject your non-interpreted nonsense, amidst your rhetoric and your worship, should be ashamed of yourself. You know better! You've read Paul's teaching and you belligerently ignore it for the sake of your spiritual appearance. You can control your mouths. 1st Cor. 14:32 tells us the spirits of prophets are subject to prophets, so it stands to reason that the lesser gifts are subject to us as well. Yet, you choose to turn away from this clear instruction and prefer pleasing your flesh, over elevating proper conduct; as well as to being concerned with potential ridicule of the Body.

So then, tongues are for a sign, <u>not to those who believe</u> but to unbelievers. But prophecy *is for a sign,* not to unbelievers but to those who believe. (*ibid* 14:22)

If tongues are for a sign to the unbeliever, as shown in Acts 2, then why do we not concern ourselves with the unbelievers among us? Secondarily, why do we make such a big hoopla out of it amongst an assembly of believers? There is absolutely no reason that your gift should be heard by another soul at all, unless it is followed up by an interpretation. If it is not interpreted, then it is not a sign and 1st Cor. 14:2-4 comes into play. You are speaking to Elohiym, and edifying yourself and uttering mysteries. So, keep it to yourself. It's distracting, confusing and potentially toxic.

There is no way anyone can validate their inability to control their tongues, unless they have been clinically diagnosed with Turrets, or some other legitimate disorder. The public use of the gift is for the Spirit to declare something on His behalf. I do not believe this is a subjective instruction. However, if you prefer to be thought of as crazy, that's your choice I suppose. In the end, it's still irresponsible and disobedient.

Just Gotta Have It

All this latter discussion is based on the presumption that the gift is legitimate. It is my belief, as well as the result of research, that much of what is considered 'tongues' are not tongues at all, but a self-engineered means of fulfilling the demand that your leaders and churchiological influences have placed upon you. There is at least one denomination that I am well aware of, that promotes the gift of tongues as "the evidence" of the baptism of the Holy Spirit. Again, shame on you and any others who propagate this falsehood. At best, it's *one* evidence of many.

All do not have gifts of healings, do they? All do not speak with tongues, do they? All do not interpret, do they? (1st Corinthians 12:30)

The answer here is an obvious no! Must I remind you that the "baptism of Jesus" was not followed with any evidence of this manifestation of the Spirit? Surely, if Jesus was filled with the Spirit at this baptismal event, and everyone receives the *evidence*, this would have been a good time for Him to preview for us what was coming to all future believers. For that matter, there is no documentation of Him ever speaking in tongues. For those of you who think this is not a good example, because this was just a 'physical' baptism, Matthew reminds us of a prophecy of Isaiah…

Behold, My Servant whom I have chosen; My beloved in whom My soul is well pleased; I will put My Spirit upon Him, and He shall proclaim justice to the gentiles. (12:18)

The phrase "put my Spirit upon" is not a physical expression of location. It implies an imputation, an impartation and an appointing. It means that Yehoshua would operate under the power of the Spirit. Whether the *baptism* of the Spirit took place at the point of this famous mikveh or not, it happened at some point; and Yehoshua is never presented as a babbler in strange tongues. Moving beyond this apparent insignificance, there is no scriptural precedent of anyone, ever, anywhere, speaking in a foreign tongue, where the hearer was *unable* to understand, through some interpretive means, what was being said. In fact, it was a rebuked misuse. Why should there be? It is not the point or plan for the gift.

It is a well understood fact by theologians, so I'm not going to reference source commentary, that there was a real problem in Corinth as to the misuse of this gift; and for the likes of me, I cannot figure out why we can't learn from their mistake. Paul wrote this instruction to deal with the false-concept (among others) that speaking in tongues made one more spiritual than one who didn't. Paul responded with…

If I speak with the tongues of men and of angels, but do not have love, I have become a noisy gong or a clanging cymbal. (*ibid* 13:1)

It has been suggested that this verse portrays Paul as someone who spoke 'Angelish', and that this verse explains and justifies the kind of tongues that are incoherent and compositionally impossible as a language.

Abuses of Power

This is a stretch of Biblical proportions, if ever there was one. What Paul is simply saying, is that even *if* he was able to speak something as lofty as 'Angelish', if it wasn't rooted and governed by love, it is meaningless and obnoxious. (The Hebrew language may be what was being considered here, as it is thought of as the language of angels; b.Chagiga 16a.)

There is a whole lot of emotionally driven support out there which endeavors to promote tongues as being legitimate, even if it has no meaning. I will not subscribe to this belief, and neither should you. Until it is revealed to me otherwise in Scripture, *and* I see it have value for the Body, I will continue with this mindset.

Counter-balancing the typical "How to Speak in Tongues" type literature out there, is a substantial amount of research done on this linguistic phenomenon. None of it bodes well, for those of you who are not speaking a legitimate language. (Unfortunately, that represents more of us than is comfortable.) Besides the occurrences in that special meeting experience (Acts 2), the one with Cornelius (Acts 10), and some implications in Corinthians, there is little other evidence that there was, or has been any continuing benefit to the non-believers among us.

Unknown to most of us, the use of language-free tongues has origins much earlier than Christianity, and not by prior believers. As a matter of fact, nonsensical tongues is still practiced among the following non-Christian religions of the world:

"...the Peyote cult among the North American Indians, the Haida Indians of the Pacific Northwest, Shamans in the Sudan, the Shango cult of the West Coast of Africa, the Shago cult in Trinidad, the Voodoo cult in Haiti, the Aborigines of South American and Australia, the aboriginal peoples of the sub-arctic regions of North America and Asia, the Shamans in Greenland, the Dyaks of Borneo, the Zor cult of Ethiopia, the Siberian shamans, the Chaco Indians of South America, the Curanderos of the Andes, the Kinka in the African Sudan, the Thonga shamans of Africa, and the Tibetan monks."[3]

In a massive study of glossolalia from a linguistic perspective, by Professor William J. Samarin, of the University of Toronto's Department of Linguistics, published after more than a decade of careful research, he rejected the view that glossolalia is xenoglossia; (def. When a foreign language is spoken by someone with no prior knowledge or training, is understandable by another person who knows that language.) Samarin concluded that glossolalia is a "pseudo-language." He defined glossolalia as, "unintelligible babbling speech that exhibits superficial phonological similarity to language, without having consistent syntagmatic structure and that is not systematically derived from or related to known language."[4]

Felicitas D. Goodman, a psychological anthropologist and linguist, engaged in a study of various English - Spanish - and Mayan-speaking Pentecostal communities in the United States and Mexico. She compared tape recordings of non-Christian rituals from Africa, Borneo, Indonesia and Japan as well. She published her results in 1972, in an extensive monograph. Goodman concludes that:

"...when all features of glossolalia were taken into consideration—that is, the segmental structure (such as sounds, syllables, phrases) and its suprasegmental elements (namely rhythm, accent, and especially overall intonation)," she concluded that there is no distinction in glossolalia between Christians and the followers of non-Christian (pagan) religions. The "association between trance and glossolalia is now accepted by many researchers as a correct assumption." writes Goodman, in the prestigious Encyclopedia of Religion (1987). Goodman also concludes that glossolalia "is actually a learned behavior, learned either unawarely, or sometimes consciously." Others have previously pointed out that direct instruction is given on how to "speak in tongues," i.e., "How to engage in glossolalia."[5]

There is an abundance of this kind of research available for those of you who are willing to study on your own. So as always, I ask you to do just that. But now, I want to share something with you from a personal perspective.

For most of my life, I have struggled greatly with this subject; and coming to terms with what my mind had been trying to tell me all that time was not easy. I have very early memories of being exposed to the 'need' to be baptized with the 'evidence' of tongues. Altar calls in my church were often for this reason. Every youth camp I attended ended each night with a compulsive request to "receive the gift". I had prayed, and prayed, and prayed to obtain this supernatural language. Not only did I simply want it, but also I admittedly did not want to be a 'lesser than' Christian, with 'lesser than' faith, as compared to most of my friends and others around me.

Many times, I begged Yeshua for hours at a time, pouring out tears in hopes that He would find me a worthy recipient. I remember a sermon that taught the benefit of speaking in tongues was that demons couldn't understand the language, so our prayers wouldn't get hung up like Daniel's did, and they'd go straight up to Heaven. I wanted my prayers to be heard too! Many around me, that I knew were heathens outside church, still seemed to have this special gift. I had glued my ears to, and fasted throughout, multi-part sermons that were delivered to "build-up" my faith enough, to get me eligible. At times, I would have unbelievable anxiety, as I stood in line to have several people lay hands on me; believing without a doubt that this would be the time; only to have my spirit crushed under the weight of my unworthiness. Other times I had peace, and knew that I would get it in due time.

Abuses of Power

I cannot remember exactly when, but there was a time when I finally gave in to the possibility that I truly had to "open my mouth and begin to speak." So I went beyond the little sounds I would normally chirp, in hopes of them becoming more complex, and began talking nonsense. I knew that it was and just didn't care. Preachers told me to do that. I figured the Spirit would make the adjustments, and kept talking "by faith". I hated the conflict within my soul, as I forcefully suppressed the truth that I was receiving no benefit or power from this action.

Over the years, as time went on, I vacillated between doing it and not doing it—from holding back in hopes that the Ruach would force my mouth open in confirmation, to pouring it out in hopes that eventually my faith in its authenticity would catch up with my skill. It was not too terribly long ago that I was willing to accept what the Scriptures had been teaching all along; that being that I didn't have the gift. I just didn't. And I was finally freed from even wanting it. The tough part was being honest enough with myself to accept the fact that somewhere along the line, I had programmed myself to believe at times that I did. Part of the freedom came through accepting the truth about the gift itself, as being a specialized and specific gift, with limited personal value, that not everyone got. Nonsense will always be nonsense no matter how you decorate it.

I am begging you pastors, teachers and evangelists, especially within charismatic circles, to stop wounding the souls of the naive. If these people need to be able to speak in a foreign tongue, to impress another person who speaks that tongue, the Ruach will give them that ability at that time. There is no scriptural teaching that expresses that it must be used all the time, or that there is any specific benefit to it other than reminding yourself that you can. (Introspective self-edification, coming by evidence of the Spirit.) Paul even wrote that tongues would cease. Maybe it's been ceasing all along, and there are but a few who have it (when needed). Sure, gifts can make you feel impressed with the fact that the Spirit resides within you. But come on, once you know...

There is/was (not sure of their current standing) a denomination that won't license you to preach within their folds, unless you say you have that gift, and that you believe everyone must have the gift if they "have the Spirit." Sorry, but how pathetic. I wonder how many people have had to lie, in order to get a license that formally enables them to perpetuate the continuation of the same said lie. If the evidence (tongues) is a 'gift' of the Spirit, then just because we see a few examples of this gift occurring at certain impartations, does not mean it's the only one that is the evidence. The word 'gift' in the Greek is the word charisma, and it covers any one of the spiritual gifts we are given. If you have any of the charismatic gifts at all, you have the "evidence" of the Spirit having baptized you, and you have been endued with power. No worries!

This silly lack of observing the basic principles laid out for us in Scripture is inhibiting our ability to influence the world. Why should we be taken seriously, when we're as well-renowned for roaring like lions, barking like dogs, laughing hysterically, shaking convulsively, and jabbering incoherently, as we are for doing good.

I know that there are a huge percentage of you who would stand defiantly against accepting this teaching, mostly because that would mean your gift might not be authentic. I know there is no way that *your* gift could be a psychological trick you've played on yourself. Just do me this favor. Next time you are speaking in tongues, pay close attention to the sounds, patterns and construct of what comes out of your mouth. Does it seem possible to be a language? Have you ever had an interpretation, or are you a person who frequently is given a message in tongues to deliver? Do the interpretations line up with the length and pattern of your message? If not, ask yourself what's going on. Might you possibly not be saying anything at all? Might some of these interpretations be fabricated by over-zealous charismatics? (Like hearing a twenty-second message in tongues be followed by a five minute interpretation.) If you refuse to accept the likelihood, how much more are you buying into? As with the presumed order of the motivational gifts being in descending order (if that fancies you), this gift is at the bottom of another of Paul's list (1st Corinthians 13:30).

I have friends and family that I know in some cases this will liberate. But I also know that in other cases, it will not. It's not easy for me to confess these things, and it won't be easy for you to either. But I have no doubt in the slightest that there are others of you out there who can fully relate to my testimony. Please, be freed! There is no shame in getting clean and coming to terms. You don't have the gift—so what! It's really not all that important anyway. If you want a gift, pray to heal. If you want a gift, pray that you may love. Be a peacemaker.

I thank God, I speak in tongues more than you all; however, in the church I desire to speak five words with my mind so that I may instruct others also, rather than ten thousand words in a tongue. (1st Corinthians 14:18 & 19)

Therefore, let one who speaks in a tongue pray that he may interpret. (14:13)

So also you, since you are zealous of spiritual *gifts*, seek to abound for the edification of the church. (14:12)

Otherwise, it will not be tongues of fire over your head, but the one residing in your mouth that burns the brightest; and it will not be just you who will get burned (figuratively). Worse yet, like Paul states at the end of this fourteenth chapter: If you ignore "the Lord's commandments," you will also be ignored.

Abuses of Power

All Blown Out of Proportion

Another manifestation of a spirit, which has become a staple in the "extra-biblical" diet of charismata, is that which has come to be known as being "slain in the Spirit".

This fainting fad, although having some nebulous scriptural support and church history, really got its burst of current popularity from a movement that began at the Toronto airport of all places, at a Vineyard affiliated church back in 1994. Actually, a lot of the absolute disregard for most of the current oddities within our churches gained momentum through this outpouring of the presence of something stemming from this movement.

The Vineyard church's founder, John Wimber, started life as a believer very familiar with oddities within the church, being initiated into the faith as a Quaker. I don't want to spend a lot of time on him as his history is easily attainable through the Vineyard website. His infatuation with the 'supernatural' is pretty clear, as he taught a class on it at Fuller Seminary in 1982. In an ironic twist of fate, this man, so affiliated with the healing ministry, died of a massive brain hemorrhage in 1977 at the young age of 63; just three years after the "Toronto Blessing" became a church house-hold name.

On Father's Day, 1995, an evangelist by the name of Steve Hill had recently returned from a powerful spiritual encounter with something, at the Holy Trinity Church in Brompton, England. This church just so happened to also be a recipient of the "Toronto Blessing". A female assistant pastor of the South-West London Vineyard met with a group of friends, many of whom were leaders of other churches, to describe her recent visit to the Toronto Airport Vineyard. As she explained her remarkable experiences with the power of God, and prayed for them to be filled with the Holy Spirit, everyone was profoundly affected. The Curate of Holy Trinity Brompton was at this recounting, and re-told what had happened to some, at his church office. He was then asked to pray the meeting's concluding prayer. He asked the Holy Spirit to fill everyone in the room. According to the church newspaper, "HTB in Focus", 12 June 1994:

> The effect was instantaneous. People fell to the ground again and again. There were remarkable scenes as the Holy Spirit touched all those present in ways few had ever experienced or seen. Staff members walking past the room were also affected. Two hours later, some of those present went to tell others in different offices and prayed with them where they found them. They too were powerfully affected by the Holy Spirit—many falling to the ground. Prayer was still continuing after 5 pm.

Although it appears I am within legal usage rights, according to the Fair Use Act, I have removed some non-critical text in these next quoted portions, in an effort to not drag people through the mud. This information originates on a document written in 1995, by someone documenting the history of the revival at Holy Trinity Church, who had recently visited Toronto Vineyard themself. With just a little searching, you can find the complete work as well.

And in the time that I was there, I have to tell you, I heard not one mention of the devil. I heard not one word about spiritual warfare. Nobody mentioned a principality or a power, and I cannot tell you how refreshing that was. And the truth is that the people there, and I ever since, have been so consumed with the person of Jesus and with the work of the kingdom that quite honestly there is no time to give any attention to the enemy or to all his works. Because the power of Jesus is so great, and the person of Jesus is so preoccupying, and our passion for Jesus is on the increase to such a degree that it is a wonderful thing.

For those of you who have ears to hear, could the problem here be any more clear? I'm bewildered. Since when does taking your spiritual armor off ever become a virtuous act? As well-meaning as this individual may be here, they have exposed themself, and I'm sure many others, of the very problem at the heart of the matter. Yehoshua never even made a vague or cloaked reference to ever turning your backside to the enemy. You can bet your exposed bottom dollar, if given a chance, he (HaSatan) will unbuckle your belt of Truth. Read these testimonies from the same letter. See if anything catches your attention.

People from all over the world are flocking to this unlikely church, the Toronto airport branch of the Vineyard Christian Fellowship, six nights a week. And every night there are astounding scenes of people shaking with laughter, slipping into a trance, falling to the floor, and crying.
Last week Bishop David ( ) from England was down here on the floor roaring like a lion," says John ( ), the church's pastor, as he explains how evangelical Christians have swarmed to Toronto like pilgrims to Lourdes.

This person has, in two paragraphs, spoken more to demonstrate a point than I could have in much more space, especially considering it being a personal, first-hand testimony. There is a strikingly clear lack of discernment in these perceptions, and hopefully you can see that. I only removed unnecessary names and words like pronouns from the text. I performed no funny business. Like I said, you can read this letter yourself, unless they discover this exposure and remove it from the site. Just in case, I saved a copy.

Abuses of Power

There are great varieties of the manifestations of the Spirit. They are breaking out both during services and outside them in homes and offices. At times, they are easy to explain and handle, and at other times they are much harder and more complicated.

Perhaps, it's because they are unjustifiable? I wish I could just cut and paste the whole document here, because it's loaded. For instance, this person also justifies these manifestations by reminding us of Jonathon Edward's wife being in a spirit-induced, insensible drunken state for 17 days. Speaking of a pastor who visited Ontario, this person said,

But he was very controlled and very all together. For a day or two. And he just soaked in the presence of the Lord. And then after two or three days he started to shake, and to rattle, and to roll, and to twitch, and to laugh, and he went home to his wife, and she said there's no way he can sleep in the same bed.

Anyone who would do any in depth study of historical revivals would soon discover that these very same manifestations have occurred many a time. But what you may not so quickly recognize is that they are often attributed to be the demise of the revivals. Being slain in the spirit may seem grand and deeply spiritual, but as in the case of glossolalia, it is often nothing more than an emotionally crippling, and spiritually handicapping experience.

And there was one middle-aged man who had been laboring as a pastor for twenty, twenty-five years. And he came to Toronto and the Lord fell on him and he became as drunk as a newt for days. And after several days he recovered himself enough to get back to the microphone, and he was asked to give a testimony, which he did, I might say, in a very incoherent fashion, and then they said to him, "May we pray for you more?" And he said, "I'd love it," and out he went, rolling around the floor as though he'd just walked out. He was just out of his mind. And it was a wonderful, wonderful thing to see.

(Uh…okay.?)

Are You Sure You Want it?

Surveying Scripture, there are several positive references to an occurrence that may be construed as being 'slain'. There are many verses that portray a response to being in a worshipful state, by prostrating one's self. There are a couple instances that show what happens when you are an enemy of Elohiym, such as a demoniac, or a soldier attempting to arrest the Son. Overall, though, we struggle to find anything concrete.

Generally, the Scriptures describe an encounter with the Living

Elohiym causing a "fell as if dead" response. It is also shown that it often requires an intervention by an angel, or by the Son of Man Himself, to restore the lost strength to the individual. Moshe and Aharon often fell *forward* with their face in the dirt, while the heathen is seen falling *backward*. Ultimately, what needs to be observed in order to perceive whether being 'slain' from a scriptural viewpoint is valid and profitable vs. sorcery or hypnotic suggestion, is the means and result.

It is my opinion that any manifestation of the supposed "Spirit," which goes beyond the boundaries of Scripture, should fall under the strictest scrutiny. Often times, these manifestations fall under the liberal label: "extra-biblical". Although when held up against Scripture they are thought of by many as being "gray-area," they are quickly given credence through the reasoning that they cannot be Satanic, because they occur around services or events that focus on Yehoshua. To say that the enemy cannot operate inside a church is about as foolish as saying HaSatan could not exist in Heaven's throne room. HaSatan was working through Balaam, while the Spirit was working through His donkey. Korah led a rebellion inside the camp surrounding the very Presence. Sha'ul the Pharisee was a murderess zealot, with intentions he thought were good for Elohiym, when in fact they were wicked. David was full of the Spirit, and yet could conceive an evil plot to murder and adulterate. I could go on and on.

We are all quick to agree that HaSatan masquerades as an angel of light, but when it comes to his ability to deceive, it's "not me or my church!" We believe in the power of persuasion, except when it's we who are being persuaded. There is a lot of pressure to "get slain," when everyone around you is having it happen to them. Actually, that's where most of our pressure to involve ourselves in questionable behavior comes from. There have been many studies done on what is called "mob psychology" and social pressure. The same pressure that is often placed on the receiving of the gift of tongues is placed upon people to be *slain*. It appears deeply spiritual. It looks like a one-on-one encounter with Adonai. People look like their having a good time, and that it would build your faith somehow. Why wouldn't you want that?

If you have been around this activity, have you ever noticed that there is some kind of understood restraint, regarding the discussion of the experience one has had, during the event? Surely, whatever is occurring has to be so overwhelming, that it is worth sharing with the rest of the Body. Why is it such a private matter? Is it because it is not supposed to be subject to interpretation? It would seem to me that a mass slaying should be followed with a public testimony of each one's gift from above.

Scriptural references to a physically crippling event with the Spirit are followed by an intensely personal, but intended for public exploit, revelation. If I'm not mistaken, manifestation gifts in general are for the edification of the Body. Since being 'slain' is not listed among the standard gifts, yet it apparently has specific and powerful effects, we must ask what it is for. If it's not a gift, but it is for the Body, what has been its modern value for the Body? Some say they have awakened healed; maybe so. Others say it's nothing but a very relaxing experience. My concern with this manifestation is that there are no regulations by which we can maintain order in its usage. The only common ground we see among its recipients is that people supposedly can't stand anymore. But is this really the case?

Upon observing and interacting with many such people, and personally being involved insofar as being the one who laid on the hands to impart it, I have rarely witnessed a genuine loss of physical ability to stand. I have seen dramatic collapses, but the great majority of the time people are laid backward carefully with fully rigid bodies. Even the collapses do not in themselves substantiate more than an emotional overload. Upon their 'awakening', they simply get up, smile, and go back to their seats. I must ask you, what could possibly have been the value in that? Again...how does that edify the Body? Most people are clearly conscious. Why do they not just lay themselves down, forward, on their face and worship Adonai?

I have heard it preached, that the reason people get slain is to allow the Spirit to have free access to you, so that you are powerless to resist, and that allows Him to have His way with you. It is said that He must do that because of our resistance to Him, while conscious. First, if that's true, getting slain would be nothing to be proud of. Second, how does this answer for the mentally impaired? I have seen a man with Down syndrome "get slain," smiling and talking the whole time he laid. Observers spoke as if it was a super-spiritual event. He was asked if he wanted to get up, and he nodded and rose. Now, for what purpose did that happen? We all know what happened there, don't we?

Another significant observance, from a scriptural standpoint, is that of the lack of examples whereby the slain one required human intervention for the event to occur. There are none! None of the examples of anything remotely resembling being slain required the application of hands, or any contact with man. It is never an event that is *imparted* to someone. The genuine article is purely a reaction to the overwhelming presence of His glory. The laying on of hands in Scripture is reserved for healing prayer, appointment to office, and impartation of ministry gifts. Also very noteworthy is that anyone else around this type of power manifestation would also react in some way.

Everyone in the upper room was impacted. Everyone on the road to Damascus acknowledged a presence. Everyone at Yehoshua's baptism saw the Dove, and heard the Father's voice. Everyone standing at Mt

Sinai saw and heard. All the soldiers who went to arrest Yehoshua were stricken as dead. All the priests of Ba'al witnessed the fire from heaven that Elijah called down. All the other encounters in Scripture, e.g., John, Ezekiel, Moses, etc., occurred in a personal encounter. Today's prayer lines to receive the gift of 'slain' seem to have a hit or miss effect.

I just simply am not one who is comfortable with the idea that Abba would not have given us a preview or instruction regarding something as significant as being 'slain'. Surely, one of the disciples at some point would have "blown" this power on someone, or "thrown" it into a crowd for effect—ultimately being recorded like so much else was. Wouldn't the Olivet discourse have been a great opportunity for Yehoshua to end His sermon with a real demonstration of power, and slay the entire crowd with a wave of His arm?

I would venture to assume that many of you who read this will have had an experience with this phenomenon. Unless you can demonstrate a valuable by-product like maturation, coming through this event in your life, I believe you were the victim of a very powerful manipulation, through the power of suggestion and/or the mesmerizing skills of the deliverer. Many of you will disagree of course, because you have personally experienced something. But this same kind of physiological response to psychological manipulation is commonplace and well-documented in other false religious circles, similar to glossolalia.

I'm not suggesting that every occurrence of being "slain" is not genuine. I am suggesting that the vast majority are not, and that if you have the ability to stand, then you should stand. If you want to lie down, lie down. If the Ruach needs to knock you out to get your attention, it's likely not because of His delight in you. In my opinion, I would suggest doing all you can to stand, thereby helping prove to yourself that if you do go down, you had no choice.

I would also strongly suggest to you that anytime you see a specific leader in charge of distributing this *manifestation*, that you watch them for other abuses of the gifts. They will often concurrently be abusing the gift of tongues and the gift of prophecy. Prior to their dispensing this "power," listen to their messages. What are they teaching? Is it doctrinally sound, or is it an array of emotionally hyping statements? Do they use a lot of repetition? Do they suggest certain lines from lyrics that they have the congregation sing over and over again? Do they assert statements that would make you feel guilty if you don't go down to "receive"? When you are down there in that line, and the man with the power is heading your way, do you watch to see if the people next to you have fallen to increase your anticipation and "faith"?

Discerning what is right and wrong, satanic or Spirit-led, flesh and fantasy, can be challenging at times; mostly because we hate to think

Abuses of Power

he can infiltrate our fellowship, or work through our leaders. It is a skill you should prayerfully desire. Never believe that HaSatan cannot infiltrate your camp! As soon as you do that, you will have given him the opportunity to build his embankment, and then covertly stay until you believe otherwise. I have been both a layer-on of hands, and a "catcher" for this deception. I, like for the gift of tongues, have beseeched the Ruach to experience this thing so that I could fully believe or reject it. I have begged for the experience for personal encouragement. I have given Adonai every reason I could think of, for it to happen to me. It never has. Until it does (and I highly doubt it will), I will reject this practice openly as predominantly a hypnotist's trick, especially when pertaining to mass occurrences. I believe it is possible that the hypnotist may be unaware of his guilt, by his/her own deception; but that is what's happening nonetheless. May He release me to experience it, with some purpose and value for the Body, if I am wrong.

"Thou Art Healed"

Of all the power gifts, I confidently believe there has been no other more written about, or preached about gift than this one—and for one obvious reason. We all at some point, and often many times, desperately need it. Actually, our very lives depend upon it. This is an extraordinarily sensitive subject, so I will not be treating it with the stern judgment I have treated other areas. But I will hopefully deal with it truthfully. To begin with, we'll quickly examine the concept of healing from its various angles.

Although we don't think about it much, all day, every day, our bodies are constantly being healed. When we sleep, there are various systems that go into effect, to refresh and restore our minds and bodies. When we are awake, as well as when challenging our bodies, there are also systems that are at work which clean, repair and sustain us as well. Complex micro-biological systems are at work within each of our living cells, repairing themselves. We also have certain cells that are programmed to go about repairing larger issues, found within the various systems of our body.

Literally, every second of every day, the pre-programmed healing functions of our body relentlessly work to repair the environmental, as well as inflicted damages that occur to us. Although it may not be construed as miraculous, what our bodies do in an attempt to awake more whole than yesterday, is nothing less than marvelous. Most all of our diseases stem from a weakness or failure of these built-in, healing systems' performance.

Then, we have interventional medicine to consider. Sometimes, the human body is incapable of repairing itself without assistance. When the built-in, Creator-designed, natural methods within the human body fail to make repairs, things like genetic mutations (e.g., cancers, birth defects, and many diseases) have free reign to debilitate us. Also, there are things which have external origins, such as: bacteria, viruses, pollutants, drugs and chemicals, radiation, and other things (like unlawful food, or unhealthy quantities of anything) that enter us and rapidly, or very slowly, and kill us from within.

The third source of physical damage we can sustain is from external impact due to adventure or accident. This area usually requires a combination of medical intervention and natural ability. For instance, medicine sets the broken bone, but the body's production and infusion of cells, minerals and molecules, bind to and bridge the break.

As the saying goes: You could do everything right, within your power, to live well, eat properly and exercise, then get up one day and while crossing the road, get hit by a car. But then there are people like George Burns, who smoked cigars and drank martinis nearly every day of his life, and yet he lived to be one hundred. If there was ever an apparently unfair part of life, it would surely be in our health department.

Every day, good and Elohiym-fearing people come down with sicknesses and diseases, and die young. The news reports on how a "fresh out of college," or "just got engaged," with "so much ahead of him," young person's life has been destroyed by a drunk driver, come out daily. Planes are crashing. Trains go off the track. Terrorism is rampant. Designer drug use is on the rise, while sexually transmitted diseases are showing up in our middle school children. Sometimes it seems like there is no more hope.

Ah, but that depends on where you place your hope. Much depends on what your expectations in this life are, and whether you still recognize we are in a fallen world or not. I, and many others I know, have recently witnessed the departure of lives that by all human reasoning should still be with us. Different types of cancers robbed a family of a father of four, and a family with a new father of one. Congenital heart problems to a young man at 36. All these men loved Yeshua, were generous and active in their church, and were getting ready to begin new seasons in their lives, with big hearts of expectation. Hundreds, if not thousands of hours of congregational prayer and support, were offered by their church families. They went through the entire battery of medical interventions available to them, with the kind of high faith and desire to live, that anyone would have been amazed at. When it comes right down to it, if anybody should have survived these tests, it just should have been them. But they didn't.

Abuses of Power

Whose Fault is it?

Soon after the loss, comes the haunting self-analysis of each family and friend's faith. "Did we pray enough? Did we really believe appropriately? Could I be the reason? Could they have swallowed just a few more pills? Did they eat the right foods and supplements? Could one more treatment of some experimental procedure have helped?" Well, could the blind from birth man that Yeshua restored his sight to, have been healed any earlier? Those of us, who have not gone through this kind of loss, can only begin to imagine the pain, the confusion, and the doubt. What really happened here? Did HaSatan do this? Does he have the power? Did Abba do this; and if so, why? Or, is there a third possibility, perhaps one that just doesn't seem good enough to be right?

Let me ask you something. Have you ever questioned Abba's logic behind allowing someone who's been raped, or the 14 year old who stupidly gave her virginity away to some guy at a party one night ("one time only") to get pregnant? But then, in contrast, the sweetest couple in the world, who all they want to do is pour out of their abundant love into offspring, have been trying for years with no success? What about the young missionary couple who had survived unbelievable hardships, only to end up dying in a plane crash on their way back to the states, for a vacation? Well, if you haven't, you are just plain odd.

What did you conclude? Typically, we end up with a pat combination answer that we draw from Scripture. It usually sounds something like: "His ways are not our ways. All things work together for good. We just have to endure our trials with joy." Although that's all true, they are not really answers; they are coping tools. People need answers and sometimes, until they get them, they hold Abba accountable and deem Him distant and cold-hearted. Then, not only have they lost someone else, they sadly begin to lose themselves and their faith. The answer to the plane crash and the unwanted pregnancy questions are pretty much the same. It probably is not the answer you are looking for either. It is—design.

Upon the completion of the sixth day of creation, the laws, principles and methods by which the universe and life operate under were established. "It was good!" It would have forever remained "good" had sin not entered the picture. There never would have been rape, plane crashes, or unwanted pregnancies. Good bacteria turned bad. Perfect genetic coding developed mutations. The need to 'toil' in the world came into the picture. However, some things did not change. The preprogrammed purpose and drive of the sperm, its ability to enter a hostile environment, find an available ovum, battle against other ambitious, like-minded competitors, didn't. The plan that upon victory, it enters the center, drop its tail, splits apart and releases 3 ft. worth of genetic information that the ovum knows exactly what to do with once in there, is still active.

The *miracle* of life is not when the blastocyst imbeds, or when the heart first starts beating, or when the umbilical cord is cut. The miracle of life is found at the most foundational levels. It is found in the forces that keep electrons in their orbit. It is found in the unfathomably exact, fine-tuning of the location of our galaxy, and the location of our solar system, and our sun with its type and distance, and our orbit, and our moon, and our own planet's mass, and our topography, and our atmosphere, and our chemistry, and our core structure, and on and on. Things have been set in motion, and it was once all perfect, and it will be again. But it is not now.

Taking the same example, what happens when a sperm and an ovum meet outside a woman's womb? Take away the love, passion or hope of the pregnancy, and simply with sterile emotion combine the two in a petri dish and what happens? Exactly what they are programmed to do is what happens. They act as if they are unconcerned with the motivation or intent; because they are. How is it that we can freeze embryos into suspended animation for long periods of time, and then upon thawing, they will pick up where they left off? Because they are *willed* to live. Please don't misunderstand me. I am in no way diminishing the *value* of human life, nor am I suggesting that YHVH has disassociated Himself from His creation. Let's see what Yeshua had to say about this subject?

Or those, the eighteen, on whom the lookout tower in Siloam fell and killed them, do you think that these were debtors more *[fig., worse sinners]* than all the *[other]* people dwelling in Jerusalem? Not at all, I say to you, _but_ if you are not repenting, you will all likewise perish. (Luke 13:4 & 5, ALT)

After establishing that premise, let's return to the example of the airplane. Homo-Sapiens are a creation, which when confined to our fully-physical dimension are not capable of flying in their natural condition. We do not have the hollow, light, bone structure, nor feathery appendages to enable flight. Summarily, humans are not designed to fly. Adonai has, however, given us the intellectual capacity for design and creativity, as His making us in His image would suppose. With experimentation and enlightenment into our physical world, we were able to unnaturally compensate for our own natural design problem and invent the air-foil. We have stepped over nature, so to speak. Working in conjunction with the physical properties of our atmosphere, we can make machinery fly— that we can get inside. We have pretty much mastered the sky, but does that make it natural? If the craft that we engineer to beat nature fails, either from entropy or design flaw, does He delight and desire for that?

Was that everyone's on board, perfectly appointed "time to go"?

A Christian scuba diver and his son went cave diving several years ago. They both died, apparently from getting stuck and ultimately running out of air. Did they die of natural causes? That depends on how you define *natural*. The need for and processing of oxygen is part of our nature. Enough lack of it, and we will die. But, was that the way they were supposed to go? Was that Yah's perfect plan, or did their actions create an opportunity to self-fulfill the prophetic mandate that we are all "appointed to die"? This is dicey material, isn't it?

A man dies at the age of sixty-three. His heart failed him after years of battling pressure and cholesterol problems. He unfortunately had a bit of a weight problem too. He was a fan of fine cuisine, and rich foods were no stranger of his. The doctors told him he was a ticking time-bomb, that he needed to exercise, and that he needed to change his eating habits. He paid no attention.

These last examples would appear to have obvious reasons for the cause of their demise, but you know people will not accept them, and will torture their minds in pursuit of the answer to the evasive, "why?" Ponder this: If someone takes their own life, quickly vs. slowly, was it their "time to go" too? Was it ultimately the Lord who took their life? We need to be consistent.

Things seem to get a little more complicated, when a seemingly unprovoked disease comes along. Consider the influenza virus. Someone is a carrier. They sneeze, or rub their nose, and shake your hand. You rub your eye and guess what—you're sick. Now, you may be healthy enough to fight it off, or you may be an elderly person who could potentially die. Because you heal from the same thing that someone else dies from, does that make the flu a consciously selective killer? Was that flu sent purposely to take the life of the weak and elderly, and leave the strong to live on? Humanistic science would say no to the "sent" part, but would argue yes to the "survival of the fittest." What about you? Let's take one more example through to its conclusion.

Most anyone can stand and jump vertically in place. Some people can barely get off the ground. Others, if they are very athletic, can reach heights of twenty-four inches, or more. Either way, in both instances, the person should come back down without doing any damage to themself.

Now, let's take the athlete and have him set up a twelve foot, A-frame ladder. He may be able to jump down from the fifth, sixth, maybe seventh rung just fine. But perhaps upon jumping from the eighth, the tendons around his ankle will give way, and the result will be injury. Was the 7th rung the end of the athlete's will, and the eighth the beginning of the Lord's; expressed through the fact He didn't stop you? Maybe there is a lesson there in common sense, or anatomical thresholds; but spiritual…I don't think so. Yet for some reason, if we build a ladder to the heavens (plane), and jump off the top rung (malfunction), the resulting incident has to be His plan. Why? Do we not carry some responsibility for our outcomes?

Here's a twist: When YHVH spoke to us and told us that honoring our parents would lengthen our lives, was that an exaggeration? Does that mean if we do, he will stop us from doing things that can result in us getting hurt, or alter the laws of physics so the planes we fly on, will never fall?

> Now may the God of peace Himself sanctify you entirely; and may your spirit and soul and body be preserved complete, without blame at the coming of our Lord Jesus Christ. (1st Thessalonians 5:23)

If we ignore the command to honor, though our spirits may be "preserved," our flesh may be corrupted, or ultimately destroyed. It's simple really. Break His moral law—have pre-marital sex and get impregnated by an irresponsible jerk—and a less than ideal situation is created. Hence, the girl was not 'saved' from the ramifications of her sinful behavior. Our salvation experience works in conjunction with our preservation process.

Maybe she didn't get pregnant, but got an STD instead. Hepatitis can kill. HIV can kill. Did Abba inflict her with that, or did she go and contract an already active virus, from someone else who already had it? After all, He did give you ample warning and instruction to avoid getting it. Wasn't that loving of Him? Perhaps you were a drug user, and though you now have entered into a relationship with Him, the damage you previously did to yourself is not going away no matter how much you pray. Do you suppose it should? He wants you healed because of His love for you, but He'd much rather have had you not need that healing in the first place. You certainly may ask, but there is no scriptural foundation for full expectation, in this life anyway.

Let's look at a very interesting portion of Scripture that many modern believers understand to be irrelevant to them. Hopefully by now, you may be willing to accept this, no matter how difficult the pill is to swallow.

> Now it shall be, if you diligently obey the LORD your God, being careful to do all His commandments which I command you today, the LORD your God will set you high above all the nations of the earth. All these blessings will come upon you and overtake you if you obey the LORD your God: Blessed *shall* you *be* in the city, and blessed *shall* you *be* in the country. Blessed *shall be* the offspring of your body and the produce of your ground and the offspring of your beasts, the increase of your herd and the young of your flock. Blessed *shall be* your

Abuses of Power

basket and your kneading bowl. Blessed *shall* you *be* when you come in, and blessed *shall* you *be* when you go out.

The LORD shall cause your enemies who rise up against you to be defeated before you; they will come out against you one way and will flee before you seven ways. The LORD will command the blessing upon you in your barns and in all that you put your hand to, and He will bless you in the land which the LORD your God gives you. The LORD will establish you as a holy people to Himself, as He swore to you, if you keep the commandments of the LORD your God and walk in His ways. So all the peoples of the earth will see that you are called by the name of the LORD, and they will be afraid of you. The LORD will make you abound in prosperity, in the offspring of your body and in the offspring of your beast and in the produce of your ground, in the land which the LORD swore to your fathers to give you. The LORD will open for you His good storehouse, the heavens, to give rain to your land in its season and to bless all the work of your hand; and you shall lend to many nations, but you shall not borrow. The LORD will make you the head and not the tail, and you only will be above, and you will not be underneath, if you listen to the commandments of the LORD your God, which I charge you today, to observe *them* carefully, and do not turn aside from any of the words which command you today, to the right or to the left, to go after other gods to serve them.

But it shall come about, if you do not obey the LORD your God, to observe to do all His commandments and His statutes with which I charge you today, that all these curses will come upon you and overtake you: Cursed *shall* you *be* in the city, and cursed *shall* you *be* in the country. Cursed *shall be* your basket and your kneading bowl. Cursed *shall be* the offspring of your body and the produce of your ground, the increase of your herd and the young of your flock. Cursed *shall* you *be* when you come in, and cursed *shall* you *be* when you go out. The LORD will send upon you curses, confusion, and rebuke, in all you undertake to do, until you are destroyed and until you perish quickly, on account of the evil of your deeds, because you have forsaken Me. The LORD will make the pestilence cling to you until He has consumed you from the land where you are entering to possess it. The LORD will smite you with consumption and with fever and with inflammation and with fiery heat and with the sword and with blight and with mildew, and they will pursue you until you perish. The heaven which is over your head shall be bronze, and the earth which is under you, iron. The LORD will make the rain of your land powder and dust; from heaven it shall come down on you until you are destroyed. The LORD shall cause you to be defeated before your enemies; you will go out one way against them, but you will flee seven ways before them, and you will be *an example of* terror to all the kingdoms of the earth. Your carcasses will be food to all birds of the sky and to the beasts of the earth, and there will be no one to frighten *them* away. The LORD will smite you with the boils of Egypt and with tumors and with the scab and with the itch, from which you cannot be healed. The LORD will smite you with madness and with blindness and with bewilderment of heart. (Deuteronomy 28:1-28)

Although there are extreme situations mentioned here, as yet to be fully seen, can we not conceive of lesser degrees as well? Look around this world and contemplate the various nations' fiscal and material states. Look at the most impoverished and disease ridden lands and examine their religious practices. We can bring all the food and medicine we want to them, but until they stop drinking raw cow's blood mixed with milk, eating spiders and snakes, bathing in the same contaminated water with the animals they worship (or believe to be their reincarnated family members), there will be no rain on their dry ground. There will be no grain in their storehouses. Their diseases will continue to spread. They starve because they honor their bulls and monkeys above their own children.

If societies would stop raping their little girls and circumcising their women, perhaps the sicknesses that plague their land would die off within a couple generations, and not continue to be spread to their victims and their unborn children. It is the right thing to feed them, and help save their bodies; it is the more right thing to instruct them in righteousness and help save their spirits. If they refuse, they will continue to suffer, and no matter how much food and money we supply them with, it will not change.

What about us? Are we following His commandments? I'm not even talking perfectly; I'm talking reasonably well. Are you disobediently filling your bodies with toxic food, and being too busy to make His Appointments? Do you sit around with swollen ankles from the gout, while licking your lips clean from the spare-rib sauce you're scarfing down, while seeking healing from Abba for your obesity-related sicknesses? Of all the miraculous healings you've read about in Scripture, stories, or have seen take place, have you ever heard of an obese person become skinny? Furthermore, there is not one example in Scripture of an instantaneous healing from any kind of self-induced illness.

Are you begging Him to heal you from the disease you have, that He has not prevented you from receiving, as a result of your outright refusal to obey Him? Are you being told you need to have more faith, when in reality it's not a faith thing at all, but an obedience thing?

I'm not suggesting here that every illness is due to your personal sin, but all illness is due to someone's; even if it's Adam's. Your job is to ensure that you have removed the obstacles of your healing out of the way, by living according to the Scriptures. If you still do not heal, then you are a victim of fallen genetics, or fallen environment, or some other repercussion of the fall. How many people are standing in a prayer line by day, desiring to be healed from emphysema and cirrhosis, yet are smoking and drinking by night? Maybe it's not so obvious. Maybe it's breaking different commandments like: lusting, coveting, character assassination, gossip, or stealing from their workplace. Maybe it's none of those things, and…"Neither this one sinned nor his parents, _but_ *[this happened]* so that the works of God should be revealed in him (John 9:3; ALT)."

It is a long accepted belief amidst Jewish thought that the various skin diseases (tsara'at; generally translated as leprosy), and the molds spoken of during the days of the wanderings and beyond, were often physical manifestations of spiritual sickness. They would start out as small legions to get one's attention, and would slowly progress until you acknowledged your sin and repented. That is why the priesthood was involved in the inspection/diagnosis/cleansing process. A priest would enter your home, or examine your flesh, and would have opportunity to examine your life.

If you were infected, in order for you to have access to the tabernacle/temple area, you had to either hide your ailment, or be clean. If you didn't repent, your ailment would grow until you could not hide it anymore, and you were required to leave the camp until you were declared clean. If you still wouldn't repent, you might find yourself outside the camp permanently. One way or the other, He was going to expose your sin.

If the sin involved your household, mold would appear on the walls. If the family wouldn't repent, the mold would grow worse until the house ultimately needed to be torn down. Either problem resulted in a state of uncleanness, and would leave you rather lonely; for you were then separated from the masses. Sin will either isolate you, get you kicked out of the camp, or ultimately leaves you homeless.

Though it stands to reason today, that we must be very careful to not automatically or always ascribe sin as the source for personal physical ailments, back then it was very likely the case. Remember, the desert wandering experience was a forty year long, miraculous intervention and sustaining by YHVH. It was a forty year long, illustrated sermon on the provisional power of the Mighty One. There would have been no reason for these infectious diseases to arise, if the Torah was adhered to. Their clothes didn't wear out, their food and water was provided, they were protected from the Sun, etc. Certainly, mold could have been kept off their fabrics also, just as it says here:

> When you enter the land of Canaan, which I give you for a possession, and I put a mark of leprosy on a house in the land of your possession. (Leviticus 14:34)

It could have been kept off the homes as well. But just because you were kicked out of the camp, didn't mean you had committed unforgivable sin. Your flesh or habitat may be being destroyed, in order to save your soul. You could die an infected person, but still end up healed in Paradise. And that has never changed.

The reason the 'healing' ministry is so popular, intriguing, and profitable is due to the "healer's" ability to duck and dodge certain scriptural truths, while using other misrepresented truths to 'lift the faith' of those in desperation. They don't have to deal with any of this other stuff. They simply tell you you're due a miracle because you're a Christian, and you have but to believe that "by His stripes you are healed!"

If you are a leader in your church, when someone asks for healing ministry, do you bother looking into his or her life to see what's going on behind the scenes? Do you ask them tough questions, or do you do them the same disservice most doctors do, by treating symptoms? Except instead of using drugs, you use heart-felt prayer, and then leave the prevention to chance. Or, do you quickly lay hands on them, hoping your prayer is powerful enough to manifest a miracle? It's possible, and I stress possible, that although many people seem so marvelous and worthy on the outside, that inside there is rebellion, or perversion, or any number of heart problems that aren't cardiac.

Sure, we should pray for our sick, but we should also minister to them as well. We need to tell people the Truth, and we need to stop hiding the truth behind a fear of hurting people's feelings. If abusing the feast of Pesach is capable of bringing sickness and death, what about everything else we do? We have to remember that there are sins of omission, as well as those of commission. It is just as much a transgression of the Law to not do something we are commanded to do, as it is to do something we have been commanded not to do.

Consider the infamous man in Mark chapter two, who was "lowered through the roof." Yeshua healed him by telling him his sins were forgiven. What was that all about? This man may well have been a walking exhibition of the results of living life against the principles of Torah. He had chronic diseases which handicapped him. If these diseases were onset by eating blood, or obtained by decadent behaviors, what would be a more appropriate way to heal him?

We shouldn't obey for the intent of blessings; but then again, don't we in some ways? We knew growing up as children, under the roofs of our parents, that obedience had its rewards. In many cases, we were taught to obey by the reward system. We also knew disobedience had its price. When we did wrong and were caught, were we surprised when we were disciplined? How much do you think you do, that goes unnoticed by the One who knows how many hairs are on your head? Why do we presume we can live contrariwise to Scripture, to do the very things we are told not to do, having been plainly warned that if we do these things there will be a price to pay—yet it should all go well with us?

Here is the sum of what we have considered so far. Sometimes

Abuses of Power

we die slowly, for ninety or more years, beginning from our birth. Sometimes we die unexpectedly. Sometimes we fall asleep and never awake. Sometimes we suffer. Sometimes our sickness is due to our sin. Sometimes our sickness is due to someone else's. So if this is true, does that allow for 'healing' to be available to everyone, and in the same way? I wonder why we never hear the man in the white suit ever say to "go and sin no more." Perhaps it's not that profitable.

This teaching in no way intends to imply that the Lord is unaware of all our goings on. He was aware of when and how we are to die, before we were even conceived. And yet, He didn't stop that from happening. Therefore, as unpopular a thought this may be, He royally decrees it. What He decrees, and what He delights in, is not always the same thing. What has got to be impressed upon us all is that He is far more interested in how we live. What we really need to understand is what Yehoshua made *possible* by His coming, death, and stripes; as far as how it relates to our healing.

Our Hope

When Yehoshua came, it is quite obvious that He did not bring with Him the New Davidic Kingdom that many were expecting the Mashiach to restore. The Great General did not come to annihilate the enemies of Israel. The scattered were not instantly gathered in. The wolf was not lying with the lamb. There was still sickness and death, wars and famines, etc. Therefore, many rejected Him due to their confused expectations of Him. In fact, the leadership of that day was so disillusioned about what the Messiah was supposed to do, they could look at a man who was raising the dead and debate how to kill him—and for fear of losing political influence, no less. They didn't want the *whole world* to follow after Him, because that would mess with their nice little power structure. They were unable to differentiate the prophecies that spoke of two different comings. (By the way, this kind of misunderstanding still happens when we misrepresent the faith to new proselytes, and they come under difficult times. Yehoshua came to do many things, only one of which was to die. He paid our spiritual debts, but getting baptized doesn't wash the balance due line off of our credit card statements.)

For four hundred or so years of silence, between the last canonized prophet Malachi and the beginning of the first century, the voice and power of Adonai had only been remembered through the words of the ancient scrolls. The Jews were under the spiritual leadership of the Pharisees, and under the legal authority of the Sanhedrin, who in their efforts to keep the Torah community together and protected, ultimately made the Torah so complicated to observe that it bound the people to religious slavery. Much of Israel had been in the Diaspora for about six hundred years now. Looking around, one could have easily questioned what the benefit of being a Jew was, considering they didn't have control over their own city, they still had the poor and the infirmed, they couldn't obey Torah fully because of Roman restriction, and it appeared there was no end of these issues in sight.

There were those who kept a watchful eye out for the coming Mashiach, but most of them were looking for Him in the wrong places, and had the wrong image in their mind of what He'd be like. So when He arrived, poor and humble, plain and inconspicuous, coming from the Galilean region, growing up to eventually hang out on the streets like a wanderer and in the taverns and with the wayward, it was all the more likely He would go unnoticed. As He began to approach the end of His ministry, He became bolder in His proclamations as to His identity. Prior to that, He remained cloaked under the prophetic title "Son of Man," and allowed for His deeds to bear the majority of the witness for Him. One of those openly revealing times, Yehoshua stood up in synagogue and read from Isaiah. You remember. He said:

The Spirit of the Lord GOD is upon me, because the LORD has anointed me to bring good news to the afflicted. He has sent me to bind up the brokenhearted; to proclaim liberty to captives and freedom to prisoners. Today, this Scripture is fulfilled in your hearing. (Isaiah 61:1)

"To bring good news to the afflicted" is an interesting statement in itself, when kept in context. It doesn't say He came to heal everyone in the physical world, right this minute. It says there is a message of hope for them. The supportive proof for this Truth is more so found in the text that directly follows that verse in Isaiah, which Yehoshua closed the scroll without reading. That following verse says this:

Isaiah 61:2, "To proclaim the favorable year of the LORD and the day of vengeance of our God; to comfort all who mourn…"

Yehoshua didn't say this portion because it wasn't time to. If you understand that the restoration of all things does not come about until after the "Last Great Day" or "the Day of Vengeance," a lot more will make sense to you.

The healing miracles that Yehoshua and the Disciples were renowned for, came to bear witness of the Truth of the gospel message that the Kingdom of YHVH was at hand. But where is this kingdom? Is it here yet? Have you been making your annual trip to Jerusalem to participate in the Feast of Tabernacles?

And it shall come to pass, that every one that is left of all the nations which came against Jerusalem shall even go up from year to year to worship the King, the LORD of hosts, and to keep the feast of tabernacles. And it shall be that whoso will not come up of all the families of the earth unto Jerusalem to worship the King, the LORD of hosts, even upon them shall be no rain. And if the family of Egypt go not up, and come not, that have no rain; there shall be the plague, wherewith the LORD will smite the heathen that come not up to keep the feast of tabernacles. This shall be the punishment of Egypt, and the punishment of all nations that come not up to keep the feast of tabernacles. In that day shall there be upon the bells of the horses, HOLINESS UNTO THE LORD; and the pots in the LORD's house shall be like the bowls before the altar. (Zechariah 14:16-20)

No, we are not living in the *restored* kingdom yet, and therefore the promises that are attributed to living perfectly according to Torah, which is when we will be able to, are not fully available to us either. As long as there is disobedience to Torah, there will be aspects of the curses for disobedience at work amongst us. In the same way that the Kingdom of YHVH is within our hearts now, as a down payment of the kingdom to come, and the sealing of the Spirit of YHVH residing in us as a "security deposit" (2nd Timothy 1:14), so were the healing miracles of Yehoshua and the Apostolic age, a down-payment of the perfect healing that is to come in the Resurrection.

Ninety-nine percent of the "miraculous" healings, that are labeled as such, are actually the product of the systems of healing Adonai has built into our bodies, or in conjunction with medical intervention. Very, very rare is the true miracle that many seek from popular "healers," as the documentation by the medical community verifies. I, unlike some denominational perspectives, believe that He does still perform miracles (I am one). But not nearly as often, or of the nature, that some TV types would lead you to believe. By His stripes, we are all healed... eventually.

If His stripes instituted a new healing dispensation, where is it? Where are the people whose cast shadow heals those on whom it falls? People would not be being born with defects; some that are never healed or improved upon through medical intervention. Macular degeneration would not occur as we age, never mind the fact we would not age at all. Healing occurred in the Tanakh many times, always by an expression of His mercy. Again, I don't want to strip you of your faith for healing, if you need it; but coming to terms with reality is more important than living in a 'blind-faith', fantasy world. This is especially true during the earlier stages of treatment, when someone might decide to shun treatment in favor of a miracle. We are a fallen people, in a fallen world, and the Messianic age is drawing near, but it is not here yet. (Contrary to what some believe.)

It is not wrong for us to believe in miracles, for they are no more difficult for YHVH to perform than keeping the Earth in orbit. However, miracles are a witness for the Gospel. We have the written Word as witness to His resurrection, which is truly where our hope is. Our problem, as finite humans, is that we are stuck here in our minds. And as much as we believe we are going to be on perpetual vacation in Paradise, we still hold on to this life as if it's all we really trust in, and all we know. It is actually in the next life, that we are shown immortality reigns over death, and every tear is wiped away.

Is your life a living witness to the Gospel? Would a miracle bear witness to the Truth in your life? Would a divine healing be in accordance with the blessing of compliance with His covenants, or would it be contrary to His Word? I know that sounds like works-based favor, but I'm not the one who invented the program.

Can a miracle happen to someone who, from a Torah perspective, doesn't "qualify"? Absolutely! And often they do, because a miracle is always a merciful gift. A miracle may happen to shake our complacency up, or get the attention of the lost. What needs to be recognized though is that the appearance of signs and wonders are often in response to the waywardness of man, and often in judgment. We should not be seeking them (Matthew 12:29). Therefore, we should not lump signs and wonders together with divine healing too readily. We should pray for miracles, but we should not get angry with the Lord if it doesn't come. We should also be careful to not too quickly accept someone's short-sighted opinion, that "you don't have enough faith."

Hear this: Prosperity is another promise of the Scriptures. Are all believers wealthy? Is it possible that some of those, not-so-well-off believers are that way because they never invested wisely? Perhaps they, with well-meaning hearts, gave it all away; leaving their future in Messiah's hands. Or, maybe they invested a bit too much in their appetites, or travel, or overly enjoyed cultural attractions. Maybe they could have been wealthier, but due to mistakes of their youth, they stunted their potential. There are many reasons why it seems that the promises available to us do not come to fruition; you just can't assume it is Adonai's fault. Anything less than strolling in the Garden with Him, is less than our potential. But thankfully, He paved the way for us to again walk in the Garden with Him. Yet endurance is required from His saints, until there is Eden again.

Do I believe that all events now are random and chaotic? No. I do believe that Adonai is still directly involved in His creation. I just believe that miracles are His interferences to temporarily reverse, or inhibit the natural course of events, more often than they are an alteration of the initial course (destiny) itself. In case that was a bit too obscure for application, I'll elaborate with this: Often, curses from above are truly the

Abuses of Power

withdrawal of blessings, more than they are directly applied evil. A blessing is how things should be ideally. A curse is the withholding of such. To be perfectly healthy and live forever was the intended, 'normal' state of mankind. Death, sickness and disease are results of the altered 'abnormality' for mankind. To be healed is to receive the gift of postponement of the altered normality. To die is our current, *natural* course. A miracle doesn't stop you from falling; it catches you on the way down. To Yah, a miracle is just an intervention. My intention is not to produce a fatalistic view, just a non-sensationalistic one.

Look at it this way. It's not always a pretty picture, but it's the truth. Our (yours and mine) very first transgression of the Law brought upon us a death sentence. Instead of Him removing us from the planet at that very moment, every day we live beyond that is a merciful deferment of our just deserve. This judgment is not based on the severity of the transgression; it is based on our rejection of his authority. That is why we should never preach messages such as: "You are going to hell because you are a _____" (insert sin here). That is not true! Anyone going into everlasting punishment is going because they don't have a Savior/Redeemer interceding on their behalf. They are going because they rejected the need for, and the work of the Messiah. That same work causes us to desire not to _____ (insert sin here).

Graciously and mercifully, Adonai has given us wisdom in nutrition, chemistry and surgery to help us cheat death's plot (which began at our birth.) Blessed be He! He's even given us the means to numb the pains found in life, and in death; but Death only barely has a sting. It has no victory! It may have no victory, but it does have purpose.

A lot of what I just said could lead you to believe that I think a lot of death occurs outside the watch and will of the Lord. I do not believe that. But I must confess that there seems to be somewhat of a mystery involved. Anyone who has experienced a death in their lives believes that as well. We often see death occurring that appears pointless. Sometimes death happens in a way that appears to show HaSatan as being more powerful than YHVH. There is no doubt that it can seem that way, but people of faith can't accept that.

What we must understand is that the Lord has made no promises regarding the means of our demise. He has only promised that He will work out believer's trials for good. Death is a loss, and it may be a waste from our perspective; but no death occurs outside the will and allowance of the Creator. It is tough to wrap our minds around; but yes, we are killed, and we kill ourselves, under His watch. Yet not all He sees, He delights in. He allows for the dynamics of life within our broken universe, and the bankruptcy of human morality, to directly participate in the fulfillment of our termination. It appears cold at times, but appearances can be deceiving.

That is why life is to be lived to the fullest. It is our testing and proving ground for eternity. How we go about dying, is just as important as how we live, because they are somewhat synonymous. A life that has ended young is far more painful to us than it is to the "victim". It should be, and is only perpetually tragic to an accountable unbeliever. It should be understood that a short life lived in a particular way is every bit as equal to a long life lived in another, from an eternal perspective.

For those of you who have lost loved ones to violent crimes, my heart goes out to you. You need to know that before I make my next statement, otherwise it may appear trite and unsympathetic. It is my belief, and take that for whatever it's worth, that…

Women received *back* their dead by resurrection; and others were tortured, not accepting their release, so that they might obtain a better resurrection. (Hebrews 11:35)

This verse tells us— and I don't know the fullness of its meaning because I've never been physically resurrected—your loved ones will be treated with some kind of special dispensation. How you go out of this world somehow effects how you go into the next. This needs to act as a consolation for some. It seems to me, that perhaps in the midst of that evil, their maintaining of faith, along with their crying out for help was actually heard and answered. Even though, it may not look that way now. I believe that there are times when the fire does not hurt, and that He numbs us with merciful intervention. There is a "better resurrection" for them, and knowing how much He loved that person/s, He will make up for anything that happened with a great healing and a great reward. If you have little more to hold onto than that, hold on for dear life.

In Conclusion

In the same way that there is a syndrome whereby victims of abuse sympathize with their abusers, and can actually have affection for them, I believe this can happen in a spiritual sense, inside our churches. We come to love our leaders, and we cannot rationalize how someone who apparently loves us, even though they may inadvertently harm us, should be rejected as our teacher. We naturally want to see the best in people, and are willing to overlook the 'gray areas' of their ministry. We tell ourselves they must not know any better, or that they don't really want to do it, or that their intentions are well-meaning, so we need to support them. Those things may be true in a typical, friend-to-friend relationship, but they are not similarly okay within a spiritual leadership scenario.

I will tell you the same thing I would tell a woman who is being abused by their husband. "Leave your abuser!" If you are a member of a church, or considering becoming one, that willfully supports and encourages such abuses as: Holy *Ghost* "car washes," the teaching that everyone must have tongues (followed up with complete disregard for appropriate order in their use), barking, clucking, uncontrollable spasmodic movements, blowing or throwing the Spirit onto people, or charismatic hysteria of any form and attributes them to the Ruach, you are likely being spiritually abused. These are not usually "signs and wonders" of the heavenly kingdom. This is more often spiritually infantile behavior, if not demonic doctrines at work. Find a place where they promote the Lover. Look to the Scriptures for guidance.

The signs of a true apostle were performed among you with all perseverance, by signs and wonders and miracles. (2nd Corinthians 12:12)

If someone is operating in power gifts, and they are not a "true apostle," then you had better know for sure what they are, and from where they are getting their power.

It is true that not every single issue has been dealt with in the fullest detail within the Scriptures, but He is the same always. And being that these 'manifestations' are a fairly recently *encouraged* occurrence, as far as the span of church history is concerned, and that He is not the author of confusion, one would have to wonder why we have them. They have little to no value! Again, I refer you to the fact that as these things more frequently appear on the scene and are embraced, simultaneously the visible church has been, and still is, veering further away from the Torah of Moses. I leave you to your conclusions as to why that might be.

12

Pandora's Box

As a result, we are no longer to be children, tossed here and there by waves and carried about by every wind of doctrine, by the trickery of men, by craftiness in deceitful scheming; but speaking the truth in love, we are to grow up in all *aspects* into Him who is the head, *even* Christ. (Ephesians 4:14 & 15)

Just when it seems like we've covered it all, along comes one last chapter. Although we will cover topics which are pertinent, borrowing a favorite saying from a good friend of mine, this chapter will be more "pan-theological". Most of these concepts will "all pan-out in the end."

There are a couple of other popular sayings I think are apropos at this time. We must be able to "agree to disagree" and "disagree without being disagreeable". There are just some things that are not worth fighting over. Doctrines are somewhat paradoxical in that they are both what bind us together, and simultaneously divide us. Some doctrines we must not waver on, and maybe even part ways over; i.e., those that relate to our redemption. Others, such as whether the Messiah will touch ground again before, during, or after the Great Tribulation of the Saints, are fine for debate; just as long as we can still have table fellowship afterward. Although these topics are not necessarily all that light and can still be controversial, I hope that in the end, this chapter will be more like the latter. After all, all this writing is starting to make me hungry.

Predestination

Sometimes I think 'densination' is actually what happens to us, when we deal with certain subjects, i.e., this one. We can really go overboard with some of our beliefs. This topic is a particularly good example, especially when we think we can fully grasp it.

The misunderstanding, or should I say "possible understandings" of it have created divisions in the Body, since the earliest years of its recognition as a variable concept. Although it is an impossibly difficult one to fully grasp, I think that one's personal perspective on it can dramatically impact the way we live and perceive our King. It's somewhat hard to come at it from a fully 'logical' angle, because the spiritual realities of the workings of Elohiym are far above human logic. There is *likely* reasoning on it though. I will give you my take on it, with my diminished capacity to understand; and be quite possibly—imperfect.

You are absolutely correct, when you believe He knows in advance, who will be saved in the end. His omniscience establishes that. He does know the ends of all beginnings. The biggest hurdle one has to jump, when dealing with this topic, is the reality that a loving and compassionate Elohiym does allow people to be born, even when He knows that they will end up in outer darkness for all eternity. For that matter, why make man at all? Why not just stick with angels? Ah, but... even those angels had the possibility of falling from grace, due to rebellion (having a form of free will). Let's revert back to chapter two, and ask why our Elohiym placed the "forbidden fruit" in the garden, knowing full-well man would succumb to its/HaSatan's temptation? Here is where it branches into both simple and complicated, at the same time.

Man is incapable of fully expressing love to Him, without obedience. I hope I have successfully established that by now. Our Abba had, and always has had, a desire for a love affair. Love is one of the few attributes the Scriptures clearly express as being what He is composed of. He can't help it. I believe all His attributes to be this way on a theological level, but He explicitly declared it about Himself this way, in His Word, to shout it out. "God is Love!" Let's go even deeper. Don't forget that before Elohiym made man, He knew long in advance we wouldn't keep our part of the covenant promises, and that He would have to sacrifice Himself in the most horrific way, to bring salvation to the world?

YHVH told Abram, in Genesis 15, to get several varieties of the approved sacrificial creatures and bring them to one place. This is the only time such a 'cutting' (b'rit) was ever made. At this time, a blood covenant was a fairly common way for two people to make a life-long agreement with each other, but only one animal would ordinarily have been necessary for this. The animal would have been split down the middle, and both parties would have symbolically walked between the two halves and pronounced something like, "If I default on my promise to you, may I become like this animal!" Then, they would have cooked the animal and shared a meal together. But notice, He does not allow Abram to walk through it! He didn't even require anything of him. Abraham took it upon himself, to fend off the foul fowl, which represented those demons that would thwart our relationship with YHVH. We see demonstrated here the fundamental principle that we are powerless to design our own covenants with Him. He makes the rules.

Elohiym puts him into a dream state instead and He proceeds to walk through the covenant seal alone. Here, He is in essence saying, "I now absolutely assure you that your generations will be innumerable, become a nation, be rescued from slavery and return to this land. This covenant is an unbreakable promise." You, as a believer, are a fulfillment of that promise!

After time passed, as was prophesied in this covenant promise, we went into slavery and were brought out by a Mighty Hand. Then more covenant agreements were made at Mt. Sinai (Exodus 19-24), this time requiring commitments on our part; and there we said, "All that YHVH asks, we will do!" But sure enough, that wasn't the case. The essence of the contract at Mt. Sinai was, "If you love me, you will obey my commandments, and I will protect and reward you." The same words used by Yehoshua himself. These commandments were how the people were to prove their faithfulness to the future coming Bridegroom, and they/we blew that as well. The scene follows up with this paraphrased summation: "If you do what I ask, you will have the best of the land and be blessed. If you don't, cursed you will be." The stage was being set for a badly needed, perfect atoner to eventually come onto the scene.

Everybody who has ever walked the Earth has in some way stood at the base of Mt. Sinai and had to answer the question, "Will you acknowledge Me and receive my goodness; or, will you reject me and accept the cursed life, now and/or later?" The book of Romans teaches us that all men are without excuse because we are accountable to our conscience. What does that mean? It means Adonai has given all mankind the capacity to know good from evil, and acknowledge the existence of Elohiym Himself. Every man was created with it already in the mind of Adonai, that each would be died for. "It is the will of Adonai that all men be saved." But without obedience, there is not genuine love. Without obedience, there may be a form of acknowledgement, but that is not what He wants. He wants a romance with a spotless bride. Think about it. Would you want to be forced to marry someone that doesn't love you, and/or desire what makes you happy?

The fact that Yehoshua sacrificed Himself on behalf of the whole creation creates a fairly weighty argument as to why people will be rejected from His kingdom. Whether or not we depend on His substitutionary sacrifice, does not dictate whether or not we are under His reign! The clay (what we all are) does not tell the Potter what to do with it! Whether your *master* is the father of lies, or Yeshua (the Truth and the Life), YHVH is the *owner* of your soul. After all, He made it. Didn't He? A servant surrenders some degree of rights to their master, and being that we all have one, none of us are wholly free. We 'will' not be forced to obey/love Him, because that would interfere with romance. However, our will to love is different from our will to obey. I'm speaking in a generalized sense, as He may well direct you for a particular function, if by using you it will fulfill His purposes. If you are not a servant of Adonai, then obedience is not even the issue anymore, and you have surrendered yourself to merely being controlled by Him. He can either "pull your strings" or "pull your plug". He can use you for a greater good; or, He can manipulate you to accomplish His will. Yes, He can!

So what is the difference then? Can't He do that to those who love Him? Absolutely! The concept of free will is always misunderstood when the principle differences between obedience and control are not considered. Neither party, the bond servant or the slave, have complete free will. We just have the "capability" to opt for which we want to be considered. We are only free to make a choice. We choose to fight the birds off, or let them carrion. None of us are the masters of our own universe! We are all created beings, by the same manufacturer. And since 'Love' is the ultimate goal, if you don't love Him, then be prepared to be pruned off the vine and cast into the fire. If you don't obey Him, how can you say you love Him? Our will has always been *subject* to Him. It's just that we might *object* to His will.

If Yeshua is the Pesach Lamb, slain before the foundation of the world, and He knew us before we were made, our outcomes are also established as well. Does the angel who presides over the Book of Life write with pencil, so that our names can be erased out, and written back in, and then erased out again continually, cyclically throughout our lives as we fall in and out of grace? I don't believe so. All our names were written in the Book before the foundations of the Earth were laid. Moshe knew it, and asked that his name be blotted out rather than Israel be destroyed. Blotting is what actually happens, not erasing, and there is a difference. A blot cannot be undone. But that's not all that was written. Psalm 139:16 tells us that everything we do, every day we live, is written down also.

That can be a little unsettling if His sovereignty is not considered to be his supreme attribute. Your days are written down in advance, yet it is you who lives them out. Even though He directs your steps, you are the walker. If He chooses to allow a stumbling block to be placed in front of you that He knows you will trip on; you are still the one who trips. However, it may very well be your tripping, that causes you to accidentally-on-purpose bump the person beside you out of the path of a landmine. But if He chooses to operate in that way, He will also be the first to help you back to your feet.

All that foundation laid—behold then, both the severity and goodness of Adonai. You are either a wild olive branch, or a natural olive branch. Either way, there is only one root. If you don't produce the fruits of repentance, you will be cut off and disposed of. Wild olive trees are, by definition, not pruned. It is only once you have been grafted that you could be cut off. The terrifying "I never knew you" comment was given as a warning to "believers," not to unbelievers.

His desire is that all should be "*saved* to the end." It doesn't say "redeemed". The redemption of all creation has been paid for. There is no unfinished work involved in the actual purchase of our souls, but the fullest expression of its accomplishment is not yet. We are all born with equal opportunity to accept our redeemer; but not all do. Some names are blotted. Some names remain. It is my belief that blotting occurs one time only. I think it is at the point of our death, and I further elaborate on that in the next topic.

We all have a destiny. We are all created. Therefore, we are all created pre-destined. Some as common vessels, some as vessels of honor, and some are to be destroyed (2nd Timothy 2:20). It isn't an easy thing to accept, but who are we to order around the potter. Look at King Saul. He was anointed as king. The Spirit fell upon him. He prophesied and became a "new man". By all impressions, it appeared as though he was *destined* for greatness. Yet, his end came with demonic torment and in suicidal failure. And look at the Pharaoh Moses had to deal with. Adonai hardened his heart so that His will would be done. He can harden and therefore soften the heart of man, as He sees fit. Be grateful all the more, when you have been elected to be softened.

The Unpardonable Sin

Talk about a widely varied concept. We can all agree that it's something none of us want to commit. Reason being, none of us want to have an unforgivable transgression hanging over us, thereby forfeiting our access to eternal paradise and communion with Him.

Let's take that notion into consideration; that of being unforgivable. We are all hopefully under the understanding that there is nothing we can do to earn our redemption. We cannot perform a particular work, or group of works, that will grant us forgiveness. Along that line, we cannot perform a particular work that will 'un-grant' us either. "All have sinned and fallen short..." If unrighteous works 'un-redeem' us, we are all doomed! Being forgiven and being redeemed are different works entirely. We need to gain a little understanding as to what exactly is blaspheming, in order to fully grasp this concept.

There are a couple of words in the Hebrew that have been translated 'blaspheme': **barak** H1288, (138c); a prim. root; *to kneel, bless*: - abundantly bless, ...to curse; and **naats**; H5006, (610d); a prim. root; *to spurn, treat with contempt*. - blaspheme, despise, spurn. In the Greek, the word is: blasphemeo G987; from *G989; to slander,* hence *to speak lightly* or *profanely of sacred things*:- be spoken of as evil.

Truly, I say to you, all sins shall be forgiven the sons of men, and whatever blasphemies they utter; but whoever blasphemes against the Holy Spirit never has forgiveness, but is guilty of an eternal sin. (Mark 3:28 & 29)

Ouch! Not good! Even the blasphemy related to the misuse of Elohiym's name, for which we "are not found guiltless" of (Exodus 20:7), apparently is still forgivable. This has to be one serious sin! So let's think about this carefully.

Many of us have verbally rejected Messiah, and then at a later point come to accept the Messiah. Would any of us suppose that these people's conversions are invalid? The Apostle Peter verbally rejected Yehoshua. Is he damned now? Or, is that not a valid question, based on the predication of Yehoshua and the Ruach not having the same caliber of deiformity? Do we really believe you can mock the name of Jesus/Yeshua, but if you used the phrase "Holy Spirit" the wrong way, you're damned? It has to be more than just a comment made in ignorance, or even rebellion. Let's do what we always should do and draw on scriptural examples, from which we can gain more understanding.

Therefore, son of man, speak to the house of Israel and say to them, thus says the Lord GOD, Yet in this your fathers have blasphemed Me by [acting treacherously against] Me. (Ezekiel 20:27)

That was the 'how'. Notice the 'why' in the next verse:

...because they had not observed My ordinances, but had rejected My statutes and had (profaned) My sabbaths, and their eyes were on the idols of their fathers. (Ezekiel 20:24)

Here are the others:

Revelation 13:6, "And he [opened his mouth in blasphemies] against God, to blaspheme His name and His tabernacle, *that is,* those who dwell in heaven. (Blasphemies are often spoken.)

1st Timothy 1:13, "…even though I was formerly a blasphemer and a persecutor and a violent aggressor. Yet I was shown mercy because I acted ignorantly in unbelief." (As we see, some blasphemies are forgivable. Here, Paul is talking about how he treated believers in Messiah; therefore, in context, this blasphemy is in regards to how he felt and spoke about the Messiah they believed in.)

Leviticus 24:11a, "The son of the Israelite woman blasphemed the Name and cursed. So they brought him to Moses." (This cursing is not the same cursing as we think of it today, as in saying a word from the list of expletives. For this curse to be associated with blasphemy, the Name (actual, not figurative for character) had to be involved in some kind of expressed abuse. A 'cuss', in our modern vernacular, in itself does not constitute a blasphemy.)

2nd Kings 19:22, "Whom have you reproached and blasphemed? And against whom have you raised *your* voice, and haughtily lifted up your eyes? Against the Holy One of Israel!" (Here we see an example of a Hebraic parallelism. The 'reproached' is comparable to the 'raising of voice'. The 'blaspheme' is comparable to the 'haughty' attitude.)

Acts 18:5 & 6, "But when Silas and Timothy came down from Macedonia, Paul *began* devoting himself completely to the word, solemnly testifying to the Jews that Jesus was the Christ. (6) But when they resisted and blasphemed, he shook out his garments and said to them, 'Your blood *be* on your own heads! I am clean. From now on, I will go to the Gentiles." (In this example, their strong rejection of Messiah is the blasphemy.)

Let's consider the expressed function of the Spirit. Is He not the one who does the work of calling us to repentance? Is He not the one who convicts us of sin? The Ruach Ha'Kodesh can be likened unto the fire of the Brazen Altar which "is to be kept burning, it shall not go out!" If we "quench" the Spirit, if we grieve Him, His presence will depart and His work can cease. If that happens, and it does happen, what hope does one have unless He returns? The difficulty here is that it is impossible for us to know for sure when that has taken place. So, I would suggest you keep stoking the flames.

You have possibly heard the saying, "If you're concerned about whether you've blasphemed the Spirit or not, you haven't!" This concept is based on the notion that upon performing this transgression, you will have surrendered your soul and therefore lost your conscience. But is this a correct notion? Are we prepared to believe that people cannot accept their redemption up until death? Their name may have been written in the Book of Life before the world was made (Psalm 139:16; Revelation 13:8 & 17:8), but that doesn't mean they knew that. At any point in our life, is it impossible to repent and receive the Messiah into our hearts? I sure hope not! Granted, their reward may be little more than their allowance into the Banquet, and eternal life (not that that's insignificant).

At what point do we know it is truly too late to seek forgiveness? Death! Upon our death, we are "out of time". If we have not repented by the moment our spirit separates from our body, we have successfully rejected the work of The Spirit, and that is irreversible. If works don't "save us," works (blasphemies) likewise don't "un-redeem" us. To reject the work of the Spirit is unforgivable. From a practicality standpoint, you can't repent of something you're not convicted about. To deny the Spirit, is to deny Yehoshua. To deny Yehoshua, is to be denied yourself (Matthew 10:33). To deny Him, is to despise and to spurn His pleading and His sacrifice for your soul. I think this passage in Numbers really depicts the essence of the issue:

But the person who does *anything* defiantly, whether he is native or an alien, that one is blaspheming the LORD; and that person shall be cut off from among his people (15:30).

If you know the truth and you continually reject it, by definition, you are unrepentant. That is quintessential defiance. In ancient Israel, a habitual transgressor would not just risk being punished, they could lose their citizenship. It is not a big leap to bring that into a current context, and see the possible risk of habitual sin affecting our heavenly citizenship.

A perfect example to consider is the thief on the crux, next to Yeshua. He was told he would be with Him in Paradise, that very day. He is like the one who was hired near the close of the working day, and ended up receiving the same wages as the one hired at the beginning. He had no working knowledge of the Law or Justification. He had no good works under his belt. He was truly our scriptural example of a "death bed (crux) conversion". In the end, all of us receive "a very great reward!" It apparently wasn't too late for him.

It is my opinion that people can set themselves up to eventually become psychopathic, and thereby surrender their souls while still in this life. In that case, only the Lord knows if his or her name gets blotted out ahead of time. But the actual, official, eternal loss is not finalized until death. To just *say* you reject Him cannot be irreversible. We have all at some point rejected Him (through disobedience) and needed restoration. Not repented of sin is the accelerant which can drive us to the 'terminal' velocity of our destiny; but death is the seal to our fate.

It is also my belief that *rejection* of any representation of Elohiym, be it the Father, the Messiah, or the Spirit, is tantamount to the same thing. I don't believe it is more wrong to blaspheme any one of their names, or authority, than any other. They all carry the same weight in my perception, when it comes to the process of salvation.

Blasphemy, then, is a term which encompasses a number of actions. It is the attributing of what is holy to an evil origin. It is the verbal rejection of Truth and propagation of lies, regarding who and what YHVH is. It is also the rejection of the Spirit's pursuit and work of conviction. Therefore, I cannot personally comprehend how anyone who loves Adonai has anything to worry about, as it should be obvious that a lover of Him would be an obeyer and respecter of Him. That being considered, it is my opinion that everyone who ends up dying while "in their sins," actually ends up blaspheming the Holy Spirit.

In all reality, people cannot know if they are in an unforgivable state (in this life). He knows the beginning from the end. To Him, of course, we are what we are. But even if He foreknows we will ultimately reject Him, His awesome mercy continues to pursue, and give opportunity, and His amazing grace forever blows the trumpet requesting our presence.

Self-Termination

Having just left a discussion regarding the notion of being unforgivable, it seems appropriate to bring up another subject with similar finality concerns. The ultimate challenge to the emotional fortitude of any family is that of a member suicide.

A woman kills herself by swallowing a whole bottle of pills. No one would openly declare that it was her "appointed" time. But how many of us do unwittingly believe that, without ever acknowledging our role in our destiny? Just because she did it the fast way, as compared to a longer, slower suicide, doesn't change the outcome. If she instead chose to give up on life by living a solitary one, being a drug user and drinking heavily until she was found dead at 56, regardless of all the information we are given regarding the dangers of a life lived that way, is it really that different?

Pandora's Box

People who commit suicide have already concluded in their hearts that their life is over. A successful suicide is not accomplished by someone who just wants attention, (unless it is a cry-out gone badly.) Many have entertained the thought that Adonai had rejected them, or turned His back to them. Many figure they personify the unlucky spin of a roulette wheel, and that all their chips were placed on the wrong number. Others may have done something that burdens them with guilt so deeply, they figure death is the only escape. Then there are those who struggle to endure through, or make others endure through, a terminal illness.

Contrary to another mainstream thought, I do not believe that suicide is the equivalent of blaspheming the Holy Spirit. I believe it can be, but not in every instance. For that reason, it is a great risk to commit and therefore I vehemently do not condone the action. You won't know the answer to whether it is blaspheming or not until you cross over, where it may then be too late.

We are not capable of judging the heart or mental health of the individual, if successful at the act, for obvious reasons. We can't perform a post-mortem interview. Is the act selfish? In most cases. Is it cowardly and weak? Maybe. But does it mean that the person does not believe they need a Savior to access Paradise? Does it mean they don't acknowledge themselves as a sinner who needs forgiveness? Does it mean they don't hope in the next life being better that the one they are leaving? The answer to these last questions is…not necessarily.

All the emotion aside, the sin committed at the point of death is murder. It is murder of oneself. But Yeshua taught that if we are angry with someone, it might be tantamount to murder. How many of us may be murderers then? And if we believe our sins (past, present, and future) were forgiven when we fell at the foot of the cross—that wonderful moment we met Him there—would not that act of self-murder be forgiven to? I purposely ask these questions somewhat rhetorically, without answering them emphatically, so as not to potentially endorse the act. Then there's those who've fallen on a sword, or given their life for a friend, in a way that preserved the life of another. It's self-killing, but we don't feel the same about that, do we?

For those of you who have lost loved ones to this, I propose to you the very real possibility that if your son or daughter had a saving knowledge of the Messiah, not I nor any religious entity should damn them to an eternal separation from Him. What they did is horrific and awful, but unforgivable goes a step beyond where we should tread. They may have maintained faith in Yeshua, but lost it for their perception of humanity.

For those of you who have or are entertaining suicidal thoughts, if you were to follow through, you are definitely gambling with your eternity. You do have one (an eternity) regardless of where it is spent. I plead with you to never take that risk. Only your conscience knows if you have any eternal hope. Your spoiled fruit will certainly cause the world to wonder. Your act will eat away at the soul of your family all their lives, and therefore you leave the world more suffering than while you were here. Ultimately, it may not only be you who pays the dearest price.

Generational Curses

Here is but another topic which has been traditionally expounded upon with great fanfare. It's always amazed me how many books have been written on one or two verses worth of material (e.g. *Prayer of Jabez*). An awful lot of material just seems to have fallen from the sky, and into the laps of some helping-hands of the Body.

This topic is no different. I believe its misunderstanding has placed a lot of undo concern and fear upon the hearts of believers. There are conferences and seminars that set out to expose the curses that we are all apparently under, and break their chains off from us. While that may be well-meaning, and intermittently successful, it is generally not how things really work. Embracing the Truth that "sets us free indeed" should always be our goal. So, if there is a generational curse, what is it, and how does one get rid of it?

And I will bless those who bless you, and the one who curses (qalal) you I will curse (arar). And in you all the families of the earth will be blessed. (Genesis 12:3)
How shall I curse (qabab) whom God has not cursed? And how can I denounce whom the LORD has not denounced? (Numbers 23:8)
But put forth Your hand now and touch all that he has; he will surely curse (barak) You to Your face. (Job 1:11)

Loosely defined; here are a few examples of about ten different words that mean "curse":

To 'qalal' is to speak strong words against.
To 'arar' is to bitterly curse, as in to bring judgment against.
To 'qabab' is to curse, as in to invoke a negative event.
To 'barak' (as a curse) is to speak blasphemously or treasonously.

The other words are verb and noun variances of these, and don't have enough significantly different meaning to list here.

When these words and their forms are examined in their various usages in Scripture, you find that there was a sincere belief and concern with the power of words to incur or project harm. A perfect example is seen in the story of Balaam (Numbers 22-24). Balak apparently had confidence in his ability to invoke harm through words, and Balaam spoke as though he did as well. The craft of sorcery is authenticated throughout Scripture as also considered genuine, and is considered abominable.

Another validation is seen in the opposite form. There are also numerous examples of invoked blessings through the spoken word; more specifically being heard from the patriarchs, over their children. Even more particularly, it is heard being given to the first-born son. Quite clearly, Scripture portrays and teaches an ability to deliver both life and death through the power of the tongue. You're familiar with the verses.

What I want you to take note of is the fact that curses and blessings come in a variety of forms. They are spoken over individuals and entire nations. They may have limited time frames, or be eternal in perspective. They may be regarding the physical realm or the spiritual. The kinds that have "generational" properties are very limited, and are even less frequently applied to a singular individual. Let us now look at nearly all the information we have regarding this type.

Thou shalt not bow down thyself to them, nor serve them: for I the LORD thy God am a jealous God, visiting the iniquity of the fathers upon the children unto the third and fourth generation of them that hate me; and shewing mercy unto thousands of them that love me, and keep my commandments. (Exodus 20:5 & 6)

Know therefore that the LORD your God, He is God, the faithful God, who keeps His covenant and His lovingkindness to a thousandth generation with those who love Him and keep His commandments. (Deuteronomy 7:9)

Arguably, even in this verse in Exodus, it may be a warning to a people group, more than just to one person. If it is something that happens to an individual family, then we are in good shape, as you'll soon see why. Judgments/curses upon nations or tribes have historically rained down on the just and the unjust alike. But, as in the cases of the Flood, and of Sodom and Gomorrah, and the Egyptian deliverance, Adonai rescued those He wanted saved, *through* the judgments.

I don't mean to disappoint anyone, but contrary to the volumes of material that have been created from this verse from Exodus (and repeated elsewhere), it is really not that complicated. If you want to know what Scripture actually reveals about generational curses, then here you go.

A "generational curse" is little more than a tendency, or predisposition towards the continuation of sinfulness (iniquity), thanks to the leadership of previous generations. It is not a hedge preventing our salvation. It doesn't even mean total ineligibility for blessing. Why? Well, whom does it affect?

"...visiting the iniquity of the fathers upon the children unto the third and fourth generation **of them that hate me**."

And because YHVH does not force man into sinfulness! Now read this translation, which just so happens to be one of my least appreciated.

"You must never worship or bow down to them, for I, the LORD your God, am a jealous God who will not share your affection with any other god! I do not leave unpunished the sins of those who hate me, but I punish the children for the sins of their parents to the third and fourth generations (NLT)."

Forgive me, but I think this verse's translation is inexcusably terrible. It is, however, an indication of the mindset of many. Even the Pharisees misunderstood this verse, exampled by the story of the blind man from birth. I can't help but wonder if that thinking is what this translation is pandering to. Isn't sin forgivable? I thought that when it was forgiven it was cast away as far as the East is from the West? So if sins, past, present and future are forgiven at our point of accepting our Redeemer, doesn't it seem a bit unjust for the Lord to punish us anyway, for something we didn't do?

Within the very same verse is the answer to this riddle. "Visiting the iniquity" is a phrase that describes the transference of disobeying Torah from parent to child. That is why the verse ends with the converse. All is well for the obedient. Also, note that the phrase, "3rd and 4th generations" is a Hebraism for "limited time," and a "thousand generations" is a Hebraism for "forever". It is not to be taken as a mathematical formula. If the verse actually was saying that He imputes sin to someone on behalf of someone else, and that sin is unforgivable and to be punished, we are all going to Hell in a hand basket.

Do you hate YHVH? Are you bowing down to idols (the context of this topic)? If not, then iniquity is not *visiting* you! The only way it is, is if you have welcomed it into your house! If your fathers were idolaters, then the "curse" was available to be upon you, as a propensity to do the same, unless you do not follow in their ways! Whatever generation that breaks the sin-cycle is eligible to come out from under it, within that very generation. Anything less than that is a deception HaSatan has pulled on you, and the only thing you need to do is "come out from under the lie!"

If they confess their iniquity and the iniquity of their forefathers, in their unfaithfulness which they committed against Me, and also in their acting with hostility against Me—I also was acting with hostility against them, to bring them into the land of their enemies—or if their uncircumcised heart becomes humbled so that they then make amends for their iniquity, then I will remember My covenant with Jacob, and I will remember also My covenant with Isaac, and My covenant with Abraham as well, and I will remember the land. (Leviticus 26:40-42)

Avraham is a perfect example. His father Terach was an idolater from Ur. Surely, nobody thinks Avraham's life is an example of generational curses at work. Avraham did not become an idolater. He got up, listened and obeyed by crossing over (becoming a Hebrew), and walked in blessing.

If your mother was an alcoholic, you probably would be wise not to drink! If your grandparents were pagans; then you worship the Lord! If your dad was a thief, you go make an honest living. If your parent(s) physically abused you, you then hug your children all the more. The only curse you are under, as a child of His, is the one you embrace. And quite frankly, we often embrace them as security blankets. We label ourselves, or we accept someone else's label, and act accordingly. So, what guarantees your accessibility to freedom from curses?

"And shewing mercy unto thousands of them (generations) that love me, and keep my commandments."

You can't actually *keep* His commandments unless you also love Him. You can only perform them. And I'm sorry, but He is not going to punish innocent children who love Him for something their parents did. What's most difficult for us to contend with is that consequences may be suffered by innocents, without it being direct discipline. This heart of the Father is clearly presented in other areas of His Word.

Fathers shall not be put to death for *their* sons, nor shall sons be put to death for *their* fathers; everyone shall be put to death for his own sin. (Deuteronomy 24:16)
No man can by any means redeem *his* brother or give to God a ransom for him. (Psalm 49:7) (That proves indulgences were a fraud.)
And His disciples asked Him, "Rabbi, who sinned, this man or his parents, that he would be born blind?' (3) Jesus answered, 'It *was* neither *that* this man sinned, nor his parents; but *it was* so that the works of God might be displayed in him." (John 9:2 & 3)
The person who sins will die. The son will not bear the punishment for the father's iniquity, nor will the father bear the punishment for the son's iniquity; the righteousness of the righteous will be upon himself, and the wickedness of the wicked will be upon himself. (Ezekiel 18:20)
But when a righteous man turns away from his righteousness, commits iniquity and does according to all the abominations that a wicked man does, will he live? All his righteous deeds which he has done will not be remembered, for

his treachery which he has committed and his sin which he has committed; for them he will die. (Ezekiel 18:24)

In Adonai's Kingdom, everyone is responsible and accountable for their own actions. This is a wonderful and just system, presided over by a same-said Judge. No one is eternally damned at birth *because* of their parents. Neither does anyone get to make excuses for their behavior based on their parents. There will be no: "But I couldn't help it. My parents..." like expressions considered as admissible evidence during judgment. Similarly, there will be nothing like: "I know My child. You couldn't stop beating your kids, because your parents..." spoken by the Judge.

Until you recognize that you are a free individual, and refuse to believe otherwise, you *will* remain shackled. Beyond that, we have to also realize that who we are, and where we are in life, is also greatly dictated by the sum of the decisions we have made along the way. Make wise decisions, and alter the course of your life. I do not believe that you can be a child of YHVH, and simultaneously be under a curse that cannot be broken. My Adonai is a Great and Mighty One; and with Him, all things are possible!

People want something super-spiritual. We often want a contrived sequence of events, along with a secret series of verses to be chanted for an allotted amount of time. I can't give those to you. Absolutely, walking it out is challenging at times. The conquest for our soul occurs in our minds, and it is a tough battle. You win this battle the same way Yehoshua did in the desert. Speak the Word, and live the Word. That is where your freedom is found. If you obey His Word, you remove yourself from the realm of curses. Obey His Word, and build a hedge around yourself. Holding fast to walking out Torah keeps you distracted from worldly lures, while actively aware of and dependent upon Him. Scripture is powerful to strengthen you. If this is not true, then Adonai is a liar.

Does all this mean there is no place for counseling or therapy? No, it does not. There is certainly a need to learn how to walk out your victory. We need skill at using the tools needed to fight back against the lies of the Adversary. The wisdom that comes from the experience of others who have discovered their own victories is immense. We simply must realize that these assistants to recovery are just that...assistants. Your victory comes straight from the power of Adonai; a power that abides within us as believers. The chains that bind us morph from metal to imagined, upon our deliverance from death to life. In an analogous way, often our bondage is similar to the phantom limb syndrome that affects amputees. We feel something that's not there. The feelings are real, yet reality says otherwise. It often takes us a long time to acclimate to how free we already are. Yet again, just like the Hebrews.

It is important to note that generational curses are not the same as demonic *possession*, although at times it may be affiliated with *oppression*. Once you've walked out from whatever curses you think you are under, curses do not come back seven-fold strong. Once you are free, you are free indeed! It is also important to consider, such as in the case of Amalek, when sons of someone were to be destroyed, it was to end a tribe or nation. Adonai has the foresight to know the destiny of all peoples, so it was not an unjust act. So then, this is as good a time as any to put your hands to the plow and never look back.

Ezekiel 18:32, "For I have no pleasure in the death of anyone who dies," declares the Lord GOD. "Therefore, repent and live."

Tribulation Fabrication

Not that it isn't going to happen. That's not what I'm implicating. However, there are some things that should be re-examined, especially in light of the popular, theo-fictional books that are so prevalent in today's marketplace. Due to the position I am about to express, I feel that these books are actually pretty harmful to the current Body, but even more so to the *potential* Body. For if by chance, these fanciful and imaginative interpretations are not the actual pattern of apocalyptic events, there are going to be a lot of people caught unawares, and the potential is there for that fact to play a supporting role in the great, "falling away" drama that is soon to come.

That ye be not soon shaken in mind, or be troubled, neither by spirit, nor by word, nor by letter as from us, as that *the day of Christ* is at hand. Let no man deceive you by any means: for *that day* shall not come, except there come a falling away first, and that man of sin be revealed, the son of perdition. (2nd Thessalonians 2:2 & 3)

And the next twenty-five thousand dollar question is: What is "that day"?

Now, of all the topics we have discussed in this book, eschatology (the study of end times) has to be on the top of the list of those which I can do no justice to in this limited space. It's an enriching endeavor to study the possibilities of the order of the end, but it's also very contentious material. I'll not spend of lot of time creatively representing the facts, because feelings and desires have little value getting involved. Similarly, the relevant verses are arguably the most interpreted-through-glosses scriptures that there are.

For those of you who are aware of the various lines of thought, and their associated arguments, you will recognize my counter arguments. They're not new. I am going to feverishly dismantle those I find discredited by Scripture, and equally support those that are. As I've stated before, I'm not interested in focusing just on the error in our midst. If we study the genuine, taking the Scripture as literally as possible, it exposes the Truth just fine; all by itself.

Blessed is he that readeth, and they that hear the words of this prophecy, and keep those things which are written therein: for the time is at hand. (Revelation 1:3)

Look at that last verse's claim: The time is "at hand." Was Yehoshua lying or confused, or was He saying that events were unfolding shortly? Some of you may think that this expression is understood to be figurative based on Yehoshua's being outside of time, and His day being equal to a thousand years. But if that was the case, then all the content that follows would have been of such ambiguity to the readers of that day, it would have been considered of questionable inspiration. They would have studied it, pondered John's cognitive state, and then kept it around for the sake of the author's notoriety. After many years going by, and nothing happening that validated it, it would have likely been shelved and forgotten.

Keeping that in mind, as well as the fact that there are various, potential candidates for the fulfillment of some of the apocalyptic prophecies that are in Scripture, we should always be careful to hesitate in our supposition that everything in apocalyptic literature is still forthcoming. Many horrible and unique events have occurred, on our march through time, which would fit quite nicely into many of the prophecies given. That is just something to consider when you embark into eschatological study. Just as it says here, some things were taking place then and some things in the future.

Therefore, write the things which you have seen, and the things which are, and the things which will take place after these things. (Revelations 1:19)

Now, for a little history lesson on the future. The concept that the "church" was somehow destined to be 'lifted away' from a coming tribulation was barely considered before the Protestant Reformation began. Consequently, most Christian denominations that have this belief are those that appeared after the Reformation. The popularization of the term 'rapture' is primarily associated with the teaching of John Nelson Darby, along with the rise of premillennialism and dispensationalism in the United States. This took place at the end of the 19th century. The rapture concept is a fairly new theology in the overall perspective of the church's lifespan. The word "rapture" comes from the Latin verb *rapere*, which means "to carry off" or "catch up". It was used in the Latin Vulgate (about 405 AD) translation of 1 Thessalonians 4:17; this being the primary biblical reference to the topic in question. It is rarely translated as such anymore.

"Then <u>we</u> who are alive and remain will be *caught up* together with them in the clouds to meet the Lord in the air, and so we shall always be with the Lord."

Notice that Paul used the pronoun "we", including himself as a possible attendee. He believed that followers would be involved, and I see no reason that we should think ourselves wiser. We will be.

Consider this: John is given a message to give to the church. This letter is distributed and upon reading, is clearly seen in these lights: A warning call for the saints, a giver of hope for the trials current and ahead, and a series of prophecies for the future Body in general. I know there are many protocols for accurate interpretation of Scripture. Often it seems prophecy must be clouded in mystery, and cannot under any circumstances just be straight forward. Couldn't it be possible though, that the purpose of this letter and its contents were to help us out? And if so, how is that possible when no one can understand it? Here is the greater question: What in the world do we (the current Body) need council and encouragement for, if we are not even going to be here during the "after these things" portion? Wasn't the letter written to the Seven Churches? You'd derive by some expositor's views, it was more directly written to the lost. Let's take a further look into obtaining prophetic insight, by listening to the one who stands in the midst of the seven lamp stands.

For the coming of the Son of Man will be just like the days of Noah. (38) For as in those days before the flood they were eating and drinking, marrying and giving in marriage, until the day that Noah entered the ark, (39) and they did not understand until the flood came and took them all away; so will the coming of the Son of Man be. (40) Then there will be two men in the field; one will be taken and one will be left. (41) Two women *will be* grinding at the mill; one will be taken and one will be left. (42) Therefore, be on the alert, for you do not know which day your Lord is coming. (43) But be sure of this, that if the head of the house had known at what time of the night the thief was coming, he would have been on the alert and would not have allowed his house to be broken into. (44) For this reason you also must be ready; for the Son of Man is coming at an hour when you do not think *He will.* (Matthew 24:37-44)

This monologue from our Messiah is one of the most commonly held supports for the rapture of the church, away from His testing. Apparently, some people are going to disappear, while others are going to remain; and not only that, but those that do remain are going to be blindsided. There are two main themes running in this commentary. The first one being that the timing of His return will be like that of previous times. The second one being that we should keep our radars active and sweeping.

As far as the first theme goes, He gives us a little insight into those days. The first thing that I want to bring to your remembrance is the fact that Noah's ark illustratively evangelized the region for some one hundred years. There was plenty of advance notice of the coming judgment. But there is something else about those days, as well as other similar days of judgment, that needs to be noticed. Noah and his family were saved *through* the flood; they were *not removed* from the earth and then brought back to it. Adonai could just as easily destroyed everyone and started over. That is the same pattern we see with the Hebrews in Egypt. The Hebrews observed the judgments that fell upon Pharaoh and the land. And the Hebrews, in kind, were observed by the Egyptians as not receiving the effects of the *most severe* plagues. The Israelites did experience the first-third of them. Lot and his family were rescued from Sodom, just before its destruction—actually, while it was happening right behind them. When judgment falls, the righteous are saved *through it*; but; not all of them, always. Sometimes there are casualties, and sometimes martyrs.

As far as the second theme goes, what is the need to "be on the alert" if we are all going to suddenly vanish? Perhaps His "coming at an hour when we do not think He will," is really because many think He's coming before the tribulation, when He's really not! He is, after all, speaking to a crowd who had not yet read the book of Revelation. Maybe, no man knows the day nor hour, up until the tribulation begins. Even if that's not what He's implying, He is giving His followers an instruction which only really makes logical sense, if they were to find themselves in an environment where looking forward to His coming has some sustaining and empowering value. Why tell us to be prepared for something we cannot possibly prepare for? Either you're redeemed or you're not, right?

"The people were eating and drinking and giving in marriage." What's wrong with that? That's not a rebuke! That's a warning to realize that things are going to seem pretty much status quo, and to not be blindsided. Isaiah and Jeremiah both speak of the end times being like labor pains. Human beings have a forty week gestation period. We know approximately when to expect a birth, but nobody can assure the hour. Since the fall of Adam, all of creation has been longing for restoration. Since Yeshua ascended, man has been in spiritual travail. How can we

Pandora's Box

point to an exact day, at when the end of a two thousand year gestation will take place? We can't! We can feel the contractions getting closer though…can't we?

One of the problems with a pre-wrath rapture is that it is, in all practicality, another dispensation-based, bad replacement theology concept. Here's the way it seems to work: Jews are bad—Christians are good. Jews stay on Earth and are punished with the heathens. Christians are rewarded and withdrawn from the time of refining. But there is a huge problem with this thinking. It's dead wrong! The Jews will embrace that gospel message well, I'm sure.

Here's another provocative questionnaire for you: Was the Holocaust punishment for the Jews still not accepting Yeshua, or was it because they are still breaking the old covenant and its stipulations? If it's the former, why did the early church, which had embraced Yeshua, undergo such persecution of its own? If it's the latter, was the holocaust a foretaste of what is coming to the entire earth (including existing believers), due to the fact that the church currently keeps the commandments even less? Moreover, was Adonai justified in allowing this, without an active, "old" covenant? Were the early believing Gentile converts persecuted because they were sinful, or righteous? The early 'believing' sect of Judaism held fast to Torah also you know.

The reason judgment (the Seventieth Week) is coming; the reason Daniel understood it's coming anyway, is because:

We have sinned, committed iniquity, acted wickedly and rebelled, even turning aside from Your commandments and ordinances. Moreover, we have not listened to Your servants the prophets, who spoke in Your name to our kings, our princes, our fathers and all the people of the land. (9:5 & 6)

Before you think these are loaded but unanswerable questions, or that Daniel wasn't referring to "us" believers (although 9:7 confirms it just fine), read this:

And they (Tribulation converts, or the church?) overcame him because of the blood of the Lamb and because of the word of their testimony, and they did not love their life even when faced with death (Faced with death? Who? The raptured church?) (12) For this reason, rejoice, O heavens and you who dwell in them. Woe to the earth and the sea, because the devil has come down to you, having great wrath, knowing that he has *only* a short time. (13) And when the dragon (beast/HaSatan's kingdom) saw that he was thrown down to the earth, he (dragon) persecuted the woman (Israel) who gave birth to the male *child* [(Messiah) brought through Israel, not the church.] (14) But the two wings of the great eagle (the Spirit) were given to the woman (Israel), so that she could fly into the wilderness to her place (Goshen--escape/hideout), where she was nourished (kept) for a time and times and half a time (3½ yrs.?), from the presence of the serpent (HaSatan). (15) And the serpent poured water like a river out of his mouth (lies, anti-Semitic ideologies, false-doctrines) after the woman, so that he might cause her to be swept away with the flood (destroyed). (16) But the earth (Divine intervention) helped the woman, and the earth opened its mouth and drank up the river which the dragon poured out of his mouth (He protects Israel). (17) So the dragon was enraged with the woman, and went off to make war with the rest of her children (Grafted-in believers), who keep the commandments (Torah) of God and hold to the testimony (Bear witness) of Jesus. (Revelation 12:11-17; reinforced in 14:12; symbolic propositions mine.)

I recognize this is just a possibility, but the last sentence says a mouthful. Who is the devil enraged with? Those who keep the commandments of YHVH (Torah)! Now, are those righteous obeyers, or unrighteous obeyers (trick question)? Did you notice that this last war is spoken of as occurring <u>after</u> the stated 3½ year period? Did you notice the saints "overcame"? Overcame what…the rapture?

In 1st Corinthians 15:51 & 52, the Apostle Paul writes:

"Behold, I show you a mystery; we shall not all sleep, but we shall all be changed, in a moment, in the twinkling of an eye, at **the last trump**: for the trumpet shall sound, and the dead shall be raised incorruptible, and we shall be changed." (Possible reference to Yom Teruah/Feast of Trumpets?)

In 1st Thessalonians 4:16 & 17, Paul also writes,

"For the Lord himself shall descend from heaven with a shout, with the voice of the archangel, and with **the trump** of God: and the dead in Christ shall rise first: Then <u>we</u> who are <u>alive and remain</u> shall be caught up together with them in the clouds, to meet the Lord in the air: and so shall we ever be with the Lord."

Let's break this down. A "last trump" will sound, and then we will be gathered to be with Him for eternity. Now, contrary to some who believe there are various definitions for the word 'last' (similar to the word 'is'), I am convinced there is only one way this verse can be read. There is only one place where there is an apocalyptic sequence of trumpets that would enable there to even be a definable "last trumpet". It also happens to be found in The Revelation. The sequence occurs within chapters eight and nine. I'm not going to copy all that text here, but if you read them, you will find that they are all judgments; and if that's the case, we're going

Pandora's Box

through at least six of them.

And I heard a voice from heaven, saying, 'Write, 'Blessed are the dead who die **in the Lord** from now on! Yes, says the Spirit. So that they may rest from their labors, for their deeds follow with them.' (Revelation 14:13)

There are apparently going to be people who lose their lives in martyrdom during this timeframe; but not just any people...believing people. So the idea that all believers get raptured, and the Spirit leaves the Earth with them, and no one can be saved from that point on is nonsense. This is even more verified by these verses:

And I saw another angel flying in midheaven, having an eternal gospel to preach to those who live on the earth, and to every nation and tribe and tongue and people. (Revelation 14:6)

What is the point of a gospel-ministering angel, if his message has no capacity to bring repentance? Look at this next portion. Who is being reaped?

Then I looked, and behold, a white cloud, and sitting on the cloud *was* one like a son of man, having a golden crown on His head and a sharp sickle in His hand. And another angel came out of the temple, crying out with a loud voice to Him who sat on the cloud, "Put in your sickle and reap, for the hour to reap has come, because the harvest of the earth is ripe. Then He who sat on the cloud swung His sickle over the earth, and the earth was reaped. (Revelation 14:14-16)

This is the reaping of righteous Israel away from the damages of Armageddon. Read these next verses to clarify, because…

Then another angel, the one who has power over fire, came out from the altar; and he called with a loud voice to him who had the sharp sickle, saying, "Put in your sharp sickle and gather the clusters from the vine of the earth, because her grapes are ripe." So the angel swung his sickle to the earth and gathered *the clusters from* the vine of the earth, and threw them into the great wine press of the wrath of God. (Revelation 14:18 & 19; destruction of the encroaching armies!)

This is not the final "Day of the Lord" component either. For the very next verse is a description of this winepress being "trodden outside the city." (Jerusalem, not the whole world.)

And the wine press was trodden outside the city, and blood came out from the wine press, up to the horses' bridles, for a distance of two hundred miles. (Revelation 14:20)

The "Day of the Lord" cannot be just the Lifting Away event! It contains it. If it is, some very credible folks have their facts twisted.

The sun will be turned into darkness and the moon into blood before the great and glorious Day of *[the]* LORD comes. (1st Corinthians 1:8) ...who also will confirm *[or, sustain]* you to the end, blameless in the day of our Lord Jesus Christ. (Acts 2:20; again mentioning being <u>preserved</u> <u>through</u>.)
But **the day of the Lord will come like a thief**, in which the heavens will pass away with a roar and the elements will be destroyed with intense heat, and the earth and its works will be burned up. Since all these things are to be destroyed in this way, what sort of people ought you to be in holy conduct and godliness, looking for and hastening the coming of the day of God, because of which the heavens will be destroyed by burning, and the elements will melt with intense heat! (2nd Peter 3:10-12)

The "**Last** Great Day" is not any event you want to be in the midst of, as an unredeemed human! And thankfully, we will not be. For that is the day we are completely removed from. This 'last' portion of *the day* is the universal restoration. Notice here that <u>this</u> is the day that we are told is coming like a thief, not the rapture!

Behold, **I am coming like a thief**. Blessed is the one who stays awake and keeps his clothes, so that he will not walk about naked and men will not see his shame. (Revelation 16:15)

If <u>He</u> is coming like a thief, and the <u>Day of Vengeance</u> is coming like a thief, then it would also stand to reason that His Second Coming is partly the "Day of the Lord", and that "day" ends with, as Isaiah states it, "The Day of Vengeance of our God."
Here is my synopsis, since I just want to bring to your attention some alternative possibilities, and can't really do more than that. The book of Revelation begins with the statement, "I was in the spirit on the Day belonging to the Lord (1:10)." Now, I realize that's likely not how your translation renders it, but that's what John's actually saying. Following that, comes the entirety of the book. It is my opinion that the only way the 'Day of the Lord' can both sneak up on us, and also be clearly definable in its end; be the day He returns, and be the day the universe is overhauled, is if the whole tribulation period, and through to the Millennial Reign as well, is *all* 'the Day'. A day is *as* a thousand (plus seven) years, right?
The Sabbath day is His day, but made for man. Prophetically speaking, there are seven days in a week, which could amount to seven thousand years. If mankind is given six thousand years (six days) to do what it wills, then the 7th, thousand year period would be His. According to the Hebrew calendar, we are in the year 5774 (2016 C.E.), and there is a

Pandora's Box

couple hundred year discrepancy. Noah was in his fifth century when he began to prepare for the end. Mankind had a one hundred year warning. At his sixth century, judgment fell from the sky. Who knows, maybe we are that close?

The "day" will sneak up on us because the first day it begins is not told to us. But for those watching, a thief loses the advantage. We know the first-coming events, but they may very well occur shortly after the 'technical' first day's start. We *can* know the seasons though.

If by now, you do not consider yourself part of Israel, I have failed at a primary objective of this book. But if you do, perhaps these verses will further open your understanding:

Fear not, **O Jacob** My servant, declares the LORD, and do not be dismayed, **O Israel**. For behold, I will save you from afar and your offspring from the land of their captivity. **And Jacob will return and will be quiet and at ease, and no one will make him afraid.** For I am with you, declares the LORD, to save you; for I will destroy completely all the nations where I have scattered you, only I will not destroy you completely. But I will chasten you justly and will by no means leave you unpunished. (Jeremiah 30:10 & 11; Has this happened yet? Does this sound conditional?)

I would like to supplement this topic with my creative *opinion* on how it could all go down. I will do it in an outline form for simplicity, and in *relative* chronological order. You can contemplate for yourselves the specific details, and I will not be mentioning every prophesied occurrence.

1. We may already be in the early stages of Jacob's Trouble.[1]

2. Wickedness becomes exceedingly wicked, while the love of many waxes cold. This figurative cold will be partnered up with a literal cold; as the winter season initiating the tribulation begins; since nobody is praying for it not to (Matthew 24:20), or will think it has begun.

3. Israel undergoes severe attacks. Israel finally gets fed up enough with America's, the UN's, and the EU's pacifistic treatment of Israel's enemies, and takes aggressive military measures to ensure its safety. They make retaliation, because their enemies are aggressively surrounding them. America looks the other way as Israel is internationally condemned for their behavior, and that is seen as an American show of weakness by Muslim extremists.

4. This gives Israel's surrounding enemies a sense of empowerment, which leads to multi-national and coordinated conflagration against Israel (Obadiah 1). The nations from the "north" are hooked into the bright idea that they have the capability of eradicating Israel. Militias engage in small assaults on the "villages without walls"

(Ezekiel 38:11). Israel takes them down without prejudice, and the global community won't support her.

5. Western nations are united under a global viewpoint that Israel is more of a threat to world peace than a participant in it. America, and its partners, aggressively campaign for a solution, which paves the way for a formal, two-state solution. Israel's enemies are dismayed by what happened, but they have no choice but to comply. They strategize that this will allow them a way to get further embedded into the land, and strengthen to fight another day. This "solution" will be backed by a seven year treaty of false peace. As part of the two-state concession, the borders are loosened enough to allow some of scattered Israel easier access to return.

6. Another part of the concession will be that the Temple rebuilding can get underway (2nd Thessalonians 2:4), or at least the Great Altar gets set up somewhere near the Temple mound. Once that option is in place, the daily services begin again. Many from Judah and scattered Israel continue to return to the land. Most do not understand the eschatological weight of the times. (It should be noted that a fully rebuilt temple is not required for the daily service to begin. A temporary tabernacle will suffice. It is the dedication of an altar that is the essential component, which is currently under construction.)

7. The Diaspora continues to reverse as international anti-Semitism further drives the return.

8. The Altar service gets underway. But shortly afterward, equating to about midway through the Tribulation, the Temple service is halted by an internationally sanctioned cease and desist; possibly provoked by its offense to creation worshipers.

9. The image of the beast gets set up (abomination causing desolation). The anti-Messiah is now staged and possibly identifiable. The restrainer, Michael the Archangel is ordered to allow HaSatan freedom to fulfill his destiny (Daniel 11 & 12). At some point, the anti-Messiah is "assassinated." But in mockery of the true Messiah, he returns to take up his position. It is warmly received.

10. Because the fastest growing, anti- any other religion is now fully supported by the governing bodies of the world, and has become the darling of the global agenda. They will be the new "useful idiots". Nazis were at least relatively isolated to their homeland. Today's version is spread throughout the world, and will be welcomed with open arms. To further make this possible, Adonai will send a strong delusion for the lies to be believed. The most obvious lie (to us believers) being that the religion of Islam is actually a religion of love and goodness (already happening). The "extremism" aspect helps to create an accepted delineation. The delusion, along with the miracles performed by the

arriving false prophet, will help fuel the great apostasy, or "falling away". Ignorance of Scripture will only help facilitate this.

11. Immediately after the beast's uprising, the two witnesses come onto the scene, and as much as it frustrates the false prophet and his followers, he can't silence their truthful proclamations. (Many believe this to be Elijah and Moses. I personally believe there is a good chance it will be Elijah and Enoch, for it is appointed that all men should die once.) The *spirit* of Elijah will have already been here, as mentioned, to restore Judah's faith (Torah) to the sons, and instill the new covenant faith upon Judah. (Malachi 4:6) Enoch appears to be the most righteous man to ever walk Earth, which would also certainly qualify him; although we know little more than that. YHVH told Moshe that He would be sending a prophet like himself, who's presumed to serve the same function, and lead the final exodus.

12. This satanic entity will also establish the "moral" compass for the one-world government, enforcing their own Torah and setting itself up to be like a totalitarian theocracy, with the answers to the world's problems. Remember how Adonai told the Israelites to destroy specific heathen nations in Canaan? Well, that will become the anti-Messiah's supportive mandate to do the same thing, but toward the wrong people (Jacob). Hitler is back! In case you are unaware of the events surrounding Antiochus Epiphanes and his assault on Jerusalem, you may want to be. Antiochus made Judaism illegal, in very likely the same way the anti-Messiah will (Books of Maccabees). As this is happening, more blind eyes will open and people will begin see the beast for who he is. Many will flee to the hills, or anywhere they can find safety, just as they did back then (Matthew 24:16). Living obediently according to the Word of the Lord, which is now being written fully on our hearts, will be the main reason believers around the world will find it difficult to hide. There are just too many signs Torah observant people give off. We have our own "marks".

13. While this is going on, and continuing beyond, believers are facing tough trials, (brought on by their rejection of the beast's name/mark, and the beast's systems, and garment laundering/testing is taking place   within the House of YHVH.) More falling away takes place as the world intensifies its hatred of the followers of the True Messiah. Anti-Semitism, as it was once known by, will be like child's play compared to the insidious venom that will be spewed. If you look at America's recent, historical example of segregationism, it becomes quite easy to understand how people won't let us "buy or sell," (or use the same bathroom, or ride on the same bus.) There are plenty of historical, political examples of father against son (civil) fighting (Mark 13:12).

14. The integrated religion of Islam, advancing terrorism, along with advancement of New Age/Order philosophies and ideologies,

population/food control, liberal socialism, Ghia science, and other economic agendas combined create the force that propels the need for a strong, universal government. The world buys the lie that this global government is a necessary institution. The "resurrected" leader is appointed to run it. This global authority readily sows the anti-Semitic/anti-Messianic propaganda required to empower all the nations to rise up against any opponents/sympathizers. America, even if it professed a desire to, will be too economically and militarily disadvantaged to thwart it (because we have turned our back on Israel.) Then, people will allow for the attempted destruction of His Chosen people. "If anyone *is destined* for captivity, to captivity he goes; if anyone kills with the sword, with the sword he must be killed. Here is the perseverance and the faith of the saints (Revelation 19:3)." Who knows, the world will probably just consider us believers to be the extremists and potential terrorists, as they instead feel pity and empathy for the genuine enemy.

15. Some severe judgments take their course (more seals are opening), but the people of the nations look toward the place of Israel's habitation (some tabernacling in the desert and mountains, some "rebels" still in the city), and see that they have been given a special measure of grace. So people continue to loathe the land and its Elohiym all the more. We are given the two wings of the great eagle, and we are given manna.

16. Some warfare, some covert infiltration and capture happen to the believers (Revelation 13:7). Some traitors of the faith cause trouble. We learn to endure and resist. It is relatively small time, but there is still more falling away. Fortunately, around the world, angels begin sealing a special group of tribesmen. I think they may be intended to act as local-level guides through what comes next.

17. Really severe judgments now fall, for the Trumpets are sounding. A strong outpouring of the Spirit is given to us to overcome (Dan 12:10). These judgments, instead of bringing repentance, bring more hatred and stubbornness—just like it did in Egypt.

18. While this is happening, the reunification of Israel is well underway. The Tribes begin to become reestablished as the House of Israel and the House of Judah are uniting and becoming reacquainted. The very desire to survive encourages this.

19. The anti-Messiah, at some point, strategically leaves Jerusalem. By doing so he will open Jerusalem up to be like a mouse trap (so he thinks), so that Adonai's people will appear to be in an isolated target zone. Surrounding nations begin to move into offensive positions around the Land. By all impressions, it looks like Israel is in real trouble (Zechariah 14:1).

20. The Pharaoh of that day gathers together his available forces, and leads a conquest intended to annihilate Israel. This will become the

battle of Armageddon. YHVH allows for some means of assassination to overtake His two prophets.

21. Yeshua sends the full measure of the spirit of Elijah to return the heart of the sons to their fathers, and takes the two houses (two branches) into His hand, and combines them to form one tree. We finally get the opportunity to meet the "One New Man," who will be led by the same Shepherd. This happens by the scales falling off the eyes of Judah (the Jews), and they receive sight to see the Messiah and embrace Him. The scales will also fall off the eyes of those in exile (Israel, and its companions: the Church), and they receive sight to embrace and obey the commandments (Torah); fulfilling the prophecy of peace coming between them (Isaiah 11:13; Ezekiel 37).

22. Being encouraged by the death of the two prophets, HaSatan is as foolish as his celebration after the death of Yeshua was. The anti-Messiah leads his armies into (without any human intervention) sudden annihilation, as Adonai intervenes with aggressive force and as suddenly as it began, the assault is over. "Surely, there is a God in Israel!" will be the reaction of those whose eyes are open to see, and they look upon the carnage. It will take seven months to clean up the bodies, and seven years to sanctify the land. This happens as He is peeling back the darkness (one of the final judgments), and ensuring "everyone sees His coming (Zechariah 14:3-5)." He then enters our dimension sitting upon His white horse.

23. An angel blasts a long tekiah on the shofar, that every creature hears. The dead 'in Him' rise from their graves. The living "in Him" are then gathered to Him. He then guards those of us, whose faith bought us our ticket out, from the impending cataclysmic finale of judgments that the earth is about to undergo, by lifting us away to where we get to watch it from our sky-box seats.

24. Those that are resurrected are given glorified bodies with which they will live throughout eternity, and return to Earth led by our Shepherd King. And those who are "caught up" are returned with pre-curse, Adamic-like bodies. He cleanses and inhabits the Temple. The Redeemed inhabit the Land whose borders are now as they were intended to be. A handful of surviving humans develop civilization outside the holy city. Temple worship *fires* back up.

25. The Beast and his prophet are then escorted kicking and screaming into punishment by Michael and Gabriel.

26. Surviving, non-resurrected mankind repopulates the Earth, outside the city (1st Corinthians 15:51)—possibly including the 144,000. I believe the *resurrected* will have a human/spirit state, like that Yeshua when He showed Himself post-resurrected. We will be able to eat, walk through walls, hopefully explore the Universe, and whatever else He allows for

(except apparently marriage and reproduction; Matthew 22:30). Those partakers of the mystery "who will not die" remain more human. They can travel within the city, but their future generations may not be able to come into it. (They may not live by faith.)

27. We partake of the Wedding Supper to celebrate our union. (Not to disappoint any of you, but He will not be serving Bratwurst or Oyster Rockefeller.)

28. For almost one thousand years, mankind experiences the peace that it's always dreamed of. But it is due to the rod of iron Messiah rules with—(peace through strength). The wolf lies down with the lamb. (Many natural things return to their pre-fallen state again.) All non-glorified mankind must obey the King, but they don't have to like it. "New covenant" and "old covenant" still co-exist—in a way like that of the first wilderness journey, except people will be far more motivated to submit. Major difference being that those of the new covenant will finally know its fullness (Isaiah 65:20-25).

29. At the end of the thousand years, HaSatan is released. He gathers up the unrighteous humans and demons, and forms his army for the "one last stand". Yeshua lifts His iron rod. The nations try to come against Israel. But, just as swiftly as before, Messiah finishes off all unfaithful humanity. Except this time, it's with fire.

30. The White Throne Judgment begins, where the damned, and the unrighteous humans who are born during the Millennium, will receive their sentence of eternal banishment from Paradise.

31. The graves of those who died in their sins, open up in the ground, and the sea gives up its own, to be judged. And so they are. Death, Sheol, HaSatan, and all those whose names are not found in the Lamb's book, are thrown into the lake of fire, with the beast and the prophet. Then we stand before Him, and receive our just deserves.

32. The universe is recalibrated. The atomic structure of all matter is scrambled and reorganized back into an entropy-free design. The genetic structures of all the selected-to-remain, living things are put back to their original mutation-free chains. (Assuming He chooses to keep the DNA-based genetic format, since DNA is for replication purposes.)

33. The New City of Jerusalem appears adorned as the Bride and settles upon the newly excavated foundation of the Earth (assuming it's a literal city.) This city will be, in essence, the capital of the universe; and from here on out is anybody's guess. Here are a couple other things to consider:

Blessed are those who wash their robes, so that they may have the right to the tree of life, and may enter by the gates into the city. **Outside** are the dogs and the sorcerers and the immoral persons and the murderers and the idolaters, and everyone who loves and practices lying. (Revelation 22:14 & 15)

Here is where eternal punishment will take place: outside the city. Remember the story of the rich man and Lazarus? Lazarus and the Rich man were within a visible distance. Think about it (literal fire or Gehenna analogy aside); forever being unable to enter the glowing city of paradise that is somehow before your eyes; forever not being able to enter into fellowship with your Creator; forever remembering the life you lived and the choices you made to get you there, will be truly horrible. That is truly Hell on Earth.

The pre-trib, rapture theory requires the belief that Messiah will visit the Earth not once more, but actually twice. Once to remove His followers from the Tribulation, and the second time on a white horse, to conquer His city's opposing forces and then take command. It is important to recognize that the Scriptures speak of Messiah's future return, in the singular only.

Let no one in any way deceive you, for <u>it will not come unless the apostasy comes first, and the man of lawlessness is revealed</u>, the son of destruction, who opposes and exalts himself above every so-called god or object of worship, so that he takes his seat in the temple of God, displaying himself as being God. (2ⁿᵈ Thessalonians 2:3 & 4)

This warning would be absolutely meaningless if it were not to be observed by the effected generation. Therefore, the "last generation" preceding His coming must see all these events take place. The apostasy is understood to be a significant 'falling away' within the believing community. The man of lawlessness is understood to be the anti-Messiah. All subjective, apocalyptic interpretation aside, we <u>must</u> see these before His return! From my perspective, these verses completely annihilate the theory of a pre-tribulational rapture, because the anti-Messiah's presence is not expected to be acknowledged until around the middle of the seven years, and <u>after</u> the building of the temple. The apostasy cannot feasibly occur until the tribulation is well under way. Otherwise, why would it happen? In case you still think you're getting out easy:

<u>Then</u> that lawless one will be revealed, whom the Lord will slay with the breath of His mouth, and bring to an end by the appearance of His coming. (2ⁿᵈ Thessalonians 2:8)

You cannot translate this verse in any way that says anything less than the anti-Messiah's temporal reign ends, upon the True Messiah's coming! His second coming ends the anti-Messiah's reign. Let me put it another way, in a more clear effort to silence the nonsense promoted by that popular series of end-time books: We are all going through the Tribulation! What is the point of the Tribulation, after all? According to

Daniel, it is to "purge, purify and refine." But that is not all. It is also for the same purpose that YHVH used ten plagues to deliver the Hebrews: "So that you pharaoh, will know the LORD." Look at this end-times prophecy in Ezekiel:

> Therefore say to the house of Israel, "Thus says the Lord GOD, It is not for your sake, O house of Israel, that I am about to act, but for My holy name, which you have profaned among the nations where you went. (23) I will vindicate the holiness of My great name which has been profaned among the nations, which you have profaned in their midst. Then the nations will know that I am the LORD (YHVH), declares the Lord GOD, when I prove Myself holy among you in their sight. (24) For I will take you from the nations, gather you from all the lands and bring you into your own land. (25) Then I will sprinkle clean water on you, and you will be clean; I will cleanse you from all your filthiness and from all your idols. (26) Moreover, I will give you a new heart and put a new spirit within you; and I will remove the heart of stone from your flesh and give you a heart of flesh. (27) I will put My Spirit within you and cause you to walk in My statutes, and you will be careful to observe My ordinances." (36:22-27)

This is a prophetic word, spoken to the scattered house of Israel. This isn't a *"when you"* prophecy; this is of the *"when He"* variety. I hope you have figured this out by now, but the house of Israel is not "Jewish" anymore. It is so mingled into the nations; it is of the nations. It is many of you, and it is I. This time is affiliated with "Jacob's Trouble," not Judah's. He is going to "prove Himself holy" among us, in front of them...so that "they will know the LORD." The Tribulation will be a global scale reproduction of what took place in Egypt, for the very same reason. And then, when we are gathered up and brought to our new promised land, we will be given hearts to follow His Laws again; and we will finally get rid of our idols. Personally, I can't wait!

The thing that concerns me greatly is how easily so many "believers" may initially be duped by this anti-Messiah. Imagine a beloved world leader standing up and saying, "No more sabbaths! No more circumcision! Jews must wear identifying clothes! Eat pig or die!" What response would that bring from an average "Christian"? "Poor Jews—stinks to be them...again." Wasn't that the typical response during Hitler's reign of terror; if people even knew what was happening? It's not as if it was very long ago.

Although some of this is my and other's understanding, that's really all I can declare it to be. However, I believe it is grounded on a more literal and less ear-tickling analysis. Sure, it would be great if we were just whooshed away into eternal bliss; but that just doesn't line up with the text, or the historical MO of Adonai. I will admit that there are varying time-line scenarios, that based on certain models, and interpretive methodology, have credence. Therefore, though I am convinced, I argue cautiously in regards to how scenarios will play out. However, I will argue vehemently against a pre-trib, mid-trib, partial-trib rapture, or the a-Millennial theory. Regardless, the "eminent return" of Messiah, as understood within the context of the rapture escape, is a fallacy. Convincing people to "get saved", by telling them He could come at any second, is irresponsible and manipulative. At the least, the Israelites had to weather the first few plagues themselves, and at least observe the rest from a distance. By preparing ourselves for the worst-case scenario, He will not come as a thief to us. Nor will we be dismayed, but only further readied.

It's obviously not in your or my favor to interpret things this way, but I can't help but "tells 'em like I reads 'em." One thing is for sure. We are to "wash our robes (Revelation 22:14)," and many will "...purify themselves, and make themselves white, and be refined (Daniel 12:10)." Will you?

Tithes and Offerings

Leviticus 27:30, "Thus all the tithe of the land, of the seed of the land or of the fruit of the tree, is the LORD'S; it is holy to the LORD."

Yes, I am that crazy. I will step on this third rail too. I figure I have already stepped in about as much "prize of the pasture" as one can absorb the stench from, so what's a little more going to hurt? We are, after all, nearing the end of the book now.

I know there are many of you out there who think that as soon as someone teaches anything other than to, "give ten percent of your pre-taxed money to the church!" they have disqualified themselves from legitimacy as a Bible teacher. That is fine. It's just not that cut and dry, as you are about to learn. Allow me to expose the different ideologies involved. What you will find when carefully examining the text is that there are legitimate differences (not discrepancies) in how the "principle" of the tithe, versus the "laws" are developed. There are clearly two sides of this coin, but the pictures on both are very similar. The thousands of years of tarnishing does make it hard to tell heads from tales.

Surely, nobody thinks tithing is a later derived, "New Testament" concept. Yet, ironically, its only appearances there involve Yehoshua's rebuking of certain Pharisees for putting their stringent tithing practices above the weightier matters of Torah, and as a proof for the superiority of the priesthood of Melchizedek (Matthew 23; Luke 11 and Hebrews 7, respectively). Tithing on cumin and mint was nice and all, but if you're a walking whitewashed tomb, all the tithing you could ever do won't buy you eternal life with Abba. I guess we have to go back to the Hebrew Scriptures again, to find out what the tithe is all about. It is important that you understand this, so that you do not succumb to charlatanism or thievery, done under the guise of pious obligation.

And Melchizedek king of Salem brought out bread and wine; now he was a priest of God Most High. (19) He blessed him and said, 'Blessed be Abram of God Most High, Possessor of heaven and earth; (20) and blessed be God Most High, Who has delivered your enemies into your hand.' He gave him a tenth of all. (Genesis 14:18-20)

Here is the first-stated appearance of a tithe mentioned in Scripture. Notice the components: You have a local king and priest represented as the recipient, a man/family who had an increase of wealth, and the base figure given of ten percent. Take note that the items transferred here were originally obtained through two methods: acquisition from others via (inheritance/war bounty; Hebrews 7:4), and through the blessing of fertility (both directly due to Yah's blessing).

This instance of giving was not adherence to a scriptural law; and, at this point, we as of yet do not have earned wages involved. (Later, war bounty required a one-fiftieth, or two percent obligatory recompense; Numbers 31:47). Also note here, that at this time we seem to be observing a fully voluntary but culturally appropriate act—a type of tribute. This is Abraham though, so as the progenitor of the people of promise, it likewise became the standard by which Adonai designed Israel's economy around. The principle of upright land dealings seen there is clearly followed throughout Abraham's life. We know earlier Bible figures made offerings as well. We just don't see the specific, ten percent figure exampled prior to this. Now, let's take a look at the next appearance: Jacob's response to his "ladder" vision.

Genesis 28:22, "This stone, which I have set up as a pillar, will be God's house, and of all that You give me I will surely give a tenth to You."

We can only presume that Ya'akov is following in his grandfather's footsteps. Beyond that, not much information is attached. Here is a more complete compilation of the laws of the tithe, according to Scripture:

Thus, all the tithe of the land, of the seed of the land or of the fruit of the tree, **is the LORD's; it is holy** to the LORD. (31) If, therefore, a man wishes to redeem part of his tithe, he shall add to it one-fifth of it. (Leviticus 27:30 & 31)

To the sons of Levi, behold, I have given **all the tithe in Israel <u>for an</u> <u>inheritance</u>**, in return <u>for their service</u> which they perform, the service of the **tent of meeting**. (Numbers 18:21; Here we see the first earnings-affiliated text in relation to tithing. Still, this is in relation to certain some ones *receiving* from the tithe. It is not a giving related instruction.)

Moreover, you shall speak **to the Levites** and say to them, 'When you take from the sons of Israel the tithe which I have given you from them for your inheritance, then you shall present an offering from it to the LORD, **a tithe of the tithe**.' (Numbers 18:26; Yes, even the priest had to tithe.)

You shall eat in the presence of the LORD your God, at the place where He chooses to establish His name, **the tithe** of your <u>grain, your new wine, your oil</u>, and the firstborn of your herd and your flock, so that you may learn to fear the LORD your God always. (Deuteronomy 14:28)

At the end of **every third year** you shall bring out all the tithe of **your produce** in that year, and shall deposit *it* **in your town**. (Deuteronomy 14:23)

When you have finished paying all the tithe **of your increase** (of produce, as seen in the above passage) in the third year, **the year of tithing**, then you shall give it to the **Levite, to the stranger, to the orphan and to the widow**, that they may **eat** in your towns and be satisfied. (Deuteronomy 26:12)

Bring the whole tithe **into the storehouse**, so that there may be **food in My house**, and test Me now in this, says the LORD of hosts, if I will not open for you the windows of heaven and pour out for you a blessing until it overflows. (Malachi 3:10)

You shall surely tithe all the produce from what you sow, which comes out of the field every year. (23) **You shall eat** in the presence of the LORD your God, at the place where He chooses to establish His name (Jerusalem), the tithe of **your grain**, your **new wine**, **your oil**, and the **firstborn** of your **herd** and your **flock**, so that you may learn to fear the LORD your God always. (24) If the distance is so great for you that you are not able to bring *the tithe*, since the place where the LORD your God chooses to set His name is too far away from you when the LORD your God **blesses** you, (25) then you shall <u>exchange it for money</u>, and bind the money in your hand and go to the place which the LORD your God chooses. (26) **You may spend the money for whatever your heart desires**: for oxen, or sheep, or wine, or strong drink, or whatever your heart desires; and there you **shall eat in the presence** of the LORD your God and rejoice, you and your household. (27) Also, you shall not neglect the Levite who is in your town, for he has no portion or inheritance among you. (28) At the **end** of **every third year**, you shall bring out all the **tithe of your produce** in that year, and shall deposit *it* **in your town**. (Deuteronomy 14:22-28)

There are a few different events going on in here, but for the sake of intent and simplicity, these verses will do nicely. A very detailed study of minchah (offerings) and ma'asrah (tithes) are beyond the scope here. I will follow up the tithe teaching with a short commentary on offerings; which are different in function. Keep in mind, the recipients of these tithing laws started out by being given the land, animals and property of the heathen peoples YHVH kicked out of Canaan. They start out similarly to the state Abraham was in, when he met with the King of Salem. (Note: My usage of the word "tithe" does not necessarily represent a law to do so. It is also used to represent it's actually meaning of ten percent.)

Curiously, after that last mention in Deuteronomy, the word 'tithe' does not reappear again until 2nd Chronicles 31:5. That is a time span of about eight hundred years! That covers the period of the Judges, the united kingdom through Solomon, up until Hezekiah comes along to rebuild and restore. Somewhat humorously, when Hezekiah tried to get things up and running again, he forgot how things were supposed to operate. Instead of the tithes being distributed amongst the thirteen Levitical cities, he had them all brought to Jerusalem, and the quantity was so overwhelming they didn't know what to do.

Agrarian peoples were to give a tithe of their harvest every year at each major crop. Every third year it was to be given to the local Levitical leadership as part of their inheritance. This last tithe was also distributed to the needy, the widow, the orphan, etc. The in-between two years, the tithe was brought to the Temple (storehouse) in Jerusalem. Growth of one's herds (His Blessing) resulted in one of every ten going to the storehouse. The grain harvests had a first tithe and a second tithe. In some cases, portions of the tithe were eaten by the tithe bringers, as seen during the pilgrimage feasts. The tithes of livestock and from the field that were too much to bring along on their journey into Jerusalem, could be sold and converted to money. This could be spent on the journey and provisions upon arrival; even the "strong drink" that accompanied the Feast of Tabernacles celebration. (Deuteronomy 14:26; which I'm sure my Baptist friends would agree, really meant root beer.)

The principle of the "increase" was based on yields that were over and above what one had ended with the previous year. In other words, when in regards to produce, all was included. Flocks and herds multiplied because of God's hand in providing good fertility and grazing land. Grain fields yielded their harvest because of God's hand in providing the right amount of sun and rain. Again, these are things we can only play a small role in, like moving the flocks around or planting seed. A good harvest or increase in flocks, as well as drought and famine, should be understood as being something the Lord is responsible for.

Although the Scriptures do not 'spell out' what an increase is, it doesn't take a Hebrew scholar to figure out. You have a parcel of land. The harvest has ended. Winter comes and the crop-bearing plants die. Now you have barren land. From this point on, anything you bring in next season is increase. A believing farmer knows their limitations in production. They can sow, plant, fertilize and water, but none of those things guarantees anything; especially when there is no seed to plant, or water to irrigate. They do what they can and hand the rest over to the Lord. So when the next harvest comes around, the farmer reaps the harvest, carefully leaving the outer corners of their field alone, and not going back through a second time, to obey the commandments; and they give ten percent of what they reap to support the Kingdom.

Things are slightly different when it comes to husbandry. If you bought a breeding pair of sheep one year, and they had one lamb, the tithe that year on your increase would be one-tenth the value of a sheep. If your flock of one hundred goats had ten kids over the year, it would seem your tithe would be one goat, based on the principle of increase. Normally, a rancher/shepherd does not start out every year with nothing, and end up with production, like the farmer. It's fairly anatomically impossible. Therefore, it is very conceivable that a rancher could start with fifty head, and end up with the same or less. Especially, considering that some of the flock was going to be eaten to survive. Or, the rancher could end up with sixty or more.

The way the herds and flocks were counted is different from the way a crop increase was calculated, because animals were counted by head. Apparently, the increase of the flock was led through a gate whereby every tenth animal was selected, marked and led away. As long as the Lord's blessing was upon the land, natural reproduction would have easily sustained the system. The tithing program was very reasonable.

Here is where my third rail electrocution will begin. Most accept the premise that the tithe is a "principle" that is in effect outside Israeli agriculture, and the temple/Levitical priesthood. Let's accept that premise, plug it into a certain scenario and see what happens.

Let's presume you live a modest and frugal life, are married, and have three children. You are not agrarian, and you make your living through a white-collar trade. You earn forty-five thousand dollars in a given year. Your expenses to survive that year were thirty-five thousand dollars (what you ate of your flock, and bartered for necessities). At the end of the year, you have ten thousand dollars remaining in savings. What do you think your tithe is: forty-five hundred dollars or one thousand dollars? What if the next year you lost your job and earned nothing. Do you pass your previous year's income through the sheep gate, and tithe upon it again?

I am not trying to trick you into answering a particular way. I'm trying to cause you to conclude that things are not always equal. If you were going to tithe on the rancher's "increase" principle, your increase that exampled year was ten thousand dollars. That is what you would tithe on. If you were going to tithe based on the farmer's increase principle, it's obviously not that simple. In either case, there are variables which we will soon discover, need to also be considered.

You have likely been taught that your tithe is to be your "first-fruits". That works well for those whose ministries require a lot of salary support. The problem with that teaching is the first-fruits offering was established only to feed the priesthood and the needy, and was only instituted upon the farming community. Also, "First-Fruits" is not a tithe, it is an offering (a sheaf of grain, etc.; Leviticus 23:10; 2nd Chronicles 31:5). The original, storehouse system of Adonai was a "need-meeting" system. It was designed to prevent starvation and to support the priesthood—that could not own land.

There is no tithe in Scripture allocated to buy luxuries for the priesthood; not one! It allowed for clothing and food for their families while in service. Did you know that most of the priesthood was on a weekly rotational serving program (2nd Chronicles 23:8 & 31:2), and otherwise engaged in income-producing, traditional trades to support their families. This enabled them to obtain the material things they wanted, that were above what was required to survive? The priesthood never was supposed to build their wealth on the backs of the citizens! The only life-long, full-time priest there was, (in the scriptural plan), was the Kohen ha'Gadol (the High Priest). All others were retired at fifty (Numbers 8:25). As highly as some may think of themselves, there is no human equal today.

Cash money was also brought into the temple, through the redemption of the first-born (of both man and animal), and the annual half-shekel used for the public sacrifice. Money was also brought it through the selling of sacrificial animals, or redeeming a tithe in cash value. And of course, if someone wanted to pledge things, or throw a mite into the pot, it was not rejected. This also allowed for some money to be available as needed for various emergencies.

If one owned a business, or worked for someone in a field like metal-smithing, they did not have a First-Fruits responsibility at all. As a matter of fact, they did not have a tithe responsibility either. Tithing was only affiliated with agriculture! There are no scriptural commandments on tithing being associated with wages, or associated with other trades.

The tithes were also collected at certain times of the year. The Free-Will and Thanksgiving offerings were given on specific days, as well as whenever one wanted. The tithe was saved up, and much of it was used to enable the fulfillment of pilgrimage obligations. Meats and grains were provided to the priesthood via the sacrifices. They did not have to buy these to eat for this reason. Tithing was never a weekly institution.

For those of you whose ministries depend on your congregation's tithes, you are aware that a small percentage of them are "faithful" to the ten percent, and are regular givers. If you'd like to see an increase in the giving, try unshackling them from the tithe error. Those who generally

Pandora's Box

give nothing because they feel that "less than ten percent is a sin, so why bother"; and those who would give grievously instead of joyfully because it's really hard on them, would be released to give more liberally and consistently. "Tithers" who just don't care to know any different, would still remain. Overall, you would probably bring more into the coffers. (Just like how the government has higher revenues after a tax-cut.) Then, take away all the unauthorized benefits of the pseudo-priesthood, and you'd really be doing well.

Although the Scriptures teach about us *becoming* a kingdom of priests, as we've already seen, that is not yet actually realized. If it was, then logically, being that all priests are fully supported by the storehouse (as twisted Torah teaches), then everyone in church should get a paycheck!

I've already written on the ministry positions, and the salary issues accompanying them, back in chapter eight. By looking at the system of giving in its original design, we can clearly see the proper allocation of the money that came into the storehouse. The priesthood was fed, and charity was distributed to the needy. So what about today? Well, there is no functioning Levitical priesthood. There is a "Five-Fold," as well as other ministries. The examples that come from our apostolic leaders, is that of being sustained by those who would bring them into their homes, and working in the world's economy as much as possible, so as to not be a burden on the Body. Scripture says they were "*worthy* of double," but you never see them collect.

As far as charity goes, the Temple and the priesthood were the storehouse and distribution center. Today, domestically, it's predominantly the federal and state government, through welfare. Everyone who pays taxes today pays reasonably toward the caring of the poor and needy—not less than anyone's normal obligation to strangers, through the annals of scriptural history. Unfortunately, much of what is distributed goes to people the Bible would not define as "the poor among you." Far too much goes to "the lazy sluggard."

It used to be that the elderly were respected in the community and not discarded. Family and community cared for the elderly, people could not rely on secular government for much of anything. The church body should help take care of its own and outsiders, above and beyond welfare; but its capacity to do so has been stunted by its self-initiated, structural changes. And when we do so, it is free to come out of the general funds. You should not need to ask for special "benevolence" donations. Benevolence should be your main account, and utilities and missions should be your sub-accounts. You want to talk about being an effective people magnet, just try having a very benevolent reputation. We are obligated to care for people; and whether voluntarily or not, through taxes, most of us do.

If you, as a minister, have people who just have to have you as their full-time leader, and you are not self-supported, your people may bless you with gifts that may add up to enough for that to be made possible. If you've got the guts, you may ask people to earmark money specifically to support you. Let's be honest, shall we? When you're up at the podium pleading for money, that's often what you're pleading for… your salaries. There would always be enough to meet the needs of your congregants, if other expenses didn't get in the way. Or, you can ask them to buy you specific things. But there is no scriptural principle for you to draw out of what is brought into the storehouse, to pay for: your car, your vacations, insurance, retirement, boats, kid's education, other big-boy toys, etc. In other words, all that comes in is appointed to care for maintaining the storehouse, and for supporting the poor and needy. Stings, I know.

I do believe, if you want to adapt the principle of the tithe to the modern day, the church could pay your grocery bill, and maybe fill your car with gas as needed. I could even see it putting decent clothes on you to preach in (a couple outfits). But, since you always get to go back home (your inheritance), that's about where it ends. If you want the church to pay for everything for you, then you'd better be prepared to never own your land (parsonage), or have property to pass down to your children. (Full-Gospel, right?) You can only have your tithe and eat it too. And by the way, all Levites received the same amount (Deuteronomy 18:8). What's it like in your church?

In case you haven't noticed by now, I'm a little concerned about Kingdom money, and I think it is extremely misappropriated. If the early church leaders were able to see the kind of wealth today's "spiritual" leaders are pulling in off the gospel, they would be horrified.

Worthy of Your Wage?

The disciples were sent out two-by-two and told by the Master Himself:

Carry no money belt, no bag, no shoes; and greet no one on the way. (Luke 10:4)
Stay in that house, eating and drinking what they give you; for the laborer is worthy of his wages. (Luke 10:7)
Whatever city you enter and they receive you, eat what is set before you. (Luke 10:8)

The parallel passage to Luke 10:7 is Matthew 10:10. In Luke, the word for 'wages' is *misthos*. This word is most always rendered 'reward'. In Matthew, the word used is *trophe*. This word is defined as *nourishment*.

Together, the image is pretty well defined. That above text is exactly what Paul was talking about here:

1st Corinthians 9:14, "So also the Lord directed those who proclaim the gospel to get their living from the gospel."

I could get technical about the meaning behind the word 'living' (zao), but he specifies and qualifies it here:

Do we not have a right to eat and drink? (1st Corinthians 9:4)
Who, at any time, serves as a soldier at his own expense? Who plants a vineyard and does not eat the fruit of it? Or who tends a flock and does not use the milk of the flock? (1st Corinthians 9:7)
Do you not know that those who perform sacred services eat the *food* of the temple, *and* those who attend regularly to the altar have their share from the altar? (1st Corinthians 9:13)

A soldier is sustained by their government. He or she doesn't (shouldn't) get rich off the war. The instructions and examples are always about provisions, not about excessiveness. For…

…If others share the right over you, do we not more? Nevertheless, <u>we did not use this right</u>, but we endure all things so that we will cause no hindrance to the gospel of Christ. (1st Corinthians 9:12)
I do not seek what is yours, but you. For children are not responsible to save up for *their* parents, but parents for *their* children. (2nd Corinthians 12:14b)

I cannot help but believe the notion of being a "hindrance to the gospel" rarely crosses the minds of far too many in positions of church leadership today.

For we are not as the rest, adulterating the word of God for financial gain, _but_ as out of integrity, _but_ as from God, we speak in the presence of God, in Christ. (2nd Corinthians 2:17, ALT)
…nor did we eat anyone's bread <u>without paying for it</u>, but with <u>labor and hardship we *kept* working</u> night and day so that we would <u>not be a burden</u> to any of you; not because we do not have the right *to this*, but in order to offer ourselves as a model for you, <u>so that you would follow our example</u>. (2nd Thessalonians 3:8 & 9)

To many, the idea of *hindrance, burden* and *compensation* being congruous terms is inconceivable. For those of you who claim this "right" for yourselves, you do realize that <u>not one</u> of the keynote personalities found in Scripture has recorded testimony that they lived solely off the coiffures of the Body. And, as Paul wrote in 1Th 4:11, people are to work with their hands (labor to earn); for if they don't, "They should not eat" (2nd Thessalonians 3:10).

Paul's <u>missionary</u> journeys were funded by a compilation of collected offerings, by various fellowships. But when he arrived, he earned his keep like anyone else. Upon the Messiah's return, Peter was found back at work fishing. I guess Yeshua forgot to explain to him all the benefits of discipleship. All-in-all, the only ones who showed any dependence on the storehouse were the apostles, and solely for ministry sake, and never for personal gain. Not one of the apostles would have considered preaching the gospel "work" to be "salaried". The <u>apostles</u> were *worthy* of double, not common lay pastors; which is really the only kind of pastor there was (should be).

Offerings

Offering is different from sacrifice, only in modern context and vernacular. From a scriptural perspective, everything given to YHVH, whether it was totally burned up, partly burned and partly consumed, or non-sacrificial property was an offering. There were mandated varieties, as well as voluntary (free will). So, like tithes, they can be obligatory. But again, what wasn't burnt up or poured out, was either brought into the storehouse for the same allocations, or eaten by the giver themself.

Offerings unto Adonai are demonstrated in Scripture as early as with Cain and Abel, and run right through the Apostolic Scriptures. Today, what we call 'offerings' are usually seen in Scripture as 'gifts' (Hebrew: *minchah*). Generally, these are 'bloodless' contributions; e.g., gold, silver, money, property, etc. Though we do not live in Israel, and have no ancient Levitical distribution center, our current responsibilities are still the same. Make sure that what we give is appropriated correctly, and not to a false, replacement priesthood.

Giving quality is often more important than quantity. This is easily understood when "offering" is recognized as a form of worship. We must care for the widow, poor and needy. Our ultimate goal is to be a living sacrifice; a poured out drink offering. This can't be done without offering out of your wellspring. If people are hungry, help them eat. Thirsty, give them drink. If they are sick, visit them. Get them medical help, if possible, and pray for them; for this is true religion. This goes for us as individuals, not the corporate church alone.

As much as certain people would like for you to think that a church building is the replacement for the Temple, it is hardly the case. Neither is the pastoral ministry the modern equivalent of the Levites. The place we gather and worship is a choice. What we do when we gather is a choice. Church is not the place He has placed His Name; it's the place *we* have placed His Name. If anything is the temple, we are... right? And if we are the temple, then we are the storehouse...right? Well, you can see where this would lead. We'd get to keep it all! I do believe we have the capacity to meet needs. That is our moral imperative. That is our free-will obligation. Through what ministry is to be decided by you. "Just eagerly remember the poor."

Out of Your Increase

There is not one example of anyone tithing on *earned* 'wages' anywhere in Scripture. But it takes a lot of money to build a Vatican.

What you earn is not necessarily increase. What you earn may create the opportunity for it though. Income tax, as we pay it, is actually more synonymous with the historical paying of tribute to the king. Sometimes the king would be benevolent; sometimes not. Sometimes the taxes were easy; sometimes they were a terrible burden. The demand for benevolence would fluctuate accordingly. It still does. If you are a poor citizen, and you are barely making it, I sincerely hope that changes.

Until it does though, it is my belief that you are not *obligated* to give anything more than your token of appreciation to the speaker at the church you attend. My belief is based on the fact that Scripture is full of references to the tithes being *for* the poor. If your teachers give you grief, or make you feel guilty, they are in error. Just because they chose to burden YHVH's kingdom with a large building/salary debt, doesn't obligate you to take that debt on. Some other attendee can cover for you, I'm sure.

If, however, you have been blessed by Him, and have had an increase in your prosperity, above what is required to meet the needs of your family, then you should consider wisely what to do with it. In accordance with Scripture, all money brought into the storehouse today is a Free Will offering. If you choose to continue calculating your charitable donations via the full ten percent formula, that is fine. As long as you understand that it is not your legal obligation, and that you are ultimately giving more than what has been asked of you. Let me demonstrate for you some modern tithe (tenth) or Free Will offering calculation scenarios, that you may want to consider framing your personal offering program around.

Example: You buy a home for one hundred thousand dollars. Five years later, you sell it for two hundred thousand dollars. Nice investment, eh? Some would tell you, you should give ten thousand dollars to your church. Some will say twenty. But did you really increase one hundred thousand dollars? How much did you have to spend to fix up and maintain that house over those five years? How much money did you spend on insurance for it? How much water did it take to keep your grass alive? How much did it cost you to buy and maintain the mortgage/s on it? How much did it cost you to sell it? What if you sold it because you had to move, and it was going to cost you $200,000 to buy a similar home? These are perfectly fair questions to ask when you're trying to figure your increase. You may have only gained around fifty thousand dollars.

Let's say you fully planned to spend that money on leisure and toys. I would completely support your decision to offer five thousand dollars first. What if though, just after the sale, you got injured so that you could not produce an income anymore? What if you spent all that money just surviving? You might have then had no increase. Or, what if right after the sale, your new investment property got its roof blown off? Your increase that year just quickly reduced. Had you tithed immediately upon income's arrival, you would not have known of your future need, and you would have then tithed excessively. I think there is a better way to translate this giving principle into this modern, economic stage.

Prayerfully, each family must determine their individual threshold of prosperity. What amount does it cost you to live a reasonable life? Perhaps you could use the average household income of a four-person family in your state or region, or maybe the poverty line? ($18,850 for a family of four.[2]) This is a highly subjective calculation, but it will be more accurate if you remove all the purely recreational expenses like: the sports package part of your Cable, non-business cell phones, toys, vacations, etc. You should also make sure you have a reasonable emergency fund, as well as contributions going into long-term retirement planning. Take that figure, which should be re-evaluated as necessary, and use it as your ceiling. If your income at the end of the year is in excess of that ceiling, calculate the difference. That is your increase. That is what would be "tithed" on.

That set-apart money can head into different directions, and this is where your giving strategy kicks in. Some money should be set aside to be spent on fulfilling the Mo'adim. (This may require a few years to assess.) Some could be set aside, possibly in an interest-bearing account, to be dedicated to benevolence and fellowship support. Then, at certain times of the year, you could enjoy searching out needs and meeting them locally; or you can give it to other charitable organizations to do it for you. Perhaps you trust the benevolence department of your fellowship.

You could also do your calculating "first-fruits" a different way. Whenever you purchase anything for your home or yourself, throughout the year that qualifies as a non-essential item, you could calculate ten percent of the value and give that amount away. Buying a 60" 4K flat screen to replace your three hundred dollar, thirty-two inch TV is not a

Pandora's Box

necessity. That plasma cannot be justifiably deducted from your increase, as being an expense within your *reasonable* life expenses. So to avoid taking the chance you convince yourself otherwise, if the TV costs you three thousand dollars, but a replacement could have cost you three hundred dollars, you should calculate the twenty-seven hundred dollar difference, reckon the two hundred and seventy dollar offering, and either give it away immediately, or put it away to be distributed later. A TV may not be the best example, as we could debate its necessity, but you get the point. Even if you earned it, Adonai provided it. It was definitely an increase, and you would *offer* on that. Plus, this kind of program will temper your spending, and keep you continually observant of your buying habits.

Every new thing that comes into your life, that is not a necessity, you could do this with. In theory, you could spend all your "income" throughout the year, and end up with nothing extra at the end. This technique ensures you don't fail in your chosen obligation, and trick yourself on paper into thinking you had no increase. Going out to eat at a nice restaurant is a non-essential as well. Designer clothes versus common label, a thirty thousand dollar car vs. a ten thousand dollar car; may all be excesses. You know when you're gratifying your flesh. You have but to take note. If you don't want to do it this way, then you should keep good books on your expenses, and know you're going to have enough at the end of the year, to meet your pledge.

As far as reinvesting your increase goes, this is a little different consideration. Let's go back to the agrarian context of the tithe. You are a rancher. You own one hundred head of cattle. You had a poor year in regards to natural reproduction, so you conceive of a plan to sell three adults to raise the money to buy six calves. At the end of the year, you have one hundred and three head, but did you have an increase? Let's say you have one hundred head, and you do have a good, reproductive year— ten calves are born to you. You want some more adults, so you trade six calves to another rancher for two bulls. You have had an increase…congratulations. But six months later, one of them dies. Sad, but it happens. At the end of the year, do you tithe on the basis of gaining four calves plus one bull; or, four calves plus two bulls?

Similarly, if you were to take the remaining capital increases you gained throughout the year and reinvested them, you should have a year to see if they were really a gainer or not. The arrangement for the tithe coming in as depicted in Scripture is an annual one; therefore, should you decide to tithe on your mutual fund type investments, that should be annually as well. Examine your portfolio at the end of your selected fiscal year; see how it grew, and tithe on the increase. Investments that are "high risk" or speculative, should be made with money that is excess and already tithed against, if possible. To take money that you've committed to His kingdom and throw it into a penny stock is not the right thing to do. Yes, it is possible that you could hit it big, and accomplish more for Him in the long run. But it is more possible you'll lose it all; which constitutes a loss in both kingdoms.

You have to see that the First Fruits offering is a completely separate concept from the "one out of each ten animals" instruction. They are taught as though they are combined together, by those who gain from the teaching, but not by those who subject themselves to the Scripture accurately. The First Fruits offering is pretty hard to convert out of its agrarian context. When you are creating your budget plan, it should be 'His' first. But that's not really the same thing. From a literal interpretation, I don't know there is a clear way to do this not being a farmer. You will just have to pray about it.

The reason why tithes were brought in once or twice a year is because you cannot really calculate your increase on a week-by-week basis. Perhaps you don't trust yourself to be responsible enough to wait that long without spending it. You could try quarterly, or set up a separate bank account. Those of you who live paycheck to paycheck, for reasons beyond your control, are already having a difficult time. How much more difficult are you making it on yourselves, when you're giving above the necessary amount to welfare, and if your own house isn't even financially in order? If you gain, then the kingdom gains. If you lose, someone else will make up for it. If I'm wrong about this teaching, then each week everyone should have their houses re-appraised, and tithe on the increased value each and every time. And if it goes backward, then what? Can you imagine how hard it would be to budget pastoral salaries, if people gave their offerings only a few times a year? They would really have to budget smart then, wouldn't they? Perhaps that is just further evidence that we are not working within a modern parallel.

If you do 'offer' faithfully, you will inevitably be making more contributions to the welfare of humanity, which of course is great. At least you have some control as to where it's going. It really is up to you to figure out how much should go to sustain your ekklesia (local storehouse) and its leaders. Your future matters to Abba. That is why He instituted a well-conceived plan to sustain everyone. We rejected His original plan, so now we are stuck in a secular and oppressive economy. Either way, if you work...you eat. If you literally *can't* work, people should help. If you just don't want to work, then you should go hungry. If you're poor (as opposed to being short of money), because your continuing lifestyle choices cause you to be that way, your giving into the Kingdom is as pointless as hiring a CPA. He owns the cattle on a thousand hills. If you're poor due to circumstances outside your control, deal with your troubles and give as you can. I can almost guarantee the famous widow's mite was not a tithe. If everyone in His kingdom followed the scriptural system, people would truly not be forsaken, or out there begging for bread. People begging for bread, have not had an increase.

Merchants of the gospel will often sell you some ear-tickling teachings on sowing and reaping. You'll hear teachings that will cause those with the least among us, to hand over their last mite; in hopes that it will somehow cause a miraculous check to show up, just in time to rescue them from foreclosure. Ever heard the one about your money multiplying by a hundred-fold? Have you ever looked at that passage (Matthew 13:8)? It has nothing to do with money! You'll hear how you should bring in your money every week, because Paul said so. Oh really?

On the first day of every week, each one of you is to <u>put aside and save, as he may prosper</u>, so that no collections be made when I come. (1st Corinthians 16:2)

Actually, he is telling them to put money aside every week, so to accumulate a gracious gift that he will pick up later, so that he doesn't have to walk around pleading; and potentially have the Body be shamed by a small gift. And what also should be noted is that this is not a tithe-related instruction. Again, it was for charity. It is an offering given "as he may prosper." He also was suggesting they do it on the first day of the week. Not because that was their day of worship (as is often supposed to be 'Sunday' Sabbath evidence), but because Paul knew financial matters were not dealt with on Shabbat. (The "every week" suggestion was simply because that's the easiest way to accumulate most effectively. The "first day" is when they would have the most money on hand; having whatever was earned during the previous week, and not having spent any on Shabbat.) Paul was not telling them to create a weekly, ministry expense depository.

You'll likewise hear teaching as wicked as that your special gift offering brought into *their* storehouse, may be the key to the healing you're praying for. They wish! (That is, of course, unless you hear the Spirit, not the TV, tell you otherwise.) Although I do believe a stingy life will have its consequences, and selfishness cannot possibly be good, such teachings are erroneous and evil, and should be exposed and corrected by the leaders who know better. If you are not normally a giving person, one gift does not make a giver, or buy favors from Abba. A mustard seed produces a mustard tree, not a money tree.

It really is interesting to consider that there was no official organization which came to your house, business, or farm and calculated your increase for you. There was no IIS (Internal Increase Service). It has always been up to the individual to assess that. The scriptural program is a voluntary honor system. The point was that giving should be done with thanksgiving and gladness. This can clearly be seen in one of the most wonderful commandments of Torah. Regarding the Feast of Tabernacles:

> ...and <u>you shall rejoice in your feast</u>, you and your son and your daughter and your male and female servants and the Levite and the stranger and the orphan and the widow who are in your towns. Seven days <u>you shall celebrate a feast</u> to the LORD your God in the place which the LORD chooses, because the LORD your God will bless you in all your produce and in all the work of your hands, <u>so that you will be altogether joyful.</u> (Deuteronomy 16:14)

> Every man shall give <u>as he is able</u>, according to the blessing of the LORD your God which he has given you. (Deuteronomy 16:17)

Again, this is subjective and undefinable. How great is that—being commanded to rejoice at a celebration of Yah's goodness and provision? It's so unfair; those burdensome olde laws. "As he is able" is the instruction for the ancients, the apostolic participants, and for us. This is the heart of all the teachings referring to giving. The above Feast of Tabernacles is one of the three pilgrimage feasts, during which Israel is to bring in their tithes and offerings.

If He had to force you to do it, then He would be forcing you as well to obey the Royal Commandments, which is not the point. No one was arrested for not bringing his or her tithe in. One might be challenged and corrected by those who discern the sin, if it was very obvious they were robbing from the storehouse. If it was kept up after a rebuke, and a formal council's corrective words, they'd likely get disfellowshipped. There is not even a prescribed punishment or sacrifice for disobedience in this area. Adonai had His way to set the record straight. It would eventually be exposed somehow; perhaps in a time of need. I'm sure this is still the case.

I find it a bit curious as well, that current church doctrine predominantly rejects the notion that we are under any kind of legal system, and yet they have chosen to hold on to the tithe, as something that transcends any covenant. Churches commonly teach the tithe as if it's a current law. They even attribute financial punishment to disobedience. If they are going to teach that this law is still in effect, they have many other laws to reconsider as well. If in order to avoid the inherent problems associated with calling the tithe "a law," by preferring to consider it a Abrahamic "principle," then they never again should preach the "Robbing God" message, or any guilt-laying message for that matter, for what Abraham brought was a customary gift! Sacrifices occurred before the law came as well, and I don't see them being done...yet!

You preachers, who play on the emotions of the weak, will one day have some serious explaining to do. If Yeshua came in the flesh to do an audit of your ministries, there would be some very uncomfortable board room meetings. Why is it that the farther we go back in time, including the days of Yeshua, despising of mammon, rejection of wealth, and voluntary poverty were the virtues of the day; but when we reverse time, we see the glorification of exactly the opposite? Today, it's taught that prosperity is the evidence of "being blessed" by the Lord. I hope that stirs some of you.

I really don't want to sound like I'm out to stick it to Adonai, by short-changing Him, because I'm definitely not. I'm well aware of Malachi's message about robbing YHVH. But I believe one of the reasons we have such a hard time providing for our own, is because we often over-plant into the wrong soil. I'm sure you've heard it said, "You can't out-give God!" That may be true, because He owns everything; but if you keep over-giving away what He's allocated to you (for you), then what? The only way He can force you not to sow into the wrong soil is to take your seed away. You're not likely to win the lottery, and He doesn't actually print currency. So why are many giving what they don't even have, to a person who doesn't need it, to do a job he's/she's not doing according to scriptural standards? If I had to venture guesses, I'd say wrong teaching, a guilty conscience, and false hopes.

Today, many very generous but poor farmers give away a lot more than He ever asked them to; expecting that maybe, somehow, one day they will walk out on their land and see a silo fall from Heaven...full of grain. For most, this just doesn't happen. Are they storing up extra treasures in Heaven? Perhaps, and that may be a consolation. Many of our elderly have sowed abundantly into charlatan ministries, all their lives, expecting their "seed" gift of a thousand dollars to someday return back a million. But now they're trying to figure out how to stretch their social-security checks out enough, to heat their homes in the wintertime. Sure, their kids should help; but what if they can't get a leg up either. Parents can barely, and rarely, leave an inheritance to their children. Who today is leaving one for their children's children? We are over-taxed, over-worked (some anyway), and over-drained by our churches, and until ministers start to bring freedom to *their* captives, that's the way it's going to remain.

Before I make my last comments, I want to interject that I acknowledge that we don't live in a perfect society, nor do we live under a theocratic government. If we did, and were true to Scripture, terrible waste and mismanagement of funds would not be draining people of their inheritances and livelihoods. We as children of Adonai have a responsibility to care for our own, regardless of what the world is doing with their own. That burdens us greatly, even to a place of seeming unfairness and serious personal sacrifice. There may not be a perfect way to deal with this topic, because unregenerate humanity always prefers the imperfect. My goal here is to expose things and maybe offer solutions; but if we don't all do our part it won't work correctly, no matter what system we use.

In Scripture's theocratic economy, there was no income tax. There was no FICA, or Family Planning Centers (abortionists killing off future contributors), no HUD, no political correctness, no AARP, no pension plans, no forty percent lawyer's fees, no 501c3's, no Dept. of Health and Human Services, no lobbyists, no WIC or Medicare, no ACLU or Affirmative Action, or over-paid, wanna-be Levites…and on and on. When it really comes down to it, just about nothing is the same except the nature of man.

There is one potential outcome from this teaching I want to shout from the rooftops. I believe there are many families out there whose philosophy and desire it is, to keep their mommies home. Except they can't, because no matter how fiscally responsible they are, they aren't able to make end's meat, on one income. If adding a five or six percent increase to your household income, by giving that much less to "the storehouse" will make the difference, and allow you mommies to stay home, then that's what you should do! Also, what you pay in taxes should not be considered "increase", so that should alleviate some of your stress as well. The cost of living may not be working in our favor, as conservative followers of The Way. Still, we may be able to overcome after all. And really, any tax-deductible value you think you are obtaining through your traditional tithe is near meaningless, unless you're doing exceptionally well for yourself anyway.

Overall, don't be stingy. Give liberally when you see needs you can help, and take care of yourself and your family first. Do not receive condemnation from any spiritual leader, in regards to an inability to give a full ten percent (unless you are a farmer in Israel). If you can only give five faithfully, and that seems good to you and the Spirit, so be it. Give with a glad hard, or don't even bother.

Giving to evangelism is nice, but it doesn't negate or cover your personal, evangelistic responsibility. Blessing your teachers and pastors is nice, but if they are robbing YHVH's storehouse, you may be an accomplice to that crime. Giving to the poor is nice, good, and necessary; but loving them into becoming a contributing member of society (when possible) and of the Kingdom, is much nicer. My hope for you is that you will always sow into only the most fertile soil; and for it, reap great harvests.

I offered those *giving* strategies for those who want a way to give with some degree of scriptural foundation. The full-spectrum of tithing is

Pandora's Box

currently impossible to transpose over to a modern context. I don't declare those methods to be a perfect alternative. The other reason I created them was because I also know that no matter how much scriptural evidence or historical record I lay out, there would be those who just cannot handle the idea that tithing is not the law they've always understood it to be. Maybe they will be useful for you; maybe not. They are a compromise. Just remember, it is possible to tithe on your cumin and your mint perfectly, but gain not a single dividend in Heaven's treasury. Who taught us that?

So what do I believe? Since you know I uphold Torah, I believe in both the laws and the principle. Like sacrifices though, tithing cannot be properly accomplished in our current, diasporal condition. So we must revert to principle. It would appear that the standards we must abide in are generosity and charitableness, with a demonstration of acknowledgment from where our provision comes, by giving Adonai some of your first fruits. Some amount definitely belongs to Him. Getting it into His hands is the tricky part.

That said…I fully support your full support, of your local fellowship. With your money, do with it as the Spirit leads your heart. If you want to meet somewhere, besides in a living room, you'll have to pay for that. If you want to not use only candles, or holler from across the room, you'll need to have power turned on. That costs money. If your group leadership has a vision you support, and want to see accomplished, then help it along. There is absolutely no sin in donating to causes you believe in; unless they are misappropriating kingdom funds. Remember, your ignorance of impropriety does not absolve you from guilt. Please, don't turn a blind eye to such important things. Your responsibility to give does not end at your tearing the check from the book.

And it shall be with regard to an inheritance for them, *that* **I am their inheritance**; and you shall give them no possession in Israel—**I am their possession.** (Ezekiel 44:28)

Marriage, Divorce, and the Ministry

Here and there, a teaching or practice pops up inside churches that just gets my goad. Granted, by this time, you've concluded I see a lot of them. There are practices/teachings that are off track, but with well-meaning intentions. Some are based on genuinely difficult passages, which could legitimately have a couple alternative meanings. But then, there are practices/teachings that I just can't help but sit in awe at how horribly bad the interpretation is, that's used to support that practice. What really drives me over the edge though, is when it is supposedly scholarly and acclaimed leaders, within certain faiths, that embrace and propagate it. It seems clear to me that (though I know not why) what Scripture actually says is just not good enough for us. We, for some reason, insist on adjusting our interpretation, according to our modern way of thinking.

Errant teachings usually require creativity in reasoning to explain them. But when they are instituted for no other reason than power and control, it is gut-wrenchingly frustrating. I can only imagine how much it must grieve the One who wrote these Scriptures, to see the original intent be twisted and counterproductive to His kingdom. Here are two illustrative scenarios you need to consider, so we can deal with one of those teachings:

1.) Two people come together in holy matrimony, but don't know the Messiah. (Marriage without the Messiah is, at best, a shadow of its potential fullness; and at the least, destined for sorrow and pain.) When the groom doesn't know his role as spiritual leader, and the bride doesn't know her role as a spiritual help mate, what are the odds? Add to that the social and economic pressures of life, children, and the natural tensions inherent in two becoming one, and divorce becomes commonplace.

2.) Two people come together in holy matrimony; and again, they don't know the Messiah. One discovers Him, and regardless of that one's efforts, the other rejects Him. The redeemed partner refuses to divorce, but the other one desires otherwise. Their lives go radically in two different directions, and eventually become very unequally yoked. What does Paul say about this?

Yet if the unbelieving one leaves, let him leave; the brother or the sister is not under bondage in such *cases,* but God has called us to peace. (16) For how do you know, O wife, whether you will save your husband? Or how do you know,

O husband, whether you will save your wife? (17) Only, as the Lord has assigned to each one, as God has called each, in this manner let him walk. And so I direct in all the churches. (1st Corinthians 7:15-17)

Apparently, there are some out there that think Paul is wrong. If the church feels that someone in this position should be punished, or that his or her gifting and calling are revoked at the time of divorce, then the freedom to release the unbelieving spouse must be a mistake. Surely, one's capacity to serve the King is more important to preserve, than one's companionship needs…right? Well?

If I'm not mistaken, aren't we all made into new creations at our conversion? How does any man have the right to deem a new creation, an old remnant? How does anyone have the right to deem something YHVH declared clean, as unclean? It's amazing to me that some of these same leaders who enforce (or at least support) the disqualifying rule, themselves

Pandora's Box

have unruly children in their homes—which disqualifies them. Actually, it's the very same verse that disqualifies them, they use to support their doctrine.

Titus 1:6, "If any be blameless, the husband of one wife, having faithful children not accused of riot or unruly."

Forgive me, but where does it talk about a divorcee anywhere in this verse? This verse, and all other verses that speak of having "one wife," while actively engaged in ministry, are all clearly speaking in quantitative regard to their current marital status; not about their past. These verses are speaking of polygamy! It is obvious, to any reasonable thinker, that if someone has a history of multiple divorces, there is a problem that needs to be handled, before they take upon themselves a role of significant, spiritual leadership. They obviously need to be examined for unfaithfulness, irresponsibility, and such things. It's very likely that if they can't keep a family together, they can't keep a kingdom family together either. But anyone who thinks that a person who has gone through a divorce is automatically disqualified from leadership, solely because it is a negative occurrence in their past, better be prepared to quit themselves, tell everyone else to quit, and then put their stones down. I've about had it with teachers/preachers who fail to let their own yeas be yeas, and nays be nays, and yet can condemn others for being part of a broken promise—and I've never even been divorced!

Although the doctrine of the RCC has glorified celibacy, the Torah of YHVH does not. In relation to the regular Levitical priests, marriage was fully endorsed. There are however regulations, and I see no reason why they should not continue to be the model for our leadership today.

Leviticus 21:7, "They shall not take a woman who is profaned by harlotry, nor shall they take a woman divorced from her husband; for he is holy to his God." (This verse must be taken with the understanding that divorce was only allowed for unfaithfulness. According to Torah, if a woman was thought by her husband to have been unfaithful, and it proves out to be false, he is not allowed to divorce her (Numbers 5).

Leviticus 21:13, "He shall take a wife in her virginity." (The High Priest must only marry a virgin. No worries here. Nobody qualifies!)

Divorce is always horrible. The tearing apart of two who have become one is always painful and destructive. It is not a practice meant to be abused. But sometimes people reject spiritual truth. No one can force another to accept Adonai. To suggest that because one spouse rejects Him, the other should pay a very high price is nonsense. As Sha'ul's teachings would suggest though, if one does choose to leave for this reason, the spiritual partner should avoid divorce if at all possible. In Messiah's eyes, you have become unified (echad) and that current partner is the only one you are qualified to be married to (assuming certain circumstances). You are not allowed to seek divorce yourself and then go off and get remarried. If you do, you will be an adulterer; as will the person you marry. I do believe that as an active adulterer, one becomes disqualified to lead a fellowship.

It is always possible that, even if it be many years later, the lost partner may remain unwed and eventually find our Messiah. As tough as it may be, you need to remain faithful to them in prayer and hope, and also be available to receive them back if such happens. But as soon as that person goes off and becomes remarried, or lies with another, they become disqualified to remarry, even if that marriage fails; for now they have become an adulterer (Deuteronomy 24; Matthew 19). You are then released.

If you are divorced, and your ex-spouse has not yet remarried, it is my conviction that until that happens you should remain hopeful of reconciliation. This is not a commandment of the Lord, but an expression of faith in the best possible scenario. Divorce is the result of sinfulness, it is not the cause. Divorce was granted by Moshe because of our sinful condition; because we are imperfect. Divorce, therefore, must exist.

It wasn't divorce that carried the death penalty, it was infidelity. The reason it carried that was due to another spiritual principle found within the physical. The people of YHVH are expected to represent Him, and covenant breaking is not His character! Marriage is a spiritual institution, bestowed upon us for far more than procreation. Marriage and covenants are issues dear to His heart. This also did not change at the cross. If you are currently being unfaithful, and you deem yourself a believer, you are wearing the mark of an adulterer. Your soul and spirit are dying. If you do not get that washed away, you will bear the consequences (1st Corinthians 6:9). Repent, turn from your wickedness—and live.

If you are the victim of ministerial rejection due to divorce (regardless of the circumstances), I apologize on behalf of the abusive and power hungry, mis-interpreters who will not. If you believe you are eligible and anointed for duty, pray that Adonai would allow you to start your own fellowship, or just serve Him as He leads. If successful, and it bear fruit, who is anyone to argue with you? If you should not accomplish it, it will be due to the state of your spirit, not your marriage. For that, He would fail it for anyone. If He does, let it go. Go find your healing, and then try again.

Pandora's Box

"Gotten Saved"

> For I am not ashamed of the gospel, for it is the power of God for <u>salvation</u> to everyone who believes, to the Jew first and also to the Greek. (Romans 1:16)

Let's take a little detour. Adonai has given us clear instructions about what not to eat, but we eat whatever and however we want, without consideration. He has also given us instructions as to how to live, but we choose to ignore many of them our whole life. We choose to create our own plan for sustenance, as well as our own plan for salvation. Let me expound on this concept.

Contrary to popular religious belief, we do not "get saved" as though it's some kind of one-time event. From a technical and theological standpoint, salvation is an ongoing work throughout our lives, and is not finalized until we, and creation, are fully restored. Otherwise, how could you, "work it out with fear and trembling"? Our redemption has been paid for in advance. We accept it and become *justified* by faith. We prove it through our good works, which are a natural by-product of living according to His instructions, which *sanctify* us. Our *salvation* occurs throughout our present lives and culminates in *glorification*, when our bodies are made immortal. It is true, from an eternal perspective, that we "are saved". But for the sake of practical application, it is an incomplete thought. The phrase "he or she *got saved* last night" is theologically incorrect, and in some ways, its misuse has done a bit of disservice in the already confusing, doctrinal area of "eternal security".

Most references to salvation found in the Apostolic Scriptures, express the ongoing work of salvation, through these conjugations:

2nd Corinthians 2:15, "for we are a sweet fragrance of Christ to God among the ones <u>being saved</u> and among the ones perishing."

Romans 5:9, "Much more then, being now justified by his blood, we <u>shall be saved</u> from wrath through him."

1st Corinthians 1:18, "For the word of the cross indeed is foolishness to the ones perishing, but to us, the ones <u>being saved</u>, it is *[the]* power of God!"

We are continually *being* saved. This leads us to another, obvious area of concern. How does this affect the issue of forgiveness? Although His blood had to be shed only once, it is constantly being applied on our behalf. Transgressions that are "under the blood" are removed from us as far as the east is from the west (Psalm 103:12). Here is the critical aspect: His blood is powerful to cleanse, from eternity past to eternity future. It will never be necessary for Him to die again. However, a forgiven sin of one's past does not necessitate automatic forgiveness of all similar future sins. It is critical that a sinner acknowledge their continual need for absolution from the Father. Forgiveness is always available, but requires an understanding of need, as well as a sense of contrition. It is my belief that a person who willfully sins because they presume the blood is being constantly applied is sadly mistaken.

Repentance is an indispensable part of forgiveness. By definition, repentance requires the cessation of willful sin. Also, if a "believer" ceases to believe (apply their faith), of what matter is the forgiveness of their past? Their present and future are not resolved. I am fully aware of alternate doctrinal viewpoints, but I adhere to Scripture's. If you accept the authority of Scripture, then you must accept all that it says.

For in the case of those who have once been enlightened and have tasted of the heavenly gift and have been made partakers of the Holy Spirit, and have tasted the good word of God and the powers of the age to come, and *then* have fallen away, it is impossible to renew them again to repentance, since they again crucify to themselves the Son of God and put Him to open shame. (Hebrews 6:4-6)

Abba has given us a plan for salvation, which is laid out all through the Scriptures. Get wisdom, seek council, live uprightly, be obedient, etc. Commandments that keep us out of trouble *save* us from life's perils. He has given us instruction in His Word designed to protect us. He has given us the means to salvation from the very beginning of time. If we choose to follow His instruction, i.e., "believe on Me," we surely are/will be saved.

Faith

I am going to make this as short and sweet as possible. There are three prominent verse texts most anyone who's been "in the faith" for any length of time should be familiar with. I feel no need to go beyond them in order to support the truth.

The first is: "Faith is the <u>assurance</u> (evidence) of things hoped for, the conviction (firm belief) of things not seen (Hebrews 11:1)." This verse is telling us something far different than what most teach. Because faith is a verb in both Hebrew and Greek, it must be acted out. That concept is lost when translating it to English. It should come as no surprise then, that it is a concept lost in the church as well. Faith is a result! It is not just the means! It is not a wish! Faith is not magical. It is not a force encapsulated within special word combinations (otherwise known as incantations). It groans when it is connected to vain repetitions.

Hebrews ch.11 is known as the "Hall of Faith". Read it, and contemplate the actions and attitudes of the characters mentioned; then you will know what scriptural faith is. Faith believes in the believable, because Yah is in charge. It doesn't pretend things are not as they seem. It doesn't deny reality. It is not frivolously wasted on lottery tickets. It does not get you a raise when you are an underachiever. Faith doesn't make you healthy, when your diet is void of nutrition, and your exercise routine consists of twelve ounce curls and getting off the couch. Faith does not believe that planting a c-note seed, in an offering plate, will somehow grow into a million dollar tree. If it does, it is attempting to harvest by mental witchcraft. Faith is inexpressible without practical expression.

When I go to flip a light switch on a wall, I *expect* the light to come on, even though I can't currently see it. Not only because I've seen it happen before, but because I have a basic understanding of electricity. But that's weak faith. When I arise before the sun, I expect to see it climb the horizon. Not so much because I've seen it before, but because "the fixed order will not depart," in order to prove that Israel will never cease to be a nation. That's a deeper faith. Standing up in the face of two thousand years of lies; believing Yah's word is still true today; teaching others to turn from their sin (to cover a multitude of my own); and knowing in the end, I will be considered an approved workman and good servant for it, requires real faith. Everything else is just nonsense.

Let me take this opportunity to unequivocally state, and repeat, that justification <u>is now,</u> and <u>has always been,</u> found through faith alone. The attempt to obtain justification through any other method is the truest form of legalism and heresy. Which leads me to the second verse: "Faith comes by hearing, and hearing by the word of Elohiym (Romans 10:17)."

Whether the word be written on pages and read, whispered in a still, small voice, or delivered via the foolishness of preaching, it is the word of the Lord that creates faith. Hearing, like faith-ing, in the Hebrew has an added dimension of meaning beyond the English. "If you have an ear to hear..." is the idiomatic phrase that Yeshua used to express this very concept. Hearing alone, without understanding and its consequential action, isn't really hearing at all. "Faith without works" is the same thing as "hearing without doing accordingly". If you "believe" without "evidence," you are no different from the demons that do likewise. Faith—is packing up your family and heading out to a country not yet disclosed. Avraham's *work* was accounted as righteousness.

Faith is doing, *because* you trust Him. As for Avraham, he leads me to my third text:

>...yet, with respect to the promise of God, he did not waver in unbelief but grew strong in faith, giving glory to God, and being fully assured that what God had promised, He was able also to perform. Therefore, IT WAS ALSO CREDITED TO HIM AS RIGHTEOUSNESS. (Romans 4:20-22)

It doesn't get much clearer than that. If you think you can be a victorious Christian by being a "believer" alone, and not an "understander," you are heading for a very difficult journey. For you to be able to "do faith," you must understand: the origins of, the prescribed method for the expression of, what the gospel of it is, and how those things affect, the faith you hold. These things are discovered in His Word. And thus begins, and ends, the circular topic at hand.

The Triune Deity

And you thought I was going to sneak out of this one. I just couldn't, even though I'd like to. After all, I teased you all the way back at the beginning. As hard as it may be to believe at this point, I am not a glutton for punishment. However, this topic can get somebody hurt. Surely, many won't agree with me. My belief is really not that complex to establish, and if you are good at reading between the lines, you likely already know from where I come.

The very first layer of my foundation is: "YHVH is One! (Deuteronomy 6:4)." Everything must agree with this statement, or it is faulty. The word 'One' in this verse is 'echad', which actually more expresses the idea of 'unified', as opposed to a definitive singularity. Technically speaking, the elohiym of the Scriptures generally represents Himself/Themselves in the plural. Elohiym and Adonai are both masculine gender plural nouns. However, there is no 'three Gods with one will and purpose' option. That is why I have a problem with the classic creed line, "God in three persons." You cannot have three persons, without three personalities. If you have one person and split them into three parts, you do not have three whole parts; you have three-thirds.

The same has to be applied to the attributes of YHVH, as we understand them. The Father of the Tanakh cannot be a ruthless dictator; while the "new" Elohiym, in the form of Yeshua, is a different character. The Father does not want to kill everyone through the Law, but the Son holds Him back with a, "Now Daddy... be nice!" waving finger of grace. If He is omnipotent, there can be no limitation to His power, even at any given time. If He is omniscient, He can never be lacking in knowledge. The same applies to His presence. If the "three parts" of Him are not equal in power and knowledge and position, then they do not each in themselves accurately reflect the God-Head. That would make The Spirit, and the Messiah, as we have seen them, less-thans. That could not be, for...

...in Him, all the fullness of Deity dwells in bodily form, and in Him you have been made complete, and He is the head over all rule and authority.

(Colossians 2:9 & 10)

and...In the beginning was the Word, and the Word was with God, and the Word was God. (John 1:1)

and...All things came into being through Him, and apart from Him nothing came into being that has come into being. (John 1:3)

and...The Word became flesh, and dwelt among us, and we saw His glory, glory as of the only begotten from the Father, full of grace and truth. (John 1:14)

and to...whom He appointed heir of all things, through whom also He made the world. And He is the radiance of His glory and the exact representation of His nature, and upholds all things by the word of His power. (Hebrews 1:2b&3a)

I cannot comprehend how people can read these verses and conclude that Yeshua is *just* a wise prophet, or super angel. "Who else has been told to go sit at the right hand of the Father (the Hebrew idiom for sharing authority)? There are a multitude of verses that can be shown to express that Yeshua and YHVH are 'echad', but one of the most powerful verses is found following a well-recognized prophecy about the Messiah. Everyone knows this one:

Behold, *the* days are coming, declares the LORD, when I will raise up for David a righteous Branch. And He will reign as king and act wisely, and do justice and righteousness in the land. (Jeremiah 23:5)

What you may gloss over is in the next, also *future looking* verse which speaks of the coming Messiah:

In His days, Judah will be saved and Israel will dwell securely; and this is His name by which He will be called, 'The LORD (YHVH) our righteousness.' (Jeremiah 23:6)

Apparently, Yeshua will one day be called YHVH. Won't that just throw some people for a loop? Something else that is rarely considered, if at all mentioned, is the fact that Yeshua was not always the Son.

I will surely tell of the decree of the LORD: He said to Me, 'You are My Son, Today I have begotten You. (Psalm 2:7).' I also will make him *my* first-born, the highest of the kings of the earth. (Psalm 89:27)

And yet, as the author of Hebrews states, He is the same yesterday, today, and forever. He became the Son, for an expression of familiarity to humanity. This also means that before all things were made, and there was only 'I Am', YHVH was not "The Father." He became the Father, for an earthly expression which we can grasp. These titles, or presentations, are simply for us to have some means of relating to Him. They correspond to events and positions which we ourselves experience within our dimension.

...and when they were come over against Mysia, they assayed to go into Bithynia; and the <u>Spirit of Jesus</u> suffered them not. (Acts 16:7)

Because you are sons, God has sent forth the <u>Spirit of His Son</u> into our hearts, crying, 'Abba! Father!' (Galatians 4:6)

So then, the question is whether these are possessive statements, or defining ones? I submit to you that they are defining. And what about these verses:

John, to the seven churches that are in Asia: Grace to you and peace, from Him who is and who was and who is to come, and from the seven Spirits who are before His throne. (Revelation 1:4)

To the angel of the church in Sardis write: He who has the seven Spirits of God... (Revelation 3:1)

And *there were* seven lamps of fire burning before the throne, which are the <u>seven Spirits of God</u>. (Revelation 4:5b)

Are these seven Spirits a defining expression as well? Actually, they are. Don't get tripped up by the translator's choice to capitalize. There are not another seven parts to YHVH, making Him into an Ennead. A likely solution is found in Isaiah 11:2:

"The Spirit of (1)the LORD will rest on Him, The spirit of (2)wisdom and (3)understanding, The spirit of (4)counsel and (5)strength, The spirit of (6)knowledge and the (7)fear of the LORD."

Isaiah was prophesying about the attributes of the Messiah. John was confirming them, and Yeshua was identifying Himself with the One of whom Isaiah spoke.

In my opening statements, I described a few differing viewpoints on the Trinity, so I'll not repeat them here. Mine does fall more in line with the last of those in their order of appearance, but there is no way to exactly describe the ungraspable. There are people who build a lot of their theology, especially those within the Jewish community (to a fault I might add), on the premise that YHVH cannot enter our time and space in the form of man, being that He transcends them all. An example of that thinking being, that the "Angel of the LORD (YHVH)," who popped up at various times, must be an angel, and could not be Yeshua in some pre-incarnate "Word" manifestation. My question to those of you in the believing community, who subscribe to this concept, is: "How do you explain Yeshua at all?" Did all the fullness of the Deity dwell therein, but not really? To the contesting community I submit this:

Who has ascended into heaven and <u>descended</u>? Who has gathered the wind in His fists? Who has wrapped the waters in His garment? Who has established all the ends of the earth? What is His name or <u>His son's</u> name? Surely you know! (Proverbs 30:4)

I am fully persuaded that Yeshua, who is the "Son of Man" expression, through which YHVH interacted with humanity, is a composite of the very same essences that have always interacted with man. Those essences created all things. They/He walked in the garden with the first man. He sealed the door of the Ark. He came and had lunch with Abraham. He wrestled all night with Jacob. His finger etched the stone tablets. His voice came down from the mountain; and twice, since Yeshua is the "Prophet like unto YHVH." If He was capable of transfiguring and ascending, why is He unable to transfigure and descend? However, the man "Yeshua" is a specific embodiment of those essences, appearing at a specific place and time. Yeshua was a hybrid deity-man on Earth. And, in order to remain consistent as the El who never changes, we could say that those appearances of deity, prior to the incarnation, were also hybrid forms of deity/substance. Moshe clearly saw YHVH, if only in a form. Can something be seen that can't possibly have access to substance? Heck, we can barely comprehend the basic atom.

My question to those in the unbelieving, "YHVH can have no physical concepts apply to Him" Jewish community is, why do you believe the story about an innocent little brother, who was loved greatly by his father, and found rejected and desired, killed by his big brother, sold and thrown into a pit, wrongly accused and convicted by governing officials, given special spiritual gifts, elevated to the highest position in the land, ended up being the savior of a nation, gathered his family unto himself, had his father bow down to him (reversal of protocol), because of being brought up out of the pit, and yet reject Yeshua as unqualified? Whatever they both touched prospered! How do you explain Yoseph (Zaphenath-paneah) at all? Is he an allegory, or a type and shadow of the Messiah?

So what is the Spirit then? It is His presence without a vessel. It is in every way YHVH, but without flesh. It is the Spirit of Yeshua, as stated in the verse above. The Apostolic Scriptures say that Yeshua made the Earth (John 1:3), but Genesis 1:2 also says the Spirit of YHVH was the force by which the creation manifested. Genesis 1:1 says it was Elohiym that made the creation. So who made it? They all did! They are all One in the same.

Just as we have a spirit, soul, and space occupying existence, so can YHVH. That is partly how we are made in His image. His soul (as it were) is the Father. His inter-dimensional, physical manifestation was Yeshua (and other possibilities—not including human "prophets," by other names, of other religions). And His Spirit is just that…spirit. Well, kind of; at least in human similarity. And that's the problem. A human comparison is just not good enough.

Scripture says Yah is Spirit, but even spirit may have substance. In our universe, all forms of energy, at their most basic level, are composed of particles. Particles cannot be made of nothing. For that matter, nothing can be made (that can be made) from nothing. Frequencies and waves both require particles and sources, to become emissions. How does anyone explain the existence of anything at all, without Yah that is? Whether or not YHVH is composed of energies which exist in, or can be measured within the confines of the laws pertaining to this physical universe or not, is certainly unknown; but He is something.

Jewish theology ascribes omnipotence to the Lord, and it recognizes that an omnipresent Spirit is at work in the world (although they can't, nor dare explain it.) So they already (with guarded hesitation, of course) must acknowledge that He can be both in and out of our physical dimension, at the same time. Didn't He brood over the Earth at its creation? Didn't He walk in Eden? Why is it such a leap to believe He could take possession of a human oocyte, at the point of ovulation, install the missing DNA sequences (that He designed to begin with), and program His personality (Seven Spirits) into it (something that science recognizes to be partly genetic, partly cranial anyhow), and essentially create a human-based clone of His essence; which would function as an ambassador to the world, with a destiny of self-sacrifice? It would in all ways be YHVH, but have self-imposed, temporary, naturally occurring limitations in its internal power structure, but be able to call upon anything He needed. Like a satellite targeting for an ICBM, they are completely independent of each other, but totally dependent. (Matthew 26:53). Remember, He did only what the Father would have Him do! This explains why Yeshua did not know the day nor hour of this universe's demise. He divested Himself of omnipotence while in human form; but it is very possible He knows now.

I could take an inexhaustible lump of clay and shape it into whatever I wanted, for as long as I wanted, and into as many things as I wanted, and it would never cease being clay. He (all three primary, *revealed* and *recognized* parts) is One, and is the Creator. He can manifest Himself anyway He wants to, as long as it does not conflict with what He is. Yeshua *was* the only thing in the universe that could be less-than and equal-to something simultaneously. Yet, even though He *was* less-than in some aspects, He was also equal-to in others! To be any part 'fully deity' is to be all part deity. Anyway, what makes our Elohiym special is not His encasement in flesh; it is His character. Fortunately, in most cases, that's true for us also.

We as humans have a triune construct, but we don't define ourselves as such. I am one person, just as you are. I am not three. I also don't have the privilege of reducing a component of myself. My flesh is my present reality, and it is of the utmost value in this life. If I lose my flesh in this world, my next reality is completely out of my hands. That was not the case for Yeshua. His human flesh ceased to function, but He never skipped a beat, nor required intervention from an outside source for continued existence (John 10:18). His exact, higher reflection was never shaken. The Word never ceased to exist, nor will His words (Matthew 24:35). It seems to me that the unfortunate by-product of this so-called separation/distinction is most often a diminished reverence for Yeshua, with an added lack of personal interaction with the Father, and an over-infatuation with His Spirit's gifts. Didn't Yeshua come to point us to Abba? Didn't He teach us to pray to "Our Father"? Yet, many Christians hardly ever do.

For many, Jesus is their high-five, break room buddy-pal; but the Father is the hot-tempered, ego-maniacal, Penthouse Boss, you carefully avoid in the break room. To others, the Spirit is a mysterious entity that is far too busy to interact with all mankind simultaneously, and responds to incantation. See if this illustrates my point: There is an existing bumper sticker that actually says, "Jesus is my Homeboy!" In my mind, that seriously lacks respect, and borders on something worse. I bet you even those who would dare apply that to their cars, would feel uncomfortable putting one on that says, "Yahweh is my Homeboy." I believe Yeshua should in every way be treated with the same fear and awe, as the High Priest treated the Shechinah over the Ark. After all, the Shechinah is of Him. HE SITS AT THE RIGHT HAND!

On any given day, I am: a father, a husband, an employee, a landscaper, handy-man, cook, etc. Does that mean I am a six-part plus creature? How we manifest ourselves, does not fully represent our construct. In chapter seven, I listed a bunch of ways YHVH has manifested Himself. Is that a complete list? Our Yah is a consuming fire; (it seems to show up around Him quite often). Is that an attribute or emanation? I am not suggesting that I know for sure, but how much more don't we know? What will be our construct once we receive glorified bodies? Will we still be three parts, or finally one perfectly harmonious creation? How much more glorified is the Creator?

Is He bigger than the universe? If so, how big is He? If He is omnipresent, there is nowhere He is not. Wouldn't that mean that all His parts are as well? All YHVH has to do is think and something will come into existence. We exist because He desires us to exist. We are His desire. Selah. YHVH wills something; Yeshua declares it to be, and the Spirit manifests it. If we were missing one of our three divisions, we would be instantly and severely incapacitated. One might suggest we would cease to exist. That is not the case with our Elohiym. Even if the representation of Adonai, which came in the form of Yeshua never manifested, YHVH would not in any way have been diminished. I would conclude therefore, that whatever YHVH is, is inseparable whenever separated.

We have a huge handicap in understanding YHVH. Our biggest problem is not merely our intellectual capacity to understand. It is the fact that our experience with existence paints an erroneous picture, because our own members are at war within ourselves. We do not have internal unity amidst our own construct. The things we want to do; we do not do. The things we do; we do not want to do. This is not the case with Elohiym. We will fully know, as we are fully known, when we are no longer at war with ourselves.

I believe (suppose) the "interaction" we see between the triune components of Elohiym is purely for our benefit, for purposes of illustration. I believe when Yeshua prayed to the Father, He was equally praying at Himself. Do I believe he really suffered? Yes. I don't believe He needed faith though. I believe He demonstrated *our* need for it. I believe when the Father spoke from Heaven at Yeshua's baptism, it was the "Word" speaking from Heaven. And I believe when Yeshua was dying on the cross, and stating "His sorrow" over being "forsaken by His Father," it was more to reference David's prophetic psaltery in general, than an actual declaration of the state of His relationship to the Father.

There are many theologians who will disagree with me on this matter. You can get in line I suppose. I can completely understand. I fully acknowledge that Scripture portrays a hierarchy of authority within the God-head, but I do not think that necessarily denotes a quantum diminishment of quality. I also think that was temporal, during his temporary visit. I tend to lean in the direction of esteeming Yeshua more highly than many others do. I'll err on the side of caution in this regard. I hope we can still be friends.

If He no longer wanted creation to exist, He would simply *will* the release of the magnetic energy which hold the electrons in orbit, around the nucleus of the atom (the *will* which I believe is the glue that holds all things together), and the elements would melt like wax. That is the power of our Elohiym.

We may be made in His image, but He is not made in ours. He has portrayed three dominant 'expressions' to us, not 'persons'. That by no means establishes an all-encompassing understanding of His construct. Therefore, explaining Him is like trying to describe how a non-living organism (a virus) can replicate itself, to a two year old. We can't even explain our own triune construct, never-mind our subconscious section. We are a mixture of eternal and mortal. He is not! We don't know where our spirit is. We don't know exactly where our soul is. It is far beyond bio-physics to ascertain, and so is He!

I believe there to be, three <u>dominant</u> expressions of YHVH. This may very well be why Ya'akov finished his blessings over his sons like this:

...from the hands of the Mighty One of Jacob (From there is the Shepherd, the Stone of Israel), from the God of your father who helps you, and by the Almighty who blesses you... (Genesis 49:24 & 25)

Here we see the Shepherd (Yeshua), the One who Helps (Spirit, a.k.a. Helper) and the Almighty (Father). And these three expressions are demonstrated in their two great roles: Redeemer and Savior. There is only one Savior for Israel, and there is only one Redeemer for Israel. In the Hebrew Scriptures, He is known as YHVH; in the Apostolic, He is Yeshua. Yeshua is the "Arm of the LORD" and He has been revealed! Hallelu-Yah! In case there is any doubt remaining as to whether Yeshua and the Father are One, I submit to you this:

And Jesus answered and said to him, 'It is said, YOU SHALL NOT PUT THE LORD (YHVH) YOUR GOD TO THE TEST.' (Luke 4:12)

This was Yeshua's response to HaSatan's test in the desert. Yeshua, in no uncertain terms, told HaSatan to not test YHVH (Deuteronomy 6:16), while telling him not to test Himself. That my friends, is a slam-dunk! But clearly, if we think He's easily definable, we don't know Him very well, do we?

Ladies and Gentlemen!

I cannot tackle everything that needs change. Neither can you. I have logs in my eyes that still need removing. So do you. But that doesn't mean that what we can see, we are to ignore. There are teachings that need serious re-examination all over the place. We need a reformation of the Reformation. Yeshua told us that tradition would be the stronghold of strongholds. And as usual, He was astutely accurate.

It is time to throw the gloves off our soft, cucumber-kiwi lotion scented hands, and get a little calloused from knocking around the bag of our great-great-great-great grandfather's church's beliefs. Each generation is responsible for its decisions and actions. We are thankful for their struggles and labors. They did what they could with what they had, at the time they were in. Religion carried many of them through very tough times. We don't need to worry about their logs anymore. They have decomposed right along beside them. If they were wrong, for crying out loud, it's okay to come clean and admit it.

Now is not the time for throwing in the towel, it is the time to sound the shofar; the horn that calls us all back into the battle. We need shepherds who will call a wolf a wolf, and pull out their sling, instead of hiding behind a rock. We need apologists who have nothing to apologize for, when they tell us like it is. Please Adonai, send them now!

In every mitzvah of the Torah, there is a piece of the puzzle of who Messiah is. Within each Mo'adim, there is a prophetic picture of the plan of redemption, salvation, and our future hope. Whether it is food or sanitation, holy days, compensation or respect of life, He is found within it somewhere. We have a real conflict when we see Yeshua all through the Torah, and say we want to know Him, yet strive to cancel His pre-incarnate revelation as to how to be like Him. It is my firm belief that you will never know your Messiah as much as is available, until you also discover Him as He revealed Himself to us, from the very beginning, as the mysterious Aleph and the Tav (the Beginning and the End) found in the Hebrew text of Genesis 1:1 (and multiple thousands of places throughout.)

Pandora's Box

Sincerely Yours,

We have talked about so many things that are held dear by most, that when held up to the light of truth, their exterior melts away and what is left is sometimes quite ugly. As I wrestled with each subject, there were times of inspiration, and times I can only hope. I am sure that somewhere I'm wrong, mostly I'm right, and that in between is a bit of probably. One thing I put full confidence in, is Yehoshua's calling out for us to seek Him like a treasure, to wash our garments, and then to walk in His shoes.

If you are disappointed that this book was not as touchy-feely as you were hoping for, I told you this was a tough-love letter from the beginning. I'm sure my motivations will be judged for the lack of times I talked about warm and fuzzy things, like clothing the homeless. Actually, it was all throughout. You just might not have clearly recognized it, through the coke-bottle glasses your religious leaders have prescribed you. Plus, you've heard that message before, I'm sure. By now, I hope you see that love and grace were likewise all throughout the Mosaic Scriptures as well. They just have to be unveiled.

You cannot possibly Love Adonai without doing His will. You cannot do His will, until you know His will. Once you know His will, you cannot help but feed the hungry, clothe the homeless, and your life will proclaim His loving-kindness and mercy. Torah demands it! Feeding the hungry in itself is good, but it can just as easily qualify as hay, wood, and stubble as it can for silver, gold, and precious stones. What defines a work's value is its root-source and selflessness. I'm trying to get to your heart and affect it, so you will live a set-apart life and produce even more good works; those that are like diamonds; those the fire won't so easily consume.

So, it is now the time for me to tackle one last topic. One that is dear to my heart. You're probably asking yourself whether or not this book will ever end. Yes, it really is coming soon. But I must ask you, "Are you part of the Bride?" I'm pretty sure you think you are, and hopefully you're correct. What you might not be aware of, however, is what the Bride actually is. I know what most people think it is, and they're not quite right. Here is what the Scriptures say about who the Bride is:

The Bride of Messiah

For Zion's sake I will not hold my peace, and for Jerusalem's sake I will not rest, until her triumph goes forth as brightness, and her salvation as a torch that burneth. And the nations shall see thy triumph, and all kings thy glory; and thou shalt be called by a new name, which the mouth of the LORD shall mark out. Thou shalt also be a crown of beauty in the hand of the LORD, and a royal diadem in the open hand of thy God. Thou shalt no more be termed 'Forsaken', neither shall thy land anymore be termed 'Desolate'; but thou shalt be called "My delight is in her," and thy land, 'Espoused'; for the LORD delighteth in thee, and thy land shall be espoused. For as a young man espoutheth a virgin, so shall thy sons espouse thee; and as the bridegroom rejoiceth over the bride, so shall thy God rejoice over thee. (Isaiah 62:1-5, JPS)

And I saw the holy city, New Jerusalem, coming down out of heaven from God, made ready as a bride adorned for her husband. (Revelation 21:2)

So, there you go. We marry the Land, YHVH marries the New City, and therefore by proxy, we marry each other. The marriage consummation is seen in the full establishment of His eternal kingdom, and His total authority over all. And notice that this occurs after the new heaven and new earth are created. Just further evidence that "the church" doesn't get removed from the Earth, and married to the Lord, and celebrate the Wedding Supper of the Lamb, while Israel stays back and undergoes judgment with the rest of humanity. What a great example of a common misconception, and how everything is worth scrutinizing.

The questions I want you to become accustomed to asking yourself are: Can I afford to be wrong? What will it cost me if I am? Am I willing to believe and obey Him, even if it seems that I'm the only one? Imagine if Noah allowed the feelings of unpopularity and aloneness, to dictate his course of action. If I've done little else, I have at least done a decent job of showing how simple misconceptions can conceivably have quite serious consequences. Listen to His Spirit when He's prodding you.

From the very first step of my veering off the wide and well-beaten path, my decisions began to cost others emotionally. In my efforts to do right, I have done what I never wanted to do. I've hurt people's feelings. I've confused and concerned them as well. I've failed at times in my witness, and I'm sure I will again. The scrutiny is even more intense than I figured it would be. Yet I must continue walking down this obviously unpopular road, and it won't always be easy to find people who'll go along with me. It will be the same for you. But you can do it!

We have all been asked to be and make disciples. That's different from "getting saved" and witnessing. It's a lot simpler to do the latter. Making disciples is another story. You do have to know your stuff, or you could actually do harm. With discipleship, there is no quick fix, and you're ultimately attempting to duplicate yourself. One, you can get in and get out of; the other will cost you time, energy, and maybe even money. Get strong, get healthy, learn the Word and go make disciples.

How do you feel about duplicating yourself? Do you think you are an imperfect, but on-track, living example of a disciple of the Messiah? The reason many of us hesitate giving the affirmative response is because we don't even live out what we do believe, never-mind dealing with the issues we are not sure of. Why are we not hungry for the Truth? Why are church pews full of defeated, depressed, and impotent believers with little-to-no understanding of the book they schlep in with them every week? Because they only know half the story! The church has brought many in, and for that we can all be thankful. The problems then develop from there. All I can say is, it's sad; and it cannot remain in its handicapped condition.

His Beloved, He loves us. He really does! But we have to change before He comes. We have to get our oil lamps burning brightly, and be devouring the words of the bread that He has baked for us. Error is everywhere! You may not come to the same conclusions many of us are coming to, but at least you'll be digging deep for yourself. Scripture may not be subject to private interpretation, but just because a million people believe one thing, doesn't make it right. History has well proven that.

The winds of false doctrine never stop blowing. There is a great apostasy on the horizon. HaSatan is playing the same game with us he's always been. If he can't get people to jump off a cliff, he'll at least get them to walk the wrong path. People—not all roads lead to life! Most lead to destruction. Listen, I don't know everything, but I do know that there is a still, whispering voice inside each of His chosen that is always trying to tell us the Truth. Sometimes it's a gut instinct. Sometimes it's a very obvious revelation. But most of the time, it's already been chiseled into stone.

Then, for what can only be a divine purpose, sometimes Adonai sends false teachers and prophets because He...

"...is testing you to find out if you love the LORD your God with all your heart and with all your soul."

And the only way you'll discern the Truth for sure, is if…

You shall follow the LORD your God and fear Him; and you shall keep His commandments, listen to His voice, serve Him, and cling to Him. (Deuteronomy 13:3 & 4)

I wish there was a quick fix for all of us. Wouldn't it be great if there was some kind of guarantee that upon accepting our Messiah, we could never be persuaded to accept lies? Here's the thing about lies. No matter how much truth is wrapped around them, it doesn't change their core substance. Granted, not every lie does the same amount of damage. An honest pastor will always tell a lot more truth, than otherwise. And when a pastor tells a falsehood, without malicious intent, he is not "a liar". But that doesn't mean the error will have no effect on people; unless they can discern otherwise, and act accordingly.

No matter what the denomination, or movement, or religion, there will always be false teachers within. Some who are predators, and some who just need to pray. Some mean well, and some mean evil. Some are tolerable amidst their ignorance; but some have to be called out and exposed. Adonai is looking for people who will work to see past all the fog, and fix their eyes on Him, and do what He did, and teach like He taught, and think like He thought. Yehoshua came to set the captives free. And by looking at what He did, it seems apparent the captives were as abundant in the synagogue/fellowship, as they were in the world. I'm not so sure that has changed much.

It's time. Let the debating begin. Let us debate the time we should begin counting the Omer, to bring us to Shavuot/Pentecost; not whether or not we should count it at all. Let us debate what we should call the fourth cup at Passover, not whether we should drink it. Let us debate what qualifies as work on Sabbath, not whether or not the Seventh day is Saturn-day or Sun-day.

Some will say all this 'technical' stuff doesn't matter, because He only looks at the heart. Well, call me crazy, but shouldn't our hearts be diligently guarding themselves from the harlots who come to steal away our faithfulness. Shouldn't a heart that desires to honor and obey its Lover, want to know for sure it's worshiping both in Spirit and in Truth?

"Don't make a mountain out of a mole hill," is another popular phrase some would say regarding these matters. Tell that to Nadab, as he didn't so much concern himself with the proper administration of ceremonial fire. "Don't let your faith be too intellectual!" Yes, I've actually been told that also. Well, I'm *not* sorry, but no matter what mystical and metaphysical properties some people ascribe to faith, true faith is built on confidence, and confidence is built on understanding—specifically the

Word.

A Torah-observant lifestyle, when incorporated into a believer's walk, has a profound effect on one's intimacy with the Father, our understanding of His heart, our awareness of His presence, and our maturity in spiritual things. If you truly want to be more like Yeshua, you really don't have a choice. You will become part of (and one of) a set-apart people. You will look forward to the coming Torah-based kingdom, instead of fearing the one I propose. You will carry a mark upon you that you cannot hide. There is little room for pew-warmers or cowards. You may think you know radical, but let me tell you there is nothing more radical than living out the calling, per His instructions versus man's. You may be misunderstood. You may be persecuted. Hmm…sound familiar?

I'd say it's not for everyone, but that's really not true. Torah is precisely for everyone. There may be arguable variations of obligation, but as a whole it is for the community of faith. For those of us who have tasted and seen, there is no other way. It is where our Messiah is found on every page. He is in every mitzvah, in every story. He is at the very heart of everything we have talked about. As soon as we forget that, we have begun to put confidence in the flesh, and in works. That is deadly error! If we would just stop elevating Paul above Moses, and study to determine they say the same things (which they do), we would tap into a Well-Spring of life, that would enable us to shoot up like oaks of righteousness, or pillars in His temple.

It's so amazing to me, that we would let one man's teachings turn the divinely given, four thousand year-old apple cart upside down, and barely think twice about it. I'm not discounting Paul, but isn't it a bit odd that somehow Yehoshua's words and Moses's words can be proven synoptic, yet Sha'ul's and Yehoshua's don't have to be? How does that work? What's even more amazing is that when it appears on the surface that they contradict, we'll more readily let Paul's confusing words supersede the Master's clear ones, than try to get them to agree. People actually think it's all right for Paul to be starting a new religion, which is actually following a new and better god, while performing signs and wonders. How excruciatingly wrong!

We are in changing times. The Jewish community's acceptance of Yeshua as Messiah is gaining momentum, as is the church's acceptance of things Hebraic. Christians are celebrating the feast days. Rabbis are engaging in theological discussion with evangelical pastors. Never since the first few centuries following the incarnation, have so many people simultaneously loved Yah's laws, and believed in the Messiah. I believe the reason it is happening is because it's prophesied to. If we believe the Bible, it has to be.

The stage is getting set up for His return, and I feel blessed to have been given this opportunity to assist. It is my goal now to reach the wayward; whether they be lost in the world, or misguided in the church. Having come to the understanding that I have, observing people try to exposit Paul's teachings, through antinomian lenses, is like watching the priests of Ba'al bleed themselves to get fire to fall. It is a most futile effort. When done, the result continues to be the arduously reconciled and inconsistent doctrines we are commonly instructed to live by. Universal accountability and adherence to Torah, along with undoing errant dispensational and replacement ideologies, is the solution to an abundance of theological imbalances. Just don't let the very same stumbling block of righteousness-by-works that Paul spoke of, in the letter to the Galatians (ch.3), be the thing you trip over yourself. Either it will crush you, or you will be broken upon it. Prefer to be broken.

It is not legalism we need to be afraid of; it's religious bondage we are to fear! Appropriately obeying Yah's commands can never be construed as legalism! As I've stated before, the opposite of legalism is illegalism. Freedom comes through rules. No society could ever consider themselves free without them. It is man who enslaves other men, not Yah or His Torah!

You can deem me a Judaizer if you like. But if you do, then so is YHVH! In ancient times, a Judaizer was the equivalent of a soul-winner, until warped and vile men came along and supplanted the title and corrupted its definition. John clearly understood this when he said:

By this we know that we love the children of God, when we love God and observe His commandments. <u>For this is the love of God</u>; that we keep His commandments; and His commandments are not burdensome. (1st John 5:2 & 3)

Do you still actually think he is talking about anything other than Torah? It does say "God" and not "Jesus", in case that somehow still differentiates their commandments in your eyes.

What's amazing is that the clear, strong message often preached is not to compromise our faith. Yet, ironically, outsiders to Torah observance are "concerned" with Law-observer's "balance". What they often don't see is...so are we! Just not in the way *they* define it. We see "balance" often used as a substitutionary term for compromise (a.k.a. partial-obedience), which is really just a repackaging of syncretism. What a sad state we have gotten ourselves into, whereby disobedience (typically substituted with "liberty") is exalted over adherence, and legalism is often the modern label for true faithfulness. Woe to us!

Torah-obedience will cause you to think about Him from the moment you awake, to when you close your eyes; from when you plan out your meals, to how you dress; even when and how you work. It affects how you schedule everything, from your day to your year; even when you rest. It teaches you how to treat others, and how to function within a Hellenistic society. It instructs you as to how you treat your sin, and how to make amends. It shows you who to follow. All of it evolves around Him. Yes, I am pretty much a Yeshua freak. Don't you want to be too? In Him, Torah never binds us with burdens we can't bear. With Him, we have real balance. We can love and obey. We have freedom!

If there is no doubt we are going to be this way eventually, why bother waiting?

So it shall be **when** all of these things have come upon you, the **blessing and the curse** which I have set before you, and you call *them* to mind **in all nations** where the LORD your God has banished you, and you **return** to the LORD your God **and obey** Him with all your heart and soul **according to all that I command you today**, you and your sons, then the LORD your God **will restore you from captivity**, and **have compassion** on you, and **will gather** you again from all the peoples where the LORD your God has scattered you. (Deuteronomy 30:1-3)

Now it will come about that in the last days, the mountain of the house of the LORD will be established as the chief of the mountains, and will be raised above the hills. And all the nations will stream to it. (3) And many peoples will come and say, "Come, let us go up to the mountain of the LORD, to the house of the God of Jacob, that He may teach us concerning His ways and that we may walk in His paths." For the law (Torah) will go forth from Zion and the word of the LORD (YHVH) from Jerusalem. (Isaiah 2:2 & 3)

If Yeshua really came to put an end to the Law, the fact that He didn't even tell His head prophets, or any others for that matter, is a problem because:

Amos 3:7, "Surely the Lord GOD does nothing unless He reveals His secret counsel to His servants the prophets."

Is it possible, that what Paul called the "mystery of lawlessness" (2nd Thessalonians 2:7) is considered mysterious because it is happening and encouraged right in our own believing back yard? After all, the reason the lost are lawless is not mysterious at all. It is time to boot that spirit out of our fellowships, and endeavor to live according to the standards set before us at the mountain; not according to the standards of this world— or even a pulpit. We need to approach this endeavor with caution and prayerfully obtained wisdom. We need to show YHVH that we desire to come out of captivity; that we want Him to come reign over us, and that we are readying ourselves for His return. Let us finish the work the reformers began, and return all the way back to Him.

You must accept Yeshua/Jesus as your personal Redeemer and King before any of these matters, matter. If you've already concluded that truth, you now have to decide what level of commitment you're willing to make to Him. You need to count the cost. I assure you, His yolk is easy and His burden is light. It is empowering to know you are living in daily obedience to Him, in real and tangible ways. Sure, you can be just part of the crowd…most do. Sure, you can learn at the pace your pastor sets for you, via the First Day's morning sermon…most do. Like Scripture analogizes it: You can stay on the bottle, but is that what you really want?

Obedience is the often shunned and usually ignored missing ingredient in the spiritual recipe for maturity and blessing. "It will be life for you." Don't be afraid of it! Lack of fearing the ramifications for disobedience is the result of a perverted grace/gospel message. I believe with full conviction that Yeshua did not come to give us a "you fill in the blanks", open-ended permission slip to live according to our own convictions. Guilt, according to the sacrificial program, as seen in Leviticus, doesn't even require awareness. Nowhere in the Bible, is the concept of being accountable only to "personal conviction" taught or supported. It is a lie originating with HaSatan and promulgated by ignorant men. It is not good enough to have knowledge of YHVH. The fact you believe in Him is helpful, but it is not what creates a saving faith. Just ask those of the wilderness generation:

When your fathers tested Me, they tried Me, though they had seen My work. For forty years I loathed *that* generation, and said they are a people who err in their heart, and they do not know My ways. (Psalm 95:9 & 10)

Moses, and the Israelites of that time alike, were obedient to Torah; but…

Psalm 103:7, "He made known His <u>ways</u> to Moses, His <u>acts</u> to the sons of Israel."

Knowing His *acts* alone, is a result of being veiled (scaled over) in the Mosaic covenant. Knowing His *ways* is the glory of the new covenant at work. He loathed that first generation because they rejected Him at the mountain, even though they agreed to do whatever He said. YHVH preferred Ya'akov to Esau, because Esau couldn't have cared less about his heritage, or the covenants of his fathers. Many of the Israelites "performed" their covenantal duties (somewhat), but they didn't love their Deliverer. They couldn't see or care about looking for the Messiah who was to come. They didn't "believe on Him."

He wants more than that. He wants your heart first, plus He wants your desire for obedience written upon it. He wanted their hearts circumcised more than their flesh. Moses was a new covenant-like believer. So were Abraham, David, Joshua & Caleb, Phinehas, the prophets, and anyone else the Spirit wooed into a love affair with Himself, and awaited the Messiah by faith. I hope you are too.

Participants in the new covenant are "new creations". When we are "born-again," we are given another opportunity to be part of the covenant people, through the better Way, through Messiah. People, who are only part of the old covenant, still are old creations, and are still in need of renewal.

Everyone must be born-again, regardless of what era they are born into. Everyone must be grafted into the Vine, and anyone can be pruned off. How we ever deduced that as a new creation we are free to live in our old ways, is a mystery. How being born-again gives us permission to live as the "old man," is equally. Here me now, as I say it again…no one ever, pre or post ascension, "got saved" by obeying Torah! That's a lie of HaSatan; created to trick believers into embracing lawlessness. If you didn't love YHVH with all your heart and soul and might, and love your neighbor as yourself, you were dead in your sin. All the rest means nothing without that foundation. That's it. End of discussion.

I firmly believe I have given you a pretty good heaping of clean meat to chew on, and I sincerely hope in some way you've been nourished by it. Truth sets us free; and he who Yeshua's truth sets free, is free indeed! It is also with truth that we will set others free as well. There is a secular, philosophical viewpoint amongst us that believes it is wrong to declare something as the ultimate truth. I strongly disagree! For you, your children's, your friend's, your spouse's, and everyone else you influence sake, please study hard and obtain it. Just don't stop there—sh'ma! Live what you discover. Draw different conclusions. Draw the same. Just make sure you have exhausted great effort to ensure the truth you live by.

Yeshua is a very nice Messiah. Yes, He has, and will again, come with healing in His wings. He is the balm of Gilead. But we have to keep in mind, and in balance, the fact that He is also coming to bring wrath and judgment, with the sword of His Word. He is not a pushover Deity, with little concern as to how people respect His authority. The Father in the Hebrew Scriptures is not some sort of opposite expression of the Son in the Apostolic Scriptures. The Law of Christ cannot be different from the Law of God, unless you wish to consider them different elohiym. Progressive revelation does not actually mean He's been changing over the years. We, and the level of our understanding, are what changes.

Perfection (completeness in maturity) is required just as much today as the Law required it "yesterday". The death sentence for sin yesterday is still fully applied today; but Yeshua paid it long ago. Thank Him that the blood that cleanses us now is much more detergent, and doesn't require systematic application. But this forgiveness of sins you have received, is not a release for you to go right back to doing the very things you were forgiven of! YHVH was not okay with the Hebrews who wanted to go back into slavery. Choosing onions and leaks, over milk and honey, is nonsensical. He was not okay with polluted worship. He did not redeem you, to bring you into the desert, to kill you. Selah! He loves you. I beg you…do not resist the work of the Spirit. He is calling us back to our fathers. Can you hear Him? It is written loud and clear to me.

Find Him through His Words, and in so doing, find yourself as well. Be obedient to what He says to you though, as is appropriate and possible, and He will reveal Himself to you in unimaginable ways. Asking to hear His voice, outside of through His Word, should not be your focus. If He needs to speak to you audibly, don't you worry; He will. If you want to get close to Him, then stick your nose to the pages. The Elohiym you are looking for is right inside the scrolls. And speaking of the scrolls, when you finish this book, I have one last homework assignment for you. Please, go read the 119th Psalm again. You have never been more ready to understand it and receive from it. Make the time to read it all at once. It is there that King David's heart toward Torah is revealed. It will absolutely confirm the basis of this work. It is why YHVH said that David was a man after His heart.

As I think back to all the times I adjusted tones, tweaked tenses and simply said, "Nope…can't put that!" I anticipated it not being a perfect work. It is not Holy Writ. I know how you theological types can be, so at times I would labor very hard, over just the right word or phrase. Often, my heart would race as I considered the potential consequences. "Did I let a statement go by, that wasn't worded quite right; which could do more harm than good?"

Something I truly worried over was the thought that many of my Christian friends and family, especially those in ministry, after reading this book, would assume that they and their churches will constantly be under my ever-judging eye. It is not I that is judging anyone, if anyone is. You are under no condemnation by me. We only have one Judge, and He has written a book on historical case precedence, from which we are to judge ourselves first. It is each our own responsibility to endeavor to obey "the law" personally. Yet, proper Torah observance does require a community effort, and was designed for a holy nation of set-apart citizens.

Another worry I still have is that some of you will be tempted to reject all of this work, for the sake of something minor. Don't do that!

And don't reject the person who led you into reading this either. If, in the end, you conclude that those of us who support the majority of this book are actually the "weaker brother," and that we have lost out on the liberties available to believers (what that may be I can't conceive), then you, being the stronger one, need to not just pity us, but restore us. However, as you can see, you'll need to be pretty persuasive. I can ease your worry though. We feel no sense of loss. You just need to consider whether you want to be construed as someone punching holes in their protective levy, or someone partnering to plug them up.

After all that's been said here, I'm sure I've perturbed people, enraged others, overloaded some and rescued a few. I hope that I'll still be welcome in my hometown, but only time will tell. Did I swing the pendulum to hard? Maybe. But the clock is ticking. I just need to ask of you a great favor. You can call me a heretic. You can call me a legalist or a Judaizer. I understand if I've upset you. I have said some difficult things; things that self-preserving people just don't say. Fortunately, a man of no reputation has little to lose. But if you're going to throw stones, please do me the favor of making them large enough to be merciful and quick.

If you are the leader of a community of believers, be very careful how you argue against these teachings. You are responsible for those sheep, and your teaching them to disobey YHVH's commandments will afford you big trouble. Should you choose to publicly refute what I've said, make darn sure it's not just your religious ego and background that are at odds with what you've read. And do me the favor of keeping my words in context. I know how tempting it is to do otherwise. You would be far better off to leave certain things you do not understand alone, than to teach the least among you to sin. Perhaps, in certain rare cases, ignorance may be bliss after all.

My Fellow Israelites,

We have a tough road ahead of us. The depth of perversion to the full gospel is daunting when honestly assessed. But do not grow weary in well-doing! There is a work going on in the spiritual realm, not started by man, nor finished by him. At best, we can help facilitate it. Be sensitive. Remember from where you came. Above all…love. Love breaks down the walls that theological argumentation cannot. If it doesn't, keep loving anyway. Their time will come, either in the here or the hereafter.

We will never have the power, wealth, or prestige that the great denominations have. It is not our path. Those of you leaders, who are in the trenches, opening your homes and showing hospitality, keep up your good work. He will send people your way, in good time. You are not unseen by the One who sees all. Just keep this in mind: don't be so torah-centric that you forget to be Christ-centric. To you scholars who are trying to apologetically justify our way, your works will get read, and noticed, and will sway the ready-tilled heart. Don't quit on us. Keep helping us to show ourselves approved.

Finally, regardless of your station, the church is where your brothers and sisters are, even when they shun your good news. Show them the grace that you have been shown. *Waywardness* isn't always *lost*.

I now would like to finish with a prayer for us all, borrowing the words of Daniel:

Alas, O Adonai, the great and awesome Elohiym, who keeps His covenant and lovingkindness for those who love Him and keep His commandments, we have sinned, committed iniquity, acted wickedly and rebelled, even turning aside from Your commandments and ordinances.

Moreover, we have not listened to Your servants the prophets, who spoke in Your name to our kings, our princes, our fathers and all the people of the land. Righteousness belongs to You, O Adonai, but to us open shame, as it is this day--to the men of Judah, the inhabitants of Jerusalem and all Israel, those who are nearby and those who are far away in all the countries to which You have driven them, because of their unfaithful deeds which they have committed against You. Open shame belongs to us, O Adonai, to our kings, our princes and our fathers, because we have sinned against You.

To Adonai our Elohiym *belong* compassion and forgiveness, for we have rebelled against Him. Nor have we obeyed the voice of YHVH our Elohiym, to walk in His teachings which He set before us through His servants the prophets. Indeed all Israel has transgressed Your torah and turned aside, not obeying Your voice. So the curse has been poured out on us, along with the oath which is written in the law of Moses the servant of Elohiym, for we have sinned against Him. Thus He has confirmed His words which He had spoken against us and against our rulers who ruled us, to bring on us great calamity; for under the whole heaven there has not been done *anything* like what was done to Jerusalem. As it is written in the torah of Moses, all this calamity has come on us. Yet we have not sought the favor of YHVH our Elohiym by turning from our iniquity and giving attention to Your truth.

Therefore, YHVH has kept the calamity in store and brought it on us, for YHVH our Elohiym is righteous with respect to all His deeds which He has done, but we have not obeyed His voice. And now, O YHVH our Elohiym, who have brought Your people out of the land of Egypt with a mighty hand and have made a name for Yourself, as it is this day—we have sinned, we have been wicked. O Adonai, in accordance with all Your righteous acts, let now Your anger and Your wrath turn away from Your city Jerusalem, Your holy mountain, for because of our sins and the iniquities of our fathers, Jerusalem and Your people *have become* a reproach to all those around us.

So now, our Elohiym, listen to the prayer of Your servant and to his supplications, and for Your sake, O Adonai, let Your face shine on Your desolate sanctuary. O my Elohiym, incline Your ear and hear! Open Your eyes and see our desolations and the city which is called by Your name. For <u>we are not presenting</u>

our supplications before You on account of any merits of our own, but on account of Your great compassion. O Adonai, hear! O Adonai, forgive! O Adonai, listen and take action! For Your own sake, O my Elohiym, do not delay, because Your city and Your people are called by Your name. (9:4-19, restored)

Shalom, and see you back at the East Gate!

Sincerely Yours

End Notes

Prologue

(1). Pauline is a term denoting affiliation with Paul the Apostle.
(2). Deuteronomy 8:15
(3). Luke 10:19
(4). Genesis 3:15
(5). Romans 16:20

Chapter One:

(1). Ken McNamara, "Embryos and Evolution," New Scientist, vol. 12416, 16 October 1999

(2). If you find yourself involved in a congregation where it appears correction is not humbly received, or not given out by the leadership to the flock, you may ultimately have to make some tough decisions. Of course, I don't want all you readers who go to these churches to just immediately up and leave. Everyone should certainly expose real problems and work to resolve it. But, if ultimately there is not a forum through which you can express general concerns or challenge doctrinal conflict, you can rest assured that is not the place for you. That's assuming of course, you're concerned with restoration.

Chapter Three:

(1) In *Dictionary of New Testament Theology* (Editor: Colin Brown), vol. 3, p. 410, after the author had critically examined all the alleged Sabbath-breaking texts, he says in conclusion, "We may conclude then, that though Jesus broke through rabbinic traditions about the sabbath, there was no annulling of the observance of the day." In the Mishnah, *Shabbath* 7, 2, we find a list of 39 specific laws the Pharisees determined were necessary for proper Sabbath-keeping. These were derived from labors that would have been involved in the creation of the Tabernacle. To an outsider, it would appear to make a burden of the Sabbath. In fact, the addition of these (and all Oral Laws), and therefore their applicability, is commonly disputed amongst various Messianic groups, due to this scriptural reference: Deut 4:2.

This very topic is an ideal representation of the need to at least appreciate the need for some Oral tradition. Malachah "Work/Creation" is a very vague concept, capable of much conjecture. Jesus was indeed opposing the Pharisees who had made the Word of Elohiym of no effect, with their burdensome oral tradition, but He wasn't opposing all Oral Tradition by-proxy. They had made the observance of the Sabbath much more of a religious exercise than God had originally commanded, but the Sabbath principle was not at issue.

The New Bible Dictionary, 1st Edition, p. 1111, explicitly refutes the allegation that the Messiah broke the Sabbath, and referring to what Messiah and His taught ones did, says as follows, "It was not wrong to eat on the Sabbath, even if the food must be obtained by plucking corn from the ears. Nor was it wrong to do good on the Sabbath day."

(2) The phrase "under the law" and "under law" is used eleven times in the Apostolic Scriptures, in the NASU translation. A very careful study of these verses is required to properly understand the usage. If you examine it, you will discover that "hupo nomos" is used to denote a subjugation to the penalties of the Law. Additionally, in some cases, "under the law" is not even the best translation, but is used to retain a thematic consistency with the bias. *Anomos*, meaning: "without law," and *en nomos*, meaning: "in the law" have very different applications and should be recognized as such. However, they are often not, and are often written as "under the law".

A great example of both the bias and the grammar issues are seen in 1 Cor 9:21: "to those who are without law (anomos), as without law, though not being without the law of God but under the law (en nomos) of Christ, so that I might win those who are without law." Here, "under the law of Christ" should have been rendered "within the law". By not doing so, the literal Greek is altered to better contrast the "law of Christ" with the "law of God". Most overlook Paul's immediately preceding comment about "not being without the law of God." The law of God is Torah! By using the phrase "within the law of Christ," he was saying that his Torah observance was now governed by Jesus's teachings, which did not annul Moses's, but diminished the authority of Oral Tradition and elevated love.

(3) The popular departmentalizing of Torah into the: Sacrificial, Civil, and Ceremonial law is not done by God, but by man. It has been done to make it easier for certain theological bends to deal with their understanding and application of Mosaic Law. It is my position that either all of Torah is still in force, or none of it is. I assert: all still is. The phrase "in force," however, does not automatically denote "must be done". Not all the Law is applicable to all people. Although some of the hidden things in Torah have been "revealed," they have not been abolished. If it could

be abolished, so could our covenants. If it all was, we wouldn't still need a savior at all!

Chapter Four

(1) I am not promoting the concept that Christians are the physical descendants of Abraham; a.k.a. his seed, a.k.a. actual lost tribes. I do not believe that. There are some who teach that *born again* believers, although it cannot be proven through lineage, are actual physical descendants of Jacob. This concept is unsubstantiatable by Scripture, and promotes a theology which conflicts with too many scriptural principles. Please don't buy into this elitist ideology if it tries to sell itself to you. This verse plainly attests to this truth:

1st Chronicles 5:1, "Now the sons of Reuben the firstborn of Israel, for he was the firstborn; but because he defiled his father's bed, his birthright was given to the sons of Joseph the son of Israel, so that he is not enrolled in the genealogy according to the birthright."

It should be understood that whether you are a physical descendent or not, you must be grafted in; whether you are circumcised or not, you must be born again.

(2) b.Shabbat 33a; b.Sotah 47b.

Chapter Five:

Pg.168, Additional Note:

There are approximately 1600 rules and regulation found in Judaism's Oral and Written Traditions (Mishnah, Talmud, Gamarra), explaining how to specifically honor the Sabbath. Over the years, differing cultures and rabbinic opinion have added to the original Scripture's rules, which far outnumber anything God specifically asked for.

The traditional justification for the validity of "adding" to Moses, and giving these laws the same level of weight, comes from the understanding that Moses wrote what he could down, but left Sinai with much more instruction that was only passed down verbally, and did not actually get written until much later. Another source for these laws came from later judgements over disputes that were presided over, by the 70 leaders. Think of Moses as the Supreme Court judge, and the 70 as regional magistrates. This "precedent" allowed for future consensus law (halachah) to be created by a minion of the leadership of a given community, and have it be passed down orally, and also be of the same caliber as, "Thus says the Lord."

Initially, much of Oral Tradition was designed to build "fences" around the Torah, like layers of difficult-to-penetrate walls you would have to break through, before you actually broke the original Law of Moses. As time moved on, the layers became quite thick indeed. In some cases, it is hard to even identify what the original law they were trying to protect is. There are several, but here is one verse that challenges one notion, and shows the need to keep restraint.

Exodus 24:4, "Moses wrote down <u>all the words</u> of the Lord. Then he arose early in the morning, and built an altar at the foot of the mountain with twelve pillars for the twelve tribes of Israel."

I do believe God's Law was firmly established; but I also believe there are legitimate implicational questions. Although it seems a natural reaction for most of the world of Christianity to blindly, and often with hostile haste, reject historical Jewish teachings, we should be careful to not. Much valuable history and understanding can be drawn from those who have carried the Oracles of God for several thousand years. It is one of the advantages Paul recognized in being Jewish, as stated in Romans chapter 3.

(1) United Bible Societies' *Greek New Testament, Fourth Revised Edition* indicates that this phrase first appears in the miniscule 1175 (p 476), which dates from the Tenth Century C.E. (p 17). The phrase *teirein town nomon* or "keep the Law" first appears in quotations of Acts 15:24 in the Apostolic Constitutions and in the writings of Amphilochius (p 467). In its list of the Greek Church Fathers, Amphilochius is listed as having died "after 394," and the Apostolic Constitutions are dated "about 380" (p 31).

(2) "During the baroque period, it took on a rayed form of a sun-monstrance with a circular window surrounded by a silver or gold frame with rays." Source: *The Dictionary of the Liturgy* by Rev. Jovian P. Lang, OFM., published and copyrighted © 1989 by Catholic Book Publishing Co., New York, ISBN 0-89942-273-X, page 436.

(3) *The Sacred Calendar of the 'God' of Israel*, A Stewarton Bible School Publication, David Loughran, p5.

(4) http://en.wikipedia.org/wiki/Gregorian_Calendar, 2005

(5) Katapauo is the usual Greek word for rest, as seen in Hebrew 4:8. Sabbatismo, used here, is a special word found only once in the NT. It is a term which was carefully chosen for its relation to observance. Thayer's Greek Definitions, #3520. It is not an allegorical term. It is quite literal.

Chapter Six:

(1) http://www.adherents.com/adh_branches.html#Christianity

(2) George Weigel, "*World religions by the numbers*," Catholic Educator's Resource Center, 2002-MAR-08, at: http://www.catholiceducation.org/

(3) Based on the UN projected world population of 6.301 billion for mid-2003.

(4) By: Richard N. Ostling, Associated Press Date: 19 May 2001 Source: Salt Lake Tribune.

http://www.sltrib.com/2001/May/05192001/Saturday/98497.htm

Chapter Seven:

(1) B. Sanhedrin 106a

(2) Alfred J. Kolatch, *Jewish Book of Why* (New York: Penguin Compass, 2003), p. 97.

(3) The fact that the rite of circumcision was given to Avraham, and not Moshe, is significant. It is, in fact, independent of the Mosaic covenant. It was/is an outward sign of rightful participation in the land deed given to Avraham's seed. To depend on it, for access to the Kingdom of Heaven, is a serious misappropriation. This is a major source for the contention over the subject in the Apostolic Letters. Understanding this, it becomes very easy to accurately interpret the oft confused, and contradictive sounding phrasing in "Circumcision is nothing, and uncircumcision is nothing. What matters is obeying God's commandments (1 Cor 7:19).

Obviously, one of God's commands is to circumcise. So, in order for this statement to make sense, we must again revert to the recognition of the word *circumcision* seen here, as being in its 1st Century context of ritual conversion (Gal 2:7; Eph 2:11). It also explains Paul's decision to allow Timothy to get circumcised. Timothy comprehended the essential, spiritual truths; but for those who don't, and undergo "conversion", "Christ prophets them nothing." Timothy was going to minister to Jews, who would have looked at him as worse than a gentile, being that he was of Jewish decent.

The Jerusalem council of Acts 15 was commenced to handle this debate. If physical circumcision could assure a place in the kingdom to come, what was the point of the cross? And, if obedience to a litany of rules, "that the fathers couldn't bear" was necessary also, why should that litany be laid on a new convert either? Circumcision (Abraham) and the Law (Moses) would ultimately be properly and gradually taught "in the synagogues, on every Shabbat." They were by no means discarded.

End Notes

Under the auspices of circumcision being intrinsically connected to ritual conversion to Judaism, and not just an external sign of connection to a specific promise, it would have been inappropriate to undergo the ritual at times. It could have born witness to a false gospel. Had a "God-fearer" undergone it, to be able to enter certain fellowships, they would have also been expected to take on the whole yolk of Torah, including the oral traditions. It wasn't long before Judaism would also require a denouncement of Christ as well.

Also noteworthy is the fact that the promise given to Abraham, was given before the rite was. Likewise, Israel was delivered from bondage before the Laws were given. Abraham was deemed righteous for his faith, not his surgery. Circumcision was a commandment given to all who desired/desire a seat at the Passover table. It was given to all who desired/desire a place in Abraham's family; all who make up the "sands of the sea, and stars in the sky." I think it's not hard to imagine that if you wanted to go out into the nations, and invite people into Abraham's family, demanding they cut their male organ *first* would greatly reduce your effectiveness. Understandably so.

(4) As previously referenced, there is a lot of mysticism associated with the Divine Name. Books such as The Zohar, the Sepher Yetzirah, and other Kabbalist works are sources that explore the subject at great length. Although I endorse the restoration of the use of His Name, I do not want it to be construed that I endorse incantational and meditative application. On the contrary, I was very concerned about the potential pitfalls of including this subject matter. Exploring Kabbalistic material to understand the mindset of Orthodox and Chassidic Jews is on par with reading the Quran to understand the Muslim faith. As a believer in Messiah Yeshua, I ask you to do so (if even you must) with great care and guarded interest. Without Yeshua, Chassidism is an astray religion of men, seeking the Divine through ritualistic behavior and pattern. It is alluring, but has its perils.

Chapter Eight:

(1) Risking more trouble, I want to be more specific. Woman can "have the floor," but it is with restriction. They must be "subjecting themselves." This means that they are not to be without oversight, but it also infers a content restriction. If a woman is given an opportunity to teach, she should not use the opportunity to bring correction to the body. It is not her place to do so.

I do not believe that women should be the spiritual heads of congregations, nor ideally...homes. I realize that an argument could be made, that a female leader, on a local level, could be subject to a male district presbytery. However, the role of the Overseer is described in Scripture as a man, for a reason. There needs to be someone at the top, or preferably a group of people, who are capable of bringing correction. The Teacher is not the highest position in the body; at least it shouldn't be. I am not opposed to a female being seated in a position of authority, within an affinity group. I think that is quite appropriate. But even in this circumstance, if the leadership of that group votes to take a corrective action against an attendee, and a man is somehow involved, a woman should bring the word to a man; but she can represent the group to a woman.

I know how old-fashioned and outdated this may sound to some of you. The modern church, as well as society, has reprogrammed our thinking on many subjects. I do not consider this to be an era-specific matter, and consider the Scriptures to be a higher authority than cultural mores.

Chapter Nine:

(1) The *Catholic Fact Book*, copyright 1986 by John Deedy, published by Thomas More Press, page 360.

(2) "Anointing", Encyclopædia Britannica, 11th ed., Vol. II, Cambridge: Cambridge University Press, 1911, pp. 79–80

(3) The Catholic Church believes they are the "true" church, founded upon their ability to trace their line of Popes back to Peter, and that Peter was the first Pope appointed by Yeshua Himself, by His word play: "Upon this rock (petra [boulder]/Petrus-Peter), I will build my church. (Matthew 16:18)"

Somehow, the clear, historical fact that James was equally the leader of the first-century, Jewish church, goes completely ignored. Also, Yeshua, in that text in Matthew, is also clearly teaching that it is upon Peter's profession (not Peter himself, as a rock is metaphoric for either/or a firm foundation, and/or the Messiah Himself) of who He is—that He will build His church. "Blessed are you, Shimon benYonah," because it was the Father who revealed the identity of the Son to him. In that way, all who come to a saving knowledge of Yeshua are blessed exactly the same way. He is re-building His ekklesia, via the Spirit imparting revelation, which leads to confession.

Chapter Ten:

(1) The Columbia Electronic Encyclopedia® Copyright © 2005, Columbia University Press. Licensed from Columbia University Press. All rights reserved.

(2) Panati's: *Extraordinary Origins of Everyday Things*, states:

a. St. Nicholas was born in the ancient Turkish town of Lycia in the fourth century. (He was sainted for his significant role in the Council of Nicea.

b. St. Nicholas was not commonly referred to during the Protestant Reformation in most European countries. However, the stories were passed on by the Dutch and the term "Santa Claus" evolves from the Dutch term for St. Nicholas.

c. The modern image of Santa Claus in the United States comes from a poem entitled "The Night Before Christmas" written by Dr. Clement Clarke Moore in 1822, which spread widely in newspapers and magazines throughout the country.

d. Moore's Santa was still a little different from the modern roly-poly version. This final version was popularized in a series of Christmas drawings that the famed cartoonist, Thomas Nast did for _Harper's Weekly_ between 1863 and 1886.

(3) The NRF 2005 Halloween Consumer Intentions and Actions Survey, conducted by BIGresearch, found that consumers are expected to spend 3.29 billion on Halloween this year.

(4) David I. Kertzer, *The Popes Against the Jews: The Vatican's Role in the Rise of Modern Anti-Semitism*, New York: Alfred A. Knopf, 2001, p. 74.

(5) I confess that I found these four origins, expressed in a variety of ways, all over the internet. I don't have a definitive source for them. I have been aware of them for many years, and it is more the supportive reasoning that I establish my perspective on.

Chapter Eleven:

(1) Mekilta de-Rabbi Ishmael on Exodus 20:2 (in the Lauterbach edition 2:234ff); Midrash Rabbah on Exodus 20:1 (Soncino edition, 3:336, where the voice of God was understood to have spoken in 70 languages, i.e., all the known languages of the nations); b. Avodah Zarah 2b.

(2) B.Shabbat 88b; e.g., Shemot Rabbah 5:9. Weissman, Moshe, *The Midrash Says, Shemos*, Bnai Yaakov Publications (1995), p.182, *citing Midrash Chazit.*

(3) Speaking in Tongues: A Cross-Cultural Study in Glossolalia by Felecitas D. Goodman, University of Chicago Press, 1972

(4) William J. Samarin, "Variation and Variables in Religious Glossolalia" Language in Society, ed. Dell Haymes, Cambridge: Cambridge University Press, 1972, pgs. 121-130

(5) Article in Journal of the American Scientific Affiliation entitled "An Ethnological Study of Glossolalia" by George J. Jennings, March 1968.

Chapter Twelve:

(1) Although "Jacob's trouble" is commonly understood as a synonym for the Great Tribulation, it is sometimes considered, from a midrashic perspective, to include the previous political and spiritual turmoil, and upheaval, eretz Yisrael must endure, before the coming of the Messiah. I agree, but also assert the whole world will be impacted as well.

Although we would like to be able to clearly structure the timelines Scripture gives us, in regards to apocalyptic events, it isn't possible. Even within the parameters we are given, there is still much speculation. I would like for you to consider something though. As I have already alluded to, it is my understanding that YHVH works through patterns and principles. The Great Tribulation, like the Exodus deliverance, is multi-purposed. As Scripture states, judgment comes upon the house of the Lord first. (1 Pet 4:17) And for all the reasons I've already mentioned, in order for that to happen, the "Church" must be present in the Earth.

I do not believe it is a coincidence that there were three sets of three strikes against Egypt, prior to the judgment; and there are three dominant sets of strikes against the Earth in Revelation: seals, bowls and vials—both ending in darkness. If it is not coincidence, then the pattern would suggest that the "Church" will have to endure the first wave of strikes as well, that being the *Seven Seals*. (Rev 6 & 8:1) Interestingly, that is where we find the infamous, *Four Horseman* discussed. An honest look at the scriptural information leaves a wide area of possibility as to the "when" and "duration" of their purposes. It is not impossible that they have begun their ride, but their journey is far from over. Upon conclusion of the seals, I believe we will be provided with our own "Goshen" to survive the remaining challenges.

(2) *Federal Register*, Vol. 69, No. 30, February 13, 2004, pp. 7336-7338)

Chapter Divisions

Chapter One:

Lies in Disguise p.21; Our War p.23; Inheritance p.25; A Couple, "What Ifs?" p.26

Chapter Two:

The Stage p.34; Then Came Death p.35; Who Fell First p.37; Shame p.39; We Fall Down p.41; A Moral Constitution p.46; An Allegorical Reality p.49

Chapter Three:

The Kingdom Corporation p.53; The Demandments p.57; Torah p.61; Just Olde Laws p.62; I Double Dare You p.66; Dual Functions of Grace p.69; Ancient Grace p.72; Repentance p.76; The Paradox of Grace P.82; Getting Testy p.85

Chapter Four:

You Can Do It! p.94; If the Staff Fits p.96; Warning to Sheep p.99; The Human Factor p.99; Blindness is Not a Virtue p.102; The New and Improved Covenant p.103; The First Covenant p.107; Just Believe? p.117; The Fire Insurance Fallacy p.118; Is it Worthy p.120; His Table p.127

Chapter Five:

Six Yummy Volts p.139; The Jerusalem Council p.144; Except to Accept p.145; Total Freedom p.148; Peter's Vision p.148; Yea, Buts… p.150; Libation or Liberation? p.158; The Appointed Times p.161; Luney Israelites p.162; He Wants to Meet with You p.169; Shabbat Shalom p.173; The Capital Offensive p.181; The Lord's Day p.183; To Shabbat or Not p.185

Chapter Six:

True North p.192; Jeroboam's Curse p.196; Take Me to Your Leader p.199; Waxed Love p.204; Christians, Christians Everywhere p.208

Chapter Seven:

Enter the Word p.214; The Missing Key p.216; Which Way Did He Go? p.217; A Name Game p.218; Forget Me Not! P.221; What's in a Name? p.224; To Be or Not to Be p.233; Identity Crisis p.238; The Church p.246; The Messianic Movement p.247; Externals p.250; Blessing of Affiliation p.257

Chapter Eight:

The Five Medicines p.262; The Apostle p.263; The Prophet p.265; The Evangelist p.266; The Teacher p.267; The Overseer p.269; The Deacon p.270; The Pastor p.271; Posturing vs. Pastoring p.272; The Minister p.273; Subject to, does NOT mean, Object to p.274; Be All You Should Be p.276; The Common Folk p.280; Ten Thous in Megawhats? P.281; The Timothy Complex p.284; Kingdom Order p.287

Chapter Nine:

Idolatry p.290; Crux-Contamination p.293; Bust or Busted p.296; Praying to Saints p.297; Hosting the Host p.298; Passover the Truth p.302; Yochanon the Mikveh Man p.307; Altar or Motives p.312; Holy Fruits of the Loom p.314; Anointing for Appointing p.315; Balder-ash p.320; Lent Up and Twisted p.323; Fat Tuesday p.326; The Fourth Cup p.327

Chapter Ten:

Selective Submission p.332; Asherah and Ba'al p.334; Ishtar to Easter p.336; The Resurrected Sun Day p.338; Further Timeline Challenges p.341; Masquerading as Mo'adim p.346; Hallowmass p.348; Norse Elven Blot p.350; Celtic Samhain p.350; Cristes Maesse p.351; Whose Mas? P.352; Trees of Worship p.358; More "Reasons for the Season" p.361; The Birthday Ritual p.367; Candles and Wishes p.369; Ach-oo; God Bless You p.370

Chapter Eleven:

Un-Motivating Gifts/Babyl-On p.376; The Indoor Storm p.380 Just Gotta Have It p.384; All Blown Out of Proportion p.390; Are you sure you want it? p.392; Thou Art Healed p.396; Whose Fault is it? p.398; Our Hope p.406

Chapter Twelve:

Predestination p.414; The Unpardonable Sin p.417; Self-Termination p.421; Generational Curses p.423; Tribulation Fabrication p.428; Tithe and Offerings p.444; Worthy of Your Wage? p.451; Offerings p.453; Out of Your Increase p.454; Marriage, Divorce and the Ministry p.462; "Gotten Saved" p.465; Faith p.467; The Triune Deity p.469

~Acknowledgments~

Of course, I want to first thank my Mashiach, who has redeemed me and by His grace has allowed me to know this, and to see past the veil.

I want to thank my parents for raising me to have knowledge of the Holy One who delivered me, and interceding for me through the times I denied Him.

I want to thank the leaders, pastors, and teachers who have served me and given me a chance to serve them. In case you didn't know, we do not see eye to eye on all things doctrinal; but you have shown me the gift of sacrifice and the love of the brethren in action. I have also seen you turn your cheek, which is often synonymous. Whether you pushed me or pulled me, He meant it for good. It is my sincere hope that you would hearken to the voices of the prophets of Israel…and return.

I want to apologize to the people of my past, who had to know my "old man". He is thankfully dead now, but sometimes I still have to kick him in the teeth.

I want to thank my friends who, through countless hours of excavating The Word with me, have helped to dig up a lot of the truth found in this book. The blisters have been oh so sweet. Thank you for your advisement, and investment, as well.

And I want to give special thanks to the courageous teachers out there today, from whose fields I have gleaned the corners—you, who against the current do choose to flow. I'm pretty sure it will be upstream until He returns; but if the river leads to a throne, last one in…

Additional Resources

I have received no financial incentive to refer these sites or sources. Also, their inclusion does not necessitate their endorsement of this book, nor my advocating of all the information found within their material content, nor their affiliated theological and doctrinal perspectives. I do not propose they advocate each other either. Not all is restored yet!

I would certainly endorse some more than others. Several are primarily reference centers and portals. After reading this book, you should be able to discern my perspective on them. As during any web based searching, for every quality teaching out there, there are several to fuel Gehenna. Please use wisdom and extreme caution, and depend greatly upon the Ruach to guide you into all Truth.

Educational Web Reference and Research:

www.ancienthebrew.com (Hebrew Language Studies)
www.darwinismrefuted.com (Creation Science)
www.FFOZ.org (Messianic Parashat Commentary and Topical Books)
www.adherents.com (World Religion Statistics)
www.godandscience.org (Creational and Apologetic Science)
www.catholic.org (Catholic Resource)
www.etymonline.com (Word Etymology)
www.askmoses.com (Rabbinical Jewish Studies)
www.wikipedia.com; www.brittanica.com (Encyclopedias)
www.mw.com; www.dictionary.com (Dictionaries)
www.bibarch.com (Biblical Archaeology)
www.bluethread.com (Hebrew Word Glossary)
www.jewishencyclopedia.com (Focused Encyclopedia)
www.Torahclass.org (In Depth Biblical Overview Study; Audio and Text)

Scriptural and Extra-Biblical Web Resources:

www.e-sword.com (Software-Based, Multi-Translation Tool)
www.blueletterbible.com (Web-based Scriptures and Commentary)
www.crosswalk.org (Web-based Scriptures and Commentary)
www.lockman.org (New American Standard Bible online)
www.scripturetext.com (Web-Based, Multi-Lingual Tool)
www.hnvbible.org (The Word English Bible; Messianic Edition)
www.audiotreasure.com (Online Audio Bible)
www.apostlesbible.com (English Version of Septuagint)
www.halakhah.com/sanhedrin (Babylonian Talmud)

Recommended Textual Resources:

The Apostle's Bible a.k.a. Modern English Translation of the Greek-Septuagint (Paul W. Esposito)
The ArtScroll Tanakh
The Babylonian Talmud (Jew's College/Soncino English Translation)
A Greek-English Lexicon of the New Testament and Other Early Christian Literature (Bauer, Danker, Arndt, Gingrich)
Brown-Driver-Briggs Hebrew and English Lexicon
The Case for a Creator (Lee Strobel)
Complete Word Study Dictionary: Old Testament & New Testament
Concise Greek-English Dictionary of New Testament Words-
(Barclay M. Newman)
The Encyclopedia of Superstitions (Christina Hole)
Expositor's Bible Commentary (Frank E. Gaebelein)
A Family Guide to Biblical Holidays (Sampson and Pierce)
The Genesis Record (Morris)
Hebrew & Aramaic Lexicon of the Old Testament-
(Koehler and Baumgartner)
Hebrew Names Version of the World English Bible
Holidays and Holy Days (Susan E. Richardson)
Holiday Symbols (Susan E. Richardson)
Holy Cow! "Does God Care About What We Eat?" (Hope Egan; FFOZ)
IVP Bible Background Commentary (Old & New Testament)
Kingdom of the Cults, Rev. & Upd. Ed. (Walter Martin)
The Jewish Book of Why (Alfred J. Kolatch)
LXX: Septuagint, New English Translation
(Albert Pietersma; University Press)
The Maker's Diet (Jordan S. Rubin)
The Mishnah (Jacob Neusner)
Nelson's Expository Dictionary of Old Testament Words
Strong's Exhaustive Concordance of the Bible
Thayer's Greek-English Lexicon of the New Testament
Too Long in the Sun (Richard Rives)
Vine's Complete Expository Dictionary of Old and New Testament-
Words